A LIBRARY OF LITERARY CRITICISM

Rita Stein
General Editor

A Library of Literary Criticism

The Ungar Publishing Company

New York

MODERN ARABIC LITERATURE

Compiled and edited by

ROGER ALLEN

To Mustafa Badawi, in gratitude

1987

The Ungar Publishing Company
370 Lexington Avenue, New York, N.Y. 10017

Library of Congress Cataloging-in-Publication Data

Modern Arabic literature.

  (A Library of literary criticism)
  Includes index.
  1. Arabic literature—20th century—History and
criticism. I. Allen, Roger M. A. II. Series.
PJ7538.M58   1986   891'.7'09005   86-5834
ISBN 0-8044-3024-1

CONTENTS

PREFACE

This volume brings together a large selection of criticism about modern Arab writers. It is, in a word, an anthology, and no anthology has ever succeeded in satisfying or catering to all its readers. Critical decisions have had to be made at almost every turn, and in this case, as in others, scholars will undoubtedly disagree about the results. Concerning this particular work I may perhaps claim double jeopardy, for not only have I made the initial selection of writers to whose works the critical writings are addressed, but I have then chosen the excerpts themselves. Using Murray Krieger's somewhat whimsical terminology, I have selected not only the "words," but also the "words about the words." As this long and involved project now nears its conclusion I would like to venture a few comments, which may be of use to the reader of this volume. They will, no doubt, be in part an apologia for the kind of book that has emerged, but I believe that they will also reflect current realities in the fields of both literary criticism and theory and some of the more practical ramifications of the present state of biobibliographical research in Arabic literature studies.

This work began as a somewhat smaller selection of authors within the framework of an anthology on three Middle Eastern literatures; that phase was completed by 1978. There followed the decision to expand the Arabic section into a complete volume in its own right, a process that has continued into 1984, although most of the materials presented here reflect a *terminus ad quem* of 1982 or earlier. That does not imply that certain selections published since 1982 are not to be found in this volume. It does, however, point up the fact that one short visit to Egypt in 1984 has not been sufficient to enable me to survey the vast amount of new material I know to be appearing throughout the Arab world. To the vagaries associated with the arrival of Arabic books in the libraries of American universities should also be added the difficult political circumstances prevailing in many Arab countries, including no fewer than three war situations as I write these words. All these essentially practical factors have impinged in one way or another on the process of preparing this volume. While not wishing to gloss over the shortcomings in bibliographical expertise that are, no doubt, reflected in this volume, I would urge upon the readers of this work the realization that it has been prepared in the United States for an English-speaking readership and has had to rely in the main on Arabic and Western resources available there.

My general aim has been to survey the most important authors and works in modern Arabic literature, taking the term "modern" to imply 20th-century from the temporal point of view and post-neoclassical from a more literary-critical aspect. Here already we have a point of considerable debate, in that this decision excludes some of the most famous authors from the earlier stages in the modern Arabic renaissance: Jūrjī Zaydān, Ahmad Shawqī, Hāfiz Ibrā-hīm, Jamīl Sidqī al-Zahāwī, Maʿrūf al-Rusāfī, Muhammad al-Muwaylihī, and so on. My own decision to exclude such authors, thus following the lead of such anthologists as Mounah Khouri and Hamid Algar in their *An Anthology of Modern Arabic Poetry* (Berkeley, University of California Press, 1974), is more a practical than a theoretical one. I am not so much concerned here with the notion of the "modern" and whether neoclassical authors can be considered "modern" (a subject to which the poet-critic Adūnīs and others have addressed themselves at length) as I am with the desire to incorporate into this work materials on some members of the newest generation of writers. In this connection I am acutely aware of two things: first that some readers will not agree with this decision concerning the neoclassicists; and second, that, as Salmā Khadra' al-Jayyūsī notes in her excellent survey *Trends and Movements in Modern Arabic Poetry* (Leiden, E. J. Brill, 1977), it is ex-tremely difficult to predict which authors, even the most popular ones, will prove to be those who endure into future generations. That Ahmad Shawqī's poetry will so endure seems to me unquestionable; that some of the works of writers included here may not is at least possible. Such, it seems to me, is the dilemma of the anthologist of "the modern."

The list of names and works included here attempts to achieve a balance, both in terms of genres discussed and of geographical areas within the Arab world. Needless to say, that has proved difficult, if not impossible. With re-gard to genres, for example, the traditional Arab predilection for poetry has prevailed for much of the period covered, although fiction, and especially short fiction, is rapidly becoming the most popular, if not the most accom-plished, medium. Drama, meanwhile, continues to develop in a lively and of-ten provocative way, but is beset by problems of censorship and governmental pressure—overt or covert—in many, if not most, of the countries within our purview. All these factors are sources of influence on the balance that has been our goal.

With regard to the question of *geographical* representation, the issue is equally complex and is colored not a little by such extrinsic issues as popula-tion, education, and sheer chauvinism. In the first place, some Arab countries are far more populous than others, and thus the number of writers and critics varies widely from country to country. Opportunities in education (and in the case of North Africa, the Maghreb, education in Arabic) will vary in availability and level according to both past colonial policies and present governmental priorities.

But probably the most significant among the external factors that have affected our ability to achieve any "balance" has been the fact that, as Muhammad Yūsuf Najm notes in his contribution to the conference volume *Arab Literature in the Writings of Scholars* (*Al-Adab al-'Arabī fī āthār al-dārisīn*, 1971), the lion's share of critical writing about modern Arabic literature has been devoted to works by Lebanese and Egyptian writers. That the writings of authors from these two nations should feature most prominently in the present work is therefore no accident, particularly in view of the additional fact that the works by writers from these two countries are also best served by bibliographical sources. In a very real sense, the entire situation is a vicious circle as far as research is concerned. I have made every effort to compensate for this situation by scouring the shelves of literary journals in Arabic in search of critical writings on authors from other Arab nations. I freely and immediately acknowledge that the results are only partially successful, but I will be rash enough to speculate that they reflect the state of publication about modern Arabic literature in general. Particularly with regard to Western research this work is a mirror of the scholarly tradition, although it may also contain implicit suggestions as to how to transform it.

Among the gaps in the current corpus of critical writing about modern Arabic literature, the most obvious and well known is that of writings by authors in the Maghreb, and particularly Algeria and Morocco. It may be the case that there is a great deal of Francophone cultural activity in the countries of the region, but many of them are now fostering a lively tradition of Arabic letters, the quality and originality of which can be partially gauged from the few examples available to Western readers in translation. With countries such as Syria and Iraq the search has been more fruitful, but has also been hampered by the unavailability or unsuitability of several studies, in the latter case because the materials were often excessively political and historical in their focus rather than critical. As is the case with the research problems connected with the Maghreb, the situation has improved considerably as a result of recent publications and, as far as possible, full use has been made of these sources in the pages that follow.

The critical writings that I have selected are themselves culled from a larger selection of such sources on each individual author. They are chosen to represent different critical attitudes and approaches and not because they represent my own views or those of anyone else. I have tried as far as possible to include contributions by the most famous critics of the modern period, from the most radical to the most traditional. Yet again, the vagaries of critical interest and publication opportunity have occasionally led to peculiar emphases and omissions in the sections that follow, but I believe that in the vast majority of cases the choices I have made and the critical opinions expressed are an accurate reflection of the impact and standing of the works discussed. A dagger at the end of a credit line indicates that I have translated the selection especially for this volume.

A comment needs to be made about information in this work concerning dates. I refer not only to the well-known fact that many works published in the Arab world do not contain a date (and sometimes, place) of publication (although I must add that the situation has improved greatly in recent years), but also to a situation illustrated best by the following anecdote. When I informed Adūnīs that I had just completed the article on him for the *Encyclopedia of World Literature in the 20th Century* (Frederick Ungar Publishing Co., revised edition, 4 vols., 1981–84) and that for that purpose needed to know his exact date of birth, he responded with a laugh that he had no idea when he was born to that degree of accuracy. With many of the authors here, not to mention their books and books about them, it has proved impossible to determine dates with any certainty. The provision of exact dates and publication details will, in many cases, have to await the availability of more biobibliographical research on modern Arabic literature (much of it now in progress), which as I have suggested above, is so needed and to which this present collection hopes to make a modest contribution.

This large work has involved the closest possible collaboration between compiler and publisher. I would like to thank the Ungar Publishing Company for affording me this opportunity; Leonard Klein, former senior editor at Ungar Publishing, who initiated this project, and Rita Stein, whose editorial eye has spotted many errors and infelicities, and who has seen the project through to its conclusion. Those errors that remain are, of course, in the traditional phrase of writers of prefaces, my own responsibility.

ROGER ALLEN

INTRODUCTION

The authors whose works are described and analyzed in this work on modern Arabic literature are heirs to a rich and varied heritage, the first manifestations of which go back to approximately the 6th century A.D., or, in Islamic terms, to the "period of ignorance" before the advent of Islam.[1] Precise details concerning dates of particular poets are difficult to ascertain and even, perhaps, inappropriate, in that the beginnings of Arabic literature—as they have come down to us—take the form of a vigorous oral poetic tradition; the poet could find patronage within his own tribe or at "courts" such as those of the Lakhmids in Iraq and the Ghassanids in Syria. The poems themselves were of varied formality and length and were of genres such as eulogy, lampoon, elegy, and boast.

With the advent of Islam this poetic tradition continued, although to the tribal and court bases were now added those of religion and even religious factionalism, including the poetry of the Shīʿī and Khārijī poets. With the rapid expansion of the domains conquered by the Muslims and the conversion of many non-Arab peoples to Islam, certain themes began to take on an identity of their own, for example, the *ghazal* (love poem), the *khamriyya* (wine poem), and the *tardiyya* (hunt poem). While the desert, its phenomena, and its way of life, continued to be reflected in the poetry (and indeed can still be sensed in certain lines of modern poetry), poets composing within the new urban and more cosmopolitan environment of the Islamic cities turned their attention to new subjects and modes of expression. A school of "moderns" (*muhdathūn*) began to emerge; these poets placed increasing emphasis on the use of tropes and poetic devices. This trend is particularly associated with the name of Abu Tammām (d. 846), but in the poetry of both his contemporaries and successors (including such famous names as al-Mutanabbī [d. 965] and al-Maʿarrī [d. 1057]) can be seen the continuing influence of *al-badīʿ*, as this new feature was called.

The emergence of an artistic prose tradition in Arabic literature is closely associated with the need felt by the secretarial class under the late Umayyad and early Abbasid caliphs to develop a system of "polite letters" for the purpose of conducting correspondence and of diverting the increasingly urbane entourage of the caliph and his governors. While writers such as Ibn Qutayba (d. 889) devoted much attention to the compilation of manuals of style and anthologies of useful and entertaining information, al-Jāhiz (d. 869), one of the towering figures in the history of Arabic literature, wrote an enormous number of books and treatises in a style that, with its clarity and conciseness, proved almost unique. Another writer who gave an early impetus to the development of Arabic prose was Ibn al-Muqaffaʿ (d. 757), who through translations from Persian and Indian sources, such as the famous *Kalīla wa-Dimna* (Kalīla and Dimna), helped in the formulation of a refined and elegant prose style. Later on, al-Hamadhānī (d. 1007) introduced a new genre, the *maqama*, into Arabic prose literature. In his hands the form was used to provide a lively insight into social life in Abbasid society through a series of somewhat picaresque episodes set in different parts of the Islamic domains. These were written in a style whose origins could be traced back to the very earliest period, namely, the rhyming prose (*sajʿ*) used by the soothsayers of pre-Islamic Arabia and also found in the earlier passages within the text of the Koran.

Alongside the literature itself there grew a tradition of philology and criticism. This was initially concerned with questions related to the text of the Koran—its verification and explication. The processes of lexicography and anthologizing that formed part of this initial stage were gradually joined by examination of particular tropes, of the principles of poetry, and of the works of individual poets or schools of poets. This activity reached its acme in the work of ʿAbd al-Qāhir al-Jurjānī (d. 1078) who—at this remarkably early date—put forward an analysis of the psychological impact of the poetic image.

Even within this great period in Arabic literature there were signs in the writings of certain critics of attempts to turn descriptive studies into prescriptive ones: al-Khalīl's analysis of the rhythms of Arabic verse into fifteen meters became the exclusive prosodic rule; the statement that poetry is "speech with rhyme and meter," suggested by some authors of works on poetics, became a slogan that poets were enjoined to follow well into the twentieth century. Authors of works on the "two arts" (poetry and prose) listed an ever-increasing number of devices, and the conceits of the *badīʿ* style and the rhyming prose of *sajʿ* led to an emphasis on form at the expense of content. This process was, of course, a gradual one, and some of the more original writers were able to avoid its worst excesses, but by the thirteenth century much of Arabic literature had degenerated into elaborate and sterile exercises in wordplay.

We noted above that among the first manifestations of Arabic literature was an oral poetic tradition. This oral dimension has always been of importance within the realm of Arabic literature, and this tradition continues right up to the present day, when some poets and storytellers may still improvise their works on public occasions. It is the storytelling aspect that seems to have provided the major "literary" product to have come down to us from the period between the fourteenth and eighteenth centuries. The famous *Thousand and One Nights* is merely one of a whole series of collections of popular tales that were put into their present form during this period. The effect of the "Arabian Nights" on the Western world is too well known to need emphasis; another such work, *The Epic of Antar*, was also translated (1819–20) into English (by Terrick Hamilton) and provides the subtitle to the Second Symphony of Rimsky-Korsakov. These collections have been largely ignored by scholars in both the Arab world and the West, but more recently, folklorists and anthropologists as well as literary scholars have begun to take an interest in them as contributions to Arabic literature. Among such scholars are some of the writers whose works are discussed in the pages that follow—Shawqī 'Abd al-Hakīm and Jabrā Ibrāhīm Jabrā, for example. The influence of these popular tales is also clearly visible in the fictional works of several other writers.

The period in which most of the authors covered in the present collection have been writing is regarded as the latter stage of a process known in Arabic as *al-nahda*, the renaissance. That process of "rebirth" implies, of course, that some previous tradition is at least moribund, if not dead. We have suggested above that, while that verdict may be appropriate for the more "formal" literary tradition, it certainly does not apply to that of popular literature. When we also acknowledge that relatively little work has been devoted to this "interim" period between the so-called classical and modern periods, it seems advisable to avoid the frequently used term "period of decadence" to describe the interim, unless the terms of reference connected with that designation are more rigorously defined.

The renaissance that the Arab world witnessed during the eighteenth century was the product of two major forces: the impact of the West and the search for and revival of the great heritage of the past. The impact of these two forces varied from one region and period to another, and in certain cases the entire process was radically changed or accelerated by political events.

While the entire Arabic-speaking region was nominally under Ottoman suzerainty, the degree of local control varied widely. In Syro-Lebanon, for example, the control was relatively direct and rigid; from a literary point of view, censorship was tight and, what was probably worse for creative writers, capricious. The Christian communities in this region had been in contact with Europe and especially Rome since the middle of the eighteenth century, and the seeds of Western thought were being introduced through missionary and educational activity. Iraq, on the other hand, lay farther to the east, and was thus rather removed from such contacts. The renaissance thus seems to have reached Iraq relatively later than other countries, although when it did, it encountered a vigorous poetic tradition, the maintenance of which may be at least partially responsible for the emergence of one of the greatest national poetic traditions in the twentieth century, beginning with the neoclassicists Jamīl al-Zahāwī and Ma'rūf al-Rusāfī and including Nāzik al-Malā'ika, Badr Shākir al-Sayyāb, 'Abd al-Wahhāb al-Bayyātī, and Buland al-Haydarī.

Egypt was jolted into an awareness of Western civilization by the French invasion under Napoleon (1798) and, from our point of view more importantly, by the corps of scholars who accompanied the expedition and participated in discussions with the *shaykhs* of al-Azhar, the mosque-university in Cairo. Napoleon's departure left a power vacuum into which stepped Muhammad 'Alī, a Turkish soldier from Albania, who took control of Egypt, founded a dynasty, and determined that Egypt should have an army like that of France. Missions were dispatched to Italy and then France to receive technical and military training. With the first such mission went Rifā'a al-Tahtāwī, a young *shaykh*, who learned French, observed French society, institutions, and morality, and on his return wrote *Takhlīs al-ibrīz fī talkhīs Bārīz* (1834; the heart's delight concerning the summary of Paris), summarizing his impressions. He was appointed head of a new Translation School, and he and his pupils soon turned their attention to literary works as well as the scientific manuals that were their major charge.

During the 1860s Egypt came under the sway of the Khedive Ismā'īl, a ruler with a passionate concern for modernization. This open atmosphere contrasted sharply with the situation in Syro-Lebanon, where a decade of civil strife during the 1850s led to a series of massacres in 1860. As a direct result of this unrest in Syro-Lebanon, numerous Christian families left their homeland and went to Egypt, Europe, and the Americas, a move that was to have a profound impact on the development of modern Arabic literature. Egypt now became the home of such famous figures in early modern Arabic literature as Jurjī Zaydān, Ya'qūb Sarrūf, and Salīm and Sulaymān al-Bustānī, to name just a few. Egypt gained considerably by this influx of literary talent—in the development of the drama and the novel and in turning an already nascent literary revival into the major focus of literary activity for several decades. One area where these new arrivals played a major role is that of the press, which gained in both impact and controversy during the latter part of the nineteenth century. The press has always played a crucial role in the dissemination of literature in Egypt; the vast majority of novels and short stories and not a few poems and plays continue to appear for the first time in newspapers and periodicals.

While these trends were taking shape in Egypt in the mid-nineteenth century, other writers, particularly in Syro-Lebanon, were concerning themselves with the rediscovery of the great classical heritage. Among the first of these was Nāsīf al-Yāzijī, who rediscovered for himself not only the poetry of al-Mutanabbī but also the *maqāmāt* (narrative in rhymed prose) of al-Harīrī

(1054–1122), the successor of al-Hamadhānī, which are reckoned among the *loci classici* of Arabic belles-lettres and of the Arabic language in general. Al-Yāzijī then produced his own *maqāmāt* under the title *Majmaʿ al-bahrayn* (1856; the meeting of the two seas). Others who concerned themselves with the question of language and style were Butrus al-Bustānī through his work on the translation of the Bible and a voluminous encyclopedia, and Ahmad Fāris al-Shidyāq, who, through his varied and energetic activities, managed to combine an interest in Europe and an intense hatred of the Christian clerical establishment in Syro-Lebanon with a somewhat recondite concern for the Arabic language. The efforts of these writers were to bear fruit later in the century when a number of neoclassicists in both prose and poetry began to produce works that made use of a precise and uncluttered style while at the same time reviving the forms and spirit of the classical period. Prominent among such figures in Egypt was Mahmūd Sāmī al-Bārūdī, who not only wrote poetry of his own but also compiled a collection of the poetry of the classical period.

Alongside this search into the past went another investigation, namely what Abu Lughod terms, in his book title, *The Arab Rediscovery of Europe* (Princeton, N.J., Princeton University Press, 1963). While Mārūn al-Naqqāsh went to Italy and learned firsthand about the European dramatic tradition, and al-Shidyāq toured all over Europe recording his impressions in *Al-Sāq ʿalā al-sāq fīma huwa al-faryāq* (1885; a punning title literally translated as: one leg over the other/the dove on the tree branch/concerning Fāris al-Shidyāq), ʿAlī Mubārak and Muhammad al-Muwaylihī sent their characters on trips to Europe. Al-Muwaylihī's depiction of the time spent by ʿĪsa ibn Hishām and the Pasha exploring Paris in 1899 in his famous *Hadīth ʿĪsa ibn Hishām* (the tale of ʿĪsa ibn Hishām) is less stimulating and coherent than the pioneering exposé of the ills of Egyptian society in the earlier chapters of that book (published in serial form between 1898 and 1902). This work, which shows the strong influence of the *maqāma* genre devised nine centuries earlier, is a good example of the kind of writing that was needed to bridge the gap between the classical tradition in its revived form and the emergence of some of the new genres imported from the West.

In the first two decades of the twentieth century, three young men from Egypt were sent to Europe, purportedly to study law: Ahmad Shawqī, the greatest of the neoclassical poets; Muhammad Husayn Haykal, journalist and *penseur*; and Tawfīq al-Hakīm, dramatist and novelist. All three were profoundly affected by their sojourn there and devoted themselves to literature and the composition of creative works that had a significant impact on the development of literary trends in Egypt.

At the extremes of these two tendencies—the advocacy and importation of Western ideas, and the revival of the language and spirit of classical Arabic literature—were fervent "modernists" and "classicists," and many of the

writers in the Arab world in the first half of this century had to face the oppro-
brium of one or other group. As early as 1898, al-Muwaylihī attacked Ahmad
Shawqī for adopting "Western" ideas in the introduction to his first collection
of poetry. Only twenty-three years later, al-Muwaylihī's pupil, ʿAbbās Mahmūd al-ʿAqqād, excoriated the same Shawqī for writing fragmented occasional verse in the traditional fashion. Jabrā Ibrāhīm Jabrā has pointed out that
developments in modern Arabic literature have occurred at such a pace that
"modernists" of earlier years often become "conservatives" in old age;[2] the
postures of both Tāhā Husayn and al-ʿAqqād in later life would seem to confirm this.

Having now sketched the background to the development of Arabic literature in the twentieth century, let us consider each genre—poetry, fiction,
and drama—in turn, and then discuss trends in literary criticism.

The earliest poet to be covered in the pages that follow is Khalīl Mutrān,
who was born in Lebanon and spent the latter part of his life in Egypt. Like al-
Bārūdī, he wrote a great deal of occasional verse in the neoclassical style governed by the traditional rules of metrification and rhyme. Of this neoclassical
"school" the most illustrious member was undoubtedly the Egyptian Ahmad
Shawqī, the "prince of poets," many of whose verses, with their superb
musicality and imagery, must be counted among the best Arabic poetry in the
traditional form. Other poets, such as the Egyptian Hāfiz Ibrāhīm and two Iraqis, Jamīl al-Zahāwī and Maʿrūf al-Rusāfī, wrote poetry that was extremely
popular because of its fiery advocacy of political causes or condemnation of
foreign domination over their countries. It should be pointed out that this neoclassical trend has continued well into the twentieth century and finds outstanding exponents in such poets as Muhammad Mahdī al-Jawāhirī of Iraq
and Badawī al-Jabal of Syria. Viewed within the strict terms of reference of
the classical tradition, much of the poetry of these writers is excellent and
continues to arouse the admiration of Arab readers and audiences. However,
it is in a real sense retrospective. What differentiates the work of Mutrān from
the neoclassicists is not so much his poetry, the bulk of which is very similar
to theirs, but rather the views he expressed *about* poetry in the introduction to
his collected works published in 1908. His advocacy of the unity of the poem
and of the need for the poet to express his own feelings in his poetry, coupled
with the subjective spark that can be detected in a few of his poems, is sufficient for him to be regarded as a bridge between neoclassicism and romanticism, or, to term him as some critics have done, a "pre-romantic."[3]

The real impetus to the development of full-blooded romanticism in Arabic poetry was provided by the poets who belong to the so-called *mahjar*
(émigré) school, those Arabs who had emigrated to the Americas and settled
in such cities as Brooklyn, Cincinnati, and Detroit as well as the major cities
of South America. Far removed from their native land and with only their col-

leagues to encourage them in their experiments in language, form, and mood, several poets proceeded to write works that introduced a significant new voice into Arabic poetry. In North America, the undisputed leader of the Bond of the Pen (the group to which the more famous poets belonged) was Jubrān Khalīl Jubrān (Kahlil Gibran), as famous for his works written in English as for those in Arabic. His leadership role was crucial in fostering the talents of some of the poets who gathered around him; his correspondence shows that he was not only in touch with his fellows in the United States but also with those like the Maʿlūf family in Brazil, one of whose members, Fawzī, is represented in the following pages. It is, one suspects, no accident that Mīkhāʾīl Nuʿayma, a prominent member of the North American group, wrote the bulk of his poetry while Jubrān was alive, and that following the latter's death in 1931 he returned to his native Lebanon.

The poetry and views of the *mahjar* school made their way back to the Middle East by normal channels but also through journals such as *Al-Sāʾih* (*The Traveler*), published by the Northern group. Poets in the Arab world itself were, of course, more directly under the influence of current critical attitudes, and the pace of experimentation was therefore slower.

In Egypt, a group of poets—ʿAbd al-Rahmān Shukrī, Ibrāhīm al-Māzinī, and ʿAbbās Mahmūd al-ʿAqqād—all strongly influenced by English romantic poetry, also advocated the need for the poet to express his own feelings rather than penning occasional verse. However, with the exception of Shukrī, they did not succeed in applying their ideas to poetry itself with any great success. The importance of al-Māzinī and al-ʿAqqād (within the realm of poetry) lies more in the effect of a work of criticism they published in 1921, *Al-Dīwān*. In it al-ʿAqqād (as noted above) launched a fierce attack on Shawqī for writing occasional poetry in which each line could be viewed as a separate entity. This group, therefore, while bringing occasional verse down from its pedestal somewhat, did not contribute in any significant way to the corpus of romantic poetry itself.

That task was taken up by a number of poets in various parts of the Arab world during the 1930s. Ahmad Zakī Abū Shādī, one of the most prolific Arab poets of all time, founded a society named after its journal, *Apollo*, in which a number of romantic poets published their verse and their views on poetry. ʿAlī Mahmūd Tāhā and the Tunisian Abū al-Qāsim al-Shābbī were among the contributors. It is somewhat ironic that al-ʿAqqād, the would-be advocate of change in *Al-Dīwān*, seems to have been more than partially responsible for the demise of *Apollo* after it dared to criticize one of his own collections of poetry.[4]

During the 1930s and 1940s romantic poetry reached a high point in the Arab world; in addition to the Apollo poets and al-Shābbī in Tunisia, mention should also be made of Ilyās Abū Shabaka and Salāh Labakī in Lebanon and Yūsuf Bashīr al-Tījānī in the Sudan. The figure of Saʿīd ʿAql presents us with a symbolist poet who strove to make a religion out of beauty and whose experiments in the use of symbols were to bear fruit among the poets of the following generation. However, ʿAql's extreme detachment from life and his views on the nature and purpose of poetry led him to be accused of "ivory-towerism," particularly in view of the discussions concerning the purpose of literature in general that occurred during the early 1950s.[5]

These discussions focused on the question of "commitment" and involved a number of the critics whose views are to be found in the present volume: Anwar al-Maʿaddāwī, Husayn Muruwwa, and Mutāʿ Safadī, for example. While the issue had been raised earlier by such writers as Amīn al-Rīḥānī, the partition of Palestine in 1948 and the ensuing events certainly gave added impetus to the message. As a result of this trauma and the developing political awareness of the Arab nations following World War II the poet was

> now expected to have a message, to maintain his artistic integrity and not to sell his wares to the highest bidder, or to serve a cause in which he did not believe, sincerity being now regarded as the prime consideration.[6]

Another change that has occurred since World War II is in the matter of form. As S. Moreh shows in great detail in his *Modern Arabic Poetry 1800–1970* (1976) experiments had been taking place for a number of years; one of the earliest pioneers in this was al-Zahāwī, mentioned above. With this fact in mind, it is rather sad that, when two poets, al-Malāʾika and al-Sayyāb, finally broke the fetters of meter and rhyme as laid down by the classical prosodists, an argument broke out as to which poet had done it first. As was probably inevitable, the "system" advocated by al-Malāʾika, based on the poetic foot rather than on the complete line, remained just that—a system. Few poets, having finally achieved a break from the constraints of preordained rules, were prepared to accept another alternative set of rules. Instead, modern poets have preferred to rely on their own sense of the musicality of words and the total association of form and content. Indeed, to Adūnīs, perhaps the most significant poet in the Arab world today, the very purpose of poetry is to innovate, to use words in unusual ways in the process of creating a new language.

Thus, among the poets writing today, there are those few who continue to compose in the traditional manner, adhering to the rules of meter and rhyme formalized in the eighth century. The overwhelming majority, however, write poems with lines of varying length, with or without rhyme and meter. Some poets—Adūnīs, Muhammad al-Māghūt, Jabrā Ibrāhīm Jabrā, and the late Tawfīq Sāyigh—write prose poems. With the exception of al-Sayyāb, whose position as a great poet seems confirmed by a wide spectrum of critical opinion, it is not yet possible to make a complete assessment of all the modern poets who have been included in this collection. They are intended, however, to be representative of the diversity of talent, choice of form, and sense of purpose that are part of the contemporary poetic tradition in the Arab world today.

The first novel in Arabic that attempted to portray contemporary Arab people within their own society in any sort of realistic fashion was *Zaynab* (Zaynab), written by Muhammad Husayn Haykal while he was in France in 1911, published anonymously in Egypt in 1913, and later acknowledged by its author. Previous to this book, works with any pretensions to the title of fiction had consisted of educational and/or reformist pieces such as the travel writings of 'Alī Mubārak and al-Muwaylihī, and the historical novels of Jurjī Zaydān, in which the author attempted to combine education and entertainment by setting numerous famous episodes from Islamic history against backgrounds with much "local color." Other writers combined an educational and reformist zeal with a tendency to sentimentality and morbid pessimism, as can be readily seen in the various essays of Mustafā Lutfī al-Manfalūtī and the early prose works of Jubrān, *'Arā' is al-murūj* (1906; *Nymphs of the Valley*, 1948), *Al-Arwāh al-mutamarrida* (1908; *Spirits Rebellious*, 1947), and *Al-Ajniha al-mukassara* (1912; *The Broken Wings*, 1957). The clear and simple style of the former and the fiery anger of the latter give these works some historical and social interest, but their reading public today is among the adolescent generation.

Zaynab also has a pervasively sentimental atmosphere—occasioned, no doubt, by Haykal's nostalgia for his home country at the time of writing. Furthermore, both the structure and the rendering of the psychological makeup of the characters evince significant flaws. Even so, the novel marks a major advance in Arabic fiction in that for the first time, it placed Egyptian characters —including women—into an Egyptian environment and situation.

The next two decades saw a number of writers setting themselves the task of producing works of fiction in which various facets of the novelistic technique would be refined and developed. The 1930s in particular was a decade in which a number of literary men tried their hand at this genre: al-Māzinī, al-Hakīm, al-'Aqqād, Mahmūd Taymūr, and Tāhā Husayn. This process has left us with a series of works that exhibit obvious faults: the excessive psychological analysis of al-'Aqqād's *Sāra* (1938; Sāra), for example, and the imbalance of the two sections of al-Hakīm's *'Awdat al-rūh* (1933; the return of the spirit). Each work, however, contributed toward the development of an awareness of the skills required to write a novel, and this experience was to be of great value to the next generation. In fact, two of the contemporary Arab world's more famous novelists, Najīb Mahfūz and Tawfīq 'Awwād, published their first novels in the final year of this same decade.

The short story witnessed a period of real growth during the 1920s. Examples had already been appearing in newspapers and periodicals, but it was during this decade that a group of young writers, including Mahmūd Taymūr and Yahyā Haqqī, began to produce collections of short stories that avoided the more anecdotal and moralistic approach of earlier writers and adopted instead the model of character portraits and sketches of situation reminiscent of European masters such as de Maupassant and the Russian story writers. This trend continued into the next decade when al-Māzinī added his own sardonic contributions to the genre and when, in 1944, Yahyā Haqqī contributed one of the masterpieces of modern Arabic short fiction with his novella *Qindīl Umm Hāshim* (the lamp of Umm Hāshim; tr. as *The Saint's Lamp*, 1973).

The preceding paragraphs have described in brief the development of fictional genres, with primary reference to Egypt. As noted earlier, many writers from other parts of the Arab world were resident in Egypt during these years, so that what emerged in the realm of fiction can be said to be the product of a multinational Arab effort. A further fact that should be borne in mind is that the dominance of French culture in both Syria and Tunisia and the relative isolation of Iraq led to the development of the fictional genres at a somewhat later stage in those countries than was the case in Egypt.[7] As will soon emerge from what follows, the complex cultural and political fabric of the Arab countries of the Middle East during recent decades has served to eradicate any such temporal differentiation.

The works of no single writer in the modern period have been the subject of so much comment in both book and article form as those of Najīb Mahfūz. The further progress of the novel genre, beginning in the 1940s, coincides with his career as a writer, and it is no exaggeration to say that his contribution to the development of the novel has been a crucial one. He began by writing three historical novels about ancient Egypt, thereby following the trend begun by Zaydān and continued by such writers as Muhammad Farīd Abū Hadīd and ʿAlī al-Jārim. Instead of following a plan to write several of these novels, however, he turned his attention to modern Egypt and produced during the 1940s a series of social-realist novels that apply well-developed novelistic techniques to the portrayal of Egyptian society during some of the most painful and difficult years of its recent history, immediately before the revolution of 1952.

During the early years of the Egyptian revolution, Mahfūz wrote no works of fiction. His monumental study of three generations of a single family, *Al-Thulāthiyya* (3 vols., 1956–57; the trilogy), was published to tremendous acclaim throughout the Arab world. However, these volumes described an era and a society that had passed. A number of other writers, prime among whom were Yūsuf Idrīs and ʿAbd al-Rahmān al-Sharqāwī, addressed the current problems of Egyptian society, and what they may initially have lacked in finesse, they made up for in the realism of their depictions of both local milieu and language. Idrīs concentrated his attentions on the short story, and in this he was joined by a number of other writers, of whom the most talented were

Yūsuf al-Shārūnī and Edward al-Kharrāt. Other writers of fiction included in this volume whose talents were beginning to emerge at this time include the Palestinians Ghassān Kanafānī and Jabrā Ibrāhīm Jabrā (whose novel *Sarākh fī layl tawīl* [cry on a long night] appeared in 1955), the Syrians ʿAbd al-Salām al-ʿUjaylī and Hannā Mīna, and the Iraqi Ghāʾib Tuʿma Farmān.

The last two decades have seen a tremendous increase in the number of excellent novels and short stories being published in the Arab world. Mahfūz and some other writers have tended to follow a pattern: In the 1960s until the 1967 war there was a concentration on the individual and the expression of ideas about revolutionary society and the world in general in a more taut and symbolic style than previously. After the 1967 débacle Mahfūz reverted to the short story in order to convey his message of civic responsibility. More recently, he has produced a further series of novels, which address themselves to issues of contemporary Egypt with varying degrees of success. Other writers of fiction also concern themselves with 1967 and its implications, although in a more direct fashion. Halīm Barakāt, the author of the prophetically named *Sittat ayyām* (1961; six days), wrote *ʿAwdat al-tāʾir ilā al-bahr* (1969; the return of the Flying Dutchman to the sea; tr. as *Days of Dust*, 1974), in which the events of those six days are recounted. Jabrā, Kanafānī, and Habībī all addressed themselves to an analysis of the Palestinian tragedy; their tone and technique may be different, but the resulting works are all poignant and artistically pleasing.

The theme of contact between East and West, seen in early works of al-Hakīm and Haqqī, was taken up again by Suhayl Idrīs in *Al-Hayy al-Lātīnī* (1953; the Latin Quarter) and presented in one of the finest Arabic novels to date, *Mawsim al-hijra ilā al-shimāl* (1966; *Season of Migration to the North*, 1969) by al-Tayyib Sālih. Haykal's depiction of the Egyptian countryside, taken up by al-Hakīm and, with strong political overtones, by al-Sharqāwī, now received a very sophisticated treatment in *Ayyām al-insān al-sabʿa* (1968; the seven days of man) by ʿAbd al-Hakīm Qāsim. A writer of both novels and short stories, Tawfīq Yūsuf ʿAwwād, seemed to be stimulated by this upsurge in creativity to write a number of works, including his most successful novel, *Tawāhīn Bayrūt* (1972; the mills of Beirut; tr. as *Death in Beirut*, 1976).

Prose literature, relegated during the classical period to second place (in bulk, at least) in comparison with poetry, has now achieved both maturity and popularity throughout the Arab world. Some genres may at times become more or less popular and available than others (often due to the lack of avenues of publication open to authors as a result of political factors), but the literary periodicals of the region continue to foster the production of fiction, while the pioneer figures have gradually withdrawn in favor of a younger, more experimental generation. Of the many authors of this generation who might have been included in this selection, we have chosen Jamāl al-Ghītānī,

Ismāʿīl Fahd Ismāʿīl, ʿAbd al-Rahmān Munīf, Zakariyaā Tāmir, and Fuʾād al-Tikirlī.

In 1963 Yūsuf Idrīs, the Egyptian author of short stories and novels who had also written some short plays, wrote a series of articles for the journal *Al-Kātib*. In them he maintained that the way in which Arabic drama had developed up until then fully justified the contention that it was derived almost entirely from European models. Within this framework many good plays had been written, but, while some of their themes and even settings may have been "local," they were nevertheless intrinsically "foreign" to the Arab experience. There was, he suggested, an indigenous dramatic tradition in Egypt, the roots of which went back many centuries. Evidence of the dramatic talents of the Egyptians could be found in a whole series of occasions when different kinds of "acting" took place, from café recitations to wedding banquets and the festivities that accompanied them. Idrīs mentions the theater-in-the-round form often involving audience comment that is known as the *sāmir* as one that could be used by modern dramatists to create an indigenous theater tradition. To prove his point, Idrīs published his highly successful and controversial play *Al-Farāfīr* (1964; *The Farfoors*, 1974) in the following year, when it was also staged to great critical acclaim.

Here again, the tension between the imported Western culture and the traditional genres of the local area is clearly evident. What is particularly significant is that the local tradition in this case is distinctly "popular" in nature, and thus, in accordance with the scholarly tendencies noted earlier, substantially neglected by literary scholars. Nor is it any accident that, of the writers who have followed the pattern suggested by Idrīs, several have a direct interest in and knowledge of the study of folklore: Shawqī ʿAbd al-Hakīm and Najīb Surūr, for example, both of whom have written plays with folkloric themes. It should also be pointed out, however, that Idrīs was writing in 1963 with the advantage of hindsight regarding the earlier dramatic tradition. In its infancy that tradition had particular problems to face, and the way in which developments occurred provided some solutions, albeit not perfect ones in some cases, to those problems.

Within this "Idrisian" framework, other writers have suggested that the dramatic medium was not unknown to the Arabs before the encounter between the Middle East and the West during the early stage of the Arabic renaissance.[8] The extent to which one is prepared to lend credence to these ideas and others—for example, the Shiʿite *taʿzīya* (a kind of Islamic "passion play") presentations and the *karagöz* (shadow play) tradition[9]—will depend on one's definitions of drama and the dramatic. Suffice it to say that modern trends in drama would suggest that a narrower definition based on dramatic subgenres will almost certainly be too restrictive for many dramatists and critics. At any rate, whatever dramatic traditions or awareness did exist in the

Arab world came into contact with the West during the first part of the nineteenth century.

Among the first attempts to stage dramatic pieces were those of Mārūn al-Naqqāsh, who used his own house in Beirut as a theater for presentations of *Al-Bakhīl* (the miser), an adaptation of Molière, and of *Abū al-Hasan*, in 1847 and 1849 respectively.[10] As with other genres, much of this initial creativity was transferred to Egypt following the 1860s, and in the latter half of the century theater troupes with such prominent Syrian names as Qabbānī and Abyad, not to mention the continuing energetic efforts of the Naqqāsh family, were added to the indigenous Egyptian theatrical tradition.

That tradition may perhaps be divided into two strands. The first can be termed the popular theater. Building on the previous tradition of the shadow puppet plays and making full use of the societal and political circumstances of the 1870s, Yaʿqūb Sanūʿ wrote a number of extremely popular plays in which he criticized the tastes and foibles of the aristocracy and particularly the Khedive (or "Headman of the Quarter," as he was known in the plays). There was also a tradition of what can only be called vaudeville, judging from contemporary accounts of which perhaps the most memorable is that of Muhammad al-Muwaylihī in the above-mentioned *Hadīth ʿĪsā ibn Hishām*; not only the standards of composition and performance but also the very familial and societal situations depicted caused al-Muwaylihī to launch into a tirade against the theater of his time on moral grounds.[11] In the works of Najīb al-Rīhānī this tradition achieved a higher level of artistry and a wider popularity, and it has continued to attract audiences right up to the present day although in recent years critics have pointed out with some justification the disparity in dramatic merit between this strand of the theatrical tradition and the more literary one.

Following the initiatives of al-Naqqāsh, numerous other writers turned their attention to the fostering of a more intellectual dramatic tradition. Initially there were numerous translations of the classics of European drama: Corneille, Racine, Molière, and Shakespeare (*Othello* being translated by Khalīl Mutrān).[12] Other works were "adapted" to the Arab milieu, and then in the early decades of this century original works based on themes both Middle Eastern and Western began to appear. An early pioneer in this was Muhammad Taymūr (the brother of Mahmūd Taymūr, who was to become famous as a writer of short stories), who composed a series of plays but died at a very early age. The great poet Ahmad Shawqī wrote the first version of a historical verse play, *ʿAlī Bey*, as early as 1894, and during the 1920s he added to his oeuvre a series of verse plays that not only gave further illustration of his poetic gifts (many extracts from them have remained popular as songs), but also provided the dramatic medium with works that discussed topics of historical significance.

The dominant figure in the development of Arabic drama until the last decade has been Tawfīq al-Hakīm, who has written over sixty plays.[13] After writing a few short plays in the 1920s, and following a visit to France, al-Hakīm proceeded to write a number of lengthy works in which stories and situations culled from a variety of sources (the Koran, *The Thousand and One Nights*, and Greek myths, for example) were used as the base for discussions of abstract philosophical ideas. These plays have always proved almost impossible to stage because of their static nature, but they have undoubtedly served to stimulate the use of the theater for the discussion of serious issues. In two collections of shorter plays al-Hakīm addressed himself to a number of societal problems, while in *Yā tāliʿ al-shajara* (1962; *The Tree Climber*, 1966) he made an important contribution to absurdist drama in Arabic.

In recent decades, the drama has become one of the principal avenues for the propagation of political and social ideas. A number of dramas and dramatists have aroused tremendous public interest and controversy; in some cases, they have also provoked the interest of the cultural apparatus of the government, not always to their advantage. Modern Arabic drama is indeed a powerful weapon, and it often finds itself blunted in certain countries for that very reason.[14]

In contemporary Arabic drama the discussion still goes on about the use of the colloquial as a means of expression in a work of literature. With regard to performance, productions today range from the traditional pattern, with the stage in front and the audience facing it, to the theater in the round advocated by Idrīs and his successors. Some writers, such as Muhammad al-Māghūt and Saʿdallāh Wannūs, write plays that involve actors supposedly presenting a play to an "audience" consisting of other actors. Wannūs in particular seems eager to break down the barriers between the stage and the theater audience; in *Haflat samar min ajl al-khāmis min Hazīrān* (1968; an evening's entertainment for the fifth of June) he has produced a work that gradually involves more and more members of the audience until the whole assembly is finally placed "under arrest" for being present at the play itself. All these facets of the contemporary theater serve to illustrate its creativity and dynamism in the Arab world today.

When we realize that many of the authors whose writings are analyzed in this volume have also been critics (and, in some cases, theoreticians) of literature, it is not surprising that the origins and development of a tradition of criticism during the modern period follow much the same lines as is the case in the genres discussed above. The same mostly healthy tension between the revival of the "classical" and the influence of the West was present from the outset, and the same social and historical circumstances have had their impact on the location and situation within which the critics write. This is again most noticeable with reference to those Syrians who emigrated to Egypt and the Americas.

The most useful survey of this subject, that of Muhammad Yūsuf Najm, begins by regretting the fact that the available sources apparently concentrate overwhelmingly on two areas, Lebanon and Egypt.[15] Later in the same article he points out that poetry has received much the largest share of *critical* attention and that, bearing in mind the relatively recent development of other genres in modern Arabic literature, this imbalance will, no doubt, change over the course of time. To fill in many of the gaps implied by this last statement requires not only culling critical materials from the literary periodicals and books of the Arab region (which has been done as far as possible for the present work), but, in certain genres and geographical regions, resorting to the daily press, in which works of literature may be reviewed for the first and only time. As Najm notes, that task must await the availability of more and better reference resources.

One of the initial tasks of the literary critic in the nineteenth century was to identify the criteria by which literature had been judged in the times of great Arab writers of the past and then demonstrate how recent writings had failed to meet those criteria. Al-Shidyāq and Butrus al-Bustānī both concerned themselves with this question, and in Egypt, Husayn al-Marsafī wrote his famous work, *Al-Wasīla al-adabiyya* (2 vols., 1872, 1875; the literary mode), which from one point of view is merely a summary of the views of the classical critics but which also cites, among others, the poetry of his contemporary, Mahmūd Sāmī al-Bārūdī, in order to show the ways in which poetry could be restored to its former glory. This essentially neoclassical approach was carried on and indeed applied by Muhammad al-Muwaylihī with both vigor and not a little contumely to the poetry of Ahmad Shawqī.[16]

The first major change in perception came, as we have suggested above, in Khalīl Mutrān's introduction to his *Dīwān*, published in 1908. Many of his aspirations were put into practice with great success by the Arab poets in America, and representatives of both that school and the Dīwān school working in Egypt made significant contributions to the development of a critical tradition. The latter group—Shukrī, al-ʿAqqād, and al-Māzinī—applied the principles of European and especially English criticism to the composition of Arabic poetry. *Al-Dīwān*, the critical work published by al-ʿAqqād and al-Māzinī in 1921, laid particular emphasis on the need for organic unity in the poem and for the creative artist to express his own feelings and emotions rather than to write occasional verse. Another great Arab writer, Mīkhā'īl Nuʿayma, set out his own ideas on poetic criticism in his equally iconoclastic work, *Al-Ghirbāl* (1923; the sieve), and then proceeded to apply them to several modern works as well as to a consideration of *Al-Dīwān* itself.

These same decades witness the emergence of one of the greatest figures in modern Arabic literature, Tāhā Husayn.[17] His study of the authenticity of the poetry of the very earliest period, *Fī al-shiʿr al-jāhilī* (on pre-Islamic poetry), first published in 1925, caused an enormous furor because it suggested, among other things, that the bulk of that poetry was actually the work of later poets. The book was withdrawn, but published in a new and expanded format in the following year. While recent research into oral literature has tended to suggest that the question of "authenticity" may not be relevant to this particular case, that does not diminish in any way the importance of this work in the history of modern Arabic criticism. In this and many other books Tāhā Husayn applied his considerable knowledge of Western literatures and criticism to the writings of numerous figures from the older tradition of Arabic literature and took a keen and avuncular interest in literary activity throughout the Arab world. The speed at which developments have taken place throughout the modern period have often served to turn champions of change in their earlier careers—like al-ʿAqqād and Tāhā Husayn—into rather conservative figures in later life. Within the broader spectrum of the development of modern Arabic criticism, however, their later disdain for many changes that occurred after World War II does not diminish the value of their contribution to the critical tradition.

Another prominent critic whose work will be found in the pages that follow is Mārūn ʿAbbūd, who in numerous books of his articles culled from newspapers and journals applied himself to the writings of his contemporaries. One writer who emerges from his criticism in a less than favorable light is none other than al-ʿAqqād *qua* poet. The latter's attempts at composing poetry about everyday subjects during the 1930s are treated with considerable scorn. During a long and productive career ʿAbbūd, like Tāhā Husayn, kept a careful eye on developments in modern Arabic literature and was not slow to apportion credit and blame as it was due.[18]

A pupil of Tāhā Husayn, Muhammad Mandūr, continued his teacher's move away from the view of criticism as something akin to a science and toward a more artistic interpretation.[19] In spite of a life marked by a considerable amount of misfortune, Mandūr was able to produce a series of excellent works that range from his doctoral thesis on classical criticism, later published as *Al-Naqd al-manhajī ʿinda al-ʿArab* (1948; methodical criticism among the Arabs) to studies of modern poetry and drama, examples of which are included in the present volume. In one of his most significant books, a collection of articles published as *Fī al-mīzān al-jadīd* (1944; weighed in the new balance), Mandūr gives courageous support to the poetry of Mīkhāʾīl Nuʿayma and Nasīb ʿArīda ("poetry in a whisper," as he terms it) in preference to the more prevalent oratorical style. After several years during which he was closely involved in Egyptian politics, Mandūr devoted himself in his later years to a number of studies of individual writers, including Khalīl Mutrān, Shawqī, and al-Māzinī. One cannot avoid the impression that, whatever the gain may have been to Egyptian politics during his middle years, there was certainly a loss to modern Arabic criticism.[20]

As has been noted above, the later 1940s saw the flowering of a new poetic tradition that rejected the canons of versification handed down for centuries. Alongside it there appeared an increasingly vigorous and vocal school of writers who advocated the need for social realism in literature under the rallying cry of commitment (*iltizām*). Among their number are many of the most important critics in the Arab world today. Needless to say, this trend can be seen in the works of certain earlier writers; in particular, the Egyptian Copt, Salāma Mūsā, both through his own work and his encouragement of younger writers (including Najīb Maḥfūz and Lewis 'Awad) provided a framework on which others could build.[21] Another writer, 'Umar al-Fākhūrī, had produced several works including *Al-Adīb fī al-sūq* (1944; the writer in the marketplace), one of whose chapters is concerned with the "ivory-tower" attitude of some of his contemporaries.[22]

In 1951 Mufīd al-Shūbashī, a disciple of Salāma Mūsā, published an article in the periodical *Al-Thaqāfa* in which he condemned the romantic notion of literature and advocated a more committed, social-realist approach. This concept of commitment has remained the predominant force in criticism since the early 1950s, and within the present work it is echoed in the writings of, among others, Maḥmūd Amīn al-'Ālim, Anwar al-Ma'addāwī, Mutā' Safadī, and Husayn Muruwwa.[23] This is not to say that all modern critics are committed to the same theories or goals, but rather that today it is a rare writer indeed who is not fully aware of his place and function within the society of which he is a part. To Adūnīs, for example, commitment is to "freedom, creativity, and change" (the motto of his periodical *Mawāqif*). The goal of poetry, in his view, is innovation (*tajdīd*), to use words in new and unfamiliar ways.[24] Adūnīs is, in fact, a fine example of the contemporary writer in the Arab world who applies his theories to every aspect of his work, as poet, editor, and anthologizer.

These few examples may help to illustrate the fact that in recent years creative writing and criticism have begun to operate on comparable levels of sophistication in the hands of some contemporary writers. Salmā al-Jayyūsī points out that this has not always been the case; she suggests that in the 1930s practice lagged behind theory in poetry and that in recent years the reverse may be the case.[25] Of all the genres where this disparity seems to show itself the most in recent years, probably none has posed such problems as the drama. We have suggested above that, bearing in mind the social and political impact that the theater may have, it is not surprising that it is often a battleground for conflicting forces within the cultural establishment in the various countries of the Middle East. However, a particular feature of recent discussions, at least in Egypt, has been the general lack of good theater criticism and the effect this lack has had on the development of the genre.[26]

Recent decades have seen an expansion in the study of modern Arabic literature in the West. Much work has been done in the fields of translation and literary history. The amount of material available for study, however, remains extremely small when compared with that of other literatures that are more commonly studied in Western educational institutions. Within this sparse situation, the amount of critical and theoretical work available is yet smaller, a fact amply borne out in the pages that follow. Scholars in both the Arab world and the West have begun to apply the techniques of modern literary theory to Arabic literature of all periods, and that will surely contribute to a greater understanding of the value of this vast and rich heritage.

NOTES

1. No attempt is made here to present a history of Arabic literature, even in summary form. The aim is rather to highlight certain significant trends, particularly those that are of interest in the light of developments in modern Arabic literature. To those who wish to know more about the history and biobibliography of Arabic literature the following works are recommended: Roger Allen, "Arabic Literature," in *The Study of the Middle East: Research in the Humanities and Social Sciences*, ed. Leonard Binder (New York: John Wiley, 1976), 399–453; Roger Allen, "Arabic Literature: Then," *Nimrod*, 24, 2 (Spring–Summer, 1981), 8–21; A. F. L. Beeston, et al., eds., *The Cambridge History of Arabic Literature, Vol. I: Arabic Literature to the End of the Umayyad Period* (Cambridge, England: Cambridge University Press, 1983); H. A. R. Gibb, *Arabic Literature* (Oxford: Clarendon Press, 1963); I. Goldziher, *A Short History of Classical Arabic Literature* (Hildesheim, West Germany: Georg Olms Verlagsbuchhandlung, 1966); R. A. Nicholson, *A Literary History of the Arabs* (Cambridge, England: Cambridge University Press, 1962).

2. Jabrā, Jabrā Ibrāhīm, "Modern Arabic Literature and the West," *Journal of Arabic Literature*, 2 (1971), 76–91.

3. See Mustafa Badawi, *A Critical Introduction to Modern Arabic Poetry* (Cambridge, England: Cambridge University Press, 1972), 68–114.

4. Salmā al-Jayyūsī, *Trends and Movements in Modern Arabic Poetry* (Leiden: E. J. Brill, 1977), 386–87.

5. Badāwi, *Critical Introduction*, 207.

6. Badawi, Introduction to *An Anthology of Modern Arabic Verse* (Oxford: Oxford University Press, 1970), ix.

7. See Hilary Kilpatrick, "The Arabic Novel—a Single Tradition?" *Journal of Arabic Literature*, 5 (1974), 98–99; and Roger Allen, *The Arabic Novel: An Historical and Critical Introduction* (Syracuse, N.Y.: Syracuse University Press, 1982), 41–45.

8. See Farouk Abdel Wahab, ed., *Modern Egyptian Drama* (Minneapolis: Bibliotheca Islamica, 1974), 9–18; and ʿAli al-Raʿi, "Some Aspects of Modern Arabic Drama," in *Studies in Modern Arabic Literature*, ed. R. C. Ostle (Warminster, England: Aris & Phillips, 1975), 172–73.

9. See Talat S. Halman, ed., *Modern Turkish Drama* (Minneapolis and Chicago: Bibliotheca Islamica, 1976), 19–28.

10. See Matti Moosa, "Naqqāsh and the Rise of the Native Arab Theatre in Syria," *Journal of Arabic Literature*, 3 (1972), 106–17.

11. See Muhammad al-Muwaylihī, *Hadīth 'Īsā ibn Hishām* (Cairo: Dār al-Qaw-miyya, 1964), 273–83, and the English translation of the passage in Muhammad al-Muwaylihī, *Hadīth 'Īsā ibn Hishām: Al-Muwaylihī's Study of Egypt during the British Occupation*, ed. and trans. Roger Allen (Albany: State University of New York Press, 1974), 826–36.

12. See Muhammad Yūsuf Najm, *Al-Masrahiyya fī al-adab al-'Arabī al-hadīth 1847–1914* (Beirut: Dār al-Thaqāfa, 1967), 245–49.

13. See Hamādī ben Halīma, *Les principaux thèmes du théâtre arabe contemporaine (de 1914 à 1960)* (Tunis: L'Université de Tunis, 1969).

14. See Lewis Awad's list of banned plays in his contribution, "Problems of the Egyptian Theatre," in *Studies in Modern Arabic Literature*, ed. R. C. Ostle, 192; also Roger Allen, "Egyptian Drama after the Revolution," *Edebiyat*, 4, 1 (1979), 97–134.

15. Muhammad Yūsuf Najm, "Al-Naqd al-adabī," in *Al-Adab al-'Arabī fī āthār al-dārisīn*, ed. Al-'Alī et al. (Beirut: Dar al-'Ilm li-al-Malāyīn, 1961), 313.

16. Roger Allen, "Poetry and Poetic Criticism at the Turn of the Century," in *Studies in Modern Arabic Literature*, ed. R. C. Ostle 1–17.

17. See David Semah, *Four Egyptian Literary Critics* (Leiden: E. J. Brill, 1973), 107–50.

18. al-Jayyūsī, *Trends and Movements*, 517–22.

19. Semah, *Four Egyptian Literary Critics*, 151–205.

20. See Najm in *Al-Adab al-'Arabī fī āthār al-dārisīn*, 357.

21. See Salāma Mūsā, *The Education of Salāma Mūsā*, trans. L. O. Schuman (Leiden: E. J. Brill, 1961).

22. See Najm in *Al-Adab al-'Arabī fī āthār al-dārisīn*, 379–80; and Jayyusi, *Trends and Movements*, 574.

23. See Badawi, *Critical Introduction*, 205–9.

24. See Issa J. Boullata, "Adonis: Revolt in Modern Arabic Poetics," *Edebiyat*, 2, 1 (1977), 1–13.

25. al-Jayyūsī, *Trends and Movements*, 370, 388.

26. Roger Allen, "Egyptian Drama and Fiction in the 1970s," *Edebiyat*, 1, 2 (1976), 228–30.

AUTHORS INCLUDED

'Abd al-Hakim, Shawqī
'Abd al-Sabūr, Salāh
Abū Mādī, Īliyyā
Abū Shabaka, Ilyās
Abū Shādī, Ahmad Zakī
Adūnīs
    (pseud. of 'Alī Ahmad Sa'īd)
al-'Ānī, Yūsuf
'Aql, Sa'īd
al-'Aqqād, 'Abbās Mahmūd
'Arīda, Nasīb
'Āshūr, Nu'mān
'Awwād, Tawfīq Yūsuf
Ayyūb, Dhū al-Nūn
Ba'albakkī, Laylā
Barakāt, Halīm
al-Bayyātī, 'Abd al-Wahhāb
Darwīsh, Mahmūd
Diyāb, Mahmūd
Faraj, Alfred
Farmān, Ghā'ib Tu'ma
al-Ghītānī, Jamāl
Habībī, Emīle
al-Hājj, Unsī
al-Hakīm, Tawfīq
Haqqī, Yahyā
Hāwī, Khalīl
al-Haydarī, Buland
Haykal, Muhammad Husayn
Hijāzī, 'Abd al-Mu'tī
Husayn, Tāhā

Idrīs, Yūsuf
Ismā'īl, Ismā'īl Fahd
Jabrā, Jabrā Ibrāhīm
Jubrān, Jubrān Khalīl
    (Kahlil Gibran)
Kanafānī, Ghassān
al-Khāl, Yūsuf
al-Kharrāt, Edward
Labakī, Salah
al-Māghūt, Muhammad
Mahfūz, Najīb
al-Malā'ika, Nāzik
al-Ma'lūf, Fawzī
al-Mas'adī, Mahmūd
al-Māzinī, Ibrāhīm
Mīna, Hannā
Munīf, 'Abd al-Rahmān
Mutrān, Khalīl
Nājī, Ibrāhīm
Nu'ayma, Mīkhā'īl
Qabbānī, Nizār
Qāsim, 'Abd al-Hakīm
al-Qāsim, Samīh
al-Rīhānī, Amīn
al-Rīhānī, Najīb
al-Rubay'ī, 'Abd al-Rahmān Majīd
Sālih, al-Tayyib
al-Sammān, Ghāda
Sāyigh, Tawfīq
al-Sayyāb, Badr Shākir
al-Shabbī, Abū al-Qāsim

al-Sharqāwī, ʿAbd al-Rahmān

al-Shārūnī, Yūsuf

Shukrī, ʿAbd al-Rahman

Surūr, Najīb

Tāhā, ʿAlī Mahmūd

Tāmir, Zakariyyā

Taymūr, Mahmūd

al-Tikirlī, Fuʾād

Tūqān, Fadwā

al-ʿUjaylī, ʿAbd al-Salām

Wahba, Saʿd al-dīn

Wannūs, Saʿdallāh

Wattār, al-Tāhir

PERIODICALS USED

Al-Ādāb (Beirut)
Al-Adīb (Beirut)
Afkār (Amman)
ʿĀlam al-fikr (Kuwait)
Arab World (New York)
Al-ʿArabiyya (Columbus, Ohio)
Azure (London)
Comparative Literature Studies (Urbana, Ill.)
Daedalus (Cambridge, Mass.)
Edebiyat (Philadelphia)
Hiwār (Beirut)
International Journal of Middle East Studies (New York)
Journal of the American Oriental Society (New Haven, Conn.)
Journal of the American Research Center in Egypt (New York)
Journal of Arabic Literature (Leiden, The Netherlands)
Al-Kātib (Cairo)
Al-Majalla (Cairo)
Al-Maʿrifa (Damascus)
Al-Masrah (Cairo)
Mawāqif (Beirut)
Mid East (Washington, D.C.)
Middle East Journal (Washington, D.C.)
Mundus Artium (Dallas)
The Muslim World (Hartford, Conn.)
Shiʿr (Beirut)
Al-Thaqāfa (Cairo)
World Literature Today (Norman, Okla.)
Al-Yasār al-ʿArabī (Paris)

ʿABD AL-HAKĪM, SHAWQĪ (?-   )

EGYPT

[In the play *Hasan and Naʿīma*] the curtain rises on an author, play producer, scenery designer, and composer. With them are two masked producers playing the Chorus, a theater critic, and spectator posing as an aware theatergoer. Next to a cup of coffee and a pack of cigarettes, each one has a copy of Shawqī ʿAbd al-Hakīm's play as he wrote it, rather than the way it was presented on stage. . . .

AUTHOR: I chose a single moment from the folktale for the characters to act out. Twenty years have passed since Naʿīma's parents killed Hasan in front of her very eyes. As the curtain goes up, they are in the midst of a crisis of conscience, particularly since Naʿīma is still reminding them of their foul deed. The parents try to shut her up by accusing her of taking part in it with them. They continue to justify the crime as a legitimate defense of their own social situation which had been jolted by Naʿīma's rushing off with Hasan. Naʿīma takes us back through flashback. . . .

CRITIC (*interrupting*): This part takes up more than fifteen pages.

AWARE THEATERGOER (*interrupting*): All this repetition goes back to . . . (*Silence*) I don't deny that, as happens in poetry, repetition can have a poetic effect on the psyche of the listener. However, I notice that Shawqī repeats things too much, so much so that the audience gets bored. Repetition makes everything seem sluggish and dull. . . .

CRITIC (*to the author*): You keep on taking us to a fateful world steeped in resignation and negativism. (*Speaking oratorically*) We must reject such things; we are no longer in a Greek society.

AWARE THEATERGOER: Personally, I don't regard myself as a supervisor of artists. Let's allow all the flowers to open and all schools of thought to debate. The genuine and authentic ones will flourish. (*Silence*) Don't forget that in the end Naʿīma refuses to submit to fate.

AUTHOR (*finishing his presentation of the play*): I would like to complete my presentation once Naʿīma has finished with her memories of her times with Hasan. A beggar enters when Naʿīma opens the big door with the bolt; she is her cousin. She tries to make Naʿīma confess. Naʿīma is undergoing a fierce internal struggle between her duty toward her butchered lover on the one hand and her blood relationship with her parents on the other. Once again Hasan appears. Na'īma accuses him and lays at least part of the blame on him. Even though he knew full well what would happen to him, he had agreed to go with her father to his home town so that he could be murdered there. Hasan stops her accusing her parents in his presence (*Everyone looks at his script*). Na'īma comes back to reality and finds the beggar still urging her to confess and testify against her parents. In this, she is helped by three neighbors who have slunk in when Na'īma opened the door. Na'īma is still being pulled this way and that. Eventually she decides to stand beside her parents. The beggar and the other women leave. The door is again locked. Eventually Na'īma opens the box to get out her dead lover's clothes. Her parents cannot stand it and go out to face the outside world and its justice. Some women come in and try to console Na'īma. They advise her to submit to her fate, but she refuses and decides to divert herself of her skin and go out into the outside world. . . .

AWARE THEATERGOER: The subject of the play is the inward-looking tendency of the tripartite family and the fear it has of the outside world. So it locks itself up inside with a big bolt and lives in pseudo-isolation, socially and psychologically cloistered.

CRITIC: There's something strange about the chorus. (He tries to think about it) A group of women and a single man; there has to be a major dramatic significance behind all that. (He thinks profoundly and then gives his opinion with a display of erudition) I regard the meaning as being. . . .

Ra'fat al-Duwayrī. *Al-Majalla*. July, 1965, pp. 87-89†

Shawqī 'Abd al-Hakīm is a writer fond of the countryside. Some years ago, he wrote a book called *Peasant Literature*, and then soon afterward, he adopted fictional forms to express his concerns about the countryside. The Pocket Theater presented two of his plays, *Shafīqa and Mitwallī* and *The Hider*, which take both their subject matter and spirit from the Egyptian countryside. Our author has not changed his tack in the novel *The Sorrows of Noah*; indeed we can easily identify in this novel the same theme as is found in *The Hider*: the camel-driver betrayed by his camel so that he is led to abandon a wife and child. If the members of the triad of father, mother, and son seem closer to the visions, symbols, and abstractions of the play, they have become more concrete in this novel and have been assigned specific names: 'Abd al-'Alīm for the father, Ghanīma for the mother, and 'Īd for the son.

With Shawqī 'Abd al-Hakīm the dramatic and novelistic styles are very close. The dramatic style relies more on monologue than on dialogue. Each character talks to himself. Even so, each character's monologue is not divorced from that of the others; as a group they form a single, new monologue, just as each musician in an orchestra plays his own instrument in the process of performing a piece of music with all the other musicians. That is because the characters are simply aspects of one and the same character: sometimes they represent misgivings and conscience, an epitome of deeply embedded traditions . . . .

In *The Sorrows of Noah* the monologue is a basic element in the narrative style. It is in the colloquial language and consists of short sentences, repeated phrases, a revealing poetic stamp which manages to exude a sense of both sorrow and bitterness. . . .

The story of the deceitful camel is but an ancillary tale in this narrative work. That much is obvious as the characters become more independent, subjective, clear and concrete than they are in the two plays.

Yūsuf al-Shārūnī. *Dirāsāt fī al-riwāya wa-al-qissa al-qasīra* (Cairo, Al-Maktaba al-Anglo-Misriyya, 1967), pp. 80–81, 83†

In his novel *The Blood of Yaʿqūb's Son* Shawqī ʿAbd al-Hakīm takes us into the authentic life of the provincial artist, from the expressive colloquial language to the kind of real life that romantic works generally avoid describing; with their lofty style they tend to be beset by the disease of contentment with everything and are written to entertain and divert rather than to deal with reality and offer a genuine service to life. Not everything in village life is good and noble . . . . Real characters are alive and fraught with contradictions, involving both good and bad to the ultimate degree.

The stream of consciousness pours forth in this work and gives us a stunning portrait of urban life in the provinces. There are masterfully artistic shifts from past to present and from one character to another, all in a language that is both simple and poetic in its lilt. The sentences are short and sharp, and the words know what they want to say and do so concisely . . . . The one situation in the novel is replete with a whole variety of scenes and emotions; life does not proceed in a straight line. Man is simply a pile of past and present and visions of the future. . . . The novel is full of all kinds of characters who are really fresh, from the village artist and the partygoer to the student who is running away after killing his sister to live with dancing girls, the local journalist with his conflicting emotions—a longing for the countryside and his bourgeois distaste for provincial customs and squalor . . . all these are genuine pictures and real aspects of provincial life, presented to us with a critical realism. . . .

If Shawqī ʿAbd al-Hakīm's novel seems to be well written and to have good technique, that is because he is a writer who has taken the trouble to learn his craft well quite apart from his literary articles. He has written about Egyptian peasant literature and has produced a collection of short stories, some short plays and another novel, *The Sorrows of Noah*. . . .

The narrative structure, which is based on stream of consciousness, rem-

iniscences, and flashbacks, moves us around rapidly. In each chapter the author develops another character and then leaves us tied to that person at the
end of the chapter as he shifts to yet another; this is an old and useful device,
one our author uses extremely well, since he keeps making us want to learn
more about the characters in his novel. When Shawqī 'Abd al-Hakīm writes
"an Egyptian novel" below the title, he really intends it to be an Egyptian
novel, flesh and blood. The narrative and the dialogue are etched from Egyptian colloquial language, chosen carefully and intelligently. The majority of
the events in the story revolve around the dancing girls and prostitutes' house;
or rather the characters branch out from there into a world that is depicted with
subtlety, to return and converge in the house once again. . . .

These, then, are the provinces as Shawqī 'Abd al-Hakīm portrays them
in *The Blood of Ya'qūb's Son*, a world in its own right with its own notions,
arts, and dramatic soirees, a countryside full of crime, loss, and the conflict of
generations.

Ahmad Muhammad 'Atiyya. Al-Ādāb. Nov., 1969,
pp. 60–61†

In *King Ma'rūf's Birthday* the performance begins with the entry of three old
women who, one supposes, are to serve as a chorus to present the characters
and events, summarizing, making judgments, and revealing the moral and
philosophical purposes of the play, that being our general expectation of the
role of choruses in drama. However, to our surprise these three women proceed to talk about things that have no bearing on the basic theme of the play.
They use a language that is neither Bedouin nor popular, nor even colloquial.
There then follows a scene backstage behind a transparent curtain involving a
funeral, something that has no relevance at all to the basic story, and that is
followed by a *mawwāl* (popular song). Then there is a caricature of the popular hero Abū Zayd al-Hilālī, the only relevance of which is that it too belongs
to the realm of folktales. We see all this before the author, Shawqī 'Abd al-
Hakīm, brings us the figure of the Queen in a scene portraying a *zār* ritual that
is also folkloric, just as the *zār* is a folk ritual. It takes us no further forward
with regard to the Queen, however; it too merely provides a folkloric atmosphere. . . .

Half an hour passes before the appearance of King Ma'rūf himself. In a
soliloquy he reveals all his concerns and his subtle and refined feelings for
humanity. The female singer then picks up the situation with another *mawwāl*. . . .

In this way, elements of popular art are interwoven into the action—stories, *mawwāls*, eulogies, even monologues—and all the while King Ma'rūf is
lost in the crowd. He is a hero who is wandering around in a void alone, destined to carry on his shoulders the burden of a play that does not rely on a
single dramatic situation. . . .

The play thus emerges as a collection of incidents unconnected by logic, one that rejects the traditions of the theater and indeed everything that goes under the heading of drama. You can remove a great deal of it without making much difference (even though a work of art, and particularly of dramatic art, is something intricate from which you should not be able to remove a single letter). . . .

The author is trying to portray the struggle between two schools of economic thought through King Maʿrūf on the one hand and the Queen, the Minister, and King ʿAwn on the other, but he does not seem to have realized, as evidenced by the shortcomings in his portrayal of economic thinking, that mysticism and capitalism are not opposites. . . .

In summary, we can say that *King Maʿrūf's Birthday* is something unique, whether we are talking about the Egyptian or world theater. A well-known principle maintains that a dramatic production is basically text and actors; indeed, in the absence of a text, we should expect something like a comedy with much improvisation, clowns or puppets, and the like. This play has destroyed that principle and brought us something new; this theatrical production is made up of two fresh elements: producer and actors.

Amīn al-ʿAyūtī. Al-Kātib. March, 1976, pp. 138–41†

ʿABD AL-SABŪR, SALĀH (1931–   )

EGYPT

In the collection *People in My Country* Salāh ʿAbd al-Sabūr has tried a large number of experiments with poetic conventions. He has used the old rhetorical tone, which is restricted in both form and sense of commitment. Within that framework he has experimented with rhyme and meter before finally settling on the single foot as his unit. Even so, he still does not seem totally settled; the connection with meter has not been severed entirely, even though he will even use different meters in a single poem. The only way we can sum up his current attitude to poetic convention is to say that, like other modernist poets, he is eager to rid it of its conventionality and make it once again a free mode of expression. . . .

ʿAbd al-Sabūr uses convention as modern writers use mythical allusions and words and expressions culled from nonpoetic reality and everyday life. . . . As we know, he is not alone in that. Such freedom of expression has become almost general among contemporary poets and has been one of the key factors in making modern poetry difficult to understand. There is no longer any preconceived format by which poet and reader can easily meet. . . .

People in My Country is a splendid example of the poet's insistence on culling materials from the current political-historical situation and on living with it. . . . In surveying the values implicit in the collection, we can see that the poet is never a coward and, in spite of his continual struggle with himself, never runs away.

However, none of the poems in the collection—as with much modern poetry—any longer . . . comes to life through that unification of poetic sound as practiced by those people who listen to it. The elements of expression in the poem now merely rely on the interior world of the poem itself. The poem now tries to preserve the poetic moment or the human situation as an integral part of itself. It can only excite emotions when the individual listener discovers the poem's particular tone.

Badr al-Dīb. *Al-Ādāb*. Aug., 1956, pp. 11–13†

The collection *People in My Country* contains thirty-one examples of modern poetry. The majority rely on a single foot as the unit of scansion and have a variety of rhymes in musical distribution. However, the poet occasionally resorts to a complete meter and continuous rhyme as a means of expressing his ideas, so much so that in some of the poems he employs the experience of modern poetry and the norms of classicism simultaneously.

Some of these poems express an inner, personal experience, while others try to record external experiences. . . . The most significant artistic feature of the collection is the capacity of the modern poetic idiom to respond to the heritage of European poetry, employing the techniques of that tradition and imitating its music, so that the poet can express through interior monologue the suffering and angst of his own self within his own culture and society. 'Abd al-Sabūr is particularly influenced by the style of T. S. Eliot—his artistic forms, the organization of the poem, and the symbolic images he uses —so much so that in places this influence becomes imitation. . . .

Our poet does not, however, limit his borrowings to T. S. Eliot, but also uses the Torah and the Koran, *The Arabian Nights* and Islamic mysticism, and the simplicity of the legends, stories, and folklore of the Egyptian countryside. From all these traditions he extracts his expressions, symbols, and imagery. . . .

The real innovation in this collection is the poet's expressing his ideas through symbolic imagery in an entirely successful integrated artistic structure and poetic form. . . . The intellectual content of the collection has aroused a question in my mind: Has the poet succeeded in recording his own self in these poems and in bridging the gap between external experience and the more personal internal experience? The critic Badr al-Dīb comments in his introduction to the collection: "The poet has not committed himself to a unified issue through which his own life and thought can be crystallized; nor has he achieved a degree of subjectivity." In other words, the duality in his experiences reflects the duality in his own self as an artist. He does not attempt to unite the two experiences so as to extract any positive values, nor does he adopt a general stance toward life and the problems of society. However, within the profundity of this experience seen through the personal narrative revealed in some of these poems, I think I can detect signs of a faith in mankind. The poet seems to be a person who can endure the fragmentation of his universe and his own inner torment within society, and who can face those givens of existence and absurdity that cause grief, alienation, deprivation, hardship, and endless repetition—face them with real sincerity, without hesitation or falsification.

As'ad Razūq. *Shi'r.* Summer, 1957, pp. 97–100†

Most critical opinion about the collection of poetry *I Say to You* resembled a funeral procession conducting modern poetry to the grave. In this procession there were those who shed real tears over the deceased, while others felt a malicious glee as they thought themselves rid of this naughty child, even while shedding some crocodile tears. Between the genuine and the crocodile tears there remained a question: Did modern poetry really die?

I am going to attempt to answer that question through discussion of Salāh 'Abd al-Sabūr's most recent collection [*I Say to You*]—in fact, through a single poem from that collection. Along with many other people, I believe it is the most beautiful and important poem in the volume and the one that casts the most light on the modern poet and modern poetry. The poem is "The Shadow and the Cross."

At a first reading of the poem, we cannot understand anything specific. However, we emerge with a certain feeling, a vague sensation inside ourselves. It is like the first moment when the piled-up snows of winter begin to melt at the first touch of the sun's warm rays. The ice cracks and separates little by little, so that small rivulets of water can flow in between them. This obscure sensation is not something we shy away from or try to set aside. It is a friendly, human feeling, a sense of distress, not a dull sense but one that is energetic and alive.

Our feelings now become clearer, and we can see that the poet is inviting us to take part in a genuine and difficult struggle, namely, facing ourselves from the inside. For the confrontation to be genuine, we have to answer the following questions frankly: What is our existence? Are we of any use in the life that we live? Are we truthful and loyal in our thoughts, behavior, and feelings? Is that the way we are, or do our bodies carry with them false spirits? Do we smile with our lips while having no notion of the real meaning of joy inside us? Do our faces shine with cleanliness and refinement, while our souls know nothing of real beauty, beauty of ideas, and profound feelings? . . .

'Abd al-Sabūr's poem expresses a human idea: the desolation and loneliness of man in the world. Man is born and experiences a variety of things: love, knowledge, pleasure, and pain. Then, at a single moment in time, he

discovers that life is full of sadness and devoid of meaning, that all these experiences are not enough to fill human life with deep and real meaning. Thus,
man finds himself alone in the face of death and oblivion. Pain and sorrow
fence him in with every step and experience, and man becomes at odds with
the world. . . .

ʿAbd al-Sabūr's poem needs greater subtlety in its artistic structure so
that the symbols can be made sufficiently clear to us, the functions of the
characters can be elucidated, and the joins between the different sections of
the poem more clearly explained. Nevertheless, this poem should be regarded
as a rare and important addition to our modern literature. It shows clearly that
modern poetry cannot die. The poem arouses vivid and powerful sensations
inside us, and the dead cannot do that. Only life can move life.

Rajāʾ al-Naqqāsh. Udabāʾ wa-mawāqif (Sidon and Beirut,
al-Maktaba al-ʿAsriyya, n.d. [1960s]),
pp. 147–49, 153, 157–59†

It must have been the dramatic possibilities of the transformation of al-Hallāj
[from Sufi mystic par excellence to social reformer] that attracted the poet
Salāh ʿAbd al-Sabūr and led him to make the transformation central to his first
verse play, *The Tragedy of al-Hallāj*. A critic is a little wary about applying to
this first experiment two terms that may seem contradictory, namely "caution" and "ambition," but it seems possible that our poet has been both cautious and ambitious in framing his first dramatic opus. His caution shows in
the way he sticks closely to the historical material, depriving himself of a
great deal of leeway for originality. The majority of his characters are historical, and the events of the play hardly venture outside the known events of al-
Hallāj's life; in fact, the action of the play includes only a few of those events.

While the poet has erred on the side of caution in the manner he has portrayed his characters and the events of the play, he has placed great reliance
on his poetic gifts. . . . Salāh's poetry has an undeniable dramatic quality, the
ability to portray conflicting ideas and emotions in close proximity with each
other; all this emerges clearly in his melodic verse. . . .

The poet's ambition shows in his attempt to write a play with classically
simple construction. In the entire play there is not a single idea that impinges
on its principal theme; indeed, there is not a single idea that is not directly related to that theme, namely the agonizing internal conflict of al-Hallāj between the glory of an inner knowledge sufficient unto itself and the battle that
this same knowledge has to wage in its quest for realization in the external
world. The play is divided in a simple fashion, too: an introduction and two
"parts." (Salāh ʿAbd al-Sabūr uses the term "part" rather than "act." It is fascinating to note that this terminology was the one used when the Arab world
first became acquainted with the dramatic medium, but I doubt very much that
our poet had such academic niceties in mind.) There are just four scenes and,

besides the principal character, al-Hallāj, only nine secondary roles. There are three symbolic characters—a Merchant, a Preacher, and a Peasant—who introduce us to the subject of the play, and a chorus of poor people and another of Sufi mystics.

Salāh 'Abd al-Sabūr deserves a great deal of credit for pursuing this path in Arabic verse drama. By so doing, he has diverged from his predecessors, except for Shawqī and 'Azīz Abāza among the "classicists" and 'Abd al-Rahmān al-Sharqāwī in the new school, and followed his own inclinations. He has not been too ambitious, but rather too cautious. As a result, we have a play that is fat in ideas but thin in dramatic potential.

Shukrī 'Ayyād. Tajārib fī al-adab wa-al-naqd (Cairo, Dār
al-Kātib al-'Arabī, 1967), pp. 151–53†

Salāh 'Abd al-Sabūr's play Laylā and Majnūn is bound to arouse a lot of discussions and arguments and certainly requires a good deal of thought and elucidation. . . .

He has chosen to make the love story a play within a play . . . with the idea that there should be no "fourth wall" between us and the love story itself, and we should remain independent as the events unfold onstage and enjoy full powers of understanding and judgment. We are thus rid of the snare of suggestion that was always there in older drama to trap the consciousness of the audience. It is similar to the Brechtian "alienation effect," although not quite the same.

In this play within a play the love story remains a fancy; it is deliberately left as a myth. It begins after the play has already started and ends before the play does. In fact, the play within a play even stops several times and on occasion withdraws into the background while the actors in it rehearse their own particular existence as characters [in the "main" play]. And that is the purpose of the play.

The actor here is not an empty shell for the story to breathe into; the story is the shell. It exists in order to reveal the inner depths of the actor and take him apart dramatically. . . .

This play, Laylā and Majnūn, is no story to be told on a bus with the appropriate sorrow and sympathy, nor one to be summarized at the beginning of critical articles. It is a part of a vivid and real existence, involving vivid and real characters who have been created with great care. What, then, is the characteristic which the people in the play have in common and which makes us join in with them, the assumption being that this is a play of characters, not of plot? Are they not a group of educated people, some of them poets, others writers, working for a newspaper? Are they not a group beset by dispute, the agony of the self and the world, the desire to work, the ability to work, the failure to achieve anything—a group which searches for a means of escape in politics or love and which eventually finds that escape in madness, in mysticism, or else in changing reality itself? They are the crafty set within which beats the inner passion of Egypt. They proceed, complacent because of the compelling thought that they are Egypt's salvation and that the savior must inevitably emerge from their ranks. . . .

At the end of the play, Ziyād comes to realize that his only course involves children and the future. He has put his finger on the secret of genuine change. . . . He has come to realize that Don Quixote's tilting at windmills, as the characters Sa'īd, Hassān, and the Professor have done, has not changed a thing: "The palace is still a palace, imperialism remains the same." Even so, he is not finished. And there are still children and a place where children can exist. There has to be a future.

Farah Sādiq Maksīm. Al-Majalla. Aug., 1971, 101–4†

The parallels between Eliot's *Murder in the Cathedral* and ['Abd] al-Sabūr's *The Tragedy of al-Hallāj* are striking. Each is in free verse and has two acts. Each deals with religious historical events which are very much part of the respective cultures and traditions of the playwrights. Both poet-playwrights interrupt their verse with passages of highly rhetorical prose, a prose which evokes their respective religious traditions: in *Murder in the Cathedral*, Eliot inserts a sermon (the "Interlude") which is almost a Christian cliché, while al-Sabūr inserts (in Act I) the kind of prose which is stylistically, semantically, and syntactically similar to what every Muslim must have heard or read in the Qur'ān and "The Traditions of Muhammad."

In both cases the true cause of death is ambiguous. In the foreground (in Eliot) stand the knights and (in al-Sabūr) the crowd which clamors for the crucifixion of al-Hallāj. Behind them stand, respectively, the shadowy figure of Eliot's King Henry, and al-Sabūr's judges who condemn al-Hallāj in a manner paralleling Pilate's judgment of Jesus. But both poets are concerned with further ramifications; the question of responsibility for, and the will to, martyrdom. Eliot introduces the question of Becket's own willingness to go to the death which looms before him; similarly, through the disciples who claim to have brought martyrdom to al-Hallāj at his own behest, al-Sabūr raises a parallel question. The will to martyrdom therefore underlies both plays at their furthest level.

The crucial issue in both plays is not the action itself but the reasons which lie behind the action. Becket's martyrdom can not be self-sought, for this would be a sin according to the teachings of Eliot's Anglo-Catholicism; yet this is Becket's most dangerous temptation, the one which rises from his own desires. In al-Sabūr's play, martyrdom has been explicitly and freely sought by al-Hallāj, who loves God so much that he sacrifices himself to Him. But as the play unfolds, the question is raised: Is it, after all, al-Hallāj's longing for his Beloved that inevitably results in his martyrdom, or is his death rather a punishment for the sin he has committed by divulging his relationship with God? Does indiscretion bring martyrdom upon al-Hallāj? The conclusion is left ambiguous. In Muslim mysticism, as we learn from the play—and indeed, from the mystic tradition itself—to divulge such a sacred secret and acclaim it publicly is indeed a sin. Yet we do not know whether al-Hallāj's judgment is by God or man, or what the motive is behind the action. In al-Sabūr, the source of the action seems to be not God but man, for the victim himself, independently of the Will of God, apparently chooses martyrdom. Yet in both cases, the poet leaves the question of essential causes ambiguous. Did Becket meet martyrdom or choose it? Was al-Hallāj's martyrdom his choice or his punishment? Neither the reader—nor the protagonist—can be sure. Both murdered men, however, rejoice in accepting their fates and reach similar ends.

Khalil Semaan. Translator's Introduction to Murder in
Baghdad (Leiden, E. J. Brill, 1972), pp. xvi–xviii

ABŪ MĀDĪ, ĪLIYYĀ (1889–1957)

LEBANON/UNITED STATES

I am extremely sorry to have to say that this purity of style in Abū Mādī's collection *The Brooks*, which [some scholars] have admired, is very faulty and is far removed from that purity and probity of style we have come to regard as normal among those writers who live in Egypt, Lebanon, and other parts of the Arab world. I am not claiming that this poet's language is nasty or objectionable, but on occasions it comes so close to being so that it almost falls into the trap. . . . One thing that must be observed and noted with regret is that this poet is really proficient and has a fertile imagination and complete understanding of what it is that he wants to say. He is successful in his fine rendering of imagery. Along with such abilities as these, we should expect a sweet and pure sound that will help him to show the power, splendor, and beauty his poetry undoubtedly contains. . . .

It is perhaps hard to fault Iliyyā Abū Mādī for his use of poetic imagery in this collection. He hardly ever tries anything different or gets himself entangled in faulty imagery that would confuse the reader, although there is a certain amount of such writing to be found. . . .

When we analyze this collection from the point of view of its phrases and meters, then we have to be far from happy with what we find; in fact, we need to be extremely reticent on this matter and even angry; at times even laughter is called for.

The poet does not bother about music in his use of meter, rhyme, or phraseology. It seems that the poetic meters become muddled in his mind sometimes, and he blends them together in an unacceptable manner. . . . If you want to see someone fooling around with the musicality of poetry, then read the poem "The Madman." You will find it is all madness. The poet's intention was to use the meter *rajaz*, play around with the end-rhymes a little, and separate each group of lines in *rajaz* meter with two lines of *hazaj* meter. . . . The result is one of total confusion, since the poet does not know his meters and phraseology properly and cannot be bothered with either. Even so, he wants to recite poetry. I cannot see how this can be viewed intelligently. I find myself totally at a loss with this type of poetry and this group of poets. They have been endowed with rich and powerful gifts and far-seeing imaginations; they are ready to become excellent poets, but they will not perfect the tools of their craft. They are either ignorant of the language or they pretend to be; and then they proceed to adopt this ignorance as a literary school of their own. I now have extreme doubts about this school of poets and their tenets. [1945]

Tāhā Husayn. *Hadīth al-Arbiʿaʾ* (Cairo, Dār al-Maʿārif,
1957), Vol III, pp. 195, 197–98, 200–201†

Abū Mādī did not begin his artistic career with a set of theories by which he could expound on his poetical point of view. He was content simply to produce a collection of poems that are significantly different in their general format from what his contemporary poets were producing. The fact is that before him the poem had no "form" in the modern sense of the word. The subject was everything. It was usually "static" and concerned an object of description fixed in place, rather than an event that lasted for some time. The distinction between "object described" and "event" is an essential element in any preliminaries to an attempt to identify the innovations Abū Mādī introduced into Arabic poetry. . . .

Since we are clearly not here simply to heap praise on Abū Mādī, it has to be admitted that in the final stage of his career he reverted to the older style and followed more traditional paths in his poetry. Artistic structures vanished and their place was taken by superficial poems containing lines that could be left out or rearranged without causing any particular damage. This led to a renewal of the belief that the subject of the poem was sacrosanct and could be quite sufficient for the creation of an artistic structure. All we have to do is compare a superb poem like "The Phoenix" with a traditional piece such as "How She Complains," in the later collection *The Thickets* in order to see the difference. The former is full of movement and life, while the latter is dull and uncontrolled, a series of verses in which each line is a separate entity. . . .

Turning to the qualities that distinguish Abū Mādī's poetry, we find that the most obvious is his intellectual bent, a tendency to use verse as a medium for thought. To him, a poem means an idea before anything else; emotion is completely secondary. In the collection *The Brooks* there is hardly any love poetry at all. The best example of the predominance of thought in his poetry is the long and famous poem "Talismans." . . .

His language is almost entirely free of metaphor, simile, or any kind of shading and coloring. His aim is to convey his meaning as certainly as possible with the most economical use of words. It is this feature that gives the words in his poetry such fixed and specific meanings, almost as though they were verses from a religious text rather than words of poetry intended to arouse the emotions and having some form of artistic effect.

Nāzik al-Malā'ika. Shiʿr. Spring, 1958, pp. 98–101†

Abū Mādī was one of those writers who succeed in conveying the message of goodness and beauty as a unified and complete whole. He pursued truth and beauty assiduously and practiced what he preached with all the strength and artistry his own genius allowed him. . . . This "message" Abū Mādī proclaimed had its own philosophy, which grew out of it. Once life's experiences had done their worst, he embraced this philosophy wholeheartedly and believed in it fervently. Taking a profound look at human society, he found that it is possible for people to determine for themselves whether they are happy or miserable; to a large degree, the fate of man depends on his view of life and on the way in which he adjusts his own behavior in accordance with that view.

The first principle of Abū Mādī's philosophy was the brotherhood of man, and of man's need of his fellow men in everything he does, great or small. As long as that is the case, then man has to learn to cooperate with his fellows, to live in harmony with them, to forgive their faults and overlook their mistakes, and to offer them the best he has. In the preface to *The Collected Poems* of Īliyyā Abū Mādī the poet expresses this idea and proceeds to apply it to himself first, as an example to others. If it were not for other people, he says, he would not be a poet. Who can he recite his poetry to, if they are not listening to him? He is a poet by virtue of others; without them, he is nothing. . . .

The second principle Abū Mādī believes in and supports with tremendous fervor is the philosophy of contentment and optimism in life. The poet seems to exhaust all the notions pertinent to this theme; he takes them as he finds them, examines the attractions they offer, and overlooks their seamier side. One of his best statements on the theme of contentment is that if man can bring himself to adopt happiness as a concept, it will bring about a big change in his view of life in general. . . . So superb a poet as Abū Mādī, whose soothing verse, attractive ideas, purity of spirit, and profound philosophical attitude to life can sweep away all the dirt inside our hearts . . . and renew our flagging resolution, deserves to retain a special place in our affections.

ʿUmar al-Disūqī. Al-Majalla. May, 1958,
pp. 104, 107, 109†

In the summer of 1916 Abū Mādī moved from Cincinnati to New York. He had hardly settled in before he began to get in touch with his fellow émigré writers who lived in New York. He continued to write poetry and to work as an editor. . . .

He established strong ties with the writers in the Bond of the Pen: Jubrān, Nuʿayma, Nasīb ʿArīda, Rashīd Ayyūb, and Nadra Haddād. He joined with them in supporting the literary group that was then using the journal *Al-Sāʾih* as a means of defining and communicating their call for innovation in both language and literature. What they were trying to do was to revive the Arabic language, to instill into it a new spirit of energy and break out of the vicious circle of tradition and imitation so that it could become an effective force in the life of the Arab people. . . .

However, as Professor George Saydah points out, this new trend did not escape the criticism of a great thinker such as Amīn al-Rīhānī, to whom the unity of the Arab people was something of overriding importance. He criticized Jubrān, Nuʿayma, Abū Mādī, and others for wasting their considerable literary gifts on spiritual philosophies and on soothing people's minds with dreams and fancies, when what the Arabs really needed was practical and effective reform. . . . In fact, in that the Arabic language is one of the most crucial elements of Arab nationalism, the émigré school did perform a very important role in introducing into both the language and literature a spirit of innovation in form and content. That spirit had a great effect on our modern literature in every part of the Arab world.

Even though Abū Mādī was influenced by this modernist trend and took part in it through his own writings, he actually never lost his own emotional contact with his homeland and the events taking place there. Once he had settled in New York, he began to serve his people, country, and language with his own pen. He published the collections *The Brooks* and *The Thickets* and founded the journal *Al-Samīr*, which he made a platform for innovation and authenticity in language and literature; it served as a voice from the New World rising to the defense where problems in the Arab world were concerned and urging the Arabs to unite in brotherhood and resist fanaticism in all shapes and forms.

ʿAbd al-ʿAzīz ʿAtīq. *Al-Ādāb.* July, 1963, pp. 6–7†

Abū Mādī was able to demonstrate for us that a revolution in form alone is not a real revolution, and that the fault lay not so much in the nature of the Arabic poem but rather in the type and level of its emotion and its ability to bring together experiences in a new way. In "The Phoenix," a poem in a single stately meter, the poet succeeds in proving that he can express the oldest of ideas in a new way without resorting to excessive variety or coloring. The theme of the poem is extremely old—the search for happiness. But the poet endows it with an attractive novelty; he portrays his anxiety and his quest, which develops and moves gradually and with great subtlety. We should note that he does not talk about happiness as the old poets did, addressing happiness in some sort of private dialogue. Rather he paints a picture of his quest for it as he moves to and fro. . . .

Abū Mādī re-created in modern Arabic poetry a number of elements that had been lost as the Arabic poem suffered much the same decline as cultural life did in general. . . . One of these was a return to the real source of poetry, namely fable, which had faded from the scene in Arabic poetry when poetry adopted the guise of a personal song for a very long period. Abū Mādī was not content merely to borrow fables from the popular tradition but went on to create his own fables that would be appropriate for each of his themes and through which he could imitate those fables his readers would find enjoyable. . . . This tendency of his shows how acute was his understanding of the psychology of the society for which he was writing his poetry. . . . He portrayed aspects of their life for them in the kinds of stories they knew and loved and created unforgettable pictures that are not merely trifling additions to popular lore but rather a real representation of the society's psychology. . . . On many occasions he deliberately chose to use the world of animals and plants. If we compare him with Ilyās Abū Shabaka, who tried to use religious fables, we can see clearly the limits Abū Mādī deliberately set for himself. While Abū Shabaka found in the religious fable a confirmation of the image of the sensual struggle between human beings, to Abū Mādī the fable was an explanation of some great social truth.

Ihsān ʿAbbās and Muhammad Najm. *Al-Shiʿr al-ʿArabī fī al-mahjar* (Beirut, Dār Sādir, 1967), pp. 146, 153–54†

Abū Mādī's poetry is essentially poetry of moods. In it we cannot discern a clear and unbroken progression, or a development in a straight line, in the poet's attitude to life. Instead, what strikes us is his eternal restlessness. There is indeed a clearly marked development in his style, for Abū Mādī's individual voice begins to make itself heard unmistakably in his volume *The Brooks*, where he announces his new conception of poetry. Addressing the reader, he says: "You are not of my party if you regard poetry to be nothing more than words and metre. Our paths will never cross and there is nothing more between us." But once Abū Mādī has attained mastery of his medium he does not adopt a consistent attitude to reality. For instance, at one point he regards the heart as the only reliable guide, at another he clearly admits its insufficiency. In one poem he runs away from the city and civilized life to seek his refuge and solace in nature. In another (as in his poem "In the Wilderness") he falls a prey to boredom and then nature is no longer capable of healing the poet's soul: its silence then is mere emptiness. But that is not because the poet prefers the noise and bustle of the city, but because the poet's feeling of *ennui* is so deeply rooted in his soul that he carries it with him wherever he goes: in such rare moments as this he cannot find his escape in nature, and even nature appears to him as hopelessly inadequate.

Abū Mādī, then, is a romantic poet throughout. The titles of his volumes indicate the extent of his interest in nature. To him nature is often a source of moral teaching in a Wordsworthian fashion. He laments the encroachment of the city upon the country as for instance in his poem "The Lost Wood," where he expresses his grief on finding that the natural scene which used to give him so much joy has disappeared and been replaced by a town and human habitation. Of course, his view of nature is highly idealized, and is synonymous with "beauty," the positive value for which alone the poet is exhorted to live (in a poem called "Live for Beauty"). As in most *Mahjar* [émigré] poetry the poet's yearning for nature is a reflection of his homesickness, a nostalgia for the Lebanon which in Abū Mādī's poetry reaches its highest degree of idealization, as, for instance, in his poem "The Poet in Heaven." Among his favourite themes is the celebration of human love against the background of harmonious nature, as in "Come" which is strongly reminiscent of Shelley's short poem "Love's Philosophy" (a poem that proved to be popular with Arab romantics), or the ennobling influence of human love and its greater efficacy than institutionalized religion and fear of hell as a means of knowing God ("The Night of Longings"). Abū Mādī's poetry is also riddled with "obstinate questionings" of the human condition: he writes about meaningless and unnecessary suffering ("The Dumb Tear"), the vanity of wordly glory ("Clay"), metaphysical doubts ("Riddles"), man's eternal restlessness ("In the Wilderness"). Although not a mystic, Abū Mādī has expressed his vague mystical longing for the ideal in a memorable poem called "The Hospitable Fire."

Mustafa Badawi. *A Critical Introduction to Modern Arabic
Poetry* (Cambridge, England, Cambridge University Press,
1975), pp. 190–91†

It is *The Brooks*, the third *dīwān* (New York, 1927), which is regarded by many as the peak of Abū Mādī's achievement, but this is true only for that type of poetry which was most typical of the *mahjar* writing. In this book he continues and develops to an extreme degree the tendency which began to appear in the second *dīwān*, namely an obsession with his individual perplexities, combined with an ever-increasing sense of loneliness and isolation. The first poem in the book—"The Phoenix"—is all mystery, constant searching, doubt, and urgent but undefined aspiration. The legendary bird is a symbol for something about which people have heard and know, which they constantly seek but which always eludes them. The object of the poet's frenzied search is referred to usually by the feminine pronoun and the whole atmosphere of evocative mystery is typical of the malaise of the individual which is such a feature of this *mahjar* verse. The search of the poet assumes cosmic proportions as he looks along numerous different courses: the life of ascetic religious piety provided no ultimate satisfaction nor did his world of visions, dreams and imagination. Throughout the poem, the mystery remains vague and unsolved.

A poem which has enjoyed a great reputation is "Talismans," perhaps the most lengthy, detailed exposition of the painful mysteries which surround the isolated figure of the poet. The sole aim and justification of this work is to express a state of confusion and perplexity, without offering any hopes of solution or indulging in deep and detailed speculation. Yet in spite of its great reputation and popularity, one feels bound to say as a work of art this is not Abū Mādī's most successful poem. It is too long and detailed to sustain the reader's interest at a consistently high level. The constant re-iteration of the answer *Lastu adrī* ["I do not know"] to the different situations becomes eventually boring as it loses its initial quite impressive effect. The poem as a whole would have benefited from a contraction in length by means of more judicious choice of the numerous details and situations. It is really a type of manifesto in verse of the various themes used by the *mahjar* writers, and probably for this reason it became a significant poem for the many poets and writers within the Arab world who found in it echoes of their own perplexity and experience.

R. C. Ostle. In R. C. Ostle, ed., *Studies in Modern Arabic Literature* (Warminster, England, Aris and Phillips, 1975), pp. 37–38

ABŪ SHABAKA, ILYĀS (1903–1947)

LEBANON

[It seems abundantly clear from Abū Shabaka's verse] that he is not writing about tumultuous sexual pleasures; he wants to avenge himself on them, he despises them. For this reason they are portrayed in woman as being the ill-omened curse of fate. He continually attacks women with the lash of his poetry, wanting them to live always in the pure light of virtue. If a woman's life is marred by some murky cloud, she will inevitably fall into a darkness without end.

His poems show, then, a variety of postures toward the physical passions in women, postures by which he attempts to portray those passions and to set dimensions and limits for them. And at the same time he establishes these limits and dimensions, he sets up all kinds of black flags to warn men of the terrible consequences of approaching the abyss.

Abū Shabaka paints the sensual greed of women in lurid and shocking detail. It is therefore incorrect for any critic to believe that it was Abū Shabaka's reading of Western literature, especially Baudelaire, that led him to compose the collection *The Serpents of Paradise*. There is a tremendous difference between the two poets and between this collection and *Les fleurs du mal*. The latter collection consists of flowers that grew and flourished in evil soil full of all sorts of psychological deviation. They describe their own author and portray his own disassociation of himself from ethical principles.

The "serpents of paradise," on the other hand, have grown up on the outside. The poet portrays the poison in them and the way they inject it into mankind. It is a portrait written by someone who neither supports nor believes in them. Indeed, he hurls imprecations at them to show how evil they are and how sinful; he demonstrates how dangerous are the things they spit out of their mouths. He is unaffected by their poison, and so he is not delirious as he talks. What he wants is for woman to stop at the border and return to her own paradise, chaste and pure.

Shawqī Dayf. *Dirāsāt fī al-shiʿr al-ʿArabī al-muʿāsir*
(Cairo, Dār al-Maʿārif, 1959), pp. 167–68†

In his collection *The Serpents of Paradise* Abū Shabaka reached the very pinnacle of his poetic achievement, penetrated to the very depths of the human soul and exposed its innermost passions. In this collection he follows Alfred de Vigny in his revenge on perfidious woman, who wallows in the mire of sin and treachery. Like Baudelaire, he describes the fiery and indomitable passions of the body. He first turned to this type of poetry when his heart was full of love for the chaste Ghalwā'. He was introduced to a woman with a child whose husband was far away. On a night of red-hot passion he made love to her. He was twenty-five at the time, and this experience and others like it inspired in him a great deal of poetry and deepened his conceptions of love, society, and life, conceptions that grew out of his own struggle between reality and idealism. . . .

While [the critic] Father Rafā'īl Nakhle believes that Abū Shabaka in *The Serpents of Paradise* has summarized his ultimate goal in life, one forged by absolute unbelief and an animal depravity, we prefer to regard this collection (without declaring Abū Shabaka or anyone else to be above sin) as being the revolt of a living conscience that has clashed with life's corrupt realities and seen its idealistic visions betrayed by the evil of other people. The poet is being true to his own romanticism when he writes that, when the poet composes, he is in fact exposing his very soul; no amount of untruth can hide it, no hypocrisy can embalm it. . . .

It should not be forgotten that his first collection, *The Lyre*, was published when he was still only twenty-three years old. While it shows the faults of a beginner, there are plenty of signs pointing to the emergence of a poetic spirit that would soon become more independent in outlook, once Abū Shabaka had read widely in French romantic poetry. *Ghalwā'* (1945) is a long poem . . . in which Abū Shabaka tells the story of his own wounded heart, his soaring dreams, and his pure and agonizing love for Olga Seraphim, who eventually became his faithful wife. In this poem, the speaker uses a romantic voice that can hardly be surpassed.

'Īsā Bullāta. *Al-Rumantiqiyya wa-ma'ālimuhā fī al-shi'r al-'Arabī al-hadīth* (Beirut, Dār al-Thaqāfa, 1960), pp. 153–55, 157–58†

It is difficult to see how the poet could go further in his rejection and condemnation of the world than he has already done in the poems we find in *The Serpents of Paradise*. The next volume he published, *Melodies*, does in fact represent a great change: the turbulence and violence of passion, the incessant inner conflict, the loud screaming voice of condemnation, the hectic imagination, have all gone. The spiritual suffering of *The Serpents* has already had a cathartic effect upon the poet, and now nature seems to be slowly healing his soul. *Melodies* is composed mainly of pastoral poems in which the simple life of Lebanese shepherds and peasants is idealized and its joys and blessings celebrated in verse characterized by exceedingly simple diction and free stanzaic form with multiple rhymes, approaching in language and music the structure of folk songs. By implication the complicated and artificial life of the city with all its vices is, of course, condemned. The volume contains songs of reapers, of winter, spring, summer, songs of the village, songs of the birds (which include the blackbird, the goldfinch, the nightingale and the mountain quail), poems on the wine press, the peasant, a village wedding and a festival. Occasionally traces of the poet's purgatorial sufferings can be felt, but the dominant mood is one of acceptance and content, the calm of mind when all passion is spent. Such calm and peace we find in the remarkable short poem "Night in the Mountains" when the trees, the river, the birds and even the wind are all tranquil while the poet hears the bells ringing in the valley beneath, "melting the spirit of the Lord in the souls of the tired ones," and he finds his own soul "bowing," his breath listening, and his love and longing rendered chaste and pure.

Mustafa Badawi. *A Critical Introduction to Modern Arabic Poetry* (Cambridge, England, Cambridge University Press, 1975), p. 155

Several factors account for the success of *Ghalwā'*, not the least among them being the novelty of its concept and its very length. The fact that Abū Shabaka set out to produce a sizable and ambitious narrative poem is significant, bearing in mind that classical Arabic literature has little, if any, epic poetry, and that this genre, though known in modern Arabic literature before Abū Shabaka, did not produce any generally acclaimed masterpieces.

However, *Ghalwā'*'s value rests mainly with its own artistic merits. Its theme embodies a juxtaposition of extreme emotional and moral situations

—sin and remorse, repulsion and love, alienation and reconciliation. The severe emotional storms that engulf the two protagonists (Ghalwā' and Shafīq, henceforth referred to as G. and S. respectively) are at times masterfully conveyed by mobilizing nature as an active participant in the drama and as a vehicle for reflecting the characters' emotions. Lebanon, its mountains, its seaboard, its villages, are all brought into play. The changing seasons are often employed as background for the shifting moods of S. and G.

Critics who have discussed *Ghalwā'* have dwelt upon many of its thematic aspects. However, too much of their attention has been given to personal matters, namely, the connection between Abū Shabaka's real life and the events in *Ghalwā'*. The fact that the female protagonist's name is composed of the same consonants as that of Abū Shabaka's beloved Olga, whom he eventually married, was often cited as evidence for the "autobiographic" nature of the poem. Moreover, there are other elements in *Ghalwā'* which are reminiscent of the poet's own life, e.g.: the setting of the poem being Zōq Mikha'īl, his native village; the death of the father while the protagonist was a boy; the fact that S. is often referred to as "the poet."

In his short introductory note to *Ghalwā'* (as well as in an article published many years before the publication of the book), Abū Shabaka makes a point of asserting that the poem reflects his life only marginally, and that in its totality it is the product of his imagination. He goes on to emphasize that its subject is the life of a community, not that of an individual; that it is Life, not a single life; and, echoing Aristotle's famous distinction, he concludes that it is "a poem, not history."

Sasson Somekh. Journal of Arabic Literature. 7, 1976,
pp. 101–2

Abū Shabaka's incandescent sense of rebellion, which was never to be extinguished, gives his emotion-racked form the characteristic of a permanently erupting volcano. Thus, in his poetry we are forever finding words like "fire," "flames," "infernoes," "volcanoes," "hell," "hellfire," especially in *Serpents of Paradise*. In a moment of extreme tension he squeezes the words out of his very heart, like some electrical discharge that explodes like thunder and lightning. . . .

He is considered an out-and-out revolutionary romantic. With his French and Arabic education, he was able to develop romantic poetry in Arabic. The poems are considered a renewal in the sphere of modern Arabic poetry, just as the poetry of Abū Nuwās is regarded as a renewal of poetic themes during the earlier Abbasid period. His innovative tendencies were such that on occasion they would recant and rebel against themselves. He rejected all literary schools and trends. As he himself would put it: "They only live on the fringes of literature, just as accident only lives on the fringes of substance, or an ephemeral dictator lives on the fringe of an abiding people." For him, poetry is "a living entity, bursting with nature and life, something which can be neither measured nor weighed." This view gives us a glimpse of his desire to escape from the requirements of traditional poetics and of his longing for the new which new poetry has finally achieved during the second half of the 20th century.

Abū Shabaka lived his life, a man in paradise, a man in hell. . . . He knew true love, the love of "Ghalwā'." After a stormy affair he was married for nine years to a woman named Olga, whose name he changed to Ghalwā'. He wrote a whole collection of poetry about her. Later he was to deny that the collection was in any way connected with reality or the truth, but critics tend to believe that his experience with her was one of the main sources of his wonderful poetry; her name was the last thing he uttered before his death.

Najjāh al-ʿAttār. Al-Ādāb. May–Dec., 1982, pp. 23, 25†

ABŪ SHĀDĪ, AHMAD ZAKĪ (1892–1955)

EGYPT

In 1927 Ahmad Zakī Abū Shādī turned to the genre of operetta . . . [and wrote] *Ihsān: An Egyptian Musical Tragedy; Ardshīr and Hayāt al-Nufūs: A Musical Love Story; The Gods: A Symbolic Operetta in Three Acts;* and *Al-Zabbā'; or, Zenobia, Queen of Palmyra: A Historical Grand Opera in Four Acts.* . . .

It is clear that Abū Shādī was fully acquainted with the development and historical sequence of art forms in the West. He must have noticed that the dramatic art had made its appearance as poetry among the ancient Greeks, the pioneers and masters of this form. In the course of time, the growth of popular spirit and the tendency of literature in general to come close to the people and serve as a natural mirror of its life without any falsification led the overwhelming majority of writers to compose plays in prose rather than verse. Our great neoclassical poet, Ahmad Shawqī, has such a limited knowledge of Western literatures that he thought poetic drama was still the predominant type in the West and the one that had to be followed. As a result, his poetic dramas are distinguished by their musicality and by his use of classical Arabic. . . .

Abū Shādī's efforts in this genre did not meet with the success their author hoped for; that much has to be admitted. It is difficult to pin down the exact reasons for this lack of popularity, and it is still the case today in Egypt and other Arab countries. We are still searching for a way to incorporate this art form into our own artistic consciousness. It is obvious that we will never be able to do so as long as we cannot decide on the artistic form we want the operetta to take. Should it be written as poetry or as music? Is the poetry to be the most basic element, with the music augmenting it, or vice versa? Or should we be trying . . . to create an indigenous and brand-new genre combining poetry and music, which we could call whatever we like? . . .

It can be said that the poetry to be found in Abū Shādī's operettas is of no less value than all the poems found in his other collections. . . . Abū Shādī had that open and free-flowing spirit that the French call the *esprit discursif*. . . . It was this spirit that lay behind his tremendous fecundity, which led to a certain degree of shallowness and lack of focus. From a writer with such a free-flowing spirit, who could compose poetry on the spot, we should not expect any evenness or fixed level of artistry. . . . Abū Shādī's knowledge was both wide and varied, and, as he continued his reading throughout his life, so did his facility for writing poetry increase, so that some of his verse sounds more like prose than poetry. . . .

In conclusion, I must say that I cannot hazard a verdict on these operettas because they were not written solely to be read or recited; they have to be sung. . . . What does need to be said is that Ahmad Zakī Abū Shādī was a pioneer in this genre, which needs to be revived.

Muhammad Mandūr. *Al-Majalla*. March, 1957, pp. 55–56, 60–61†

Abū Shādī longed for freedom in his homeland and during his exile joined with the political activists in their struggle for Egyptian independence.

He also strove for freedom in poetry and aimed at ridding it of the trammels of tradition. He imbued poetry with new splendors it had never known before in both the ideas he expressed and the format he used. He tended to use free verse; he expressed its virtues thus: "Even though it is tied to the notion of verse, it still permits variation in accordance with the positioning and inspiration of the words being used. Thus, the restraints are less rigorous than those applied in blank verse. Both types of poetry abandon rhyme and a strong dislike of any kind of incongruity." He wrote several fine examples of free verse and invited others to do the same. His call was answered by writers such as Khalīl Shaybūb, Muhammad Farīd Abū Hadīd, and Mustafā ʿAbd al-Latīf al-Sahartī. . . .

He was fully aware of the political intrigues that enmeshed his beloved country and drew attention to them in his poetry. . . . The poem entitled "The Comedy," from his collection *The Spring*, is one of the best examples of this type. In it he portrays a period when Egypt had to exist with its thoughts and ideas suppressed, the year 1933. . . . During the last part of his period in Egypt, before he emigrated to America, Abū Shādī castigated the policies advocated by the palace and by the politicians who supported the king. The king was angered; Abū Shādī's university position came under fire, and he was denied the deanship of the College of Medicine at Alexandria University (where

he was assistant dean). His salary was also affected, and he found work opportunities closed to him. Eventually, he decided to emigrate and left his
homeland, taking with him the burdens of a half century, the pains, the sorrows, the memories, and the hardships. . . .

It was a different Abū Shādī who emigrated this time, an old man considerably changed from the young man who had gone to England years before.
. . . His spirit was weakened and his hopes had been shattered. Even so, the
spark of freedom in this man had not dimmed, and he continued to excoriate
the tyrannical king and his aides in poetry that was sometimes revolutionary,
sometimes sarcastic, while the hypocrites in Egypt kept on breathing fire and
pouring their egregious hatred on this stubborn man, just in order to please
their brutal overlord.

Hasan Kāmil al-Sayrafī. *Al-Majalla*. May, 1958,
pp. 94, 95, 97†

He was one of the proponents of personal experience, something on which he
wrote excellently. Even though he was a man of science, his poetry is full of
delicate emotion. He acknowledges his debt to [Khalīl] Mutrān as a teacher
and is unstinting in his appreciation of him, unlike many others. He says that
Mutrān was both a friend and teacher to him thirty years before, when Abū
Shādī was a young man, and that he was guided by Mutrān. The older poet's
effect on his verse is profound, he says, because it goes back to his early days
as a writer and has stayed with him at every stage of his life and career. If his
works now show an obvious independence, they represent at the same time a
natural continuity in artistry, which he gleaned as a young man from Mutrān,
the great teacher. In his later years, he says, he still cherishes this heritage and
thinks of his youth and his first teacher with the greatest of affection.

Abū Shādī's output is very large, showing both abundance and variety.
The poems are many-sided, and not all of them are romantic. His romanticism
shows most in his descriptions of nature and the ever-changing seasons with
which the poet merges himself. It can also be seen in the way he praises love.
Abū Shādī makes frequent mention of the idea of alienation in his poetry. An
explanation for this is that his own society treated him so badly because of his
progressive ideas, his reformist principles, his liberal tendencies, and his desire for innovation that he found it difficult to work and earn a living. He suffered at the hands of reactionaries who banded together against both him and
his poetry. In 1946 he was forced to leave Egypt and emigrate to America.
Even so, he still kept up his insistence on the defense of human values, and
his call for intellectual freedom, social justice, democratic principles and
peace. His personal involvement in poetry did not prevent him from taking a
full and conscious part in the national struggle, and it is to that aspect of his
life that the realistic trend in his works should be traced.

Abū Shādī campaigned for artistic originality, poetic instinct, genuine emotion, and a total lack of any mannerisms or falsification. He believed that there had to be a sound artistic balance between idea and style in the poem. The lines had to be welded into an artistic unity, the mainstays of which were personal experience and lively sensibility.

'Īsā Bullāta. *Al-Rumantiqiyya wa-ma'ālimuhā fī al-shi'r al-'Arabī al-hadīth* (Beirut, Dār al-Thaqāfa, 1960), pp. 121–23†

The descriptive aspect of Abū Shādī's poetry shows a variety of moods. He described everything he set eyes on. He composed as quickly as he received impressions, and was as eager to learn about new things as he was to give vent to his own art. He would look at a scene, find out about it, and convert it into poetry. This rapidity of composition may well have caused his poetry to lose a certain quality they would have had if the poet had culled experiences and then allowed them to mature; it probably also did not allow him the opportunity to revise and polish his poems. This, in fact, is a general feature of his poetry. He tries to justify the phenomenon by ascribing to himself originality and profundity and a startling ability to assimilate and digest his experiences at great speed. We must admit that a great deal of Abū Shādī's verse shows tremendous poetic talent, genuine craftsmanship, and depth of feeling. And yet this phenomenon, the failure to review his work, can still be felt in the majority of his poetry. It seems to go back to Abū Shādī's own organic makeup, and his nervousness in particular. If this rapid pace of composition has resulted in any good qualities, they can be seen in the flood of descriptive poetry we can find in Abū Shādī's works, and above all in the collection *The Weeping Twilight* (1926).

His descriptive technique shows a great deal of variety, and several new features are evident that were not to be found in older descriptive poetry. The poet is not content to describe merely external phenomena of nature or the purely spatial aspects of their beauty. He delves deep inside them and contemplates the relationships among the phenomena, imparting his own feelings and sensibilities to nature as he fuses with it and mingles with its outward aspects. . . .

The contemplative aspect of Abū Shādī's poetry is particularly important because it shows his innovations clearly. We can see a number of the original ideas and new phrases he acquired from his scientific studies. Innovative poets earlier in the century (such as Shukrī, al-'Aqqād, al-Māzinī, and the émigré school in America) started this innovative trend, but Abū Shādī continued it and added a number of concepts and phrases to the lexicon of modern Arabic poetry.

Abū Shādī's contemplative poetry has a mystical and philosophical aspect. It is poetry in which the poet throws doubt on accepted values and tries to be rid of them. He wrote a great deal of this poetry, in which he contemplates existence and oblivion and asks questions about mankind and the world: who fashioned it all? . . .

Turning to the poetry of emotion, we can say that such a title can apply to all his poetry because the circumstances of his life decreed that such should be the case. . . . Abū Shādī began his emotional life with a cruel blow that shattered his dreams and put an end to all his hopes, turning his emotional poetry into something morose and tearful. . . . But Abū Shādī was to remain faithful to his love until the very end of his life. Even so, this fidelity did not prevent him from loving woman in her various guises. He could love her as a voluptuous body, he could love her for her ideas and refinement, as a wife to look after him and organize his life, as a small child who would whisper in his ear, or as a fancy that would waft through his imagination. He would then paint an inspired poetic image. His many collections of poetry are full of examples of this kind of emotional poetry.

ʿAbd al-ʿAzīz al-Disūqī. Jamāʿat Abūllū wa-atharuhā fī al-shiʿr al-ḥadīth (Cairo, Jāmiʿat al-Duwal al-ʿArabiyya, 1960), pp. 225–26, 235, 238†

In the 1920s Abū Shādī undertook a radical experiment that he termed "free poetry" or "free verse." Other poets imitated the idea, but it fell into oblivion. The idea was to combine a number of different meters in a single poem. However, this mixture was achieved without any artistic or semantic justification that could explain the sudden shifts from one meter to another. Abū Shādī and others (such as Khalīl Shaybūb) were unable to create an original musical structure. In fact, they totally destroyed the aesthetics of stress. Nevertheless, this attempt to combine meters established the fact that poets sensed that changes would have to be made in the forms of Arabic poetry, and in fact, poets began in the 1920s to bring about changes in form although they were not to have any success until the end of the 1940s.

There seem to be three major artistic reasons why this was so. In the first place, Arabic poetry was not ready on the artistic level to accept any radical change in technique until the 1940s. The classical Arabic poem, which had achieved its acme in the first decades of this century, had to be allowed to wear itself out by a great deal of repetition, and the old form had to lose the position of respect it held in people's minds. Second, poetic experiments in the first half of this century had shown that the poetic form inherited from the past was deeply embedded in the artistic sensibilities of the Arabs and would therefore resist any hasty attempts at experiment. The Arab poet had to bring about changes in all the other elements of the poem first, in language, imagery, tone, themes, emotion, and the attitude of the poet to life, before he could deal with form. The musical sensibilities within poetry established over ten centuries on the basis of meter, homogeneity, the strict and mechanical division of the poetry into two halves, and the insistence on a unified rhyme scheme—these had not yet been superseded. This century's poets needed three generations of listening to the music of Western poetry before their ears were ready to accept a new music for Arabic poetry, one that ran counter to its old rigid divisions and strict mechanics. Third, any change in the form of the Arabic poem did not simply need an opportune moment within in artistic development but also the emergence of some outstanding poetic talents. And that did not happen until the end of the 1940s.

Salmā al-Jayyūsī. ʿĀlam al-fikr. July–Sept., 1973, p. 330†

In 1927 or 1929 Abū Shādī published his largest and perhaps most important collection of poems, *The Weeping Twilight*, which contained some bold but immature experiments in blank and free verse. He wrote his first free poem in 1926, the year which witnessed the appearance of Harriet Monroe's work *Poets and Their Art*, which seems to have had a decisive influence in encouraging him to experiment with free verse. The poem was significantly called "The Artist" and was introduced thus:

> ". . . the following poem is an example of blank verse combined with another type of verse called *free verse* (Shiʿr hurr) in which the poet not only frees himself from the rhyme but also mixes the metres according to the requirements of the occasion." (*The Weeping Twilight*, p. 535).

The poem is printed without any mark to show the caesura and the divisions of the lines, though these still follow the old classical structure of the two-hemistich line. This seems to suggest that the reader is asked to read the lines as undivided units, that is, without breaking them into two equal halves. But such a reading, which might have been found possible by Abū Shādī, is not easily permitted by the old metrical structure of the lines.

On its first appearance the poem seems to have shocked its readers, accustomed as they were to poems composed in one metre, and this doubtless prevented them from seeing the reason behind its new or free technique and the form in which it was printed. Yet the four metres that it employees, *al-tawīl*, *al-mutaqārib*, *al-basīt* and *al-mujathth*, are not altogether alien to each other. . . .

An interesting feature of the poem may be found in the relationship between its free metrical technique and the concept of art which it implies. The artist is depicted as a man in search of the secret of life or existence for which he must then find a means of expression. To him art is an assertion of life and a revelation of beauty. It is also the power which frees man from his earthly bonds and wordly interests and raises him to a position parallel to that of God. The whole poem seems to centre around the idea of artistic expression and the search after beauty which is at the same time a search after freedom and life.

Art or beauty is conceived as something inseparable from freedom, and the artist as the apostle of beauty, life and freedom. Here lies the apparent link between the theme of the poem and its free technique.

A. M. K. Zubaidi. *Journal of Arabic Literature*. 5, 1974,
pp. 17, 20

Quite a different spirit lay behind the poetry and activities of the man whose career in Egypt was to culminate in the founding of the Apollo society: Ahmad Zakī Abū Shādī. This is the other main group of poets within the Arab world usually associated with subjective, romantic poetry akin to that which Ilyā Abū Mādī and his colleagues brought to such a peak in the *mahjar*. The broad-mindedness of the man and the aims which he hoped his society would pursue are indicated by the fact that Ahmad Shawqī became the first President in 1932, even though the style and way of life with which he had been identified were doubtless alien to the more progressive members of the group. The key word to associate with Abū Shādī and his colleagues is that of co-operation between writers who did not necessarily have the same ideas or objectives in poetry. Because poetry was still very much one of the voices of society, perhaps Abū Shādī saw Apollo as an attempt to bridge the gap between those whose cultural and political orientations were increasingly at variance. This interpretation would seem to correspond with the character and intentions of the man himself, one who hoped that poetry would be a means of communication open to the different sections of society, and perhaps even a means of bringing them together. His early *dīwāns* of the mid-20s represent a broad range of themes and styles: there are many of the lyrical love poems of the type one would normally associate with the Apollo society (*Zaynab*, 1924), but there are numerous pieces on political and social change, poems of patriotism and nationalism, and "occasional" poetry in the most traditional sense. He acknowledges his debt to Shawqī, to Hāfiz, to Mutrān, as well as to European poetry. (See the *dīwāns* Poems of Egypt, 1924, and Groans and Echoes, 1925.)

His huge tome *The Weeping Twilight* was published in 1926–27, containing more than thirteen hundred pages of poetry. In view of their drastic variations in quality, the only reasonable explanation which one can derive from the innumerable prefaces and poems contained in this book is that their author considered poetry as a possible means of linking together the increasing ramifications of modern life. He seems to have feared the break-down in communications between different sections of society as it became more complex and as the Islamic way of life in all its traditional forms came increasingly under attack, or did not respond positively and intelligently to the demands being made of it. For him, poetry had to be firmly rooted in its society, it must take account of and reflect its religion, its patriotism, and its modernising processes. It had to play its part in preserving the position of the Qur'ān, traditional literature, and the purity of the Arabic language.

For Abū Shādī, the poet is a prophet who must be constantly in accord with the needs and tastes of his times. He goes in fear of the situation in which the poet could become estranged from his people by speaking in a language and terms which they do not understand.

R. C. Ostle. In R. C. Ostle, ed., *Studies in Modern Arabic Literature* (Warminster, England, Aris and Phillips, 1975), pp. 42–43

In fact, Abū Shādī was persuaded to adopt free verse by his desire for a new, simple, and personal style, for a new music and rhythm which enabled him to discard the sonorous conventional form, its declamatory tone, and the simple statement of the results of the poetic experience . . . and to avoid refined and highly rhetorical poetic diction. He wanted to probe his inner world and sub-conscious, to use symbols and images in order to convey the environment of his experience. He advocated freedom of expression and the employment of new techniques and forms, according to the dictates of poetic experience and the talent of the poet.

His search was for a form which was more liberal in employing prosody, allowed more freedom of expression, contained new music, and allowed the poet to choose the right form for his poetic experience.

Abū Shādī preferred free verse to blank verse because he found that the former is a better medium for epic, drama, and narrative poetry, since it is unrhymed and more flexible. It enables the poet to vary the rhythm according to the thought and emotion, and to use the exact expression to convey his intention.

Besides, he realized that the conventional form tended to enslave the poet. The conventional metre entices him to use the style, rhythm, and tech-niques rooted deep in his subconscious mind, dictates the rhythm, diction, and style, and subdues the poet's originality and personality. By discovering a new medium it would be possible to avoid what he called "the similarity in words and meanings." Even when great poets such as Shawqī and Mutrān dealt with the same theme, they used the same words and thoughts, when composing in the same metre. . . .

Abū Shādī argued that the real test of poetic and artistic ability is its man-ifestation in the poet's strong inventive and independent personality, which moulds the poetic form according to the dictation of poetic experience. It does not lie in the application of the ready-made form of classical poetry and repeti-tion of the classical poetic diction and rhetoric, whether consciously or un-consciously. He declared that it was of great benefit to Arabic poetry that it should be enriched with new and original style, techniques, and form by introducing blank and free verse, rather than to be content with the mere imitation of classical poets in their hackneyed form and rhetoric.

S. Moreh. *Modern Arabic Poetry 1800–1979* (Leiden, E. J. Brill, 1976), pp. 162–64

ADŪNĪS (ʿALĪ AHMAD SAʿĪD, 1930–   )

SYRIA/LEBANON

In Adūnīs's *First Poems* there is a preoccupation with the experience of poetic creation. Every poem in the collection gives us a feeling of the anxieties of creation; we are faced with a world within which the poet's heart is beating. Adūnīs's poetry is no intellectual game; it attempts nothing less than to create a more human world. . . .

In *First Poems* Adūnīs surveys the world with confidence and love; he celebrates the world with all the joy of childhood. To him it is perpetual childhood. . . .

Adūnīs writes about woman in a way completely different from any poet before him. He places her and her relationships with man above the level of mere sensual instinct. She becomes a symbol of love and renewal. She is not just a physical being, but life itself, the earth, fertility. She is childhood, motherhood, and continuity in this world of ours. To Adūnīs, woman is not an individual being; she is woman in absolute terms. . . .

To Adūnīs, form and technique have no independent value, as they did for his predecessors, who devote especial attention to verbal ornamentation. Form to Adūnīs is not some garment to put on content as decoration so that it will look nice. In his concept of form, words are atmosphere and music; they are experience. . . .

Adūnīs has broken away from the confines of traditional forms and has begun to devise new ones that conform to his own new theories of existence. He has not broken away completely in this collection; in fact, he is still under the influence of the pulse of rhyme and external music of the traditional canons of poetry. But we get the feeling that he has set forth on a road that will lead increasingly toward new rhythms and internal music emerging from the harmony of the artistic unity in the poem both as a whole and in its several parts. . . .

Up until now, Adūnīs has achieved—in both poetic form and content—what few other poets have done. He has an intellectual personality, which only a few great poets possess. What this implies is that he is preoccupied with intellectual issues. They are not abstract or isolated from time and place, but rather emerge from the essence of his own living reality. As with any great poet, his value lies in the fact that he discusses these problems from a new viewpoint and with a new understanding. As a result he devises new formulations for them.

Khuzāmā Sabrī. *Shiʿr*. Spring, 1957, pp. 75, 79–80†

Barely a year has passed since the appearance of Adūnīs's *First Poems*, and here we are with another collection [*Leaves in the Wind*]. . . . Perhaps the first question we should ask, therefore, is where the poet now stands in comparison to his earlier works; what is his present attitude to those universal burdens that so preoccupied his attention in *First Poems*.

This new collection contains poems written between 1956 and 1958. It soon becomes obvious that the questions we have just raised are appropriate only with regard to those poems that have some connection with each other, poems marked by the sincerity of their poetic artistry and a genuine concern with the existential problems with which the poet deals in this new collection. . . . In *First Poems* there was — as we have seen — an overriding concern with the questions of poverty and death, doubt and conviction. In that framework we heard hardly any echo of the frightening sound of emptiness. In this second collection, on the other hand, it rears its head very stubbornly. It takes two terrible forms: personal emptiness, which besets mankind during his hours of bitter loneliness; and collective emptiness, when the feeling becomes concentrated in proportion to the concentration of people and is reflected through the sorrows and joys they have in common. This collective emptiness can appear in a number of guises: a general tendency to doubt, lingering resentment, and an all-encompassing egotism. . . . In spite of this emptiness, which makes the poet groan, he does not give in completely. In fact, he escapes from its clutches and achieves fertility after total aridity, creativity after stagnation, victory after defeat, and life after death. Through all this he gives us evidence of his faith in the wonder and wealth of life and its limitless ability to put on a new veil every day.

At any rate, that is the rule of life according to our poet, as seen in "Hymn of Resurrection." The Phoenix in life and death is simply an expression of the mechanism of eternal renewal: death followed by life, aridity followed by fertility, ashes of fires from which anemones grow. The blood of life starts pulsing once again in the veins of living creatures. . . .

This is the way Adūnīs appears in his latest collection, as he touches upon a number of universal dilemmas that seem to be seething within him: loneliness, emptiness, despair, disillusion, and belief in the renewal and richness of life, with its enigmas that baffle madmen and intellectuals alike.

In praise of the poet, it is sufficient for us to say that in this collection he has gone beyond the problems of poverty, death, the body, and anxiety. He has yet to rid himself of his universal burdens, however. In this collection they prey on him again; and these problems may be even more complicated than those in the first collection. They are certainly more frightening. Can there be any more powerful evidence of spiritual maturity than the fact that a poet is prepared to risk tackling the most difficult and recalcitrant problems?

Mājid Fakhrī. *Shiʿr*. Summer–Fall, 1958, pp. 70–71, 73–74†

[In discussing *The Songs of Mihyār of Damascus*] we will deal first with the negative side of rejection as presented by the poet. It is sufficient to note that our poet rejects the heavens, gods, tyrants, sand, and veils [of classical poetry]. In most cases, the reader can work out the inner significances of these symbols and words and supply them with a certain amount of dimension and positivism. We are not concerned here with clarifying and crystallizing these meanings and nothing else. We have to deal with the causes of rejection. Rejection is not simply saying "No." Above all, it is a new world with its own values, feelings, and ideas fermenting deep down inside. For that reason, the poet finds himself a stranger in the world of other people. . . .

In the name of creation Adūnīs insists on the following values: First, individuality: the poet wishes to be an individual, to have his own viewpoint and his own personal style . . . Second, renewal: in Adūnīs's poetry this is not some ephemeral quality, but its very lifeblood. The poet is advancing toward the future; he is the "Knight of Strange Words," words unfamiliar to ears, minds, and hearts alike . . . Third, freedom: through this he creates, becomes distinct, and renews. Real salvation—if there is such a thing—is something internal; on that basis, boundaries begin to dissolve between man and reality after a long period when he was only able to look at them through the spectacles of tradition or of religious and political communities. . . . Fourth, the spirit of childhood: Adūnīs's insistence on this is a sign of his desire to reject previous ideas and visions of reality as it is. . . . Fifth, sincerity: the poet has decided to be sincere. He embraces the world, naked inside and outside. The barriers between him and his self on the one hand and him and the world on the other have been demolished. He will deceive neither his own self nor the world. . . .

Sixth, the intellect: the poet's loyalty to sincerity forces him to be faithful to knowledge, and that in turn makes him resort to the intellect . . . and at this point we have to say that the influence of the intellect on Adūnīs's poetry reaches such a high pitch at times that we come to feel as though we are being bombarded by analysis and abstraction. . . . Seventh, intuition: Adūnīs believes that intuition is part of the essence of poetry. Thus, we find that his poetry is a flood of sensations and mystical visions. . . . Eighth, rebirth: poetry to Adūnīs is not simply creation, but a creator as well. Poetry is a gift of life and a renewal of it at the same time. . . .

Through these values . . . Adūnīs rejects the classical heritage, in other words, the heavens, gods, tyrants, sand, and veils. . . . To summarize, creation is the poet's world. Anything that fences that process in or clashes with it has to be rejected.

Halīm Barakāt. Shi'r. Summer, 1962, pp. 114–18†

The aim of poetry is no longer to arouse the reader's emotions or to shake the hearer's senses. Modern poetry now strives for something beyond merely attracting the heart of the reader or listener. Above all else, it is striving to speak to the reader's mind and stimulate his conscious faculties. *The Book of Metamorphosis and Migration in the Regions of Day and Night* is an example of this kind of poetry, which is as far removed as possible from any attempt to arouse the emotions of the reader. The work is full of symbols, allusions, implicit statements and allegories. The only way to unravel them is for the reader to use all his perceptive powers and cultural knowledge at every stage.

In this volume, as in its predecessor, *Songs of Mihyār of Damascus*, we are indeed far removed from the theories of the school that proclaimed, in the name of [Henri] Bergson, that the aim of art was to drug the conscious powers of the reader. . . . We are equally far from the concepts that Sa'īd 'Aql tried to impose on Lebanese poetry when he said, about thirty years ago in his lectures at the American University in Beirut, that poetry is a state of unconsciousness, that it can be communicated to the reader only in one of two ways: either by paralyzing the reader's consciousness and taking him into the state of unconsciousness that the poet achieved when the poem was created, or by supplying intoxicating music.

Adūnīs is in the forefront of those poets who want to turn poetry away from the notion of achieving this subtle stupor that leads to the paralysis of the consciousness through sounds and intoxicating music. In his two latest collections, particularly, and through all the theorizing that has grown up around his works, he has worked with other poets (especially Khalīl Hāwī) to put poetry in the category of intellectual and philosophical knowledge, something that requires an alert intellect on the part of the reader and a direct link with intuition on the part of the poet. In spite of Adūnīs's and his wife, Khālida's, insistence on the importance of intuition in poetic creation, we see our poet tending—perhaps unintentionally—to give his poetry a cerebral and intellectual stamp. This tendency does not emerge solely in his attempts to expand the realm of poetic experience to metaphysical problems that in the past were the province of philosophers and thinkers: questions of life and death, God, the spirit and the body, and human destiny. It can also be seen in the way he turns his back on the usual modes of speech, his rejection of traditional clarity and logical sequencing as found in everyday language; also in his continuing attempts to draw the reader into unknown regions of the world where no poetry has ever dared to explore. He is forever trying to remind us that there is no continuing conformity between the world around us and the ways in which we describe it and the connections that bind us to it.

'Alī Saʿd. *Al-Ādāb*. Jan., 1967, pp. 18–19†

Adūnīs begins *The Book of Metamorphosis and Migration in the Regions of Day and Night* with the words: "I must journey in the garden of ashes among its hidden trees." We realize from the outset that this is going to be an enigmatic journey into the recesses of the soul, into regions of a world surrounded by a veil of estrangement—all this in order to elicit a *cri de cœur* from one in agony because of alienation, denial, and a sense of homelessness. These three themes have filled the poet's mind with images of terror and alarm, so that his poetry is a personal projection of the terror with which these visions are filled. . . .

In the general poetic sense of the word, the journey is simply a change in the gloomy face of a world in which the poet lives and a solution to a crisis that is stifling the voice deep down inside him. The journey implies leaving the foul din he complains of, to ascend toward the turrets of dreams where the lost truth lies.

We keep roaming around among Adūnīs's poetic designs so that we can get to know the continents of his emigration and the position of his transformations among the towers of ascent and descent in the regions of body and soul. The poet's profound poetic sensibilities are presented through genuine mystical situations and far-reaching visions, which he achieves through an intense fusion with the spirit of the world. He brings to his poetry a language drawn from this strange world in which he wanders, a language of personal preoccupation. For this reason, we often find that it is not a little obscure. . . .

The towers of the mystical dream to which the poet lifts his soul weigh down his thoughts with notions of death and birth. Through death he achieves his victory, in that the face that terrifies him fades and vanishes; through life he can restore the original face to the world, to life, to mankind.

Adūnīs feels a strong affinity with the notions of birth, death, rebirth, and resurrection. These are symbols of tremendous impact, laden with meanings and suggestions . . . which he uses a great deal in his poetry. . . .

I wanted to say that this new collection represents a new step in the course of modern Arabic poetry. It is, in fact, a definitive change from the narrow, restricted worlds against whose solid walls the visions of the majority of our poets found themselves crashing. . . . It is a transformation in the sense of a flood of profound cultural utterances loaded with a veritable outpouring from the poet's soul on its long journey.

Mājid Sālih al-Sāmarrānī. *Afkār*. April, 1967, pp. 100, 102–3†

Adūnīs may well have been as fascinated as the majority of poets by the call of surrealism, a vogue that reached the Arab world in the 1950s. Since surrealism in its Parisian form was a revolutionary protest against French poetry, it should undoubtedly be regarded within our milieu as a rejection, a revolution, and an expression of opposition. Our poetic heritage had proceeded slowly and deliberately in moving from one idea and notion to another. It had all, without exception, originated within the milieu of the conscious, without there being any attempt to penetrate the realm of the unconscious. Classical poetry shunned the surprising and exciting in favor of the normal and usual. In most periods the poetic idiom was venerated much more than the poetic impulse, so much so that surrealism appears to be in total opposition to the traditions of classical Arabic poetry. . . .

Surrealism does not pay a great deal of attention to form or concepts. It is the art of expressing the absolute by means of the absolute. For that reason, it may be that it was a social protest as well as an artistic protest against traditions and the classical heritage. . . .

The poem "The Mirror of the Road and the History of the Branches" [in *The Stage and the Mirrors*], is the best representative of the surrealist school after it had taken root; surrealism totally dominates the poem. The only thing the reader can possibly get from the poem is a state of confession and self-discovery, all in a new language that is very difficult to grasp. This language relies on stripping words of their surface meanings and giving them suggestive ones instead, and then on creating a kind of striking link between things. It is extremely difficult, however, for us to read it as we do expressionist poetry (in all its different guises) or symbolist poetry. With those, all we have to do is to discover what it is that is symbolized and then proceed securely on our way. The pages of the poem are now open to us just as the petals of a rose open up. . . .

I am sure that the reader of this collection will not fail to discover the extreme novelty in Adūnīs's poetic lexicon and then will be able to assess a further contribution he has made to modern Arabic poetry. One question that still has to be asked as we finish reading this important collection is: Is surrealism an experiment or the end of the road? I am inclined to think that it is an experiment that can benefit modern Arabic poetry by jolting it a little out of forms that have become fossilized in a mere twenty years of creativity, and by opening new worlds it has never entered before. In this regard, Adūnīs is the first one to steal the divine fire and disclose it to other poets. Surrealism is not the end of the road.

Salāh 'Abd al-Sabūr. Al-Majalla. May, 1968, pp. 37–38†

Adūnīs provides us with poetry and mysticism at the same time; he offers us things to listen to and contemplate. He suggests that his words deal with important issues of our times and that what he says has a prophetic bent to it that we have to verify carefully. More important, Adūnīs always promises to give us poetry, poetry as experiment, magic, excitement, alarm, delight. The collection *The Stage and the Mirrors* is rich in all these things. Indeed, it almost persuades us as readers to share in the mystical rapture, the unusual dream, and the journey to the eighth heaven. If we stumble in our rapture or if we are unable to fly in dimensions beyond our usual span, then the fault is ours. For the poet is moving and pushing us. The rest is up to us. . . .

However, Adūnīs occasionally (and to an increasing extent) slinks into the foliage of the branches and disappears into opaque notions that prevent us from seeing his vision. The only way we have of knowing that he is still there is that we can hear him moving, the sound of the branches as they rustle, and an occasional shout from him. . . . We are afraid that wild animals may catch him.

The biggest of these wild beasts in his poetry is verbal opacity, which does not persuade us that it is either intellectual, symbolic, or sensual. It is like an iron garment a man puts on that prevents him from dancing when he would really like to. Instead of the words being feathers in the poet's wings, they become ropes in a snare set to catch him. This is just the first of a number of contradictions we notice in *The Stage and the Mirrors*. . . .

To what extent is this collection modern? Here, too, we find a contradiction, without knowing whether there is an acceptable resolution. Adūnīs's repeated visions are loaded with a painful historical perception, which forces him to use a language that, however excellent it may be, is one of the past thousand years. But it is also a language marked by new styles of creation. Stripped of its verbal repetitions, it has a symbolic freshness to which its saturation in the past gives a particular richness. However, the balance between the Middle Ages and our own century is an uneasy one. The poet is, of course, eager to make his vision an allegory of our times today. But since the vision staggers under its own mystical burdens, it cannot escape from that precise backward-looking classical attitude it rejects and stumbles into something close to generalization. It hardly ever reaches the heart of the modern city, with its psychological and spiritual problems; when it does, it is only by a circuitous route or through an occasional reference to revolution. . . .

This is a feature of Adūnīs's last three collections, *Songs of Mihyār of Damascus, The Book of Metamorphosis and Migration in the Regions of Day and Night*, and *The Stage and the Mirrors*. In all of them we note a trend to create images with a spontaneous freedom usually close to surrealism. It is the freedom of the mystical position that transcends both mind and logic in an attempt to provide us with something more profound and wonderful. . . .

The Stage and the Mirrors, then, is the poet's own stage as one of the heroes of the age. He reveals to us his own incredible narcissism as he sets up the mirrors of his own self in front of us, trying in the process to smash all other mirrors so that we can look at existence and history, in fact civilization as a whole, through his mirror.

The volume does not, however, bring us to a final sense of repose because the attempt is fraught with contradictions. . . . We are left with the worry that the poet's own mirrors, which he is continually talking about setting up and smashing, are in fact shattered, with their fragments reflecting light in all directions. The figure of the hero fits into this framework only in a divided and incongruous fashion.

Jabrā Ibrāhīm Jabrā. *Shiʿr*. Fall, 1968,
pp. 113, 122–23, 125†

In his latest poem, "This Is My Name," Adūnīs broaches a number of questions. From the very first glance, the poem seems new and unusual in the way the words are arranged. When we begin to read, we are startled by the arrangement of sounds, in other words, the metrical pattern. What is particularly striking is that the poem uses established metrical feet, and yet, from the formal point of view, it is not at all clear when one unit of sound (usually termed the hemistich or line) comes to an end and the next one begins. Apart from the musical sections, the reader is left to work it all out for himself. The next problem posed by this division of sounds is that, while the poem is nothing out of the ordinary from the point of view of meters, it keeps on shifting at those curves in the road of poetic sound, the poetic feet that are common to two closely related meters. . . .

This poem marks the destruction of the principle of poetic stability, of methodology, and classicism. It proclaims the canon of change: every single poem must transcend all previous successes in poetry, including those of the poet himself. Each poem will then become a new land to be added to the known world. Thus, there can be no relaxation, no pause for breath, no final form—instead, continuous, ever-renewing creativity, unending risks bursting forth. . . .

Heidegger's statement that "the poem is an encounter" seems particularly appropriate to this poem. It is an encounter in the domains of fire and madness, in that moving moment that is the present, in that caldron that is the depths of the poet's soul. In this caldron the personal encounters the objective and universal, the egotistical meets the absolute. Many characters intersect through the poet's own personality; many voices traverse his own. This much we learn when we find out the identity of the speaker in the poem. . . . "This is My Name" is an entry into the atmospheric world of Adūnīs. If we choose to go in, we find that the objective has penetrated to the very core of the poet and settled there, but in a fiery or magical guise. This poem leads us on step by step; it is that obscure key which gradually takes us down into the interior of Adūnīs so that we can find "a city beneath his sorrows," a city beyond the froth of emotion and the veils of trifles. There we find the real sorrows which gnaw at him and the visions that live deep down inside him. . . .

What will Adūnīs do after this poem? Will this ferocious forward movement push him to silence or something akin to it? Or will he be able to break through the wall, one the reader may not be able to pierce? Is there any choice? He will write many poems before he finds one to match this one, which torments him so. It seems probable that he will continue to discover the world of madness, all the worlds of madness, worlds of change and unity, worlds of division, before the window of salvation looms through the wall of silence.

Khālida Saʿīd. *Mawāqif.* Feb., 1970,
pp. 250, 254, 257–58, 269–71†

In his Paris thesis entitled *Stability and Change: An Investigation of Classicism and Creativity among the Arabs*, Adūnīs suggests that Arab Islamic life recognized two principal modes of thinking and action: the continuing or stable mode, and the changing mode. He goes on to say that the connection between the two was not a dialectical one involving an exchange of influences or give and take. Rather, it was one of conflict and contrast, a relationship between two parties, each of which denied the other.

The first of the two is the stable mode. It is the one that has governed Arab life and been dominant (and the one that gives expression to the nature of the Arab mind). . . . In the realm of literature, this mode appears in the way rhetoric and poetry criticize themselves, and literature becomes a science whose aim is instruction. It can also be seen in the dominance of the ethical factor in literature over the artistic, in the looking backward to earlier times, and to the pre-Islamic period in particular, and the view of that period as being the most ideal. Then there is the rejection of innovation (which follows from the retrospective attitude) and any infringement of the "rules," a hostility to metaphor similar to the hostility of religious thought toward interpretation. From this last stance stems the adherence to the obvious, received word as word from the ancients. . . .

The second mode is the changing one. It is the direct antithesis of the first, and denies it, although this denial has no effect on the first mode. Because of this denial, the changing mode suffers a great deal of misery and oppression, and it suffers defeat under the heavy burden of intellectual, religious, and political repression. . . . In the realm of literature this mode shows itself in its defiance of the pre-Islamic canons of poetry, and in its placing the artistic factor in literature ahead of any social goals it may have; it also emphasizes a general return to life and to a consideration of it as the major source of literature rather than referring to social values and prevailing ethical norms.

We find ourselves substantially agreeing with Adūnīs concerning the existence of these two trends. He has done a good job in analyzing the facets of each one and has thereby made a valuable contribution to the study of the Arab heritage in the fields of religion, literature, and politics. Where we disagree with him is in the way he treats them as two parallel lines that do not meet and the way he denies the dialectical relationship between them. . . .

This work by Adūnīs tackles a basic problem in our lives, and it has important echoes in both our present and future. This problem is the search for a way out of the sterility besetting contemporary life. A quest for originality has to be the first goal in our cultural and educational efforts. No other problem is more important; once it is solved, nothing else will be as difficult.

'Abdallāh 'Abd al-Dā'im. *Al-Ādāb*. March, 1973,
pp. 10–11, 81

Adūnīs's first experiments were with language. His use of words is far from ordinary and his poetic lexicon is extremely rich. He is a daring adventurer who has achieved his own personal poetic style and introduced words and phrases that have never before been used in a poetic context: "magnesium," "essence of glass," "vinegar honey." Adūnīs is a poet of suggestion and mystical incandescence. In his poetry, words lose their basic meanings and take on new relationships; he stands at the halfway point between poetry and philosophy. The language of poetry has been given a rich supply of mystical and philosophical phrases by him. At their best his words can be brilliant and exciting; they strike one with their very novelty, originality, and peculiar usage and send a poetic shiver down the spine. At their worst they tend toward abstraction and sometimes seem to need that infectious warmth that characterizes the poetic diction of al-Sayyāb. Without doubt, Adūnīs is pursuing his career in poetry with confidence, drawing his language from everything around him—elements of nature, instruments, inanimate objects, emotions—and from all mankind's experiences, be they religious, political, or personal. His greatest experimentation comes in the relationship of words to each other, and they are new and surprising.

Adūnīs has undoubtedly moved far away from writing direct poetry, in which the words are arranged according to logic. His poetry remains one of the most important experiments in the attempt to create a new poetic lexicon far removed from the old poetic language, on the one hand, and the language of ordinary speech, on the other. His exciting and successful experiment shows very clearly how dangerous it is to stick to a set of rigid critical principles. His writings show an almost total lack of any attempt to revert to the language of ordinary speech or that of the colloquial dialects. In this he has many followers. Adūnīs is a poet of conflict and contradictions, but the greatest contradiction of all is the radical difference between the way he uses the language of poetry and his theory about the Arabic language. He believes that Arabic is in need of vitality; repeating the words of Jacques Berque, he says that "it is the language of descending to life, not rising up to it." Even so, his lexicon is totally classical while being at the same time new and original.

Salmā al-Jayyūsī. *'Ālam al-fikr*. July–Sept., 1973, p. 350†

According to Adūnīs, he was the writer of the first *qasīdat nathr* [prose poem], doing so in 1958, when he translated a poem by Saint-John Perse. This translation exposed him to energies and ways of expression which metre could not supply. Influenced by this translation, Adūnīs wrote his first *qasīdat nathr*, "The Unity of Despair" ("Wahdah al-ya's"). He also discussed this new genre in the study group of *Shi'r*. Like Saint-John Perse, his vision, too, is universal, roving over the past and its buried civilizations. His images and vocabulary are precise, clear, simple, but sometimes unusual and exotic. His poetry is distinguished by historical images, and clear symbols which reflect the tragic past and present of his country, the invasions of foreign races such as the Mongols, the destruction and stagnation which it underwent, the enslaved present: "You capricious map of wheat, petrol and ports. You gazelle stabbed in the heart and waists, when your wounds heal. . . . No friend, no hope. All of them barbarians, spitting on the word and devouring the children. . . . They export to you the bombs, heavy artillery and tanks; they educate for you youths who kill their fathers while they laugh. . . . They steal from you the wheat and the word [*kalima*], the cotton and the word, the oil and the word. . . ."

Adūnīs describes the past of his country as "Seven centuries and another seven more, we sought under the boughs of magic; and live over a carpet of dancing, when the nether garments are swept away, the wool (*al-sūf*) conceives a miracle, the locusts of spirit enjoy the good graces of her spring. . . . In which sea-brooks we wash this part of our history, which is wrapped with turbans, soiled with the sweat of Dervishes, perfumed with the musk of spinsters and widows who are returning from pilgrimage?"

The poet is waiting for the wind and rain to carry away the sand, and wash the ruins and the history of his people. He is waiting for the future when a new leader comes and changes the present: "A brown-skinned man will rise from the sea in the garments of divinity. . . . Teach rejection (*rafd*), and confer new names, and under his eyelids the eagle of the future is getting ready. . . ." In the last line of this *poème en prose* the poet says "My homeland is not complete yet, my spirit is far off, I have no sovereignty."

S. Moreh. *Modern Arabic Poetry 1800–1970* (Leiden,
E. J. Brill, 1976), pp. 305–6

Concern with form is an important aspect of Adonis's poetics. Form, however, must not be understood to be anything apart from content. In fact form and content are fused together in an indivisible unity. The vision of the poet has to be embodied in words to become a poem, and the words have to be set up in a certain structure to become an aesthetic creation. Therefore the poet's vision is ultimately the form which his poem takes. But for Adonis there is not any one definite structure that is absolute and necessary. Each poem has its own structural form that is the outcome of the thematic expression of the poet's vision.

There are no words and no structures that are more poetic or less poetic than others. All words, and all structures are permissible in the poet's creative search for a new way to express his thought and emotion. As long as the world is a changing world that remains undefined and in need of being constantly uncovered, the poet will have to use ever-new forms to express the human condition. Adonis says, "The modern poem will never reside in any form. It will always endeavor to escape from all kinds of imprisonment in definite meters or rhythms so that it may more comprehensively suggest the feeling of a surging essence that cannot be perceived with completeness and finality, namely, the essence of our present age, the essence of man." Thus the form of the poem is its mode of existence as a created aesthetic expression of the poet's vision in a particular situation at a particular time and place, i.e., after a particular experience. Adonis's call is not for a chaos of form, but rather for the paramount necessity of exploration which must remain above all possible forms. He does not accept ready models of form any more than he accepts preconceived principles of technique, because doing so would stifle the vision and cramp the creativity of the poet. The form of a poem develops and grows as its themes are being expressed. It has no existence apart from the poem, and it has no aesthetic reality except in the presence of the poem as an organic unit and as a whole; each part of it is integrated in the whole semantically and structurally, deriving its meaning and aesthetic value from the whole. . . .

Another significant aspect of the poet's creativity, in Adonis's view, is his use of words. While language is given as a social and cultural heritage, its use by the poet remains open to creative ways of composition. A word usually has a definite meaning, but in poetry it transcends its meaning to a wider and deeper connotation because of the associational power with which the creative poet charges it as he places it evocatively in a new context. It thereby becomes, according to Adonis, "a womb for a new fertility." In this sense, the whole body of the national language is not an absolute entity given once and for all, but rather an entity that remains in a constant state of becoming. A poet has to bring out words from their ancient darkness, flood them with a sudden light, change their relationships, and enlarge their dimensions. He has to make language say what language has not learned to say, and capture what it has not been accustomed to capture. Thus the new poem is not "a verbal mosaic," not even "a verbal chemistry," but rather what Adonis calls "an emotive chemistry"—emotion being taken to mean an existential state whereby sensibility and the intellect unite as they project the modern human condition.

Issa J. Boullata. *Edebiyat.* 2, 1, 1977, pp. 2–4

The intensity of the struggle of the modern has never been greater than it has been over the last twenty years, and it has never been greater in the work of any poet than it has been in the work of Adonis, who has stood constantly (since co-founding with Yūsuf al-Khāl the poetry review *Shiʿr* in 1957, and founding *Mawāqif* in 1968) at the very forefront of modernism and modern poetry. To the *Shiʿr* period dates some of his most violent poetry of rejection (*rafd*), a badly misunderstood word which came to designate the work and attitudes of a number of poets who gathered around *Shiʿr* and its founders.

Both as a theorist and a poet, Adonis is the writer with the greatest influence on Arabic poetry today, although perhaps not the most widely read. Sophisticated, erudite, widely read in Arabic and European literature, with a deep vision of Arabic culture and the forces which have shaped it, of man and God, man in history and man in culture, he has a dazzling linguistic flair and power. A rebel and force of destruction ("A mine for civilization: this is my name"), but also a force of positive rejection with a tormenting love for his culture and his country, he is certainly one of the greatest poets in the history of the language, and one of the finest makers of a poetic phrase since al-Buhturi in the ninth century. . . .

For Adonis the poem becomes a microcosm through which he can redefine the world and recreate it in his own image. By violating the accepted standards of poeticality and poetic structure, he is violating the structure of the world as inherited and accepted by the culture. He has revolutionized the poem totally, from the levels of its elementary constituents—the nature of words and their semantic value—to the rhythm, structure and tone of the poem. The simple lyric in his early poetry, with its echoes of earlier romantic imagery and vocabulary and with its linear, one-dimensional structure, has given way as early as *Songs of Mihyār of Damascus*, and even a little earlier, to the complex multi-dimensional poem, often dramatic and permeated by oppositions and paradoxes embodying the contradictory forces which have shaped the history of the culture. The personal "I" of the early poems has similarly given way to the impersonal, cultural "I" embodying a multiplicity of forces, dreams, hallucinations, and the will to transcend the stagnation and morbidity of the culture. This complexity and the violation of the established order have been as powerfully embodied on the level of imagery, syntax and, especially, rhythm, as on the level of structure. Gradually, but firmly, Adonis has been moving towards the "total poem," which is more preoccupied with creating the rhythm, syntax, forms, and images capable of embodying its own reality than with any popular or accepted or appealing aesthetic criteria. His later poetry, especially poems such as "This Is My Name,"

"Singular in the Plural Form," have dismayed some admirers and brought forth accusations of total obscurity (to which he has responded very recently in his latest published poem). But for me at least, these later poems represent not only his greatest achievement but the very highest achievement of modern Arabic poetry as a whole.

Kamal Abu Deeb. Mundus Artium. 10, 1, 1977,
pp. 165–67

AL-'ĀNĪ, YŪSUF (1927–   )

IRAQ

What gives al-'Ānī a particular importance is that, being a truly humane artist, he is prepared to profit from his own mistakes and those of his fellow artists in the theater. His own skill in this regard parallels that of his colleague in drama, Najīb al-Rīhānī, even though they are separated by both distance and a relative difference in circumstances and goals. The élan that characterizes his works . . . has been created to a large degree by the aims, content, and techniques used in his successful plays. . . . With his troupe he has shown a constant attention to things from which Arab, and specifically, Iraqi people could benefit. For example, al-'Ānī has made it clear that the colloquial dialect is capable of supporting his philosophy and constructive ideas about the future; more than that, it has an innate sparkle, and it almost bursts with openness and with psychological and mythological creativeness. Furthermore, it is the language that is closest to the minds of the common people. Al-'Ānī has written all his plays in this language, showing great insistence and perseverance in the process and carrying thereby the burden of progressive realism. It is these features that have given his works their authenticity and also contribute to their cogent calls and suggestions for social change. In all fairness, however, we must add that this authenticity is not confined to questions of form but involve themes and content as well. . . .

All this is by way of introduction to the play *The Cost of Medicine* . . . , which, I confess, seems to be set apart from al-'Ānī's previous plays, which are marked by sarcastic comedy. The story tells of a father who has to live through two traumatic experiences: one of his sons is close to death because the family does not have enough money to buy medicine for him; his other son, meanwhile, who works in a hotel, is put in prison for stealing the wages he is due from the safe of the hotel where he works in order to buy the medicine for his sick brother. . . .

With this tragic work, al-'Ānī has proved that he is not merely a successful comic actor and playwright, but one who has also mastered realism and can use it to express human values. He has been able here to exploit the tragic medium for the benefit of the true expression of reality and the greater good of others. In spite of the serious faults in some of his works . . . he has successfully pursued the role of an artist in society here by helping in its development. For, as he himself has put it, "the artist's role is not just to make people laugh."

Jalīl Kamāl al-dīn. Al-Ādāb. May, 1957, pp. 78–80†

The feature that distinguishes the works of al-'Ānī from those of other contemporary Iraqi dramatists is that he has consciously adopted a successful form of popular art, benefiting thereby from the achievements of progressive and modernist artists in the West, as well as from his own work as an actor.

Al-'Ānī may put on the stage scenes that are photographically realistic; in so doing, however, he does not allow himself to become bogged down in the pedantries of being literal but goes beyond that to incorporate specific ideas. Similarly, we may regard al-'Ānī's plays as being extremely local because his own unique tableaux are particular to Iraq and Iraqis and may not be found in other countries. And yet we find that his local color is merely the means he uses to bring out something of universal human value. We certainly will not find al-'Ānī's characters anywhere else than in Iraqi society. But what they have to say in his plays speaks to the vast majority of people all over the world.

If we take a closer look at some of al-'Ānī's characters, such as Umm Shākir, Kawthar, and al-Khāl, in his play I'm Your Mother, Shākir . . . , we find that they are not merely symbols but palpable realities that can be seen here and there throughout Iraqi society. We respond to them, hate them, and sympathize with them because they acquire a real essence of their own within the play. And just as that part is real for us, so is the fact that the characters talk in the particular dialect of our country. . . . In I'm Your Mother, Shākir, for example, there is a struggle on the public level between the people and the authorities and on the private personal level between Shākir al-Sayyāb, the educated lawyer, and his family on the one hand, and the rulers of Iraq on the other. In the end both Shākir and his brother die. Even so, the fight goes on at the public level between Umm Shākir and the tyrannical authorities.

One of the most significant features of al-'Ānī's plays is the subtlety of his dialogue and the extreme skill with which he chooses words for his characters to speak. His dialogues are always authentic, express the different facets of the particular character, and are appropriate to their way of thinking and character traits. When Umm Shākir talks about national problems, for example, her understanding of the issues corresponds to the extent of her knowledge on the subject, and the words used are completely appropriate to the character whom the author is trying to portray. Umm Shākir is an Iraqi mother without a great deal of education, naïve and simple; and she loves her chil-

dren. She is not just Umm Shākir but a universal mother, as the doctor in the
play puts it.

'Umar al-Tālib. *Al-Masrahiyya al-'Arabiyya fī al-'Irāq*
(Baghdad, Matba'at Nu'mān, 1971), pp. 190–91, 192†

Al-'Ānī's writing career can be subdivided into two major phases. The first is
from the 1950s to the 1960s. . . . Among the most important principles of this
period is what we might term "directness," whether in topic or presentation on
stage. In these plays the events have a direct impact in that they are a reflection of the life of the people; each play addresses itself to a problem or even
more than one problem in their lives. It is also "direct" in that it faces without
any circumlocution or equivocation those forces that are antithetical to the development of the people. He attacks these forces in an open, courageous manner with a clear Marxist orientation. From the situation of the characters in the
drama he is able at certain times to distill the spontaneous spirit of popular
comedy, and at others an aspect of the day-to-day tragedy of such a miserable
existence. . . .

The second phase ranges from the 1960s into the 1970s. We call it "the
experimental phase." . . . There are relatively few plays during this period,
and so we can discuss some of them in detail. . . . The play entitled *The Key*
goes beyond others of this phase in its indirect approach. Al-'Ānī makes use
of a plot based on a popular children's tale known in slightly different forms
throughout the Arab world. Al-'Ānī's indirect approach has broadened the
plot in space, time, and scope, since the author concluded correctly that he
could hold his audience's attention longer by expanding the more original aspects of the play. This is in contrast with his plays from the first period, with
all their bustle of activity and large number of characters. The structure no
longer relies on stereotyped characters; other types of character are now introduced. . . . In order to bring about this "indirectness" of approach, al-'Ānī has
shown a great deal of artistry in plotting the events of the play, in making use
of history, and in introducing into the dialogue the spirit of poetry, singing,
and dancing.

Banyān Sālih. *Al-Ādāb*. March, 1972, pp. 65–66†

Al-'Ānī wrote the play *The Key* between 1967 and 1968—in other words,
twelve years after *I'm Your Mother, Shākir*. In this play we find him preoccupied with mankind and the issues it faces, and in particular the progressivist
side of man, something we always encounter in his works. Here, however, he
chooses to adopt a total approach to art, one that suits any environment and
any time frame, since he speaks about man by dealing with individuals.

He chooses a current popular song similar to those found in many Arab
countries and proceeds to follow it through to its conclusion. In this way he
reaches an unavoidable decision which is artistic and humanist at one and the

same time: you cannot live your life on the basis of illusion. The long chain of promises the song contains do not lead to the desired goal that Hīrān and Hīrā, two of the characters, sing about: that Hīrā should have a child, and that the child should be able to enjoy a sufficient degree of security—as the father stipulates.

Hīrān and Hīrā set out on a journey of investigation. Their companion Nawār goes with them, although he is not convinced that there is any point to the journey in the first place. Stage by stage, the two main characters discover that they are chasing illusions. . . .

We are dealing, then, with a morality play, a journey of inquiry and enlightenment. It is all couched in a framework that provides a successful dramatic presentation for everyone to enjoy. As with all al-'Ānī's works, the major purpose is to direct mankind toward those means by which progress may be achieved. Victory is always guaranteed in the end, but, as we have seen, it is not the kind of preordained conquest about which so many plays with social themes tell us. Victory in this case is not easily attained. Mere exertion will not be enough. What is needed is to select with care the goal of those exertions and the means of achieving that goal.

This is a general or comprehensive play that can be performed easily and with great success; it should be presented not only in the Arab world, but also in theaters throughout the world, provided that the production is appropriate.

'Alī al-Rā'ī. *Al-Masrah fī al-'ālam al-'Arabī*, Silsilat 'ālam al-ma'rifa, No. 25 (Kuwait, Al-Majlis al-Watanī li- al-Thaqāfa wa-al-Funūn wa al-Ādāb, 1980), pp. 362–63, 365†

'AQL, SA'ĪD (1912–   )

LEBANON

Fifteen years ago or more, Sa'īd 'Aql promised to publish this collection; at that time it was supposed to have the title *The Intoxicated Moment*. However, *Rindalā* was eventually chosen for the name of this long-awaited volume, which has a charm and suggestiveness quite apart from the sweetness of the name. Wafts of scent flit through the air at the sound of the name.

I have long wanted to write about Sa'īd 'Aql and his influence on modern Arabic poetry, ever since I read [the verse plays] *The Daughter of Jephtha*, *The Magdalen*, and *Cadmus*. Now, with the appearance of this collection, I have the opportunity to talk about his works. . . .

Symbolism made its entry into Arabic poetry in Lebanon. There it nourished poetry with lush and beautiful colors and supplemented its imagination with new embellishments and similes. Perhaps it was in the very nature of Lebanon . . . to reveal to its poets an obscure world in which light and darkness are in ferment and in which clarity and obscurity struggle for supremacy. . . . Around the genius of ʿAql himself there grew up a circle of poets whose stars began to shine in the poetic firmament. . . . These included Amīn Nakhla . . . Yūsuf Ghusūb . . . Ilyās Zakariyyā . . . Salāh Labakī, and Yūsuf al-Khāl. However, Saʿīd ʿAql, who was at the center of this circle, imbued poetry and poetic drama with a new spirit and gave both genres a totally new quality; through his flights of imagination and his use of words and ideas. . . .

ʿAql's poetry shows how melody, perfume, passion, and shivers of delight can all blend together in a magical accord. This blend is undoubtedly derived in part from French symbolist poetry. The poem "Fire" is full of descriptions of lust and burning passion . . . and one can detect within it a hint of the fiery and tempestuous emotions of Baudelaire. In fact, one feels in the majority of poems in [Rindalā] that ʿAql is like Baudelaire in his concern with perfume and flowers. . . .

Most of these poems have already been published in periodicals. The poet has made changes, however, adding things here and taking a number of things out there. I have noticed this tendency to change and correct things ever since The Magdalen was published first in Al-Mashriq and then as a book with a number of alterations. This process may point to a poet who is beset by worry and is always seeking perfection. Even so, I have been poring over the pages of this collection with a certain amount of regret, searching for some of the lines that still excite me as I remember them. But they are no longer there, or else they have lost the old wording I found so pleasing. The new words in his poetry have made his style more restrained and luminescent after so much correction and adjustment; all of which shows him to be a genuine servant of poetry who is used to polishing and honing his lines, so much so that signs of his efforts and craft appear in the finished product.

Badīʿ Haqqī. Al-Adīb. Sept., 1950, pp. 57–58†

To anyone who followed the development of SaʿīdʿAql's poetry in his collections, his plays, and the poems he had published in newspapers, it is obvious that his most innovative period was between 1932 and 1937. In that period he wrote The Magdalen and The Daughter of Jephtha, and most of his personal poems appeared in Al-Makshūf, Al-Mashriq, and Al-Jumhūr. At the same time his artistry crystallized into one based on the value of the psychological image and on suggestion, with neither clarification or resolution. The Magdalen was the work that more clearly embodied his new artistry because it was the one that showed the least correction and polishing in an attempt to realize the theories he had learned from [Paul] Valéry, [Henri] Bergson, and others. . . .

ʿAql makes considerable use of the colorings seen by the eye as a me-

dium for conveying internal colors that are perceived only by the imagination
and interior vision. Desires, according to Sa'īd 'Aql, are "blue, then white."
We can appreciate that dreams are a psychological state which each one of us
experiences internally but which cannot be seen. 'Aql sees the color of his
dream and then colors it according to the psychological situation, under the
influence of the separation between the world of the self on the inside and the
world of feelings on the outside. He adopts a direct approach, which obliter-
ates the boundaries separating the senses and their specific natures. The process also frees the poet from the bonds of logic and the twists and turns he has
to make in order to reach understanding. From internal feelings it moves to
the scene on the outside, to which it gives concrete form. We can almost
imagine that feelings and dramatic scene have been discovered in a single psychological moment. Thus, the poet uses one to describe the other, just as if he
were talking about one thing. He has no sensation of moving from the stage of
inner suffering to the outer, corporeal stage.

Genuine symbolism involves an artistic experiment whereby there are no
longer any boundaries between content and form. They are united in a psychological vision through which the distinctions between the worlds of nature
and the mind are removed. . . .

If anyone makes the effort to compare *The Magdalen* and *Rindalā* with
More Beautiful Than You? No!, it should be clear enough that 'Aql has not
really shown any internal development in either his artistry or psychological
approach. There is unbroken thread connecting *The Magdalen* to the most recent collections, namely the descriptive aspect, where he becomes excessively intellectual and exaggerates in his attempts to put into words what he
sees in woman. *The Magdalen* . . . is really no different from some of the
poems in *Rindalā*, and in much the same way there is no profound difference
between all these and some of the new beloveds who appear in his latest collection, *More Beautiful Than You? No!*

Īliyyā Hāwī. *Al-Ādāb*. June, 1961, pp. 28, 43†

I do not go along with the general view that Sa'īd 'Aql's experimentation in
poetry is tinged antagonism toward Arab nationalism, that it serves as an
agent of foreign imperialism. However, I do think it is likely that this experimentation of his fell victim to a violent stage in our literature as it responded
to the sedateness, fossilization, and reaction that has kept Arabic poetry in a
state of decline for a long time. Reactions are often characterized by inflation
and exaggeration. Sa'īd 'Aql, for example, dreams of using the Latin alphabet
as a means of salvation in the face of the torment of the Arabic alphabet, but
he ends up falling into the trap of a banal formalism by starting his experiments with the lowest level of the verbal element in the linguistic patterning of
the poem itself. . . .

Something else that Sa'īd 'Aql and his followers forget or pretend to forget in their laziness and general lassitude is that, by removing the question of diction from all the other elements that go to make up the poem, he and they are transforming their experiments into hollow mummies. . . . As a result ʿAql ends up with a work diametrically opposed to what he had in mind in undertaking his experiments with poetry, namely that they should be quintessentially "Lebanese." He has exchanged the means for the ends and vice versa. His goal is thus lost in the mists of a cloudy vision. It has to be admitted, however, that the dramatic experiment in *Cadmus* and the experiments with language in *Yārā* number among the most successful attempts at providing the colloquial language with a great potential to unlock the gates of man's passions. Even so, the path Saʿīd ʿAql has followed once again confirms that the gates remain firmly closed.

Ghālī Shukrī. *Shiʿrunā al-hadīth: Ilā ayn?* (Cairo, Dār
al-Maʿārif, 1968), pp. 70–71†

The symbolist movement in Arabic poetry tried to emulate the views of French writers such as Mallarmé, Paul Valéry, and Abbé Henri Bremond without being able to become fully immersed in the essence of their aesthetic philosophy. Saʿīd ʿAql is undoubtedly the greatest representative of this school. In the introduction to *The Magdalen* he emphasized the fact that poetry should not inform; on the contrary, it should hint and allude. Like other symbolists, he insisted on the illogical and intuitive perception of the world. The subject of poetry, he announced, is music. The poet of this school is dissociated from ordinary life and from any concern with the ambiguities of the age. In this school, the relationship between the poet and society reaches a low point. Subservience to rhetoric, the narration of stories, addressing the masses, aiming homilies and advice at the world—all this is rejected. Poetry is neither wisdom, prophecy, nor valor. It is a rare anthem that venerates the highest ideal in beauty. This, then, is the holy ground of art with which Saʿīd ʿAql challenges the world, displaying at times an arrogance akin to pomposity. Ideas, images, and emotions, he announces, are all products of consciousness. Poetry comes before them and is outside them. In insisting that the elements of consciousness "play no role in poetry," he contends that poetry is for an intellectual elite, a select class that can appreciate it. Prose, he says, is for schoolchildren.

Saʿīd ʿAql polishes his verses with extreme care and hones his expressions with much subtlety. In *The Magdalen* there are dozens of words picked like rare jewels. *The Magdalen* is a spring of abundant water, not for any religious associations but for the worship of beauty. ʿAql's love of the ideal of beauty in woman remains something unusual in modern Arabic poetry, although after the 1950s it was no longer appropriate to the wrathful spirit of the period. Even so, he continued writing in his usual way as if the world had not changed at all. ʿAql's experience is most like a remarkable truce in the competition between two other schools: first, the romantics who were engaged in an exhausting quest for an identity that the poets had not yet discovered; second, the school of new poetry, the poets of which were striving to find an identity that was lost and dissipated. The first group was eventually torn apart by despair, laments, escapism, and fragile dreams. The second pledged itself to a vision of rejection, rebellion, terror, and wounded arrogance. 'Aql's poetry, which lies in between these two schools, seems to us to be outside the bounds of time as we know it. He continued to live in an ivory tower, cutting gleaming jewels and polishing pearly phrases. His persistent struggle for serenity and his incredible insistence on a literary system so totally at variance with the nervous mood that characterized the period after the June War of 1967— these are features of 'Aql's views. The modern poets felt a natural aversion to 'Aql's experiment in aesthetics, but they nevertheless exploited it to the full. 'Aql gave them poetry free of the instability of the romantics—the padding and general languor, the nebulous and imprecise use of words. The best poetry written since 1967 is poetry of symbols, allusion, and conciseness. Those poets are as indebted for that to Sa'īd 'Aql as they are to the symbolists of the nineteenth century in the West.

Salmā al-Jayyūsī. 'Ālam al-fikr. Sept., 1973, p. 320†

AL-'AQQĀD, 'ABBĀS MAHMŪD (1889–1964)

EGYPT

Passerby is the latest production of the poetic equivalent of the Ford automobile plant. In it our professor 'Abbās has various topics in mind, as usual, and puts them into "words with meter and rhyme" so as to make them Egyptian literature. . . . Now he has started hitting his readers with a comprehensive coverage of the house, as though he is the landlord, apparently believing that by so doing he is creating some Egyptian literature. He seems to think that Beirut, Haifa, Damascus, Baghdad, Jidda, and so on do not have houses for rent, hotels where people of all races stay, clothes pressers, and shop windows, all these being the stuff of *Passerby*. . . . He talks about "The Train," "The Quarter," "The Dinar," and does not forget "The Clothes Presser on Sunday Night," a poem that would make Mary Magdalen laugh at the foot of the cross. . . .

Al-'Aqqād's aim in all this seems to be to carry on Egypt's mission through poetry. But has he really done that? Do these subjects really represent that mission? Does innovation consist in describing the Pyramids?

Al-'Aqqad seems to regard expression as nothing; he tries to create it but is unable to do so. . . . Poetry, in Shelley's words, relies on truth and beauty;

if our friend were to know the truth, his poetry is devoid of beauty. Shelley also says that the language of poets should have a particular color, an echo of music that suits the sound of the words. Without it, he says, there is no poetry. Is there any of this in al-ʿAqqād's poetry? . . .

According to al-ʿAqqād, the poet is someone who declares that he loves truth and beauty, and that is all. It is as though poetry merely consists in a statement of faith like the creed to Christians or the *shahāda* to Muslims. . . . Al-ʿAqqād composes with his mind, and the mind does not create immortal poetry. His concern with unity . . . does not make art. The truly inspired poet creates unity without even thinking about it. Al-ʿAqqād is a child playing with a butterfly, catching it just as people who collect insects do in order to study them scientifically. The poet contemplates his butterflies and describes them in admiration. [1937?]

Mārūn ʿAbbūd. ʿAlā al-mihakk (Beirut, Dār al-Thaqāfa, 1970), pp. 223–24, 226, 232–35†

One of the most significant hallmarks of [al-ʿAqqād's] work is his grasp of Western thought. He displays this trait from his very first collection [*Morning Wakes*] and makes no attempt to conceal it. The fourth poem in that collection is a version in Arabic of a poem by Shakespeare entitled "Venus and the Corpse of Adonis." As we proceed through the collection, we come across an extract from *Romeo and Juliet*, an extract by the English poet Cowper entitled "The Rose," and another from Pope called "Fate."

These translations are no more than a sign of his erudition in Western literatures. . . . Even so, he could dispense with this Western approach and with his own Arabic literary heritage in order to discover himself, his own personality, and his modern Egyptian spirit. That spirit shows in his works in two tendencies in particular: first, a concern with pharaonic monuments and praise for ancient Egyptian civilization—as seen in his poems "Uns al-Wujūd" and "The Statue of Ramses"; second, descriptions of Egyptian political and nationalist sentiments—among the best of which is "The Day of Return," celebrating the return from exile of the great nationalist leader Saʿd Zaghlūl. . . .

Another hallmark of this first collection is al-ʿAqqād's concern with the organic unity of each poem. [In contrast to the neoclassical poetry of the early years of the century], the ringing tones of his poems are no longer dissipated among a whole variety of topics. Now there is a common thread that ties them all together so that each verse has its own designated place in the poem; it is a part of the whole, a member of one body. It is now difficult to put any verse in a different place or to remove it from the poem.

Aided by his wide knowledge of Western literatures, al-ʿAqqād also fostered the concept of the general structure of the poem. We are not referring so much to the verbal structure as to the ideas. He filled his poems with thoughts and fresh intellectual ideas, applying them to everything around him, always subordinating himself to the laws of logic. . . .

These features of his first collection . . . can also be seen as important motifs in his subsequent volumes. In *The Inspiration of Forty* the major themes are thoughts about life, love, and nature. In *The Gift of the Plover* he composed a large number of poems about this Egyptian bird, which fills the night air of the Nile Valley with its sweet songs and touching melodies. . . .

Al-ʿAqqād is an important figure in modern Egyptian poetry. He may even be the most dedicated of all to the idea of innovation, since it was based on a full grasp of Western and Arabic literatures and the derivation therefrom of a new image of the poet—his spirit, his people, and his personality. It must be said, however, that he sometimes goes too far in forming new ideas, so much so that his poetry comes close to being prosaic because of the large amount of logic and clarification involved.

Shawqī Dayf. Al-Adab al-ʿArabī al-muʿāsir fī Misr (Cairo, Dār al-Maʿārif, 1957), pp. 141–45†

Al-ʿAqqād, together with Ibrāhīm ʿAbd al-Qādir al-Māzinī, the Copt writer Salāma Mūsā, and a few others, formed what might be called—from its initial inspiration—the English school of writers, in contrast to the French school of Tāhā Husayn, Haykal, al-Hakīm, and their contemporaries. Al-ʿAqqād was born to a middle-income family in Aswan, where he received his primary education, and began, but never finished, his secondary education in government schools. At the age of fourteen he moved to Cairo where he held miscellaneous jobs with the government while beginning to educate himself by intelligent and well-selected reading in classical Arabic literature and in English and German literature and thought. Al-ʿAqqād has never stopped educating himself and, paradoxically, this has become both his greatest asset and most conspicuous liability.

In the years after 1910, al-ʿAqqād had progressed sufficiently in his education to become a teacher in a college preparatory school and to make a notable contribution to the evolution of modern Arabic literature. At the school he had met al-Māzinī and had begun a long and fruitful intellectual association with him. The two men, together with ʿAbd al-Rahmān Shukrī, founded a new school of poetry which revolted openly against Shawqī and Hāfiz, the two deities who had reigned unchallenged over the Arabic poetry revival for many years. Al-ʿAqqād and his friends assailed the work of the titans as formal, haphazard in its choice of themes, lacking, both in its totality and in its individual parts, unity of structure and meaning, insincere, seeking to impress the reader with verbal *tours de force* and unlikely or exaggerated imagery, rather than to communicate to him deeply sensed moods or feelings or securely grasped thoughts. In its place the three men advocated and promoted what they called "subjective" or "expressive poetry" such as that contained in the collections of poems which they published in 1911, 1913, 1914, 1916, and thereafter. Their criticism did not, of course, stop people from continuing to read and enjoy Shawqī and Hāfiz, but the influence of the new poetic concepts became so pervasive that even the two veteran poets modified their later work to bring it into accord with them.

Nadav Safran. *Egypt in Search of Political Community*
(Cambridge, Mass., Harvard University Press, 1961),
pp. 135–36

Was al-'Aqqād really a gifted poet with his own authentic poetic impulses and a poet's vision of life and existence? Or was he simply a great writer who could not stand the idea of not entering the arena of poetry, and so made his way around in it and wrote a total of nine collections? . . .

The feud between al-'Aqqād and [the neoclassicist] Shawqī (1868–1932) was one of the most bitter literary quarrels of the previous era. Shawqī was at the height of his prestige, a great poet acknowledged as such by most Arab poets, an establishment figure, a member of the wealthy class, close to the royal family and ministers as well as other influential people. In a word, Shawqī received the fruits of eternity while still alive. Al-'Aqqād, on the other hand, was a young man of about thirty, a brilliant journalist of the Wafd Party, avid reader of Western literature, especially English, and at the same time an energetic poet who had published a collection or two.

The book called *The Dīwān: A Book on Criticism and Literature*, written by al-'Aqqād and [Ibrāhīm] al-Māzinī, was the first attempt at practical criticism in our modern literary period, and it caused a storm at the time of its publication the like of which no other critical work has aroused ever since. . . . The book was more destructive than constructive. It made a great deal of noise in order to try to shake the very bases of Shawqī's reputation. Even so, I get the impression that al-'Aqqād's attitude towards Shawqī softened in later years. . . .

Al-'Aqqād's most adventurous collection is *Passerby*, in which he tries to take his subjects from daily life. He talks about the clothes pressers' holiday on Sundays, he discusses the inhabitants of the house in their own language, he describes the cars speeding by and the traffic policeman, and other things close to us all. It might have been possible for al-'Aqqād to make these topics poetic if he had been able to distinguish between prose and verse treatment. He chose prosaic subjects and talked about them in a prosaic manner. The result is a palpable failure; only the Introduction is worth recording. In my opinion, the reason for this failure is that al-'Aqqād thought things out first and planned his collection before writing the poetry. The impulse may have come from some idea he had read about or a theory he had come across during his wide readings, and these ideas and theories may have had as their starting point the tendency of much recent European poetry to move away from figures of speech and traditional ideas and instead to pattern its threads according to the events of everyday life. However, there is all the difference in the world between the innovations attempted by Eliot or Aragon and those of al-'Aqqād.

Salāh 'Abd al-Sabūr. *Mādhā yabqā minhum li-al-tārīkh*
(Cairo, Dār al-Kātib al-'Arabī, 1968), pp. 51–52, 73–74†

The plot of *Sāra* can be presented straightforwardly, although that is not what Al-'Aqqād did. As he wrote it, the novel falls into three parts from the point of view of chronological sequence: end, middle, and beginning and end, and this structure makes it difficult for the reader to form a clear picture of the two principal characters. He is introduced to them in the second or third act, when the cloud of Hammām's suspicion overshadows all Sāra's actions except those right at the beginning of their friendship, and Hammām's role as hero and narrator makes his point of view pervasive. Al-'Aqqād's technique of making a generalisation and then supporting it with a description of a particular incident also makes for a fragmented presentation of personality. . . .

Sāra is not only interesting because it expresses the conservative reaction to the movement for the emancipation of women, which was just then achieving one of its great victories with the entry of women into the university, nor because it reveals the extremes to which Al-'Aqqād's dislike and contempt of the other sex went. The mood of the novel is one of doubt, and, although the particular occasion for it is the behaviour of Sāra, Hammām appears to find little cause for confidence in other things. At least if negative evidence may serve as a guide, there is no trace of deep religious feelings or philosophical conviction in Hammām's character, and he does not appear to have a coherent picture of society as it is or as he would like it to be. He cannot even form a consistent idea of what women ought to be like, and consequently when he describes Hind, who is a contrast to Sāra, he finds her equally unsatisfactory although she exhibits opposite characteristics. It is possible to consider *Sāra* as an expression of the confusion in which Egyptian intellectuals found themselves during the thirties, when the ideals which inspired the nationalist movement had lost their hold, and when Western culture had penetrated Egyptian society, or at least part of it, enough to destroy confidence in traditional patterns of life without them yet being replaced by anything more suited to modern conditions. Thus in *Sāra* the only relationship in which Hammām feels completely at ease is his friendship with Amīn, the man who volunteers to watch Sāra; the explanation is that in this relationship no demands are made on him. Community of interests is what binds the two men together, and in their intellectual pursuits they can ignore the realities of a confused and dis-

turbed society and either escape into fantasies or evolve theoretical solutions
to their problems. There is something of both these elements in this novel.

Hilary Kilpatrick. *The Modern Egyptian Novel* (London,
Ithaca Press, 1974), pp. 30, 34–35

Among 'Aqqād's most interesting poems are those dealing with "demons." In
"The Demons' Contest," which is written in a stanzaic form based upon a
skillful use of the *muwashshah*, Satan, the chief devil, holds a contest among
the devils in an attempt to prove which of them is worthy of controlling the
Kingdom of Hell. The contest in which Pride, Envy, Despair, Regret, Lust,
Sloth and Dissemblance participate is easily won by Dissemblance. Here the
vices are personified in a manner reminiscent of the treatment of the Deadly
Sins in the western poetic tradition. A much better-known poem is "A Devil's
Biography," which is also written in an interesting and more satisfactory
form, the quatrain, which contributes towards the rapid movement of the
story. It is a long narrative poem of over a hundred quatrains and it tells the
story of a demon who grew bored with his job of tempting human beings to
their perdition, since he saw that they were all alike, more to be pitied than to
be envied, and that in his view there was no difference between the so-called
good and bad. He repents, and God accepts his repentence and settles him in
heaven in the company of angels, but he soon resents having to sing the
praises of the Lord and he aspires to be as exalted as God himself. He rebels,
and God immediately turns him into a stone statue. But even in his final state
he still exercises an evil influence, for as a statue of perfect beauty he has the
power to bewitch the beholder. The poem is interesting on account of the view
of mankind it reveals and which, according to the poet, is coloured by the despair engendered in him by the shocking events of the First World War. Although the devil, clearly a mouthpiece of the author, says that all mankind is
to be pitied, it is not because he believes that men are innocent: on the contrary, when he was on earth the worst trick the devil could devise to play on
mankind was to invent the word "right" (*haqq*, which means both Truth and
Right) in the name of which all human action was justified. The poet makes a
repeated profession of faith and belief in God; yet it is not without significance that the charm and lure of the statue, which is seen by him simply as a
work of art, is related to the wiles of the devil. Although one should not drive
the point too far, it seems that 'Aqqād's view of art and the creative imagination is somewhat similar to 'Abd al-Rahmān Shukrī's, which . . . involves
some degree of moral danger. That 'Aqqād was drawn to the supernatural in
this manner seems to be, at least in part, the result of his reading in English literature; we know that he was familiar with Milton's *Paradise Lost* and with
the writings of Joseph Addison, whose papers in *The Spectator* on the Pleasures of the Imagination reveal the common eighteenth-century view of the

imagination which limited its creativity largely to the invention of supernatural characters.

Mustafa Badawi. *A Critical Introduction to Modern Arabic Poetry* (Cambridge, England, Cambridge University Press, 1975), pp. 112–13

ʿARĪDA, NASĪB (1887–1946)

LEBANON/UNITED STATES

The first thing I look for in a poet is scope—scope in thought, in emotion, and in skill with words. Only then do I look at the external techniques of his poetry. Readers can have no doubts about the scope in Nasīb ʿArīda's poetry, unless they cannot see beyond their own noses or trip over the illusions of their own shoes. His poetic methods combine generous amounts of smoothness and fluency and a certain economy in the use of words with a touch of complexity, coarseness, and exaggeration in phraseology. The words of his that show the most smoothness and fluency are the ones in which he moves away from a single rhyme scheme to a multiple one. However, whether he is sticking to a single rhyme in the same poem or using several, you find him occasionally neglecting his genuine talent and making do with an unsuitable word, an inappropriate metaphor, or an image that is not completely developed or well delineated. In the collection *Despairing Spirits* there are a number of poems you read and then say to yourself: "If only he had avoided that word or rhyme, if only he had left out that line or that phrase, if only he had not permitted himself such a license, then it would really have been a jewel of a poem."

All this makes some of the poems in the collection seem like a chain of lofty, spacious mountain peaks immediately followed by a series of narrow, gloomy depressions. Nevertheless, it cannot be denied that Nasīb ʿArīda provides his reader with an arresting mental picture even though it may be obscure or faulty. And I can add that the lofty peaks in his poetry are far more numerous than the depressions. If we came across such faults in a collection of the second or third rank, we would accept them as things to be expected in volumes of that quality. But when we find them in a collection of the quality of *Despairing Spirits*, we begin to wonder, since they seem so out of place and unsuited to the beautiful spirit of the collection. . . .

There are some poets whose works are so attractive that no sooner have you read the opening line of one of their poems than you find yourself immediately drawn from line to line and from poem to poem, and all this almost in spite of yourself. It is as though you have entered a magical palace in which every room is a separate palace in its own right and every door leads to another. These are the poets whose poetry has scope. Among them is the poet of mute bewilderment, Nasīb ʿArīda, speaking, solitary, lamenting, skeptical, ascetic, mystical, rightly guided and himself serving as guide.

Mīkhāʾīl Nuʿayma. *Al-Ghirbāl* (Beirut, Dār al-Sādir, 1964),
pp. 142–44†

He was beset by sorrow and felt that his life was full of pain and grief. But instead of recording his sorrows in a gentle complaint or in tones of grief and nostalgia mixed with a little hope and radiance, we find him losing patience entirely with this sorrow and the problems that pile up on top of him. This impatience induces in him a tendency to bitter pessimism and despair and a general defiant attitude toward life and people around him. . . . His collection *Despairing Spirits* is perhaps the only one by an Arab-American poet in which there is not the slightest glimmer of hope and no sign of joy or laughter. A single look at the title index is sufficient to convince you of this fact: "The Poet Talks"; "Drink Alone"; "Return, Heart"; "Sleep and Death"; "Between Storms and Desires"; "Leave Me Alone" . . . and so on, all of them subjects that arouse sympathy and pity. Even a poem called "At a Happy Gathering" is just a collection of painful groans and sad complaints. . . .

One of the major causes of ʿArīda's despair, pessimism, and anxiety was his feeling of disgust at people around him and the way they treated him. He seems to have been insecure with all of them. Hence, he lived a life of solitude and seclusion far away from people, the life of a mystical recluse whose only companions were his own perplexed verses and anxious thoughts. These notions of loneliness abound in his poetry. He is always avoiding groups of people and is extremely introspective. He describes this loneliness to his readers, a feeling that stays with him even when he is having a drink, an occasion that forces him to sit with other people. . . .

One thing that particularly annoyed him was the low ethical values he saw in people. Their love of money shocked him deeply, and this prompted another tendency in him, namely a defiance of all the conventions of material existence around him and a revolt against any principles and beliefs that ran directly counter to those of the Arabs, with their ideals of generosity, tolerance, and nobility.

Nādira Sarrāj. *Shuʿarāʾ al-rābita al-qalamiyya* (Cairo, Dār
al-Maʿārif, 1964), pp. 350–53, 356†

In appreciating Nasīb ʿArīda's poetry it is important to bear in mind the phases of his career, whose development seems to depend more on philosophical growth than on movement in any particular artistic direction. We believe that the hidden power within Nasīb ʿArīda's poetry can be understood clearly only when this gradual change in outlook and in his attitude toward life is clearly understood. This slow change is the secret behind the completion of the poetic structure the poet began to build in 1912 and finished in 1927. Every poem, if separated from this large structure, loses something (if only a little), a certain degree of fluency. For that reason, Nasīb 'Arīda's poetry is in fact that collection of images gathered around his own psychological self as he moves from one of these phases to another. It is a poetry that has a strong and direct connection with the growth of his own self. . . . Above all else he is a poet who lives to record psychological movement, which is something that occurs in segments. If it is to be seen as it really is, then it must be seen as a whole. The remarkable thing is that Nasīb 'Arīda's poetry does not have a single peak during each of the three different phases of his career but a number of them. They are evident, however, only to someone who takes the trouble to study his poetry throughout its growth and development.

While Nasīb 'Arīda's life may prompt a comparison with the way a tree grows—coming into leaf, opening, then withering away and dying—his poetry can tolerate no such comparisons. The closest we can come to it is a comparison with a well. You can draw water from it time after time. This process in itself allows an even closer comparison. When the water gatherer becomes tired, he puts his bucket on one side and has a rest. After a while he resumes his task with renewed energy, a new bucket, and a new rope. Just read poems like "O Soul, Who Are We?" and others and you will see the poet emptying bucket after bucket of bewilderment locked up inside him. After a while all this lifting of water tires him out and he takes a rest. The reason is that the poem is not born inside him; it does not extend its roots there nor does it spring out like Athena from the head of Zeus. It is more a question of rising and ebbing, give and take, action and reaction. It is a portrait of the struggle or a history of it, not an analysis of its causes and effects.

Ihsān 'Abbās and Muhammad Yūsuf Najm. *Al-Shiʿr al-ʿArabī fī al-mahjar* (Beirut, Dār Sādir, 1967), pp. 209–10†

A poet of lesser importance, Nasīb 'Arīda, another member of Al-Rabīta [the bond of the pen], nonetheless played an important role in the development of modern Arabic poetry. In the first place he was a pure Romantic who, without indulging in sentimentalism, brought a permanent change in several fundamental aspects of poetry. While Īlyā Abū Mādī alternated between the old, loud, exhibitionistic tone, and the private and more subdued one characteristic of later poetry, Nasīb 'Arīda achieved a more permanent change of tone. Because he abhorred didacticism, his tone is soft and subdued, the tone of a poet who is given to meditation, and who indulges in introspective explorations and soliloquies within his own soul. . . .

His one collection of poems, *Despairing Spirits*, came out shortly after his sudden death in 1946. He must be remembered as a poet of introspection and of spiritual moods, who explored the world of the subconscious. In this he has come a long way from poets like Ahmad Shawqī, who lived in the public eye and were constantly conscious of their roles as public figures. With 'Arīda, the divorce of poetry from the platform is complete, and the private voice of the poet finds its freest and most uninhibited expression. Although 'Arīda did write on national questions, he never really concerned himself in any major way with the problems of the world outside. Yet, despite this, his subjects are of universal and permanent value, hampered only by the inadequacy of his poetic talent to support the depth and richness of his theme.

Salmā al-Jayyūsī. *Trends and Movements in Modern Arabic Poetry* (Leiden, E. J. Brill, 1977), pp. 135, 137–38

'ĀSHŪR, NU'MĀN (?–   )

EGYPT

Nu'mān 'Āshūr's outstanding work is *The Middle-of-the-Road Family*. The story concerns the bourgeois family of a baker who dies, leaving a little money and a lot of debts. The inheritance causes continual rows among the lazy and selfish members of the family who survive him. The chief character in the play is the old family servant, al-Tawwāf, who is in his seventies. He has spent his entire life toiling in bare feet to make money for the baker. He has also undertaken to bring up all the members of this "middle-of-the-road family," from childhood to adolescence and maturity, accompanying them to school and telling them genie stories. All his life, al-Tawwāf has had but one ambition, and that is to wear a pair of shoes. He has always walked barefoot, and he is afraid that he will die without ever having worn a pair of shoes. When he hears that there has been a revolution to restore justice to the poor, his hopes rise. He goes to each member of the family, one after the other, but they all seem totally indifferent to his modest request. In fact, they are so self-centered and uncharitable that they even scoff at the old man and his simple dreams for himself. Eventually, one of them feels sorry for him and buys him a pair of shoes. Unfortunately, the shoes do not fit properly. They hurt him, and he cannot wear them. So al-Tawwāf comes into this world and then leaves it with no shoes on his feet, even though there has been a revolution in Egypt.

The story is rather like *Death of a Salesman* by Arthur Miller; here the protagonist spends his life wandering around the city selling bread. He too harbors no feelings of bitterness and believes that his masters are good people. But the disappointment portrayed by Nu'mān 'Āshūr is less of a misfortune than what occurs in Miller's play, although it certainly touches a sympathetic nerve in us.

Lewis ʿAwad. Al-Kātib. Sept., 1964, p. 57†

The realistic trend in Egyptian drama that came into being during the clamor for revolutionary social change rapidly found itself faced with a dangerous crisis. Changes within the society came so thick and fast that it was impossible to keep up with them or to give expression to their various aspects. Nevertheless, some dramatists tried to do so, among them the leader of the new realistic school, Nuʿmān ʿĀshūr. Such changes are reflected in some of the plays he wrote after *The People Downstairs*, for example, *The Movie's a Mess* and *The Female Sex*. These plays were not successful, however, because they dealt with problems that had already become obsolete because of the rapid progress being made. Faced with these dilemmas, the artist became like Don Quixote, battling nonexistent foes and imagining that windmills were really hostile armies preparing to do battle with him. This sort of artistic situation does not offer any opportunities to affect the conscience of the audience or to leave a lasting impression on the artistic life of the country.

Nuʿmān ʿAshūr had already scored his greatest success with his first play, *The People Downstairs*. In it, through the play's hero, Professor Ragāʾī, he had proclaimed his slogan that the aristocracy had failed and was finished. The professor watches his old world collapsing around him and lives entirely on his own illusions and fancies; day by day he begins to discover that he is part of the ruins of a vanishing social class, and that a new class is emerging, taking control of its own existence and giving enthusiastic expression to its own new values.

This theme accounts for the success of *The People Downstairs*. It was a profound expression of the downfall of the old aristocracy and the birth and emergence of the new class fostered by the revolutionary struggle. *The People Downstairs* echoed these events and was simply a confirmation of the same issues and ideas.

Ragāʾ al-Naqqāsh. Introduction to Mahmūd Diyāb,
Al-Zawbaʿa; Al-Gharīb (Cairo, Dār al-Kātib al-ʿArabī,
1967), pp. 7–8†

Nuʿmān ʿĀshūr has had a tremendous influence as the pioneer in social-realist drama in Egypt. It is no exaggeration to say that he has opened the door to a new trend that has had a great impact on the younger generation in the theater. . . .

He has been heavily influenced by the writings of Bernard Shaw; what he admires especially about Shaw is the way he involved himself in political protests as a member of the Fabian Society. ʿĀshūr has been imprisoned no fewer than eight times. According to what he tells us, he has always been put in prison along with the leftists even though he never did anything politically to warrant imprisonment, and is, rather, a strong advocate of cultural and intellectual action. When the great theatrical figure Najīb al-Rīhānī died in 1949, he started writing about Rīhānī's dramas. From then on he became committed to the theater, although he did not isolate himself from politics altogether. He continued to live in the company of other people, and he was inspired to write some short stories, even though all his readings were in the realm of the drama. It was from Bernard Shaw that he found out how to express himself through dialogue. . . .

Gradually his skill in developing both form and content grew. He believed that the new had to encompass some aspects of the old as well as the present in order to blend into a new and totally different form. . . . 'Āshūr was much influenced by his background in dramatic literature and took a great deal from al-Rīhānī as he tried to combine elements of the written text as a literary work and the drama as an artistic performance on stage. As he points out, he is no occasional writer. He did not feel able to write about the setback of 1967 or the fighting in 1973. His connections with the National Theater began when Ahmad Hamrūsh was director. His plays began to be produced by this company; among them was *The People Upstairs*, which turned out to be the goose that laid the golden egg as far as the National Theater was concerned.

And when 'Āshūr presented his play *The Movie's a Mess*, his aim was to protest against the intellectual bankruptcy of the Egyptian film industry and to expose the way things really were in the Egyptian cinema. Film critics, producers, and directors immediately launched fierce attacks on him . . . and performances were stopped. 'Āshūr was summoned before the Minister of Culture and was dismissed from the Ministry of Culture and from government service.

al-Sayyid Hāfiz. Al-Kātib. Aug., 1975, pp. 114, 116–18†

If [Tawfīq] al-Hakīm's plays have been described and criticized as plays to be read rather than acted, then 'Āshūr's drama displays an opposite tendency. Many critics have found fault with his use of the colloquial language, not because of the wide argument over the use of that type of language in principle, but rather because the language which he did use was blunt and unattractive. Other authors in the drama and other genres had used the colloquial language earlier, and it was gaining a slow but steady acceptance as a *literary* medium in which plays could be written. On the evidence of this play and others which followed it, however, 'Āshūr did not succeed (or perhaps was not interested) in transcending the barrier whereby drama written in the colloquial could become enduring literature. . . .

Between 1957 and 1962, 'Āshūr produced two other plays of social import, *The Movie's a Mess* (1958), a searing and apparently unwise attack on one of the sacred cows of the Egyptian cultural establishment, the cinema (which led to ʿĀshūr's being fired from his job and essentially ostracized for a time), and *The Female Sex* (1959), an investigation of polygamy and the problems which it poses. These plays too were popular successes, but critics continued to comment on the lack of character development and of any sense of plot, especially in the last two cited above. Social realism came ever more to the forefront in these works. In *The Flour Mill* (1962) it almost reaches the level of slogans. In this play ʿĀshūr leaves both the urban situation and comedy behind and takes us to a village in which there is a struggle between the village authorities, who are exploiting the peasantry, and the peasants themselves, who gradually discover that the flour mill is in fact their property; the peasants thereafter take control of the situation. To the problem of the extremely didactic nature of this play was added an ambivalence over its production on stage. ʿĀshūr conceived of it as an operetta; one of the characters is a *maddāh* (singer), and there was much singing in the production. However, even though ʿĀshūr's social realism is at its peak in this play, the producer, Najīb Surūr (whom we will encounter later as a playwright), chose to stage the play with its large cast in a Brechtian fashion, using a chorus and stark (actually black and white) contrasts between the different levels of involvement in the villagers' situation. As Bahāʾ Tāhir, the critic of *Al-Kātib*, noted, the portrayal of the Egyptian countryside needed more subtlety than this.

Roger Allen. *Edebiyat*. 4, 1, 1979, pp. 102–3

'AWWĀD, TAWFĪQ YŪSUF (1911–   )

LEBANON

The Loaf is splendid and lively and has such an effect that it is almost impossible to summarize. Without fear of exaggeration we can say that this novel, with its important subject [the resistance by the people of Syria-Lebanon to the Turks during World War I], is one of the finest Arabic novels to date and has broad implications. The subject is especially relevant at this particular stage in Arab history, when nationalist sentiments are beginning to make themselves heard in various Arab-world countries. In presenting various possibilities and opening up new horizons it is a momentous subject. *The Loaf* extols not just a major event in contemporary Arab history but also a whole series of equally important events taking place today. It even extends the subject into the future. The "Arab revolution" is not over yet; imperialism still holds sway, independence has not yet come, and the struggle still goes on. Arabs of all nations are still striving for a loaf of bread. Thus, *The Loaf* is a marvelous rallying cry for independence and freedom. . . .

I have two criticisms of this work. The first is that the first part has a lot of details that do not all fit in with the requirements of the narrative. As a result, it is somewhat boring. The second is that the author intervenes in a few instances to explain some of the action, disrupting the flow of the narrative. . . . Even so, these faults do not diminish the excellence of *The Loaf*. . . . It merits a high place in the list of Arabic novels for the way it balances psychological analysis and dramatic sensitivity.

Suhayl Idrīs. *Al-Ādāb*. Feb., 1957, pp. 13–15†

In the introduction to [*The Tourist and the Guide*] the author asks: "Is this a play? If so, I want the actors to be on the level of gods among mankind. At any rate, they should be greater than the gods of Baalbek." This statement clearly shows that the author does not want his play to be of the usual kind. Its only connection with realism is in the way the dialogue is fashioned. And dialogue alone does not make a drama. . . .

The Tourist and the Guide belongs to the trend of intellectual drama of which Tawfīq al-Hakīm is the acknowledged pioneer in the Arab world. Intellectual dialogue pervades this work. It is for that reason that the author wants the actors to be gods. There is nothing unusual about this; in the ancient Greek theater actors portrayed gods, and gods and men mingled in the same world without any differentiation. Even so, 'Awwād is eager to explore lofty philosophical problems faced by mankind, problems in which the gods may have a part and which may cause them some anxiety in their secluded world.

The characters consist of a tourist who has come from the farthest corner of the world to see the ruins at Baalbek; the guide, who has to keep on telling tourists the same old things; the sculptor, whose hand and chisel are used in making the statues; and a man who is a symbol of the people of the future. The place is the temple at Baalbek, and the time is the present.

Instead of dividing the play into acts in the usual way, the author gives the play three sections: Arrival, Visit, Return. . . . From the point of view of artistic form, the work is not bursting with action or full of restless movement. However, its skillful nonstop dialogue makes up for this lack. Even though the dialogue is full of the discussion of ideas, it has color and flashes of imagery. The lofty strains of poetry endow it with a sweetness of sound. . . .

Earlier in his career, Tawfīq Yūsuf 'Awwād gave us successful works of fiction. Now he has added to his list this play, which shows a writer of great maturity in his thought as well as his use of language and imagery.

Khalīl al-Hindāwī. *Al-Maʿrifa*. No. 32, 1964, pp. 146–47, 152†

When Tamīma, the heroine of *The Mills of Beirut*, leaves her village and comes to Beirut to complete her university education, the experiment of the Lebanese novelist Tawfīq Yūsuf 'Awwād begins. His aim is to observe the cultural transformation that modern Lebanese society is undergoing, with all the complexities of that process and all the obstacles and difficulties. The artist is someone who knows how to choose his own subject for a novel. 'Awwād has bolstered his own conscious choice in this case with a long experience of both life and art, experience captured for us by the pen of a narrative artist of great sensitivity who is aware of the subtleties and fluctuations in the larger picture. In so doing he is following in the footsteps of the great realists and painting a picture in the colors of life itself. The painting is a panorama of modern life in Lebanon that strikes a careful balance between two facets: a bold historical document on the one hand, and a penetrating poetic understanding of the inclinations and struggles of the characters on the other. And even though these characters may in fact represent social fashions, moral positions, and ideas in conflict, they are still far from being mere intellectual abstractions. They manage to preserve their full realistic value and their own past, which extends into a present based on an environment whose circumstances, contradictions, and deep-rooted history constitute a major, almost crucial, element in the actions of the characters. . . .

This work is an end and a new beginning. . . . *The Mills of Beirut* is both original and masterful. It combines two elements in one work: the novel as a stimulating work of creative imagination and a faithful historical document supported by citations that summarize the most significant features of modern Lebanese thought. Through this well-balanced combination it also becomes a brilliant work of literature and an outstanding addition to the history of the contemporary Arabic novel.

'Abd al-Jabbār 'Abbās. Al-Ādāb. March, 1973, 39, 41†

Tawfīq 'Awwād's second novel, *Death in Beirut* [i.e., *The Mills of Beirut*], describes with great insight, sympathy and understanding the basic problems that confronted Lebanese youth in the aftermath of the Six-Day War of 1967 and the Israeli raids on Fedayeen strongholds in southern Lebanon. The precarious balance of religious communities in Lebanon, the role of the Fedayeen, the university environment and the fortunes of young people from conservative communities are all interwoven into the tragic and passionate story of the Shiite Moslem girl Tamima Nassour, the focal character of the novel, who hails from the primitive Moslem community in the village of Mahdiyya in southern Lebanon.

Lured by the bright lights of Beirut, Tamima Nassour is caught up in student demonstrations, wounded and finally rescued by the Maronite Hani Raai. In her dismay and disillusionment after her seduction by the ruthless rebel writer Ramzi Raad, she begins to nurture her relationship with Hani. She takes a part-time job, goes to the Teacher Training College and becomes involved in student activist groups. The reaction of her no-good brother Jaber and his squandering of the family fortune, the passes made at her by Akram

Bey Jurdi in Madame Rose Khoury's "house," her growing intimacy with the
Christian Mary Abu-Khalil, and above all the efflorescence of her idyllic love
for Hani constitute the bulk of the novel, which culminates with Hani's rejec-
tion of her when she confesses her past to him. She then joins the Fedayeen.
One cannot help but notice the similarity between the fortunes of Tamima
Nassour and those of her prototype, Tess Durbeyfield.

The third-person omniscient point of view adopted throughout the novel
—except for those moments when we are allowed to peer into Tamima's
diary—enables ʿAwwad to explore the issues at stake in the "boiling
cooking-pot" that is Beirut. ʿAwwād does not rely on authorial comment to
make his point, but rather on dramatic situations and human relationships of
potential conflict and violence: e.g., the Shiite Moslem Tamima seduced by
the fiery rebel writer, Tamima in love with the Maronite Hani from Deir Mutil
in northern Lebanon, the Christian Mary Abu-Khalil engaged to the Moslem
Akram. In this way ʿAwwād avoids being overly didactic or political. However, the narrative point of view he adopts leads him sometimes to explore in
some detail the fate of people whose fortunes are tangential to Tamima.
Ramzi Raad's long monologue on the death of Madame Khoury, Zennoub's
suicide and the Mary Abu-Khalil/Akram Bey Jurdi episode are cases in point.

The novel is not without its own poetry. In fact, one striking feature is
ʿAwwād's use of vivid poetic images. During her seduction—a scene rather
daringly and boldly described, at least insofar as Arabic literature is concerned—Tamima "felt as if she were borne in some strange vessel ploughing
through the sea. The waves were its snorting horses, her heartbeats the thunder of their hooves, and her panting their panting breath as they galloped
on." . . .

Death in Beirut is a moving novel well worth reading, for it explores relationships of people in a troubled community and gives, with much accuracy,
the bases for the terrible and tragic events in Lebanon that followed its publication in Arabic in 1972.

A. F. Cassis. *World Literature Today*. Autumn,
1977, p. 675

Tawfīq Yūsuf ʿAwwād's *The Mills of Beirut* is a case in point [in discussing
novels that deal with the protagonist's initiation into urban life]. His protagonist Tamīma leaves her village to settle in Beirut. Like many, she is attracted
to al-Hamrā Street where vice is rampant and debauchery is evident everywhere. Meant as an initiation into metropolitan life, this experience is the opposite of the purgatorial journey, for her innocence is gradually abandoned in
this corrupt urban milieu. ʿAwwād follows her career through conflicting circumstances, as she succumbs to or resists, temptation, focusing throughout on
his protagonist's inner feelings and social manners. After a series of setbacks
and disenchantments, Tamīma becomes wiser, realizing that her own freedom

makes no sense apart from the freedom of others. Instead of searching for personal solutions to social problems, she joins the forces of revolution and change, projected in a mysterious figure whom she calls "the man." "As soon as I walk along with him," she concludes, "I shall no longer speak of myself as Tamīma Nasūr." This decision, however, rather than being an act indicating an ideological maturity, seems too contrived to suit the general structural and thematic pattern of 'Awwād's *Mills*.

As a dissenter, 'Awwād's Tamīma has demonstrated some emotional and intellectual growth brought about by a determined effort to see through falsification and deceit. But in accordance with the prevailing conventions of ideological commitment, 'Awwād decides to end Tamīma's career on a note of self-effacement which is inconsistent with her intellectual growth.

Muhsin Jassim Ali. Journal of Arabic Literature. 14,
1983, 81–82

AYYŪB, DHŪ AL-NŪN (1908–   )

IRAQ

Ayyūb says that his stories gain in value according to the amount of analysis he weaves into the fabric; in so doing he attempts to gather up different strands to depict complex phenomena, and to bring to light the hidden factors that influence events. And that is precisely what he does. In fact, at some points he goes to such lengths in this analysis and categorization that the reader gets bored with the whole thing and skips over lines and even entire pages just to get away from the whole process. This may be the major fault with this writer: a short story becomes a sociological work, and only someone who is used to such heavy reading can tolerate all the effort involved. . . .

His collection *The Toilers*, which he dedicated to the struggling masses of workers and peasants, provides many pictures of life in Iraq that shock and jolt the reader. In fact, he does this so well that the reader at times is moved to tears and at other times is infuriated at the actions of those people who treat the "toilers" so meanly and expose them to such misery and hardship and even to death. But the reason for this success is not hard to find. The author himself has lived in similar circumstances, and thus what he has to relate to us is based on hard experience.

"Boatman," for example, is told by the narrator through a series of letters he sends to a friend; it is one of the best stories in the collection. The narrator is a boatman with a wife and five children, who, like him, survive on a diet of barley and maize bread. They see their father only a few days a year, when he brings his boat their way, pulling it himself for the most part rather than riding in it. . . .

In my opinion, Ayyūb's weakest collection of short stories is *Empty Glory*. It certainly shows clearly how frank and courageous he was prepared to be in writing disparagingly about the prime minister and in criticizing the military and civil court systems—all of which led to Ayyūb's dismissal from the civil service and eventual trial. But even so, this volume seems more akin to a collection of newspaper articles than of genuine short stories.

Jamīl Saʿīd. *Nazārāt fī al-tayyārāt al-adabiyya al-hadītha fī
al-ʿIrāq* (Cairo, Maʿhad al-Dirāsāt al-ʿĀliya, 1954),
pp. 28–29, 31–33†

Ayyūb believes in literature with a message; the novel, in his view, is neither written nor read for its own sake but as a means of reforming society . . . and it is for this reason that the genre must be connected with society. The local color in his novels is the bridge he builds between the present reality, which he loathes, and the socialist future for which he hopes. . . . Deep down Ayyūb is convinced that the social struggle must come to fruition and that eventually human virtues will win their struggle; the characters who people his novels are continually expressing these views. . . .

We can say that Ayyūb is the pioneer of the new school of realism in Iraq, which developed after World War II and swept aside all other trends in Iraqi fiction. His pioneering is particularly evident in the short story, since Ayyūb chooses his characters from among those classes of society who find themselves faced with a daily battle merely to stay alive. These stories are characterized by a stamp of local color exemplified by extremely realistic pictures of the life of the common people, which gives some of these stories a profoundly moving humane quality. They are distinguished by their sincerity, by their fidelity to real life, by the link the author sees between literature and his homeland, and by the way he illustrates the essential characteristics of that homeland and the people who live there. His stories are irrevocably bound to the Iraqi soil; they deal with reality, and they discuss simple people within the borders of Iraq living in the present time. In all of them there is a strong belief that man is a noble creature forever aspiring to achieve a free and happy life. Ayyūb conveys the idea that in spite of all the obstacles that exploiters and rulers of various kinds put in the path of people to prevent their reaching their goals, and all the regulations imposed by governments for the benefit of the exploiting class, the common man is still able to fulfill his desires.

In saying that there is a distinctly humane side to Ayyūb's writing we are not implying that it has the profundity that elevates literature to a high level, but rather the sense of empathy and the belief in democratic socialism that have been an intrinsic part of him since his earliest upbringing. He feels the

strongest affection for the lowest class of people in Iraqi society; he marvels at
their unsullied naïveté and their noble yet simple convictions; he grieves over
their ignorance and the idea that they should feel content with the life of humiliation they have to lead; and he feels pain at the thought of their everlasting
silence.

ʿUmar al-Tālib. *Al-Fann al-qasasī fī al-adab al-ʿIraqī
al-hadīth* (Najaf, Iraq, Matbaʿat Nuʿmān, 1971),
pp. 284–86†

[Ayyūb's] style shows traces of the influence of the popular tale. He is very
methodical in his way of thinking: each collection brings together stories that
belong to the same sort of environment, a result of his careful sorting and
sifting. Thus, his first collection, *Prophets of Culture*, focuses on educators
—teachers and administrators. . . . It gives us a vivid and painful portrait of
the lives teachers lead in Iraq. There can be little doubt that these educators,
who expend a great deal of effort in the process of molding new generations,
have to put up with a great deal of hardship and mistreatment. Iraqi society
does not regard them with any deference or respect. People still behave in a
backward fashion; they were brought up in the fear of authority and punishment and are unable to appreciate that with a sense of dignity and respect
comes an awareness of the value of learning and those who teach it. To all this
can be added the bureaucracy that extends from the school principal, the in-
spector, and the ministry supervisor to the junior administrator who regards
himself as superior to any teacher. . . .

In this collection Ayyūb gives a picture of how pervasive hypocrisy, deceit, and graft are in the fabric of Iraqi cultural and administrative life. He has
tried to give his readers a genuine view of the events, the bizarre personalities,
the administrative structures, and the governmental regulations and social
conventions that fall within his purview. He succeeds to a large degree in
showing up the faults of this society, particularly in his description of the civil
servants in the Ministry of Education and its heads of departments who are un-
willing to face the facts.

In his collection *The Tower of Babel* he extends his treatment to include
an exposé of opportunism and false modesty in the performance of administrative functions. He proceeds to criticize governmental bureaucracy, nepo-
tism, the influence of families and tribes on the governmental process, and the
way people are given administrative posts without any consideration of ethical
values or intellectual qualifications. . . .

In his literary works Ayyūb dealt with the problems of Iraq as he lived
through them. He portrayed them in a variety of ways, using a beautiful and
ironic style. His stories had a wide influence on a generation of young edu-

cated people. We all read them and discussed them in detail, since he succeeded in dealing with the problems that were affecting us all.

Yūsuf ʿIzz al-dīn. *Al-qissa fī al-ʿIrāq* (Cairo, Maʿhad
al-Buhūth wa-al-Dirāsāt al-ʿArabiyya, 1974),
pp. 136–37, 141†

Ayyūb's novel *Hand, Earth, and Water* inevitably calls to mind his earliest
short stories, which had a direct link with social and political life in his country and which aimed to present a detailed picture of what that life was like.
This process required explanations and comments. Consequently, *Hand,
Earth, and Water* pays little attention to the usual requirements of an artistic
novel . . . ; instead we have the courageous stance of an author who is prepared to expose things that others are not willing to. The work thus attains an
aura that attracts a large number of readers. . . .

All the characters in the novel are portrayed in accordance with these priorities. They speak with a single logic, and they all use the same language.
For a large part of the time it is impossible for the reader to distinguish among
them. . . . The author distributes the dialogue among them by alternation; this
method is obviously used to achieve his goal of explaining and elucidating
the points he wants to emphasize. Thus, there is very little difference in the
speech of the various characters. For example, Mājid, the attorney who is the
hero of the novel, Doctor Husām and his fiancée Hayfāʾ, who are Mājid's
partners in the agricultural project, and Saniyya, the character who is thrust by
the author into the midst of the novel without any preliminaries merely to express certain economic and political views and who becomes Mājid's fiancée, then wife and partner in his unsuccessful project—all these characters speak with one and the same voice. And the same thing happens with the
peasants, who number among the novel's main characters. Occasionally the
way the dialogue is distributed among the characters by the author becomes
laughable, as, for example, when, in a discussion about the high price of
bread, he passes over the older participants in the novel to use a young servant
girl who hangs on every word Mājid says; she discusses the subject in terms
that could be used only by someone of a much more mature intelligence. As a
result of all this the characters seem to blend into each other, and the reader
cannot detect any clear differentiations most of the time. This feature is exac-
erbated by the fact that the author does not bother to go into any detail about
the characters' personalities or to analyze their moods. . . . As a result they remain strangers to us; we hardly get to know them, and therefore we feel no
sympathy for them. Above all we find no plausible reason for their different
attitudes.

ʿAbd al-Ilāh Ahmad. *Al-Adab al-qasasī fī al-ʿIrāq*
(Baghdad, Wizārat al-Iʿlām, 1977), pp. 220–21†

[Dhū al-Nūn Ayyūb's novel *Doctor Ibrāhīm*] also treats one of the major themes of the *nahda* to which we alluded above: the impact of Western culture on those Arabs who go to Europe to study and the return to their homeland. The work paints a sordid picture of opportunism, as a young Iraqi with a Persian father is sent to England for his university education, totally assimilates British values, marries an English girl and acquires a doctorate. He then returns home, and by peddling influence and prejudice manages to secure himself a position in the Ministry of Agriculture. He joins all the right societies and organisations in order to gain the attention of his Minister and of the British, and then proceeds to acquire as much prestige and money as he can, mostly at the expense of his colleagues. When their enmity towards him and his own awareness of his political vulnerability reaches a certain point, he transfers his funds out of the country and takes out American citizenship. Once again, the socio-critical purpose of this work is not handled with the subtlety of some later works, but we are led to believe that Ayyūb himself was made to suffer internal exile in Iraq as a result of departmental intrigue. This fact, together with the historical circumstances in which the novel was conceived, no doubt contributed to the somewhat excessive fervour with which the author portrays the evil qualities of his hero.

Roger Allen. *The Arabic Novel: An Historical and Critical Introduction* (Syracuse, N.Y., Syracuse University Press, 1982), p. 54

BAʿALBAKKĪ, LAYLĀ (1936?-   )

LEBANON

I Live is the story of a young girl who introduces herself to us as she knows herself. She also takes us into unknown recesses of herself, areas she does not know but wants to find out about. We set out on a journey of discovery inside the world of a young virgin, an unknown world in which the author assumes the role of an experienced guide, one who shares with you everything such girls know and feel, and who then goes on to join in investigating the things they do not know or find impossible to understand. There is no attempt to suppress what the guide knows or to claim to know things that are not known, as is the case with guides in museums and at monuments!

In this novel Laylā Baʿalbakkī declares open revolt, the revolt of girls of the Middle East against their present reality. She rebels against the emptiness of life . . . and everything that is tawdry about our social relationships and the way people think. She rebels against her colleagues who fool around with no sense of direction, who lust after money and look for it wherever they can. She rebels against young men in the Arab world, even those who have been educated and have gone to university, young men who cannot think about girls without seeing a bed in their mind's eye. Finally, she rebels against the home because it is a prison even though the bars may be made of gold; it seems to be a home for her family but not for herself. . . .

Laylā Baʿalbakkī is a tremendous talent. We will not term her (as some have) the "Arab Françoise Sagan" because we do not want her to be that, but simply Laylā Baʿalbakkī. We want her to achieve her potential as a citizen and a writer, a young girl who may fall in love or dream of so doing; who may marry or dream of marriage. But along with that, she should produce ideas, art, or literature too. We need more works like *I Live*, and better works at that. . . . so let her persevere and continue her literary production. She should think of herself as being at the beginning of the road. If she thinks she has achieved her goal, she will in fact be finished without ever reaching that goal or pinnacle in her career.

Anīs Sāyigh. Al-Ādāb. May, 1958, pp. 59–61†

In [the short-story collection *Spaceship of Tenderness to the Moon*] we encounter the personality of Laylā Baʿalbakkī along with the same basic constituents that appeared in *I Live*. There is also a tangible advance in poetic sensibility, in use of imagery, in style, and in the attainment of maturity during the inevitable and necessary crisis through which the author goes.

The pivot of her "problem"—if the expression can be used—is the relationship of Middle Eastern women to men, linked to the development of their selves and their search for freedom within the current social and moral ambience. However, this problem (which can be characterized as a "general" one) loses its general status and any abstract intellectual framework it may have. With Laylā Baʿalbakkī it takes shape in the personality of an individual with her own feelings, someone who lives with the outside world. . . . The various strands in the personality of this author are embodied in a kind of dialectic of opposites found in society, and, in fact, in the individual as well, and in every single aspect of nature, with its varying seasons.

In the stories of *Spaceship of Tenderness to the Moon* the author dwells on the internal events and concentrates on the self, with its tragic problems and willful attempts to escape, to break loose. We see that she has tried to combine this internal drama, in which she may be either angry or submissive, and the external drama, where all this effusion of life either meets or separates, harmonizes or clashes . . . an effusion that divides into two streams, one of despair and pain, the other of optimism and happiness. . . .

With her nervous, sensitive, poetic, colorful style, full of imagery, this writer has thrown some light on the limits of the problem. Her story goes on a journey with her, on a nighttime adventure. It stays close by her when she looks at a mist and a beautiful scene in nature, when she trembles at a sudden encounter with a face in the crowd or probes the depths of banal reality with a rapid glance. We can say that she is herself the pivot of her story and the focus of the enigma it contains.

Hānī Abū Sālih. Hiwār. No. 8, 1964, pp. 133–34†

The novel *Disfigured Gods* by the Lebanese writer Layla Ba'albakkī treats the idea of past and future on the level of personal relationships. What is it that brings together Mīrā, the young girl of twenty-two, and Nadīm, the history professor who is over forty. It is just that they live in the same building; the older man feels a craving for youth, while the young girl discovers an obscure feeling of ease in consorting with a man who is her father's age. Both of them are fighting devils from their past. Mīrā lives with the thought of her father, who died of a heart attack; she believes that she will die the same way. The dead man is still the master of the house, which he rules from a picture hanging on the wall. Her mother sits by the picture every day and talks to it any time something serious happens, as though she is the priestess of some idol god. Nadīm lives with the idea that his wife left him. He has led a life full of women and has grown tired of it all. Now he dreams of a modest house and a faithful woman who will not invite men to come and visit her because he will be able to satisfy her every need and desire. He likes to imagine himself as a happy father with lots of children. But 'Ā'ida, his wife, let him down; she was not a virgin.

Each of these characters needs the other. The young girl restores a sense of youth to the middle-aged man, while he in turn releases her from slavery to her own father. Then the abandoned wife becomes pregnant. She has taken advantage of a drunken moment when Nadīm is raving about Mīrā in a stupor, taken him to bed, and held him in her arms "like a sick baby." The young girl, meanwhile, has been cured of her fear of "the violet cloud" which, she fears, will carry her away as it did her father. She has come to know happiness. She falls in love with a young man of her own age and they decide to get married. . . .

However, while life opens its arms to the young girl, who manages to obliterate the image of the past from her imagination, oblivion and languor envelop the middle-aged man, who remains bound to his past, its passions and disappointments. 'Ā'ida has died during childbirth, the baby has been put into an oxygen tent, and Mīrā has left the building. All that is left for Nadīm is the bottle so that he cannot open his eyes and see the light.

Shukrī 'Ayyād. 'Ālam al-fikr. Oct.–Dec., 1972,
pp. 637–38†

The defiant mood of Lina—the protagonist of Laylā Ba'albakkī in her novel *I Live* (1958)—is deeply rooted in her egoistic assertion of her individual

freedom. Her strong feelings and ideas spring from a point of view which focuses on her ego to the almost total exclusion of social reality. What is at issue
for her is her personal problems. [Georg] Lukács' characterization of modernist literature applies here. He points out that the process of negation of history
takes "two different forms in modernist literature. First, the hero is strictly
confined within the limits of his own experiences. There is not for him . . .
any preexisting reality beyond his own self. . . . Second, the hero himself is
without personal history. He is thrown into the world: meaninglessly, unfath-
omably." Lina proudly proclaims her separation and self-sufficiency by con-
templating the following analogy: "I am a luxurious palace. . . . It has everything necessary for the sustenance and reproduction of life; it needs no help
from the outside world. . . . the wall around it is high and separated from the
road by a moat. I am an autonomous world whose course of life is not influenced a bit by any outside event which does not spring from my ego." Being
preoccupied with her self to the point of narcissism and almost totally engaged
in the nurturing of her ego, Lina pays little attention to others, "to those
strange creatures who slide on the outer surface of my life." It is consistent
with such a view that she has no interest in politics: "I simply confess that I do
not have the mind to find a solution to the problem of Palestine, Kashmir, or
Algeria. What worries me . . . is how to walk for the first time with my shoes
that raise me seven centimeters above the ground. Will they break as I rush
into the streets?" Let no one be tempted into believing that the author's intention here is simply to expose Lina's trivialities. The intent is to shock and defy
the society. That is, without doubt, the crux of the matter. The defiance is
most intense when directed against the family. Lina despises her father and
his wealth, and shows ambivalence (reflected in feelings of pity and disgust)
toward her mother.

Halīm Barakāt. *Visions of Social Reality in the
Contemporary Arab Novel* (Washington, D.C.,
Center for Contemporary Arab Studies, 1977),
pp. 23–24

The public prosecutor of the Court of Appeals called the author, Laylā ʿAlī
Baʿalbakkī, in accordance with item 532 of the criminal law, accusing her of
harming the public morality in her book recently published under the title
A Space Ship of Tenderness to the Moon. The public prosecutor of the Court
of Appeals, Mr. Saʿīd al-Barjāwī, assigned the case to the court in charge of
monitoring publication (Makhamat al-Matbūʿāt). The trial of Miss Baʿalbakkī
was ordered to begin. Under item 532 the public prosecutor demanded the imprisonment of Miss Baʿalbakkī for a sentence of one to six months plus a fine
of ten to one hundred liras. . . .

The author's purpose and intention. Now the court proposed to examine
in some detail the stories in the defendant's book *A Space Ship of Tenderness
to the Moon* in order to determine whether the author's intention was serious,

or whether it was simply to divert the reader and to arouse his sexual desires and thus harm the public morality. First, let us consider the defendant herself, Laylā ʿAlī Baʿalbakkī, the daughter of a conservative Lebanese village family, who left her home and traveled to Paris, where she remained for some time, in an environment totally different from that of her own people. As she lived in this strange environment, she observed the people's life styles, their confusions, their troubles, their silences. Each day she tried to learn more about this new society, to discover its particular truths. Trained from childhood in letters, coming from a tradition which used words to express enlightened thoughts, Laylā ʿAlī Baʿalbakkī was moved to put down on paper the things she had seen and felt in her real and her subsequent imaginary trips to the strange society in Paris, and thus she wrote the book in question, *A Space Ship of Tenderness to the Moon*. . . .

Therefore, after all these points have been considered, the court views the defendant Laylā ʿAlī Baʿalbakkī and her book *A Space Ship of Tenderness to the Moon* as follows: Her intention was to portray, realistically and truthfully, her characters as she saw them moving on the bare stage of life. She gave to acts and emotions their accurate names in order to dramatize the idea which she was presenting. Just as a human being exposes his real self in front of a mirror in order to see clearly, and hopefully improve, its faults and its uglinesses, so does the book in question use realism to help the reader see life more clearly. The stories in question do not arouse sexual instincts or harm public morality. The work is to be seen rather as a serious creative effort, a call to set people free from their narrow environments, a call for all of us to face the naked truth and its ramifications, to see good and evil and to learn to choose between them, not with eyes closed with the trachoma of tradition that has woven a veil of ignorance around us, but with eyes wide open toward the light.

And therefore, the court finds that, since such efforts do not constitute a crime which is subject to punishment, the court's judgment is that all procedures against the defendant, Laylā ʿAlī Baʿalbakkī, should cease immediately. [Aug. 23, 1964]

> Court decision. In Elizabeth Warnock Fernea and Basima
> Qattan Bezirgan, eds., *Middle Eastern Muslim Women*
> *Speak* (Austin, University of Texas Press, 1977),
> pp. 280–81, 287–89

BARAKĀT, HALĪM (1933–   )

LEBANON

In *Six Days* Halīm Barakāt broaches the subject of belonging in the life of the current generation. Najīb Mahfūz had already addressed himself to the ques-

tion in his *Trilogy* . . . and now here is Halīm Barakāt adding a new element to
the crisis, namely cultural backwardness.

The fact is that the crisis of freedom and the tragedy of cultural backwardness in the Arab world are among the most significant factors affecting
the problem of "belonging" in our country. The essential difference between
us and the West at the moment is that we have arrived at our present cultural
situation because of a staggering heritage of backwardness in the face of
world civilization. We are also heirs to undemocratic traditions in our mode of
government. The Arab conscience can no longer avoid "committing itself" to
certain social theories and political and economic solutions. . . .

The author of this novel uses interior monologue, personal reminiscences, dreams, and all the other devices needed to express ideas about past,
present, and future within a short time frame. . . . The major event in *Six Days*
is the ordeal of Dayr al-Bahr in the face of enemy threats: either the village
surrenders, or else it will be wiped off the face of the earth, to quote the first
line of the novel. . . .

Halīm Barakāt places all his characters in a single crisis within a short
time period and in a place surrounded by danger; in other words, during the
most crucial event in the life of each of them. He then chooses from among
these characters the one who is most worried and crisis-prone . . . and puts
him in the midst of a unique situation. He falls into enemy hands and suffers
terrible mental and physical torture. What should his position be? Should he
confess what he knows and save himself so that he can go back to his girl-
friend? Or does his "honor" hang on this one key moment in his life? The protagonist of this work finds himself clinging to the essential concept that is inseparable from his own particular concerns, namely that of freedom. His
country's freedom is the same as his own personal freedom. And so he endures the torture stoically and without emotion.

Ghālī Shukrī. Al-Majalla. July, 1963, pp. 124–26†

A work by Lebanon's Halīm Barakāt heralds the beginning of the Arabic political novel in the best sense of the term. Set against the Arab debacle in
Palestine, *Six Days* marks the approaching communion of the heroic act and
the tragic experience in the Arabic novel. Halīm Barakāt weaves his novel
around the inner sensibility and inner conflicts of his protagonist, Suhayl.

The six days represent the lease on life that the superior forces of the enemy grant the inhabitants of the small hamlet of Dayr al-Bahr in their ultimatum to surrender or face annihilation. During these six days, Barakāt, through
his protagonist, portrays the crisis faced by the Arab intellectual of that period. The crisis is expressed in all its religious, social, and cultural ramifications. Suhayl defies destiny by struggling against insurmountable odds to up-
hold his ideals, to be true in his love, and to save his land. He experiences
pain, torture, and despair. "It may be hard to commit suicide but it is even

harder to face life. Suicide is a passing protest whereas life is a continuing act of protest," he declares.

He joins the partisans in an engagement against the enemy even though he harbors great doubts about the worthiness of their cause, for the partisans are defending a kind of life and society that he despises. He loves Nahidah, a victim of irrational and outmoded social and religious conventions. Winning her seems as hopeless as victory in battle. But he remains in the thick of both these battles. Why? That is what he asks himself and tries to resolve. "Why does he love her? To forget boredom. Why does he expose himself to death? To forget boredom. Why defy? To forget boredom. He did not mean what he said about the blessings of death. He wishes only to overcome boredom."

Suhayl is captured by the enemy. Despite the torture he suffers at their hands, he refuses to betray the defense plans of his hamlet. He thinks only of his colleagues and of Nahidah, who, toward the end of the novel, rebels against her parents and runs away to join him only to learn that he has disappeared and is believed to have been killed. The enemy attacks before the ultimatum has expired and takes the hamlet by surprise. Suhayl's colleagues, in a desperate maneuver to defend the village, are all killed.

Written in direct, staccato-like sentences, *Six Days* reflects the development of a new stylistic technique and a higher level of perfection in the Arabic novel. Barakāt's work is comparable in craftsmanship and spirit to Marguerite Duras' *Moderato Cantabile*. It is a genuine work, fashioned out of the raw material around which it is woven—the sweet breath of nature that envelops Dayr al-Bahr and the sweaty bodies of its inhabitants. The leading characters are tragic loners who, amid the ruins of their place and time, must bear the agony and conflict created by their acute sensitivity.

George Sfeir. *Daedalus*. Fall, 1966, pp. 956–57

Halīm Barakāt clearly reveals himself in the thoughts and reactions of his principal characters. His latest work, the novel *Return of the Sailor* [i.e., *Flying Dutchman*] *to the Sea*, published in Beirut early this summer, is of extraordinary interest. In it he draws a comparison between the Arabs and the flying Dutchman of legend and the Wagner opera. The Arabs, like the sailor, are decreed by the fates to wander till eternity in search of a lover true to death who will break the spell and allow a return to their homeland.

The novel covers the period from the fifth to the twentieth of June, 1967. The outbreak, development and conclusion of the war are seen through the minds of Ramzi Safady, a professor at the American University of Beirut, and half-a-dozen minor characters set in various locations close to the old borders of Israel.

Their mood changes, of course, from optimism mixed with varying degrees of doubt and foreboding to the utter despair and hopelessness of the final outcome. The lightning speed of the war, the skillful use of surprise, airpower and napalm by the Israelis are shown to be the immediate reasons for the Arabs' defeat, but the self-deception and disorganization of the Arab governments and ineffectiveness of Arab intellectuals are seen as the root causes of the disaster.

The hero's feelings are so clearly autobiographical and the incidents so obviously related to reported events, that the work is polemic as well as fiction. Halīm Barakāt is clearly deeply influenced by the work of Kahlil Gibran—an earlier work has two passages of quotation from the latter's *Prophet*.

Trevor Le Gassick. *Mid East*. Oct., 1969, pp. 14–15

In my opinion, the value of this novel [*The Return of the Flying Dutchman to the Sea*] lies in its reliance on a new artistic style, without which the work would be worthless. We therefore find ourselves faced with a novel that belongs to a new trend in Arabic novel writing, one that rejects traditional methods of construction, character portrayal, and even sentence structure. It strives to create a new technique that shows the influences of innovative methods of novel writing in the West and also of current cinematic styles.

The Return of the Flying Dutchman to the Sea is divided into three sections. Since this novel—any novel—depends entirely on the concept of time (that is, time is one of the major elements in its structure and creation), time in this novel follows the rhythm set by the chapters and their subdivisions. Even so, the author relies on external time, historical time. And so the first part begins on the eleventh of June and ends on the twentieth; the second starts on the fifth of June and goes through to the tenth; with the third, we return to the point where the novel began, from the eleventh to the twentieth of June. Actually, the first and third sections should be regarded as an introduction and conclusion to the second part, which is the real core of the work. This central section takes its rhythm from time as well; it is divided into six days, the six days of the well-known war. . . .

At the end of the novel, the hero is eager to change and transform everything around him. He wants to have roots and a shadow. However, the author leaves all that in the realms of hope alone; in all likelihood, the character, the present situation, and the past of this educated protagonist will prevent him from achieving these hopes.

To sum up, we find ourselves here with a novel that is new in its content, its structural technique, and its tense and vivid style. Even though the protagonist is a character who simply watches the events and is affected by them rather than having an effect on them, the author still manages to use this and other characters—especially the Palestinian ones—and the events he describes for us to give artistic expression to the disastrous setback the Arabs suffered in the June war of 1967. In achieving such a success the author is helped considerably by his own broad cultural background and his new narrative method.

George Sālim. *Al-Ma'rifa*. March, 1972,
pp. 147–48, 153–54†

Like Flaubert, Barakāt, in *Days of Dust* [i.e., *The Return of the Flying Dutchman to the Sea*] examines responses in Beirut to an Arab political calamity which ought to be understood in terms of failure, not in those of an enemy's victory. Unlike Flaubert, Barakāt shows a genuine kindness to his cast of actors; he has none of Flaubert's bitter indictment of an entire generation. Whereas in *L'éducation sentimentale* sentiment and fantasy are associated with the important failure at which Frédéric Moreau and Deslauriers finally arrive, in Barakāt's novel sentiment is employed to heighten the human poignancy of the disaster. For Barakāt disappointment and dislocation can always be made intelligible if they are commented on with reference to justificatory passion. The images of sea and fire, as well as the sequences using the *Flying Dutchman* figure, are instruments of clarification employed to increase the disaster's universality, and its tragic shades.

Barakāt's use of the scene shares with Mahfouz' technique the interest in intense particularity; indeed, it shares with Barakāt's classic study (done jointly with Peter Dodd) of the 1967 Palestinian refugee exodus, the practiced sociologist's focus on those minutiae of everyday life that compose man's large-scale activity. Yet Barakāt's scene is dominated by the almost hateful sequence of six days. This short succession of moments dominates the action off-stage, but in the novel Barakāt amplifies these days into a wide-ranging geographical and emotional voyage. His blurring of space-time distinctions, the montage effect of rapid scene-change, the carefully chosen cross-section of characters from Beirut to Amman to the West Bank, all these argue a sometimes uncertain balance between the social scientist's deliberateness and the novelist's inventiveness. Unlike both Flaubert and Mahfouz, Barakāt takes, I think, a decidedly softer position on Arab contemporaneity in the throes of a major disaster. For him, the scene is an arena for continual struggle. Even though Arab history is a repetition of Biblical history, Barakāt's principal character, Ramzy, judges it also as a field for potential victory. There is none of that bitter attitude toward repetition that animates Flaubert's work or Marx's *18th Brumaire of Louis Napoleon* or, for that matter, Mahfouz' post-1967 work. For in the end Barakāt is a novelist of good will; and this is his interest.

Edward Said. Introduction to Halīm Barakāt, *Days of Dust*
(Wilmette, Ill., Medina Press International, 1974),
pp. xxxi–xxxii

AL-BAYYĀTĪ, 'ABD AL-WAHHĀB (1926–   )

IRAQ

The collection *Broken Pitchers* wavers between phoney existentialism, despairing romanticism, and obscure realism. It draws its imagery from outside society and from the noisy confusion of fantasy. Thus, each reader of the collection emerges with a different and unclear picture of the poet's personality. It is vague and impressionistic, like a mirror that reflects things, but in a distorted fashion because it has not been polished properly. As a poet, al-Bayyātī is subject to a number of influences; he copies and imitates others. There are two exceptions, which number among the best poems in all of modern Arabic poetry, "The Corsair" and "The South Wind." . . .

When al-Bayyātī "borrows" atmosphere and expressions from poems by other writers, he knows in advance that he will be found out sooner or later. Sometimes, he resorts to a clever ruse as a way of warding off the possible consequences before they actually happen. Every time he steals a phrase from some other poet, he precedes it with a colon so as to show that a quotation is to follow. He then puts quotation marks at both the beginning and end of the citation, so much so that the reader ends up completely confused as to what is meant by these punctuation marks. Is the poet, you wonder, using these marks to indicate that everything between them is an insertion, or something entirely different? Those who know absolutely nothing about it extol this "poetic artistry" to the skies. But those who know the real reason for this literary pilfering can say that the man is admitting that everything between quotation marks is not by him! However, we come to realize that some things that have been taken from other poets are not put between quotation marks, other "borrowings" have been tampered with, and some lines that are placed within quotation marks are in fact by al-Bayyātī. When all that comes to be known, we realize what the poet is trying to do. . . .

I will not prolong this discussion any further. The collection contains few images of the social environment and evinces an odd incompatibility among the images that are used. One example will serve as a representative of many others: "My dead friends, pouring forth like the waters of a heaving river." I do not understand how there can be any congruity between dead people in a state of oblivion and silence and the headlong rush of a river. This kind of incongruity is a feature of the entire collection.

Kāzim Jawād. Al-Ādāb. July, 1954, pp. 34, 36†

Al-Bayyātī has tried to a certain extent to match the achievement of Baudelaire, particularly in pictures of folly and wasted effort taken from the experiences of everyday life. But al-Bayyātī differs from Baudelaire in one important social fact, namely that he is not a city poet. In all the images he creates

he is the son of the village who can see all its shortcomings and feel the tribulations of its inhabitants, those good folk with their dreams. Al-Bayyātī does
talk about the city; it is just like the city of Baudelaire and Eliot, a "blind
beast" or a deadly abyss that swallows up everyone in it and turns individuals
into dwarfs. But al-Bayyātī takes these images of the city from the outside,
since he lives with village images. The reader does not have to exert much effort in order to discover the way the village spirit predominates in the collection *Broken Pitchers*—through the similes he uses, the characters, the scenes,
and the events. A quick review of the similes will show us the extent to which
he has exploited the atmosphere of the village and derived forceful symbols
from its animals and insects: flies, dogs, wolves, foxes, cats, snails, spiders,
rabbits, rats, and so on. There are pictures of birds and plants as well, but the
ones of animals have more force because animal images can be larger and
clearer symbols than those of plants. Figs pure and simple are probably just
figs, whereas dogs and their howling can be used to represent a number of
ideas.

It may be this technique that enables the language of ordinary speech to
enter the realm of poetic sound. It is in this regard that al-Bayyātī and Eliot
coincide with each other and diverge from the imagists in their use of suggestion and symbols and in making the movement of the image similar to that of
the psyche. In this al-Bayyātī is, almost of necessity, less abstruse than Eliot,
since he is less concerned with the interior workings of the mind and the conflicting currents hidden deep down inside us, reluctant to delve into religious
motivations, and less influenced by the French symbolist school. With al-
Bayyātī, association does not always produce facts for the mind, but more often a list of exterior aspects of the picture. In remembering Paris, for example, the following things come to his mind: the tombs of Mirabeau and Robes-
pierre, the snow, the darkness, the beggars, the coughing of a sick child, and
the boats. All that such a list shows is a mind hovering around the external aspects of the total image. In describing the village he will remember the yoke,
the plow, the field, and the oak tree—things the eye picks up but which have
value only because the suggestive images they arouse are connected with the
scene as a whole.

Al-Bayyātī's connection with Eliot is undoubtedly very close, whether it
be a direct one or through a more circuitous route. The general technique in
Eliot's poems influenced al-Bayyātī's poetry, especially in its reliance on a
type of invention whereby fables and citations from older preserved materials
are used in the corpus of the poem until they come to be like bricks that fit in
perfectly with the general structure. . . .

Al-Bayyātī's personality has begun, with this tendency toward greater
freedom, to exert its independence and to state its own philosophy. The reason for this development can be ascribed to the difference between al-Bayyātī
and Eliot with regard to religious belief, that being the area on which Eliot

concentrates in his own poetry. Al-Bayyātī on the other hand has, to a large degree, ignored the subject. His personages spit in the face of heaven and only cry out to heaven in times of extreme weakness. Al-Bayyātī's characters feel no sense of sin or have any inner mental struggle caused by guilt. The only exception is when the sin is directed by an individual against society. . . . To al-Bayyātī sin is not something religious, it is a social deficiency. The worst sin of all is to sell your conscience. It may have been this feeling that made it possible for al-Bayyātī to diverge from Eliot, although he never completely eradicated his connection with him and his philosophy.

Ihsān ʿAbbās. *ʿAbd al-Wahhāb al-Bayyātī wa-al-shiʿr al-ʿIrāqī al-hadīth* (Beirut, Dār Beirut, 1955), pp. 22–24, 26–27†

This past week I have visited a number of places: Iraq, Palestine, Marseilles in France, Madrid, Chicago, Tehran, China, Syria, Morocco, Tunisia, and Algeria. I really wanted to spend some more time in Warsaw, too, after I had flown there on the wings of love through the poems of ʿAbd al-Wahhāb al-Bayyātī. His poetry, with its freedom, its quasi-universality, and its inclusiveness takes you—albeit through the senses alone—to North Africa and China and makes you feel present—if only to a minor extent—in those countries. For al-Bayyātī has read widely, studies daily events closely, and follows all the political news and international developments. To this he adds his experience at forming an image, his quick imagination, his receptivity to excitement, and his capacity for suggestion. The fact is that al-Bayyātī's poetic gifts are based on a comprehensive human emotion that does not differentiate among races, colors, or religions. Its affection spans everyone on the face of the earth, since "humanist" poets like al-Bayyātī believe that the earth is not something to divide one person from another. People near and far, yellow, black, and white, can only be treated as equals.

Thus, it is humanity that is the binding force in al-Bayyātī's latest collection, *Glory to Children and the Olive*. This theme would be rather dull if it were not for the poet's revolutionary nature. . . . Usually, sympathy for the poor, destitute, wronged, struggling people of the earth is not sufficient to produce good poetry. Many poets here and there have devoted poems to these oppressed people and have not been able to bring a tear to the eye or strike a spark. It is just the opposite with al-Bayyātī. His psychological background is rich, although I personally believe (without any personal acquaintance with him) that he has some profound psychological problems, the most significant of which is an inferiority complex.

Unsī al-Ḥājj. *Shiʿr*. Spring, 1957, pp. 80–81†

The work of al-Bayyātī is reckoned to be a contemporary peak in realistic literature among the Arabs, not only because he has a grasp of humanistic

knowledge and the course of history and consults them both, but also because his talents and burning emotion transcend form and current topics and
reach out with depth and intelligence to more far-reaching horizons and problems. These are the questions posed by our own clamorous and complex reality, the age that is on the brink of discarding and burying our entire culture
and all our possessions in the abyss of appalling death, although from an opposite viewpoint, this age is almost bringing genuine freedom to fruition for
mankind and society! . . .

In the collection *Fire and Words* there are two main questions preoccu-
pying the poet's sentiments . . . and in which all the psychological, emotional, and poetic strands and tendencies come together: death and freedom.
They are the most significant of this age's psychological problems, and our
poet tackles them both with a fiery veracity.

Al-Bayyātī penetrates into this terrible question of death, something man
has avoided discussing in detail throughout the ages—until the twentieth century, that is. And yet, in spite of the suffering and bitterness involved in the
subject, he does not dissolve into soporifics or lose his connection with life.
He hates death because he loves life so much, that most marvelous gift of existence! . . .

Before talking about freedom, I would like to record that the poet's understanding of the function of language in poetry has the utmost importance.
To him it is concise and suggestive. . . . Words are a rich and fertile world,
and thus the choice of which ones to use requires a tremendous talent. . . .

The freedom al-Bayyātī has to be sad and to subject his feelings to psychological scrutiny lends his diction a special musicality and a wonderful
sense of sincerity, authenticity, and artistry that come from the heart. The
sense of alienation that colors his life, and the feeling of loss and anxiety in
the face of a dire fate, give his poetry its warmth and poetic mastery. He does
not use any predetermined measure to sketch these feelings, but lets them
speak for themselves about sorrow.

Jīlī ʿAbd al-Rahmān. *Al-Ādāb*. Jan., 1965, pp. 34, 36†

I do not know what it is that ties al-Bayyātī's poems together. Probably nothing. They are all disconnected. Their structure is secondary, and the collection [*The Book of Poverty and Revolution*] seems devoid of frame or edges.
We will therefore concentrate on the quest for understanding of the parts that
make up the whole. . . .

Our poet likes to laugh at the past. This laugh is a shout of defiance; it
may perhaps be negative. But he is a compulsive innovator. [In a group of six
poems about the medieval martyr al-Hallāj (d. 922), whose life is used as an
allegory for contemporary Arab politics], the sultan's jester is no longer his
servant; he has become his daughter's lover. . . . The sultan here is a symbol
of the upper echelons—justice, morality, the prevailing political system. Al-

82   AL-BAYYĀTĪ, 'ABD AL-WAHHĀB

Bayyātī is poor, from the lower social stratum, where all the production, toiling, and building occur. He is disputatious in his poetry and rarely resorts to analytical verse. He announces his revolt calmly: "I just said a couple of words to the sultan: 'You're a coward!'"

He is a poet of deep revolutionary convictions, the poet of the hungry making their way to the fields, the threshing floors, the factories; the poet of cultural modernization, of awareness; the witness of a generation taking vengeance on all jesters (who mock their masters), swindlers, middlemen, occupiers, and tricksters. He is the great Islamic mystic al-Hallāj on trial; he is Christ crucified. But he is also different from both of them. For, whereas the former writes about the soul, and the latter about resurrection and deification, al-Bayyātī's theme is poverty and material revolution. . . .

Al-Bayyātī is extremely clear, a realist who can reach his people with well-fashioned, living words, effective and able to convey spiritual experiences that spring from the cultural birth-pangs our great people have to endure. . . . He delves into the popular memory in order to get to our heritage, and then tries to change its images and ideas so as to plant new seeds in people's hearts. Thus the words become creative, becoming a firm and thoughtful force. He is searching for a new raincloud which will wash away the nightmare of servitude and misery from his heart and alter the face of the Tigris, the creative river that is not fulfilling its proper role. When water and people meet, then movement and vigor will be kindled in everything. Al-Bayyātī's poetry is a call to reach the real homeland, the new homeland far away in the distance.

Khalīl Ahmad Khalīl. Al-Ādāb. Dec., 1965, pp. 24–25†

Bayyātī's most recent volume, *Love Poems on the Seven Gates of the World* (1971), includes among the personae or masks the Muslim mystic Ibn al-ʿArabī and the Arab lover Waddāh al-Yaman, as well as poems addressed to the Muslim jurist Shāfiʿī and to Ikhnatun. Now the mystical and surrealistic elements become dominant features of his style, in many places to the point of unintelligibility. A more moderate example of this style is the last poem in the collection, entitled "The Nightmare," which in five sections asserts the poet's faith in the value of the struggle and dissent in art and in life, and the continuity of the spirit of revolution despite the fall of revolutionaries. . . .

Although Bayyātī himself may hotly deny it, it is most likely that one of the factors that have led to his change of style is the growing influence of Adūnīs's poetry, which . . . reveals a mystical outlook, and which seeks to destroy all logical connections, relies heavily on surrealistic imagery and resorts to the use of masks. In this respect Adūnīs's influence helped to strengthen and confirm whatever effect on his poetry was exercised by Bayyātī's earlier fascination with the work of Marxists like Mayakovsky,

Aragon, Éluard and Neruda, which, besides being Marxist, was also either futuristic or surrealistic or opaquely symbolist.

Mustafa Badawi. *A Critical Introduction to Modern Arabic Poetry* (Cambridge, England, Cambridge University Press, 1975), pp. 215–16

Al-Bayyātī has shown a growing interest in the use of the archetype. A poet's universal vision, al-Bayyātī explains, depends on three things: an objective understanding of the paradoxes of existence, a discovery of the logic of history and a dynamic involvement with the events of his own time. From the appearance of his second collection, *Broken Pitchers* (1954), al-Bayyātī showed a cosmic sense, and sought to unify human struggle everywhere. As a Marxist, he forged links with famous left-wing poets such as Nazim Hikmet, Pablo Neruda, Mayakovski, Lorca, Aragon and Éluard. Even at the zenith of Arab Nationalism in the 'fifties, he showed a genuine preoccupation with the struggle for freedom all over the world. The broad cosmic outlook which, at the beginning, preoccupied itself more with contemporary times, has persisted in his poetry, but has been greatly enriched by a growing historical sense that has been developing deeper in him, simultaneously as it did with various other major poets in the Arab world. Myths, historical events and recorded stories of bygone days are incorporated into the texture of many of his poems seeking unity with present-day archetypes, and some are vested with qualities that surpass their basic historical descriptions in order to make their material rich enough for the creation of the archetype. However, al-Bayyātī, in what seems to be a very diligent search for historical material, sometimes toys with his findings too drastically for success.

Salmā al-Jayyūsī. In R. C. Ostle, ed., *Studies in Modern Arabic Literature* (Warminster, England, Aris and Phillips, 1975), p. 60

Like Arab nationalists, [the Arab Socialist poets] backed the national revolutions of some Arab groups, especially the Algerians, against European domination. They discussed current political and social problems in the Arab and the international spheres, and praised the achievements of the Soviet Union and other Communist countries. However, as we have seen, they also derived their images from Christian symbols and Greek mythology, as did the Russian poet Boris Pasternak. . . .

Another resemblance between the nationalist and the Socialist poets is that both groups believe that European culture has reached its zenith, and is now in the process of corruption and decay. But the Communist poets do not say whether they consider the Soviet Union part of the decadent Western culture or not.

Al-Bayyātī, in his collection *Words Which Do Not Die* (Beirut, 1960), in the group of poems which he called "Poems from Vienna," said in "The Western Civilization" that it was corrupt like a prostitute who had missed her train and found herself naked in the night of Europe dying in the cold and rain.

Like the nationalist poets in their attacks on Europe, al-Bayyātī also quoted Western thinkers and poets who criticized European civilization. In his "Old Europe" he used T. S. Eliot's poem "The Hollow Men" to emphasize the spiritual emptiness of Europe and to mock its civilization. In another poem, "To T. S. Eliot," he ridiculed the damned waste land of the British writer, that it contained no poet, no love, no martyrs, no drop of water, no windmill. Eliot's land is the land of foreigners and evils. He invites Eliot to see the real struggle for life in the Arab countries.

S. Moreh. *Modern Arabic Poetry 1800–1970* (Leiden,
E. J. Brill, 1976), pp. 270–71

DARWĪSH, MAHMŪD (1942–   )

PALESTINE

The most attractive aspect of Darwīsh's poetic world is his particular "human vision," which is reflected in the structure of the poem. He sees people and things in a way in which all the elements are intermingled. In a single poem he will talk about his beloved, and then in another section of the same poem we will find that the beloved has been transformed into another concept, the homeland, and then again to sister and mother. Thus, the concepts of love, homeland, freedom, and nature are completely blended together; they possess similar features. The poet views his homeland through the transparent emotion of love; he sees his land through the feelings of motherhood. There are no longer boundaries between things; in his poetry we find a kind of "unity of existence." . . .

In the poem "A Lover from Palestine" [in the collection of the same name] we come face to face with this particular vision. The poet talks about his beloved, but we soon realize that he is moving from his beloved to his homeland. Then he combines the two, but we do not feel that his beloved is in any way separate from his homeland. . . . The talk is of love, but it is a love that is sad and wounded, as is everything in a sad and wounded country. . . . He is a lover who sees in his beloved's eyes reminders of his own deprivation and his tremendous responsibility. He is no usual lover; he is a lover from Palestine. . . .

In Darwīsh's poetry we encounter a number of symbols, the most important and frequent being that of the Cross; it appears in the majority of his poems. The poet certainly has a number of artistic and intellectual reasons for this, the most significant of which is that he is living in Palestine, the land of the Messiah. The tragedy of Christ is compared with the cross on which the Jews wanted to crucify Him. The cross is compared with both old and modern Palestine in that the Jews in Israel want to crucify Palestine and everything in it and to put an end to both it and its people. For someone who lives through this tragedy on a daily basis . . . there is obviously good reason for using the symbol of the cross to express that tragedy. . . .

Darwīsh is considered one of five major poets of the modern generation who have used the cross as a symbol; the others are Badr Shākir al-Sayyāb, Adūnīs, Salāḥ ʿAbd al-Sabūr, and Khalīl Hāwī. I can state my opinion quite frankly that Darwīsh, through his own experiences and sufferings, comes closest to artistic and emotional conviction in his use of this symbol.

Rajāʾ al-Naqqāsh. Al-Ādāb. Feb., 1968, pp. 5–6, 56–57†

The thing that strikes one about Mahmūd Darwīsh—apart, of course, from his tremendous talent and his commitment to the value of commitment itself as something that can enrich a work of art rather than spoil it—is the very speed with which he has developed, something extremely rare among poets of repute, in his case, rather like the touch of a magic wand.

In a relatively short period between 1961 and 1963, when Darwīsh was between twenty-one and twenty-three years old, something important and unusual happened on the level of the poet's artistry; in one burst it gained in both range and depth. It was a major step forward for him and seemed almost like some kind of transmigration. A rather colorless poet who seemed only concerned with scratches on the surface . . . suddenly began to pour out poetry in a flood. Profoundly aware, this poetry viewed things from a solid stance with complete self-confidence and, above all else, was able day by day to affirm its correctness and profundity.

Needless to say, Darwīsh has been able to continue his development after this basic leap forward, but the later development was merely the natural form that maturity and fullness of vision would normally take. . . . In comparison with his development between 1961 and 1963 it hardly merits investigation. The earlier stage was a kind of discovery that propelled the poet to a totally different level in both form and content. . . .

In fact, there have been two extremely important "leaps forward" in Darwīsh's poetry; and he is not yet thirty years old. The first was when Darwīsh "chose" to turn to a more comprehensive and radical vision; this is the more important of the two and the one that causes the most surprise. The second one, which began to take shape in the aftermath of the June war of 1967, is also important, even though it is proceeding on its natural and gradual course. When Darwīsh at the beginning of the 1960s saw woman, trees, horses, rocks, and grass as the homeland, the question was reflected in his poetry as a "choice." After June 1967 it seems that he has stopped "seeing," since, in and of himself, he has become an indivisible part of the whole; the process of fusion has reached its peak.

The story of Mahmūd Darwīsh over the last ten years is a curious and surprising one, in that it involves a combination of those two contrasting elements, Marxism and Islamic mysticism.

Ghassān Kanafānī. Al-Ādāb. March, 1969, pp. 27, 29†

This attachment to the land is an affirmation of identity against persistent attempts by the colonial settler state to rob him of such identity by expropriating more and more of his land. Through this affirmation, a new meaning emerges from the use of the word *Palestine*. It is not only the homeland of those poets; it is also their land threatened by government takeover. Still a third dimension is added when their love for a woman is identified with their love for the land and for Palestine. The merging of the three concepts is exemplified in the poetry of Mahmūd Darwīsh, "A Lover from Palestine." . . .

The land, like the woman and the homeland, becomes a symbol of dignity, life, and the future: a symbol of humanity and manhood. The merging of the three is an act of resistance and a declaration of opposition. The olive and orange trees are particularly poignant symbols of the love for the land, the homeland. The farmer plants and cares for these trees with the expectation of getting fruit, which represents life and hope; but this age-long relationship was shattered with a tragic loss of blood. . . .

The use of the land as a symbol of struggle against the negation, to presume the identity of the Arab in Israel, gives a new meaning to Arab nationalism. The latter, in addition to legitimizing the struggle for independence from foreign dominations, becomes a question of spiritual survival for the individual himself, a struggle against the alienation that the Palestinian poet feels in his own land, and which he tries to overcome by affirming his Arab identity. Mahmūd Darwīsh stresses this affirmation in his "Identity Card," a poem which could not have been written in any Arab country; but in Israel, it is not only a picture of the struggle, but part of it.

Naseer Aruri and Edmund Ghareeb, eds. Introduction to
Enemy of the Sun: Poetry of Palestinian Resistance
(Washington, D.C., Drum and Spear Press,
1970), pp. xxxiv–xxxvi

In his recent collection *Sparrows Are Dying in Galilee* [Darwīsh] achieves a fully rounded poetic and artistic form, if such an expression can be used; his poetry has its own particular flavor. There is also a shift from a gleaming clarity to an opacity of great beauty and to an excellent use of symbols and myths to express the poet's emotions, a poet who feels such sorrows of long experience deep down inside himself that he seems to acquire the wisdom of old age, with its acknowledgment of bitter reality. . . .

The latest poems reflect the experience of prolonged practice. The artistic structure of the poem is now well planned, and all of the sections blend in with each other. The poet's musicality is often closest to that of free verse in those of his images that are most developed and brilliant, although the reader may feel a little dismayed by a certain amount of disjointedness in expression at times and some obscurity in the use of symbols. Even though we may perhaps detect the influence of al-Bayyātī in some of these more diaphanous poetic images, when we survey the history of this poet's development since he published his first poems we come to realize that we are facing a productive poet who has opened his emotions to life in spite of all the bitter conditions in the shadow of which all this poetry has been written.

This poet is not satisfied by the stage he has reached at any one time; he continues to look for new psychological and artistic horizons. In his poetry we can detect a clear line of development that should achieve a good deal of distinction and brilliance if he can persevere with it and support it with some new experiences of mankind. The nationalist experience in its direct form cannot remain for long as the source of inspiration for any poet without that talent losing its liveliness and resorting to repetitions and stereotyped expressions. The poet who wishes to keep on conveying the nationalist message in successful works of art must search continually for new modes of expression in fiction, drama, and poetry and draw attention to the common tragedies faced by all humanity and the community of feeling about them everywhere. . . . Some of this Mahmūd Darwīsh has tried to achieve, and yet his talent does not seem to include within it a sufficient degree of creativity.

ʿAbd al-Qādir al-Qitt. Al-Majalla. March, 1971, p. 9†

There are certain recurrent images in these poems whose significance isn't limited to the idiosyncratic concerns of the poet or to the mysterious personal source of his creativity. In the West we are accustomed to finding that a contemporary poet's most pregnant images are those which conduct us into his underworld, bring us into contact with the deep sources of his energy, with the semi-articulate matrix of the poems. In Darwīsh's poems these *leitmotive*, although protean, are consistently and invariably public. It is in the superstructures of the poems that we find personal notes and references.

This has a number of consequences. It means that Darwīsh can use a kind of shorthand. The presence of this familiar system makes it easy for him to set up echoes in the furthest reaches of Arab classical literature, tradition, and mythology. It makes possible "classic" ironies which are almost certainly going to be lost on most readers of translations. To appreciate the significance of this one must imagine T. S. Eliot, for example, to be familiar and loved in the market places where, in addition, his lines will be heard in the vernacular of proverb and epigrams. This doesn't mean that there is no controversy over Darwīsh's poems. It means that the controversy is not the prerogative of those with "higher education." At the same time, we shouldn't imagine that analysis of the poems' matrix is going to provide the equivalent of an ordinary Arab reader's response. We will extract an echo of the old blind Syrian poet Abu'l-ʿAlā al-Maʿarrī, who died nine hundred years ago. To the ordinary Arab reader, the tradition is *current*: he perceives it primarily as a tone, not as detail. Translation of these poems provides only half an equation. The other half does not consist merely in making the crossing to another culture, but in making the crossing to another order of culture.

There are two related groups of imagery, that of wounds and that of martyrdom and earth, which, with their ramifications, shape the matrix of most of these poems. These images lead us to a persistent inversion of expected values and responses associated with what the images stand for. This duality, in turn, leads us to see a crux in Darwīsh the poet, which while it has antecedents, helps us to understand how Darwīsh is so much a poet "of his time."

Ian Wedde and Fawwaz Tuqan. Introduction to Mahmoud Darwīsh, *Selected Poems* (Cheadle, England, Carcanet Press, 1973), pp. 7–8

Exile, banishment—these are the objective realities that are the topics of Mahmūd Darwīsh's investigation in his most recent collection, *Attempt Number 7*. In striving to grasp the external dimension of the subject, he is really aiming to gain an artistic grasp on this exile once it has managed to penetrate into his inner self as a result of everyday experience. . . . In this collection, Darwīsh is not merely reflecting and embodying disaster; he is embodying his own sense of calamity in that the Arab people in general have not been able to transcend the disaster. Put a different way, he is stunned by our present circumstances after becoming acquainted with them at first hand, penetrating their innermost secrets and being affected by them in a direct fashion. It is here that we meet Darwīsh in his exile face to face. It is on this ground alone that we can explain the factors that prompted him to write the poem "Sirhān Drinking Coffee in California." More than any other title, this poem's is the one that can best define for us the political psychology of this distressed poet. . . .

This subject, which we have seen as the basic starting point for an understanding of this collection, *Attempt Number 7*, also serves the same function for his previous collection, *I Love You or I Do Not Love You*, in that it serves as a preparation for the present collection. In much the same way, this present collection is both a completion and extension of the previous one, something that can be gleaned from a study of the poetry itself. . . .

It is obvious that the change Darwīsh has made from a simple technique to a more complicated one has of necessity led to a greater complexity in the meanings the words convey on the one hand, and to an increasingly intricate use of expression and style on the other. In fact, the relationship between development in language use and consciousness is one of cause and effect. . . . Thus we find that Darwīsh's vocabulary of the 1960s has undergone a radical change and become completely new. Now we find words such as "sea," "river," "water," "shore," "mirrors." . . .

Why, one may ask, is this "attempt" called "number 7"? Some people have observed that this is the seventh collection of Darwīsh's poetry, and that of course is reasonable. However, something more profound than that may be indicated. The revolution that has been Darwīsh's overriding concern is now the seventh in a series of attempts by the Palestinian people; it has been preceded by six others: in 1919, 1921, 1929, 1933, 1936–39, and 1948. So "*Attempt Number 7*" is not just Darwīsh's; it is that of the Palestinian people as a whole.

Yūsuf al-Yūsuf. Al-Ādāb. Nov., 1974, pp. 24, 27–28, 30†

DIYĀB, MAHMŪD (1932–   )

EGYPT

Mahmūd Diyāb was in the vanguard of the second generation of realist dramatists. *The Storm* is the most outstanding realistic play to have freed itself from the problems of the realistic trend and to have taken full advantage of previous efforts in the same direction. It has thus emerged as a fully developed work of art; in fact, it is certainly one of the most sophisticated works of art yet to appear in modern Egyptian drama.

The playwright does not resort in this play to a discussion of the urgent issues that can change as fast as social conditions themselves change. He has been able to create for us the world of the village, with its problems and many complexities. By means of this microcosm the problems of mankind can be surveyed with the maximum of profundity and seriousness. When you take an unhurried look at this play, you realize that Diyāb has been able to give it two distinct levels, as with any authentic work of art: the first level is the direct one, and the second is the more profound interior one. The first level is the portrayal of the village with its complex relationships. This involves both the wrongdoers and the wronged, the people who trample on other people's rights and the poor devils who suffer as a result, the rumors with which the life of the village is filled and the vicious and grave effect they have on it; the poor and the rich, the wise and intelligent who try to build a decent life in the vil-

lage, sometimes succeeding, other times failing. This is the external picture of
the village that *The Storm* manages to depict with a total and subtle clarity. . . .

This play succeeds in arousing with a tremendous philosophical profundity a spirit of responsibility in mankind. Every crime on this earth, in any human society, is not simply the result of one individual's evil intentions; everyone is responsible, all of us bear the obligation to see justice done within the
context of human reality and to prevent crime. This play manages to strike
home with these ideas without any falsification or distortion of either thoughts
or situations. If we regard the village in *The Storm* as the world or society, we
come to realize that the play arouses in us a sense of responsibility for what
goes on in this world. The crimes that are committed in international society
are not simply the responsibility of the criminal but also of those who fail to
resist him, to stand up to him, and to take a firm position. If international
crimes are allowed to continue because of the negative attitudes of some and
the distortions of others, then the result will be destruction and disaster for everyone, and the world will face a dire future.

Rajā' al-Naqqāsh. Introduction to Mahmūd Diyāb, *Al-
Zawbaʿa; Al-gharīb* (Cairo, Dār al-Kātib al-ʿArabī,
1967), pp. 19, 25†

Shade on the Other Side is a long novel by Mahmūd Diyāb, who has previously published a collection of short stories and a play as yet unpublished,
which won the Language Academy Prize. Thus, Diyāb has so far tried his artistic talents in the drama, short story, and novel.

The most noticeable thing about this work is the obvious differences between it and the short story collection, differences that show a clear and rapid
development in his narrative skill. The majority of stories can be subsumed
under the general heading of realistic literature in that they deal with the problems of the underprivileged classes and the way their feelings are trodden on
as they attempt to earn some sort of living. In *Shade on the Other Side* the
whole direction shifts. The work is what may be termed existential literature.
It deals with the educated class and the way ideas can be shattered in the process of adopting a metaphysical position toward existence in general and the
problem of freedom in particular.

It is not just this subject that distinguishes this novel, but its narrative
form as well. It is written in the form of a quartet, each part being narrated by
an individual character from his own point of view, as he describes the events
he has witnessed. This is the format we find in *The Man Who Lost His
Shadow* by Fathī Ghānim, an example from our own modern literature, in
which it is a new form. There are, of course, many examples of this kind of
writing in Western narrative fiction, for example *The Sound and the Fury* by
Faulkner, *The School for Wives* by André Gide, *The Alexandria Quartet* of
Lawrence Durrell, and many others. . . .

The hero of the novel, Jamīl, is very like Meursault, the hero of Camus's novel *The Stranger*. Like him, Jamīl is concerned only with the present. Both of them are thrown into environments that are strange to them; both reject all customs and start looking at themselves and everything around them with a bitter gaze. They live the life of someone who could not care less— that is their crime. However, in *The Stranger* Meursault eventually wakes up to the fact that other people exist, when he comes to face death. On the day of his execution he wants to see lots of spectators waiting to see him and hurl hateful insults at him so that he will not find his own loneliness unbearable. Jamīl in Diyāb's novel is left at the end without waking up, since he has not yet had to face the sentence of execution.

Yūsuf al-Shārūnī. *Dirāsāt fi al-riwāya wa-al-qissa al-qasīra* (Cairo, Al-Maktaba al-Anglo-Misriyya, 1967), pp. 72–73, 79†

In *Harvest Nights* we go back to the same village as in *The Storm*. . . . People now concentrate on sowing and reaping, and things have quieted down. But there are still sorrows, troubles, hopes, happiness, joy, and consolation. Life keeps them all occupied, and they make use of a night at harvest time to act out their life. They invite an audience so that they can lay their life out in front of them. . . .

Mahmūd Diyāb manages with quiet and humble persistence to construct a peasant play without pretensions, and does not interpose himself between his actors and the audience. He uses as his mouthpiece Hassān al-Ghāwī, who has his own particular existence and role in the play. He is not just a mouthpiece who relays the author's viewpoint. Hassān invites us to see a play the people are going to present as a way of spending time on summer nights. Through the play, the interplay between art and life, and the reaction and effect each of these have on the other, a plot that is complicated and simple at one and the same time develops. It is complicated because it relies on this interplay between the two elements of art and life. The simplicity lies in the fact that it is presented to us in an easy fashion without our having to be bothered with explanations and symbols. Mahmūd Diyāb has succeeded in putting his fingers on the pulse of contemporary Egyptian village life and in transferring it to the stage so that we can live it again for ourselves, and he has done so with a complex spontaneity. . . . I would like to conclude by saying that with this play Mahmūd Diyāb has made a new and valuable addition to Egyptian drama and has assured himself a place of honor on its stage.

Fārūq 'Abd al-Wahhāb. *Al-Masrah*. Jan., 1967, p. 67†

The setting of [*The Storm*] is totally provincial and authentic: a village in the Sharqiyya province of Egypt. The local nature of the setting is considerably aided by the use of what we may term the non-urban colloquial dialect, a fac-

tor which, no doubt, contributed to the play's extreme popularity when it was
presented in the provinces. We are not only set in the midst of this village, but
also in the thick of a situation pregnant with antagonisms, hatred and opportunism. The focus of the plot is Husayn Abū Shāma, a character who never
appears. Some twenty years earlier, he had been framed for a crime which he
did not commit, and many men in the village, either through lying or with-
holding testimony, are implicated in the process of having him imprisoned for
almost twenty years. One of the village watchmen admits at the beginning of
the second act that "the whole village was calling him a thief, and so, when
they asked us if he really was, we said yes." In other words, Husayn is the
victim of a vicious combination of conspiracy and herd instinct. A young man
of the village wonders out loud how people can live with themselves under
such conditions. . . .

One of the splendid features of this fine work is the way in which the
events which have occurred in the past are made known to the audience gradually through the developing tensions of the play itself. However, the import of
the play is clear enough. Shaykh Yūnus, who represents the moral conscience
of the village, has been consistently ignored for years. It takes the kind of fear
induced by this situation to get the village to sense the need for corporate responsibility. The whole community has participated in the wrong done to
Husayn and his family, and, as the tension mounts, we witness the village trying to purge itself. The process is made even more complex and interesting by
the fact that another murder takes place during the corporate purge, thus allowing us to gauge how sincere the village's resolution is. Not even Sālih
emerges very well from this moral dilemma.

To those critics for whom the introduction of the absurd drama into
Egypt was becoming a vogue, this play of Diyāb constituted a welcome return
to realism. The leading figures in the drama are well portrayed, and the clash
of characters and the sudden changes in demeanor are all skillfully handled as
the tension builds up towards the denouement. And, as we noted above, the
language provides yet another dimension to the realism of the setting. *The
Storm* thus presents the audience with a convincing picture of an Egyptian village, and at the same time addresses itself through the development and resolution of a situation to the broader questions of justice and responsibility; it is
a combination which is both accomplished and enjoyable.

Roger Allen. *Edebiyat.* 4, 1, 1979, pp. 118–20

FARAJ, ALFRED (?–   )

EGYPT

In *The Barber of Baghdad* Alfred Faraj has succeeded in extracting from the
text of *The Thousand and One Nights* a character rich in possibilities for dra-

matic treatment: the nosy barber. He has made this character the subject of two short plays, the first of which gets its main idea from *The Thousand and One Nights* while the second comes from the book *Good Deeds and the Opposite* by al-Jāhiz (d. 869). He has removed all unnecessary excess from the two tales and added more than he has taken out without causing either of them to lose the particular flavor of our popular Arab heritage. He has thereby confirmed that our heritage is full of limitless treasures that are just waiting for someone to bring them back to life and brush the dust off them as Faraj has done with these two tales.

While the author has given these stories a successful dramatic treatment, he has still managed to preserve from the formal point of view the pattern of the popular tale, which relies so much on coincidence. The Caliph enters at the crucial moment to restore everyone's rights after they have come to despair of ever getting justice. This happens in both plays and thus gives them a bond of similarity quite apart from the fact that Abū Fudūl, the barber, appears in both plays. The other connection between the two plays is the lengthy poetic monologue with which the second play begins and which serves to tie the two works together.

Both plays are a rich store of ideas with regard to their social content. Our naïve, nosy barber of Baghdad is used to uncover all the injustices and corrupt practices of the rulers. He is put in the midst of the wronged and oppressed and proceeds to seek justice for them through trickery, chance, and the just ruler who gives him a guarantee of safety and immunity. After all this, the barber is subjected to nothing but blame and abuse. In both plays the curtain comes down with the barber being pelted with a hail of boots on his head as punishment for his nosiness and interference in things that are none of his business. But, in spite of everything, you can rest assured that in the next plays he will behave in exactly the same way. He is the type who feels compelled to do good; he cannot restrain himself from interfering in matters that are no concern of his so as to rid people of oppression and wrongdoing.

I have said "in the next plays" above because I feel that this character is so rich and has so many artistic possibilities that he can serve as an excellent dramatic model on which a number of other successful plays can be based.

Fu'ād Duwwāra. *Al-Majalla*. March, 1964, pp. 56–57†

Sulaymān al-Halabī is the latest play by Alfred Faraj whose previous works include *Pharaoh's Fall* and *The Barber of Baghdad* along with a number of shorter plays. *Sulaymān al-Halabī* has, in my opinion, a number of dramatic themes that stem basically from the type of play it is. It is a historical drama, and for that reason it is realistic. It portrays a series of situations and events during the French invasion of Egypt (1798) and the effect they have on Egypt and its people. Alfred Faraj has taken a slice out of this historical period and used it to portray the Azhar Mosque and its popular movement under the leadership of Shaykh Muhammad Abū al-Anwār al-Sādāt against the colonialist

Kleber. He shows the injustice of the French commander and the heroism of the Egyptian people, the tyranny they suffered and the sacrifices they made. Eventually, when things reach a crisis point, a young student from the Azhar appears on the scene who is destined to put an end to Kleber, the arrogant source of all the injustice and tyranny.

From this thread of historical events that the author has selected emerge a number of motifs: one is the character of Kleber; connected with this subject and acting as a counterpoint to him are the secret organizations formed to repel the invasion, headed by shaykhs of the Azhar such as al-Sādāt, al-Sharqāwī, and others. . . . Sulaymān emerges from the focus of the struggle, the point of tension between the two main forces. He thus represents a large number of young Egyptians at the time of the French invasion. . . .

Sulaymān moves with great speed because he believes he is being hounded down. He is tormented by the idea of murder, by the fear that the assassination of Kleber may be a crime. . . . He is running away from the specter of this crime of his. . . .

Sulaymān's feeling that he is being hounded dictates to the author the form the play should take; or perhaps we can express this idea better by saying that the artistic work has adopted the form that is most suitable to the content. And the content here consists of a nervous, worried person who thinks he is being chased as a result of his psychological, emotional, cultural, and political makeup on the one hand, and the political crisis of the popular revolt against the French on the other hand. The play is thus in the form of forty-five scenes that portray the events in the chase . . . and the rapidity with which they change serve the purpose of the play extremely well.

'Azīz Sulaymān. *Al-Masrah*. Feb., 1966, pp. 50, 52†

In the play *Policeman and Thieves*, the author derives material from Brecht, the master of the epic theater. He allows some employees in the General Consumer Organization, where the action of the drama takes place, to tell us the story as a chorus would do in Brecht. However, Faraj does not simply copy Brecht all down the line, but simply makes use of his general idea and then branches out on his own. His style in this play is to make use of caricature to show up minute details, and sneak particular phrases in as a way of addressing the audience's reason rather than their emotions. The aim is to suggest what they ought to be doing when faced with similar situations that arise in the course of the grind of daily life. In the play, society—here a microcosm of all societies—is divided into two groups as Fahīm, the hero of the play, explains. People in our country, he says, are either policemen or thieves. The policemen, ever watchful, are the people; the thieves are the forces of reaction, opportunism, and exploitation. . . . This play, then, can be considered a direct invitation to the mass of the people to become aware of what is going on in their lives. . . .

If this educational and well-intentioned play were not as excessively realistic as it is, it would not have met with such popular approval. The dialogue, too, is marked by a respectable degree of conscious wit, of a rather intellectual stamp. Even though the author has taken great trouble to draw his characters convincingly, this intellectual aura so dominates the general shape of the play that it is difficult to regard the characters as being flesh-and-blood people; they seem to represent more abstract ideas. The sense of idea seems to have predominated over the sense of character. . . . Each character is an idea, and each idea has a label that is the name of the character. Fahīm Nazīh Amīn, ("sensible, pure, reliable") is the hero of the play; . . . Tawfīq al-Sālik ("Success the Operator") "operates" in stealing, graft, pilfering, and so on. . . . All these characters give us a useful lesson about the need to protect the things we have gained through the revolution.

Khayrī Shalabī. Al-Masrah. June, 1966, pp. 82–83†

The play *Prince Sālim* takes the form of an investigation. The subject of the trial is the history of society and its rulers. In the beginning we see a prince who refuses to mount the throne he is entitled to. He considers it to be stained with blood and weighed down by crimes that cannot be expunged. He asks the people around him, his mother, grandfather, sister, and aunt, to explain the various bloodbaths they have witnessed. The mother, Jalīla, provides her testimony, and, with that as an introduction, we go back into the past. The present and past then intermingle in a series of scenes, the focal point of which is this royal investigation that the prince is conducting around the throne. . . .

This play is rich in themes. While the most obvious of these is certainly the question of justice and rule, this does not mean that the play does not also make other points, with their own dimensions and profundities. Yet again, the ability to incorporate several themes into a single coherent experience through a number of different visions is what gives enduring value to a dramatic work of art. I believe that *Prince Sālim* will endure as one of the finest additions to our dramatic heritage.

The play would not be so rich were it not for the fact that it shows all the hallmarks of a good play: firm structure, lively characters, compact poetic dialogue. . . . However, we should also point out what is probably the principal fault with this play, namely that, although the play has many excellent things in it, there is at times a tendency to exaggerate, and the quality is uneven overall. Take the dialogue, for example. Alfred Faraj has a genuine gift for creating dramatic dialogue. In this play, he is at his best; there are sections where the dialogue is so compact and crystal clear that it becomes pure dramatic poetry. . . . But on occasion this very same feature becomes its opposite in that the dialogue becomes more ostentatious and "dramatic" than is required. . . . In *Prince Sālim* Alfred Faraj has given us a new work which is both authentic and cohesive.

Bahā' al-Tāhir. Al-Kātib. Jan., 1968, pp. 120, 124–26†

About five years [after the first production of *The Barber of Baghdad*], Alfred Faraj was to make more mature use of the [*Thousand and One*] *Nights* in his significant play *'Alī Jannāh al-Tabrīzī and His Follower Quffa'*. Here again the two tales from the *Nights* are merged together, this time into one play, to that of the character of a dreamer who comes to a town and pretends he is the richest man alive. He claims that he has a caravan extending over all the way from Baghdad, heavily laden with rich merchandise and precious jewels. As 'Alī Jannāh is a remarkably persuasive man, all are soon taken in. Traders lend him money without reserve, and the king agrees to let him marry his only daughter, on the strength of his vaunted wealth. 'Alī gives to the poor most of the money he borrows, thus effecting marked social and economic change. In the end, when it is discovered that no caravan exists, 'Alī has barely time to flee, taking away with him the royal princess who has discovered hidden merits in him more precious than the wealth he does not possess.

The play raises many questions: to what extent can dreams be considered either lies or truths? Is a revolutionary who bases his beliefs on a myth and succeeds in creating good social change to be considered a prophet or an imposter? What is illusion and what is reality? The two attempts by Faraj have done more to point out the importance of tapping traditional sources for drama than some of the theorisation that was afoot at the time. They also proved, through success with the critics and at the box office, that going back to the sources can be good sound business, as well as added richness for Arabic drama. They, alongside other efforts by other dramatists, have shown that the search for identity, and the desire to move nearer the sources do not merely represent hankering after new literary and dramatic fashions. They have to do with that deep-rooted desire to remove resentment and make good the loss of centuries which many Arab playwrights felt as their duty.

'Alī al-Rā'ī. In R. C. Ostle, ed., *Studies in Modern Arabic
Literature* (Warminster, England, Aris and Phillips,
1975), p. 175

FARMĀN, GHĀ'IB TU'MA (1927-   )

IRAQ

The Palm Tree and the Neighbors may well be the first serious Iraqi novel. It comes in the wake of the work of Mahmūd al-Sayyid, who is rightly considered to have made the first attempts at producing an Iraqi novel, as well as short stories. The novel of Farmān has also been preceded by other works termed "novels," but in fact, they have not really shown any of the artistic features that make a narrative into a real novel.

Readers have been aware of Ghāʾib Tuʿma Farmān as a writer of fiction since 1955, when he produced his first collection of stories, *Millstone Harvest*. That was an excellent start, containing successful stories such as "A Picture." Then a second collection was published called *Another Child*. Lately we have seen him emerge as a novelist; few other Iraqis seem prepared to venture into this field. In fact, before *The Palm Tree and the Neighbors* there do not seem to be any Iraqi novels worthy of the name. . . .

Many novelists tend to concentrate on a single character or perhaps two. Through their behavior and their relationships with others we come to learn about other characters, who are really only supporting players to the protagonists. Then there are other novels where we cannot single out any one or two characters and where the majority of characters seem to represent a similar sphere within the structure; *Anna Karenina* can perhaps be regarded as an example of this type of novel. In *The Palm Tree and the Neighbors* we find an example of this method of structuring and character portrayal, especially in the first part up to chapter twenty-seven. At that part, the author becomes preoccupied with a single character, Husayn, who shows a remarkable development in the final chapters. In fact, he becomes the only character from that point to the final page. I can see no justification for this turn in the plot structure. Without any preliminaries—Husayn has not taken a major role in the majority of the earlier sections—this change in narrative development simply takes over. The author could have given a better portrayal of and shown the development of another character alongside Husayn, the one who is the cause of this dramatic change, namely Tamādir, who runs away with the gardener. . . .

The Palm Tree and the Neighbors is marked by a subtle poetic quality evident on almost every page. I got the impression that Farmān must have tried his hand at poetry at one time or another and done it very well. . . . I have decided to leave out of consideration here the particular problem raised by the use of the Iraqi colloquial dialect in the dialogue of the novel. The reason for my decision is a simple one: I am still at a loss as to how to deal with this question of dialogue. All I can say at the moment is that I am happy to accept works in either the colloquial or literary language.

Hasab al-Shaykh Jaʿfar. Al-Ādāb. Aug., 1966,
pp. 45–46, 61†

The way the author has developed from his earlier short stories to his novels gives a clear demonstration of his thought processes and of the way his themes are tied to the life of his country. He comments on the underlying principles of his own society and contemporary life in a way that impels him to develop his own authentic and dynamic creativity.

[*The Palm Tree and the Neighbors*] shows his concern with humanity in general, even though the author tends to place his subjects in a purely local setting and to use it as the source of inspiration for his subject matter. He gives true expression to the realities of his society and human values, in the process conveying vividly the goings-on on the local level of society—small incidents and major events—the people, and their way of speaking. The characters are selected from a world that is never far removed from the environs of the Iraqi city. . . . The author concentrates on the internal aspects of these characters, analyzing their emotions and inner feelings, although he does not ignore the purely external features. . . . There is an important artistic element in the way he portrays these characters so successfully and reveals their inner aspects, and that is his use of the character's point of view. The author sees through the eyes of the characters, thinks with their minds, and feels with their feelings. . . .

Style is an inseparable aspect of what the author is trying to present here. Thus, similes and metaphors are rarely used, since the author prefers to illustrate a particular psychological state of mind without having to resort to comparisons or a plethora of images to achieve the effect. This is particularly noticeable in the portrayal of Mustafā's feelings, for example. . . .

The dialogue is realistic and stems from the characters themselves; it reveals aspects of them and carries their own particular hallmarks. In his use of dialogue the author has stayed strictly within the bounds of the characters as portrayed. He does not allow them to speak in ways that do not suit them. The dialogue allows each character to reveal aspects of his thought, whether it be through conversation with another character or through an interior monologue. In no case does the cadence of the speech rise too far above that of normal common language. In fact, this author is distinguished by the skillful way he is able to create atmosphere through the use of dialogue.

'Umar al-Tālib. Al-Fann al-qasasī fī al-adab al-ʿIrāqī
al-hadīth (Baghdad, Matbaʿat Nuʿmān, 1971),
pp. 329–30, 343–46†

[*Five Voices*] consists of a presentation of five characters and a study of their daily lives at home, in the street, and at work. The author records their feelings, opinions, and attitudes, conveys the atmosphere in which they all live, and gives a picture of the evenings they spend together in the cafés of Baghdad, achieving oblivion by drinking wine and trying to forget reality, their own private tragedies, the general sense of futility that overwhelms them, and their inability to change the world around them.

What gives these characters their particular dimensions and makes us feel that we are dealing with a novel rather than cameos of a series of characters is the inclusion of a number of events that give the novel its own interior movement; through these events the characters develop until they reach the end, which is both realistic and plausible.

The first of these events may be Saʿīd's discovery of the detail concerning the tragic life of their friend, Hamīd, a tragedy that occupies a sizable portion of the novel. Saʿīd discovers a letter among those sent in to the complaints column in the newspaper where he works. The writer of the letter asks him to help her and visit her house so that he can see the conditions she has to live in. . . . After a great deal of hesitation Saʿīd does go, only to find out about the realities of the life of his friend Hamīd, whose wife has written him the letter. . . .

The second important event in the novel occurs when the river floods its banks, inundating and destroying homes and sweeping people to their deaths. These five intellectuals rush to help students and other citizens in setting up barricades against the swirling waters. All this serves as a means of exposing them to the realities of life. . . .

At the end of the novel it is Hamīd who faces the direct situation. The departure of his wife leaves him with a feeling of desolation and loneliness. He no longer has with him the person who shared his life and was always at his beck and call, while his girl friend in the office has discovered from her relative, the doctor who treated Hamīd's child, that Hamīd was married all the time. She has thus rejected both his past behavior and his offer of marriage. . . .

The impact and value of this novel lies in the authentic way it explores the psychology of the characters and the subtle realism used to portray their way of life and their behavior. . . . It gives us a vivid picture of the situation in Iraq during the regime of Nūrī al-Saʿīd and provides a clear condemnation of that period on both the political and social planes.

Jūrj Sālim. *Al-Mughāmara al-riwāʾiyya* (Damascus,
Manshūrāt Ittihād al-kuttāb al-ʿArab,
1973), pp. 147–49†

Ghāʾib Tuʿma Farmān's novel *Five Voices* provides a realistic picture of those times [just before the revolution of 1958] as seen through the eyes of five characters drawn from the intellectual, bourgeois class. The author assigns a number from one to five to each character and then introduces them in turn. The first is Saʿīd, a young man in his twenties who works on the complaints column of the newspaper *al-Nās*. The second is Ibrāhīm, the editor-in-chief of the newspaper. . . . The other three "voices" are, in turn, ʿAbd al-Khāliq, Sharīf, a would-be poet and philanderer, and lastly Hamīd, a senior bank official. The frequent meetings between these five characters in bars, restaurants, buses and so on allow for discussions on a wide variety of topics of local and international interest: Palestine, the Arab League, Guatemala; the alienation of intellectuals, the virtues of city and provincial living, the rights of women. Indeed, this aspiration for a realistic setting and treatment is often carried too far, as for example when Saʿīd retraces his steps back to the places of his youth in an extended passage. The novel does, however, have a central focus to its plot. Saʿīd receives an anonymous letter at his office concerning the plight of a housewife who is being maltreated by her husband. Research reveals that the husband is none other than Hamīd himself, something which causes considerable embarrassment to the entire group. Eventually Halīma, Hamīd's wife (or Najāt, as she is called in the initial letter to Saʿīd), returns to her home town of Karbalāʾ. At the end of the work, Hamīd has been rejected by the girl at the bank with whom he has been flirting throughout the sorry episode with his wife, and Sharīf the poet has been thrown out by his prostitute girl friend, Sabriyya. According to the canons of social realism, we are to assume that the opportunists and philanderers have been given their just deserts. With the closing of the newspaper, Saʿīd takes that decision adopted by so many young Arab intellectuals who find themselves at odds with the authorities, namely to leave the country, and the work ends with him saying farewell to his father.

A particularly interesting aspect of this novel is its narrative technique. The majority of chapters deal with one of the five characters, but on two occasions the canvas expands to incorporate all five at once. The narrative throughout is told in the third person, so that the portrait of each individual remains more external than is the case in, for example, Mahfūz's *Miramar* or Jabrā's *The Ship*, other examples of what Diyāʾ al-Sharqāwī terms *riwāyāt sawtiyya* [novels of voices]. However, even if Farmān does not exploit the potentialities of the "novel of voices" to the full, his novel is a convincing portrait of Iraqi society at a crucial period in its modern history, and the final chapter in which the five voices are merged depicts that tantalising mixture of despair and hope which characterised the period immediately prior to the revolution of 1958.

Roger Allen. *The Arabic Novel: An Historical and Critical*
Introduction (Syracuse, N.Y., Syracuse University Press,
1982), pp. 75–77

AL-GHĪTĀNĪ, JAMĀL (1945?–   )

EGYPT

Al-Ghītānī is a talented artist with a gift for bringing together the different aspects of reality. He has a rare and highly developed sensitivity in the way he selects from its various convulsions and probes deeply into the misgivings and scruples revealed there. . . .

If al-Ghītānī hurls his characters into a constricting, Kafkaesque hell on earth, he still provides them with the ability to dream. For that very reason, his characters are overwhelmed by a strong and bitter sense of tragedy, the source of which is their feeling that they all deserve to achieve their own sense of integration, while at the same time they long for freedom and the emergence of ideal values. . . .

The principal feature that has dominated the reality of Egyptian life in recent times finds itself represented in the systematic elimination of all the achievements of the people of the country under the slogan of "opening up to foreign investment" (*infitāh*). We have also seen the assault of foreign capitalism on our country, and the revelations of official papers; the realities behind the factors involved in the October War and the exploitation of the blood of thousands of citizens have thus been exposed. Al-Ghītānī manages [in his novel *Remembrance of What Is Past*] to put his finger squarely on this particular feature of our life and to focus his spotlight on its numerous ramifications. In so doing, he makes use of all the artistic means at his disposal and digs his way to the very bottom in order to reveal to us phenomena and destinies in all their clarity.

In so doing he resorts to the fragmentation of imagination, history, and documentation. He breaks up time by using the memory and imagination as the key to reality. But al-Ghītānī's imagination differs from other people's, filled as theirs usually are with diaphanous sprites, dreams, and floating visions, in that his imaginary world is harshly landscaped, fierce in its objectivity and as cruel and violent as its source material. He fragments and imagines, and the whole collection of debris is tied together by history and documentation. We are therefore faced with a structured pile of rubble and a documentary imagination.

'Abd al-Razzāq 'Īd. Al-Yasār al-'Arabī. June, 1979, p. 30†

Although *The Events in the Za'farānī Quarter* is full of subtle historical allusions and provides minute details of events in the quarter, it reveals the external time frame only through a passing reference found in two widely separated points in the novel. . . . We find ourselves at the end of 1971 or in 1972, in other words, at the time immediately after Nasserism. The author is eager to establish this temporal definition so that he can use the novel as a token of an era or a stage; in fact, more than that, as a means of recording an attitude toward that time period. . . .

The novel offers a vision at once integrated and at odds with itself. One point of view is that of the oppressor, and another, that of the oppressed. Yet we find these two aspects are involved with each other. Even though the point of this involvement is the search for a better world, the interaction is both negative and fantastic and is achieved on a level of magic and fable, despite the fact that it has at the same time a tragic and serious side to it that arouses sympathy and a bitter sense of irony. . . .

The novel takes the form of extremely detailed reportage, in its precise chronologies and in particulars of events both external and internal, real and imaginary. Thus, the work is not divided into chapters, but rather into dossiers, memoirs, reports, telegrams, news items, and journalists' investigations. Through the dossiers we are able to follow the development of events and characters within the quarter while the reports, telegrams, and investigations take us out of the quarter into the outside world.

We thus follow the structure of the novel on more than one level: at times it is through the point of view of the author himself in the form of external narrative or else as an attempt at interpretation; at other times it is via the internalized view of one of the characters; at still others it is through reports, telegrams, and dry documents. However, in spite of the various levels of narration, the overall stamp is that of reportage, although the styles of the various narratives differ in spite of their common stamp. . . .

In some of the scenes of this novel we get the impression of the exaggerations of caricature, particularly in its aspects of fable and the absurd. This all may be deliberate, an attempt to fragment this fabulous, absurd aspect by sheer exaggeration so as to make clear that it is precisely fabulous and absurd. At the same time, it may be an expressionist means of revealing the ugliness of reality and its actual absurdity. This expressionist style may well be one of the principal distinguishing features of al-Ghītānī's writings in both his novel and short stories.

Mahmūd Amīn al-'Ālim. Al-Ādāb. Feb.–March,
1980, pp. 20, 23†

One of the most original contributors to the fictional genres is Jamāl al-Ghītānī, who has written a number of novels and short-story collections. One of the most interesting from the technical point of view is *Al-Zīnī Barakāt* (written c. 1971). The novel is at first appearance entirely historical in focus; indeed it is set in the decade immediately before the Ottoman conquest of Egypt in 1516. Barakāt is the *muhtasib* responsible for the supervision of public morals, and his presence is felt by everyone although he never actually participates in the action of the novel as a character. Al-Ghītānī chooses this format, with its use of actual historical texts [and] parodies of religious and secular pronouncements, to put together a montage which gives an accurate picture not only of an earlier period in history but also of Egypt in the 1960s, a country . . . "asked to sacrifice its freedom for a fragile and corrupt establishment."

Al-Ghītānī is more direct in his concern with the present in his collection of short stories, *Ground to Ground* (1972). Several of them are concerned with soldiers at the front, while "The Mongols" combines a reference to past history with an application to the present in much the same way as *Al-Zīnī Barakāt* does.

Roger Allen. Middle East Journal. Winter, 1981, p. 38

Parody . . . is exemplified by the historical novel of Jamāl al-Ghītānī, *Al-Zīnī Barakāt*. Parody is related to what Gérard Genette calls *transtextualité*, that is, the set of relations that link a text to other texts. These relations can be of different types. Parody as a particular type of transtextuality aims at imitating a text; it is a device which emphasizes the "literarité" of literature, since its main aim is to destroy the mimetic illusion, and [it] does not aim at imitating nature but at imitating literature; by doing this it destroys the realist illusion and comes as a reaction to the realist concept of art.

In Jamāl al-Ghītānī's novel, the hypotext (the text imitated) is the chronicle of the Egyptian historiographer Ibn Iyās, *Badā'i' al-zuhūr fī waqā'i' al-duhūr* [*Spectacular Flowers Concerning Events of the Ages*]. In the novel the author puts in parallel two texts, his own and Ibn Iyās's, and by doing this he puts in parallel the ideological, social and cultural postulates of two epochs: Egypt under the Mamelukes' rule at the time of the Ottoman conquest and Egypt of 1967 at the time of the military collapse.

The interest of this technique is that this parallel is carried out through a formal literary parody, that is, the imitation of the historical discourse of Ibn Iyās. . . .

We find two main axes in the novel: the axis of resemblance and the axis of difference, and from their merging appears the paradox and the irony. The movement is a dialectic motion of ebb and flow which goes from literal quotations of the hypotext to the most modern techniques of narrated monologue.

The axis of resemblance centers around the linguistic structure of the text at the micro-level. The author tries to stay as close as possible to the linguistic register of Ibn Iyās. This is done by quoting whole passages of the *Badā'i' al-zuhūr*, the three most important passages quoted being the departure of al-Ghūrī for Syria, the beating of al-Zīnī Barakāt by the disciples of Shaykh Su'ūd and his imprisonment in his house, and the defeat of al-Ghūrī at Marj Dābiq and his death. The author moves one step further from the hypotext by using "formulas" taken from the hypotext and integrating them in the narrative. . . .

But while Jamāl al-Ghītānī observed the techniques of Ibn Iyās at the microstructural level, he reversed them at the macrostructural level of the novel's units, i.e., years, divided into months and into days in which the subunit is the event; all the events are on the same level of importance and are given the same textual space: the death of a sultan, the rise of the water of the Nile or the fixing of the prices on the markets. In the novel of Jamāl al-Ghītānī the narrative structure follows on the large narrative structure the same pattern: that of years covering the years between 912h to 922h. But the sub-units are that of the characters. Each narrative section carries the name of one of the major protagonists. The characters are five: a mijāwir at al-Azhar, Sa'īd al-Juhaynī; Shaykh Su'ūd, one of the 'ulamā' of al-Ashar; Zakariyya Ibn Rādī, the head of the Diwan of the Bassāsīn; a Venetian travelogue [sic], Visconti Gianotti; [and al-Zīnī Barakāt himself]. These characters are presented to the reader through the technique of the "narrated interior monologue," the narrative material, that is, the events, being presented through the filter of the consciousness of the character and not through an omniscient narrator. Thus the text of Ibn Iyās, which is a monophonic text, becomes here a polyphonic one.

Ceza Draz. *Journal of Arabic Literature*. 12,
1981, pp. 142–44

HABĪBĪ, EMĪLE (1921–   )

ISRAEL (PALESTINIAN)

The Peculiar Events Surrounding the Disappearance of the Ill-Starred Saʿīd the Pessoptimist is one of those novels that demand close scrutiny, since it is—rightly—reckoned to be one of the monuments in the development of the Arabic novel. Within a huge framework Emīle Habībī presents a world brimming over with confusion, chaos, and a whole variety of jumbled and clashing emotions, all this revealed with all the starkness of a documentary. Feelings of love, hope, despair, a sense of contact or a sense of distance, and bitter sarcasm combine to convey terrible pain. The scenes in the novel are not really "scenes" in the usual sense of the word but more like flashes and glimpses clustered around each other so as to give us in the end a mosaic through which the author attempts to tell us the history of the Palestinian people's experience during the British occupation and then the establishment of the state of Israel, the various invasions, and lastly the Black September in Amman. The author is endowed with a penetrating vision that permits him to give the reader a comprehensive and detailed picture of his subject, conveyed with subtlety and profundity. The obvious love he feels for his subject, coupled with his artistic abilities, enables him to make use of a number of devices that demonstrate an unusual technical mastery.

Perhaps the first thing that attracts the reader's attention is the brilliant narrative that takes the subject to its utmost limits. The course of events is influenced here by the extensive concerns of Saʿīd the pessoptimist and the multitudinous ways through which he expends his energies during a life filled with a variety of events and many strange happenings. It is undoubtedly true that the effect this brilliant narrative technique has on the ordinary reader or indeed the critic at the second or even third reading of the work is to arouse his intense interest and a desire to read on. And so he continues from one moment to the next, captivated by the unusual character of Saʿīd, who operates under a carefully perfected "cover" of naïveté and simple-mindedness. In the same way, the reader comes to admire the author's ability to pull together all the strands of his story and to combine the elements of analysis, criticism and judgment within the framework of a story into a compact and integral structure.

Shukrī ʿAzīz Mādī. Inʿikās hazīmat Hazīrān ʿalā al-riwāya al-ʿArabiyya (Beirut, Al-muʾassasa al-ʿArabiyya li-al-dirāsāt wa-al-nashr, 1978), pp. 183–84†

While distinctively Arabic in flavor, there is [in *The Peculiar Events Surrounding the Disappearance of the Ill-Starred Saʿīd the Pessoptimist*] much that seems derived from European literature. Here and there one senses the influence of Brecht, and the extremely short chapters, essential to the structure, and their pungent and paradoxical titles are openly paralleled on Voltaire. The relationship here is closer than that of mere outward form, and the evident similarities in character and modes of thinking, utterance and action between the heroes of *Candide* or *Zadig* and Saʿīd himself are striking. The lucklessness, the innocence of their relationships with women, the foolish optimism, tactlessness and gullibility these characters share are remarkably similar. The inner structures are comparable too. The author's extreme verbal restraint, in certain passages, and the rapidity with which he moves from joke to joke, understating and relying on the reader's imagination and quickness of mind to supply a detailed context to appreciate wherein the humor and the tragedy lie, are precisely in the style and spirit of the great French sceptic. What more appropriate summation of Saʿīd's character and life experience could be made than Voltaire's passing comment that, "Zadig's bad luck was due really to his good luck and, above all, to his merit."

Habībī's gift for comedy pervades this work, and he achieves his humorous effects from both situation development and characterization. Much amusement comes from his sense for the incongruous. How ludicrous it seems for the young Saʿīd, immediately following his infiltration from Lebanon, to sit so at ease in the headquarters of the Military Governor entirely relaxed and confident because of his knowledge that he was taller than the high Israeli official! Some of the scenes are pure slapstick, as for example when Saʿīd, rushing to clean his apartment for his meeting with Yuʿād, makes the cigarette-butt-filled toilet overflow all over the floor! The scene where he refuses, feigning sleep, to respond to her invitation to her bedroom that night is followed by an equally funny one next morning when he desperately tries to persuade her to make love even when the soldiers are banging incessantly on the apartment door. Such incidents are Chaplinesque in quality, and it is not surprising that there is talk in the Arab world of rendering this work into a film.

It is in his portrayal of his central figure that Habībī's gifts are most evident. His Saʿīd the Palestinian is the epitome of the anti-hero, perhaps the most finely drawn in modern Arabic literature. Complex to the point of inconsistency (and therefore very human), he is a gentle and poetic man, as we see from his image-rich comments on the natural beauty of his homeland, despite his insensitivity to the feelings of others and his cowardly and obsessive concern for his own self-preservation. The reader is constantly baffled to determine whether he is indeed the most incredible "ass," or whether his ludicrously transparent attempts to "act smart" that make his idiocy all the more patent are in fact deliberate camouflage. . . .

For all the mixture of puckish wit and bitter sarcasm that Habībī directs at his Arab compatriots, within Israel and outside, his major concern in this work is clearly to underline the essential tragedy of the lot of his "Palestinian Everyman" Saʿīd. Despite the latter's cardinal fault of over-dependency on others and the faults of character, of traditions and of contemporary policies of the Arabs, the major blame for their circumstances is applied squarely against the Israelis; the only positive judgment that could be made for them, we are told early in the work, is that they have not proved so utterly brutal as the country's conquerors were in earlier times. The belief that the Israeli authorities would not defile the sanctity of places of worship is justified, we learn, only by the fact that ". . . they have plenty of room on the outside." And when his old principal tells Saʿīd that the Israelis were not, after all, mere foreign invaders, Crusaders or even Mamelukes, but ". . . people returning to their own country after an absence of 2,000 years," Saʿīd's innocently amazed response, "My, what prodigious memories they do have," succinctly expresses the author's sarcasm.

Trevor Le Gassick. Middle East Journal. Spring,
1980, pp. 219–20, 222

Emīle Habībī . . . [has attempted] in two works to show the bitter ironies of daily life in Israel for the Arab citizens of that country. While *Sextet on the Six Days* is a bittersweet description of six separate encounters between Arabs in Israel and their relatives in neighbouring states, his later work, *The Peculiar Events Surrounding the Disappearance of the Ill-Starred Saʿīd the Pessoptimist,* is not only a wonderfully sardonic account of life in Israel, but, as the wordiness of the title suggests, an evocation of the picaresque *maqāma* genre initiated in the tenth century by al-Hamadhānī and revived in modern times by al-Muwaylihī. In fact, Saʿīd's claim in the first chapter to have encountered extraterrestrial beings sets up precisely the same narrative distancing based on either time or space which had been used as a device by both al-Muwaylihī and Hāfiz Ibrāhīm in their criticism of society earlier in the century. The work is subdivided into three books, the first and last given the girl's name Yuʿād, a word implying "return," while the central book is entitled "Bāqiya," also a girl's name with the sense of "remaining"; the significance of this choice of titles need not be emphasised. However, the work succeeds in its purpose of giving us a kaleidoscopic view of the life of an Arab in Israel through the use of extremely short chapters which afford ample opportunity for changes of pace and scene and encourage terse and sardonic comment. The result of this montage is a truly picaresque and sometimes farcical work of fiction which manages to show great originality while conveying its often bitter message with a tragicomic force.

Roger Allen. *The Arabic Novel: An Historical and Critical Introduction* (Syracuse, N.Y., Syracuse University Press, 1982), pp. 66–67

In his *Sextet on the Six Days*, Emīle Habībī manages to pull together in six integrated tableaux a large nexus of human relationships centered around the themes of the land and struggle. The reality of the occupation is the starting point, and from there the author proceeds to tell us in a colloquial style very close to that of the heritage of popular narrative how people's relationships with the sheer reality of the occupation developed. Eventually this idea leads him to the revolutionary stance through which he is united in his struggle with the people of Leningrad in their battle against the Nazi invasion. There is no one single event to bring these separate tableaux into a unity, nor does the author attempt to provide them all with a unifying thread. The unity they do possess comes from two elements: first, from the very reality on whose soil, as it were, it grows, in that it is entirely derived from the land of occupied Palestine, and all the events are concerned with relationships with the occupation; and second, from the variety of different movements that lead in combination to a single chant, a unified call for resistance, all couched in the simplest of popular forms, which have the greatest impact and efficacy. . . .

In this fashion the various movements are blended into a single chant, one that uses a language capable of reaching the popular consciousness and that can proceed to focus it anew so that the more stalwart and combative values begin to emerge. This is achieved on two levels: first, that of the narrator, who brings the whole subject into focus, and who, through his explanations and reassessments within the mythic framework, brings us close to the age of childhood, with its sense of wonder, and yet at the same time takes us far from it in the fostering of the consciousness of a practicing freedom-fighter; second, the deliberate intrusion of the author's voice in the course of the narrative itself, something that produces a didactic element emerging from within the relationships themselves and not from the outside. This intrusion takes on certain aspects of a diversion whose aim is to bring us back to the main point at hand in case we forget it while becoming absorbed in the story itself. . . .

These two levels fuse within the mythic structure of the story. Emīle Habībī steers clear of folklore by resorting to myth. Myth here brings with it the ability to join things together, to weave a realistic connection that makes of this novel a unique tapestry within the tradition of the Arabic novel. The most important thing about this work in our view is that it is the only novelistic work that comes from the occupied territories themselves. Emīle Habībī thus joins Tawfīq Fayyād and the poets of the occupied territories in presenting to us an integrated literary tradition with its own particular qualities.

Ilyās Khūrī. *Tajribat al-bahth ʿan ufq*, Palestine Essays,

No. 44 (Beirut, Palestine Research Center, 1974),

pp. 47–50†

AL-HĀJJ, UNSĪ (1937–   )

LEBANON

Unsī al-Hājj has become engrossed in his violent revolution against anything that is usual or classical and in his fierce aspiration and longing for free and independent thought, which is to be founded on the ruins of the collective thought of old. He has gone to such extremes in this tendency that he refuses to use any word whose meaning he recognizes. He fashions words in such a way as to obtain new meanings that no one else is aware of, and for no other reason than that no one else can understand them. His purpose in writing is not so that others may understand.

Unsī al-Hājj wants revolutionary ideas to pour forth like a flood and to flash like lightning. He wants for those ideas a word or words that do not come from dictionaries. Consequently, he has become a captive of his own recalcitrant tendencies, imprisoned by his own revolutionary ideas. He has thus lost his freedom, the very thing that justifies his revolution and defiance. In much the same way he has gone too far in his statements of independence and revolution, to such a degree that he has abandoned and revolted against the idea of "beauty."

Why all this? Because the search for and sense of beauty is something that brings art and its practitioners together. As regards its procedure within the framework of revolution, art is a kind of ready-made sense. After all, people, however high- or low-brow they may be, will always search for beauty in everything according to their own criteria. As long as things are that way, then why shouldn't our writer look for beauty where other people do not usually look? Why shouldn't he look for it in ugliness? One may even find some beauty in ugliness.

However, in his collection *Never*, Unsī al-Hājj has carried this too far. He has started seeking ugliness as an end in itself; perhaps by so doing he is deceiving the slaves of beauty, those who adhere to the notion of "ready-made feelings."

Nahād Khayyāta. *Shiʿr*. Winter, 1963, pp. 98–99†

The Past of the Days to Come is the title of the poet's third collection of poetry. . . . The title is indeed odd; it implies the past, but I am not sure whether anything else is involved. Some of our writers seem nowadays to prefer meaninglessness to meaning. Unsī al-Hājj, however, is not one of them. His collection is a gift to himself; "to me," to quote the poet. What this means is that he has finally decided to come to terms with himself alone. This is an unnatural stance for a social being to adopt, since one of the conditions for the existence of the individual is the establishment of living relationships and exchanges. Unsī does not deny that fact either, but seems nevertheless determined to live with himself in a combination of narcissism and masochism. . . .

Unsī al-Hājj is a poet of quest and damnation, of "I" and sex, a poet of the "distant shore" who hates and attacks any poet who is direct. In his writings he delves deep into things, trying to see himself, something that is scientifically impossible. However, we will endeavor to understand how he sees himself. He himself says that, when all the contradictions are considered, he is no longer any good at anything, even lying. He is proclaiming his own downfall, since lying—an essentially negative, defiant, and hostile posture —grows out of a number of objective circumstances, such as upbringing and education. . . . His relationships with women are like a bomb to a house, totally destructive. . . . We see Unsī as a man of passion, violence, and individualism who never stops attacking, whatever the consequences may be and for any reason at all. Needless to say, this is not in any way natural behavior. He tries to show himself off in some usual way, and that is normally termed ostentation; he has to be seen and to do anything to see that no one else is like him. . . .

Unsī shows us his attitudes and relationships with great candor. . . . There is no truth, no hope; the man is cancerous. When he finds his country to be as constricting as his poetry, he does not show any affection for it, share in its tragedy, or lighten its painful burdens. Instead he pours out his hatred and pounces on it like a demon. This is the principal difference between a poet of commitment such as Al-Bayyātī and a poet of dissolution like Unsī al-Hājj.

Khalīl Ahmad Khalīl. Al-Ādāb. Dec., 1965, pp. 26–27†

In *The Severed Head*, Unsī al-Hājj branched out still further with his thought, his senses, and his body, playing with ideas under the stimulus of the forces in the world around him. He scorns the old devices completely, and so there is no longer any connection with the image as it was or with previous notions of emotion. That pure blue dome in Lebanese, and in fact all Arabic poetry, that offered shade to group after group and kept them fettered for a long time has now been defaced. Al-Hājj has put graffiti all over it and filled it with blatant scrawlings that project him directly into the fold of poetic culture as it really is, and of poetry that moves forward, develops, and proceeds toward discovery.

In following these lines and scrawlings through, he has been fully aware and alert, loyal to his own principles, and ever curious. In his collection *Never* he embarked on an experiment in language that, like glue, found stuck to it elements of sickness, hallucination, dry humor, diffuse pleasures, and sad, painful memories. Now, in *The Severed Head*, we see him cleaning up to a certain extent. He is wiping some of this valuable dust off himself, and in, from, and all around the book hallowed, yet infidel perfumes arise. Here we have that unique blend that is his alone, characterized by language, image, emotion, and "a line of blue passion." Through everything he does and produces, he confirms that he is creating forms without parallel or equal, even though many people around him are attempting to create such forms. . . .

The insistence of Unsī al-Hājj on using prose is such that it has now become part of the essence of poetry. It is no longer regarded with distaste because it is an easy way out or uncontrolled. It is now used a lot after being employed rather scantily at first. Along with some of his colleagues, Unsī al-Hājj has been involved in the enrichment of this new movement. . . . In this revival of prose most of the credit belongs to Al-Hājj as the major participant and outstanding creative talent who can take a moving spark from a word, expression, or idea and then ride on it like a horseman. He takes it into the skies, and in so doing he demolishes any obstacles, devises new paths and steps, and always reaches the heart; and that is where he finds the young girl hiding, the long-desired face, and the conclusive moment.

Shawqī Abū Shaqrā. *Shiʿr*. Winter–Spring, 1967,
pp. 152–54†

Al-Hājj's concepts of prose poetry are largely expressed in the introduction to his collection of prose poems *Never*, which clearly reflects his adoption of the French *poème en prose* techniques as developed by the French symbolists and surrealists and as most thoroughly analyzed and formulated in Suzanne Bernard's scholarly work *Le poème en prose de Baudelaire jusqu'à nos jours*. . . .

Reproducing almost verbatim most of the basic concepts outlined in Bernard's work, al-Hājj believes that there is nothing final in poetry and that, as long as the poet's work is always subject to his internal experience, no laws, conventions, prosodic systems and forms should become "eternal" poetic absolutes which inhibit his innate freedom and prevent him from expressing his innermost experiences and position in the world, truly, fully, and freely. Toward this end, and in order to give fresh perspective to his word and to his position in the world, the poet must discover a new language and a new form that are most suitable to him as a means of poetic expression or ends of artistic creation.

The prose poem according to al-Hājj at this time is the most recent language and form on the ladder of the contemporary Arab poet's aspiration. With regard to the structure of the prose poem, al-Hājj enumerates the basic concepts of intent, intemporality, brevity, and unity as defined by Bernard.

Issa J. Boullata. Edebiyat. 1, 2, 1976, pp. 133–35

Among those who have been influenced by the French *poème en prose* is Unsī al-Hājj, to whom it is a medium to express his revolt against the holiness of the Arabic language and its cultural heritage, and to challenge the stagnation in Arab life and its narrowness of view. The preface to his collection of *poèmes en prose, Never,* can be considered a manifesto of the new trend in poetry. In it al-Hājj distinguished between prose and poetry. Poetry can be without metre provided it has emotional tension and evocative and suggestive images, while a versification with metre and rhyme is prosaic, explanatory, logical, informative, and demonstrative, because metre and rhyme are an external and ready-made music, of which a talented poet has no need. Afraid of progress, the conservatives in their battle with the progressives, [propound] the arguments of the continuity of history, the holiness of the language, the needs of the Arab people and the political, social and spiritual conditions of the Arabs in order to preserve stagnation, to delay the revolution in intellectual and emotional life.

Al-Hājj added: "A thousand years of pressure, a thousand years we are slaves, ignorant and superficial. In order to be saved, we have . . . to stand in front of this wall and break through it." Al-Hājj continued that in the face of this conservative life in the Arab world, in schools, and among the Arab writers there are two ways, suffocation or madness. By madness the rebel conquers and lets his voice be heard. In order that any revolutionary attempts will be able to stand against those who challenge them with the weapons of politics, racialism and sectarianism, nothing helps but absolute sincerity. Those who are trying to break the thousand years have to destroy and destroy. They might be killed but they will have been able to tell the truth to those who want to make decadence dominant.

S. Moreh. Modern Arabic Poetry, 1800–1970
(Leiden, E. J. Brill, 1976), pp. 306–7

AL-HAKĪM, TAWFĪQ (1898?–   )

EGYPT

The Return of the Spirit is written in the only style that can be considered suitable to the theme: an easy, uncomplicated, authentic style that conveys conversation through its spirit and describes and speaks in such a way that the readers, about and for whom it was written, can understand it. However, this has displeased Ibrāhīm al-Māzinī, who has attacked it for its grammatical errors, its poor style, and its reliance on the colloquial language. It is only natural that al-Māzinī would base his criticism on style; for some writers that is their only pretext for being alive! Ideas to them mean nothing at all! All a stylist has to do, for example, is to go to one of the works of Galsworthy, say, transfer it word for word, step by step, and then give it an Egyptian flavor when he has finished and claim it as his own. . . . Many people have said (and many others will follow) that there are grammatical mistakes; but then, what writings in Egypt are entirely free of grammatical errors? Al-Hakīm does not claim to be a grammarian, or that his story is a model of style. His only aim is to be entirely natural, unforced, and unpretentious. . . .

Why do we always have to flinch when faced with the truth and reality? The colloquial is a living language; there are dictionaries and lexicons in print that you can find in England! From time to time some loyal supporters make good use of it; who today would dare attack 'Uthmān Jalāl for having used it? What does al-Māzinī want? Should fiction be an accurate and close reflection that readers can identify with, or should it fumble its way around and lose its spirit, fit for neither man nor beast? . . .

The question of the classical written language and the spoken colloquial is still with us. The conservatives do not show a sufficient regard for the people, and the rebels have not sufficient power to fight. We are thus faced with a tricky problem. Let it continue that way until God grants a solution. Meanwhile, it is pure hypocrisy to use the issue of the colloquial as an offensive weapon in criticism, ignoring in the process all ideas and benefits, and any desire for reform, quite apart from the fidelity and sincerity in the work and signs of life and maturity. [1930s?]

Yahyā Haqqī. *Khatawāt fī al-naqd* (Cairo, Maktaba Dār
al-'Urūba, n.d. [1961?]), pp. 104–5†

In *Pygmalion* we see Tawfīq al-Hakīm using a legend of Greek origin to treat an issue we can believe concerns the author, the problem of life, which the artist can find no way of avoiding however much success he may have; life is forever catching up with him and demanding its rights. The Greeks realized that too, and so one of their legends was to the effect that on the island of Crete a superb artist decided not to marry in order to devote his life to art. . . . Aphrodite, the goddess of love, was annoyed by his arrogance and made him fall in love with a statue of his own making called Galatea. . . . When Pygmalion falls in love with the statue and asks the goddess to breathe the spirit of life into her, the goddess's heart softens and Pygmalion marries his Galatea. . . .

Al-Hakīm's artistic muse wishes to embody both sides of the struggle going on inside him. Thus, he resorts to another Greek legend, that of Narcissus, . . . who knew that he was beautiful and was always looking at himself in the mirror.

In combining Pygmalion and Narcissus, al-Hakīm has two characters who represent the two aspects of the artist's existence: one, life, from which he must take his share as does every human being, the other art, to which the artist wants to devote all his energies. Now we see Narcissus running away with Galatea. And yet Pygmalion is not troubled by jealousy, since Narcissus is a part of himself. It is no more than the victory of life at one stage in the career of the author or artist. And it is a victory that does no harm to art, since art and life now go hand in hand, Galatea with Narcissus.

This, then, is the way Pygmalion's life goes through all its complications at al-Hakīm's hands. He wavers between life and art; at times, he feels happy and secure with Galatea the woman, and at other times he reverts to his longing for Galatea the statue. . . .

If only al-Hakīm had the ability to stir the emotions and leave lasting impressions, the ability of a poet such as Shelley to choose images and compose sonorous verse, or the ability of Shaw to breathe life and perception into reality. If only his heart and imagination could be a match for his intellect!

Muhammad Mandūr. *Fī al-mīzān al-jadīd* (Cairo, Maktabat Nahdat Misr, n.d. [1944?]), pp. 14–15, 19†

Scheherazade, like *The People of the Cave*, represents a new art form in our modern literature. I cannot claim that it represents the highest ideal in drama or anything close to it. But I will say that it is a carefully wrought work of art, enjoyable, subtly crafted, and certainly worthy of a long life. In this play, I cannot fault al-Hakīm's grammatical usage and his long-windedness at certain points, as I did with *The People of the Cave*. He seems to have revised this work with care. . . . Given the basic requirements of the stage, I cannot really find any fault. The blending of a work of literature and a text suitable for stage performance has been handled with obvious success. However, it would be impossible to have this work acted in Egypt at the moment for two extremely obvious reasons. The story is too highbrow for most of the audiences who flock to the theater; only the intelligentsia would get any enjoyment out of this play. . . . The second reason is that actors who could perform this play as it needs to be and could present it faithfully in a way that would be appropriate to its beauty and precision do not exist in Egypt yet. Actors who are genuinely cultured and educated are still extremely few in number. It is therefore a play to be read rather than acted; it may even benefit from that fact. In the whole of modern Arabic literature I know of no work that shows a similar inclination on the part of the author to direct his ideas at the mind and feelings of the reader at one and the same time, and in fact, to aim them at the mind more than at the feelings. The play discusses nothing less than that all too simple question that has baffled philosophers for ages: what is truth? What can it possibly be? I think you will agree with me when I say that this type of Platonic dialogue was not really designed for the theater, and particularly not for the Egyptian theater. . . .

I trust that our words of praise will spur Tawfīq al-Hakīm on so that he will work at his craft and perfect the tools he needs for it. He needs to exert a great deal of effort, to study hard . . . to read a great deal of philosophy and perfect his use of language so that it can be a proper vehicle for expressing his views and ideas. [1945]

Tāhā Husayn. *Fusūl fī al-adab wa-al-naqd* (Cairo, Dār al-Ma'ārif, 1969), pp. 103–6†

Critics may differ when talking about Tawfīq al-Hakīm's huge output, his different styles, and his varying levels of quality. But nothing can be allowed to detract from the tremendous status he has in contemporary Arabic literature. He has even succeeded in moving beyond the borders of the Arabic-speaking world. Many of his plays have been translated into English, French, Russian, Italian, Spanish, Swedish, and other languages. The literary community throughout the world has come to see him as representing a splendid renaissance in contemporary Arabic literature. His success is clearly visible in the realm of dramatic literature, of which he is generally regarded as one of the originators in Arabic; he is the creator of prose drama just as the poet Ahmad Shawqī is of verse drama.

To assess the benefits he has brought to our contemporary dramatic literature, all we have to do is to see how he has been able to raise its standards from cheapness to real artistry. Comedy, for example, is no longer what it used to be: puns, clowning around on the stage, all for no other purpose than to get a laugh. Comedy has moved up in the world, and is now used to reveal the contradictions in life and personal and social behavior; it is now a combination of seriousness and amusement. It can now use laughter and sarcasm as a very effective device for putting right whatever is wrong or ineffective. Al-Hakīm's comedies make use of laughter as a potent social weapon.

With his intellectual drama Tawfīq al-Hakīm has created a lasting literature that deals with a large number of enduring human questions. . . . He does all this with a poetic spirit, wit, and attention to good dialogue that give his dramas all the deftness, beauty, and magic of great literature. More recently, he has turned his outstanding artistic and literary talents to the service of his own people—their present life and the revolution that it brought about. He has now written a series of plays with a definite social or political purpose. In them he has responded to the revolution and its consequences with all his humanistic and artistic capacities.

Muhammad Mandūr. *Al-Majalla.* June, 1962, p. 21†

Tawfīq al-Hakīm has been accused for some time of living in an ivory tower. His plays, some people claim, deal with intellectual issues that have little or no connection with real life. But even if this accusation were accurate, there would be no cause to fault al-Hakīm for the way he writes. This type of intellectual drama has an important place in all world literatures, and yet it is almost completely lacking from our own Arabic literature if we exclude al-Hakīm's output.

In any case, al-Hakīm's plays are not all abstract dramas of ideas, as some people claim. Anyone who has any doubts about the truth of that statement should read the large number of plays he has published in the volume entitled *Theater of Society*. Then they will see for themselves how our "ivory tower writer" manages to come down from the heights to the real world of daily life and how successful he is in putting the problems of contemporary life into a fully rounded dramatic form that combines comedy and tragedy. In all this, al-Hakīm above all shows a profound social conscience and an ability to penetrate to the very depths of the human soul.

In one of these plays, *I Want to Kill*, we encounter the false emotions that some of our social conditions and relationships force on us. Two people are faithfully married to each other, and each would sacrifice himself or herself for love of the other. . . . When disaster strikes, when they are both faced with death as a deranged neighbor threatens them with a gun, all their phony, superficial feelings vanish to reveal the true nature of their relationship, with all its disgusting selfishness. Each of these two "devoted" married people is eager to let the other die in order to stay alive.

Another play, *Boss Kandūz's Building*, shows someone who has made a lot of money from war profiteering and knows how to make good use of his wealth to marry off his ugly daughters. The play demonstrates that the greedy husbands of the girls are marrying his building and not his daughters. This play is particularly successful in its comic effects and in the way the characters are appropriately and truthfully drawn.

A third play, *Courtly Love*, revolves around an incredibly miserly pasha who has the desperate adoration of a courtly lover toward his own wealth. He cannot bear the thought of reaching out and touching it, or of anyone else's doing so either. For this "courtly love" of his, he sacrifices everything in order that his money should not be touched: love, ministerial position, influence, and all the joys and pleasures of life.

Fu'ād Dawwāra. *Fī al-naqd al-masraḥī* (Cairo, Dār al-Miṣriyya li-al-Ta'līf wa-al-Tarjama, 1963), pp. 270–71†

This play, *The Predicament*, has aroused a great deal of argument and discussion even before the completion of the serial publication of all five acts over the last five weeks. . . . In his introduction to the play Tawfīq al-Hakīm takes up the same age-old problem, that of the classical, written language versus the colloquial, spoken one. The author of *Equilibriumism*, who published his marvelous novel *The Return of the Spirit* in the 1930s, has now produced several plays and other literary works with the dialogue in the colloquial. . . .

If the play *The Deal* managed to put al-Hakīm's ideas about a third language [somewhere between the written language and the colloquial dialect] into practice (even though there were a few colloquial words and expressions scattered about), then *The Predicament* is a truly exceptional work in the colloquial language. . . .

This play also represents a new phase in al-Hakīm's dramatic writing, in that the scenery has been simplified to the extent that the play can be put on anywhere without a pressing need for a stage, decor, and special clothes. It thus constitutes an extension of the efforts al-Hakīm made in *The Deal* to bring the drama deep into the countryside and right into factories. All the acts in the play can be performed against one very simple backdrop. . . .

What does al-Hakīm wish to achieve through this long play in five acts? Does he not want the world of ideas to come into contact with reality, or to try new experiments? In the play Doctor Yahyā gets into a predicament when he tries to create a theoretical base for his research on the solid turf of reality. This is the only impression we are left with at the conclusion of al-Hakīm's latest play. If his object in the play *Shams al-Nahār* was to extol work in a way suited to socialist thought and the ideals of the new Arab socialist society, then in this play he seems to be pursuing some utopian tack involving the separation of thought from reality. . . .

What has our great writer Tawfīq al-Hakīm been doing? After attacking the colloquial language both in the introduction and postscript, he then turns around and writes an excellent work in the colloquial! He wants to establish for our benefit how noble is the world of thought, but then advocates its separation from reality. Why is al-Hakīm pursuing this course, which has led him to fall into "the Predicament"?

Ahmad Muhammad ʿAtiyya. Al-Ādāb. June, 1965,
pp. 26–28†

The dialogue between the relative virtues of East and West (speaking in a cultural rather than a political sense) is recurrent in the Arabic writing of the past fifty years. It has assumed varying forms: soul versus mind, spiritualism versus materialism, humanism versus mechanization—with the East laying sole claim to the first of the contending concepts and the West (Europe and America) invariably identified with the second.

Al-Hakīm indulges in this argument in his major novel *The Return of the Spirit*, or *The Resurrection*. Here the dialogue is between two Europeans, a Britisher and a Frenchman, rather than between a European and an Easterner. It is almost as if al-Hakīm seeks to produce objective outside evidence to prove the superiority of the Eastern soul vis-à-vis the European mind, which, according to the author, is all that Europe can brag about. "Europe's strength lies in its mind, that limited instrument which one has to augment by will power. Egypt's strength lies in its heart, which is limitless."

In *The Resurrection* al-Hakīm again sends his protagonist on a journey, this time into the national past of his own land in search of the spiritual and cultural sources of his national ethos. Al-Hakīm maintains that this ethos derives from the residue of the ancient culture and that it is still present and alive in his people's consciousness. "I do not have a recent past. I am compelled to penetrate the ancient past which is about to disappear under the sands of time," says al-Hakīm.

The protagonist in *The Resurrection* is the son of rich landowners. He fails both in mitigating his parents' contempt (particularly his mother's) for the peasants who work for them and in ignoring the suspicions aroused in him by rumors about the girl he loved. Eventually he finds satisfaction and fulfillment in revolutionary acts against the alien rulers of his land. In the revolution, al-Hakīm seems to be saying, Egypt finds her resurrection. He borrows his symbolism from the oldest known Egyptian script, "The Book of the Dead," and applies it to the modern reawakening of Egypt that the revolution of 1919 represents.

George Sfeir. *Daedalus*. Fall, 1966, pp. 944–45

The Sultan's Dilemma is no less of an intellectual play than *The People of the Cave*. We should note that, to al-Hakīm, intellectual drama was not something he wrote purely to be read and not acted. It was a deliberate attempt, a conscious experiment, aimed at binding together dramatic literature and the cultural heritage of the Arabs. We can well appreciate quite how much the success of this venture means not only to the author's art, but also to our dramatic literature as a whole. The "closet drama" phase that al-Hakīm's works passed through was merely a prelude to the transformation of this genre into genuine drama, drama to be acted. . . .

If al-Hakīm was trying in *The People of the Cave* to create "intellectual tragedy" in Arabic, then in *The Sultan's Dilemma* he has tried with greater success to create "intellectual comedy." It is within this latter framework that we must examine this play.

Two observations need to be made. The first is that a sultan in a dilemma is a character who cannot possibly exist; we have never seen, nor will we see, a ruler who will submit to the rule of law unless he is forced to do so. But that is precisely what the sultan in this play does. Second, the "conflict" in this play does not extend beyond the end of the first act. The other two acts are merely codas to the initial conflict. The fact of the matter is that al-Hakīm would not have been able to produce his work in the way he wanted if these two observations were not valid. What he has done is to use history as a source for a tale about the conflict between a Mameluke sultan and the chief judge. The judge insists that the sultan is a slave and therefore cannot be the ruler of free subjects. Another writer might well have seen this story as an example of the struggle between the people and a tyrannical ruler, using it to produce a version of our history with a revolutionary content to it. However, Tawfīq al-Hakīm has chosen to transform the tale into a concept that is almost entirely divorced from any time frame. He is concerned with power and truth, and proceeds to construct his play on that basis.

Shukrī ʿAyyād. *Tajārib fī al-adab wa-al-naqd* (Cairo,
Dār al-Kātib al-ʿArabī, 1967), pp. 98–101†

Within the framework of the play *The Sultan's Dilemma* there lurk a number of opinions to which Tawfīq al-Hakīm adheres. They are easy enough to deduce. The most obvious is the one he emphasizes in the introduction to the play, the opinion that the problems of life and the world cannot be solved by resorting to force and violence (= the sword). The only solution is the law. If we follow its dictates, we will be safe. . . . Nevertheless, al-Hakīm goes on to make it clear that following this policy is by no means easy; there are thorns and spikes all the way along the road. In the play we see the sultan enduring humiliation, being sold at a public auction, and then being forced to spend the night with a woman in a house of ill repute. But all works out well in the end. . . . Just as Scheherazade in the play of that name was victorious over King Shāhrayār, so in this play the madam wins over her sultan. He tells her that he will never forget the night he has spent in her company when he served as her slave. In both situations there occurs a spiritual submission on the part of the king. Both men submit to the woman involved with their mind and soul. Each one loves the woman and at her hands is raised to the level of inspiration. . . . Al-Hakīm may even have had this idea in mind when he makes the sultan and the madam mention Scheherazade and her situation in *The Thousand and One Nights*. The sultan is actually so affected by the forceful personality of the madam that he likens her not so much to Scheherazade as to King Shāhrayār, with all his tyrannical power; the sultan feels that *she* is the one who is in full control of the situation. But she rapidly rejects this notion and resumes her gentle femininity. . . .

In this play al-Hakīm has succeeded in combining lively dramatic movement, forceful ideas, a variety of characters, and excellent dialogue. He has been able to make the events peak expressively and clarify important philosophical concepts and intellectual problems: placing justice and the law over personal interest safeguarded by force of arms; the connection of goodness and decent morals with beauty and love; and the relationship of freedom to ethics. All these questions have elevated this play to a very high level and assured it a lofty place in al-Hakīm's dramatic output.

Nāzik al-Malāʾika. *Al-Ādāb*. Jan., 1970, pp. 23–24†

Al-Hakīm, one of the most versatile Arab literary figures, is perhaps the most important Arab dramatist if only because of the number of plays he wrote and the varied themes he chose, and because of his innovations in Arab dramatic literature—in particular, the refinement of the dialogue as a literary vehicle. Al-Hakīm's *King Oedipus* belongs to his abstract "intellectual" theater (*al-Masrah al-Dhihnī*), which is defined by him as the stage inside the mind. "My dramatis personae are ideas in struggle," he said. "They are dressed in symbols and move in the world of abstract meanings." The intellectual plays are not supposed to be stageable, but for *King Oedipus*, unlike his *Scheherazade, The Seven Sleepers of Ephesus* [i.e., *The People of the Cave*], or *Pygmalion*, stageability is made possible by emphasizing action as well as dialogue. . . .

It is obvious that al-Hakīm has changed the myth as many others have done before or after him and has adopted it so as to conform to his own conceptions and aims. However, the deviations introduced by him correspond not merely to an author's desire for innovations in style and dramatic action but to deeper philosophical beliefs. . . .

In the very beginning of the first act, al-Hakīm presents a kind of prologue wherein the background of the Oedipus myth is given. But there is more in this background than a simple narrative. The theme of the tragedy is set and the philosophical orientation established. It is not the attempt of Oedipus to evade his destiny and avoid committing the two deadly sins of patricide and incest that moves him to act, but the desire to search for his origin and identity. Al-Hakīm apparently considered the problem of identity as more important for our times than the problem of sin. Knowledge of one's identity saves and not the evasion of one's destiny. But this interest in a more modern theme led al-Hakīm necessarily to contradictions and to the presentation of an image of a hero whom nobody, except perverts perhaps, would care to identify themselves with or look up to. Gone is the very real humanity of the Sophoclean Oedipus, manifest in his sincere desire to avoid committing sin and his weakness in the face of an ineluctable destiny and unmerciful gods. This change detracts greatly from any possible sympathy we might develop for the hero of the play. The hero has little choice; his values do not morally oblige him to affirm his freedom to choose a path of his own, fatal to him, yes, but by this very act of choice he would enhance his humanity and raise himself closer to the gods.

George Atiyeh. In *Festschrift für Michael de Ferdinandy*
(Wiesbaden, G. Pressler, 1972), pp. 137–39

One of al-Hakīm's most interesting novels is written in the form of a journal, *Diary of a Provincial Public Prosecutor* (1937), a novel already translated into French, English and Spanish. The author draws on his experience as a district attorney in the provinces and the readers find it difficult to discriminate between fact and fiction concerning the narrator himself. He is naturally involved in the narrative but as a spectator, an outsider who has to deal with murder, theft and witnesses in the daily round of his work.

The novel gives a mercilessly revealing picture of the seedy side, or rather the darker aspect of rural life. It seems to involve most inhabitants of the village and is apparently the major concern of the government officials stationed in the provinces.

The few days covered by the journal (11th to 23rd of October) reveal the hopeless gap between the district attorney and the environment of his office. He finds it almost impossible to get through to the peasants he has to deal with. He understands his colleagues, the other government officials well enough, and has created a rich gallery of such types. But the peasants remain a closed mystery, as impenetrable as the double crime he investigates in the course of those twelve days. He finally closes the file in despair, washing his hands of the whole business.

This ending is, of course, unsatisfactory and so are the endings of most of al-Hakīm's novels. Technically, the novels are far from perfect, but he was a true pioneer. He could see he was treading virgin soil in this field and could not stop to perfect his technique. He opened new roads and explored possibilities of various kinds of experience which he added to the domain of the Arabic novel. Other authors soon followed in his steps. When he saw them walking on surer ground, he turned back to his old love and major concern—the drama.

Fatma Moussa-Mahmoud. *The Arabic Novel in Egypt*
1914–1970 (Cairo, Egyptian General Book
Organization, 1973), pp. 29–30

The Return of the Spirit is a wonderfully romantic expression of that nationalist philosophy of rebirth which inspired the revolution of 1919, and for this and its portrayal of the life of a lower-middle-class household in Cairo it has earned the admiration of successive generations of Egyptian readers. Combined with picturesque observation is the idea, expressed symbolically, of the revival of past glories, the unification of the nation and the expulsion of foreign oppressors. Much of the book is concerned with this: Muhsin and his uncles represent the Egyptian people, and Saniya Isis, the regeneration force. As critics have noted, the characters unfortunately do not live up to their symbolic value; Saniya, for example, is an ordinary girl with little thought of anything but teasing the neighbours and getting married, and al-Hakīm cannot reconcile this realistic but commonplace character with the great idea she is supposed to represent.

The problem of finding satisfactory vehicles for the symbolism he wants to express leads al-Hakīm to adopt unexpected attitudes in contradiction to ones which he supports in later novels. There is little social criticism in the novel, which is chiefly concerned with amusing descriptions of life in Muhsin's uncles' house, or when it rises to a more serious level, with the idea of expelling the foreign rulers because they are foreigners. What strikes the reader is the negative social criticism, a glorification of conditions which might be expected to horrify, and the origin of this phenomenon is the author's desire to represent "cette intimité chaleureuse, cette ferveur que l'Égypte puise dans sa fertilité" [this warm intimacy, this fervor that Egypt derives from its fertility] (J. Berque) through the fellah, that link between the Pharaohs and the present day.

Hilary Kilpatrick. The Modern Egyptian Novel
(London, Ithaca Press, 1974), pp. 41–42

Al-Hakīm's stay in France convinced him that the Arab theatre had had a false start, or at least a terribly immature one at the hands of the Naqqāshes. The tradition which they started in 1848, he felt, led to an almost complete divorce of the theatre from literature, so much so that even the poet Ahmad Shawqī gave very little thought to publishing his plays. Al-Hakīm believed that only a return to "the source of drama," that is, the works of the ancient Greek masters, could rectify the situation. Such a return could not be accomplished simply by translating their works into Arabic, but required assimilating the Greek experience in drama, without, in the meantime, shedding one's character completely or losing oneself in one's model. Writing in retrospect in the Introduction to his *King Oedipus*, al-Hakīm gives an illustration from his own experience with Sophocles's tragedy. Although on an intellectual level he could understand and appreciate the conflict in the play, when he started thinking of writing his own version, his sensibility, both as a Muslim and as an Oriental man, rejected the idea that the gods could plot something so mean. So, he changed the play around, making Tiresias the chief culprit in the tragedy.

By writing *The People of the Cave* shortly after his return from Paris, al-Hakīm aimed at "introducing the element of tragedy to an Arabic-Islamic theme." In so doing, he says, "my purpose was not merely to take a story from the Glorious Book and to cast it in dramatic form, [but] rather to look at our Islamic mythology with the eyes of Greek tragedy, [hence] bringing about a fusion of the two mentalities and literatures."

Farouk Abdel Wahab. Modern Egyptian Drama
(Minneapolis and Chicago, Bibliotheca Islamica,
1974), pp. 29–30

When in his searching years Tawfīq al-Hakīm appears to us so obsessed with the idea of forging for himself a dramatic style and with opening up for Arabic literature a new medium, we have the feeling that he is aware, albeit in theoretically quite broad terms, of this very problem. His first intimations of accomplishment, conveyed so well in his *The Flower of Life*, come with the writing of *The People of the Cave*, where a new, more individually deter-

mined, more internally motivated idiom makes its appearance. This idiom is
not borrowed in *genre* terms, brought in from some other context, recognizable by other stylistic traits. It seems, tentatively, perhaps but quite indica-
tively, to be originating in the action of the play itself. This may have been the
realization which gave Tawfīq al-Hakīm the feeling of having found "his
style." Today we see perhaps a little more clearly, realizing that *The People of
the Cave* specifically is as yet quite a "styleless" work as far as the language
itself is concerned. At the same time it is unmistakably a work where for the
first time in the history of Arabic dramatic literature conceived and executed
in the *fushā* [the classical language], an effective fusion of dramatic action
and language takes place. It is, therefore, rather than the achievement of a
personal style, the achievement of a play.

> Jaroslav Stetkevych. In R. C. Ostle, ed., *Studies in Modern
> Arabic Literature* (Warminster, England, Aris and Phillips,
> 1975), p. 159

Tawfīq al-Hakīm . . . took tentative steps in the drama in the twenties, but it
was in the mid-thirties that he achieved renown as a playwright: to this day he
remains the premier writer for the stage (like Rīhānī, he has a Cairo theater
named after him). Writing always in prose, both literary and colloquial, al-
Hakīm has used historical and mythical themes, *Arabian Nights* settings, and
the local contemporary scene: he has written symbolist drama, realistic drama
(mainly comedy of situation and drama of social problems) and one very successful surrealist play. His characters are rarely memorable individuals, but
they play their parts in a clash of ideas which is less purely cerebral, and more
poetic, than Shavian drama; his inherited and borrowed themes are employed
to express, or at least to display, philosophical concepts. His mastery of language and stagecraft and his manipulation of the varying tensions and rhythms
of a dramatic unfolding are concealed by the smoothness and apparent ease of
his achievement, but are very clear to anyone who has come to grips with any
of his works. . . .

In the preface to his book on the Egyptian theater from 1955 to 1971,
Mahmūd Amīn al-ʿĀlim speaks of a "new beginning to Egyptian theatrical
creativity." It is a fact, however, that Tawfīq al-Hakīm, who had dominated
theatrical writing during the previous twenty years, continued to play an important part, not as a stultified survival, but as a vigorous imagination which
continued to develop and to experiment. Al-Hakīm is responsible for the best-
written and most successful Absurdist play of the sixties, *The Tree Climber*:
in his preface to the play, indeed, he makes the very interesting remark that he
was familiar with the French surrealist theater in his student days in Paris in
the 1920s, but that, much as he appreciated it, when he began to write he de-

cided that the Egyptian public was not yet ripe for such art. Forty years later, the sensibility of the public had caught up with that of the artist.

Mahmoud Manzalaoui. Arabic Writing Today: The Drama
(Cairo, American Research Center in Egypt, 1977),
pp. 29–30

The theme of The People of the Cave, then, is man's struggle with time, a theme which Tawfīq al-Hakīm contrives to relate to his romantic, nationalistic idea of an unchanging corpus of distinctively Egyptian thought which has resisted all invaders, and which is based on the Nile, with its rhythm of alternate death and resurrection. (This idea is developed at greater length in the novel The Return of the Spirit.) Despite this elaborate theorising, however, it is difficult to find very much specifically Egyptian about the play. The story itself is not Egyptian, the scene is set not in Egypt but in Tarsus, and there is only one brief reference to the ancient Egyptians, as the disillusioned Marnūsh reflects on the hopelessness of man's struggle against time. The idea of "resurrection," of "revival," of nahda, is as relevant to the rest of the Arab world (and to many places outside) as it is to Egypt; and indeed, al-Hakīm seems rather to emphasise the universality of this theme by introducing the parallel Japanese legend of Urashima into the play (an insertion for which there is little or no dramatic justification); and Gallius, Prīscā's tutor, points out explicitly that the story is found amongst every people.

In fact, as Tawfīq al-Hakīm himself admits in the introduction to The Tree Climber, the play's roots lie not so much in Egypt (either in the Islamic or in the ancient Egyptian tradition) as in the European tradition of intellectual drama with which he had come into contact during his stay in Paris from 1925 to 1928; and, of those playwrights whose work he saw performed during that period, it is perhaps Pirandello whose influence is most apparent in al-Hakīm's drama. Here Tawfīq al-Hakīm was breaking entirely new ground, for in addition to being the first Arab playwright to use Qur'ānic material as a basis for serious drama, he was introducing a previously unknown philosophical note into the Arab theatre.

Paul Starkey. Journal of Arabic Literature. 8, 1977,
pp. 137–38

Tawfīq al-Hakīm attempts to place his modern drama into the context of the Arabo-Muslim literary tradition. In early articles he had often addressed the problems of the origins of art and literature . . . but a long period of development was needed to serve as preface to the appearance of Oedipus the King in 1949 before we see him dealing in detail with the origins of his own drama. It is true that at that time there were very few serious studies on the subject of the absence of theater within the classical Arabic literary tradition. In this

book we find al-Hakīm firmly underlining his conviction that Islam in no way
hindered the transfer of Greek tragedy into Arab civilization. Rather, he emphasizes the difficulties in understanding legends and mythology, also pointing out that people did not read tragedies in those days. . . .

Thus, what Tawfīq al-Hakīm had in mind was to introduce the element
of the tragic into an Arabo-Muslim subject. It can be confirmed with pleasure
that *The People of the Cave* has come to be regarded as Arabic literature. In
addition, the ideas that are suggested in *King Oedipus* are merely an extension
of the ideas of Muslim philosophers. He often refers back to this aspect of renewal in Arabic literature and to its original characteristics, such as the art of
caricature found in the works of al-Jāhiz (d. 869), which provided him with
inspiration. In al-Hakīm's opinion there is absolutely no need to feel inferior
to Europe on this subject. Thus, we find ourselves constantly encountering
this need for self-justification. Such is the case with *Shahrazād [Schehera-
zade]*, where he claims to be disparaging Darwin's evolutionary theory; above
all he finds it necessary in dealing with this science to resort to the traditional
Muslim scholars and even to the reasons for Muhammad's prophetic message.

Jean Fontaine. *Mort-resurrection: Une lecture de
Tawfīq al-Hakīm* (Tunis, Éditions Bouslama, 1978),
pp. 36–38†

HAQQĪ, YAHYĀ (1905–   )

EGYPT

Yahyā Haqqī is not a prolific writer. Each year he may produce two short stories. His favorite rallying cry is for a style that shows subtle verbal precision.
One of the objects of his researches in that process has been color: the precise
definition of colors attracts a great deal of the storyteller's attention.

To Haqqī, the word, with all its subtlety, integrity, and efficacy, is at one
with the intended meaning, an experiment in expression. Yahyā Haqqī's style
is a lively one in which the words all convey much more meaning than can be
provided by the letters on their own. In trying to achieve the precision that is
his permanent goal he is completely against using older expressions like "even
though . . ." and so on to link sentences together; to him they seem to be
treating the reader like a baby who always protests to the person who is holding his hand in case he falls down. Haqqī wants an intellectual relationship
with his reader, as is the case for writers in the West. He will sometimes write
the same sentence tens of times until he feels that it is right and fits into its
place well. The seemingly free-flowing spontaneity of his writing may lead
the reader to be entirely unaware of this continual and difficult process. The

reader may even feel that Haqqī has no difficulty in expressing himself in the way he does, but, as he says in an article in *Al-Ādāb* (July 1960), he may write a single sentence of a line and a half over thirty-five times and will put it into its proper place only when he feels that it comes out spontaneously the way he wants it to be.

This intense concern with precision and definition works well in the long story, in which a certain prolixity is part of the nature of the genre. In the short story, however, his technique is to use the form to describe obscure aspects of life that no one else can be bothered with. Haqqī loves to pause for a while, investigate things, and then reflect on it all in a great deal of analysis and detail. All this is done in a gentle tone of sadness that cannot fail to affect both the Eastern writer and reader.

Ni'māt Ahmad Fu'ād. *Al-Majalla*. Sept., 1960, pp. 25–26†

Yahyā Haqqī is a fiction writer of long standing; he has been writing for over thirty years now. He was in the vanguard of a group of young people who set out to found a new Egyptian literature during the national renaissance, which aimed at reshaping the Egyptian personality in a variety of environments. These young men decided to use fiction as the framework within which this new Egyptian literature would come into being. . . .

The novel we are dealing with here is *Slept Well!* . . . which gives us a picture of a village the railway has not yet reached. The villagers are quiescent and lethargic; some of them manage to find some relief at a tavern, where they spend most of the night gossiping and drinking wine. The village stays this way until the railway comes. Then they get a new headman in the village. The tavern is closed, a spirit of seriousness and industry takes over, and the age of reform sets in.

This story is covered by a veil of symbolism: the village represents the Egyptian people, lazy, disdainful, and dull. The tavern is a symbol of the frivolous attitude that prevails in Egyptian life. The train is everything that Egypt has taken in as part of its renaissance and reform; the headman who modernizes the village and wakens the villagers represents the leadership that produced the era of revolution and liberation. . . .

The novel operates on a high intellectual level. The author has imbued it with his own exceptional cultural background and his broad experience with the realities of life. He shows great sophistication in the way he explores people's personalities, and endows the story with some marvelous descriptions and lovely language, both in direct comment and through the mouths of the characters themselves. It has to be admitted that sometimes these ideas seem too sophisticated for the intellectual level of the villagers! . . .

This story gives a picture of two periods, one characterized by frivolity, the other by seriousness. The reader will find that the two sections are marked by different styles: the first is a picture of life presented in an attractive, artistic form; the second is a treatment of the concept of reform in a precise, socially aware form.

Mahmūd Taymūr. *Munājayāt li-al-kutub wa-al-kuttāb*
(Cairo, Dār al-Jīl, 1962), pp. 9–11, 15–16†

"Antar and Juliette" [in the collection of the same name]—these are two names that seem so familiar to us that we can hardly doubt that the story will be about chivalry, bravery, and love. . . . Imagine our surprise, then, to discover that the story is not a love story at all; it is about two dogs! It is a touching story that may seem almost familiar if you like dogs. Haqqī tells this story in order to make us interested in two different modes of life, two types of thought, of sentiment and reaction. Antar and Juliette exist in the story because there are dogs with and without collars and licenses, but above all because there are people who grow fond of domestic animals without being able to afford the license that can offer at the least the minimum of protection and save the animal from the pound. . . .

For the author of *The Lamp of Umm Hāshim* and *Leave It to Allah*, . . . a story is a living, independent entity in its own right, a particular world through which the author proposes to travel and which he will depict for us. Haqqī is not concerned with initiating the reader into any particular universe with its own principles and laws, its realities and implications, and its tragedies and joys. The subject only matters crucially in the very particular cases of detective stories or adventures, and, besides that, in the writings of authors who can tell us stories only as narratives.

For Haqqī, the subject is a pretext, an occasion, an invitation, a means. The real goal is to be found elsewhere: rapid impressions, a savory detail, a comparison, a metaphor, an image, all of which make us dream and intrigue us. . . . Haqqī is like Flaubert (and he knows his works intimately) in believing that a novel or story is "a manner of living" or even "a type of existence"; it is not written for everyone. . . .

If each story is an independent work, Haqqī observes, what can possibly guarantee that a collection of such diverse entities will have even a minimum of unity? Haqqī himself poses the question and seems to expect that critics will be the only ones able to reply. . . . I can say to Yahyā Haqqī that his sensitivity as a writer, the qualities of his emotion, his power of concentration, his artistic ability to interpret everything he sees and hears, and his sense of humor, become inherent elements of his lively and direct style. Their very consistency guarantees that everything he writes will have force, grace, and unity.

Raymond Francis. *Aspects de la littérature arabe
contemporaine* (Beirut, Dar Al-Maaref, 1963),
pp. 229–30, 232–36†

For his story "The Lamp of Umm Hāshim" [in the collection of the same name] Haqqī chose the symbolic style. On one level, this involves the events that constitute the plot and happen to the characters. But on a more profound level, this technique has far-reaching implications. Ismāʿīl is the dynamic spirit of Egypt in its renaissance. Fāṭima al-Nabawiyya is traditional Egypt standing on a solid foundation of history and heritage. Mary represents modern Europe, proud and confident in its technology but without faith or particular concern for mankind. The mosque stands for faith, and the lamp itself represents the form faith takes. The implication of the story on this level is that Egypt will reject the modern spirit if the intent is to impose anything on it mechanically from the outside. On the other hand, it will accept this spirit if the approach shows the appropriate respect for heritage and for style and if it makes an attempt to blend in rather than simply dominating everything else. . . .

We will never be able to appreciate fully what happens in "The Lamp of Umm Hāshim" unless we realize one crucial point, and that is that everything in the story has as its aim to show the spiritual events in the life of Ismāʿīl. . . . The importance of this fact becomes much clearer when we come to consider the artistic merits of the work. The move from the realistic to the symbolic level corresponds exactly with the spiritual happenings Ismāʿīl finds himself experiencing. . . . In "The Lamp of Umm Hāshim" material events are reduced to a basic minimum beyond which one cannot go. This gives the work at least two primary characteristics: first, it has an intense focus and a rapidity of movement; second, the spiritual movement in the story is made even clearer since there are no material descriptions or events to prevent such a movement or stop it from being clearly visible to people reading the story. We should add to this the fact that as an artist Haqqī leans toward poetic expression, in other words the use of images. This is of all forms of expression the one that is most focused and economical in its use of words. . . .

This work demonstrates an important critical principle: namely that the content of a work of art is the thing that should define its form and techniques. . . . "The Lamp of Umm Hāshim" is an excellent example of the organic connection between form and content. By that, we imply that, above all, it is a perfect work of art.

ʿAlī al-Rāʿī. Dirāsāt fī al-riwāya al-Miṣriyya (Cairo,
Al-Muʾassasat al-Miṣriyya al-ʿĀmma li-al-Taʾlīf
wa-al-Tarjama wa-al-Ṭibāʿa wa-al-Nashr, 1964?),
pp. 166, 177, 180, 187–88†

In Leave It to Allah . . . the man no less than the artist is clearly revealed through his style; for of no other of our writers would it be truer to say that "the style is the man." Yahyā Haqqī's choice of words and expressions strewn with colloquialisms, and his vivid imagery taken from everyday life, establish his immediate appeal. The impression that his writing creates is that of a sensitive observer who misses nothing in the world around him, be it man, animal or nature. In his approach to his material, whether he is discussing criminals, who appear to have a strange fascination for him, or circus animals and humble beasts of burden, such as the common donkey, he is without affectation and, above all, compassionate. This human and highly civilised writer allows his feelings to flow with a naturalness matched by the easy rhythm of his style, so that an effect of spontaneity is achieved in spite of what he has said about the innumerable revisions he has made of his writings. Such revisions explain the meagreness of his output, but they also account for its distinctive literary merit. Haqqī is an artist with a sense of vocation, apparent in the sincerity and truth of his work as well as in its disciplined form. So unassuming himself, he dislikes all that is loud and histrionic, in writing as in life. "It is enough for me," he says, "if these memoirs emerge as a dialogue between me and myself."

Nur Sherif. *About Arabic Books* (Beirut, Beirut Arab
University, 1970), pp. 19–20

The Lamp of Umm Hāshim is a collection of short stories by the distinguished Egyptian writer Yahyā Haqqī. . . . Because of their peculiar mixture of realism and fantasy, their humour and poetry, the strange and haunting note of mysticism that runs through them, and not least because of their impassioned and artistically faultless style of writing, these tales have already attained the position of a classic in modern Arabic literature. Moreover, they are all rich in cultural and sociological significance: in this respect the most interesting perhaps is the story which gives the collection its name, a novella which occupies half the volume.

Besides conveying the feel of traditional life in Cairo at the turn of the century, and indeed for many years to come, the tale of "The Lamp of Umm Hāshim" belongs to the type of writing which in the field of the novel is known as the *Bildungsroman,* i.e., the type that deals with the education of the protagonist. The main character, Ismāʿīl, is a man who finds himself at the crossroads of civilization. He was brought up on traditional Muslim culture, which in its basic features remained largely medieval. But as a young man of impressionable years he was heavily subjected to the influence of modern western culture, for he spent a number of years in England studying medicine. The work treats in detail Ismāʿīl's early background in traditional Cairo, then in a brief manner his experiences in Europe, and finally what he decides to make of his life when he returns to his native country. It traces the spiritual development of this young man and the change that takes place in his social, moral and mental attitudes. In so doing it indirectly places one set of cultural values in juxtaposition to another, illustrates the tension and dramatic clash between them and ends up with pointing to a possible resolution or synthesis.

The work, therefore, is a deeply moving account of the devastating effect upon the soul of a sensitive and intelligent young man when he is caught in the clash between two different sets of cultural values.

Mustafa Badawi. *Journal of Arabic Literature.* 1, 1970, pp. 145–46

Yahyā Haqqī's important work *People in the Shade* contains more than twenty essays from his own diaries. If all his essays were gathered together, they could, no doubt, fill twenty full volumes of this type. Yahyā Haqqī is one of those authors who has been honored by the government with the State Appreciation Prize, but even so, his works are extremely hard to find. These rare and amazing memoirs were scattered over the pages of numerous newspapers and were just waiting for some hand to reach out, open them up, and blow the dust of oblivion off them. We are very much the beneficiaries of this. . . .

The book contains a unified collection of journals revolving around people in the shade in all their variety, around the untapped perspectives that remain in the shade, and around the virgin worlds that have to move far away from the shade. It is around this threefold, homogeneous focus that the author's journals and tableaux revolve. It gives us a broad picture of the people in the shade, those people who prefer to be simply cogs in the machinery of life, which never stops moving, those who give everything they have and yet get nothing back from life at all, not even a small gesture. These bit-part actors on the stage of life are the abiding concern of Yahyā Haqqī in this book, because they are the real producers of life with all its headlong movement. The genii may perform miracles, but it is the ordinary players alone who give life its continuity and who thus carry on the miracle of miracles, survival. . . .

Yahyā Haqqī is inordinately fond of parenthetical sentences in his works. I think the reason for this lies in his close adherence to the spirit of Egypt and his unique style of both expression and thought. It is also the result of his extreme concern with the inner secrets of those two languages, the classical and the colloquial. This book contains examples of both that are treasures. This is a literary work of a rare kind; it offers a service to Arabic prose and celebrates the Arabic language. . . .

Sabrī Hāfiz. *Al-Ādāb.* Sept., 1971, pp. 36–37, 41†

HĀWĪ, KHALĪL (1925–1982)

LEBANON

Khalīl Hāwī is a serious poet who takes great pains to produce marvelous poetry and succeeds to a large degree. There are, however, some things I need to say. The poet forgets the primary virtue of the symbolist school, which is self-control. The seductive quality of words seems to lead him to use them with a number of different meanings, and that in turn nullifies his symbols.

For example, he uses the symbol of fire with four separate meanings in four places in the poem "Sindbad's Eighth Journey" [in *The Flute and the Wind*]. . . . The same comment can be made about snow, which he associates in the fourth and fifth sections with the idea of purity and in the ninth section with the idea of death and oblivion. Salt in some places symbolizes perdition and ruin; elsewhere it implies love and brotherhood.

The poet then does not concentrate his symbols. That is the first point.

The second is that the poet's efforts to turn the more prosaic stages of his experience into poetry are very dull; I refer especially to the first and third sections, which are full of detail that could easily be shortened and revised. The Arabic expressions used here are very colorless.

In the second section the poet gives a picture of the dominance of outdated social customs on our society. Hāwī alludes to Federico García Lorca's play *Blood Wedding,* in which two lovers are forced by social convention to marry people whom they do not love. On the wedding night, the young man leaves his bride, goes to his beloved, and snatches her from the arms of her husband. They run away to the mountains where he kills her and then commits suicide. Hāwī tells the story of the poet Dīk al-Jinn, who killed his beautiful wife when he heard she was being unfaithful and then spent the rest of his life grieving over her. Frankly, I do not see the need to include the Lorca allusion here; the tale of Dīk al-Jinn is quite sufficient to convey the notion of the corruption of current social customs, and in any case all the symbols in this section are fixed and well known, as so they must be, since the subject of discussion is a series of perceived social issues.

What I fear most of all is that the poet's Arabic cultural awareness is inferior to his European, especially when we discover errors in scansion within the poem. . . . Even so, these comments cannot diminish the value that "Sindbad's Eighth Journey" undoubtedly has, or the amount of effort Khalīl Hāwī has spent on it.

ʿAbd al-Muʿtī Hijāzī. *Al-Ādāb.* June, 1960,
pp. 71–72†

The poems in *The Flute and the Wind* are of particular importance because they represent the pinnacle achieved thus far by genuinely existential poetry in Arabic literature. In *The Flute and the Wind* the experience is a cultural one echoing anxiety and fragmentation, which arouse feelings of despair and uncertainty. They force the poet to wander over the world's great oceans like Sindbad in the hope that the winds of fate may eventually blow him back to some haven of certainty.

The imagery in *The Flute and the Wind* is certainly more complex and

opaque than what we have encountered in *River of Ashes*. . . . Khalīl Hāwī
knows no respite or inactivity. We see his poetry developing and adapting itself under the influence of the metaphysical anxiety that besets his life. The
conditions he describes in his poetry are simply stages in the experience he is
going through. After seeing him endure boredom with the feelings of someone rolling in dust and mud, we now see him moving on to a new stage that
grows out of the first and is at the same time an attempt to escape from it and
overcome it. The poet has endeavored to throttle his feelings of anger, boredom, and inanity. The only way out he can see is utter indifference and indo-
lence. . . . He has succeeded in giving concrete form to this situation just as he
did in previous works, through sensory phenomena that serve at the same time
as symbols of internal sensations and of stimuli. . . .

   In the poem "Faces of Sindbad" the poet goes through a struggle with
time, old age, and a fear of decay. In "The Flute and the Wind" the struggle
involves fidelity to his art and the fulfillment of his self and his ideals. The
poem contains a number of internal voices within the experience, but two
sounds overpower all the others: the first is the sound of the wind or rather its
player; the second is the sound of the flute, a doleful, funereal sound. The
wind . . . is a symbol of revolution, the life force, and liberation from the fetters of reality. . . . while the flute continues to wail and moan. . . . The poem,
then, is an expression of the experience of release, purification, and detachment in the process of attaining absolute purity in the artistic experience. The
poet thus seems like Nietzsche's Zarathustra, who manages to purge and pu-
rify himself of all the banes of humanity, except, that is, for the bane of sympathy for the concerns and tragedies of other people.

Īliyyā al-Hāwī. Al-Ādāb. April, 1961,
pp. 19–20, 22–23†

   In *River of Ashes* Hāwī is almost another al-Bayyātī, a Lebanese version of
the Iraqi poet. Al-Bayyātī's *Broken Pitchers,* with its inspirations and premises, finds itself reflected in a number of poems in this collection. . . . But it is
clear that Hāwī imbues it with his own spirit. He neither transcribes nor copies; it is just that the poems display the same gifts within the same basic
framework; in fact, the two poets undoubtedly read each other's works. . . .

   In *River of Ashes* the poet is searching for truth, or rather, for the radiance of salvation. To the poet truth means the beginning of salvation. He rejects the materialistic and unpoetic world that surrounds him and does its best
to stifle the poetry of song. Beirut overlooks the sea, and the sea licks its feet
morning and night. The city has dank taverns, "paltry festivities," and a
whole stock of woes that beset any number of people, particularly those who
are most sensitive and refined in their spiritual makeup. There is also stunning
beauty to be seen in Beirut, but it is sometimes, or rather often, murdered by a
fistful of money or a glass of whiskey. From time to time Beirut also has visits

from battleships, fleets carrying demons. From time to time too the poet's phoenix catches fire and burns, but with no resurrection and no salvation! . . .

The poet has surveyed Eliot and the heritage of the modern West more than seems necessary. His nerves are on edge "like those of Nāzik," a reference to the Iraqi poetess Nāzik al-Malā'ika, a writer of great sensitivity. The poet finds himself faced by two worlds, the old and the new. But what is the point of either? The old world gives us dervishes, drugs, opium in its various guises, while the new world brings us the West, fleets of warships, demons, and the atom. Where does all that leave the poet's mariner (in "The Mariner and the Dervish")? And what of truth? . . . The poet's mariner rejects the East of the dervish and also the West of the demon. . . . Is he uncommitted, a romantic, or just crazy? He is indeed uncommitted as far as the East and West are concerned; he does not acknowledge either of them, even though he is a product of both. He is a romantic because he is forever wandering. But he is not crazy, unless his perpetual wandering can be reckoned as madness, a never-ending quest for truth and the radiance of salvation.

Jalīl Kamāl al-dīn. *Al-Shiʿr al-ʿArabī al-hadīth* (Beirut, Dār al-ʿIlm li-al-Malāyin, 1964), pp. 404, 406†

In all three of Hāwī's collections of poetry [*River of Ashes, The Flute and the Wind,* and *The Threshing Floors of Hunger*] the unifying factor is that he bears on his shoulders an enormous sense of responsibility for our present cultural era. By that I mean first, the revolution, which has had its effect on the traditional poetic forms when they were no longer able to respond to the complex and intricate experiences of the age; and second, the serious preoccupation with human philosophical problems that is required of anyone in this modern age who takes a practical view of things.

Khalīl Hāwī's poetry takes on the responsibility of this revolution in form and of this human preoccupation with all the skill of one who is fully prepared to succeed in his task. And indeed he has succeeded to a large degree. He has managed to create new Arabic forms that have the ring of authenticity to them in addition to their origins in popular tradition. These forms are powerful enough to comprehend a broad vision, highly suggestive imagery, and vital symbols, no matter how profound or lofty the contemporary poet may be in his use of the dimensions of imagination, emotion, and intellect, or how prolific he may wish to be in his introduction of symbols laden with mythical and cultural signification. . . .

Through his poetry, Hāwī has used the elements of the musicality of words and all the dimensions of emotion to pound on the door of intellectual and philosophical life. He has penetrated into the anxieties of people who are enduring the intensity of this modern life and all its problems, but he has done it through the language of poetry, with visions, symbols, and suggestions. . . .

How do we categorize the anxieties treated in Khalīl Hāwī's poetry? In his three collections, from *River of Ashes* through *The Threshing Floors of Hunger,* we find him wading through the flood of that existential struggle between various cosmic and cultural inevitabilities and the desire for freedom and release from the domination of those inevitabilities over mankind. In this process we see him creating in himself . . . a world in which the wind of terror rages, where murky caves are dug, and in whose deserts the flame and fertility of life is burned to a cinder. Life is a river of ashes from death and decay, piles of rotting corpses—corpses of ideas, traditions, civilizations, and human beings. . . .

The Threshing Floors of Hunger is a towering artistic monument of our modern poetry. The last poem in the collection, "Lazarus 1962," is the chief architectural feature of this monument. We may, and indeed, we do find something new here. The name Lazarus has not been associated with the year 1962 in this poem at random; what, one wonders, does the poet intend by such an association? Many ideas come to mind as we read the title and then recall the year 1962 and the events that occurred in the Arab world. If we combine these events and the story of the raising of Lazarus as recounted in the Biblical story, then we have to assume that the first thoughts that occur to us are correct, namely that the poet is here treating the idea of the expected revival in the life of the Arabs through the events of the year which he links to the name Lazarus. . . .

Husayn Muruwwa. *Dirāsāt naqdiyya fi daw' al-manhaj al-wāqiʿī* (Beirut, Maktabat al-Maʿārif, 1965), pp. 379–81, 406–7†

Hāwī's skilful manipulation of rhythm in his poems makes it difficult for the occasional reader to recognize. For example, one gets the notion that a different metre is used in sections V and IX of "Lazarus: 1962," but on a closer look, the reader realizes that the metre is the same as in other sections.

In brief, Hāwī's choice of the metres is close to the Arabic song and dirge, and his exploitation of their variations brought his poetry closer to conversational language and enabled him to express in the same metre serious and light subjects.

But Hāwī's innovations are not restricted to rhythm, metre or language; his philosophy of symbolism had a new and far-reaching impact on the poets of today. His predecessors, it is true, had used emotional symbols in their poetry, but while most of their attempts concentrated on the evocation of emotional association, Hāwī's endeavours have successfully exploited intellectual as well as emotional symbols and associations. On the one hand, most of his predecessors and contemporaries employed subjective symbols in the tradition of Mallarmé; these were merely metaphors that had limited associations. On the other hand, Hāwī, like W. B. Yeats and the great French symbolists, employs universal as well as subjective symbols, in order to supply his verse with a frame of reference which carries the reader beyond the world of the senses, "the threshold of waking life."

Moreover, Hāwī uses symbols to emancipate poetry from the element of narration and to achieve organic unity in his poems. . . . Hāwī discovers his symbols in his country's ancient folk legends and religious heritage, because these supply the reader and the poet with an "objective correlative" that produces an empathy between them. Hāwī also borrows his symbols from the world around him, where some people suffer from intellectual indigestion and many from dishonesty and perversity. Only very occasionally does he borrow his symbols from his own life; Sinbad, for example, is at once the adventurous sailor, the Arab who searches for ideal life, the poet in his quest for a meaningful identity with his world, and the helpless victim of his circumstances.

The symbol then, according to Hāwī, binds the poet's imaginative perception with the subtleties of rhythm, form, and imagery, and produces an "objective correlative" that is capable of evoking many associations.

> Adnan Haydar. *Khalīl Hāwī's "Bayādir al-jūʿ" ("The Threshing-Floors of Hunger")* (Beirut, The American University in Beirut, 1969), pp. xxxiv–xxxv, xxxix

The Threshing Floors of Hunger, with its three poems, is a single poetic experience, with "Lazarus 1962" as its pinnacle. The first poem, "The Cave," deals with the tragedy of sterility, emptiness, and the inability to change reality where time turns to stone and minutes become whole eras. . . . The second poem, "The Genie on the Shore," symbolizes the condition of basic innocence personified by a gypsy girl who lives her life as a response to the volcanic urges that stir within her. The poet portrays the pains of innocence in the face of pseudoknowledge, as the gypsy girl, the symbol of innocence and vitality, is turned into a gray-haired old woman after coming into contact with the artificial civilization that strangles vitality.

"Lazarus 1962" is the apex of this poetic experiment. The poem represents the tragedy of the Arab people in its painful endurance of a perverted revival, which is even worse than death itself. The poet uses the figure of Lazarus from the Gospels; Lazarus dies, and Christ raises him from the grave three days later. In this poem, however, Lazarus is given new dimensions in that the poem represents the tragedy of death and a distorted revival of Arab culture. Thus coincidentals are united with the whole, the sensory and the abstract come together. History in its entirety is presented in poetic symbols; the vision is fused with the theme and then the total, sensory symbol (as Hegel terms it) emerges. . . . Through the interplay of the Lazarus figure with the other characters in the poem, especially his wife, the symbol begins to expand through songs and sensual images that carry their own symbolic suggestions;

for the central symbol can enjoy an existence of its own and a freedom of movement in accordance with its own particular nature. Lazarus symbolizes the Arab people enduring the pain of a deformed resurrection when it has proved impossible to change their own twisted reality. He changes from a freedom fighter into a spy. He manages to pull his wife down into his own hell; evil conquers good, and all hope of a genuine revival dies. The desire for death has complete control over Lazarus, so much so that Christ, the symbol of transcendental power, cannot restore life to him because transcendental miracles come from the outside, while genuine resurrection must be triggered from within. This, then, is a picture of the death of Arab civilization: the wife symbolizes the civilization that is dragged down to the hell of the grave. "Lazarus 1962" was thus a poem about the defeat before the defeat (as the poet puts it), since it predicted the 1967 débacle before it happened. That disaster was the inevitable consequence of decadence. Hence the poem is a picture of the interconnectedness of man and culture.

Rītā ʿAwad. *Al-Ādāb*. Jan., 1974, p. 39†

Very different in mood is Hāwī's third volume, *The Threshing Floors of Hunger*. The first poem in the volume, "The Cave," depicts the poet's impatience because the prophetic vision has not yet been realized and the miracle which he had expected at the end of *The River of Ashes* is taking such a long time to happen, if it will happen at all. "The Cave" is probably one of the most eloquent poetic statements in modern Arabic, expressing fruitless waiting that borders on despair. In "The Female Demon [i.e., Genie] of the Shore" Hāwī shows how innocence and spontaneity are misled and destroyed by sophistication and religious fanaticism. But it is in the last work in this volume, the long poem "Lazarus 1962," that the poet's bitter disappointment in his earlier vision is expressed. Here we find some of the most disillusioned and most powerful poetry written in Arabic since the Second World War, and it is in this poem that Hāwī attains the height of his rhetoric, particularly in the opening of the poem entitled "The Bottomless Pit." Using a modified version of the biblical story of Lazarus as a scaffolding for his poem, Hāwī records his disenchantment with the dream of Arab revival, and shows how when values die in the soul of the leader of the struggle, the hero becomes a tyrant. This is a very pessimistic poem which in its unrelieved gloom can be compared only to some of Sayyāb's works.

Mustafa Badawi. *A Critical Introduction to Modern Arabic Poetry* (Cambridge, England, Cambridge University Press, 1975), pp. 249–50

Khalīl Hāwī thinks in images, relying mostly on metaphors and symbols. He has great ability in producing vivid, precise images. . . . Like Adūnīs, his poetry is informed by ideas, and it is again the voice of the cultured intellectual, thinking and interpreting experience in terms of its equivalent in thought. . . .

Indeed, it is to the poet's credit that despite this intellectual basis to most of his poems, he is able to portray a spirit torn with anguish and anxiety. But the reader is constantly aware of the poet talking at a high level of consciousness, and is haunted by the feeling that this poetry does not portray, in fact cannot be portraying life as it is really lived, but rather a certain premeditated attitude which has worked its way to the poet's spiritual experience. This is especially so in his two last *dīwāns, The Flute and the Wind* and *The Threshing Floors of Hunger.*

But the greatest drawback to his imagery is his frequent use of excessively repellent images. . . . He endlessly fills his poems with metaphors to convey the meanings of decay, corruption and revulsion. . . . There is nothing wrong with rage in poetry, but in Hāwī's poetry it is excessive. This is a sorry defect, which can immediately alienate a reader who might accept it in one poem but when it permeates entire *dīwāns,* feels inadequate to cope with it, not only emotionally and aesthetically, but also intellectually.

> Salmā al-Jayyūsī. *Trends and Movements in Modern Arabic*
> *Poetry* (Leiden, E. J. Brill, 1977), pp. 697–98

AL-HAYDARĪ, BULAND (1926–   )

IRAQ

Buland al-Haydarī's poetry has an emotional streak that shows the influence of Īliyyā Abū Mādī and his colleagues in the American émigré school. But in al-Haydarī's case this streak is blended with touches of gloom and yearning that seem overwhelmed by a sense of failure and despair. Al-Haydarī has brought to life a sensitive spirit and a heart bursting with hopes, but it is only a short while before he is stricken by bitter realities; the melodies his lips have hardly had time to intone are changed into doleful elegies mourning the loss of youth and renouncing love and happiness. . . . Gradually, however, this aspect of his writing disappears as another begins to emerge: cries of revolution and a denial of the value of life. This aspect of his writings shows a direct spiritual connection with Baudelaire and Ilyās Abū Shabaka. He finds himself fettered by the chains of the body as it rolls in the dust, in a hell seething with animal urges, aflame with burning passions, drunk with wine that only leaves a bitter taste in the mouth. . . .

Buland al-Haydarī is a gifted poet, and a fine example for the children of his own generation, who seem so restive in their ideas and feelings and continue to wander aimlessly in the valleys of doubt. Through World War II he has witnessed the struggle of human civilization during critical moments of its bloody history, and has emerged from this experience with feelings of renunciation and rejection, and a bitter, mocking revolutionary attitude. If, as an experienced practitioner myself, I did not realize that poets never ask questions about their inspiration, I would suggest to the author of this collection, *The Throb of Clay,* that he slow down a little and take things at a gentler pace. . . . I do not know for sure whether the above comparison with Baudelaire is appropriate, but what I am sure about is that al-Haydarī is still a young man and has a bright future in front of him in the realm of poetry.

Mīr Basrī. *Al-Adīb.* 6, 9, 1947, pp. 52–53†

In his collection *Songs of the Dead City, and Other Poems* Buland al-Haydarī emerges as a poet who writes about women. Sometimes they are portrayed in much the same way as they were in Abū Shabaka's poetry; in the poem "Semiramis," in fact, things are even more extreme than in Abū Shabaka, as woman becomes a symbol of animal instincts and fiery passion. The night belongs to her, and only opens its eyes to see a tiny candle shedding its tears perfumed with light so as to illumine the darkness of two naked bodies lying on a bed that sways to their rhythm. They are Ninyas and his mother, Semiramis. On the bed of passion the body ignores the sanctity of motherhood. Did the portrayal of woman reach limits such as these in the poetry of Abū Shabaka? A mere question mark we wish to put into the reader's mind! What, one wonders, can have led our poet to place woman in such a position? Could it have been the result of some bitter experience, as was the case with Abū Shabaka and his poetry, or has al-Haydarī simply been influenced by the Lebanese school of poetry? I would suggest that the poet's life incorporates both aspects. . . .

Whatever the case may be, our Iraqi poet admits in his poem "Angry Nature" that his life has seen some strange upheavals. . . . At first we can find few poems that make no mention of woman or some specter of her presence. But little by little she begins to disappear, and her role becomes more restricted, until she is just one element in the poem whose presence is justified by the ideas and feelings about life, death, and time, which he unfolds through her. Finally, he banishes her from some of the poems altogether. . . .

Buland al-Haydarī begins the collection as a symbolist, but then settles on a new realism: a big, poetic picture that grows from the inside with the various parts of it adhering; simplicity in expression; and a weary chant playing to both emotion and intellect in an atmosphere of inspiration that dissolves in a mist of pessimism and dark sentiment. This is the atmosphere that distinguishes Buland al-Haydarī from his colleagues among contemporary poets.

Nadhīr al-ʿAzma. *Shiʿr.* Autumn, 1957, pp. 98, 101–2†

Buland al-Haydarī is right to call his new collection of poems *Footsteps in a Strange Land,* since it really does portray slow, rapid [sic] steps in worlds of exile. I say "worlds" rather than world because Buland al-Haydarī's exile comprises more than one world, since he has had more than one exile.

In the first period of his poetic life his exile involved his artistic and spiritual feelings; only when he was divorced from them was there any sense of clarity. The details of "the streets" would seem obscure, and a silent, tragic darkness would loom in front of him. While we are on the subject, silence plays a notable role in Buland's poetry. It is the symbol he prefers to use most often to depict his interior world, with its "moving" stillness and its "talking" silence. Stillness and silence, then, are expressions of the experience of bewilderment springing from deep down inside him, struggling toward a dawn as its passes and does not pass. He waits for it, and it comes without him seeing it; he flounders, bewildered, in a silent darkness. . . .

In this period of bewilderment, "silence" in its symbolic form represents the power of defiance in the face of "the story of the soil," the tale of man who comes from the earth and the dust. . . .

The writer's poetic temperament is faced with violent internal tensions at this stage of his career. Obscure desires that are in conflict with the traditional poetic mold, both in form and content, keep erupting within him. . . . This mold, these conventions, however, adamantly refuse, at this point in the poet's career, to let themselves be destroyed by the struggle going on between them and the poet himself. For that reason, we notice that the poetry of this stage in al-Haydarī's career observes poetic conventions by sticking to the usual meters and to rhyme as well, at least in part. It is satisfied with other gains, which may perhaps be considered as among the first victories for contemporary Arabic poetry, at least at that time. Of these, the most important is that Buland can adapt his poetry so as to carry these emotional pulses liberated from rhetorical tone coloring, pulses that move forward with a spontaneous force created from within the poetic event itself.

Husayn Muruwwa. *Dirāsāt naqdiyya fī daw' al-manhaj al-wāqi'ī* (Beirut, Maktabat al-Ma'ārif, 1965), pp. 337, 344†

Through Buland al-Haydarī's latest poetical "journey" we find ourselves faced with a new and entirely different vision on the part of the poet. A new face appears, one that before has seemed pallid, alarmed, and hesitant during the course of its long poetical voyage leading up to *Journey of the Yellow Letters.* This new face is proud, stern, pugnacious, and forbidding, the face of a revolutionary poet, one who is fully aware of and committed to the problems and fate of mankind, to his concerns, victories, defeats, and desires. . . . Instead of the frightening pessimism and the sense of defeat and impotence in the face of a wall of impossibility, the poet's feeling of exile has now acquired a new tone, one of aspiration and revolutionary optimism steeped in a mixture of anger, defiance, and opening up to revolutionary man.

The revolutionary voice of the poet that emerges in this collection also reveals a distinctive artistic and intellectual maturity. This can be discerned in the newly aware vision of the poet, in the transparent tone of purity that used to flounder in a fog of anxiety, fragmentation, and exile, and lastly, in the development of the poet's means of expression and technique in constructing his experiences in poetry.

The birth of this new poetic voice is not something that has happened suddenly. It is the direct result of a process of development in art, ideology and life itself through which the poet has passed. This latest collection proves beyond a doubt that al-Haydarī has now gone beyond his previous works and now stands on the threshold of a new stage in his poetic development. . . .No longer is he the poet of sex and neat, aristocratic verbiage searching for musical rhythms as in *The Throb of Clay*. . . . This new stage in al-Haydarī's career leads us to look with reassurance and confidence at this poet who has at last managed to live his own ideological and revolutionary commitment with a sense of profundity and spontaneity.

Fādil Thāmir. *Al-Ādāb*. April, 1969, pp. 50–51†

This new long poem, *Dialogue across Three Dimensions,* represents a significant advance and a new birth [for al-Haydarī] when compared with his other works. In fact, this poem is an important new addition to the corpus of modern Arabic poetry in general. Buland al-Haydarī, I believe, has not previously shown such a marvelous and stunning sense of planning in the formation of his vision or revealed such new potentialities for the creative imagination. In this epic poem, with its three voices, you get the feeling that the poet has seized the tiller of the language and learned how to manage and maneuver it; not a single word or letter seems to be out of place. There is no repetition of phrases, no trite clichés, no harping on images until they are stone dead, no chasing after rare words, no digressions, and no frills. He makes you feel that the language is being created in his hands especially for this particular poem. . . .

Buland has finally emerged in this long poem from the lyric enclave that has continued to hold sway over Arabic poetry. He has constructed this type of complex and involved creation that is difficult to define precisely in terms of either epic or drama. If one can say that the epic is still as lost in our modern poetry as it was in the ancient period, Buland has still managed to construct such a thing in this poem after imbuing it with a touch of modernity and contemporaneity. He has been able to inject into this work some of the givens of the cultured poet talking psychologically, philosophically, and even politically, without foisting those givens onto the artistry in the poem. He has embarked on this difficult path with extreme caution so that his ideas and culture would not spoil the luminosity of the esthetic charge that must be present in a piece of writing if it is to be considered poetry. He may well have achieved that most difficult of equations: poetry and thought. And yet neither half of the equation mars the other. As evidence of all this we may point out that you cannot translate the ideas in this long poem; the only way you can explain it is by reading it. . . .

If innocence is the natural environment for the creation of poetry with a great poet like Nizār Qabbānī, then Buland al-Haydarī operates in a different world. He assures us that culture can serve as another environment for the creation of marvelous poetry.

Khālid al-Barādiʿī. Al-Ādāb. July, 1974, p. 60†

HAYKAL, MUHAMMAD HUSAYN (1888–1956)

EGYPT

The development of Egyptian life in its various aspects is Dr. Haykal's overriding concern in this collection, *Egyptian Stories,* just as it was in the vast majority of his other works.

If there is a unifying theme to be found from beginning to end, from *Zaynab* of 1914 to *She Was Created Thus* of 1955, from "Ibīs" of the 1920s to the other stories in this collection, then that theme is a particular concern with Egyptian life in its different guises and forms. In *Zaynab* he deals with the countryside, its open nature, its rigid customs, and its pure, chaste love. *She Was Created Thus* deals with Cairo society and shows the changes brought about by urban development and progress. In both cases, Haykal shows extreme concern with the portrayal of Egyptian life.

The same holds true for Haykal's short stories. "Semiramis" and "Aphrodite" draw their inspiration from Pharaonic history, while "Shaykh Hasan," "The Rule of Love," and others take their theme from the realities of our contemporary life. In all of these works destiny plays a large role, thus affording great prominence to the emotional tragedies that are so appropriate for the short story and that provide an intrinsically Egyptian stamp to these literary works. . . .

There are also stories derived from our present historical circumstances. "Crown Witness" allows Dr. Haykal to portray the heavy imprint of the British military occupation during the Egyptian revolution of 1919 and the way in which methods of extreme oppression were applied against nationalists at the time. . . . In "Legacy" he touches on the question of family endowments, which caused any number of Egyptian families a great deal of suffering and which people had been clamoring to have cancelled since the beginning of the century. Haykal takes the opportunity to show many aspects of the life and customs of our society.

Ahmad Haykal. Introduction to Muhammad Husayn
Haykal, Qisas Misriyya (Cairo, Maktabat al-Nahda
al-Misriyya, 1969), pp. i–iii†

The importance of *Zaynab* as an early novel does not lie in the unresolved conflict between the individual and social mores, for that has remained unresolved for many decades after *Zaynab*. It lies rather in the detailed picture of country life the novelist so faithfully portrays. Though the author obviously belonged to the land-owning class, he could depict the lives of poor peasants with sympathy but without the conventional gloss of sentimentality often associated with pastoral scenes. The work in the fields, the household tasks of the older women, the regular rounds of filling the pitchers with water at the canal or river, the peasants' talk on all kinds of occasions, all that is faithfully and vividly depicted in this early novel. Haykal was one of the first to imitate the peasants' speech. It is true he found it necessary at the beginning to apologize to his educated readers for this lapse from classical norms, but he saw to it that his peasants were real enough. . . .

Zaynab marks the beginning of the Egyptian novel as a new literary form, but stands on rather a lonely pinnacle as an early but abortive start. It could have been the author's reluctance to put his name to a work of fiction, or the country's preoccupation with the political struggle and series of setbacks that followed the Revolution of 1919. Whatever the cause, the fact remains that no novel of equal interest or importance as *Zaynab* was published in Egypt before the early Thirties.

Fatma Moussa-Mahmoud. The Arabic Novel in Egypt
(Cairo, General Egyptian Book Organization, 1973),
pp. 22–24

Zaynab was written while Haykal was abroad, and the strain of nostalgia in it is marked, although the romanticism fashionable at the time must share the responsibility for the lyrical descriptions of the countryside and the idealised vision of the peasants. At the time of its publication, 1914, the only forms of creative writing which were considered respectable were poetry and historical novels of an educational nature, but *Zaynab* is far from being an example of escapist, *vie en rose* fiction. It is not only a description of rural life and customs, as the subtitle *Rural Scenes and Customs* would suggest, but a story of the loves of five people connected with the village, and the central figure in this situation is not the peasant girl after whom the book is named, but the son of the wealthy landowner, Hamid, who returns from his studies in Cairo to spend the summer with his family. . . .

When Haykal published his novel he established in Egyptian fiction many of the themes which were to be important later on: the countryside, both as background and as an independent element, the position of women, above all the dilemma of the intellectual, especially at the beginning of a period of change. He may later have despised his youthful writings, but if he believed in the sentence Hamid quotes from Qasim Amin—"The pleasure which gives life value is that man should be an active force leaving a lasting effect on the world"—he should perhaps have considered *Zaynab* as the source of his greatest pleasure.

Hilary Kilpatrick. The Modern Egyptian Novel (London,
Ithaca Press, 1974), pp. 21, 26

[For Haykal,] literature was important mainly in so far as it provided historical or sociological evidence, and for its capacity to influence national life. Even in articles dealing with literature, he paid practically no attention to its artistic values, the beauty it embodied, and the pleasure it aroused. In his Introduction to Shawqī's *Dīwān*, for instance, he dwelt on the poet's intellectual background, his loyalty to the Ottomans as the defenders of the Islamic state, his mastery of the Arabic language and his ability to revitalize old words; but he said practically nothing about his poetic talent or his contribution to modern Arabic poetry. Similarly, the Introduction he wrote for *Al-ʿAbbāsa*, one of Abāza's plays, gave nothing more than an account of the relationship between the family of the Barmakids and the Abbasid caliphs, and the reasons for the execution of Jaʿfar in the time of al-Rashīd. This account was followed by a very brief summary of the play. Typically enough, Haykal concluded that since the public was still enjoying the play, the "poetic excellence" it achieved spoke for itself.

Haykal's articles on literary subjects, however, may be said to have exerted some influence on the evolution of literature in modern Egypt. He took part in general discussions about the state of poetry and the novel, suggesting a remedy for their many weaknesses. His call for the Egyptian poets to depict their own lives and experiences, and to desist from imitating ancient models, does not seem to have gone unheard. This call might have been one of the factors that induced the rise in the thirties of a new poetic school, usually referred to as the Apollo group, which provided Egyptian poetry with the stimulus of a variety of individualistic talent.

David Semah. Four Egyptian Literary Critics (Leiden,
E. J. Brill, 1974), pp. 101–2

She Was Created Thus is a novel whose faults are more obvious than its merits. It is much too long with excessively detailed descriptions, particularly of the heroine's moods. Its characters act at times with contradictory motives whose inspiration remains illogical and unexplained; the first husband's per-

sistence in assisting the widow despite his wife's objection is the prime example. Haykal does not retain control of the novel or of himself throughout,
changing tenses as the heroine intrudes on her reminiscences written in the
present tense to comment from the point of old age; in the epilogue he shoulders the heroine aside to comment on his own life in terms that have no relation to the heroine's experiences.

The lesson Haykal intended to impart to the leaders of "the new stage"
was hardly a model of clarity or generosity. On the one hand he suggested that
no lessons could be drawn as fate rather than choice decreed events; on the
other hand the new rulers reflected the triumph of irrationality owing to the intellectual's enforced submission to mass whims in his hope of guiding them
towards progress. The latter was his own delusion, symbolized in the novel by
the heroine's turning to Islam. That these "aids" should be obscured by the
novel's length and Haykal's manipulation of the final chapters to suggest the
heroine has found contentment in Islam suggests a deliberate cynicism in his
treatment of these themes and a likely assumption that the new leaders would
miss the point. More than being a lesson, *She Was Created Thus* is an indul-
gent exercise in self-pity and a more subdued mea culpa for Haykal's past attempt to manipulate Islam and popular whims which resulted in his own sub-
jection to mass will.

Charles D. Smith. *Edebiyat.* 1, 2, 1976, pp. 194–95

HIJĀZĪ, AHMAD 'ABD AL-MU'TĪ (1935–   )

EGYPT

Hijāzī represents an Arab generation in transition. The best proof of that statement may lie in his poem "The Year Sixteen" [in *City with No Heart*]. We notice that he has tried to rid himself of all romantic melancholy and has taken a
vow to keep well away from the vortex of introspection, from weeping, and
from the trials and fancies of adolescence, so that he can escape into the light
and emerge into the larger context of life, thus embracing joy, faith, and
struggle. He confesses that, for a while, he was a prisoner of imagination . . .
but then goes on to declare resolutely that he is no longer in such a prison and
has found a means of escape through opening up to the world as a whole. But,
one wonders, is he right? The poetry in this collection [*City with No Heart*],
including those poems where he intends to sing of the joys of life and to talk
about faith, are clothed with precisely that sorrowful adolescent garb that the
poet has suggested with such confidence that we beware of and go beyond. It
is this particular kind of sorrow that is one of the hallmarks of this collection;
the whole work exudes the same feeling. The beauty of this emotion lies in the

fact that it is clearly spontaneous and genuine, with no suspicion of any artificiality on the poet's part, "willing himself to be sad."

The poet has transcended the adolescent phase, but even so, he is still sad. Thus, for him it has not been enough to be struck by the sorrows of adolescence. The experience that was supposed to resolve his problem for him has not succeeded in doing so. He still has a problem, and it seems insoluble. The poet, then, is a sad "singer," not, as he himself intended, a happy man. He may even have intended to show some joy, but his path is paved with grief. He longs for a revival, believes in Arab nationalism, and is proud of his leader, Nasser. However, poems like "Socialism," "Struggles of Ideology," and "Panegyric" cannot persuade us that Hijāzī is a great epic poet, the poet of revival, socialism, and bravery. Actually, however hard both he and the introduction to the collection by Rajā' al-Naqqāsh tried to convince us otherwise, Hijāzī remains the *romantic* poet of revival, socialism, and Arab nationalism.

Unsī al-Hājj. Shiʿr. Spring, 1959, pp. 106–7†

In Hijāzī's eyes the story of mankind and the city can be summarized as the story of man wandering in the wilderness, a stranger. He is, at one and the same time, crusher and crushed. In the city he is not moved by any natural or organic forces; instead, he finds himself tied to rapid and continuous transition. . . . Thus, whereas to [the neoclassicist] Ahmad Shawqī the city could be considered as the center of public events, where public life could be seen in the open, a meeting place where all kinds of colorful and brilliant people could be encountered, Hijāzī looks on it as the very image of internal and social oppression. . . .

One thing that sets ʿAbd al-Muʿtī Hijāzī's poetry apart is that he always ties the concept of the village to words. It is very difficult to find a passage where he talks about the village and what goes on there without him mentioning "the word," which to the Semitic Arab sensibility is still an essential part of existence, with all the innocence of Eden before the Fall. "Nights in the village are full of words," he tells us, while in the city "Doesn't man know how to speak?" and "People are always silent." To the sensibility of rural people, words "perfect" nature, while silence is "death" and "plunder." And so, like the village itself, the word is a means of escape from decline and oblivion. . . .

The city, then, is a place of sorrows; it exudes "soft winds of putrefaction." To him the streets are deserted because "he is alone in the big city." In the countryside there is "expanse," while in the city people crowd each other and grow plants in brass pots. Through our own estrangement in filthy, barbaric cities we lose our own village and our innocence. The essence of the poet's attitude toward the city in all phases of his writing is therefore a search for the countryside, for a return to innocence.

Munāf Mansūr. Al-Ādāb. April, 1974, pp. 43–44†

Hijāzī's attitude to the city later [after *City with No Heart*] loses something of its intensity in the two subsequent volumes: *There Remained Only Confession* (1965) and *Elegy on the Handsome Life* (1973). This is due partly to the fact that the poet was no longer the bewildered newcomer to Cairo, but had grown more accustomed to fairly complex urban living, partly to the measure of recognition he had received, which made him feel less of an outsider. He was now in fact writing songs for the Arab Socialist Union in which he hoped to find the answer to problems of urban life. . . .

In his later poetry Hijāzī became increasingly interested in Arab nationalism. In the preface to his poem "Aurès," which was inspired by the Algerian revolution and attained great popularity, he wrote (1959): "I have found in the idea of Arab nationalism an embodiment of the spirit of the people, as well as my own personal salvation from a violent intellectual crisis which nearly drove me to a psychological breakdown." Like other Arab poets he was drawn to Paul Éluard because of his political position: in "Aurès" he quotes from a poem in which Éluard laments the death of a man belonging to the French Resistance who had been shot by the German Nazis.

Hijāzī is a committed Arab nationalist and a Nasserite who wrote more than one poem on Nasser in which he gave expression to his feelings of hero-worship. This is particularly true of his moving elegies on Nasser in "The Journey Has Begun" and the title poem of the last volume, "An Elegy on the Handsome Life." In his recent poetry Hijāzī too shows the dominant influence of surrealism, in his tendency to break down logical sequence and his predilection for surprising imagery.

Mustafa Badawi. *A Critical Introduction to Modern Arabic Poetry* (Cambridge, England, Cambridge University Press, 1975), pp. 218–19

When we attempt to analyze the content of the poem ["The Sea and the Volcano," in *Elegy on the Handsome Life*], the first thing that strikes us is that the voices that compose its artistic fabric are intermingled. Sometimes the voice simply supplies general narrative description; another voice is in a more individual lyrical mode, and varies in accordance with the different situations; a third voice is epic, rebellious, and adamant. We therefore find ourselves faced with a new kind of complex poem, one in which the lyric and epic styles are mixed. Our age is not one for epics, however. On the societal plane, this is not the age of the individual hero, but rather one of the masses as hero and of the people in resistance. On the artistic plane, heroic epics have died out as a form, and the personal lyric has declined. The two types—epic and lyric— have blended into a contemporary poetry, the result of which is the long complex poem. And so it is that in "The Sea and the Volcano" we find the epic quality represented in situations that record the heroism of the people and not the individual.

Hijāzī has used this technique in previous poems, for example, "Baghdad and Death" and "Syria and the Winds" from the collection *City with No Heart,* and the collection *Aurès,* about the Algerian revolution, one of the best examples of this type of poetry. These poems represent a continuum as far as the poet himself is concerned; through them he gives expression to an artistic need that reflects an awareness of changing reality.

Tāhā Wādī. *Jamāliyyāt al-qasīda al-muʿāsira* (Cairo, Dār al-Maʿārif, 1982), p. 27†

HUSAYN, TĀHĀ (1889–1973)

EGYPT

Tāhā Husayn's style is that of simplicity yet without the loss of linguistic beauty and classical references. In a sense he is neither modern nor classical but a remarkable combination of both. He answers, perhaps better than any other contemporary author, the question of the importance of Western ideas as over against Eastern ideas in modern Arabic writing. His answer to this question is an ingenuous inclusion of both rather than avoiding one or the other. While he was so thoroughly schooled in French writing he also realizes that Arabic writing cannot be divorced from its literary heritage. There is, hanging over every writer of Arabic, a tremendous influence of the classical norms of good language; more so, it seems, than in any other language. The Qur'ān and the great prose classics of the past, whose style may be considered to be too archaic for direct imitation in the 20th century, still stand as literary ideals and cast their influence upon the modern writer. This explains an essential characteristic of Arabic style. Ancient Arabic literature, beginning with pre-Islamic poetry and the Qur'ān, was designed to be heard in the first instance and not written. Hence, in Arabic literature interest is in the sound of the language— the oral beauty of the composition. This interest often supersedes, or strongly competes with, care for the thought content. Tāhā Husayn has an especially keen sense for the sound of words and the music of language, enhanced no doubt by his blindness. He is careful in the choice of words and the balance of phrases. He maintains a perfection of classical grammar. There is in his style a touch of dignity and formality without loss of directness and simplicity.

There is no doubt that his memory, filled as it is with so much of great Arabic literature, gives him a readiness of vocabulary and of classical allusion which makes for much of the charm of the style. He is in no way pedantic or seeking to present strange words. The vocabulary and phraseology are neither archaic nor ornate, yet have a slightly elevated tone and a richness of connotation which gives beauty and grace to the writing.

Kermit Schoonover. *Muslim World.* Oct., 1955, pp. 367–68

It is clear that Tāhā Husayn has some valuable assets as a story-teller. Not the least of these is his command of words. He also has to a marked degree the ability to recount his personal experiences with simplicity, truth, and communicative emotion. It need not be pointed out how much of his story-telling consists of reminiscences, and indeed the narrator in him is never very far from becoming a participant: when Adīb [in *Adīb*] jokingly tells him to remove his shoes before entering his sanctum, he is reminded of a number of mosques which he used to enter barefoot, and of the courses which he attended there; he writes long introductions or interrupts a story to state his opinion or even to explain his approach to story-telling; and even in stories intended to be impersonal, such as *Dreams of Scheherazade,* he exclaims "Even if he (Shahryār) open his soul to us, we shall not know whether he is happy or not," or "How do you expect me to describe the indescribable?" involuntarily revealing his consciousness both of himself and of his reader. Paradoxically, another virtue of his is the objectivity, the accuracy of his character studies and of his descriptions of the physical or social environment. Except in *The Call of the Plover,* which does not profess to be factual, he does not project the thoughts, emotions, and reactions of a Westernised intellectual into rustic characters. The secret of this apparent objectivity is that he seldom creates, or even analyses; he brings individuals and even entire communities to life by cumulative description of their characteristics and activities, much as a television beam reproduces a picture by scanning it spot after spot.

Pierre Cachia. *Tāhā Husayn: His Place in the Egyptian Literary Renaissance* (London, Luzac & Co., 1956), pp. 200–201

The novel *The Tree of Misery* can be set apart from all the other works of our great author in that it gives us part of his own life's experiences. He has provided a complete narrative framework, and there is thus no need for the kind of sarcasm he levels at critics in the Introduction to *The Tortured on the Earth* for their demanding the particular facets and elements that make up a story. In his comments he was careful to point out that he does not write stories; he quotes conversations. The stories in *The Tortured on the Earth* and much else of what he has written are closer to being narrative conversations than artistic stories *per se. The Tree of Misery* is a narrative work in which we can sense Tāhā Husayn's refined literary taste at work. No fair critic can deny that it has great value as a story, unless, that is, he has not read it.

In this novel the author is concerned with a group of people; no one character plays the role of hero at the expense of the others. In this respect, Tāhā Husayn may even have anticipated the works of the young Najīb Mahfūz. This group of people operates within the sphere of influence of the chief of an order of Sūfī mystics who holds a spiritual control over them. The story gives a precise and wonderful picture of the hold which the leader has over them and of their total submission to his will. . . .

The style the author uses in this work involves a lot of repetition and such a delight in the melody of words that it even takes over the passages of conversation as well; there is no distinction among conversation, description, and analysis. The author never puts into the mouth of a single character the kind of language that is closest to his or her characteristics, and yet he still manages to bewitch us to such an extent that we overlook the need for a kind of language more closely related to the characters.

'Abbās Khidr. *Qisas a'jabatnī* (Cairo, Dār al-Fikr al-'Arabī,
1961), pp. 38–39, 45†

Two observations can be made about Tāhā Husayn as a novelist: the first is about the role digressions play in his works; the second concerns his efforts to remain in contact with his readers. "Plot," in the narrowest sense of the term, is not something of paramount importance to Tāhā Husayn, and, as a result, his characters are not above stopping in their tracks in order to investigate some particular thing, to look it over at leisure, and then describe it to us in considerable detail. No one tries to hurry them along, especially the author himself. They have all the time in the world. After all, life is not simply the sum total of the things one does, but rather the thread that ties together moments in time. Is it not essential to pay most attention to beings and things? The heroes of Tāhā Husayn's novels have this trait to such a degree that it sharpens their sense of observation and triggers their feelings. All the usual digressions that, when introduced into a work of art without any skill, run the risk of disrupting the harmonious development of a narrative, succeed in Tāhā Husayn's works in making the very atmosphere of the novel more realistic or more lively, as the case may be. . . .

With regard to the author's direct interventions in the narrative (in the same form as we find them in the works of Stendhal, Gide, and Jean-Paul Sartre), we find that they seem to have no other goal (however paradoxical this may sound) than to call the writer to task for standing back in the face of the heroes who act within the novels. On close analysis we come to realize that, from the novelist's viewpoint, they show a particular concern on the part of the novelist that the characters be left free to behave as they intend, to react in accordance with their temperament and psychology; in a word, to live out before our very eyes the adventure in which they find themselves involved. I feel that we can even push this a little further and state that Tāhā Husayn intervenes in his narratives not as author, but, however odd this may seem at first, as reader.

Raymond Francis. *Aspects de la littérature arabe
contemporaine* (Beirut, Dar al-Maaref, 1963),
pp. 30–31†

Adīb is Tāhā Husayn's best novel and the one that comes closest to the ideal of narrative art in that it has succeeded in escaping from the trammels of Tāhā

Husayn's non-narrative style. The subject of the work is too large to be hidden beneath mere decoration, while the genuine, realistic characters have too much life in them to have their voices suppressed by the music of Tāhā Husayn's style. . . .

The subject is the meeting of Eastern intellectual with Western civilization, as an Egyptian leaves behind the haven of Upper Egypt and the environs of Al-Azhar and frequents instead the squares and streets of Paris. He exchanges yellowing, decaying books for concentrated study and amusement in Paris. This is a subject that has preoccupied the majority of Arab writers who have been able to visit Paris. I would not be exaggerating if I said that by following this thread alone in the works of Tawfīq al-Hakīm, Tāhā Husayn, . . . Haykal, . . . and others, we can probably get a fair reflection of the trends and currents that appeared during the period. . . .

It is difficult to summarize any particular point of view that Tāhā Husayn develops in this works. He certainly does not blame his friend who has traveled to Paris, and indeed, he may even be reckoned to be trying to arouse sympathy for him when he offers excuses for the man's divorcing his country-girl wife and for his love of the great city, which has surprised him with its fascinations.

However, Tāhā Husayn gives his friend's tale a painful ending as he shows him totally at a loss, dangling in mid-air between an earth he has left behind and a sky he cannot reach.

Salāh ʿAbd al-Sabūr. *Mādhā yabqā minhum li-al-tārīkh*
(Cairo, Dār al-Kātib al-ʿArabī, 1968), pp. 15, 19–20†

When *The Tortured on the Earth* first appeared as individual essays and sketches little notice was taken of the seditious nature of the contents. But when there was an attempt to collect and publish them in book form, those who "feared justice" also feared the impact of such a damning document, written with the eloquent pen of a master stylist. The passionate anger and bitterness to which Tāhā Husayn gave vent appear to have disturbed the ruling class who sensed, in such highly inflammable material, a threat to their position. The *Tortured on the Earth* therefore was banned in Egypt and first published in Lebanon. Egypt had to undergo a revolution before the work was allowed publication in 1955. The marked change in the attitude of the authorities to this work is in itself an indication of the basic change in the whole social and economic structure of the country, long overdue and finally brought about.

The Tortured on the Earth has become a social document of the pre-Revolutionary era. It presents a portrait of life in the countryside among the poorest of the poor, a people so destitute that they hardly recognised the fact of their wretchedness; for poverty means ignorance which, coupled with a fatalistic attitude to life, leads to a total unawareness of one's rights as a human being. The characters dealt with in these sketches, all types representing the millions of have-nots, are so taken up with eking out a bare subsistence that they have no time to consider their plight on earth, even had they the ability to do so.

Nur Sherif. *About Arabic Books* (Beirut, Beirut Arab
University, 1970), pp. 11–12

The novel *The Call of the Plover* lacks a great deal of "realism of presentation," which similar romantic works possess. Not only do all the characters speak in the same style of classical Arabic, but there is nothing to indicate the approximate date at which the events of the novel occur, and the town in which the main part of the action takes place is not named. Even such an important character as the irrigation engineer who is the indirect cause of Hanādī's death, and who marries the heroine Āmina, remains nameless. In addition to this some details of the action are improbable. . . .

Among the most serious of the plot's weaknesses is firstly that the reason given for the man driving his sister and her family from her home is inadequate. Given the social conditions of a village in Upper Egypt, one might expect that if instead the sister had been caught with a man, she would have been killed by a member of her family and her husband might have had to leave the village to save his face. But it is difficult to imagine a man, merely because his brother-in-law is disgraced and killed, driving out his sister, "a single woman with a share of beauty which would make men desire her and would entice the shameless to her, with two wretched girls who are good at hardly anything." . . .

It seems that the author here is principally concerned with presenting an ethical and social message: he intends to make people aware of the crimes committed in the name of honour, and wishes perhaps to indicate that love should take the place of revenge. His concern with the message, however, leads him to create these unlikely situations, the improbability of which is often more strongly felt because of the absence of realistic detail, and to force his characters to behave unnaturally.

Hamdī Sakkūt. *The Egyptian Novel and Its Main Trends
1913–1952* (Cairo, American University in Cairo Press,
1971), pp. 33–34

What is it that gives the two volumes of *The Days* their enduring value? The two parts (published [in book form] in 1929 and 1939) are made up of quite ordinary pictures of life in an Egyptian village and in the environment of al-Azhar Mosque at the end of the nineteenth and the beginning of the twentieth centuries. It is undoubtedly true that the bitter personal experiences that Tāhā Husayn went through do give certain parts of the book an extremely touching appeal, but in the majority of the chapters there is absolutely no mention of the sufferings he endured. And yet, that does not diminish its artistic value.

We have to look elsewhere, then, for some more general reason for the book's merits.

Are we to say that it is the work's artistic form? Or is it Tāhā Husayn's style? But neither form nor style can exist on its own without there being some specific posture that the author adopts as his own. In *The Days,* the posture Tāhā Husayn adopts is that of an educated Egyptian who has been attracted by European civilization, but who still retains deep down inside himself the sensibilities of a country boy in one of the villages of Minyā and also of a young student in the neighborhood of al-Azhar. The way Tāhā Husayn defines this posture for us at the end of each part is especially novel and charming. It is the light drawn from modern culture that discloses the dimensions and different shades of his treasured memories. But for that light, his store of memories from earlier times would have little or no value. By all this, I not only imply that the narrative form in which *The Days* is written is new to Arabic and that the frankness with which he reveals his family and personal reminiscences is something quite unusual in Arabic writing and society in general, but also that the critical tone that can be detected throughout the work, and that leaves its mark on the author's style—without in any way spoiling the emotional impact—would not be there if it were not for the author's wide-ranging outlook.

Shukrī ʿAyyād. *ʿĀlam al-fikr.* Nov., 1972, p. 621†

Like the other writers of the generation of '89 Tāhā Husayn was strongly influenced by nineteenth-century French romanticism, and this has been detrimental to his intention of writing novels which illustrate a moral or describe social change. In addition his lack of familiarity with the genre hampered him from expressing his ideas effectively. It is, however, possible to discern his preoccupations; the position of the intellectual between East and West, neither of which receive his complete approval, the importance of education, the belief in progress. He restricts himself in the discussion and application of them to a narrow section of society, the rural middle class of traders and the urban intellectuals, and he does not extend his analysis to other groups. Even when talking about the small-town merchants he reveals a lack of insight into the lives and thoughts of his characters, so that he refers to the traders who have come from Cairo and undermined the business of the local shopkeepers as "devils," leaving the reader with the impression that he has a feeling of superiority towards the simple people of the provinces. The description of the train, "this new invention which came from Cairo some time ago, iron travelling on iron and sending smoke and dust in front of it," is another attempt to observe through the eyes of his characters, and a particularly inept one, since railways were introduced even into Upper Egypt by the 1870s. There is a superiority on the part of the writer which recalls that expressed by Amina [in *The Call of the Plover*] when she maintains to her mother and sister that she has a better understanding of life than they do. The explanation is perhaps that Tāhā Husayn was sent away from home to study when he was too young fully to understand the way of life of people in the provinces, although he does not realise this and writes as a straightforward outsider like Tawfīq al-Hakīm.

Hilary Kilpatrick. *The Modern Egyptian Novel* (London,
Ithaca Press, 1974), p. 40

This third volume of *The Days* was published only some six months before Tāhā Husayn's death, in October 1973, at the age of eighty-four. It is thus the work of long retrospect. The writer adopts the curious device of almost always referring to himself in the third person, as "the youth," or "that young man." Only very rarely does he use the first person and then, it would appear, only because momentarily he forgets his habit in excitement. Similarly, the name of the owner of "that sweet voice," first his reader-helper, then his fiancée and finally his wife, is never revealed. Even after daughter and son are born to her, the reader is not allowed to share the secret. In a blind writer one cannot expect descriptions outside the aural.

Yet this idiosyncrasy is in line with that quality of personal objectification which goes with sightlessness: it is an inward seeing of oneself in a sharpened egocentric situation precisely because one is denied the comfort of visually exchangeable transactions in society. In so far as sight imbues one's handling of oneself, so deprivation of it interiorises oneself in, as it were, a visual anonymity.

However, these psychic reaches of the story remain wholly in the narrative realm. *A Passage to France* reflects only on the handicaps of blindness, not on the ultimate mystery of suffering.

Kenneth Cragg. Introduction to Tāhā Husayn, *A Passage to
France* (Leiden, E. J. Brill, 1976), pp. xii–xiv

Anyone who has read the stories and novels of Tāhā Husayn can see quite clearly for themselves that his fictional writings cannot be divorced from his other activities, be they literary or political. Each of his fictional works is an individual cry against social injustice and a call for reform. And now, we suddenly find ourselves presented with an unfinished work entitled *Beyond the River,* which Tāhā Husayn was apparently prevented from completing for some reason or other. . . . In his introduction to the book, Dr. [Ahmad Hasan] al-Zayyāt states that Tāhā Husayn began to publish chapters of this work in the periodical *Al-Kātib al-Misrī* [The Egyptian Writer] in November 1946. It apparently aroused some people's anger . . . but Dr. al-Zayyāt goes on to say that the novel is incomplete, even though the author gives no indication at the end of the chapters that the story is to continue.

Now that I have read the book, I am prepared to state that there seems to be nothing missing; I can see no reason to consider it incomplete. The story itself makes it clear that Tāhā Husayn did not stop writing at a particular point in order to rouse the reader's expectations or to resume the writing of it at a later date, but simply because the story had achieved its purpose at that point. It is possible that Tāhā Husayn did plan to write more, but he never did so. In my opinion, the reason for that is that the artistic form he uses in this work had given him everything it had to offer. The reader is quite capable of deducing from the narrative a complete picture of Arab life at the time it was written and a specific point of view. There is no need of any further events. In fact, the ending of the story as it now stands can be considered in my opinion as a warning of the tremendous period of trial that Arabs are still living through, right up to the present day.

Khayrī Shalabī. *Al-Kātib*. Jan., 1976, pp. 137–38†

IDRĪS, YŪSUF (1927–   )

EGYPT

The first talent Yūsuf Idrīs shows [in his short-story collection *The Cheapest Nights*] is precisely that he has realized the need to remain within the limits of a genuinely popular literature, while at the same time making sure that he does not get involved in various odds and ends of subjects that are both vulgar and uninteresting. . . . Now, it is extremely hard to use a slum or an Arab café, a wasteland or a hovel as a setting for the action of a story without seeing the place exert some kind of influence and without putting ideas into the mouths of the characters that may jar in a written text, however broad the terms of reference may be. Among the things that have helped Idrīs overcome this problem is that he differentiates between the language his characters speak and the one he uses to tell the story each time he intervenes in the narrative. This technique, which is not without subtlety or appropriateness, contributes in a major way to the realism of the work and allows us to appreciate fully the writer's qualities and the purity of expression to which he has recourse when it is required. . . .

The second talent Idrīs shows in this work, as far as I am concerned, is the simplicity of its subjects. I am avoiding the word "plots" deliberately, since, strictly speaking, nothing happens in any of the twenty-one stories before us. Only in very rare circumstances does the reader wonder what is going to happen to so-and-so, how this character will achieve his goal, or how that one will get out of his difficult circumstances. We are merely introduced to a certain number of characters, who are perfectly portrayed and allowed to share their lives with us for as long as the story lasts. It seems, then, that Yūsuf Idrīs is narrowing his novelist's art, if one can speak in those terms, so as to give as truthful a picture as possible of the most visible traits of his characters

without investigating in any depth the motives that make them act in the way
they do or the problems that can trouble them.

> Raymond Francis. *Aspects de la littérature arabe*
> *contemporaine* (Beirut, Dar al-Maaref, 1963),
> pp. 148–50†

The novel *The Sin* deals with the question of sin as a product of urban society.
The young girl, Sanā', starts work in a government department and in a very
short time finds out that she has become part of a world that is quite different
from her own: her colleagues, she notices, demand enormous amounts of
money from department clients for doing special favors for them. Needless to
say, her colleagues try to get her to join their little group, but she adamantly
refuses. Even when her own brother is not allowed by his school to take an
examination because he has not paid the fees, she still resists the temptation. . . . Eventually, however, Sanā' comes to feel that what she is doing is
like trying to fumigate a brothel. It is a comical scene; there is nothing heroic
about it. At one and the same time she gives in to the hundred pounds that
have been placed in her drawer, and also gives in to the advances of Muhammad al-Jindī. Her own psychological tragedy seems a reflection of her social
tragedy.

It is too hasty a verdict to maintain that the intellectual substance in this
novel has spoiled it as a work of art. Every great artist plans the intellectual
content of his works of art; that is, he lays down the general framework before
going on to the more particular questions of composition. The intellectual
component in *The Sin* probably aims at that Idrisian equation that says that human beings are a product of their social environment. In a startling way,
Idrīs follows every single psychological qualm Sanā' has and every aspect of
her external behavior. He shows tremendous precision in his choice of minute
details that give every single scene its *raison d'être*. And then comes the basic
contradiction in Yūsuf Idrīs's works: all this detail does not provide us with a
complete view of what society should be, but simply leaves us with a set of
abstractions floundering in absolute generalities.

> Ghālī Shukrī. *Hiwār*. No. 2, 1963, p. 115†

[*The Terrestrial Comedy*] is written in a mixture of styles. Some parts seem
like the theater of the absurd, which challenges both mind and logic. Other
parts are more reminiscent of the kinds of play that would have been seen in
the Middle Ages, in which the characters are simply embodiments of ideas
and ethical values. The play also mixes narrative and oratory. Into the latter
the author has stuffed all his ideas and all the results of his reading, rather like
a student who puts down everything he knows on an exam paper without bothering to check what question was actually asked. The answer is thus lost
among hundreds of other sentences that are entirely unnecessary.

Doctor Yūsuf Idrīs could have communicated his ideas to the audience with ease and in a pleasant atmosphere if he had only made his play about half as long as it is now. The play might then have been full of life and movement, instead of being turned into a debating hall at several points, one in which the actors themselves were yawning (as actually happened). The fault is not theirs. The time that each one of them has to wait before performing his role is intolerably long.

Another point is that the only voice that keeps talking throughout this play is that of Yūsuf Idrīs himself, and it is an angry voice, so much so that some people have tried to relate this play to the "angry young man" type of theater.

It has been suggested that this play is full of new ideas and expresses the author's new vision. This new vision has been the inspiration for this play from start to finish. I frankly do not believe that this applies to *The Terrestrial Comedy,* since the first act seems to me to be simply a dramatic preparation for the story "Beyond the Realm of the Intellect," which Yūsuf Idrīs published in 1961.

Shafīq Majallī. *Al-Masrah.* March, 1966, p. 26†

Dr. Yūsuf Idrīs is completely justified when he says that he is a writer who never repeats himself. He is always surprising the public with his new works. He began by establishing himself as one of our foremost short-story writers; he may even be the best we have. Then he turned his attention to the theater. Having established his reputation as one of the leaders and staunch advocates of the social realist school, he then proceeded to divest himself of all that and of any other "school" approach and entered an experimental phase. In all respects this has resulted in a series of works that have aroused a great deal of argument, ranging from enthusiastic support to outright rejection. However, the list of rejectionists now includes the supporters of the realist school, the supporters of art for art's sake, and opponents of the use of the colloquial language and of any kind of experimentation. As a result, Dr. Yūsuf Idrīs finds himself beset by a kind of comprehensive opposition.

The odd thing about the situation is that all those who oppose him now begin by pointing out that Yūsuf Idrīs is one of our most brilliant writers. They talk about his older works, and then go on to say that each new work is a further failure. Needless to say, the reasons vary from one writer to the next. This situation may help to explain why Idrīs feels so bitter toward critics, and I have to admit that I think he has every right to feel bitter. This is probably not the place to talk at length about the problems affecting our literary-critical environment, but I will say at this point that all Yūsuf Idrīs's most recent works have yet to receive a genuinely perceptive and objective evaluation.

Bahā' Tāhir. *Al-Kātib.* April, 1966, p. 146†

The novel [*The Taboo*] gives an astonishing insight into individual peasant characters, for Idrīs seems to have grasped the peasant psychology which so many of his predecessors missed. The short novel is alive with characters of peasants and overseers. The traditional Coptic clerk has a daughter, Linda, who is considered the beauty of the village, simply because her skin is whiter than the other women's. The village idiot is treated kindly because he is the clerk's brother. The head steward has his plump wife and a spoilt son who spends hours on the canal bank pretending to shoot pigeons, when he is really watching Linda's window for any sign of his beloved. The daily round of work on the estate, in the offices and in the fields is depicted by someone who really knows it inside out. The crowd of strangers pouring into the estate by the lorry-load, their excitement at the prospect of earning regular wages of six piastres a day for a few weeks and the details of their long working day, all are concretely evoked in the reader's imagination. The predicament of ʿAzīza, the peasant woman who gives birth to an illegitimate baby in the evening, and goes to work under the burning sun next morning, with all her entourage of disabled husband and hungry children is tragic in every sense. Her death is given wide significance by the change it causes in the relations between villagers and "strangers," and further still by the superstition that springs round the spot of her worst ordeal. A tree which grows there on the bank of the canal is enshrined by the simple peasants; barren women seek its hallowed shade and chew its leaves and twigs as a cure for the worst curse that can afflict an Oriental female. The obvious conclusion is left unstated. "Was ʿAzīza a sinner—or a saint?" Having shared the author's rich vision, one can hardly draw a line between one and the other.

Fatma Moussa-Mahmoud. *The Arabic Novel in Egypt*
(Cairo, General Egyptian Book Organization, 1973),
pp. 45–46

With *The Farfoors* in 1964, Yūsuf Idrīs made a significant contribution to the Egyptian theatre's search for roots and identity. In a series of three articles entitled "Towards an Egyptian Theatre," and in the introduction he wrote for the play two years later, Yūsuf Idrīs blasted those who recognized only the European forms of drama or who believed that those were the universal forms, and that for an Egyptian or a Kenyan or a Vietnamese to write a play, all he had to do was to take the ready-made moulds fashioned in Europe and pour into them an Egyptian or a Kenyan or a Vietnamese content. All peoples, he argues, have always had one dramatic form or another, and he called for exploring those forms and experimenting with them in order to arrive at a genuine national theatre. Not only would such theatres stand side by side with the European, but would help enrich drama all over the world. In Egypt, Yūsuf Idrīs called particularly for exploring such popular forms of drama as mimicry, *aragoz* (the shadow play), and dervish dances, which he believed to be the genuine expression of the dramatic impulse of the people.

Whether or not we agree with Idrīs's point of view, there is no doubt whatsoever that *The Farfoors,* whether it is the most apt illustration of his theoretical speculations or not, represents a fantastic leap forward from the type of drama he wrote prior to it. Ironically enough, by turning away from the social realism of his earlier years, Idrīs managed in *The Farfoors* to give more edge to the ideas he wanted to communicate and to reach a far greater number of people than he ever did before.

Farouk Abdel Wahab. *Modern Egyptian Drama*
(Minneapolis and Chicago, Bibliotheca Islamica,
1974), pp. 36–37

Yūsuf Idrīs presented the first realistic solution to the crisis [in Egyptian fiction, in which sentimental and melodramatic stories predominated], starting from his belief that the trend of escapist dreams had distorted the correct path of the Egyptian short story. To end the alienation between the short story and reality, it was vital to adopt the vision of the Egyptian character and its style of expression. The Egyptian personality during this period had begun to overtake the state of depression and frustration which followed the war, as it advanced along the path which culminated in the abolition of the 1936 treaty, the beginning of the armed struggle in the canal region, and the ending of the monarchy and the occupation. At that stage, the Egyptian personality began to reassert its control over its destiny, after it had suffered a post-war semi-dictatorship from the palace, and the exploitation of the occupation.

During this period Yūsuf Idrīs began to understand the real depth of the Egyptian personality as he adopted the vision and approach of its most typical, and authentic characters—the *Felāheen.* He began through their customs, way of life, rituals, and traditions, to present new artistic realms. He adopted their love of story telling and their special style of narration, returning to folkloric roots different from the roots of the classical Arabic tradition on which the pioneers of the Egyptian short story had relied. He was thus able to depict new realms, new questions, new themes, and new social groups from the village and the city, which had not previously been treated in the Egyptian short story. Yūsuf Idrīs expressed in his stories the striving of the Egyptian personality to face the external world, because all the enemies and problems of the Egyptian personality were at this time external ones. It seemed that this style and this solution was the true answer to the crisis of the Egyptian short story.

Sabrī Hāfiz. In R. C. Ostle, ed., *Studies in Modern Arabic
Literature* (Warminster, England, Aris and Phillips,
1975), pp. 103–4

Idrīs came out with his very interesting play called *The Farfoors,* which was
presented by the Cairo National Theatre in the season 1963–64. In the preface
to the printed play Idrīs told his readers that by writing *The Farfoors* he aimed
at raising Arabic popular drama to the artistic and aesthetic levels achieved by
world drama. In this he was decidedly successful. In parts the play reminds
one of the comic discussions of Aristophanes' plays. In others it is an approxi-
mation of some of the techniques of the Roman and Italian popular comedy.
Like these it makes use of the comic duet of stupid master and intelligent
slave, or servant, to shed ironic light on very many things indeed. These range
from the plight of humanity at large, the inadequacies of various political ré-
gimes, to more personal matters concerning the marriage, birth and death of
some characters taken from everyday life in Cairo.

The Farfoors makes considerable use of characters and situations taken
from Egyptian popular comedy, such as the hen-pecked husband and his
sharp-tongued wife; the match of abuse in which characters in Arabic popular
comedy readily indulge, and which never fails to produce delicious laughter,
as well as some slap-stick comedy and various comedy numbers. In all this,
Idrīs has notably achieved his aim of raising Egyptian popular comedy to
higher levels. All the same he does not prove his main contention that the
Sāmir form [based on theater-in-the-round, often involving audience comment and/or participation] is able to induce that rare state of mind in its audiences in which actor and spectator become one. This amalgam never actually
took place in any of the performances. Writer and director alike had to content
themselves with a compromise: actors pretended to be spectators and were put
in the stalls and boxes to give the illusion of intercourse between audience and
performers.

ʿAlī al-Rāʿī. In R. C. Ostle, ed., *Studies in Modern Arabic
Literature* (Warminster, England, Aris and Phillips,
1975), pp. 167–68

"City Dregs" takes the shape of a detective story: the judge discovers the loss
of his watch, eliminates the suspects until he decides that Shuhrat must be
guilty, and then plans his journey to recover it, with the help of his friend
Sharaf, an impoverished actor who is to pretend to be a policeman, and Far-
ghalī, who comes from the same area as Shuhrat. The description of his sexual
relationship with Shuhrat only forms the recapitulation in the centre of the
narrative but it explains, most pertinently, the exact nature and extent of his
separation from Shuhrat and all the people like her, and demonstrates the
emptiness and hypocrisy of his own values. The natural climax of the story is
not in the death of their sexual relationship, but in their confrontation in
Shuhrat's house, when he "takes her to the window, and he looks out, and she
looks out, and he says, 'Officer,' and Sharaf says, 'Yes, sir' . . . and almost
laughs," and then they go back into the room, and he threatens her with "a

year in prison" if she does not hand back the watch, and in the end she takes it from a broken glass in the cupboard and gives it to him.

Idrīs traces the intricacies of cause and effect in the details of the relationship between Shuhrat and ʿAbd Allah, a relationship which is more a confrontation, and has its blueprints in stories like "The Fourth Case" [in *Isn't That So?*] (where a complacent young doctor has his first contact with a woman "criminal"). Then with a skilled and delicate sense of proportion he steps back to describe the complete and tragic division between their ways of life with the dispassionate intensity of one who has been involved with, and has identified with, both sides and is able to create an image which does not impart a subjective impression, but forces the reader to imagine those aspects which he does not know from experience, and to share in the conflict.

Catherine Cobham. Journal of Arabic Literature. 6, 1975,
pp. 87–88

In Idrīs' recent stories there is a sharp increase of paradoxical and oxymoron-like collocations. This increase, too, seems to have occurred in the mid-sixties. Truly enough, paradoxical expressions can also be found in Idrīs' early works. However, both in the quantity of these collocations, i.e., the frequency of their appearance, as well as in their literary function, there is a great difference between the two stages. In the first stage we find, for instance, such oxymorons as "the victory of defeat," which is, incidentally, the title of one of the stories included in the volume *The Black Soldier* (1962). But such expressions seem to be few and far between at this stage. In the second stage, the frequency of paradoxical expressions is far greater. We can even find stories so densely loaded with such collocations that the very quantity becomes a new quality. This applies to such stories as "The Plaything" [in *The Language of Screams*] . . . .

As for the employment of these collocations, an expression like "the victory of defeat" is of a rather straightforward denotative value. "Defeat" here is "death," and its victory merely refers to the death of the beloved protagonist whose friends had hoped against hope for his recovery. In contradistinction, the paradoxical expressions in the second stage often have an unmistakably connotative value. In other words, the paradox which is conveyed by them is a complex one, loaded with shades of meaning. Most of these incongruous collocations seem to emanate from a background of the absurd and reflect a breakdown of logic. Such paradoxical expressions as "your top bottom" or "your bottom that is a top," or "the radiations of the invisible light" are hardly an indication of a plain paradoxical situation whose poles can be easily isolated and identified. Rather, the incongruity is deeply rooted in the nature of things, in the core of human existence.

Sasson Somekh. Journal of Arabic Literature. 6, 1975,
pp. 97–98

With "The Omitted Letter" we come to one of Idrīs' most effective expressions of the conditions of modern man; it is a veritable tragicomedy about his position in and response to the kind of existence governed by the demands of technology and administrative bureaucracy. There is much in this story which is amusing. It is a flea which keeps Ahmad Rashwān, the ultimate in punctilious civil servants, awake and thereby provokes the incredible and crucial question as to how he differs from his own typewriter. Everything about the company, from its fancy glass doors, to the posturings of Ahmad's boss and the upward and downward movement of the mouse-like figure of the Director-General as he swivels his chair, all these things are portrayed with a generous dose of sarcasm. And yet, the essential question is a real and critical one: is modern man being dominated by the machines which are supposed to help him; does he have any freedom of choice, can he exert any initiative? These are the issues which Ahmad resolves to settle for himself when he refuses to insert into a typed document a letter which he has deliberately left out as an assertion of his own individuality. Needless to say, the company bureaucracy, in the form of Abd al-Latīf, his boss, is quick to inform Ahmad that he has no individuality. Abd al-Latīf makes no concessions to Ahmad's feelings as he makes this fact brutally clear to him, but the Director-General tries a more gentle approach. Everyone has to obey orders, he tells Ahmad, even the Director-General himself. But by now, Ahmad has become obsessed by the notion of the dignity of mankind and his own superiority over his colleagues, and continues his defiance. After he is fired, he discovers that the typewriter key for the letter which he has deliberately left out is not working and rushes to tell his boss. As a final blow to Ahmad's crusade for individual rights, his boss tells him that machines can be repaired; we are left to infer that defiant employees who insist on asserting their individuality are fired.

Roger Allen. Introduction to *In the Eye of the Beholder:*
Tales of Egyptian Life from the Writings of Yūsuf Idrīs
(Chicago, Bibliotheca Islamica, 1978), pp. xxiii–xxiv

ISMĀ'ĪL, ISMĀ'ĪL FAHD (?–   )

IRAQ

This novel [*The Sky Was Blue*] records events of a time that grows along with the characters themselves; or perhaps we should say that it is the characters who grow through it. The protagonist is running away. The basis of his escapist philosophy is that he rejects the miserable reality in which he lives, as well as his wife, whose only function is to have sex and get pregnant, a simple woman who cowers in a corner, the very personification of a restricted and closed vision. It is this perception that sets the hero on his way, since as a first step he asks himself whether he can tolerate all the irritation that goes with living with this ignorant woman. If he contents himself with remaining silent, his freedom will be compromised. This is the first way his own liberty is being strangled. As he realizes the extent of his tragedy in all its profundity, he sees two possible paths before him: either he has to compromise his liberty and humanity, or else he has to face the situation frankly and announce his total rejection of this false marriage, in the process rebelling against the arid silence it imposes. Then, he thinks, he will really be able to grasp his true dimensions as a human being within a new time frame created by this direct confrontation with his own realities—so long, that is, as the confrontation itself is really the principal expression of his own sincerity and sense of loss. It is in this way that he goes in search of an alternative, and he finds it in the person of the girl with the blue dress. . . .

However, within this framework of challenge and escape, time has a negative connection with the other characters in this story: the officer, the wife, and the lover. The author has made use of the character of the hero without any limitations or caution. The use of the association of ideas in the treatment of both events and characters loses a great deal of its esthetic appeal, since in this case it is not accompanied by an objective awareness that brings with it a series of spatial and temporal dimensions; in this novel the association of ideas becomes merely a traditional flashback technique, if the term can be applied here at all. In a novel like this, time should have been the principal prop for the work as a whole, motivating all the characters involved. . . . But as the critic Yāsīn al-Nusayr observes: "The fact is that the whole novel converts the other characters—the officer, the wife, and the lover—into characters without fully rounded features; we know about them only through the hero himself. What of the wounded officer; does he not have some past experiences that need to be presented? And how about the submissive wife?" The technique of association, the primary distinctive feature of the novel, should have registered the temporal dimension for the other characters by means of a temporal dialectic that would tie past and present together.

Ya'rub Maḥmūd al-Sa'īdī. Al-Ādāb. Dec., 1970,
pp. 78–79†

In *The Rope* we are confronted with an experience of a new kind. Kāzim 'Abīd is a perfectly normal member of society who one day happens to write a poem lampooning 'Abd al-Karīm Qāsim. He is put in prison and fired from his job, even though he places an announcement in the newspapers disavowing the poem. He tries to run away to Kuwait, but fails and returns to his home, where he now has to face total ostracism. As a result he turns to burglary as a trade and solves his problem in his own unique fashion. . . .

The novel proceeds on a single level, that of a direct relationship with the quest for work and honor. The protagonist is forever trying to breach the wall of reality by various methods. It is the prevailing political situation (involving coercion and intolerance) that forces him to take up a life of stealing once his adventure in Kuwait has come to a fruitless end. However, he steals only from the houses of police officers. His wife—who serves as the author's own voice in this work—comes to the conclusion that this particular kind of work is an expression of his own leftist immaturity.

The novel operates in two separate time frames, one involving the events of the present, the other retrospective. In this way the associations are turned into mere expressions of direct memories from the past, and as such they are actually unnecessary. What they do is to freeze the present action as we wait for a whole panoply of memories from the past to move by. The novel's format certainly does not require this technique. The protagonist is an ordinary person incapable of undertaking continuous self-analysis. When the author makes Kāzim ʿAbīd stop his activities as a burglar as a result of the romanticized events in the novel, the result does not fit in with the growth of the character as the novel itself has protrayed it, namely, as a man realistically drawn who has been wounded by life and as a result is unable to find any meaning in things. . . .

In all four novels in this quartet [*The Sky Was Blue, The Light Swamps, The Rope* and *The Other Shores*] we notice that the author insists on using two lines to develop relationships: the first is the narration of normal events, where he makes use of the usual novelistic techniques—in other words, we find ourselves presented with understandable relationships that proceed in a logical and clear progression; the second resorts to the use of associations whereby internal parallels to the external world are set up or else are left to serve merely as memories of the past.

Ilyās Khūrī. *Tajribat al-bahth ʿan ufq* (Beirut, Palestine Essays No. 44, 1974), pp. 94–96†

In his quartet of novels Ismāʿīl Fahd Ismāʿīl establishes the leadership role of the working class. In the first three novels he sets out to examine reality and all the futility, coercion, and backwardness it contains. . . . In *The Sky Was Blue* we are dealing with a member of the petite bourgeoisie who runs up against reality but is incapable of seeing the possibilities it contains for transcending his current situation. So he runs away from his homeland, his relationships, and his past. . . . The tale of the wounded officer completes the tableau by revealing to us the mentality of the ruling military regime and showing how backward it is. In *The Light Swamps* we find Humayda condemned to hard labor for a crime he committed by accident, although the accident that landed him in prison had its own societal roots and causes (namely the *crime d'honneur*). In *The Rope* we see an extreme leftist who has failed and lost all hope of achieving his dreams, and so chooses, on emerging from prison, to work out his own salvation on an individual basis. However, he eventually rids himself of this disease of frustration through an artificial ending inconsistent with the novel's structure.

At the conclusion of *The Other Shores* the characters are given specific class identities and clear and final affiliations. The author gathers together characters from the previous three novels and also borrows the character of Karīm al-Basrī from 'Abd al-Raḥmān al-Rubay'ī's novel *The Tattoo*. . . .

Fahd Ismā'īl makes copious use of the association technique in these works, and employs it to good advantage so that both the internal and external worlds blend into each other. However, the obtrusive nature of the ideas expressed, on the one hand, and the author's insistence on using this technique, on the other, serve to deprive the reader of a good deal of external description of life in general. It can certainly be said that characters like Ahmad 'Abdallāh and Ja'far 'Alī are not the kind to stay in the reader's mind for very long, quite apart from the fact that the author does not allow himself to get close to the internal life of the character. In *The Other Shores* the movement of the novel is restricted for most of the time to the way the factory is being directed; the major focus of attention is the way intellectuals as symbols are subjected to scrutiny. It would have been better to depict the concerns of the workers inside the factory itself and in their daily lives. That would have provided a better link with the revolutionary vision of the work.

Shukrī 'Azīz Mādī. *In'ikās hazīmat Hazīrān 'alā al-riwāya al-'Arabiyya* (Cairo, Al-Mu'assasa al-'Arabiyya li-al-Dirāsāt wa-al-Nashr, 1978), pp 143–45†

"This poet novelist," says the Egyptian colloquial poet 'Abd al-Raḥmān al-Abnūdī, "sorrowful, forceful and well versed in our problems, has succeeded in blending his own public and private experiences in a way which is incredibly simple and spontaneous." Behind any such simplicity and spontaneity there is always the work of a literary craftsman, and that is certainly the case here. Ismā'īl's four novels may represent one of the most ambitious projects yet undertaken in the tradition of the contemporary Arabic novel, and it must be admitted at the outset that the result is only partially successful. However, that should in no way be allowed to detract from the considerable merits of individual novels in the group, most particularly in specific aspects of technique; of those we would single out the treatment of time, together with the investigation of the different levels of consciousness in the major character who is the focus of attention in each of the first three novels. . . .

A significant place in any assessment of the impact of these works must be given to Ismā'īl's use of language. Rare indeed are any excursions into a prolix narrative style in these novels; the emphasis is on short utterances, often in the form of exclamations or, on a more inward mental level, the terse cerebrations of the stream of consciousness. This technique is particularly obvious at the beginning of the novels where the reader is often left in a suspense of anonymity and mystery until the scattered segments of narrative begin gradually to provide a background against which to view the mental ramblings of the major characters. From the stylistic point of view, it seems to be no accident that the comments on the back cover of the first novel come from three *poets*, ʿAbd al-Wahhāb al-Bayyātī, Salāh ʿAbd al-Sabūr and—already quoted—ʿAbd al-Rahmān al-Abnūdī. The language throughout remains a fully grammatical, standard written Arabic; in the rare occasions where he uses a colloquial word, it is placed within quotation marks and given a specific footnote. The style which emerges, however, is no ordinary narrative prose; the extreme economy of diction which Ismāʿīl chooses as the best means of transmitting his multilayered projection of the inner mind of his characters forces him to use his words with all the artistry of a prose poet or craftsman of the shortest of short stories.

It is this great talent of Ismāʿīl to use words to convey mood as accurately and effectively as reality, and indeed to fuse the two together, which makes this series of novels such a notable contribution to the contemporary tradition of the Arabic novel. Nor should this literary estimate of their value leave unstated the fact that they provide from within a vivid portrait of Iraq during the 1960s. That is the stated goal of the author, and he achieves it with great distinction.

Roger Allen. *The Arabic Novel: An Historical and Critical Introduction* (Syracuse, N.Y., Syracuse University Press, 1982), pp. 144–45, 155–56

JABRĀ, JABRĀ IBRĀHĪM (1919–   )

PALESTINE

The first thing that you notice about *Cry on a Long Night* is the smooth style; you cannot but enjoy it as you continue to devour it page after page. When you become aware of the fact that an odd kind of intoxication has come over you, you may even feel inclined to scoff at the author. However, if you take the trouble to read it again even though you may have disparaged it, a sarcastic smile will again show itself on your face, accompanied this time by admiration; this time, though, the sarcasm will be directed at yourself, not at the author.

Talking about style prompts us to ask the question whether Jabrā has been influenced by the style of William Faulkner, whose works he has analyzed recently [and translated]. . . . The story concerns a journalist who, in addition to his normal work, is engaged in writing a comprehensive history of an aristocratic, blueblood family at the request of one ʿInāyat Hanem. Fate wills—it plays its role in the story—that the journalist is himself in love with a girl from a good family. Under a pine tree where they have taken shelter from the rain, he takes off his coat and puts it around her. He persuades her to go to his home to dry her clothes and she agrees. . . .

In spite of the insignificance of the events in the story, the novel does treat an interesting subject, an existential one dealing with relationships between people. It reminds us of Faulkner's *The Sound and the Fury*, which treats a theme very similar to Jabrā's.

Like any great artist, Jabrā leaves you to get what you most enjoy out of the work through his treatment of the subject. In revealing the relationship between the two major poles in life, man and woman, Jabrā expresses his views with daring. He conceals nothing and shows no signs of fear. In the words of his characters he reveals his own opinions . . . , striving to show the effect that marital infidelity can have on a man's life. The behavior of the protagonist reflects this with great clarity.

ʿĀdil al-Aʿwar. Al-Ādāb. July, 1956, pp. 37–38†

There is a tremendous sense of desolation in *The Closed Circuit* by Jabrā Ibrāhīm Jabrā, whose first collection was called *Tammūz in the City*. Jabrā is one of the very few poets who have given poetic creativity in the Arab world a new format that is both subtle and dynamic. They have also given it a new content, and so the modern poem has started to convey a contemporary human point of view and has a format that interacts with that point of view through the content. Jabrā may well have begun his wanderings in the wilderness when he lost his Tammūz in the city. It all began in the first collection, where Tammūz is the savior god of fertility, a man crucified at the edge of the city, dangling from its pillars, cast out in its cafés. Here is the first stage in the process of loss. How could he be brought back to life? How could one search for him? Only *The Closed Circuit* remains, and from it he begins with a single step his long journey into the wilderness. His poetry is a clarion call for hypocrisy, yielding to every kind of deceit! . . .

In Jabrā's poetry the city is a cesspool, an abyss in life. There Tammūz was crucified. Hands are nailed to windows and doors; blood gushes from houses. There is no one around to stain what is blood-smeared with love instead. . . . There is noise in his poetry too. It gives you the feeling of a kind of internal gnawing that stimulates your destructive instincts to the ultimate degree, all for the sake of looking under heaps and piles for what you have lost and want to rebuild. And then, when you finally wake up, you find that all you have, apart from being awake, is the remnant of a song. This noise has turned into a deafening cry. . . .

Jabrā's generation has produced a new poetry, and he is one of the leaders of this generation. This poetry marks the beginning of a movement that has stimulated the fertility of literary currents as a whole. *The Closed Circuit* is Jabrā's most authentic and integral poetic experiment to date, and clearer in its content [than his previous work]. It comes after *Tammūz in the City* to confirm that modern poetry is not satisfied with pattern or form as its whole *raison d'être* or as a reason for abandoning traditional metrical canons. It is to provide a modern content relevant to the era of modern crises that Arab people are living through in the twentieth century.

Riyāḍ Najīb al-Rayyis. *Hiwār*. No. 11–12,
1964, pp. 208–9†

Cry on a Long Night was written by Jabrā in Jerusalem in 1946, but it was not published until 1955 in Baghdad. So are we to regard it as a product of the 1940s, as part of the crest between the 1940s and 1950s, or as belonging to the late 1950s? In general, it seems to belong to the final category, the implication being that we are following the history of its publication rather than its writing. But then, there is nothing odd about that. Many progressive works have to wait for publication until the atmosphere is right to receive them. *Cry on a Long Night* is one such work. It is true that the subject of revolution against outdated customs is something that has kept novelists busy since the early days of the genre's appearance in the Arab world. One has only to think of *Broken Wings* by Khalīl Jubrān [Kahlil Gibran] and *Ibrahim the Author* by Ibrāhīm al-Māzinī. But in the present phase this particular revolution has adopted a clear posture, just like someone who turns his back on you and moves off in a totally different and conflicting direction. This is the posture adopted in *Cry on a Long Night*. The protagonist, Amīn, belongs to a group of angry young intellectuals who disavow love because they believe it is hypocritical and that it allows woman to work her wiles as a response to the demands of the flesh; they despise wealth because it brings along with it leisure and frivolity. . . .

The theme of transition from past to future is so clear in this work that all we need to do is to describe the major thrust of the novel. The fact that there is no frank discussion of the West here should not concern us. Both reader and author know very well that a stubborn attachment to the past is one of the features of the reaction with which Arab civilization faced the onslaught of the culture of the West. That does not mean that all trends in the present and toward the future have to imply a surrender to Western civilization; rather, what is suggested is a confidence in the ability of the Arabs to face both present and future. That is the way it is in this novel.

Shukrī ʿAyyād. *ʿĀlam al-fikr*. Oct.–Dec.
1972, pp. 630, 632–33†

I would like to detail three features that give *The Ship* its value within the development of the Arabic novel. First of all, there is the rich and varied cultural background we get from the pages of the novel, covering a number of subjects. The characters discuss life in a number of conversations that are full of profound thoughts and experiences. They discuss philosophy and religion very seriously and with considerable authority, thus revealing the author's

wide and comprehensive learning in philosophy, theology, literature, painting, sculpture, archeology, and myth, unparalleled in the modern Arabic
novel.

The second point to note is the new technique Jabrā Ibrāhīm Jabrā introduces to the Arabic novel . . . in choosing such a complex method of unfolding the novel's plot and portraying all the characters: he relies on the internal consciousness of each speaker to provide the necessary information, and
he breaks up the presentations into separate sections. This process takes us
backward in time with each character before we reach the final tragedy, the
dénouement of the novel itself. If anything, this novel reminds us of the work
of Faulkner, especially *As I Lay Dying*.

Finally, we must also mention the style Jabrā uses in this novel. It is brilliant and luminous. The words are possessed of a particular weight and are ex-
ceptionally suited to expressing the necessary emotions. In this work, the
style rises above mere prose and the journalistic style of reportage in which so
many Arabic novels are written. Imagery plays a large role here in both stylistic expression and the conveyance of meaning. Sentences seem to overflow
with a richness of vocabulary full of tremendous linguistic potentialities. The
novelist is here restoring to both style and language their role in the composition of literature and in artistic creativity, a role that has been forgotten.

Jurj Sālim. *Al-Ādāb*. July, 1972, p. 66†

Jabrā's novel *Hunters on a Narrow Street* has the same feel about it as the
great classical novels in world literature. The characters, events, and ideas in
such works branch out in interlocking directions, and yet each character and
each idea manages to maintain its own individual pulse and allows us to feel
the sense of the worlds about which the author is writing. We then see that we
are faced with a great writer who is completely able to deal with his characters, events, and ideas in a confident and calm fashion. He feels no need to
falsify or fabricate things. So much is this so that the reader comes to realize
that the novel's hero is none other than the author himself and that the characters are genuine models with whom he has lived for such a long time that he
can write about them in this lively and subtle way. Jabrā Ibrāhīm Jabrā has, no
doubt, also realized this fact. In his short dedication at the beginning of the
book, he points out that the novel is not the story of his life in Baghdad, and
that there is no connection between the characters and any living being. But
whatever Jabrā may have to say about his hero and the other characters, the
novel is still an expression of his own experiences and cannot in any way be
divorced from him as a human being and writer with his own particular views
and vision. . . .

Even though this novel can be reckoned one of the few that bear the unmistakable flavor of the country in which it was written (Iraq), it also tries to
offer examples of the situation in the Arab world that led up to the defeat of
1948, especially since the events take place one year after the defeat itself.

Jabrā strips down a number of outmoded models and ideas and exposes them mercilessly. He adopts the device of talking about sex and the significance of the word "honor" among the Arabs and uses that as a key to all the other questions he surveys and discusses in the novel. It is no accident that Jamīl Farrān begins his adventures in the new city at the brothel that serves as the key to open up the city to him. . . .

Whatever Jabrā's aim may be with this work—to create a superb novel or a history of a particular political phase—he has managed to give us an exceptional novel analyzing in detail the reality that has dominated our life as Arabs for a long time; indeed, vestiges of it may still be with us.

'Azmī Khamīs. *Afkār*. July, 1976, pp. 48–50, 52†

The Ship by Jabrā Ibrāhīm Jabrā, a Palestinian writer residing in Iraq, is an important novel of nonconfrontation. It offers a dark perspective on society and man in the Arab East. In a highly prearranged manner, several bourgeois characters from Iraq, Kuwait, Syria, Lebanon, Egypt, and other countries meet on a tourist ship. As events unfold, we discover that the journey over the Mediterranean is another improvisation on means of escape from reality. Each of the male and female characters from diverse countries has failed in one way or another—love, politics, liberation, marriage, art, or self-assertion. . . .

The fact of the matter, however, is that they are escaping from repressive systems, traditions, routines, other people, and even themselves. These characters are greatly tormented by society and its contradictions: big money, ownership, marriage, children, and above all the pressures to conform and keep silent in an age of injustice, domination, hypocrisy, and opportunism. . . .

Stylistically, *The Ship* is well-planned and neatly integrated. Characters, events, ideas, and plots evolve slowly and spontaneously. The inner world and intimate secrets of the major characters are unravelled more through what each narrates about others than through what they say about themselves. The multidimensional nature of human experience and behavior is effectively revealed through artistic use of symbols, poetic imagery, free association, and legends. One significant shortcoming, however, is the imposition of the author on his characters. It seems that each character represents different aspects and concerns of the author. Wadī' 'Assāf, for instance, is a successful businessman, but (like the author) his main preoccupation is painting and literary as well as philosophical argumentation. The author tells us through Wadī' 'Assāf that "there are no solutions in art. The issue is what is important." Nothing is said, however, about the significance of the issues to be raised.

Halīm Barakāt. *Visions of Social Reality in the
Contemporary Arab Novel* (Washington, D.C.,
Institute of Arab Development, Georgetown
University, 1977), pp. 21, 23

At first sight, [*The Search for Walīd Masʿūd*] would appear to be a novel of ideas, dealing with Walīd's disenchantment with social and cultural life and his consequent participation in armed struggle against the Zionist occupation of Palestine. But a careful study of this work shows that Jabrā is playing on the enthusiasm for the Palestinian cause. Walīd's mysterious disappearance is treated as in a detective novel but the search soon becomes a search for meaning in a complicated social and cultural bourgeois experience. The discovery of Walīd's taped farewell provokes conjectures, explanations and further problems, leading in a very intricate manner to each participant's past and present expectations and attainments being revealed, with the views and actions of others as seen, mostly, through Walīd's eyes, which happen also to be the author's eyes. The search for Walīd leads to such revelations as his love-affairs, his distrust of institutionalized culture and ideology, and his disillusionment with bourgeois egoism and selfishness at a time so disastrous for the Palestinians. But instead of evoking some philosophy of action and resistance, this search leads to an artistic creation, similar to Scheherazade's involuted work, which is the novel itself. Indeed, the studied nature of the language of the taped farewell reveals a meticulous concern with diction that aspires to attain the effectiveness of ritual, enchantment and magic. In this, Jabrā's work invites comparison not only with Tennyson's island of Shalott and palace of art, but also with Oscar Wilde's escape into a private world of aesthetic poignancy. Indeed, the reader feels at times that Jabrā's work uses the national issue only as a convention that is identical with marriages and recognition scenes in traditional novels.

For all this Jabrā's novel substantiates the thesis that the modern Arab novelist is searching for an identity of his own, which surely corresponds to a general rational search for a philosophy of life that restores the Arab's pride in himself and his past to counterbalance the predominance of Western culture.

Muhsin Jassim Ali. *Journal of Arabic Literature*. 14, 1983,
p. 82

JUBRĀN, JUBRĀN KHALĪL (KAHLIL GIBRAN, 1883–1931)

LEBANON/UNITED STATES

Jubrān's romanticism made him want things for both literature and society that were completely different from the aspirations of his predecessors. He wanted literature to be a genuine expression of life and a faithful picture of the writer's soul. He wanted it to be completely free of anything that would make it artificial and contrived, to be unsullied by any of the stains of traditionalism and free of all the trammels of enslavement to the past. He wanted literature to stop bothering about the outside shell of things, the superficial gloss, and to plunge straight into the essential core so that it could disclose the hidden se-crets of the human heart. He was eager for literature to break out of the mode that used common language and an outmoded style; he wanted it to open up to a new kind of phraseology, daring and elegant, using a style both brilliant and refined. He wanted literature to take wing and fly into the firmament of the creative imagination, abandoning worn-out images and metaphors and adopt-ing instead more original tropes of all kinds. Jubrān hoped to see literature purified by the fire of emotion and revealed through the illumination of thought; he wanted to see it as a living literature. . . .

Jubrān was certainly the first great Arab romantic. He took literature away from the ambience of sycophancy, flattery, and cheap praise and at the same time rescued it from the abyss of lethargy, inertia, and blind imitation of the past. He raised it to new heights of soaring freedom and creativity and gave it the means to express the most profound feelings and desires of the hu-man spirit.

> ʿĪsā Bullāta. *Al-Rūmantiqiyya wa-maʿālimuhā fī al-shiʿr al-*
> *ʿArabī al-hadīth* (Beirut, Dar al-Thaqafa,
> 1960), pp. 100–101, 106–7†

Another factor in Gibran's narratives which makes for an effect of uniformity is the constant use of poetical prose for all the characters' utterances, which are either lyrical rhapsodies or rhetorical sermons, and in the narration as well, so that the tone never varies materially. Perhaps he regarded poetical prose as an element of beauty which would soften his explicit didacticism and make it more acceptable, not realizing that he was thereby violating the prin-ciple of the *vraisemblable*. This being so, the narrative stands or falls by its appeal as poetry, and not by any intrinsic virtue it may possess. It is evident that this was Gibran's intention, since the poetical element in his narratives became more and more marked as time went on. The last of the three books of narratives, *Broken Wings,* is poetical through and through. In the four drafts for this work kept in his museum, the alterations Gibran made clearly show his determination to eliminate every last shred of the prosaic and keep the style at a high poetical level. This, it seems, entailed the elimination of the unpoetical elements in the personal experience he was depicting—his first love—and the addition of many exceedingly poetical situations. . . .

His ambition to be poetical made him indulge more than ever in lyrics and sermons on various subjects, and so *Broken Wings,* although it contains no more action than the other narratives, is very much longer than any of them. After *Broken Wings* his interest in the narrative diminished; he took it up casually from time to time, and finally dropped it completely. Perhaps he was convinced by then that the parable was better suited to his didactic purpose.

Khalīl Hāwī. *Kahlil Gibran: His Background, Character and Works* (Beirut, American University in Beirut, 1963), pp. 247–48

In *Nymphs of the Valley* and *Spirits Rebellious* we see pictures of precisely that disturbed existence against which Jubrān rebelled. There we find the canon laws and regulations, in all their rigidity, that he hated so much. In two stories, "Warda al-Hānī," and "The Bride's Bed," he vents his spleen against the makers of such rules and expresses his opposition to this way of marrying off young girls in the Arab East, just as though they are pieces of merchandise to be bartered for. Here we see an old man with one foot in the grave marrying a young girl in the prime of her youth and beauty; in another story, a girl is forced to marry a complete stranger with whom she has not the slightest connection, whom she has never set eyes on, and toward whom she feels no inclination whatsoever. What eventually happens in such cases? They either divorce or break up, or else the unlucky person dies of grief. In "Khalīl the Heretic" and "Jonathan the Madman" we see Jubrān poking fun at the religious establishment that appropriates people's money and property, which they have struggled so hard to earn. And then all that people get in return is rejection and deprivation.

Returning to *Broken Wings* we see that in the story of Salmā Karāma, Jubrān again attacks men of religion and all outmoded religious customs. That leads him to rebel against all laws and customs mankind has ever chosen to put into force. Signs of this can be seen in the books and articles he produced from then on. Furthermore, Salmā's death has a profound effect on his view of the kind of life man lives and hardly has the chance to enjoy before death and separation bring it to an end. Students of Jubrān's later life and circumstances will notice the profound effect death had on him when his younger sister, Sultāna, was taken from him while he was in Paris.

Nādira Sarrāj. *Shuʿarā' al-Rābita al-Qalamiyya* (Cairo, Dār al-Maʿārif, 1964), p. 279†

Jubrān is the uncontested leader of the émigré school in America. Mikhā'īl Nuʿayma moved in the same general direction, but he never managed to achieve the range Jubrān did. Nuʿayma could use his imagination, but he never allowed it to break loose and always kept it within the bounds of reality.

Jubrān went through three distinct phases. The first is that of *A Tear and a Smile,* the essay period. If you look closely at these works, you will notice in their style elements borrowed from the writings of earlier great prose writers such as [Ahmad Fāris] al-Shidyāq, Adīb Ishāq, and Nīkūlā Haddād, but

Jubrān's style is neat and smooth, unlike the severe style of these earlier authors. . . . It differs from their style too in the incredible imagination of Jubrān. He is a painter in his use of expressions rather than an author, as though he is using a paintbrush and not a pen. . . .

The second phase is that of the novel and short story. Here Jubrān shows only a slight change from the style of *A Tear and a Smile,* although he does move perceptibly toward realism, since story and dialogue are transformed without involving a total flight into the ethereal world of the imagination. Jubrān's stories—in fact, his works as a whole—are based on the idea of love. The love of flesh and bone is the focal point for Jubrān, and it is around it that his grinding millstone revolves. . . .

The third phase involves the emergence of his philosophy, where he expressed his thoughts in English. Wanting to bring to America the mystical notions of the East, he wrote in English *The Madman, The Forerunner, The Prophet, Jesus, the Son of Man,* and *Earth Gods*; in the last of these, Jubrān's use of symbolism reaches its peak. . . .

His influence on the Bond of the Pen in America and those who followed this group of writers is still perceptible. All the members of the group thought and expressed themselves in ways similar to his own. Jubrān's essay "The Grave Digger" and Nuʿayma's poem "My Brother" might as well be from the same source even though their form is different. They were all bound together by a belief in eternal life. . . .

The leader of the émigré school was a forceful personality with elements of defiance. He was an Arab from the East. He did not write in order to westernize the East, but the opposite; he wished to be a messenger to the West. He was that rare and exceptional person who can preserve his own coloring because he has no need of any of the colors to be picked up in a strange environment.

Mārūn ʿAbbūd. *Mujaddidūna wa-mujtarrūna* (Beirut, Dār
al-Thaqāfa, 1968), pp. 241–46†

Jubrān came on to the scene like a wind blowing in the face of the "renaissance" trend, which represented a tendency to focus on a point of light in the past, an attitude of acceptance, reverence, and hence, of imitation. Jubrān came along with a different view of the concept of "renaissance," one that sees the process as one of giving back to a people its power to interact, to create, and to review. This particular phase was marked by a crisis of confrontation between the void in Arab culture on the one hand and the inroads of Western culture on the other. That in turn led to a reaction and a withdrawal into the past and a stubborn adherence to it as something that could distinguish it from the West.

It was Jubrān, steeped through and through in Eastern culture, who opened himself up to world cultures without any inferiority or superiority complexes. He was able to show that Eastern Arab culture, with its elements of Islam, Christianity, and paganism, was fully able to meet other cultures, to borrow and assimilate, and to enrich itself thereby. He totally rejected the notion of cultural historical discontinuity and advocated integration and continuity.

Through his connection with world literature, Jubrān never used anything trite and overly familiar, things that produce neither fruit nor movement. His choice always fell on living sources that represent a large portion of the basis of modern culture (the New Testament, Greek and Chaldean mythology, Egyptian mythology—*The Book of the Dead*—mysticism, Shakespeare, Blake, Nietzsche, Ibsen, Bergson, Jung . . .). He found himself within the heritage of protest and rejection, in the writings of the amazing, the unheard-of, the limitless, among "the Arab colossi" whose spirits were limitless in a strange way because "they had not lost the primitive vision of man."

Khālida Saʿīd. Mawāqif. June, 1970, p. 4†

Processions, Gibran's long poem in Arabic, is a dialogue between two voices. Upon close analysis, the two voices seem to belong to one and the same man: another of those Gibranian madmen, or men who have become Gods unto themselves. This man would at one time cast his eyes downwards at people living at the bottom of the tower, and consequently raise his voice in derision and sarcasm, poking fun at their unreality, satirizing their Gods, creeds and practices, and ridiculing their values, ever doomed, blind as they are, to be at loggerheads. At another instant he would turn his eyes to his own sublime world beyond good and evil, where dualities interpenetrate giving way to unity, and then he would raise his voice in praise of life absolute and universal.

To achieve self-fulfilment is to achieve serenity and peace. That Gibran and his heroes are still mad Gods, grave-diggers and enemies of mankind, filled with bitterness despite their claim of having arrived at the summit of life's tower, reveals that Gibran's self-fulfilment throughout this second stage of his work is still a matter of wishful thinking and make-believe rather than an accomplished fact. Too preoccupied with his own painful loneliness in his transcendental quest, Gibran the madman or superman, it seems, has failed hitherto not only to feel the joy of self-realization at the summit, but also to recognize the tragedy of his fellow-men supposedly lost in the mire down below. Consequently instead of love and compassion, people could only inspire in him bitterness and disgust.

Nadim Naimy. Journal of Arabic Literature. 5,
1974, pp. 61–62

From Nuʿaima's lengthy study of Jibran, first published in 1934, it is clear how important and extensive Jibran's influence was on the rest of North

American *Mahjar* poets. Jibran's output is enormous. Besides painting, he wrote essays, short stories, books of meditations, poems both in traditional forms and in *vers libre,* as well as much poetic prose with strongly marked biblical echoes. He wrote both in Arabic and in English: he is, in fact, one of the few Arabs who managed to produce best sellers in English. Most readers of English, especially in America, must have come across copies of his book *The Prophet,* a work of fairly popular mysticism: by 1958 it had sold a million copies.

As an *Arabic* poet it must be admitted that, interesting as he is, Jibran does not occupy a very high rank, and that is partly because of his exceedingly small output, partly because of what some regard as excessive sentimentality, but chiefly in the opinion of most Arab critics because of his rather weak Arabic style. Nevertheless, because of his great influence on *Mahjar* poetry, it is necessary to pause for a while and examine his poetry. His fame as a poet rests chiefly on his long poem *The Processions,* which was first published in New York in 1918. . . .

Although structurally the poem is interesting, in that it rejects the monorhyme *qasida* form, a feature which is to be found in the work of most of the *Mahjar* poets, it is mainly in its ideas and themes that *The Processions* occupies such a crucial position in the poetry of *Mahjar.* In it, in fact, we find most of the themes with which the *Mahjar* poets dealt, some of them more successfully than Jibran. *The Processions* is a philosophical poem treating metaphysical and moral questions, like the problem of good and evil, the relation between the soul and the body, the problem of happiness, of social and political institutions, of what man has made of man.

Mustafa Badawi. *A Critical Introduction to Modern Arabic Poetry* (Cambridge, England, Cambridge University Press, 1975), pp. 182–83.

Of the other talented Arab-American poets the most important was Jubrān Khalīl Jubrān. Having been uprooted by emigration from Lebanon to the United States (Boston and New York), he was influenced by the romantic literature of the West, by the American transcendentalists, especially Emerson, and by such poets as Longfellow, Whittier, and Whitman. He was also nurtured by Western ideas and influences such as those of Nietzsche, Blake, and Rodin, and by the Bible as well as by recollections of Eastern mysticism. These disparate influences were blended and internalized in Jubrān and the genuinely original literary and artistic creations that resulted were his unique contribution to the development of modern Arabic letters. The difficulties of form were largely resolved by the "Jubranic style" that he created in his poetic prose and prose poems, which proved to be a milestone in the history not only of Arabic poetry but of Arabic letters generally. Although he was much less concerned with the form than with the content of his work, Jubrān was essentially engaged in a struggle to achieve the organic unity required in the creation of all great poetry. He clearly achieved this in most of his work where he was able to create "a language within a language" and to break down the barriers of form between prose and poetry. He created this new mode of expression in the belief that the innate freedom of poets to seek fresh molds and styles cannot, even in the Arabic language, be expressed in arbitrary prosodic rules and conventions. The primary task of the poet, as Jubrān defined it, is to use language effectively, his own language, the only language which is to him authentic.

I am certain, whether it is called poetic prose or prose poetry, that a substantial part of Jubrān's writings in Arabic constitute in their heightened language, subtly varied rhythmical flow, and fascinating imagery, some of the richest and most individualized free verse forms in modern Arabic poetry.

Mounah Khouri. *Edebiyat.* 1, 2, 1976, p. 131

In his constant efforts to achieve a Biblical balance of language, pouring forth adjectives often in rather unfamiliar ways, Gibrān resorts to another device: the image. His images run into each other like brilliantly coloured dyes, a rest to the imagination and the eyes after some of the hackneyed and overused images of revived Classicism. The metaphors and similes are interwoven with the clarity of a lucid mind behind them, and one's sense of the impassioned conviction of the writer is heightened, as well as of the irrepressible fascination of Gibrān, the painter, with colour and variety. His images evoke feelings, not through stock responses but by a highly emotional, new but familiar, way of describing his object. By familiar here is meant that Gibrān in his images uses, on the whole, words and pictures which, although many are new, can be readily accepted by the reader or hearer.

Gibrān's imagery is often highly symbolic. In fact Gibrān's symbols, of which the forest, the sea and the night are the most important, anticipated more the Symbolism of some of the poets of the 'fifties and 'sixties rather than the Symbolism of poets such as Saʿīd ʿAql, who flourished in the late 'thirties and 'forties and who looked to French nineteenth-century Symbolism. The former use symbols, as Gibrān did, to denote a point of reference, to represent more richly and concretely, a basic idea. The latter use sounds and symbols to evoke impressions and meanings in a magical, suggestive method. Great stress is laid on the inner music of the words and their evocative power. Gibrān's insistence on complete elucidation of his ideas, moreover, separates him still further from the Symbolists who care nothing or little for making themselves intellectually understood.

Salmā al-Jayyūsī. *Trends and Movements in Modern Arabic Poetry* (Leiden, E. J. Brill, 1977), pp. 101–2

Throughout his career, Gibran had little relationship, if any at all, with his immediate precursors, the neo-classicists. His inspiration, as poet and artist, had its roots in Western theories of art and literature, Western philosophy, the Bible, as well as Eastern philosophy, and perhaps, to a lesser extent, the Qur'ān and the works of the great classical Arab poets. The distance that separated him from the Arab world offered him the necessary freedom to formulate his ideas on art and literature and to question the position of the Arab neo-classicists without having to answer directly to traditional dogma or suffer the censure of the traditionalists. When his ideas and literary compositions became known in the Arab world, his influence was considered by some to be an affront to Islamic culture, and was accepted not without reticence by others. Today, however, Gibran's influence has pervaded all modern Arabic poetry and has initiated the inevitable successive transformations that we are witnessing.

Gibran dreamt of changing life. He was, as Adūnīs puts it, "our first annunciation from the land of poetry." He succeeded in assimilating a unique blend of Western and Eastern thought into an ideology, shaping his whole outlook on life and literature. He supplanted the intellectual flashes and the aphorisms of traditional Arabic poetry with metaphors that grow, expand, and attain hidden truths of a world above this world. His metaphors are in constant metamorphosis. The soul becomes a tree, the tree the universe; the nymphs of the valley materialize into dancers tripping on waves; or the poet himself becomes a prophet, a Christ-like figure changing from the recesses of time to save the crucified world. His metaphors are not fettered by finite logic. They are the spiritual visions of prophets, far removed from the naive similes and metaphors of many classical poets which, by and large, suffered horizontal expansion and dilution. His imagery creates its own mythology, and by so doing multiplies and deepens its allusions. His was the dream of man, wherever he may be, the dream of that of many Western poets before him. All this was a new way of discontinuing with the tradition, a successful attempt at producing difference. If Gibran's anxiety of influence is not as strong as it is in the case of the stronger Arab poets, it is because his tradition remained at some remove from him. His anxiety rather is the anxiety of influencing, of having to give away one's most precious achievement to those after him.

Adnan Haydar. Al-ʿArabiyya. Spring–Autumn, 1981, p. 54

KANAFĀNĪ, GHASSĀN (1936–1972)

PALESTINE

Ghassān Kanafānī is the only novelist and story writer who clearly concentrates his entire attention on the Palestinian question. His situation is the same as that of the poets in the Occupied Territories; he is there too, and not in exile. This is the impression I gain from reading his works; it is something that must be recorded as a particular feature of his writing. . . . However, after reading *Returning to Haifa,* I would like to put down some comments I have to make as a reader of his works. . . .

This novel is a document for the prosecution that leaves absolutely no room for compromise. In that way it is exactly like *Men in the Sun,* where in every situation the men flounder around on their futile road to perdition. But this work is more in the form of documentation, by which I mean that the developments in the Palestinian question are faithfully put on record right up to the resistance.

How can an author manage to include such a documentary approach in a work of art? In creating a work of art there is a huge difference between simplicity and triteness. In the case of the first, the author finds himself faced with exactly the same problems as he would if he were choosing a more complex structural form. . . . Whether the work is to be simple or complex, the work needs all the creative skills of the author in its preparation; in either case, the process is far removed from being merely trite.

It is this fact that seems to have escaped Ghassān Kanafānī with respect to his latest novel. He has already had experience with the construction of a complex work with an internal symphonic structure of its own. The amount of effort he put into *What Is Left for You*—generally agreed to be his most significant work thus far—is quite clear. However, after that book he did not continue along the same narrative tack, perhaps for some intellectual reason connected with his relationship with the public. In addition, he did not continue that same obvious effort mentioned above. In his first choice, he is of course free, but in the second he most certainly is not. The conditions under which an author chooses a narrative technique are based on his intellectual circumstances and on his own vision of the relationship between form and content, as well as a number of other wishes he may have. However, the work of art must also be bound by the author's readiness to use his creative talents so as to apply his best efforts to such matters as structure and technique.

Fawzī Karīm. Al-Ādāb. Oct., 1970, p. 65†

In the collection of short stories entitled *Umm Saʿd* Ghassān Kanafānī shows us quite clearly that the major character, Umm Saʿd, while she may be a genuine Palestinian character in her own right, nevertheless represents Palestine as a whole. She comes from the ranks of the struggling masses from whom the revolutionary has to learn, those same people who have suffered all the bitterness of defeat. [As Kanafānī says in his introduction to the collection,] "As far as I am concerned, it is for that reason that her voice always sounded like that of the class of Palestinians who had to pay dearly for the defeat." Umm Saʿd represents the Palestinian vision in the aftermath of the defeat, showing resolution instead of collapse, and resolution to resist with weapons rather than mere words. In fact, she has come to loathe the sound of oratory: "The war started on the radio, and that's how it finished too. When it was all over, I got up to switch it off." The great hope Umm Saʿd sees lies in her son's going away to fight for the liberation of the Occupied Homeland. The Hope for the future as far as Palestine (Umm Saʿd) is concerned lies in a new generation of young men who will fight in spite of all odds, a generation of violence and blood. . . .

In this work, Ghassān Kanafānī is eager to combine two separate approaches, the realistic and the symbolic. Thus, at one moment he shows us Umm Saʿd affectionate, loving, anxious for her son and longing to feed him herself. And then, we see her as the great mother, the symbol of Palestine standing tall in spite of twenty years of exile, banishment, and life in tents.

To sum up, Kanafānī has shown us in this short-story collection the way in which the Palestinian revolution has altered the attitude of the Palestinians to their life, ideas, and daily routine.

Ahmad Muhammad ʿAtiyya. *Al-Ādāb*. Aug.,
1972, pp. 87–88†

How far should the Arabs hold themselves responsible for the disasters that have beset them in Palestine? This remains an open question during the period we are discussing. It requires of Arabs that they look inside themselves and review their situation. . . . The Arab novel has recorded, among other positions, the could-not-care-less attitude that has been a direct cause for the disasters that have already occurred and continue to happen. Ghassān Kanafānī's novel *Men in the Sun* (1963) is a splendid example of this process.

It portrays the attempt of three Palestinian refugees to get from Jordan to Kuwait by way of Iraq. Each of them has a different story. There is a middle-aged man who has waited for ten years to return to his house and field. When the period seems to be growing longer and longer and the family is exasperated by the lack of sustenance, he sees no alternative but to look for some other means of support. Then there is a young man who is being forced by his uncle to look for a livelihood so that he can marry his cousin, to whom he has been engaged since her birth simply because they were both born on the same day. He himself has to move on in any case because he is accused of conspiracy against the forces of law and order in the town where he lives. Finally, there is a young lad aged sixteen whose elder brother has stopped supporting the family and whose father divorced his mother because he found another wife who could guarantee him a more settled life. . . .

They are picked up by another Palestinian who has a job as a driver of a water-tank truck owned by an influential man. . . . He suggests a plan to his three fellow countrymen: he will carry them on top of the tank until they are fifty meters from the border, then they will get into the tank; it will be as hot

as hell, but they will not have to stay there for more than five minutes while
he crosses the border; then they can get out again fifty meters beyond the other
border. . . . However, when the driver does reach a safe place over the border,
twenty-one minutes have passed, and the three Palestinians are lifeless bodies. . . .

In this novel, the writer is trying to say: "Look, here is the disaster of
Palestine, this is the tangible reality, far from all the speeches and slogans. It
is all passivity, procrastination, and indifference. The knocking on the interior
walls of the tank is a symbol of the fact that the disaster has to be faced with
rejection and revolution instead of weakness and surrender."

Shukrī ʿAyyād. ʿĀlam al-fikr. Oct.–Dec.,
1972, pp. 643–45†

For Kanafānī a scene is centrally the convenience given to the writer by the
general novelistic tradition; what he uses in order to present the action, therefore, is a device which, displaced from the tradition that can take it for
granted, ironically comments on the rudimentary struggles facing the Palestinian. He must make the present; unlike the Stendhalian or Dickensian case,
the present is not an imaginative luxury but a literal existential necessity. A
scene barely accommodates him. If anything, then, Kanafānī's use of the
scene turns it from a novelistic device which anyone can recognize into a
provocation. The paradox of contemporaneity for the Palestinian is very sharp
indeed. If the present cannot be "given" simply (that is, if time will not allow
him either to differentiate clearly between his past and his present or to connect them, it is because the disaster, unmentioned except as an episode hidden
within episodes, prevents continuity), it is intelligible only as *achievement*.
[In *Men in the Sun*,] only if the men can manage to pull themselves out of
limbo into Kuwait can they *be* in any sense more than mere biological duration, in which earth and sky are an uncertain confirmation of *general* life. Because they must live—in order ultimately to die—the scene prods them into
action, which in turn will provide writer and reader with the material for "fiction." This is the other side of the paradox: a scene is made for the novel, but
out of material whose portrayal in the present signifies the psychological, political, and aesthetic result of the disaster.

Edward Said. Introduction to Halīm Barakāt, *Days of Dust*
(Wilmette, Ill., Medina University Press International,
1974), p. xxiv

What Is Left for You is a work of ambitious technical complexity, and the
treatment of the desert in it differs significantly from that found in the earlier
novel [*Men in the Sun*]. On the factual level, the action takes place at night,
and so the most fearful aspect of the desert, its heat, is not mentioned except
at the end, when the sun rises and the coming day's inferno is evoked. The

desert is here immense and mysterious, "too vast to be loved or hated. It was not completely silent, and he could feel it like a huge body, breathing audibly." "Nothing could come as a surprise in this expanse, nothing could ever be anything but small, obvious and familiar in this vast world, wide open to everything." The qualities of immensity and silence frequently recur, and the comparison with a body is developed. The cold wind which rises as the sun sets blows across the heart of the desert. When Hāmid, trying to hide from the headlamps of a passing car, presses himself into it, the desert trembles like a virgin. Most unexpected, perhaps, is the parallel between the desert, that most arid part of the globe, and the mother whom Hāmid is seeking. . . .

Clearly Kanafānī's view of the desert, as it is revealed in these novels, is far from that of the pre-Islamic or Abbasid poets. He lacks the beduin's familiarity with the landscape and his ability to discern the lie of the land, the imperceptible variations in an apparently monotonous expanse of sand or rock, the watercourses, the traces of vegetation and the sharply observed scenes of animal life which enhance the old *qasīdas*. He is interested in the desert from the point of view of the city-dweller who feels no sympathy for its rigours, even when these must be endured for a specific purpose, but at the same time its stark beauty strikes a responsive chord in him and he appreciates its possibilities as a symbol. Whether the classical or pre-Islamic poets were using it as a symbol also is beyond the scope of this paper to discuss, but it cannot be denied that Kanafānī gives it a new value.

Hilary Kilpatrick. *Journal of Arabic Literature*. 7,
1976, pp. 59–60

AL-KHĀL, YŪSUF (1917–   )

LEBANON

The collection *The Deserted Well,* with all its different poems, is actually one poem within which one finds variation in the process of discovery of the sterility in the psyche of both the individual and society and a cry for rebirth. The earth and water are Tammūz; Tammūz is Christ; and Christ is man. This symbolic equation is the basis of almost every poem, although each individual poem is a new experiment with the different parts of the basic equation. . . .

In *The Golden Bough,* Sir James Frazer points out that Semitic poetry contains a great deal of comparison of the life of man to plants. The ancients, too, did not regard this as a mere poetic image, either; as far as they were concerned, the comparison was close to reality. All nature was one, and its various parts and manifestations were of a unified essence. The forces of fertility and aridity in man, animals, and plants are one and the same; their source is earth and water. . . .

In Yūsuf al-Khāl's poetry—as with other Tammūz poets such as Adū-nīs, Badr Shākir al-Sayyāb, and Khalīl Hāwī—this ancient Semitic notion appears again. . . . Yūsuf al-Khāl penetrates deep into dead cities in the search for the life of man and plants, combining the two according to the old Semitic custom and extracting from mankind's earliest experiences an image for the experience of contemporary man with all its nakedness, loss, and loneliness. . . .

All this represents a rare poetic vision within the tradition of creative writing in the modern Arab world, a religious vision that can be fully appreciated only by a few after much effort, deprivation, and rebellion. It seems to me that now that Yūsuf al-Khāl has left behind him the sexual feelings best expressed in the poem "Hirūdiyā," he is engaged with a sensibility both richer and more abundant; it is accompanied by an imagination that reminds me of the English metaphysical poets. His work now embodies suffering as much as it does pleasure. He makes of both a religious problem with the most profound philosophical dimensions. In his work we find a symbol of this generation's sufferings, its fearsome misfortunes, and its great aspirations for the future.

Jabrā Ibrāhīm Jabrā. *Al-Hurriyya wa-al-tūfān* (Beirut, Dār
Majallat Shiʻr, 1960), pp. 31–32, 33–34, 42†

I believe that, since Yūsuf al-Khāl abandoned the traditional poetic forms, he has been trying to edge closer to the language of everyday conversation just as Pound and Eliot tried to do in their "intellectual" poetry. I think he has had more success in his metered poetry (and his articles) than he has in his prose poems, where he has insisted on stripping his language of all artifice without managing to achieve the transition to a genuinely realistic orality. His orality is still decorous and comes closer to being an intellectual monologue rather than a spontaneous effort in which the rapid flow of living language is mixed with jokes, sarcasm, and graceful expressions. With regard to sarcasm, we come across delicate touches of ridicule in his poetry directed at fatalism and pain. The latter brings to his face a look of contempt rather than a howl of anguish. Fate seems stupid enough to deserve to have its back broken under the overwhelming weight of freedom of choice. . . .

It is obvious that *Poems at Forty* goes further toward revealing certain facts about Yūsuf al-Khāl, the poet and the man, than *The Deserted Well*. This applies particularly to the love poems, which have a fragrance he has avoided until now: here he treats woman as a woman rather than merely as a cover, a device, or a symbol for some other topic. The theory which gives art precedence over the artist and which is implemented in *The Deserted Well* finds its influence much reduced in the later collection. This fact does not show itself so much in the content as in the technique. By that we imply that we still remain ignorant of the poet's experiences and personal problems, although he does give us a glimpse of some of them. His style, on the other hand, shows something essential, namely that the poet is now tired of adventure and deep penetration into things; the whirlwind of his own unrestrained energies has left him with a headache and a desire to settle down and believe in the existence of concrete realities and principles.

Unsī al-Hājj. *Shiʿr*. Autumn, 1961, pp. 100–101†

Al-Khāl's best-known poem is that which gives the volume its title, "The Forsaken [i.e., "Deserted"] Well." Superficially, it is the story of the poet's neighbour and old friend Ibrahim, an ordinary man in the eyes of the world which is not aware of his existence, but whose belief that his death might bring about peace and plenty, remove injustice and put an end to evil and misery on the earth, prompts him to walk straight into the enemy fire, totally deaf to the warning and the advice given to him to seek safe refuge in a nearby shelter. The verdict of the world is that he was simply mad, but the poet knows otherwise. The poem is clearly a modern variation on the theme of crucifixion, and it emphasizes the need for the deliberate act of self-sacrifice to revive society. Ibrahim is the poet and the man of vision who in the pursuit of his ideal runs counter to self-interest, with the result that he is taken by lesser mortals, men of cruder substance, to be mad. However, by making Ibrahim an ordinary man in a sense, the poet asserts his hope in the salvation of his culture: we only have to turn to the well we have forsaken, the inner spiritual depths within each of us; it is an arduous process demanding nothing less than total self-abnegation, but, nevertheless, it is possible. The same theme is treated in "Memento Mori" where the need for self-sacrifice is further emphasized.

The water image is not accidental in "The Forsaken Well"; it is part of the contrast between water and desert, life and death, which is to be found in the work of Khal just as much as in that of Adūnīs, Hāwī and al-Sayyāb, and which plainly has an ultimately religious (and anthropological) significance.

Mustafa Badawi. *A Critical Introduction to Modern Arabic Poetry* (Cambridge, England, Cambridge University Press, 1975), p. 243

After eight years of activity, the magazine *Shiʿr* was suspended. In the chief article of the last issue (vol. VIII, nos. 31–2, 1964), al-Khāl declared that the established new movement towards which his magazine had paved the way had arrived at a new stage. The new movement realized now that the change in form, which was brought about by the change in the purport of modern life, had affected only the metre, an effect which was not sufficient to convey the poetic experience in a spontaneous, lively and original way.

According to al-Khāl what al-Malā'ika . . . prophesied, that the new form would soon lose its vitality, has already happened, but it will not lead to what al-Malā'ika presumed, to the return to the conventional form. . . .

Al-Khāl believed that the main problem is linguistic, to make the vivid daily colloquial speech the basis of the written literary language. Only by doing so will Arabic poetry be revived and maintain its existence. . . .

With the reappearance of *Shi'r* magazine [in 1967], *qaṣīdat al-nathr* [the prose poem], the new trend of modern Arabic poetry, gained fresh life. Yet even at the end of 1969, Yūsuf al-Khāl was not sanguine about the condition of the new movement. Al-Khāl saw the reactionary movement in Arabic poetry which took place at the end of 1964 as a result of the decline in Arab life. The reason for this reaction in Arabic poetry towards the past and ages of decline is the predominance of engagement (*iltizām*) literature in the Arab world. It also reflects, according to al-Khāl, the Arab spiritual inferiority which has been the source of the continuous Arab physical defeats in the last thousand years. He found that false revolution is the purport of Arab life, and the engagement in literature which the Arabs adopted from Sartre was misunderstood and misused. It became a weapon against free thinking and true and genuine art.

S. Moreh. *Modern Arabic Poetry 1800–1970* (Leiden,
E. J. Brill, 1976), pp. 284, 287–88

AL-KHARRĀT, EDWARD (1926–   )

EGYPT

Edward al-Kharrāt has taken great trouble to record the date of each of his stories in the collection *High Walls*. We discover that the stories were written over a period of about fifteen years. Some of them seem to have been begun in 1943 and 1944. Then the author gave up writing for more than ten years and resumed only in 1955. In spite of this long hiatus, we can still detect similarities among the majority of characters in the twelve stories.

The most obvious feature is that the author views his characters from the inside more than from the outside. The psychological makeup of these characters is locked up within high walls that prevent them from interacting with other people. Some walls stand between husband and wife, others between one colleague and another, between father and son, and so on.

The protagonist of the first story, "High Walls," is a husband who has been married for five years, and yet there are walls that keep him apart from his wife. He feels that he was been abandoned on some final retreat into seclusion with no hope of salvation. All he asks of his love is that it help him demolish the walls of his loneliness. Even so, he has the nagging sensation that there is no point to it all. . . .

This is the way Edward al-Kharrāt uses his poetic style to describe the feeling of isolation and the desperate desire to get rid of it. His poetic style combines aspects of existentialism and surrealism at different times, in addition to his own wide learning. The scene soon shifts to a café where the husband starts playing backgammon with an acquaintance. We find the same walls standing between his colleague and himself; indeed, the main character even feels a hatred toward the other man. . . . When we discover that this other man who is sitting with him in the café is the main character's own self (the other man is described as having the same face and the same psyche), we realize that Edward al-Kharrāt perceives a sense of enmity, alienation, and hatred between a man and his own self. . . .

"Inside the Wall" may well be the best story in the collection. Haniyya is a young widow who lives in the Egyptian countryside. A wall stands between her and her dead husband, to the extent that she does not feel that his assaults on her were an attack on her person. The only thing she has is something quite insignificant, namely a feeling of sympathy toward this abandoned creature [her aged mother] nestling in her arms. There is no real difference between this story, "High Walls," and most of the other stories. It, too, shows a world closed on itself. There was this body, the author tells us, that filled the entire world. Nothing existed outside it. The room, the street, people, the sky, all these, to the wife's obscure sensibilities, were merely dimensions that kept her body confined and delimited its boundaries. There was nothing beyond these boundaries; the whole world lay inside the bounds of the one thing that was hers, hers alone, her entire fortune. That thing was her own body. She wrapped it in her long garment and wallowed in the privacy of its internal folds.

Rumors start to build up because of Haniyya's relationship with a peasant who tends her acreage in the village. One of her relatives comes to invite her next day to settle up the season's accounts and discuss some agricultural matters. Three of her relatives are waiting for her in the garden. When she arrives, she is slightly surprised because she has never noticed the covered passageway before, those low, wide walls, broken up at the ends and covered with dry palm branches. She never noticed any of this before. These walls too stood between her and her relatives, and so they have put an end to her while she struggled with them in vain.

Edward al-Kharrāt, through stories such as these, takes us inside his high walls to begin a journey inside the mind of man. With him we reach basic geological levels where we find sex, instinct, and brutality. All this comes to us in a copious poetic style that expresses the visions of this interior world and the emotions, agitations, and desires clamoring within it.

Yūsuf al-Shārūnī. *Dirāsāt fī al-riwāya wa-al-qissa al-qasīra* (Cairo, Al-Maktaba al-Anglo-Misriyya, 1967), pp. 164–66, 169–70†

The fact is that Edward al-Kharrāt's stories deal with that ancient struggle that literature has been talking about since time immemorial, the same struggle that can be seen with even greater clarity and candor in the works of the French existentialists, and particularly Camus, namely that between man and civilization, between societal norms and individual identity. It is through this struggle that one sees embodied the continuity of the relationship between societal and individual sensibility. . . . We have to define al-Kharrāt's attitude toward this struggle, the way he visualizes it, and the characteristics of the concept that he applies to one or another aspect of this ancient and eternal struggle. From the very beginning, we can note that Edward's protagonist is no condensation of the anxieties of a generation as a whole, nor does he attempt to achieve his ambitions by going beyond the obstacles of materialism and transcending the confines of the unjust norms society imposes. Rather he is a loud paean to individualism wherever it occurs, to isolationism, to the process of switching off all events and societal values. . . .

Edward al-Kharrāt's world is a night world in which we never come across daylight matters such as work, the sun, feelings, and obvious emotions. This does not imply that work, the sun, feelings and emotions are totally absent from the horizon of his protagonists altogether. They do have a place in their lives, but it is only a secondary one with no real value. When this secondary existence is transformed into a real, cogent, and moving presence of its own, it takes on the features of a terrifying nightmare.

Sabrī Hāfiz. *Al-Ādāb*. May, 1969, pp. 44–45†

With the publication of [the anthology] *Gallery '68* littérateurs of the far left have been able for the first time in the history of our modern Arabic literature to forge a way through to the reading public and to interact with traditional literary currents. This is an entirely healthy phenomenon, one which we should be glad about and try to expand so that continual renewal and growth can be guaranteed for our literature. . . . The principal feature of *Gallery '68* . . . is its relative closeness to the usual literary traditions. The reader will not find himself confronted by a totally strange style. . . . In fact, there is an obvious connection between many of the stories here and those of writers of an earlier period whose works are well known, such as Yūsuf Idrīs, Yūsuf al-Shārūnī, and Fathī Ghānim.

One of the writers who is a link between these two generations is Edward al-Kharrāt, in that his own style had matured before the decade of the 1960s.

The story published in this particular anthology does not represent an essential change from the stories in *High Walls,* even though there does tend to be a greater control of the means of expression.

Edward al-Kharrāt achieves the acme of his "angle of vision" or point of view in the story "The End of the Road." This technique is not new in his own works, nor can it be reckoned an innovation in story-writing in general during the last ten years. It is the kind of style that the American writer Henry James used at the beginning of the century; thereafter the existentialists gave it a philosophical content, clearly seen in Camus's novel *The Stranger.* This style is known to us from Edward al-Kharrāt's first collection, but he has never before devoted himself to it as much as he has in this most recent story. The language is completely subordinated to the process of conveying the protagonist's sensibilities to the reader, or, more accurately, of making the reader live within those sensibilities.

Shukrī ʿAyyād. *Al-Majalla.* June 1969, pp. 94–95†

The stories contained in Edward al-Kharrāt's second collection, *Hours of Arrogance,* rely basically on description. From this we can form a clear impression of his ability to weave his stories with a unique, highly individual descriptive thread. In some descriptive passages al-Kharrāt creates imaginary worlds where nature finds itself subordinated to spontaneous rules. The protagonists gradually become entangled in a web of illusions without any basis in reality, even though they themselves may think that they are indeed real. This, of course, is nothing new in the works of al-Kharrāt; it appears in his first collection, *High Walls . . . .*

I do not believe we are pushing matters too far if we suggest that human existence leaves its traces on the whole of nature all around it; material objects bear the imprint of mankind, who comes into contact with them. If this idea applies to a table, a chair, and plants in fields or gardens, does it also apply *ad infinitum* to nature and existence in the larger sense, to clouds, rain, stars, and storms?

The stories in *Hours of Arrogance* are, from the point of view of description, an answer to that question. For al-Kharrāt, nature is neither a framework nor an arena nor a stage set. Rather it is a set of characters acting in a drama, each with a particular role and a sense of close harmony with mankind. The sky and the sea, as al-Kharrāt himself puts it, are not natural phenomena so much as simultaneously symbols and happenings. . . .

Edward al-Kharrāt's attitude toward description leads to the question as to whether literature's attitude toward the universe is a mechanical one, like photography, for example. The literary image cannot be a photographic one, since literature is a vision, not merely a process of receiving or recording something. . . . A scientific image, however perfect, will always need a literary one as well in that the littérateur can achieve dimensions unknown to the scientific image through his own creation. As al-Kharrāt puts it, the literary image is somewhat akin to prophecy and the aspirations of philosophers.

Na'īm 'Atiyya. *Al-Kātib*. May, 1975, pp. 126–27, 130†

LABAKĪ, SALĀH (1906–1955)

LEBANON

It seems as though the author of *From the Depths of the Mountain* has the teachings of Plato etched deep in his heart. His fables in this volume emerge replete with the notion of good and beauty. The lights of Lebanon shine forth here, bringing to the ancient world a mission of civilization, spirit, love, and peace. The poem entitled "The Wandering Melody" symbolizes the all-encompassing love with which the heart of Lebanon is full so that it is able to sow fertility in the land and produce civilization. . . . In this way the fables in this collection sing the praises of Lebanese civilization and the beauty of its land and sky, creating a link with the stories of the peoples and beliefs of the past without losing the particular originality of the poet. . . .

This is most noticeable in the story of Cain and Abel. One wonders what idea in the mind of the author inspired him to build his fable on a version that contradicts the story as told in the Old Testament and elsewhere. It may be that this very same idea lurks within each of us; we may even mention it without realizing what it is we are really implying, or else we may investigate its origins and development in detail. Often we hear a really awful discordant song that hurts our ears, and quite spontaneously we will say: "That's the voice of Cain!" How, one wonders, did this particular image come to take hold in our minds when nothing in the Old Testament or other accounts suggests it? . . . Whatever the case may be, we have adopted the story from the ancients with no particular reason. Now here comes Salāh Labakī to draw it to our attention once more through his own fable. Such accounts have often been able to explain any number of customs, beliefs, and practices among different peoples.

Butrus al-Bustānī. Introduction to Salāh Labakī, *Min a'māq al-jabal* (Beirut, Manshūrāt Dār al-Makshūf, 1945), pp. 9, 11, 13–15†

Salāh's poetry is not "crafted" so that you approach it wondering how strictly it has been put together like a row of stones. Rather it has emerged like a violet or an elder tree. . . . Since he is a poet in everything he does, I will not permit myself to talk about him as a human being. As a prose writer he is forever in quest of beauty, while as a political force he insists on banishing ugliness. Every act of will he undertakes is a poem in its own right. . . .

His cadences are simultaneously lofty and tender, making beautiful things even more beautiful. Once his pen has treated anything, it becomes more than a mere thing. He seems a friend of most of them, a colleague in life, a boon companion. He travels from the serenity of the hills—which seem to be just earth and stone anywhere else but Lebanon—to the panic of a branch beneath a nightingale and the violence of passion in the heart, that passion that seems to have no name in languages other than ours! . . .

If Salāh as a politician was a man of principle, then as a poet he espoused perfume, night, hills, and roaring waves. With him we learned how to sniff a handful of earth and venerate it and how to spot a crack in the sea beyond a sail, a crack that would lead us to a kingdom we had built there at the ends of the earth as broad as the aspiration in our hearts.

When Salāh sings, our hearts feel warm; it is almost as though we are not aware that what he is saying is in verse, but rather that he is talking to us.

Sa'īd 'Aql. Introduction to Salāh Labakī, Sa'm [Disgust]
(Beirut, Manshūrāt al-Thaqāfa al-Lubnāniyya,
1949), pp. 10–12, 14†

Salāh followed his poetic instincts and made use of his impeccable taste. He refused to abandon the excellent form, carefully selected diction, and magical musicality of the old poetic tradition, but managed to adhere to the ideas of the modern school in his concept of poetry, his humanistic mission in life, his feelings of loyalty toward it, and his desire to express a love of beauty and truth, which are the perennial preoccupations of the poet. His poetry in general, and especially "The Moon's Cradle" and "Promises," [the title poems of two collections] must be considered among the purest, subtlest, and sincerest from the point of view of emotion, thought, excellence of form, and economy of phrase. These two are good enough, in fact, to be reckoned along with the best of classical Lebanese poetry.

Some of his poems, on the other hand, and particularly the longer ones, seem to me to be experiments in which he is trying his hand at complex structure and obscure images and phraseology. In this regard he seems rather like a musician who spends some time every day relaxing his fingers on a musical instrument. Even so, these poems are not lacking in sincerity of expression and poetic feeling, nor in that sense of love that predominates in all of them, particularly where Lebanon itself is concerned.

Yūsuf Ghusūb. Introduction to Salāh Labakī, Ghurabā'
[Strangers] (Beirut, Dār Rīhānī li-al-Tibā'a wa-al-Nashr,
1956), pp. 6–7†

Salāh Labakī is the poet of the spirit and of intimate disclosures, beset by passions, consumed by dreams, and racked by despair. His poetry emerges like a

confession or a prayer and is steeped in melancholy and remorse. He is a romantic by inclination, an esthete in style, and his works are a blend of profound emotion and subtle beauty. . . .

His romantic bent gives his poetry a particular stamp in its subject matter, style, and imagery, but he keeps a firm control on his sentiments and attitudes and does not allow them to take over or be the subject of improvised
compositions. Instead he remains within the serious limits of a humanistic vision and only makes use of emotion to deepen and intensify the experience
rather than descending to the level of mere amusement, bombast, and zeal.

The subject of his poetry in the main is love, a topic in which he immerses himself with a great deal of empathy; through it images and scenes
from nature are portrayed alongside some of the usual topics favored by romantics, such as night, evening, spring, winter, rain, storms, birds, roses,
and similar things. And as long as the poet experiences life's trials as a romantic, then there will inevitably be reference to his dreams, troubles, and despair; faced with life and death he will at times be conciliatory, and at other
times rebellious and defiant. In his last collection [*Strangers*] he tends toward
longer poems, with cantos to be recited one after another, in which he expresses his views in general on man, life, God, and fate. His long poem *Disgust* was composed shortly before his death.

Īliyyā al-Hāwī. *Salāḥ Labakī shāʿir al-rūḥ wa-al-bawḥ*
(Beirut, Dār al-Kitāb al-Lubnānī, n.d. [1970s?]), pp. 5–6†

AL-MĀGHŪT, MUHAMMAD (1934–   )

SYRIA

Sadness in the Moonlight is a collection of poetry that does not rely on the traditional criteria of meter and rhyme. The majority of readers in Arab countries
will not call the contents of this collection poetry at all. All sorts of phrases
can be used: prose poetry, poetic prose, artistic prose. Even so, people tend to
like it and enjoy reading it, not because it is prose dealing with particular subjects or telling a story or narrative, but rather because the material in it is poetic. Yet people still refuse to term it poetry. This is a normal point of view
with regard to average readers. However, the critic should be bolder and call
things what they really are. For that reason, I myself consider this "poetic
prose" to be poetry. . . .

With Muhammad al-Māghūt the poem is full of images laid out alongside each other. They do not follow a straight line or the old mode of orderly
presentation. That may, perhaps, be considered one of the beauties of these
poems. They do not follow the modern circular method either. The images are
scattered without orbiting around any particular pivot. They seem like scat-

tered impressions that throw the reader off in various directions. This feature
is especially apparent in the two long poems "The Dead Man" and "The Murder." If Muhammad al-Māghūt had a firm grasp of his poetic art, he could
have gained a great deal by transforming this disjointedness into a style all his
own. Jabrā Ibrāhīm Jabrā, for example, makes use of this diversified technique, but keeps it under firm control and directs it along the channels he
wishes to follow. . . . With Muhammad al-Māghūt, on the other hand, the
poem is like a beautiful palace where the gleaming stones and delicate pillars
have been laid down in no particular order; when it leaves your conscious
mind, all that remains are some images of its parts, not of the whole.

Khuzāmā Sabrī (Khālida Saʿīd). Shiʿr. Summer,
1959, pp. 94, 98–99†

Muhammad al-Māghūt is immensely gifted as a poet. He is the prince of the
prose poem—if I may be allowed to borrow that designation for a while as a
means of specification; he has no rivals for that title. From his very first poetic
compositions he has produced images and symbols that display a truly amazing talent. He has managed to transform the ordinary pedestrian patterns of
speech into poetry.

He can be considered as a poet who is as much concerned with poverty as
he is with fragmentation and alienation, that kind of alienation he feels is imposed on him both inside and outside his own homeland. Force of circumstances also makes him be, as it were, a Catholic in the midst of a Protestant
church choir. The tunes do not suit him, and he cannot synchronize the
rhythm. He dislikes the words of the hymn very much, and so turns to reading
the Psalms on his own; no one hears him as he continues his chanting.

Life does not provide him with any of the many things he wants. Even
his eyebrows are foes facing off against each other. Funerals fill the streets,
workers tumble from the highest floors, and small graves fall like dew on the
hats and coats of everyone. All he wishes to do is to eat, drink, and die.

In his poetry Muhammad al-Māghūt has fashioned strange and unusual
poetic imagery. His images are exclusively his own; he has made them, he
alone has devised them. They are bitter, vicious images, fragmentary and
evocative; they spring up and slap you in the face. This kind of imagery
intensifies the richness of the poetic experience in his works. All his experiences are with the minutiae of everyday life, unveiled and unadorned. He is a
fugitive, forever being hounded down, a Bedouin with no tent, a vagrant with
no pavement.

Riyāḍ Najīb al-Rayyis. Hiwār. No. 11–12, 1964, p. 211†

Has Muhammad al-Māghūt's play The Hunchback Sparrow carried him off
on its wings after the reception of his first collection of poetry, Sadness in the
Moonlight, had lifted him as a genuine poet on to the poetic throne as a poet
of alienation, poverty, and wandering who loved freedom?

Al-Māghūt has not changed. He is still the genuine poet who lives in some city or other, dozing in the cafés, dreaming in the alleys, longing for packs of cigarettes, making love, yearning for the nipple of his mother's breast, searching in the bosoms of women as he also does for a loaf of bread and freedom, his body burning with sensuality. In spite of all that, however, and his own move from Beirut to Damascus—accompanied by a reputation as a genuinely gifted poet—he now finds himself locked in by his second collection of poetry, *Room with Millions of Walls*. There is no real artistic development from *Sadness in the Moonlight* either in style or poetic experience. What is more significant is that *Sadness in the Moonlight* is the more forceful in expression.

The problem with Muhammad al-Māghūt lies in his enormous innate gifts. Unlike the French poet Rimbaud, he never dreams of gold; he has no desire to penetrate geographical barriers and plunge into the arteries of the wide world and get lost in them.

Lately, al-Māghūt has started resorting to a new device, even though he remains in the same place, involves himself in the same psychological problems, and speaks through the voice of the same characters. He has begun to pour his poetry into a theatrical mold so as to break down the "terrifying wall" of creativity. Muhammad al-Māghūt's *The Hunchback Sparrow* cannot fly very far.

It is a poetic play, but you can find in either of his poetry collections verse and artistry of a much higher caliber than you will find in this play. The poetry emerges like prose, ordinary prose that you expect to hear on news broadcasts. The imagery is direct and flat. . . .

I would recommend to Muhammad al-Māghūt . . . that he revise *The Hunchback Sparrow* starting from the second scene. . . . I say that because I consider the play to be a very courageous and important literary work that treats the political and social climate we in the Arab world have been living in for a number of years.

Laylā Baʿalbakkī. *Shiʿr*. Winter–Spring,
1967, pp. 156–58†

[There is] what might be called the neo-Senecan Absurdism of *The Hunchback Sparrow,* a prose play by a poet [Muhammad al-Māghūt] who is not a stage practitioner, and who uses every startling linguistic and dramatic device to bring home his message: from extending or distorting the meaning of his words, through the polyvalent symbolism of the birds, to the final shooting on-stage, by the National Firing Squad, of two totally innocent small children, condemned, in the Judge's words, "in view of their tender years" . . . to be "shot with small-bore rifles." . . .

Inhumanity, injustice, and the physical and psychological degradations induced by torture are the sombre themes of this play, which, in its verse passages, attains a chorus effect by turns anguished, despairing, cynical, and full of sorrow. The court scene (Act IV scene I) must be among the most savagely Swiftian scenes written in the name of human rights since the death of Brecht. When the Accused tells his little son that life is all ahead of him, the Boy, already schooled by fear and despair, responds with "I'm going to kill myself tonight." Yet this brutal and unnerving play leaves one, as do others in this volume, with a larger sense of the supreme worth of humane values, of the preciousness of ordinary life which, even though it is dull, once threatened is infinitely worth protecting. It is the victims who signal to us through their agony and force us to reassert our humanity.

> Mahmoud Manzalaoui and Andrew Parkin. Introduction to
> *Arabic Writing Today: The Drama* (Cairo, American
> Research Center in Egypt, 1977), pp. 42, 51–52

MAHFŪZ, NAJĪB (1911–   )

EGYPT

In all the works of Najīb Mahfūz, from *The Mockery of the Fates*, the first of the three historical novels in which the events are derived from the history of ancient Egypt, through his social and psychological stories (including the mighty *Trilogy*), and right up until his most recent novel, *The Quail and Autumn*, the events of which end five years after the Egyptian revolution of 1952, we feel internal links that bind them all together. It is not merely the natural kind of relationship that ties the works of a single author together. Rather, it seems to me more like the principal themes in a whole variety of musical compositions, which differ from each other in a number of ways but which nevertheless rely on some constant element that makes its own profound echoes heard in all the works of that particular author. Perhaps they are the major problems the author continues to face with his probing questions in one work after another. He may never find an answer to these questions, but even so, the response may itself be contained in the process of asking the question through his own artistic experiment.

As we survey the long novelistic journey of this great writer, time and again we find ourselves confronted with situations and characters of the same type. The fabric out of which they are fashioned hardly seems to change, and yet this outstanding novelist is able to create them afresh—or almost so—on every occasion. Such is his artistic skill that he can place his characters into a new and dynamic context that so commands our attention that any echoes of past works are shut out.

These types of situations and characters, then, are not simply repetitions of a single theme, but, if our analysis is correct, fixed poles around which a series of ever-regenerating experiences revolve. With each new work, these poles reach out to new horizons. Perhaps this tireless activity on all sides may reveal profundities and new dimensions that were not clearly visible before.

Edward al-Kharrāt. *Al-Majalla*. Jan., 1963, pp. 16–17†

Najīb Mahfūz's artistic standards continue to preserve their own basic values. His method of portraying the psychological dimensions of his characters, the way he shows spatial dimensions as a material framework for events and situations, and his technique of employing a human example as a symbol of a particular problem—these are the special features that continue to mark his novels. If any change is to be seen, then it lies in the presentation of the interior monologue in a new way based on the notion of recording psychological movement directly before any developmental process and also on the portrayal of events from the inside rather than the outside. This is clearly seen in the incident when Fahmī, the hero of this long novel, *Bayn al-Qasrayn*, is killed in a demonstration.

However, the major forward step this most recent novel has taken lies in the realm of the awareness that the author exhibits toward the problems of his age. After exploring a particular problem from a single time period by giving a cross-section of society at a fixed point in a generation, Mahfūz has now expanded the range of his artistic presentation and focused on the problems of the age over a span of three generations: one living before the 1919 revolution, another that lived with it and through it, and a third generation that came afterward and laid the groundwork for the popular uprisings that occurred in the revolution of 1952. By means of an extended cross-section spread over three complete generations (using a variety of viewpoints in the process, somewhat like a tributary of a river that helps the overall flow of the river toward the sea), Mahfūz shows us the family of Al-Sayyid Ahmad ʿAbd al-Jawwād, the grocer in Al-Nahhāsīn, along with all his sons and grandsons. This family serves as a genuine human symbol of Egyptian society during an extended historical period in terms of social, political, and intellectual development.

Anwar al-Maʿaddāwī. *Kalimāt fī al-adab* (Beirut, Al-Maktaba al-ʿAsriyya, 1966), pp. 36–37†

The prostitute is a familiar figure in many of Mahfūz's novels. In *A Beginning and an End*, published in 1949, her name is Sanaʾ, and in *The Quail and Autumn*, published in 1962, she is Riri. Invariably she is a woman compelled by dire need and unfortunate circumstances to accept this degrading fate. But at the crucial moment in the story the reader always discovers how loving, loyal, and uncompromising she can be. One wonders whether in the person of this downtrodden, contemptible prostitute Mahfūz is not chastising the state of morals in Arab society today where, in the face of stringent conventions, hypocrisy is not unknown.

Mahfūz is also vitally concerned with socialism and religion. "For some," he says, "socialism could be the elimination of obstacles that stand in the way of God's justice." In saying this,, Mahfūz, the realist and the socialist, is reconciled with his religious background. To Islam and to Marxism, history and the building of the good society are important. Islam's acute consciousness of the transcendental imbues it, however, with a morality repudiated by the atheism of Marxism. Atheism has failed to establish itself in Arab thought and literature; God is alive in all his glory. When Rushdi ʿAkef, Mahfūz's protagonist in *Khan al-Khalīlī*, finds himself face to face with death as a result of an incurable disease, he seeks solace in the Koran, in the Word of God. And when Ahmad ʿAkef goes to the Department of Health to obtain the necessary release for the burial of his brother, he is appalled by the cold routine approach of the government official who receives his request and processes the papers. "How could he," Ahmad ʿAkef complains, "approach death in this nonchalant way when it is the greatest event in the world."

George Sfeir. *Daedalus*. Fall, 1966, pp. 950–51

"The Mosque in the Alley" [in *God's World*] is a new and important experiment in the realm of the short story; in it Najīb Mahfūz shows himself to be at the very height of his creative powers. In his hands the short story becomes a pliant artistic form that allows itself to be sculpted with his chisel. The new dimensions in it are confined only by the author's own perceptions of the terms of reference and potentialities of the short story genre. . . . It is quite impossible to summarize this story without destroying the basic framework around which it is built. This story shows a perfect command of technique, and for that reason it is impossible to give a proper summary of it without describing that technique in some detail.

The title of the story itself, "The Mosque in the Alley," gives the basic foundation of this technique, namely place. A mosque is situated at the head of an alley in olden times and joins on to another alley where all sorts of thugs and criminals consort. The second aspect of this technique is Najīb Mahfūz's remarkable creativity, and in particular the way the tableaux switch backward and forward between the mosque and the alley. In the mosque itself we find Shaykh ʿAbd Rabbihi, who is still disgruntled since being appointed imām of this particular mosque. Close by, ʿAmm Hasanayn, the sugar-juice vendor, seems—at least to the shaykh—to be the only decent man or even the only normal person in the entire alley. . . .

Najīb Mahfūz has given us here a short story in every sense of the word. The style is firm and cuts like a diamond. Every single sentence in the story seems like a stone that forms part of a necklace. The imagery is completely fused into the dynamism of the story itself. The way in which the scenes follow one another is not based on any chronological order so much as on artistic logic, the logic of the similarities and contrasts between what is going on in the mosque and the alley. . . . In this story, Najīb Mahfūz has certainly benefited from the notion of cinema montage as much as he has from his own literary training. His tremendous creative gifts have ensured that this story, in spite of its brevity, will be counted among his very best works.

Shukrī ʿAyyād. *Tajārib fī al-adab wa-al-naqd* (Cairo, Dār
al-Kātib al-ʿArabī, 1967), pp. 234–35, 236–37†

The Vagrant is the fifth in the series of novels that mark Mahfūz's latest phase, which began with *Children of Our Quarter*. This phase is marked by particular features in both form and content. The most important of these is conciseness: the avoidance of precise detail, the focusing on a single event, a small number of characters, and a concern with intellectual problems rather than social circumstances and historical aspects of any situation. Thus, in Najīb Mahfūz's previous phase of realism, life always came ahead of intellectual significance, whereas in the new phase of his realism, the latter comes ahead of the events that give expression to it. Along with this trend, we can see a lack of adherence to any temporal rules, the mixture of dreams with reality, and a greater use of the conscience. In most parts of these novels, the consciousness of the narrator is to be connected with that of the principal character, and yet the speaker will either address himself or talk about himself. It is the same with the interior monologue, which presupposes that there is a listener, whereupon it becomes the unspoken speech that is closest to being spoken; in other words, somewhat akin to the kind of words we repeat to ourselves before considering writing or talking to other people, where occasionally a spoken word will interpose itself in the form of an actual dialogue or else some sort of version of one.

These, then, are the features of this new novel, although it must be said that the author's knowledge of these new techniques has made him yet more proficient and effective in this work than before.

However, the main thing that attracts our attention is the connection between the content of *The Vagrant* and the stimuli for the new literary phase in which Najīb Mahfūz has published his last five novels. Mahfūz has often stated that the change in the political situation in 1952 made him review his writing from the point of view of both form and content. On this particular point we can see the crisis of ʿUmar al-Hamzāwī, the hero of *The Vagrant*, coinciding with that of the author, although the latter has managed to transcend his own crisis by resuming his writing career and discussing the whole thing. . . .

Yūsuf al-Shārūnī. *Dirāsāt fī al-riwāya wa-al-qissa al-
Qasīra* (Cairo, Al-Maktaba al-Anglo-Misriyya,
1967), pp. 27–28†

The Thief and the Hounds, which is one of Najīb Mahfūz's relatively more recent novels, is an example of the "new realism." It is an expression of the meaning of life as the novelist sees it, a personal vision of man's fate in a deterministic universe, which is no less dark and pessimistic than Thomas Hardy's vision. Man, as he appears in this little compact allegory, is a defenceless tormented victim from the moment of his birth to the moment of his death. The fate of Said Mahran, the central character in the novel, is sealed when he is born the son of humble parents . . . His attitude to society is determined by its inhumanity to him during the formative years of his life. When he grows up he becomes the leader of a gang for robbing the rich. He is caught and thrown into prison. With his release he is plunged back once again into the greater prison of society, where he finds himself face to face with the treacherous and heartless. . . .

The whole novel grows out of the inner existence of the central character, frequently presented through the modern medium of the interior monologue. Chronological time breaks down, and the reader is constantly moving backwards and forwards in time and place, wherever Said's thoughts and feelings may lead him. . . .

This technical handling of the character draws our sympathy which goes out to him as it does to Dickens's and Dostoievsky's lonely criminals. We are relieved only at the end when the "torment of the long wait in the dark" is over, and the nightmare of life recedes in death. But this is not before the hunt, which has been on since birth, becomes fiercer and more intense in Said's last bid for freedom and light. Pursued throughout life by the hounds, he is finally trapped by them and killed.

Nur Sherif. *About Arabic Books* (Beirut, Beirut Arab
University, 1970), pp. 75–76, 80–81

The Children of Our Quarter is an audacious departure from the author's familiar style. However, it loses much of its literary value because of the imbalance between the form and the content. The resort to allegory does not really lend greater profundity to the ideas. The revolt against plain realism which was smouldering for quite a while in Mahfūz's works, together with his well-known passion for the mysteries of life, combine to precipitate an amazing turn in the author's career. Yet the first product of this new style is too abstract and too prosaic to satisfy the demands of so ambitious an edifice as that which the author aimed at erecting.

Nevertheless this novel (if novel it is) is essential to anyone who seeks to discover the way Mahfūz sees our world as a whole and, moreover, the world in which he could like to live. The outlook, as it emerges from [the work] is highly gloomy. In fact never before in his works has the author been so sad. Here on the whole we are presented with a history of a world that has always been harsh to its people and never, since Adham's explusion from the Big

House (= the Garden of Eden), has his posterity been able to enjoy a moment of bliss. Truly enough, the reason for our misery lies essentially in the prevalence of unjust social and political orders. An all-out social revolution whereby science and wealth can be put to the service of the people of the "Quarter" is the only possible way of breaking loose. As things are, however, there is but slight hope for such a dream to be realized. We live in a Godless world, and the reins are as tightly held in the hands of the ruthless superpower (or powers) as they have ever been. The revolt of science was buried alive. There is a glimmer of hope, though; the people are now waiting for a dauntless science-conscious revolutionary to emerge and overthrow the tyrants.

Sasson Somekh. *The Changing Rhythm* (Leiden, E. J. Brill, 1973), pp. 153–54

The title of his first novel with a modern setting [*Modern Cairo*] is symbolic of this change of direction [a shift from historical novels about ancient Egypt to novels with a more social-realist orientation], and its content is equally indicative; this is the story of three university students looking for work and facing the outside world for the first time. It is a simple book in many ways, lacking the intricate background of lower-middle-class Cairene life which Mahfūz introduced in later novels.

The transformation of Egyptian society from traditional to modern has already gone far by the 1930's; Cairo University is a witness to this, as is the presence of recently admitted girl students, and modernisation is the issue which Mahfūz uses to introduce his principal characters. Types representative of their period, their personalities are already formed: Ma'mun Ridwan, the strict Muslim, 'Ali Taha, who has shed his religion for materialism and a belief in science and western civilisation, Mahjub 'Abd al-Daim, who has no ethical principles, being the classic *je m'en foutiste*. It is this last, amoral and impelled by his poverty-stricken background to sacrifice almost everything in pursuit of success and wealth, whom Mahfūz takes as the central figure in his story, and through him and the others Mahfūz introduces several of the themes which are repeated in the other Cairene novels: poverty, ambition, corruption, the search for a meaningful philosophy of life, and on another level the intervention of fate. . . .

The force of Mahfūz's indictment of Egyptian society is such that one can understand why he had difficulty in getting it past the censors. Yet the reader is left with a certain feeling of dissatisfaction, for two reasons. First, as in many novels, a disproportionate role is given to Fate. By itself this would not matter, but in conjunction with the second flaw, that of unexpectedly making Mahjub the hero after presenting the three friends in equal detail at the beginning of the book, it is disquieting. Mahfūz's concentration on the "lost" member of the trio suggests a consuming interest in the darker aspects of his society, while his frequent need to resort to a *deus ex machina* when portraying his hero's rise and fall shows that his artistic abilities are not equal to the task he has set himself, or else that his conception of the character is somewhat artificial. Possibly he began writing the novel with one plan in mind and later changed it, but his giving the book this slant can only be explained in terms of his pessimism.

Hilary Kilpatrick. The Modern Egyptian Novel (London,
Ithaca Press, 1974), pp. 73, 75

Certainly the most brilliant writing produced during the past generation, Mahfūz's collection of short stories and playlets *Under the Bus Shelter* (1969), was written in the months immediately following the 1967 June War. As with most of Mahfūz's other work, the collection is composed of short scenes, although now the scene has a special new character: instead of being part of a prospective continuity in the making, each individual scene is shot through with the desolation of extreme, and hence Egyptian, loneliness. The scene therefore is a sort of national clinical process. Things take place with the utmost medical clarity, yet their general opacity, their terrifying impingement on every ordinary citizen, their defiance of ordinary, lay understanding, the swift succession of inexplicably triggered events, all these cut off the action (always minutely Egyptian) from understanding or, more interestingly, from the possibility of a universal Arab explanation. Mahfūz's world turns Egypt into a vast hospital whose boundaries are the various military fronts, and whose patients are, equally, soldiers and citizens. The author presents his cases silently; no explanations or apologies are given. A curious, perhaps obsessive, theme in this collection as well as in Mahfūz's 1973 novel of no-war no-peace Egypt, *Love in the Rain*, is the cinema. The scenes in which films are being made, where directors are being sought for their help in solving some specially difficult problem of interpretation, in which citizens are seen changing into actors, are common. When Egyptian involvement in Palestine or Yemen is mentioned, it is always by way of journalism or the cinema. Arab problems must be mediated by the layers of Egyptian reality that surround everyday life like the walls of a clinic, or the protection of a cinema studio.

Edward Said. Introduction to Halīm Barakāt, Days of Dust
(Wilmette, Ill., Medina Press International, 1974),
pp. xxx–xxxi

Najīb Mahfūz, in a short novella "Story with No Beginning and No End," which is also the title of the collection of stories in which it appears, gives us a more complex and elaborate treatment of the interrelated themes of religion and politics, and the crisis of faith. The novella is in nine parts, and it depends heavily on dialogue to carry the action forward. Philosophical speculations and a spiritual ambience form the background for the story, upon which political overtones are superimposed. The story without directly tracing the history of a whole family, that of Al-Akram the central figure, delves into the psyches of representatives of three successive generations. Mahfūz's intimate familiarity with his subject matter enables him to conjure up those characters and trace their development and/or moral deterioration in a highly intricate design. . . .

In "Story with No Beginning and No End" Mahfūz traces as it were the emergence of the revolt of man. ʿAlī ʿUways is the Prometheus who dared defy the gods. He is not, however, depicted as an abstract personification but is very much the existential man in that he translates his revolt into action and achieves the change desired. . . .

ʿUways plunges into "concrete action" to change a state of affairs imposed upon him. His uprising is also directed against the notion of the godhead, and results in God's defeat and his surrender to human recriminations. Al-Akram, that deposed God, is like Sartre's Jupiter in *The Flies*, a god who bargains and compromises with his creations. There is nothing divine or godly about him; indeed, he is conceived strictly in human terms.

Mona Mikhail. Journal of Arabic Literature. 5,
1974, pp. 152, 157

In the novel *Miramar*, artistic form gives rise to an entirely new technique which Najīb Mahfūz tries out for the first time in his artistic career. This technique relies on telling the same story a number of times from the perspective of the major characters in the novel. ʿĀmir Wajdī, an old retired journalist, starts off by giving an account of the events and situations that arise in the Pension Miramar. He does this through his own eyes, thus reflecting his own past, his education, and his psychological makeup. In giving us his picture he also makes use of his contacts with the other characters and his personal experiences with them. In other words, this character's past and present and even his view of the future—all these dramatic strands find themselves in a continual process of interaction throughout the course of the novel. The same approach is used with Husnī ʿAllām, a young man who comes to the Pension Miramar from Tanta to escape from his own large, feudal family and to acclimatize himself to the new realities of Egyptian society under the revolution. . . .

Some readers may imagine that telling the same story four times from the viewpoint of four separate characters would tend to be boring, since the novelist has nothing new to add to the basic framework of the story itself. Events, situations, and characters are just the way they are. But this opinion does not hold up when there are so many angles from which one may look at the story and when the whole impact may alter from one character to the next. It is just like a symphony, where there may be themes and basic motifs that are repeated from one movement to another, yet the different rhythms and the number of variations on these motifs manage to avoid any feeling of monotony or repetition. Thus, the gentle, slow, and regular rhythm we find in ʿĀmir Wajdī's section is suddenly transformed into harsh and rapid tones when we are introduced to the psychological dimensions that motivate Husnī ʿAllām, the young man who wants to take revenge on the new society while at the same time making a not very serious attempt to live with it.

Nabīl Rāghib. *Qadiyyat al-shakl al-fannī ʿinda Najīb Mahfūz*
(Cairo, Al-Hay'a al-Misriyya al-ʿĀmma li-al-Kitāb,
1975), pp. 333, 337–38†

The stories written after the war [of 1967] are noticeably different from those written earlier, both in technique and in content. This phase of Mahfūz's writing can be termed political, because these later stories are almost entirely political and topical in content. This makes them more difficult for non-Eygptians to appreciate. But even Egyptian readers find these stories extremely obscure, because Mahfūz relies so heavily on symbolism and the use of the absurd that, while the general message of a story may be grasped, the significance of details is sometimes not at all clear. Critics, on the whole, have avoided commenting on these later collections, and have hesitated to offer any interpretations.

In addition to this use of symbolism and the absurd, we find that Mahfūz has increased his use of dramatic dialogue. The vast majority of these later stories are written almost entirely in dialogue. . . .

The title story from *Black Cat Tavern* . . . was written after the war, and gives an indication of the new trend in Mahfūz's writing. This story is somewhat obscure. The regular customers of the Black Cat Tavern suddenly notice a large and powerful stranger wearing black, who blocks the exit from the tavern. Threateningly, he refuses to let them leave, because he thinks they heard him reveal his "secret" (*hikāya*). They can't understand what he is talking about, and, finding themselves imprisoned, drink themselves stupid. They begin to come to after a while, but they can't remember who and where they are. They recall that there was talk of some secret, to which the black cat is the clue. Did not their ancestors worship the cat, who sat one day at the door of a prison cell and revealed the secret and made threats. But what is the secret? The cat was once a god, then he became just an ordinary cat, because he revealed the secret. Their discussion is interrupted by the shouting of the head waiter at the black-clothed stranger, who is now humbly and sadly clearing and wiping tables. This story appears to refer to the position of the Egyptian Government before and after the '67 defeat.

Hamdi Sakkut. In R. C. Ostle, ed., *Studies in Modern
Arabic Literature* (Warminster, England, Aris and
Phillips, 1975), pp. 122–23

The most important theme which these novels [of the 1960s] emphasize is that of the obsessive search for freedom in a world which seems to have been abandoned by God and surrenders its reason and logic to an inverted law. "The novel hero's psychology is demonic; the objectivity of the novel is the mature man's knowledge that meaning can never quite penetrate reality, but that, without meaning, reality would disintegrate into the nothingness of inessentiality." This general feature takes in Mahfūz's novels the form of a profound quest to render rational the irrational world around the hero, or rather the anti-hero. Therefore the novels tell the adventures of interiority, of the soul that goes to find itself, that seeks adventures in order to be proved and tested by them, and by proving itself to find its own essence. But, painfully, these adventures end without dissipating the clouds of discontent and uncertainty, and their only outcome is to underline the validity and solidity of the inverted law which governs external reality. Most of these six novels may be classed as novels of psychological development in which "the hero becomes temporarily isolated from society on an active quest of self and the source of his being." But in most of Mahfūz's novels isolation is not temporary any more, it becomes a permanent condition, the progress of the psyche, which very often involves a gradual elimination of hope and a corresponding weakening of the protagonist's confidence in himself, is towards more intensive isolation culminating perhaps in death or martyrdom. It may also involve a futile, if not absurd, criminal act entailing the death of an innocent while evildoers may escape punishment, which provides a means of consolidating the psychological and social state of siege, and of strengthening the elements of absurdity in these novels.

Sabri Hafiz. *Journal of Arabic Literature.* 7, 1976, p. 73

The impact of Mahfūz's works is further undermined by his use of mystifying allegories and riddles instead of artistic symbolism. The aim in the first form is to insulate or mask the critical message. On the other hand, artistic symbolism aims not to hide but to inspire, enrich, create a poetic climate, and transcend the limited and particular and embrace universal human experience without loss of concreteness and uniqueness. Mystifying symbolism (as reflected in Mahfūz's allegories and riddles) is often used by writers in repressive societies to escape risks and censorship. In this sense, they become a form of self-censorship. [The title stories of] *The Black Cat Tavern* (1968) and *Honeymoon* (1971) are excellent cases in point. . . . The characters (who represent the Egyptian people or a segment of them) are harassed by a strange, tough, and brutal man who behaves as if the tavern in the first story or the apartment in the second (both the tavern and the apartment standing for the country) are his own private property. Less mystifying symbols are also used by Mahfūz to represent specific noted persons, political figures, and agencies, or Egypt as a country, but they fail to embrace universalism and particularity simultaneously. The author himself may have sensed such a failure, because he resorts in the same stories to direct and explicit expressions of some aspects of his message but after making sure of maintaining his safe distance. Thus, man is portrayed in these stories and others as (1) haunted by a brutal force, (2) uncertain of the nature and sources of his plight, (3) always entangled in some kind of difficulty (*warta*), (4) forced into compliance and passivity, and (5) desperately waiting for a savior.

Halīm Barakāt. Visions of Social Reality in the Contemporary
Arab Novel (Washington, D.C., Institute of Arab
Development, Georgetown University, 1977, p. 18

One has the feeling that Mahfūz has read extensively in the literature of Kafka, Ionesco, Becket and probably Jean Genet. *Chatter on the Nile* (1966) is a novel of the absurd, where the absurd is also socially involved. It pictures the mind and activity (or inactivity) of a group of pseudo-intellectuals in Cairo who can find no redeeming hope in the existing system and seek oblivion, sedation and solace from their alienation by smoking hashish, practicing sex and chattering, with a certain amount of detachedness, on the various aspects of contemporary life. Every night they meet on a boat on the Nile, where an ageless servant looks after them and procures hashish and women for them. Their female companions are like them, lacking in a healthy, constructive attitude towards society. Sex is given and taken freely, a sex devoid of love and tenderness, exchanged almost with *ennui*. The *ennui* is a basic attitude in the novel, and the whole work is a magnification of human impotence. . . .

Chatter on the Nile symbolizes the end of all quest. Even the woman journalist who comes "in quest" of information is corrupted by the characters of the boat and loses interest in her objective. Time has stopped completely in this novel, and it is only the accident which kills the innocent unknown pedestrian that brings about any action. However, the action here is a negative one, for in deciding to go to the police about the accident, Anīs Zaki is not doing an act of conscience, but an act of revenge intended to destroy even the static uninvolved world of the boat where he and his friends had found sedation and false peace. The characters in this novel are a mixture at once of the victim, the alienated hero and the anti-hero.

Salmā al-Jayyūsī. Mundus Artium. 10, 1, 1977, pp. 46–47

Al-Karnak is Mahfūz's shortest novel. If we leave out the illustrations and blank pages, it covers 90 pages. It is subdivided into four sections of varying lengths. The first, entitled "Qurunfula," sets the scene at the Al-Karnak Café, introduces the names of all the characters, and in effect tells the outlines of the entire story, such as it is. The second and third sections, "Ismā'īl al-Shaykh" and "Zaynab Diyāb," consist of lengthy conversations between the narrator and these two characters individually. They succeed in filling in several of the gaps in information left in the outline to be found in the first section and in particular give a more vivid picture of the shadowy figure of Khālid Safwān. The events described in these two sections are important to the reader's understanding of the narrative in the first section, but the means by which they are conveyed seems rather transparent and contrived. There are passages of dialogue in which Ismāʿīl and Zaynab exchange comments with the narrator on their fate in prison and their relationship with each other and with Hilmī Hamāda. These are interspersed with connecting passages in which the narrator conveys his impressions to the reader or fills in gaps of information before returning to the same conversation again or even to one from a different occasion. As a result of this process, we feel that the narrator and Ismāʿīl or Zaynab are in a sort of spatial vacuum, with little connection to the scene at the café created in the first section. . . .

We noted above that *Al-Karnak* was, like *Love in the Rain*, closely concerned with politics. In the former case, it is not perhaps an exaggeration to term it a political document. Yet again, Mahfūz uses the format of the novel to express certain political realities and to explore the possibilities for the future. More specifically, his frank treatment of the subject of the torture of political prisoners in the 1960s reflects the changing attitudes in Egypt after the death of ʿAbd al-Nāsir and the beginning of the Sādāt regime. This short work has recently been made into a highly opportunistic and propagandistic film. Whatever doubts one may have about its artistic value, it has certainly touched a most responsive nerve in the people of Sādāt's Egypt of 1976.

Roger Allen. Journal of the American Research Center in
Egypt. 14, 1977, pp. 106–7

The novel [*Midaqq Alley*] does not revolve around a group of individuals, but rather around an entire alley. It moves across time and space to reveal to us the alley's social relationships, values, morals, and shifting sympathies as the characters are tested in the crucible of poverty and war.

The novelist does not present the character of Hamīda to us at the beginning of the work. He makes the events turn on all the contradictions in the alley until we finally come to her as representative of the social phenomena to be found within the alley's confines. There are, for example, the piety and honesty of al-Sayyid Radwān al-Husaynī; the corruption and immorality of Muʿallim Kirsha, the head of a large family but also a drug addict; and the rich lecher al-Sayyid Salīm ʿUlwān. Ultimately, abject poverty seems to be the lot of almost all the people of the alley. Also present is the mystical love for the family of the Prophet, a love exemplified by Shaykh Darwīsh, who is forever whispering confidences to the Saint Sayyida Zaynab. . . . We also note the presence of idealized love (ʿAbbās's love for Hamīda), and, in contrast, the vileness of the pimp Ibrāhīm Faraj's school for prostitutes.

Into this broad canvas of turbulence the author, through simple narrative description, introduces Hamīda. . . . But Mahfūz goes beyond mere description of her physical appearance and psychological makeup; he provides great insight into her complex character by rendering conversations between her and the other characters, and particularly with her adoptive mother. We hear Hamīda declaring her dislike of the alley and everyone in it. . . . Hamīda's lively and revealing conversations show us the various aspects of her character; they suggest to us that she is indeed "some type of devil" and tailor-made to be "a born prostitute," which is the way Ibrāhīm Faraj actually describes her.

Tāhā Wādī. *Sūrat al-mar'a fī al-riwāya al-muʿāsira* (Cairo, Dar al-Maʿārif, 1980), pp. 259–60†

AL-MALĀ'IKA, NĀZIK (1923–   )

IRAQ

Nāzik al-Malā'ika is endowed with a profundity of emotion, a breadth of vision, and a purity of conscience that give her unique qualities as a poet. Her artistic gifts and her ability to use language allow her to soar. She is able to use her talents to give the most honest and successful analyses of her own self, revealing to us the sights and perceptions that haunt her and the painful events she has witnessed. She immerses herself in terrifying visions and then distills them into an atmosphere of melancholy and bitter suffering. It is in this sense of anxiety that the secret of her creativity lies, along with her fertile gift for expression and a breadth of imagination that makes full use of her own fervent emotions and marvelous poetic imagery. In her love she finds herself rapidly stricken by devastating failure; a stream of ideas begins to flow from the profound depths of her soul. Sentiments pour forth, responding to her agitated thoughts and the whims and fancies of her mind. She gives inspiring expression to a very genuine experience that makes you feel the profound fervor of artistic truth and the clash of sentiments. . . .

Nāzik al-Malā'ika also concerns herself with the problems of human existence, showing her usual skill and subtlety. She pours her realism into an attractive artistic mold and then gives artistic expression to her feelings. . . . Unlike some of our writers, she is not prepared to live in an ivory tower . . . but stands in the forefront of contemporary poets who are proclaiming the birth of a new age in which social problems will be aired and portrayed in unprecedented ways. This will be a genuinely humanist literature that will deserve to survive from one era to the next, since it conforms with the dynamic

principles of development and is totally free of any artificiality or narrowness
of vision.

Khidr ʿAbbās al-Sāliḥī. *Al-Ādāb*. Dec., 1958, pp. 22–23†

I would like to say a few words about the love poetry of Nāzik al-Malā'ika.
When I use the term "Sūfī poetry," what I actually mean is the kind of love
poetry she herself writes. Nāzik al-Malā'ika does not tell us in this kind of poetry anything of particular importance about her private life or about the "passions" of the members of her sex. After all, excellent poetry should be neither
a psychological or social document. There is no inherent contradiction in the
statement that poetry can tell us far more about the person who wrote it than
can be gleaned from talking about personality. Good poetry is neither masculine nor feminine. It is true that in her first collection and a few weak poems
from her other collections there may be a few obscure references to her experiences in life. However, we only pause at these rather weak examples of her
depiction of her life when we want to find out how she has come to mold the
more productive experiences of her better poems; once we have that information, that is enough of such weak poems.

She does not tell us a great deal about any love affairs hidden in the recesses of the past; her total concern is to tell us about the present and future.
From the point of view of poetry, all that concerns her about these past experiences is that they were idealistic and short-lived. And it is precisely this that
makes the whole thing so suitable for transformation in the poet's consciousness into a Sūfī mystical experience, particularly when it is linked to that inward contemplation that sees in the self the "secret of nature." In this way,
pain, anger, sorrow, and contempt are changed into a burning desire for the
return of the moment in the past, the ideal moment, the overwhelming sense
(but without any feeling of revolt) of the deep abyss separating lover from beloved; and that is the essence of the mystical experience.

Nāzik does not achieve this stage in one move. Indeed, it would be futile
and even laughable to conceive of her moving upward gradually like a pupil
moving from one class to another. We can see that this mystical experience
has allowed her to escape from the prison of the self through self-contempla-
tion and to liberate herself from the past by adhering to it. This has given her
poetry a new psychological richness, so much so, in fact, that it has almost
brought her—as with others—to a stage of sterility and bankruptcy.

Shukrī ʿAyyād. *Al-Ādāb*. March, 1966, pp. 41–42†

The collection *Lover of the Night* contains both poetry and straight narrative.
This fact stems from her own fierce sensibilities: she is eager to say everything and hide nothing. And so you will find fine expressions alongside others
of much less worth. But, you may say, that is the way it is with all things at
the time of birth; that is one of nature's rules. Great classical poets like Abū

Tammām and Ibn al-Rūmī pointed this fact out. Nevertheless, I choose to differ with both of them; to me the laws of art require that early faults should be
exposed and strangled at birth. . . .

Most poets get their sustenance from the world around them . . . but
Nāzik draws her poetic inspiration from within her own heart and soul. When
she describes the scene of the horse stumbling in the street . . . she chooses to
portray only that part of the total scene which touches her own sensibilities
and strikes a chord of sympathy within her. In such a picture what she has
seen is a reflected image of her own self. . . .

To turn to her poetic technique, she has succeeded admirably in getting
away from the confines of rhyme. Her poems consist of couplets, quatrains,
and so on, but you will not find more than two poems in the entire collection
with the same rhyme scheme. It is the same with the meters. Most of the
poems use the *khafīf* pattern [one of the traditional meters], which is particularly appropriate for the expression of grief. But you are not conscious of this
correspondence of form and content as you read because this most sensitive
poet holds your attention principally by describing the sufferings she endures.
So you suffer with her.

There are few images in her poetry, but she makes up for this with her
own fiery spirit, which produces an emotional revolt without parallel among
Arab women poets. This revolt of the mind and the heart takes her attention
away from the external world. . . . I believe that her hatred of the world
springs from her love of it. If you read through the complete collection from
beginning to end—including her translations of works by foreign poets—you
will find that it revolves around one single emotion. In fact, it seems that you
are faced with an *idée fixe* that has enabled her to go into her theme thoroughly.

Mārūn ʿAbbūd. *Mujaddidūna wa-mujtarrūna* (Beirut, Dār
al-Thaqāfa, 1968), pp. 221–22†

It would be a mistake to impose on Nāzik al-Malāʾika's poetry the criteria applied to committed poets. In her four collections, Nāzik is, in her own words,
a free poet who "expresses the sentiments of her life and records the strange
feelings of her own soul." That is not to say that she disavows commitment.
She has written poems within the realm of social sensibility and has dealt with
the questions of the hour in a manner that displays a burning national feeling
and her own humanitarian attitudes. We need only point to her seething poem
"To Wash Away Dishonor" in the collection *The Bottom of the Wave* to demonstrate what we mean. However, she does not impose the idea of commitment on herself, nor does she believe that poetry can endure being tied to a
particular school or topic. She has expressed this view very clearly in the introduction to *Splinters and Ashes*, where she says: "In poetry, the golden rule
is that it has no rules." In her view the poet is only a poet if he has his own
special identity, since that identity is the secret behind his individuality and

creativity. He can borrow new styles on condition that he mold them so as to express his own individual personality and his own private world.

In the case of Nāzik al-Malā'ika, the world she writes about is certainly her own private world. There may be images in it that are familiar enough, but the notion of "I" looks down on us from every direction. Her poetry represents a violent revolt against the old poetic tradition. Her immersion in the identity of the self is a reaction against homiletic poetry and occasional verse, with their rhetorical style; it is a withdrawal into the world of the imagination and the unknown, of nature and song.

Rose Ghurayyib. Shiʿr. Spring, 1968, pp. 117–18†

It was undoubtedly the Iraqi poetess Nāzik al-Malā'ika who, first in the introduction to her collection *Splinters and Ashes* and later in her book *Problems of Contemporary Poetry* (1962), laid the theoretical foundations for the development of this new form [of free verse]. Al-Malā'ika was concerned with freeing Arabic poetry from the regularity characteristic of the traditional forms. With the single line of verse as the basic unit of the *qasīda* pattern, the molds of Arabic poetry imposed their form on the content and quite often deprived the resulting poetical composition of its vital effect. Thus al-Malā'ika advocated the need for a free verse, in which the meter is based upon the unit of the *tafʿīlah* (foot) and the freedom of the poet is secured through his right to vary the *tafʿīlāt* (feet) or the lengths of his lines as he feels most appropriate for the expression of his message. However, she limited the range of this freedom by requiring that the *tafʿīlāt* in the lines be completely similar. This meant that, of the sixteen traditional meters, only seven (*Kāmil, Ramal, Hazaj, Rajaz, Mutaqārib, Khafīf,* and *Wāfir*), which are based on the repetition of a single *tafʿīlah*, could be used by the free-verse poets. The other meters were considered inappropriate for this type of poetry. Furthermore, al-Malā'ika insisted on the use of rhyme in free verse for its rhythmical and organizational value in the making of a poem.

These are, in broad lines, al-Malā'ika's basic principles for the development of free verse. Many poets and critics rejected them on the assumption that they were arbitrary rules no less rigid than those of al-Khalīl's (d. 791) prosodic system. Other poets modified them by using combined meters in their compositions or by inventing their own *tafʿīlāt*. In his criticism of al-Malā'ika's theories, Muhammad al-Nuwayhī, a prominent Egyptian critic, advocated the shift of the basis of modern Arabic verse from its traditional quantitative structure to the accentual pattern of English poetry.

Mounah A. Khouri and Hamid Algar. Introduction to An Anthology of Modern Arabic Poetry (Berkeley, University of California Press, 1974), pp. 16–17

In the recent edition of her Collected Works, her two-volume *Diwan* of 1970, Mala'ika published for the first time her long poem *Life's Tragedy* which runs to 1200 lines (in rhyming couplets), written between 1945 and 1946, together with two revised but incomplete versions of the poem composed in the same form of verse in 1950 and in 1965, and entitled respectively *Song for Man I* and *Song for Man II*. The poem, clearly influenced by Abu Madi's "Riddles" and Taha's "God and the Poet," is, as Mala'ika herself was aware in the introduction, an extremely romantic work, the title of which indicates the extent of her pessimism and her agonizing sense of life as an overwhelmingly painful riddle. The theme is the poet's quest for happiness, which is occasioned by the sufferings of the Second World War and which drives her to seek it in vain, first in the palaces of the rich, then in the monasteries of the ascetics, the dens of sinners, in the simple life of the shepherd and the peasant, among poets and lovers, until finally the poet finds her rest in the presence of God who, as in the conclusion to Taha's poem, provides the answer. There is nothing in the least unusual or surprising in the young Mala'ika writing such a poem on a theme of this type in the mid 1940s. What is obviously significant and indicative of her apparently permanent romantic cast of mind is that she should later on feel the need to go back to the poem and to revise it at two different periods of her life. As she says in the introduction, comparison between the styles of writing might give the reader an idea of her poetic development. Indeed the diction of the latest version is much less unabashedly romantic than that of the earliest one, although the earliest version would seem to be much more successful because in it the language is more in keeping with a theme that belongs to the heart of the romantic tradition in modern Arabic poetry.

> Mustafa Badawi. *A Critical Introduction to Modern Arabic Poetry* (Cambridge, England, Cambridge University Press, 1975), pp. 228–29

AL-MA'LŪF, FAWZĪ (1899–1930)

LEBANON/BRAZIL

The poem "On the Carpet of the Wind" is a simple story, but it has a wonderful simplicity; it is relatively short, too, but that very brevity gives the poem a particular quality. . . . The poet flies into the sky for a few minutes and then descends to the earth once again; that is all there is to it. This is the idea that has inspired this poem, a particularly simple kind of fancy that might occur to almost anyone. But when you look at the way it has inspired this particular poet, you discover that it is excellent indeed. The odd thing is that the poet does not spend any time at all describing the plane in which he is flying; there is nothing that could be thought of as modern. . . . Even so, the poem's beauty does not come from the descriptions in it, but rather from the simple philosophical imagination that can elevate man, through an old and well-known philosophy with no particular innovation to it, to his own higher level of spirituality without any sign of strain or effort during the long ascent.

The poem is divided into sections and arranged in subsections called cantos. These are devised in a totally natural and logical fashion that gives a symmetry and appearance of order to the whole thing. Within the sense of unity thus created there is injected a forceful liveliness and movement that correspond to the forces of life itself. . . .

It is worthwhile to consider the musicality that bursts forth from all of these cantos, with their phrases, tropes and strange imagery presented to you with such daring. They sound like voices from afar heard through the music of the poetry as the poet wishes you to hear them. You do not, however, realize this fact, but merely enjoy what you hear; you come to like it and find it reassuring. [1945]

Tāhā Husayn. Hadīth al-Arbiʿāʾ, Vol. III (Cairo, Dār al-
Maʿārif, 1957), pp. 181, 183†

While the star of the Bond of the Pen was waxing strong in North America, there was a delicate romantic voice to be heard in South America too, that of the poet Fawzī al-Maʿlūf. He was a person who seems to have lived his life among people only corporeally. His soul remained suspended somewhere beyond the firmament, ever ready to embrace the world of visions and dreams. He found living among his fellow human beings such a painful experience that his most original and eloquent poetry is concerned with the sufferings his soul endured on its own; they pulsate with a lofty pessimism even though Fawzī himself lived a life of prosperity and ease. All he could see in life was its misfortunes and then death, which brought everything to an end. . . .

The only cause we can find for such pessimism is Fawzī's own refined sensibility, which was shattered by the evils of mankind. There is also another factor, which we can trace to a failure in love that deeply wounded his sensitive soul. His *Collected Poems* is full of chaste and noble love poetry that clearly shows his own fervor. However, the poems are not flights of fancy; the beloved emerges as a cruel and flippant woman, while Fawzī himself seems both devoted to her and tortured by the experience. . . . For example, his poem "On the Minaret of Beirut" describes a meeting with his beloved late one afternoon. They are standing on a minaret overlooking the sea. After giving a wonderful description of the sunset and nightfall, Fawzī describes the love which the two are keeping hidden without being able to talk about it. . . .

It is easy to appreciate the pain that a sensitive poet might feel when such an ardent love as this is a failure. When this element is combined with the clash of his own lofty idealism and genteel morality with the avaricious materialism of people and their hurtful corruption, it is perhaps possible to explain his profound pessimism.

'Īsā Bullāta. *Al-Rūmantiqiyya wa-ma'ālimuha fī al-Shi'r al-'Arabī al-hadīth* (Beirut, Dār al-Thaqāfa, 1960), pp. 146–49†

In the poem "The Lebanese Girl" Fawzī plays on the nationalist theme and bewails the fate of Lebanon beset by French occupation after so many years of Ottoman domination. The sufferings under the French make the Lebanese nostalgic for the Ottoman period, in spite of all the tyranny and injustice it involved. The longings of the poet so far away are frustrated. He wants to hear the songs of his homeland, to feast his eyes on its seashore and its cedars, to quench his thirst with its sweet waters, and to breathe its bracing air. But there are strangers, interlopers, in his beloved Lebanon, and they manage to stop him from achieving these, his dearest wishes. . . .

His *Collected Poems* . . . contains only eleven that are either love poems *per se* or else come in varying degrees within the framework of the love poem. The small number of such poems raises the question as to whether they are the only response to the fervent passions of our poet as a young man.

It is quite obvious from the outset that any sensitive, graceful, and elegant poet such as Fawzī al-Ma'lūf feels the stirrings of youthful passion in his veins. He cannot have written so little love poetry. It seems probable, therefore, that he wrote a great deal more than has been published in his collected verse, and that he either tore up or burned much of it, as many poets are in the habit of doing.

As an example of the poems that *are* in the collection, the one entitled "Distant Clouds" is a clear and delicate picture of the spiritual hunger Fawzī al-Ma'lūf feels. He is addressing his beloved who has doubts about his love. He talks of his amorous glances, his passionate groans, which waft in her direction on the passing breeze, the rapid beating of his heart, and so on . . . the kinds of things that point to a sensitive love rather than a purely sexual hunger.

Hārith Tāhā al-Rāwī. *Afkār*. Nov., 1966, pp. 51, 53, 54–55†

Although the Southern contribution [i.e., that of Arab émigrés in South America] in general could be regarded as a fresher version of the neo-Classical school, some poetic works stand out for their originality and novelty. The most important work of Fawzī al-Ma'lūf, his long poem "On the Carpet of the Wind," could well have belonged to the Northern [North American] contribution. Its involvement with the "soul" and its ultimate freedom; with life's absolute slavery, its shackles and burdens; with the dualism of good and evil; its distinctly abstract atmosphere, are definitely more aligned to the thematic adventures and attitudes of the Northern poets. The poet imagines himself going on a journey over the clouds, where he meets his soul and rejoices in the union. Exhortations against the evil of man on earth are uttered without hesitancy or compassion. The pessimistic tone of the poem and its imaginary framework are directly Romantic. When it was first published in 1929 in *Al-Muqtataf*, its originality immediately attracted the attention of readers in the Arab world. The premature death of the poet in 1930 focussed further attention on his work and many articles were written on him and on the poem. "On the Carpet of the Wind" was also translated into several European languages. . . .

Despite its purely imaginative content, the poem strikes an authentic note which gives it a special place in modern Arabic poetry and which has contributed to the high esteem in which its author was held among the poets of his day. In its pessimism there is a heart-catching element which gives it a note different from that found in the works of others such as Gibrān and the poet's brother Shafīq. The flow of its rhythm is a fine example of fluidity and smoothness, and it shows great harmony in its words and phrases.

Salmā al-Jayyūsī. Trends and Movements in Modern Arabic
Poetry (Leiden, E. J. Brill, 1977), pp. 72–73

AL-MAS'ADĪ, MAHMŪD (1911–   )

TUNISIA

Our author [Mahmūd al-Mas'adī] has been influenced by both French and Arabic literature and also by his Tunisian homeland and the kind of life that existed there in the days before independence. [*The Dam*] gives us an excellent picture of all these types of influence. The author is in despair, or seems to be so. He is driven by hope, imagination, and his own human nature to create, experiment, and innovate. He expends much energy, tolerates hardships, and suffers all kinds of pain and tribulation. Once he feels certain that he has reached his goal and achieved success, everything he has created and designed and all the results of his innovative efforts disappear as though they had never been and no effort had been expended or trials suffered. . . .

The author has adopted the symbolic mode as his form of expression and does not seem interested in writing philosophy pure and simple but prefers to write literary philosophy or to create a philosophical literature. With that in mind, his use of poetic expression to portray his ideas through symbol and allusion seems appropriate. He has been more successful in achieving this goal than any other contemporary Arab symbolist author. The reason for that seems to be that symbolist writers in Arab countries, in spite of their great va-

riety, have not yet succeeded in getting the Arabic language itself to conform
to their creative purpose, and as a result they are still in the experimental
stage.

Al-Mas'adī, on the other hand, has succeeded in enlisting the language
to his cause, and indeed, it has responded to his call without resistance or objection. Indeed, I will go further and suggest that it has responded too readily by allowing him to feed on it and by tempting him into exploiting and
overusing it.

Tāhā Husayn. *Min adabinā al-muʿāsir* (Beirut, Dār al-
Ādāb, 1958), pp. 113–14, 115–16†

The theme of the ancient mariner and the sea, enriched by so many voyages of
adventure across the uncharted worlds of the ocean, has on more than one occasion provided a lively source of inspiration for contemporary Arab poets
and authors. . . .

Mahmūd al-Mas'adī's work, *Sindbad in Quest of Purity*, thus owes a
great deal of its initial impact to the collection of *The Thousand and One
Nights*, or, in other words to Arabo-Muslim culture. But behind the tormented
expression of al-Mas'adī's Sindbad there lurks a modern Sindbad who is
racked by the unsatisfied quests of such authors as Charles Baudelaire in "The
Voyage," Arthur Rimbaud in *The Drunken Boat* and *A Season in Hell*, and
Gérard de Nerval in *Aurelia* and *The Daughters of Fire*. . . .

Upon reading this work many people have found fault with Mahmūd al-
Mas'adī's lack of commitment to an Arab world that is going through a number of changes and even revolutions. It is true that al-Mas'adī remains an ide-
alist who is taken with beautiful ideas, but that does not mean that he has a
negative or outsider's attitude to the world that emerges from his works. . . .
In spite of everything, one cannot avoid being touched when one listens to the
savage, wrenching cries of a man in quest of himself.

Al-Mas'adī's great originality lies in his attractive style. Above all it is a
purist's language. A follower of Mallarmé, al-Mas'adī tries to give new
meaning to the communal language. From the *Lisān al-ʿArab* dictionary of the
African Ibn Manzūr [d. 1311] or the language of the famous *muʿallaqāt*
poems [of the pre-Islamic period] he culls curious and rare words with which
to dazzle us. . . . Here one finds the language of the desert, those epithets describing camels that so delight the reader of the ancient poetry, whether authentic or not.

Ferid Ghazi. *Le roman et la nouvelle en Tunisie* (Tunis,
Maison Tunisienne de l'Édition, 1970), pp. 42, 44, 45†

A reading of Najīb Mahfūz's novel *The Thief and the Dogs* reminded me immediately of another work, Mahmūd al-Mas'adī's *The Dam*, with its portrayal

of a world of futility (as Tāhā Husayn has pointed out in his review of the work) seen through the events portrayed and the characters' dialogue. . . . Ghaylān, who does not believe in laws, boundaries, obstacles, or death is merely a symbol of revolution and struggle as a solution to existentialist complexes. Maymūna is the woman of the possible who loves life as it is and relishes existence for all its faults; she serves as a symbol of submission and obedience to reality and of confidence in the prevailing laws. Sāhabbā' (the Goddess) is the goddess of aridity and drought and serves as a symbol for the religious solution to the dilemma, one that rejects confrontation and resorts instead to withdrawal and submission to absolute will through acts of devotion and mystical evanescence. . . . In *The Dam* al-Mas'adī has set about portraying the hero, as well as the other characters, through their intellectual and psychological aspects only, and as a result these characters emerge as being somewhat strange and detached from the level of our own human domain. That may, of course, be a result of the atmosphere of fable with which the author provides the work from the very beginning, so that it can serve as an arena for the portrayal of their actions and a stage on which the elements of their existence can be brought to fruition.

Abū Zayyān al-Sa'dī. *Fī al-adab al-Tūnisī al-mu'āsir*
(Tunis, Mu'assassat 'Abd al-Karīm ibn 'Abdallāh,
1974), pp. 136–37†

The most significant event in the literary history of Tunisia in the 20th century was the appearance of the play *The Dam* by the Tunisian playwright Mahmūd al-Mas'adī, published in 1955. In form it belongs to the genre of drama, but actually it is a pseudodrama. It is extremely doubtful whether it was composed to be acted onstage. In fact, it is really a portrait of a particular approach to the events of life, or more accurately, a philosophical play intended only for reading . . .

The symbolic mode allows for the portrayal of conflict between opposites: heart and mind, freedom and fate, art and life. On the one hand, *The Dam* uses an expressionist, symbolic framework to convey the notion of the uselessness of man's struggle against fate; on the other, it is a testament to the nobility of the struggle for the cause of individual thought and shows a confidence in the goals of the individual's struggle even in the face of predestined and unavoidable death. . . .

The play is written in a very literary style that achieves its effects through the use of the traditional devices of imagery. To the basic framework of the plot the playwright adds a number of events from the history of the Arabs; a dam really was destroyed in the Yemen in ancient times. . . . This ability to blend together such disparate elements is not merely the sign of an unusual work but one of genius. A philosophical awareness of the struggle between ideals and reality leads the author to the idea of the need for a struggle against evil even at the price of self-sacrifice.

Radwān Ibrāhīm. Al-Taʿrīf bi-al-adab al-Tūnisī (Tunis, Dār
al-ʿArabiyya li-al-Kitāb, 1977), pp. 66–69†

The Dam does not fall into any of the recognized categories of literary form, even though it is usually thought of as a play because of its division into eight scenes and the fact that the majority of the text consists of dialogue between the various characters. Yet these elements of the drama structure are frequently transformed into something which has a closer resemblance to a narrative form. This is because of the existence of quite lengthy prose passages which take the place of what would be stage directions in a normal play. Most of this work is surrealistic in its action and atmosphere, and these prose passages play an important part in sustaining the surrealism: they are as charged with poetic allusion and imagery as any of the dialogue, and because of their genuine and deliberate literary qualities they become an integral part of the work. . . .

It is interesting to note that the dialogue does not pose artistic problems as it does in so many plays and narratives in modern Arabic. The problems are avoided because the level of the work from beginning to end is one of surrealism, symbolism, elevated flights of the imagination, and argument about sophisticated intellectual concepts. It is far removed from the mundane, the realistic, or in terms of language, the colloquial. There are occasions when the text approaches the realm of blank verse, particularly in the utterances of the *hawātif*, the echoing voices which mock the statements of Ghaylān, and extol the power and might of Sāhabbāʾ. Reference has already been made to al-Masʿadī's frequent use of language in order to symbolize different literary and religious traditions in Arabic, usually for purposes of satire and irony. Thus, what for many are the limitations, the archaisms, and the deficiencies of literary Arabic, are turned by him into highly creative elements of a work of literature which sacrifices nothing of the modernity and relevance of its message.

Robin Ostle. Journal of Arabic Literature.
8, 1977, pp. 161–62

AL-MĀZINĪ, IBRĀHĪM ʿABD AL-QĀDIR (1890–1949)

EGYPT

Al-Māzinī never wrote any of his stories *ex nihilo*; nor were they fabrications of his imagination. Each one derives its material from something he has seen, heard, or experienced. In fact, the hero of his two major novels, *Ibrāhīm the Author* and *Ibrāhīm Again*, is none other than al-Māzinī himself. I do not think we would be going too far if we suggested that he is the hero of the majority of stories that he wrote. He is, after all, the focal point of many of his articles, memoirs describing his work as a journalist, his various experiences in life, and his social relationships; indeed, we can say that al-Māzinī's oeuvre consists wholly of poetry, prose, stories, and literary articles of a personal nature. In spite of all this, however, al-Māzinī was able to use his God-given gifts and his poetic spirit—not to mention the witty and ironic outlook he derived from life—to give his writings an especially human stamp that should guarantee their survival. . . .

A general feature of al-Māzinī's novels and short stories is that they are never concerned with events and avoid branching out into the realms of the imagination. It was his decision not to concern himself with the narration of events, but instead to concentrate on analysis of people and on portraits of individual characters. In fact, a large number of his "stories" are, from the strictly artistic point of view, hardly stories at all; rather, they are fictional articles with no structure to them and none of the formal features normally associated with the short story. They are either memoirs or narratives of experiences of an extremely basic type, around which are clustered a whole host of psychological probings and analyses.

Muhammad Mandūr. Ibrāhīm al-Māzinī (Cairo, Matba'a
Nahdat Misr, 1954), pp. 67–69†

One of the most remarkable features of al-Māzinī's style is his use of dialogue. If we compare his approach with that of Tawfīq al-Hakīm, we find that al-Hakīm is very involved with dialogue and proceeds to record it wherever he encounters it; he even writes down what he hears in the street, linking everything together in such a way that it always leads to the planned conclusion and the desired result. That is not natural. With al-Māzinī on the other hand, the major characteristic in this regard, as in other aspects of his writing, is simplicity . . . ; there is no formality, fabrication, or artificiality. The whole thing is presented exactly as it would happen in normal daily life, changing from one topic to another without your being able to guess what the eventual outcome will be. . . .

With al-Hakīm's dialogue you are presented with a wonderfully cooked meal. Al-Māzinī, on the other hand, gives you a fresh piece of fruit that looks, tastes, and smells marvelous. . . . Al-Māzinī's dialogues are really poetic tableaux using simple language. He has read the Arabic dictionary thoroughly and that gives him the necessary confidence to use colloquial phrases and words. In my opinion at least, his use of dialogue is the most outstanding yet in Arabic. . . .

At the beginning of his writing career, he used a very pure and formal style with lofty phrases that reminded one of [ʿAbd al-Qāhir] al-Jurjānī [the great 11th-century Arab critic] and al-Sharīf al-Radī [an 11th-century poet]. Then his style became more mellow and began to adapt itself to the spirit of the era; he molded it to the demands of journalism, which he preferred to schoolteaching. Al-Māzinī was well aware of this facet in himself, which he wrote about as follows: "Most people think I was influenced by al-Jāhiz [a 9th-century writer] at first; that is true. But it is more accurate to state that I was fascinated by al-Jurjānī's style at that time. However, that period has long since passed—thank God!"

Niʿmat Fuʾād. Adab al-Māzinī (Cairo, Muʾassasat al-Khānjī, 1961), pp. 284–86†

Some readers and critics find the novel *Ibrāhīm the Author* strange, for the reason that it is not a single story but three interwoven love stories. The protagonist of the three stories is Ibrāhīm, and the three main female characters are, in order, Mary, the nurse; Shūshū, the young girl who is all shyness and inexperience; and Laylā, the woman of experience who enjoys life and love to the full, has complete control over her own affairs, and embarks on any new venture fully aware of what she is doing.

Ibrāhīm becomes involved in the three love stories in succession, and sometimes they almost overlap. Ibrāhīm almost comes to believe that two different types of love are filling his heart or that he loves two women at once. When he realizes that these feelings are true, he falls into despair, but manages to devise the excuse that no one can know the secrets of the human heart or how it really functions. So what is there to stop him loving two women at the same time? He loves his mother, his country, and his work, and they are all different kinds of love. . . .

At the end of *Ibrāhīm the Author*, the hero has emerged from his three amorous adventures just as he went into them. In fact, he may even be more bitter and despairing than before. He could have followed each of the experiences through to a happy end, found some rest for himself, and settled down to a quiet existence, but he usually finds some pretext or other for not doing so. It may be that he is too weak to carry any experience through to the end.

Some people may imagine that the three love stories make up the core and essence of the story, and that Mary, Shūshū, and Laylā are the heroines of this sentimental novel. But the fact of the matter is that there is just one hero and that is Ibrāhīm. Actually, even though the novel is full of the theme of love, it is not a love story so much as a psychological one, which sheds a kind of light on a particular type of person represented by the character of Ibrāhīm. This human exemplar can be a symbol and key to a greater understanding of the other characters. In fact, it can serve as a general example, along the lines of Shakespeare's Hamlet and Stendhal's Julien Sorel in *The Red and the Black*. He reflects the malady of the age, which could be detected in a large segment of educated Egyptians in the first half of the twentieth century, particularly those who were not involved in political life and who remained indifferent to the victories and defeats that would crowd the front pages every day. These people were by nature individualists, and their feelings developed from within themselves. They were able to hear only the echo of their own voices. . . .

So why does Ibrāhīm reject love, which symbolizes home and family? He does so because he is rejecting life itself; because he cannot see his life leading anywhere. The world of books has corrupted his real thinking processes; his scope of vision is so wide that, like Hamlet, he is unable to make a choice between right and wrong, good and evil, intelligence and stupidity.

Salāh ʿAbd al-Sabūr. Mādhā yabqā minhum li-al-tārīkh
(Cairo, Dār al-Kātib al-ʿArabī, 1968),
pp. 135, 141–42, 145†

More than any other novel by al-Māzinī, this one [*Starting All Over Again*] is deeply rooted in social reality. The plot alone is fanciful, but the details of the work are those of everyday life. In fact the life of a middle-class Egyptian family breathes through every line. The dialogue, all written in literary Arabic, is a model of what dialogue in the Arabic novel should be like: here the problem of the duality of the Arabic language has virtually vanished, for while remaining faithful to the spoken idiom to the point of reflecting its minute rhythms, it has the polish and elegance of literary Arabic. The characters are all alive, sketchily, but sensitively drawn, as in a Rembrandt etching, although, as is to be expected, it is the character of the narrator that is most vividly delineated. Here the author's great humanity, his affection and tolerance, his irony and urbanity of spirit are amply illustrated. Original both in conception and execution, this work of fantasy which, however, is rich in Freudian overtones, ranks among the great works of humour in any literature. It provides a sensitive, though perhaps a little limited, comment on the human comedy, a comment which according to one symbolical interpretation, was inspired primarily by the author's fear of death.

No doubt *Starting All Over Again* is much shorter than al-Māzinī's other novels, and it is perhaps legitimate to argue that it is too thin to be regarded as a great novel. Indeed, despite its exciting story it has no plot in the proper sense. There is no complication of divergent threads, no building up to a climax to be followed by a dénouement. Instead, there are variations on a main theme, much elaboration of a basic situation. The work is indeed tightly organized, in the sense that all the events illustrate different facets of the same situation or that they are all written with an eye on it. But the relation between the episodes remains essentially a *post hoc* rather than a *propter hoc* relation. In this respect it is more of a tale than a novel.

Mustafa Badawi. Journal of Arabic Literature.
4, 1973, p. 144

Whatever the particular reasons for al-Māzinī's treatment of women in these novels [*Ibrāhīm the Author* and *Ibrāhīm Again*], the result has a general significance. While his view of women may be compared to that of earlier writers as far back as the classical period, there are important differences, brought about by changes in society. Ibrāhīm looks to girls for entertainment and intellectual companionship, and he is attracted to those who have some education and may work for a living, while their physical appearance often appears to be unimportant. He would find those who have not been to school inadequate, for he wants to be understood enough to be admired. The hidden tension in this situation is never brought out, because the author does not realise that women who are educated will rarely be content with the kind of life which their grandmothers led, that they are less passive, more inclined to form their own opinions. Equally important is the fact that by setting out his view of women and their relationship to men in these two novels, the author has revealed his attitude to one radical change in his society. For him the emancipation of women means their education and consequent ability to follow an intelligent conversation; intellectuals are thus able to discuss with them ideas acquired from abroad. When it comes to the structure of personal relationships, however, there is little change from the old ways; seclusion may be at an end, but the woman's position of inferiority has not altered. The contradiction between European thought and the traditional Middle Eastern organisation of society, a contradiction which still exists in many aspects of Egyptian life, stands out clearly. The fact that the author has not perceived it is hardly surprising, given his lack of consciousness of social conditions.

Hilary Kilpatrick. *The Modern Egyptian Novel* (London, Ithaca Press, 1974), pp. 29–30

In his poetry, al-Māzinī was the most apparently Romantic of the Dīwān group. In its expression of Romantic pessimism and rebellious sentiment, this poetry of the self was in complete contrast with the objective poetry where the personality of the poet disappears behind the public façade. In all other features, however, al-Māzinī's poetry differed little from the traditional poetry. His diction, his phraseology, his general poetic structure, still had the strength and traditional resonance of the neo-Classical poetry with none of ['Abd al-Rahmān] Shukrī's faltering phraseology and hesitant expression. There is no attempt to bring about a change in diction, and his language is based on a firm Classical foundation, which not even his direct appreciation of certain English poems with their new themes, was to affect. His poetry, for all its Romantic features, failed to influence in any important way the Romantic trend in Arabic poetry.

The enthusiasm manifested in al-Māzinī's early writing on poetry seems to have been inspired by outside factors rather than by a permanent drive. Criticism with al-Māzinī was a passing attraction, the result of an impressionable mind fascinated with the world of ideas and theories, as he himself admitted. In fact his career, perhaps more than that of any other man of letters of his generation, is a proof of the influence of imported Western theories at that time on the young writer, and the need that was felt for a new kind of theory and for forging links with foreign and more progressive fields. As a result of his falling early under the influence of Shukrī, who was predominantly a poet, al-Māzinī took to poetry and poetic criticism, his true talent—he became later the best humorous writer in modern Arabic literature—remaining dormant until the mid-twenties. His final change of tone from the emotional and erratic to the sarcastic and humorous is a good example of a literary talent finally emerging from the labyrinth of imported ideas and methods.

Salmā al-Jayyūsī. Trends and Movements in Modern Arabic
Poetry (Leiden, E. J. Brill, 1977), pp. 162–63

Reading al-Māzinī's books and essays, we can see clearly that sarcasm is a distinct and intrinsic aspect of his style; it is never absent, be it in his conversations, his essays, his stories, or his other works; his conversations with friends and family are full of sarcasm, his stories are filled with satirical situations, his characters all tend to be treated ironically by him and often use joking expressions, and any conflict between characters is more often than not expressed through an exchange of sarcastic comments.

All of al-Māzinī's essays show this endearing trait, which lends them a particular tone and timbre. Indeed, some of them can be considered as outright comedy, for example, those in his collections *The Magic Box, Carry On!*, and *Spider's Webs*. Most of these revolve around al-Māzinī himself and his memories of childhood and adolescence. Everything he writes about— scenes from nature, his travels, people he visits, a group of people he happens to meet by chance, an accident he passes—are treated with the same sarcastic style; he never passes over any situation without finding in it something he can use to crack a joke or make a sarcastic comment. Indeed, sarcasm is the essence of his style.

Hāmid ʿAbduh al-Hawwāl. Al-Sakhariyya fī adab al-Māzinī
(Cairo, Al-Hayʾa al-Misriyya al-ʿĀmma li-al-Kitāb, 1982),
pp. 220–21†

MĪNA, HANNĀ (1924–   )

SYRIA

The novel, *The Sail and the Storm* actually focuses its attention to a large degree on the character of al-Turūsī. The many events with which the novel seethes are merely a means of exposing the protagonist's personal characteristics. He is that sailor forever bound by an enduring love for the sea; having spent the majority of his life on it, he has come to know it and face it. He has traveled from port to port and been involved in numerous adventures at sea. If we want to be a little more precise, we can say that the novel is in fact a study of this character and his life on land, from the time when his boat *al-Mansūra* founders until he returns to the sea once again in a new boat. In the time between the loss of his old boat and the beginning of his new voyages, broad social and human vistas open up. We see the café for sailors al-Turūsī has opened in order to earn a livelihood, and we also see the port workers and fishermen. Beyond all this the novel gives us a picture of a social reality based on class exploitation and the struggle of political groups against each other. There is also the struggle of the Syrian people against French imperialism during a tense period in Syria's history, namely during the Second World War. . . .

Hannā Mīna conveys this rich fictional world to us with all the skill of a great novelist. He knows how to draw all the strands of the novel and its characters together and how to grab hold of the reader and gain control of his feelings. I think the reason for this lies, on the one hand, in the tremendous sense of sympathy the novelist shows toward his hero, and on the other, in his use of realistic details. Indeed, it is the facet of realism that most attracts the attention of the student of this particular work, and it lies in the brilliant way the novelist portrays the protagonist and other characters who populate the work. The effect is also conveyed through the way their conversations are rendered simply and spontaneously: that is, what they say, how they behave when talking, and the ordinary language they use to express a whole spectrum of human emotions. The same can be said of the way in which Mīna portrays the daily life of the sailors and fishermen, with their arguments and fights, and also the life of the harbor workers and the wretched conditions in which they have to work, the influential racketeers and their conflicts with each other, and lastly the struggle against French imperialism. . . .

The Sail and the Storm is a story about manhood, a novel of chivalry with all the values and ideals that word implies. The realistic mode that the author has insistently endeavored to employ in the work gradually gives way to a more idealized image of mankind, which we can regard as a higher type of human being. In fact, the author brings his hero into something close to a fabled world, so that we can legitimately ask whether a hero of this kind really exists in spite of all the realistic detail the novelist has put into his work.

Jūrj Sālim. *Al-Mughāmara al-riwāʾiyya* (Damascus,
Manshūrāt Ittihād al-Kuttāb al-ʿArab,
1973), pp. 91, 94–95†

The novels of Hannā Mīna present us with a broad world dominated by an insistence on coming to terms with reality. That is achieved through revolutionary activity. The socialist revolution is the goal that Mīna's world sets itself, but the path to be followed in reaching that goal is complex and tortuous. It leads to revolutionary activity in the context of a real and absolute sense of solidarity with the working class. Coming to terms with reality, then, is not the same thing as acceptance of it. It involves a call to change it, a change that will come through revolution, but it is a call that will emerge from the context of societal relationships and an awareness of reality and its struggles. It is from this point of view that Mīna's novels assume their tremendous importance. They form the only integrated attempt in modern Arabic literature to reach the moment of revolutionary activity within the milieu of the working class. In his earlier novel, *The Sail and the Storm*, Mīna succeeded in giving an excellent portrayal of the sufferings of the populace through the character of al-Turūsī. Now he has moved on to deal directly with the whole range of this experience by incorporating the bourgeois intellectual within the populist activity. . . .

In *The Snow Comes In through the Window* we discover that the novel is a conduit for the vision of reality through revolutionary operations. The work itself attempts to record revolutionary activities in Syria and Lebanon through scenes that are both rich and full of contradictions. Even so, they proceed along a straight line, the two ends of which consist of culture (the petit-bourgeois intellectual) and activity (the proletariat). In between the two we find a Christian sense of a God who can heal the wounds of thousands and serve as an intensified redemption for a long journey of agony and suffering. A thaw sets in, and the men begin to perceive that the future holds promise, that they can alter the way they see life, that they can re-create life in a new form. . . .

Mīna works hard to reveal change through the medium of societal relationships. His heroes are realistic and have their feet planted firmly in the soil of their homelands and in the right social environment, and it is from there that they search for the doors that will lead to the revolution to come. And when he resorts to using Christian poetic language, he makes sure to integrate it within the overall structure of his novel; in that way he can use allusions that transcend the particular moment and interpolate themselves into the dimensions of the future.

Ilyās Khūrī. Tajribat al-bahth 'an ufq (Beirut, Palestine
Essays No. 44, 1974), pp. 87–88, 92†

Sun on a Cloudy Day is a work so full of ideas, allusions, and symbols that the reader may find himself at a loss in determining a single topic for the novel as a whole. Is it concerned with the struggle against the class enemy through an analogy with the struggle against the national enemy? Or is it an attempt to search for the self and, through a search for the meaning of life, to elevate the self through resistance, revolution, and mobility from one class to another? The fact of the matter is that all these ideas are drawn together within this novel in a close-knit format that cannot be subdivided. The one thing about which there can be no argument, however, is that *Sun on a Cloudy Day* is a work about class conflict.

In presenting two differing breeds of mankind—those who live in lofty mansions and palaces and the poor people in their wretched hovels—the novelist attempts to expose the attitudes of the bourgeoisie and expose them as they really are: how they oppress the masses and come to terms with the occupying French forces. From the very first pages of the book the reader becomes aware of the author's sympathy for the poor, who are continually attacking the occupation forces. . . . The struggle between the two groups is a bitter one. The fight against the colonial occupation is inevitably compared with that against the bourgeois class who live in the shade of French protection and exploit the poor workers and peasants. At this point a legitimate question that could be asked is, Why did the author choose the period of French occupation, and why did he make a historical period a framework for his vision and attitudes, knowing full well that he had done precisely the same in his previous novels? The importance of *Sun on a Cloudy Day* lies in the fact that it is tied closely to the time period in which it appeared, namely the aftermath of the June War of 1967, when the external enemy was still oppressing the land and expropriating the country's resources. Although the time period in which the novel is set is not the same period in which it appeared, there is a close correspondence between these two periods, to the extent that it seems that the author has provided history with characters and events from the present in an attempt to stress the fact that the ruling bourgeois class sees its interests best represented in placing itself in a position directly opposed to the hopes and welfare of the poor masses. . . .

As we have said above, this is a novel about class conflict, and as such the kind of struggle the author tries to convey assumes a greater significance than the individuals involved, whatever their class or ideological affiliations may be. Mīna draws his characters with tremendous artistry. He does not use names, but allows their various aspects to emerge; we come to know them through the way the events develop, through their work and place of residence, and through the social and political situation all around them.

Shukrī ʿAzīz Mādī. Inʿikās hazīmat Hazīrān ʿalā al-riwāya al-ʿArabiyya (Beirut, Al-Muʾassasa al-ʿArabiyya li-al-Dirāsāt wa-al-Nashr, 1978), pp. 137–38, 142†

The problem I am addressing here consists of identifying the narrator or narrators of the novel *Fragments of Pictures* and defining the status of each narrator vis-à-vis the others.

We can start by saying that there are a number of narrators in *Fragments of Pictures*. The narrator who signs his name under the dedication "To Mariannā Mikhāʾīl Dhakūr, my mother. Hannā" should be reckoned as the first one. He is the only one who reveals his identity at the outset of the story. At this point, however, we have to be sure not to confuse the primary narrator, who tells the story, with the other narrators, who are actually imaginary characters into whose personae the storyteller is transformed without actually becoming any of them.

The storyteller, or primary narrator, as we have called him, who reveals his identity by signing his name "Hannā," looks down upon us from the very first page, and does not even give us his name [in the narrative proper]. He makes use of the first-person pronoun as a symbol of his total presence. . . . In fact, this "I" actually serves as the second narrator, assuming the burden of narrating *Fragments of Pictures* until the last page. . . .

However, this second narrator is not the first and last in *Fragments of Pictures*. There exists another, third narrator, who speaks in the third person. This occurs whenever the second narrator ceases to speak in the first person, or, in other words, whenever the events being narrated have a direct bearing on either the second or primary narrator. . . .

Beyond all these there is also a fourth, the mother, who narrates a sizable portion of the events. This mother-narrator reveals to the child-narrator numerous facts and secrets of life. . . .

The primary narrator who placed his name under the dedication of *Fragments of Pictures* wanted to be the first and last narrator. But our reading of the novel has established that there are a number of narrators of different kinds and with varying degrees of significance.

Maurice Abū Nādir. *Al-Alsuniyya wa-al-naqd al-adabī* (Beirut, Dār al-Nahār li-al-Nashr, 1979), pp. 109–13†

Hannā Mīna's novel *Blue Lamps* (1954) appeared during a decade when the notion of commitment was very much to the fore, and it suffers a good deal because the political message is allowed to predominate over the presentation of characters and events. In fact, the ending of the novel follows the tradition of the romantic novel, with the heroine Randa dying of tuberculosis, while her beloved, Fāris, the freedom fighter who has joined the army in order to earn enough money to get married, is killed fighting in Libya. The echo of Haykal's *Zaynab* of many decades earlier seems particularly strong.

Mīna's second novel, *The Sail and the Storm* (1966), is a much more accomplished work. As in Halīm Barakāt's *The Return of the Flying Dutchman to the Sea*, set during the 1967 defeat, we are here dealing with the return to the sea, but in the case of Mīna's novel it is not a condemnation to a continuing exile but rather an aspiration on the hero's part to rejoin the element in which he feels most at home, a theme which several critics have connected with Hemingway's *The Old Man and the Sea*. Al-Turūsī, the major character of this work, has lost his ship at sea and opened a café in the Syrian town of Lādhiqiyya or Lattakia, a community racked by civil unrest and nationalist activity. For him, this period on land is a time of alienation, but it is also a time during which he becomes aware of the injustices suffered by his fellow men, the porters and dockers in the harbour who have to carry prodigious loads under the merciless scrutiny of the local racketeers and their thugs. In a brutal fight, al-Turūsī defeats one of these thugs and thus symbolically confronts the social injustices of his homeland. The café now becomes an even greater focus for the activity of the local nationalist groups. Al-Turūsī even goes into the business of smuggling arms to resistance groups. But the event which acts as the catalyst for his exile on land is a violent storm in which he rescues another sailor, al-Rahūmī, from his sinking boat. After many years of alienation, the hero is now given the opportunity to return to his natural environment, the sea, where the turbulence and unpredictability reflect the societal conditions on land which he has worked so hard to combat and defeat. This novel and others by Mīna take as their theme the quest for freedom on the part of his fellow-countrymen. In the earlier works this tends to be an external quest: freedom from oppression, colonial rule and exploitation, whereas in more recent works the quest has involved more internal factors, release from the burdens of the heritage of the past and from the feelings of alienation of the present. In all this, Mīna has continued to use a vivid realism which makes no concessions to such devices as flashback or stream-of-consciousness in order to recall the past. The narrative sequence is uncomplicated and the impact is often similar to the heroic saga, something to which even more emphasis is given in *The Sail and the Storm* by the way in which the major character is presented.

Roger Allen. *The Arabic Novel: An Historical and Critical Introduction* (Syracuse, N.Y., Syracuse University Press, 1982), pp. 72–73

MUNĪF, ʿABD AL-RAHMĀN (1930s?–)

SAUDI ARABIA (RESIDENT OF IRAQ, THEN FRANCE)

The Trees and the Assassination of Marzūq is a novel in which ʿAbd al-Rahmān Munīf manages to capture the moment of collision between an intellectual and reality through the relationship of Mansūr with Ilyās Nakhla. The meeting takes place in a train, and the memory of the past comes full circle. Ilyās Nakhla is outside of official society; he cannot understand why people insist on cutting down trees. The tree in this instance is a symbol for contact with the soil, a symbol of endurance and continuity. When it is cut down, the relationships that tie things together are lost. Ilyās Nakhla wanders around from one job to another, looking for a woman. But there can be no woman for him after the death of Hanna, the only real tree in Ilyās Nakhla's life. For him women are in the domain of impossible relationships. . . .

Ilyās Nakhla represents the model of a man totally absorbed in the popular milieu; he breathes its air and feels it coursing through his veins. He is a living symbol of the impossibility of conducting any kind of dialogue with a repressive society that is, in effect, a police state. That is what Mansūr 'Abd al-Salām declares, he being the educated mirror image of Ilyās. Mansūr goes to Europe to study and then comes home again to become a professor. After he is drafted into the army he becomes a part of the 1967 defeat. He voices his grievances along with the rest of the people, but the forces of repression crush the people mercilessly. Mansūr finds himself thrown out of his job. He finds that he can no longer remain in contact with other people. When he lifts up his head, all the instruments of repression are set in motion and eject him from society. He becomes alienated from his homeland. . . .

The novel tells us that the intellectual who is unable to fuse with reality in the course of changing it cannot escape from his own failures on an individual basis. When the end of the process turns out to be madness, he should try once again and face up to reality. This forms the structure of the novel, and Munīf presents it to us in a convincing classical format that is extremely lucid and in a style very close to poetry.

Ilyās Khūrī. *Tajribat al-bahth 'an ufq* (Beirut, Palestine Essays No. 44, 1974), pp. 106–7†

I do not know of any other Arab novelist who relishes, and indeed even suffers from, such a fierce and passionate sensitivity to nature as 'Abd al-Rahmān Munīf. Earth, trees, animals and birds, all these are to be found in his novels, and they give them vigor, energy, and a particular flavor. They seem to be as important as the characters themselves, and in fact, the characters sometimes become truly rounded only through the mediation of the nature around them; they seem to be extensions of it. This sensitivity toward nature is a part of his spatial sense: it does not matter whether the place consists of the suffocating atmosphere of a gloomy city prison, as in *East of the Mediterranean*, or the vast expanses of the countryside where feet can sink in the mud, lungs can breathe in the air, and faces turn toward the sun and rain, as in *The Trees and the Assassination of Marzūq* and *When We Abandoned the Bridge*. This spatial dimension grabs hold of the reader and pulls him into the fray, each time underlining its presence and significance. *Endings* is 'Abd al-Rahmān Munīf's most recent novel (1978), and, unlike his other novels, it is distinguished—among its numerous qualities—by the author's ability yet again to convey to the reader this appreciation for nature in a truly lively fashion. He uses it to intensify an experience that may well be unfamiliar to the reader, but gradually it penetrates ever deeper into the reader's mind. It then comes to represent in the mind something fleeting and intangible which the reader could not have defined or grasped before but which is now within reach. . . .

However we read this novel, we find ourselves continually moving along parallel lines of events and symbols. On the level of events, the novel takes us back to the experiences of the people of the village of al-Tība, their attachment to their roots and their perpetual confusion in the face of love and death involving humans, animals, and birds. On the symbolic level, the novel allows us to discover things about people wherever they may live, and about their attachment to those obscure forces in the universe that make of love and death the most potent and fruitful elements in the whole of nature.

Al-Tība, with all its dogs, gazelles, crows, pigeons, and flocks of grouse shooting up into the sky like scudding clouds is of some higher order; it belongs to the realm of experience and dream. It represents every village we have known, not merely in our own consciousness and surface experiences, but in the deepest recesses of our subconscious. . . .

Jabrā Ibrāhīm Jabrā. Yanābī' al-ru'yā (Beirut, Al-
Mu'assasa al-'Arabiyya li-al-Dirāsāt wa-al-Nashr,
1979), pp. 36, 40†

Dr. 'Abd al-Rahmān Munīf's latest novel, Race of the Long Distances: A Journey to the East, is one of those works that take an important event in a Middle East country and make it the principal focus of the story. In this case the event chosen by Munīf is the nationalization of Iranian oil production in 1952, at the time Mossadegh was Prime Minister, and the ensuing struggle between England and the United States with regard to control over the area. Even though the author does not mention the name of the Prime Minister anywhere in the novel, or for that matter, the name of the country where the nationalization occurs, we can deduce from the course of events about which we read, the results that ensue, and the fate that awaits "the aged man" that the country in question is Iran, that the "aged man" is Mossadegh, and that the Americans were behind the entire operation. . . .

The events of the novel are conveyed by way of reports and recollections. In other words, no events are presented through the actions and behavior of the characters in the novel themselves, but rather through the information we are given by the character of Peter McDonald. This, however, is not necessarily a primary fault in the composition of a novel, for there are numerous novels that rely on this method.

The other principal characters in the story are Ridā 'Abbās Safrāwī, Muhammad Mīrzā, Ashraf Āyatallāh, and Shīrīn. We are not able to establish any precise details about them through the novel. Once again, everything we know comes from the information provided by this Peter McDonald. . . . He can be regarded as the major character in the work in that he serves as the main narrator from start to finish. The figure of Shīrīn also plays a direct role—at least in McDonald's sex life—and the shadow of her presence is to be found in most parts of the novel. As a result, these two characters leave behind some residual effect that enables us to define their surface characteristics, if nothing else. . . .

Novels that focus primarily on important historical events are much fewer in number than those that treat questions of sentiment or society. This generalization applies to non-Arabic novelistic traditions, but it is especially true about Arabic novels. Thus, we may rightly say that *Race of the Long Distances: A Journey to the East* is indeed a pioneering work in this difficult genre.

ʿAbdallāh Niyāzī. *Adwāʾ waʾāfāq.* Feb. 6, 1980†

Recent structural analyses of a number of poems from the pre-Islamic period have shown with great clarity that the traditional notion that the *qaṣīda* possess no unity of purpose can no longer be justified; these studies show clearly that the unifying thread which runs through these poems is based on a series of oppositions involving lack and the elimination of lack, of "plerosis" and "kenosis." . . . These interpretations and others like them inevitably come to mind upon a first reading of the novel *Endings* (1978) by ʿAbd al-Rahmān Munīf. . . .

The emphasis on the desert, intense heat, the dangers of travel, the search for food, all these features and others set this novel apart from others written in Arabic. Novels written by Arab authors have tended to a large degree to take as their subjects the city and its inhabitants and particularly the bourgeoisie, thus emulating at least the initial stages in the development of most of the Western novel traditions. There have, of course, also been novels which deal with life in the countryside, from the very early *Zaynab* to ʿAbd al-Hakīm Qāsim's *The Seven Days of Man*; there have also been novels, parts of which have been set in the desert, Ghassān Kanafānī's *Men in the Sun* for one. However, I am not aware of any other novel in Arabic which devotes its attention so unswervingly to a depiction of this particular segment of contemporary Arab society.

The setting of the novel is the village of al-Tība, which is situated right on the edge of the desert. The hardships implicit in this rugged life serve to create strong bonds between the inhabitants of the village and also to bring back home in times of crisis those sons of the community who have decided to seek their fortunes elsewhere, and particularly in the "big city." . . .

The principal character is the community as a whole. The actions of individuals are portrayed, but their import is seen within the framework of the larger picture, namely the village as a unit. Whatever characterisation they receive emerges from the description of their actions, and not from any attempt at internal analysis or still less from dialogue, of which there is comparatively little. In fact, the reader is supplied with only four names of characters in a work which covers one hundred and eighty-seven pages.

This then is very much a novel of environment, but that does not mean that there is no action at all. In fact, the manner in which a series of flashbacks recalling previous momentous occasions in the history of the village are re-counted serves to lend the narrative certain elements of the folktale which are entirely appropriate to the situation of the novel.

Roger Allen. The Arabic Novel: An Historical and Critical
Introduction (Syracuse, N.Y., Syracuse University Press,
1982), pp. 156–58

Another variation upon this narrative technique [interior monologue] is Munīf's handling of his protagonist's experience of political belief, imprison-ment and torture, escape and exile, and eventual return, imprisonment and death in *East of the Mediterranean* (1977). As the title indicates, no specific country in the region is identified; ironically, however, it may well apply to all countries passing through political conflicts or falling under totalitarian governments and despotic rulers. In this novel, Munīf places his protagonist Rajab in very trying circumstances, which are, nevertheless, not surprising to those acquainted with the sufferings of intellectuals and political groups in Third World countries. After initial reluctance, Rajab thinks of writing about the experiences has just undergone, despite his feeling that "words, seem at certain moments and quite often, like leaves in early winter: yellow and pale, blown by the wind, to be trodden later by feet. The written word is no longer a living thing, capable of doing something." To present a many-sided view of his own experience, Rajab asks his sister to co-operate in depicting her own fears and expectations, including as well her own husband's and children's re-actions, describing thereby the nature of the sufferings undergone by many, "East of the Mediterranean." Munīf, in fact, begins his novel with a quotation from the Declaration of Human Rights, which calls for the treatment of indi-viduals as human beings entitled to freedom and respect.

Muhsin Jassim Ali. Journal of Arabic Literature.
14, 1983, p. 74

MUTRĀN, KHALĪL (1872–1949)

LEBANON/EGYPT

A poet can make use of the power of words to create his own private universe separate from the normal world in which we live. When we look at Mutrān's poetry, we discover that his diction is appropriate to the subject and shines forth brilliantly in his poetry. For powerful causes he could choose forceful phrases, while, if the occasion was more refined, his words would be gentle and soft. . . .

In Mutrān's poetry, the sentence was a complete unit chosen as such. Sometimes there might be a certain terseness, but it was the kind that would cause no intelligent reader any trouble or difficulty; in any case, it lent his poetry a particular beauty and brilliance, since such brevity imparts a tremendous rhetorical power to poetry, as any students of the subject will realize. . . .

His sentences use words in a metaphorical way on a number of occasions, and this affords his style both power and beauty. It permits him to avoid using poor wording and filling up the line with empty verbiage. Mutrān frequently resorts to inverting or shifting normal word order. He also makes use of antithesis and various other tropes. Particular attention is given to the construction of sentences and the connections between them. No single line of poetry is a unit in itself; Mutrān regards the entire poem as a complete unit and keeps a special watch on the way sentences are divided and joined together, including the use of particles to show causation and circumstance. . . .

Mutrān's sentences have an easy flow to them; there is no complication about them, and no pitfalls are involved. This, of course, is one of the characteristics of all great literature.

Jamāl al-dīn al-Ramādī. Khalīl Mutrān: Shāʿir al-aqtār al-ʿArabiyya (Cairo, Dār al-Maʿārif, n.d. [1955?]), pp. 211, 213†

Anyone who looks at Mutrān's poetry in its various guises cannot but appreciate his excellence as a poet and as an inspiring teacher and guide. He created such new vistas of contemplation, sensibility, and even mysticism that he deserved to be called the "first creative poet in modern Arabic literature."

Arabic poetry was by no means lacking in representatives of the realistic school, or in examples of empirical knowledge and philosophical ideals. Neither Mutrān nor any of those who followed him can claim any originality on that score. . . . What Mutrān and his pupils did bring to poetry was something greater: they formed a school of genuine artistic freedom that paid due respect to the artist's own personality and honored the complete independence of art from all kinds of artificiality, embellishment, and superficial elegance, from any type of servitude that words or the fetters of classicism might impose on art or the artist, fetters not sanctioned by either natural beauty or authentic art.

Mutrān lent his full support to the concept of the unity of the poem and to the personality of the artist. He reinforced the artist's mission just as democracy bolsters the rights of man. This opened wide the doors of life and revealed new vistas for the imagination. Everything in existence, be it big or small, now emerged as a poetic subject that could and should be treated in an artistic fashion whenever the poet felt himself able to interact with the object. . . . He convinced the poets of his school that each one of them had an exemplary mission to fulfill. The poet's function was not just to string words together or to exploit opportunities to chant occasional verse. They had to lead the way in thought, to be emissaries of emotion, preachers of reform, and epitomes of faith for not only their own generation but those that followed it.

Ahmad Zakī Abū Shādī. Qadāyā al-shiʿr al-muʿāsir (Cairo,
Al-Muʾassasa al-Misriyya li-al-Tibāʿa al-Hadītha,
1959?), pp. 56–57†

Mutrān is a romantic, and yet he is not quite as free of the trammels of society as Jubrān. Jubrān, after all, lived in America, far from the influence of Arab society. He had no need to go along with the demands of that society in any way at all. Mutrān, on the other hand, was living in Egypt, where at the beginning of the century a good deal of reactionary thought could be found. Additionally, he was a sensitive man and much preferred being polite and smoothing things over to angering other people. If you look at his *Collected Poems* you will be surprised by the number of poems of the traditional types, such as eulogy, elegy, congratulations, and other types of occasional verse. These poems have little value apart from their historical interest.

If you concentrate on the other poems of Mutrān, where he was free to give full rein to his own temperament, you will find romantic poetry of real excellence. . . . Take, for example, the poem "The Weeping Lion," which he wrote in the suburb, Modern Cairo, to which he retired soon after it was founded. The romantic features are self-evident, the most significant being the sense of alienation from other people Mutrān feels, a feeling that leads him to keep his distance from them and withdraw into his own self in order to deal with its injuries. . . .

You can also find Mutrān's romanticism in his narrative poetry, a genre to which he made a most original contribution; I would mention particularly the poems about lovers, which resemble the ballad poetry of Western literature. There are many examples of this in his works; one of the best is the one entitled "The Martyr Embryo." The same romantic spirit can also be seen in Mutrān's desire to go back to the happy past, and especially to the days of youthful innocence, times that were full of play and laughter and free of sorrows and cares.

ʿĪsā Bullāta. Al-Rūmantiqiyya wa-maʿālimuhā fī al-shiʿr al-
ʿArabī al-hadīth (Beirut, Dār al-Thaqāfa,
1960), pp. 107–8, 111, 116†

Mutrān was no less cultured than [Ahmad] Shawqī and showed an equal concern with the problems of Arab countries and the events that occurred there. He was eager to direct the thought of the younger Arab generation to everything he regarded as worthwhile and valuable from the ethical point of view. He is at his most individual in his attempt at epic and in his historical writings. What is immediately obvious is his reliance on reality to put forward the views he wishes to express and to convey his poetic message.

Mutrān wrote poetry about love, and demonstrated great variety in the way he deals with it. He uses more than one situation, incident and story to convey his feelings about this human emotion, which may be considered as the focal point of any poetics. In his love poems, he was eager to extol "moral beauty" and to show the most subtle and secret of its concepts and images.

Mutrān also wrote nature poetry. So much love and concern does he show for mountains, rivers, trees, and valleys that we get a clear impression of the tremendous attachment he felt for his homeland, Lebanon; in fact, fleeting visions about Lebanon predominate over all other aspects of beauty in his poetry. . . . His work is full of memories of Zahle, Beirut, and the villages of Lebanon scattered like tiny dots of magical beauty all over the hills and vales of the country. . . .

Finally, he wrote a sizable amount on the subject of freedom. This "mistress" received a great deal of his attention and effort throughout his life, and to the end of his days he would spend time supporting this cause and offering resistance to its enemies.

ʿAbd al-Latīf Sharāra. *Khalīl Mutrān* (Beirut, Dār Sādir, 1964), pp. 53–55†

The poem "The Evening," written in Alexandria in 1902, represents one of the important landmarks in the development of lyrical poetry in modern Arabic; here the deep personal feelings of the poet come through even more strongly and impressively, and there is a complete identification of the poet's troubled state with the surrounding scenery, which is quite remarkable for the poetry of this period. The poem is carefully divided into sections varying in mood and intensity like the parts of some melancholy song. . . .

As many poets had done before him, Mutrān muses on the frailty of man, and the inevitability of his suffering, as he addresses the stars which look like flowers in the sky. Then in the final three sections there is a dramatic increase in intensity as the poet realizes that it is foolish to try to escape from himself and his troubles simply by moving from place to place, but he must contend with his sadness, his useless passion and the turmoil of his thoughts all alone. . . .

This is the beginning of a deep and moving identification between his own inner turmoil and the surrounding scene. In the scene of the setting sun which he contemplates, the poet sees reflexions of his own problems: it is a struggle between night and day not unlike that within himself; the bright certainty of the light becomes shot through with dark, gloomy shafts of doubt, and the visible tangible world is blotted out until the dawn of a new day ef-

232   MUTRĀN, KAHLĪL

fects a type of resurrection. The vivid, moving colours of the sunset evoke an
image of his own tortured thoughts as he thinks of the woman he loved. . . .
    The climax of this pathetic fallacy comes as he watches the shafts of light
play over dark hills and through clouds, forming glistening effects similar to
the light reflected in his tear drops. The whole of creation weeps with him as
he watches this symbol of the ebbing of his own life and vigour.

Robin Ostle. Journal of Arabic Literature.
2, 1971, pp. 121–22

The first major change [from the classical and neoclassical tradition of Arabic
poetry] manifested itself in the poetry of the Lebanese-Egyptian poet Khalīl
Mutrān, whose individual talent and solid training in both classical Arabic tradition and French letters and culture combined to inspire his innovations and
qualify him for the decisive role he played in modernizing Arabic poetry. Like
Shawqī and other contemporaries, Mutrān was able to create a new poetic
style characterized by its refinement, correctness and classical purity. But unlike their poetry, the best of his compositions reveal distinctive concepts and
values never before adopted. Among these were his concern with the principles of organic unity and contextual structure in a poem, as well as his tendency to be moderately lyrical, individualistic, introspective and expressive
of his private vision. Armed with his notion of poetry as a conscious art, he
rejected the extreme form of neoclassic rationalism and moved in his poetry
toward a stronger emotional conception of taste. Under the direct influence of
the French romantics, particularly Hugo's poetic narratives, Musset's lyrics,
and Baudelaire's <i>Les fleurs du mal</i>, he developed in a significant part of his
work the first romantic trend in contemporary Arabic verse.
    Focussing in his poetry on the primacy of meaning, Mutrān attacked des-
potism, tyranny, class distinction, ignorance, and social injustice and championed the cause of progress, national freedom and liberal thought in his age.
    In view of his deep concern with the principle of organic unity which de-
termines the internal coordination and emerging unity of texture in a poetical
composition, he became fully aware of the severe limitations of the Arabic
prosodic system. In order to pinpoint these limitations, he ventured to create
the longest poem of its kind in the history of Arab letters, . . . his four-
hundred line, epic-like, monometered, monorhymed poem called "Nero."

Mounah A. Khouri and Hamid Algar. Introduction to An
Anthology of Modern Arabic Poetry (Berkeley, University
of California Press, 1974), p. 7

The main revolution which he brought about in Arabic poetry was a change in
the internal form of the poem. He demanded that a poem should have organic

unity and not the external form of fixed rhyme and metre through which a number of individual verses dealing with different themes are connected. He wanted the poem to be a pattern which combines images, meanings, ideas and words, blended together in a lively way and dealing with a single theme. . . .

Mutrān was deeply influenced by the Romantic movement in French literature and tried to introduce its criteria into Arabic poetry. The Romantic influence can be seen clearly in his emotional and love poetry as well as in his romantic tales and his poems devoted to the description of nature. Some of these poems reveal a deep and complex relationship between nature and his mind. In his emotional and love poetry in which is reflected his melancholy, despair and sadness, he expressed himself with intense subjective identification with nature, describing the outer and inner atmosphere.

In his romantic tales and "epic" poetry, nature was never used for its own sake alone, but as part of a spiritual or moral feeling or as an emotional image. Thus in dealing with these themes he was predominantly objective. In his long romantic narrative "The Martyr Embryo" Mutrān described a young man seducing his beloved. . . .

He thus portrayed the despicable action through the vivid image of daybreak, whereas in conventional Arabic poetry the beauty of nature is described accurately without discussing its reflection in, or its deep and complex relationship with the poet's mind and emotions. His romantic tendencies can also be seen in the poems which he dedicated to desperate lovers who committed suicide, or in which he lamented young people who died tragically in the full bloom of their youth.

S. Moreh. Modern Arabic Poetry 1800–1970 (Leiden,
E. J. Brill, 1976), pp. 59–60

It is clear, then, that Mutrān's Romantic tendencies were offset to an extent by his Classical sense of balance, by too much deliberation and by an occasional tepidity of tone and emotion. He was unable, therefore, to generate a current of Romanticism in Arabic poetry, but his poetry had given the first signs of basic change and heralded the Romantic trend through his great interest in nature, his choice of Romantic themes in his narratives and his open call for experimentation. . . .

In short, one may say that Mutrān, in spite of his important contribution to poetry at the beginning of the century, did little to add any revivifying warmth of feeling to the poetry of his time. But in his work a wider range of interest, power of imagination and a certain originality are to be found. The element of imagination was so strong in his poetry that it is safe to say that he laid the basis of much of the imaginative work produced in the 'twenties and 'thirties. He was precocious in his early definition of his aims and in his discovery of a new field of poetic experience. What is dramatic about his experiment is not his poetry so much as the courage of his deliberate attempt to undertake the double task of seeking continuity with an Arab literary past while moving towards untouched fields against the tide of strongly entrenched traditions.

Mutrān had led the way towards several aspects of innovation but had stayed all his life at the periphery of his own experiment. His greatest and most original contribution to Arabic poetry was made at the beginning of his career. He must be remembered as the herald of a new awareness in Arabic poetry, even if he was unable to project his argument with force.

Salmā al-Jayyūsī. *Trends and Movements in Modern Arabic Poetry* (Leiden, E. J. Brill, 1977), pp. 63–64

NĀJĪ, IBRĀHĪM (1893–1953)

EGYPT

Ibrāhīm Nājī is reckoned to be one of Khalīl Mutrān's most faithful students in his advocacy of the unity of the poem and also in the purely emotional tendency in his writings. His poetry consists of living pictures of his emotional experiences and artistic feelings.

As we have noted, the hallmarks of this tendency are a resort to nature and a direct communion with it; even further, a process of fusion with it. In this realm, Nājī's only rival is Khalīl Mutrān himself. One of Nājī's best poems is the one entitled "The Mirage." . . . In this poem Nājī mingles his own self with nature. He envisages himself gradually sinking into the quicksands of life, consumed by thirst and destroyed by care. . . .

One outstanding feature of the poetry of Ibrāhīm Nājī is the feeling of despair and alienation he communicates; in this, his poetry is like that of ʿAlī Mahmūd Tāhā and the European Romantics, who themselves resorted to isolation and had similar feelings of loneliness and estrangement. However, it seems that Nājī's feelings were more profound than those of ʿAlī Mahmūd Tāhā, since the latter in later years turned his thoughts to more sensual pleasures, whereas Nājī was more moderate. He devoted himself to the service of all kinds of people, whether he knew them or not, and applied his skill as a doctor to treating all sorts of sickness.

Nājī's poetry, then, shows evidence of an authentic talent and exalted status within the general lyrical trend and the entertaining narrative of emotion. It is poetry of great creativity, bursting with élan, liveliness, and innovation, and free of the trammels of artificiality and banality.

Jamāl al-dīn al-Ramādī. *Khalīl Mutrān shāʿir al-aqtār al-ʿArabiyya* (Cairo, Dār al-Maʿārif, n.d. [c. 1960]), pp. 325–28, 333–34†

Of all the poets of his generation Nājī was the one who came closest to fulfilling the spirit of the ideas which were disseminated by the group of romantic innovators in Egypt, and especially the Apollo Group. . . .

Nājī was the only poet who really appreciated the essence of romanticism
and dealt with it as an incessant stream or a link in a chain of innovative
movements that Europe had witnessed in society, science, and art from the
industrial revolution until World War I. . . . He may well have been the only
poet of his generation who read Eliot both as a poet and critic from the beginning of the 1940s. . . .

If we exclude from Nājī's collected poetry all the occasional verse, then
his poetry can be considered to be something completely new in modern Arabic poetry. The reason for this is that he may be the only poet of his generation
who refused to put some kind of mask over his poetry. Quite the contrary, he
made it his business to show it as it really was. Poets before him had either
emerged as clever companions at court, or reforming leaders, or as poets in a
state of distraction. Nājī preferred to appear without any veil or pretence
whatsoever. . . .

Nājī did not write his poetry first and then make us look at life through it.
He asked us instead to learn about life first in order to know his poetry well.
This helps to explain why it is that our affection for his writings begins after
we have become emotionally mature. Nājī's poetry emerges from life; that of
his colleagues comes to it from above.

Ahmad ʿAbd al-Muʿtī Hijāzī. Al-Ādāb. March,
1970, pp. 22–24†

In his justly celebrated poem "The Return" we find the religious imagery, the
desert, the journey, the nights and the wounded bird. In it Nājī skilfully uses
the old outworn classical convention, that of weeping over the desolate encampment of the beloved, but in a manner, typical of the great artist he is, in
which at his touch the dead convention springs to life again. It acquires immediate relevance and becomes an adequate medium for the expression of a thoroughly modern sensibility. This is done in a subtle fashion. In the first place,
although the poet returns to the place once inhabited by his beloved, it is not
the ruins of a deserted encampment in the desert. It is clearly a house in a city,
with a hall or a drawing room, a staircase and a door (in fact we do know that
it is a house situated in one of the main streets of Cairo). But the delineation
is left deliberately vague and no further details are given; we are only told
enough to make us see that the poet is writing about a real personal experience
and not merely engaged in a literary exercise in poetic imitation. Yet the total
situation of the poet, mournfully returning to the vacant site which had once
been occupied by his beloved, together with the use of the term talal (ruin),
ensures that in the mind of his reader an emotional charge is released, the
feelings aroused by the long-established tradition of nasib [erotic prelude]

brought into play. Secondly, the whole scene is internalized, for when we reach the last quatrain of the poem where the poet describes himself as "a wanderer, eternally exiled in the world of my grief" we realize that the ruins he talks about may not be an external reality so much as a vision in the poet's mind. This possibility makes the poem undeniably an expression of a modern sensibility. Thirdly, the poet's manner of evolving imagery is somewhat alien to the older tradition. For instance, that night should crouch like a camel is a traditional enough image, but it is not traditional to make the shades of night flit in the hall. Moreover, for the poet to feel the breath of Weariness/Despair filling the air or to see with his own eyes Decay weaving cobwebs with its hands, or to hear the footsteps of Time and the sound of Loneliness climbing the stairs, argues an unusual and a daring power of personification, too individualistic for the main body of the Arabic tradition.

> Mustafa Badawi. *A Critical Introduction to Modern Arabic Poetry* (Cambridge, England, Cambridge University Press, 1975), pp. 135–36

Nājī's main asset was his capacity to achieve a tenderness, a compassion and a personal touch unrivalled yet among his contemporaries. This was greatly helped by the melodiousness of his verse. A great lyricism is achieved which gives fluidity and music to his poetry.

Nājī's poetry, moreover, revolved mostly around his experience of love. Through this it released the current of feeling and arrived at great emotional veracity. His several poems of occasion (eulogies, congratulations, elegies, satire and other themes) can be regarded as remnants of traditionalism that had persisted in the poetic tradition. But they were not authentic representatives of Nājī's talent. In fact, his poetry, as [Muhammad] Mandūr agrees, was on the whole sincere and original, and one can dismiss these poems as mere versification outside the main stream of the poet's creativity. It was the liberation of the emotion of love and yearning for woman that gave Nājī his popularity. He had responded in his poetry to the suppressed emotions of the younger generation of the time, which was thirsty for love. His achievement, Mandūr asserts, was that he was able to make out of these current feelings a fine art. . . .

Nājī remains one of the cornerstones of modern Romanticism in Egypt. He simplified and modernized the language of poetry. He opened the way to emotional veracity and true experience, and enriched modern imagery. He also achieved a remarkable change of tone in poetry and, above all, he restored to Arabic love poetry a tenderness, a sustained devotion and a direct, uncomplicated, even humble approach unknown since the days of the bedouin Umayyad poets.

> Salmā al-Jayyūsī. *Trends and Movements in Modern Arabic Poetry* (Leiden, E. J. Brill, 1977), pp. 395–97

Nājī's literary legacy is a large one, but we will deal here only with his poetic output as seen in the four volumes of his *Collected Works: Behind the Clouds* (1934), *Cairo Nights* (1944), *In the Temple of Night* and *The Wounded Bird* (both 1953). If we try to discover the poet's attitudes through his poetry, we find that the literary experience can be explained on more than one semantic level; in fact it gives expression to a whole group of interlocking semantic and intellectual voices. . . .

Anyone who reads the poetry of Nājī—that great romantic—will soon discover that the entire collection consists of a single poem which is in essence "a prayer at the temple of love." As a result, the collected poetry turns into a set of variations on a single theme, a sad song sung over and over again to a beloved who has departed and to a beauty that is no more. Hope still haunts him, and anguish continues to jog his memory. The poet lives his artistic life creating poetry under such inspiration and giving form to his artistic experiences as he waits for what is lost to return. . . . Nājī's experience in poetry emerges as a perfect circle that, in spite of the number of poems he wrote, expresses just one intellectual point and then revolves around it: the poet has an idealized vision of love and the spiritual relationship with the beloved; he relishes intimate conversation with her apparition from afar and clings to her even if she turns him away, remains aloof, or abandons him.

Tāhā Wādī. *Jamāliyyāt al-qasīda al-muʿāsira* (Cairo, Dār
al-Maʿārif, 1982), pp. 184–86†

NUʿAYMA (or NAIMY), MĪKHĀʾĪL (1889–   )

LEBANON/UNITED STATES

Nuʿayma's "My Brother" is a nationalist poem composed toward the end of World War I or shortly afterward. It falls, then, into that category of literature called occasional poetry, about which there is frequent discussion as to whether it can be considered literature that will stand the test of time or not. When the particular circumstances surrounding its composition fade from view, will it too vanish into oblivion or will it stay with us? Indeed, if the latter is the case, what kind of remnant will it be? Something like a historical document gathering dust in archives, or a lasting work of literature that will live forever and continue to stir the hearts of men. . . .

In the first stanza we notice a unity that leads the reader toward its conclusion, thus producing a most satisfactory effect. Notice how the reader is led into the imagery in such a way as to participate with the author in the experience. When the nations of the West boast about their deeds, revere their dead, and honor their heroes, we should neither extol the victors nor feel any malicious glee toward the vanquished, since we have no part in either situation. . . . See how well the entire atmosphere is conveyed and how powerfully the poet leads up to it.

Thus, I the reader become a partner in humanity with "my brother"; we are close to each other. When I am near him, he can whisper to me, since I will still be able to hear him. His gentle voice can touch me in a direct and forceful way as he conveys his powerful feelings; he can do this because he is able to choose the appropriate wording that will make the maximum use of emotion.

Muhammad Mandūr. *Fī al-mīzān al-jadīd* (Cairo, Matbaʿa Nahdat Misr, n.d. [1944]), pp. 69–70†

The way Nuʿayma portrays the conditions of his own soul and the evil and good impulses that contend for it can only stem from a profound belief in the spiritual world. He is no materialist like Abū Mādī. In fact, Nuʿayma totally shuns materialism; one might even say that he does not believe in anything that could be called material. All material phenomena in life, as far as he is concerned, originate in the higher self. . . .

We have, then, a poet with his particular mystical dreams. This enables him to face the trials of life with a serene countenance. In fact, he even regards these trials as one of the necessities of life, which everyone has to learn to accept, just as they do the good things in life. He almost seems to be telling us that there is neither good nor evil, but simply life itself, just as the Creator of existence has planned it for us. We have to accept His will and His wishes. We are a part of His order, an order based on these two contrasting aspects. We should not accept one without the other. Life in general and our own total sense of it will not be fulfilled unless it shuttles between good and evil, joy and sorrow. . . .

One of the finest poems portraying the psychological tension he feels with regard to the spiritual path hidden deep inside him, which he is anxious to clear, is "The Wanderer," [in *Murmurs of the Eyelids*]. He begins by telling us that he is lost, far away, seared by the fires of his own life, hopes, and desires. The heavens have put a distance between him and them. Have his passions and the demands of his body prevailed, he wonders. Or does the victory belong to his thoughts and the doubts of his mind? Or could it be that his heart and its feelings have fallen short of the task? He is unable to answer these questions.

Shawqī Dayf. *Dirāsāt fī al-shiʿr al-ʿArabī al-muʿāsir* (Cairo, Dār al-Maʿārif, 1953; 2nd ed., 1959), pp. 222–23†

To Mīkhāʾīl Nuʿayma our society is desiccated and cruel. . . . a society with no feelings, one that suffocates everyone and kills all inventiveness. Nationalism, religion, principles, and ideals, none of these things can save man from being driven inexorably into the dry, cruel earth. In this society, man is not really man; there is no freedom and no struggle to survive. He is merely the ossified product of the society itself. This sense of desiccation we feel is amplified by the dry style the author uses, a rigid style that seems to be carved out of rock. There is no emotion to it, no fancy, no warmth. . . .

Life, as Nu'ayma puts it in the story "Notables" [in the collection of the same name], is just like a book known only from its title; to him, life's own title is desiccation. In this story, the desiccation takes the form of the sky holding back its rain at the proper time and then providing it in abundance when it is not wanted. . . . In the story "Sattūt's Struggle" we see another manifestation of this dryness in that Sattūt had not been blessed with any children (to quote the story) and had seen her husband taken from her after only ten years of marriage. . . .

The title story is undoubtedly the most accomplished and mature of the stories in *Notables*. Indeed, it may well be one of the best modern Arabic short stories altogether. . . .

I do have two criticisms of this collection. The first is that some of the stories lack the necessary level of artistic maturity one expects, as well as a sense of the unity of time, which is so essential to any short story. However, the author does compensate somewhat for this latter flaw through the unity of the predominant emotion. My second criticism is that some of the stories seem to range beyond what is probable in the realm of general relationships between human beings, as for example in the stories "Truthful" and "A Wayfarer."

Jūrj Tarābīshī. Al-Ādāb. March, 1957, pp. 60–62†

Mīkhā'īl Nu'ayma seems to have taken upon himself for some time now to add a new work of his own each year to the library of works of modern Arabic literature, a work in which he once again emphasizes that particular existential and contemplative quality that has become so much the hallmark of his literary works and his thought. This hallmark numbers among its characteristics a humanist tendency that wavers between realism and beatific vision and a poetic style that can display all the liveliness of the Arabic language as well as its vigorous and expressive momentum. All the author's intellectual and emotional features are evident through his use of this language.

This new work, *Marginalia*, carries a certain external meaning through its title and has a new artistic form. But even so, it does not in any way move outside the general frameworks of ideas we have come to find in the other works of Nu'ayma. This particular work has a general framework that contains significant philosophical thoughts, ideas, and notions, which the author proceeds to review in various guises and through a number of portraits. . . .

I do not think that the narrative form the author has chosen to use for his ideas and notions in this work can really be considered as the short story. The pieces in the collection are not short stories in the genuine artistic sense of the word, but rather narrations of events in which intellectual concerns predominate and determine the format most suitable to the purpose at hand. That is to say, the artistic purpose is secondary; in the author's view its only real purpose is to make it easier to convey his ideas. . . .

It has to be admitted that some of the stories in this collection, such as "The Village Philosopher" and "Professor," simply do not match the intellectual or artistic standards of the other stories. Both of them involve superficial and hackneyed topics, in addition to which they both treat their subject in an extremely direct manner more akin to that of a mere report. There is no poetic imagery, no intellectual or philosophical dimension in either of these two examples from this collection.

Husayn Muruwwa. *Dirāsāt naqdiyya fī daw' al-manhaj al-wāqi'ī* (Beirut, Maktabat al-Ma'ārif, 1961), pp. 47, 55–56†

Naimy's masterpiece in *Once Upon a Time* is undoubtedly "Her New Year," written in 1914. . . .

The story as a whole does not simply tell about characters and things; it attempts to bring them alive for the reader. Any real attempt to summarise it therefore cannot stop short of rewriting it. Abu Nāssīf is not characterised in terms of what he says or does but in terms of how he actually lives, his social position, his world and particularly his crisis. He is characterised from the inside. So is the midwife, greatly perturbed as to how to face Abu Nāssīf with the evil news. Even 'Ayrūn is not defined in terms of exterior physical dimensions, but through what it psychologically means to living people in terms of delicious wine, beautiful maidens, generous cows and awe-inspiring Shaikh.

In "Her New Year," as in the rest of his short stories in *Once Upon a Time*, Naimy can be described as a realist: but a realist in the nineteenth century Russian sense. He is not only interested in reflecting what people actually do or say but mainly in bringing alive the psychological shades and implications beneath people's deeds and utterances. This is how in Naimy's stories, as in those of his Russian teachers, particularly Chekhov, Dostoyevsky and Gogol, we are so introduced to the character's intimate inner self that we are no longer capable, though horrified by the deeds, of hating the doers. It is always when we judge the doer by the deed that we are made to hate him, but once the deed is seen in its primordial stirring in the inner selves of people who are as basically human as we are, we are instantly disarmed of hatred and left in a position where we are either to pity or to laugh, or even to "smile through tears."

This type of realism accounts much for the success of *Once Upon a Time* in general and of "Her New Year" in particular. Through it, as can be seen, Naimy is enabled, like any successful artist, to instruct without teaching, to

moralise without preaching, and to be infinitely human without sentimentalism.

Nadim Naimy. *Mikhail Naimy: An Introduction* (Beirut,
American University in Beirut, 1967), pp. 153, 155–56

With his play *Job*, Nuʿayma is coming to market in much the same way as a
village peddler who brings only one kind of produce each year; sometimes it
may be sour, while at others it may be more sweet, but it always comes from
the same place. . . . *Job*, then, appears on the market as an extension of everything Nuʿayma has written up until now. At first glance, we can detect the
hero of this play in his various stories. In "Memoirs of the Man with the Pitted
Face," the major character is just like Job, yearning to be set free, to be liberated from the stranglehold of the earth. . . .

This play is so written that it almost does not merit the designation
"play." There is nothing particularly connected with the dramatic medium
about it. The lengthy pauses and four "acts" are used by the author to expound
on his belief in the unity of life and to spread the good word to mankind trium-
phant in the person of Job. For Nuʿayma in this play, the ideas are the meat of
the whole work, and not the actions. The actions are used merely to move the
reader from one concept to another. In fact, in one of the acts, Job does not
move at all; this lack of action really paralyzes the play and makes it very dull.
While this play shares with Greek tragedy the idea of the *deus ex machina*,
whereby the gods involve themselves and impose their will on mankind in
some mysterious way, it is clear in both *Job* and Greek tragedy that man is
very much the loser. It is precisely this atmosphere that elicits respect for the
characters in the play. . . .

The style in this play is simple and excellent; there is no artificiality to
the language as it flows along with the soul of one immersed in the heady spiritual experience of mysticism. The ideas that emerge are a faithful blending of
those pulsating within Nuʿayma himself, but they are merely a further mulling
over of what he has written about many times before.

ʿUmar Shiblī. *Al-Ādāb*. Oct., 1967, pp. 55, 57†

Nuʿayma turned his back on the traditional subjects of classical poetry: there
is no panegyric, no eulogy or self-praise in his poetry. Instead we find poems
expressing the poet's innermost thoughts and feelings, and more specifically
those related to his spiritual life. In this respect Nuʿayma's verse is purely subjective. Significantly enough it was his reading of the work of the Russian Romantic poet Lermontov (who was heavily influenced by western Romanticism
and especially by Byron) which aroused in him an overwhelming desire to
compose poetry. Yet in Nuʿayma poetry there is little turbulence or vehemence of passion, which is not the same thing as saying that it is devoid of
feeling. On the contrary, there is a strange and almost other-worldly serenity

in his best poems, unmatched elsewhere. Even when he writes about the conflict between good and evil (as, for instance, in his poems "Good and Evil" or "The Conflict," which he wrote when he was involved in a passionate love affair with a married American woman), the tone of the writing is muted and low: there is no feeling of conflict, but an account of conflict given by someone who has made up his mind about the universe and whose vision of life remains undisturbed. When he writes about "Autumn Leaves" we do not find the "wildness" of the "West Wind." It is not an accident that one of his best-known nature poems is about a frozen river. The vehemence and aggressiveness of the critic, the author of *The Sieve*, are totally absent from his poetry. Instead there are quiet meditations on the passing or the coming year ("From Time's Book"), the gentle nostalgia of the poet for his childhood and for his native village ("The Echo of Bells"), and a simple, but poignant devotional feeling that runs through most of his poems (as in, for instance, "Prayers" and "The Lost Traveller"). Indeed, like the rest of the *Mahjar* romantics, Nuʿayma raises the heart above the head, imagination above reason: he is alarmed when he finds that his heart is not capable of feeling (as for instance in "The Frozen River") and rejoices when it is awake once more ("The Heart Was Awakened"), but compared with other romantics like Abū Shabaka, Shabbī or Abū Mādī, Nuʿayma's feelings, though deep, never reach the point of overflowing.

Mustafa Badawi. *A Critical Introduction to Modern Arabic Poetry* (Cambridge, England, Cambridge University Press, 1975), pp. 187–88

Nuʿayma's technique of story-telling bears witness to his acquaintance with prerevolutionary Russian prose. His early stories have a more balanced construction than the firstlings in fiction of the great authors of his time, such as Mahmūd Taymūr and Tāhā Husayn. The latter frequently leave the main track of their stories and novels to indulge in some side-line expositions which may or may not have anything to do with the story as such. Nuʿayma's stories develop along a straight line, and extraneous matter is not allowed to slip in. The *dénouement* is prepared for in the preceding scenes, but here Nuʿayma does not always escape from being a little over-explicit in the preparation. When a person is on the verge of committing suicide, or is to die through an accident, invariably a number of references to death and dying precede the fatal act. . . .

Nuʿayma has a tendency to account for everything that happens in his stories. Nothing takes place without a perhaps over-explicit preparation. In some stories this has led to curious consequences. The shepherd [in "The Bancarolia," i.e., the baccalaureate], e.g., gathers a handful of the excrement of his sheep after he has sold the herd to finance his son's studies in America. Eight years later, the son, who has finished his studies and who has earned his living for a few years, finds himself out of a job. The father meets his request for financial support with part of the eight-year-old dung; the rest of the excrement is plastered over the baccalaureate diploma. . . .

The language used in Nuʿayma's writings is a modern variant of the classical Arabic language. Rhymed prose phrases, still popular in the first decades of the twentieth century, are almost absent, as are other archaisms. The colloquial language is limited to isolated words. This, however, has not always been the case. In the original versions of the early stories, as far as can be established, Nuʿayma made use of colloquial language for the dialogues in the same way as Haykal did in his *Zaynab*. Nuʿayma, however, limited the use of the colloquial to illiterate persons, whereas literate persons were given the speech of literary language, regardless of their interlocutors. The hybrid character of this solution may have caused Nuʿayma to rephrase the dialect clauses in a language more consistent with that of the other parts of the stories. The play *Fathers and Sons* escaped this fate, and the introduction, in which Nuʿayma discusses the problems and adduces arguments for his option, has remained unchanged. Nuʿayma's knowledge of, and admiration for, Russian literature until 1912 may have influenced him in his choice of a common and simple language.

C. Nijland. *Mīkhāʾīl Nuʿaymah, Promotor* [sic] *of the
Arabic Literary Revival* (Istanbul, Netherlands Historical-
Archeological Institute, 1975), pp. 59–61, 63

Nuʿayma's poetry was new. The novelty was both in the content and in the technique. His thematic adventures, however, were mostly of the meditative kind, saved only by an ardour of emotion which proves an authentic spiritual tendency. All his poems, except "My Brother" were of the directly subjective type expressing the poet's inner personal experience, spiritual and emotional. "My Brother" could well belong to the poetry of the 'fifties, with its social consciousness expressed through the personal consciousness of the poet. It is important to note Nuʿayma's tendency to write about a true experience, an element lacking in the poetry of the neo-Classicists, including much of Mutrān's.

The authenticity of his meditative basis is also significant when set alongside similar poetry of the North Mahjar. Nuʿayma's influence on his fellow writers was considerable, although his own spiritual attitude was in turn enriched by Gibrān's pervasive influence. His spiritual themes, which steadily increased in their meditative attitude until they gave mystical expression to his beliefs, were accepted by the Arab world without much effort, despite their novelty. Nuʿayma was writing his poetry during one of the most exciting periods in modern Arab literary history, when it was possible to impose on the reading public a great variety of themes, as long as they did not touch the basic dogma of religion, the sanctity of the heritage or the jealously guarded code of honour. The first four decades of the century are marked by a rare freedom to experiment, by what can be termed an "individual sensibility."

The main change achieved by Nuʿayma through his poetry was a change in the poetic tone. The achievement of this new, subdued tone was a real victory for poetry. The great resonance of the neo-Classical poetry has gone. Even Gibrān's passionate rhetoricism seems pompous and pretentious compared with the gentle and rather sad tones of Nuʿayma's poetry which flows like the ripples of a gentle stream, which three decades later was to move M. Mandūr, Egypt's foremost critic in the 'forties. Nuʿayma confirmed Gibrān's adoption of Nature as an object of spiritual love and spiritual experience. His spirit merged in it with awe and wonder, finding it evocative of emotions and spiritual yearnings.

Salmā al-Jayyūsī. Trends and Movements in Modern Arabic
Poetry (Leiden, E. J. Brill, 1977), pp. 118–19

QABBĀNĪ, NIZĀR (1923–   )

SYRIA

All the poetry of Qabbānī that we have read so far shows an excellent poetic sense; the imagination is daring, the use of symbols is creative, and there is to it a lilting musical quality that is fascinating. All these refined characteristics we find fused into the various conceits concerning women, fused in a remarkable and engaging fashion.

Whatever may be the inclinations of this poet at the moment, there is absolutely no doubt in my mind that his sense of nationalism, humanism, and the long-established patriotic feelings of his famous family will make themselves evident in his poetry sometime in the future when age and experience have both afforded him a little more maturity. The poetry he is writing at the moment is not concerned merely with beauty in the abstract. The way he writes about the beauty of women in his poetry represents an unusual turn to a natural source of inspiration that tends to be avoided in less developed societies because of their isolation and the veil. When the poet sings of the beauty of nature, with its different colors and images, his work displays a splendid artistic richness. . . .

We have already acknowledged that Qabbānī's poetry shows a delicate artistry that makes clear his genuine excellence as a poet and his authenticity as a writer. Even so, we have to point out that it seems extremely unlikely to us that his poetry will be read in every household as long as his own connection with the life we lead, indeed the life to which we all aspire, is so limited.

Ahmad Zakī Abū Shādī. Qadāyā al-shiʿr al-muʿāsir (Cairo,
Al-Sharika al-ʿArabiyya li-al-Tibāʿa wa-al-Nashr, n.d.
[1959?]), pp. 131–32, 136†

From time to time Nizār attempts to rid himself of the restraints of realism and to rebel against the tenets of description that are forever talking about what we comprehend, see, and feel, so that he can turn to other dimensions which are shrouded in darkness and which are to be experienced rather than understood, envisaged rather than seen, and touched by our intuitions rather than our senses. In the poem "River of Sorrows" he tries to talk about the hopelessnes and misery of life and the deplorable tyranny of fate. . . . I should quickly point out that the majority of poems in his latest collection, *Darling*, show a fixation with the idea of fidelity. It is as if they all flow from some secret wound inside himself, or as if the force of his instinctive emotions has died down somewhat; the things that in the past would rattle his nerves do not disturb him now, and his horizon has cleared to reveal a fierce sense of void and pointlessness, a painful feeling that things have run away from him and done a rapid *volte face*. . . .

In the final analysis, the problem with Nizār Qabbānī is not that he lacks talent; he is indeed a talented poet. However, he is also limited and artistically underdeveloped. He does not possess the education and culture required of a modern poet. Nor does he have any really profound experience of the realities of existence, since there is in him no definitive bond to such realities, something that in the mind of the true artist links art with the destiny of the human race. If there were such a bond he could raise his efforts from the level of mere coincidentals to an all-inclusive totality, his style from that of mere simile to true symbolism, and from an improvised, accidental unity in the line to a complete organic unity that grows and comes to fruition from within the poem itself.

Īliyyā al-Hāwī. *Al-Ādāb.* Jan., 1962, pp. 49, 55†

From the time of his first collection, *The Brunette Told Me*, the voice of man has always been present in the works of Nizār, in his mentality, his consciousness, and his hidden self (as Professor Salāma Mūsā would put it). But that voice was continually strangled. The poet was going through a raging adolescence and feeling all its forceful passions. His own intellectual stance had not yet been defined or crystallized. He was living his life as a person who was open to women in a manner that showed a fierce and passionate emotion. Even so, the poet was not prepared to accept all women; he was prepared to reject certain women of different kinds. This rejection in the poet was to develop as time went on. He moved from a purely personal approach to the question to a more objective one. From a colorless song lost within the vast expanse of what may be termed Qabbānī's "womanizing" poems we can see a development toward a song with a specific color of its own; it is more emotional and human, it shows a process of blending the self and the object, the private and public. Even though the number of such poems is extremely small, they do exist. . . .

In my view, the vast majority of the poems in Nizār Qabbānī's first four collections (*The Brunette Told Me, Childhood of a Breast, Samba,* and *You Are Mine*) are merely segments of one long poem, or perhaps chapters in Nizār's long verse epic on the subject of women. There hardly seems to be any difference between one poem and the next. If there is a difference, it is very insignificant and is certainly not large enough to bear close scrutiny. The music and the words may change somewhat, but the spirit remains one and the same.

Jalīl Kamāl al-dīn. Al-Shiʿr al-ʿArabī al-hadīth (Beirut, Dār al-ʿIlm li-al-Malāyīn, 1964), pp. 310, 366†

If the important thing is for poetry to stay with us while the poets themselves die, then Nizār Qabbānī will certainly occupy a large number of pages in the history of Arabic poetry during the last twenty years. If, on the other hand, it is the poets who should remain with us, then he will take up only a few pages indeed. As it is, the most important thing is surely that the poetry should survive. To be fair to Qabbānī, we should point out that, when he first unsheathed his poetic sword to face the giants who were seated on the thrones of literary reaction in the Arab world, his weapon was indeed small and kept snapping in two. He would simply unsheathe another one from his new lexicon of words and proceed to beat the conservative face of Damascus with it, knocking off as he went along the tops of the hubble-bubbles in all the cafés of its ancient quarters. But, as time went on, this vocabulary of his became rather like ammunition for an obsolete weapon, one that was no longer suitable for the age of modern poetry. The era had seen an expansion, but the poet himself had not changed.

Between Qabbānī's first collection, *The Brunette Told Me* (1944), and his latest, *Drawing with Words* (1966), the poet has spent twenty-three years without altering a single word from the lexicon he has been carrying around for so long, nor has he made any changes in the topics and poetic styles for which he is generally known. He now finds himself beset by the real poetic revolution, with new poets and new words with which his lexicon is unfamiliar. And its swords are longer and more effective than his ancient tiny weapon.

Nizār Qabbānī has tried to stop the clock at the things he came to know in his youth. . . . He has stood there waiting for women to come and go without realizing that time has escaped from his clutches and the revolution he was fostering has now been taken over by others who have achieved new and uncharted regions of excellence and poetic creativity.

Riyāḍ Najīb al-Rayyis. Shiʿr. Winter/Spring, 1967, pp. 159–60†

Before the setback of 1967 Nizār Qabbānī was a famous poet who had acquired a large number of admirers; at the same time, he was also rejected by a fair number of cultured people in his own country. Since the setback Nizār has astonished both admirers and detractors alike on two occasions.

The first of these is the complete reversal in his poetry, from the point of view of both topic and depth of vision. Before the setback, his subject matter revolved entirely around women, and not just women, but women with an absolute, ideal beauty. . . . After the setback, there is a total collapse of his old world; his earlier voice disappears, and he discards his Don Juan guise. He reappears as a moralist. Qabbānī again becomes a controversial figure, but this time the point is not to analyze his poetry but to determine whether the homiletic posture of the moralist he has now adopted is a legitimate one or not. . . . All the row over this particular issue has served to obscure any discussion of the poet's attitude and of his new voice, as seen in poems such as "Marginalia on the Notebook of the Setback," "The Actors," "Interrogation," "Fath," "To the Poets of the Occupied Territories," and "Jerusalem."

In parts of "Fath" and "Jerusalem," and also in a poem like "Granada," composed before the setback, Qabbānī succeeds in achieving an organic fusion of the voices of the poet and the moralist. He has been able to open up to reality and achieve a union with it without appearing to be a judge and preacher. Instead, he has relied on suggestion, that being the poet's major method and tool. In the poem "Diaries of a Woman Who Could Not Care Less," he tries to achieve this same fusion in an area where he can unleash his greatest abilities. He wants to be poet and revolutionary at one and the same time, not a poet at one moment and a preacher the next. He wants to achieve a peace between the illusory, cartoonish, superficial world in which he was living before June 1967 and the world after that setback.

'Abd al-Muhsin Tāhā Badr. Al-Ādāb. Feb.,
1969, pp. 11–13†

It is an undeniable fact that Qabbānī's love poems are repetitious, in the sense that the themes are fairly limited. The poet's artistic talent is only deployed in the variations. This stress on variations at the expense of themes, if judged by Western critical values and artistic standards, may be branded as lacking in poetic skill or devoid of artistic imagination. But these Western critics should always keep in mind that Nizār Qabbānī, although influenced and inspired by Western culture and despite his vociferous preachings in its favor, is first and foremost an *Arab* poet of Near Eastern culture and Near Eastern background, addressing himself to an *Arab* audience imbued with Near Eastern values and artistic standards. The application of foreign standard of literary criticism, be they Western or otherwise, as criteria for judging Qabbānī's poetic skill or effectiveness, should be handled with care because they are bound to be misleading.

Qabbānī's excellence, then, lies in his manner of dealing with the variations on his theme. This is where his originality lies and where he displays the qualities of a gifted and delicate poet. His style is easy and flowing. His artistic ideal is that "art should lift up the veil from tragedy without seeking solutions." Qabbānī touches upon his subject with the tenderness and delicacy of a butterfly. He seems more like a painter using his brush than a poet his pen. He has aptly entitled one of his poetic collections *Drawing with Words* (1966). Qabbānī *paints* a scene, seeking neither cause nor effect. Like Wordsworth, he wants to transmit his feelings to the heart of the reader as an immediate excitement.

Arieh Loya. Muslim World. Jan., 1973, p. 51

When I read Qabbānī's poem "Bread, Hashish, and Moon" in 1954 for the first time, I was struck by the new direction it was taking and by the abstract expressions. . . . However, in general I was not attracted either intellectually or psychologically by Qabbānī's early poetry. In fact, I left him to wander on his own and to become engrossed in his own particular journeys; as Amīn al-Rīhānī would put it, "he had said his word and then left." All this does not imply that I ignored his poem "Does He Think?" when it appeared, nor did I fail to see the poem "Baghdad" and in fact analyze and assess it at the time of the Baghdad festival in 1962.

In the wake of the setback of 1967, I noticed, as did everyone else, that Qabbānī changed his posture from one of concern with women, sex, and beauty to an intense concern with laying bare political realities, with ascribing blame where it was due, and with self-criticism. This significant change was represented by his poems "Marginalia on the Notebook of the Setback" and then by the poem "The Actors" and others that came after; they were all symptoms of an intense reaction. . . .

Nizār Qabbānī does not "belong" to any particular poetic school; he does not feel that such a posture affords him a way to practice freedom of thought and rejection of all kinds of classicism and prejudice. Thus his visions on every issue and event are his own. He has his own personal theory whereby he elucidates whatever emotions and ideas may be stirring inside him. In all this, man alone is the pivot and focus of his concern. . . .

Qabbānī is clearly creative in his use of ideas and concepts, and an innovator in his style and technique. A concern with truth is the basis of his art; continual discovery is the focus of his attention. He has thus been able to derive new concepts from well-trodden paths, ideas that had been left there on the ground, as it were—living concepts, pulsating with life. . . . This is a sign of genuine art.

Wahīd al-dīn Bahā' al-dīn. Al-Adīb. June,
1974, pp. 16, 18†

Qabbānī had attained enormous popularity across the whole Arab world through his love poetry, in which he expressed his amorous feelings in a sensuous and elegant vocabulary, of great simplicity and immediate appeal. His collections of poems, which are numerous, often ran into six or seven impressions. From the date of publication of his earliest volume in 1944, until 1955, love and woman remained his main themes, although his attitude to woman gradually changed. In the first volume, it was one of sexual starvation (which according to the poet was typical of the whole of his generation), a mode heavily influenced by the Abū Shabaka of *The Serpents of Paradise* and by the growing gap between the poet's readings in Baudelaire, Rimbaud and Verlaine and his own experience of conservative Damascus society. With his departure for Cairo, where he worked in the diplomatic service (1945–48) and was exposed to the sophisticated social life of diplomats, he began to develop a more "aesthetic" interest in women, his crude sensuality giving place to civilized and refined eroticism which marks some of the poems in his second and third volumes, where he describes in loving detail society women with their dress, jewels and perfume. His subsequent service in London deepened his experience and sharpened his awareness of the complexity of human relationships. A note of melancholy begins to creep into his verse, but even in his mature period love and women remained his primary concern. He would write a poem such as "Her Birthday" [in the collection *Poems*] where the poet's sole problem upon receiving a card from his mistress informing him of her birthday was what present to give her. From this type of verse which, despite its elegance of phrase in the original Arabic, suffers from a limited range and a narrow sensibility that borders on the sentimental and adolescent, Qabbānī suddenly moves on to a more responsible and adult poetry which reveals real concern with social and political issues, such as his outspoken criticism in his "Bread, Hashish and Moon" of an Arab society that lives in daydreams and a world of pleasant sensations invoked by drugs. . . .

> Mustafa Badawi. *A Critical Introduction to Modern Arabic Poetry* (Cambridge, England, Cambridge University Press, 1975), pp. 221–22

QĀSIM, 'ABD AL-HAKĪM (1935–   )

EGYPT

In his short story "The Journey" 'Abd al-Hakīm Qāsim describes a country woman who is in the habit of traveling to the nearby city whenever she needs something she can get only there and whenever she feels a yearning to visit the shrine of Al-Sayyid Badawī, the "saint of God." From sunrise to sunset, this woman, who is unnamed in the story, goes through the experience of this journey. At dawn and just before getting on the train she sees her husband in an entirely new light; after all, she is going on a journey. . . .

In this story, life itself is the main character. The author shows us the psychological impact on the woman of the journey, with all its unfamiliarity, and depicts her exposure to the wiles and wickedness of the world. When her yearnings get the better of her, this woman yields to the temptation to travel. It is the connection between the woman and the unfamiliar outside world that attracts 'Abd al-Hakīm's attention, and within that connection it is the moment of unfamiliarity on which he focuses, even though it may only last for a second in the life of the individual. The relationship of the individual to the external world is the general theme of 'Abd al-Hakīm's experience, and within that framework, the impact of that relationship on the psychological makeup of the individual. The external world is forever impinging on the individual, attacking him, but he does not run away. Instead he searches for some refuge where he can renew his strength in order to come back again, whenever the need or the longing is felt again or when the passions begin to stir. . . .

'Abd al-Hakīm realizes that the basic problem for the realist artist in our age—and in our society as well—is the question of the search for a bridge between the individual and the world. If the "collective revolution" was for previous realists the way to solve the problem of the freedom of the community (that being a revolution achieved outside the individual), then the search for the identity of the individual or his specific "individuality" is the way to confirm that the humanity of the revolution itself is as complete as possible. Realism in our age is as much concerned with the individual as it is with the community. It is searching for a way to bring about a meeting of the two, even though that meeting may involve a struggle before it is achieved.

Sāmī Khashaba. Al-Ādāb. Oct., 1965, pp. 76–77†

The novel *The Seven Days of Man*, by the young writer 'Abd al-Hakīm Qāsim, presents a contemporary view of the village. The most important thing about this view may be the fusion of self and subject. The author in this work does not impose some external problem on the village—that is, some personal problem that has nothing to do with the village itself. The village is not turned into the unfortunate vehicle for some intellectual concept or a mere tool for the propagation of some idea or other. The author tries to view the village faithfully, as it really is, and to probe its inner secrets.

In his novel he is no stranger on a visit looking from the sidelines and maintaining his neutrality. Nor is he a judge handing down verdicts of innocence and guilt. He belongs to the village world and is a part of it, irretrievably linked to everything that goes on there. He does not survey it from on high or look down from an ivory tower. We cannot even use the normal terminology and say that he sympathizes with the village world, since he does even more than that by actually belonging to it and being part of it.

Because he sees the village on the village level, he does not make legendary heroes, people who can perform miracles, out of the men who live there, nor does he regard them as mere samples to be examined, people sick in mind and body, exemplars of poverty, ignorance, and disease. He simply sees them as they are, loving them all the while because he cannot separate himself from them. Even so, his love for them does not lead him to picture things in bright glowing colors. He endeavors to deal with them as they are, with all their faults and qualities.

From his point of view, the village people love, dream, desire, and complain. And, since he wants to portray them as they are, he does not apply a static vision to the village but sees it as a developing world. Since he wants his picture of the village to be realistic, he does not make the description one-sided, a mere political view, a struggle with the authorities in the light of which all the other facets of life in the village dwindle away to nothing. He wants to show the village from all angles, and so he does not choose a period when passions are roused to a fury and people are struggling and resisting authority, a backdrop against which the life of ordinary people fades away forever. He chooses instead a quiescent time when the village is leading a normal and regular existence with no inflamed passions and no excitement. But in spite of the superficial normality, life is still full of vigor and richness. ʿAbd al-Hakīm Qāsim's view of the village has as its aim to observe the process of change hidden beneath the surface normality of village life. He observes the way the details of village life operate and fuse together so as to form a special world with its own particular stamp: special values and fixed patterns of behavior and of economic and social relationships. He continues to observe this microcosm as it is subjected to the process of change when the light surrounding this little universe begins to dim and weakness begins to show in the links binding it all together. After this begins the gradual process of the disintegration and collapse of this world.

Since the author's view is so profound and authentic, he does not subject his world to any crushing blows or sudden, dramatic convulsions that would make it lose its equilibrium in an unexpected and unjustifiable fashion. The collapse of this old world and the emergence of the new world happen as the result of changes that gradually build up until they achieve the desired transformation.

ʿAbd al-Muhsin Tāhā Badr. Al-Riwāʾī wa-al-ard (Cairo,
Dār al-Maʿārif, 1971), pp. 189–90†

In the novel *The Seven Days of Man*, the "seven days" follow one another, fuse together, and reach a climax when "Man" achieves the height of his emotional involvement [at a festival of a Muslim "saint"] in the chapter "The Great Night." Next morning comes "The Farewell," and then he finishes his days or else is left by time on "The Road," a corpse abandoned without mercy. If this is the external structure of ʿAbd al-Hakīm Qāsim's novel, the internal structure shows us the different levels in the "days of Man."

In spite of the sequential movement made clear by the seven chapter titles, the story is not narrated as a sequence of events that proceeds from one chapter to the next. It is based on the element of selected illustrations of repeated events, regular routines, formal scenes, and fixed expressions and litanies. It is through this technique of choosing motifs to illustrate these cyclical occurences that the continuity and the temporal dimension in the journey of the "seven days" becomes clear.

This temporal dimension covered within these "seven days" also incorporates the psychological development in time of the boy ʿAbd al-ʿAzīz. This begins with the initial stirrings of his consciousness as a small, affectionate creature crouching alongside his father, Al-Ḥājj Karīm, and takes us through to the accomplishment of his own self-awareness and his escape from the vortex of the "seven days" and from the world of Al-Ḥājj Karīm and his dervish mystics. . . . It is the development of ʿAbd al-ʿAzīz's awareness that embodies the movement and action of time in the end. Without that we cannot appreciate the cyclical movement that keeps on repeating itself without any essential change.

Nājī Najīb. *Al-Ādāb*. Oct., 1972, p. 65†

[In *The Seven Days of Man*] Qāsim conveys the process of change from the peasant ways of life, established from time immemorial, to the values and attitudes of those with a modern education through the person of ʿAbd al-ʿAzīz, who has autobiographical elements: beginning by accepting the values for which his father stands without question, he ends by seeing the peasants from outside, as town-dwellers see them. The theme of change from the traditional to the modern is by now a well-worn one in Egyptian literature; in particular, *The Trilogy* of Najīb Mahfūz has treated it, and Qāsim can be said to complement that work by describing the process in its rural setting. . . .

What is interesting is the way in which the author sees peasant life as almost unconnected with other aspects of the country; except for the saint's birthday and the visit of the shaikh to the village it might be a self-contained unit, for which the government does very little except provide education. Clearly the novel is set in the period after 1952, since there are references to Cooperative Associations and feudalism and to international politicians such as Khrushchev, but the relationship between the peasants and the administration has not changed basically since the 1930's and the situation which Tawfīq al-Hakīm describes in *Diary of a Public Prosecutor*. Qāsim himself holds the view that there has not been a radical change in Egypt since the revolution, because the prerequisites for this, a realistic appraisal of the country's situation and a recognition that reform must take place from within, are not present. There has been a tendency to entrust decisions to individuals, and the masses have not been involved in constructing a new society. The first step is for Egyptians to accept their past and the people from whom they come, and to remember them when they set about the task of rebuilding their country.

With *The Seven Days of Man* the author has made an important contribution to this self-critical approach which he advocates; other writers have described the peasants with sympathy from outside, but he has gone further in portraying the way they see themselves and the conflicts suffered by one of them who comes to see his people as an outsider, and who can appreciate the changes which are taking place in their beliefs and attitudes.

Hilary Kilpatrick. *The Modern Egyptian Novel* (London,
Ithaca Press, 1974), pp. 141, 147

AL-QĀSIM, SAMĪH (1939–   )

PALESTINE

The emergence of Samīh al-Qāsim as a poet of the Druze community in Israel was an event of major significance. He is very prolific, and in his poetry we find him adhering to a clear and explicit position: he believes that Palestine is Arab territory and totally rejects the Israeli occupation of it. If you read the numerous works of poets in the occupied territories, you will find that Samīh al-Qāsim stands in the forefront in the way he gives expression to anger and revolution. By way of example, we find in the poetry of his friend and fellow freedom-fighter Mahmūd Darwīsh a certain tendency to live in the future as he sees it and believes in it. With his own feelings and imaginative gifts he can transcend all the circumstances, difficulties, griefs, and sufferings of the present in order to focus his attention on the future of Arab Palestine, one he envisages to be full of dreams of freedom and released from all chains and difficulties. Samīh al-Qāsim, on the other hand, adopts a quite different posture. He sees all the trials and difficulties; he can see the tragedy that has beset the Arab people and their land, and his anger bursts out in the form of fiery, violent poetry.

If we can call Mahmūd Darwīsh the poet of revolutionary optimism, then the nearest we can come to a definition of Samīh al-Qāsim is to say that he is the poet of revolutionary anger. His poetry is full of wrath; defiance spreads its roots through every line he writes, and a fire burns continually in every letter. He is a raging storm blowing on the grim Palestinian reality, wanting to demolish everything in front of him in order to bring some justice back into life after it has become full of oppression and tragedy.

Rajā' al-Naqqāsh. *Udabā' mu'āsirūn* (Cairo, Al-Maktaba
al-Anglo-Misriyya, 1968), p. 266†

Like [Mahmūd] Darwīsh, Samīh Qāsim tells the story of his homeland and his people forcefully. He exalts Arabism, describes the conditions in Palestine, and decries injustice. Unlike Darwīsh, who was expelled from his village and forced to become an "internal" refugee, Qāsim has never had this experience, but his Druze background has placed a special emphasis on at least two prominent themes in his poetry. Qāsim has attempted to demonstrate that, in spite of the special position in which the Israeli government has placed its Druze minority, and the special privileges given to them for cooperating with the authorities, they are still part of the Arab nation. Hence one notices in Qāsim's poetry an almost continual reassurance of his commitment to the Arab cause and a categorical rejection of any possible compromise. However, the influence of this background by no means tarnishes the sincerity of his resistance to the official policies of the state. This theme is central to his poetry.

Qāsim's poetry also hammers on another chronic difficulty of the Arabs, forced unemployment. Economic pressure is exercised by the military government as a punitive device against those who speak or write against the regime. This intimidation for political reasons is most effective against teachers and civil servants, as teaching is the major employment of the Arab intelligentsia. Samīh Qāsim himself was a public school teacher who was dismissed for political reasons. His poetry is therefore a testimony to his on-going commitment. . . .

In response to pressures to relinquish his struggle, Qāsim renews his determination. In speaking to those who have given up the struggle as futile, he invokes their memories, their courage, and his hope for eventual justice. To those Jews who pressure him to abandon his course, he invokes the commandment of love, which is forcefully illustrated in a dialogue between two Israelis—an Arab and a Jew. . . . In his prayerful moods, one senses a feeling almost of resignation, as if the poet has lost hope in man's justice toward his fellow man.

Emile Nakhleh. *Arab World*. Feb., 1970, pp. 34, 36

Anyone who reads Samīh al-Qāsim's collections of poetry comes to feel that he is a candid poet who never hides his own commitment and his views on religion and politics in abstruse verbiage. With his own broad horizons he tries to avoid falling into the snare of a single, enclosed experience and to go beyond that to different themes, even though they may have a firm tie to the concept of poetry of resistance in their overall nature. . . .

His first collection, *Songs of the Alleys*, contains two exceptional poems, "Sound of Lost Paradise" and "Antigone." The first has an air of obscurity and vagueness about it; if it were not for the title of the poem, you would have no idea what sound the poet was talking about. Perhaps it is the sound of old memories, or else of loved ones who have passed away. . . . The beauty of this particular poem does not, of course, reside solely in the poet's use of the kind of phrases the romantics may have used to excess: night, stars, winds, birds, and clouds. Rather it is the poetic image the poet has fashioned out of these words. He is keen for the particular image to remain surrounded by a misty and undefined obscurity. For that reason there is no need for melody and song; it is just a medley of numerous open-hearted beings whose nature is to expand, to move, and to be able to arouse feelings of passion and longing in the human heart. . . . The second of these poems relies on the Greek legend of Antigone, who led her father Oedipus into exile as an atonement for his sin, whereby he fulfilled the will of the fates without realizing it. . . . Throughout the entire length of the poem we hardly encounter a single complex image or metaphorical expression. There are simply short, daring thrusts from an artist who couches his style in a marvelous spontaneity. . . .

The poet is not overconcerned with love, not so much because he is naturally averse to it, but rather because he does not know on whom to bestow it when life is devoid of love. . . . In the few poems in which he does speak of love, it is mingled with a sense of tragedy and loss, so that the experience comes to have two complementary aspects of equal importance. In his poem "To Whom Shall I Give You?" from his collection *Blood on My Hands* he recalls the memory of a dear love which started when he was still young and which followed him through the various stages of his life until it drowned in the vast ocean of this cruel life. . . . But perhaps the best of the love poems in which he combines love and loss is "Come Now, Let Us Draw a Rainbow Together," from the collection *The Fall of Masks*, in which love appears to be a means of escape from tragedy and a boost to hope, although, with all that, the poem still does not lose that profound sense of dejection.

'Abd al-Qādir al-Qitt. *Al-Majalla*. April, 1971, pp. 2, 5–7†

In all of his *Elegies* Samīh al-Qāsim relies on the religious heritage prevalent in the East, something that can be considered part of the psychological and social makeup of each individual member of the society. However, he does not make use of this heritage in the same way as some of his predecessors have done, by simply inserting a few scriptural verses or religious stories in their poetry. Samīh al-Qāsim takes over the language of the Koran and the Old and New Testaments as he intones his elegies and laments. This gives his poems a rare touch of humanity that succeeds in touching the reader's sensibilities in two distinct ways: first, there is the bitter feeling of sadness, and then this sadness is mingled with an equally bitter sarcasm, which is not above looking upon the wounds the homeland is suffering and feeling a sense of anger at what is happening. The two paths then come together and are channeled in a single direction, namely to incite people to action . . . and that is what eventually happens. . . .

The poet is able to adapt the religious style, with its maxims and homiletic statements, to his poetry through a brilliant and effective diction, which is applied to the various emotional levels of the poems: sorrow, calling to account, derision. . . .

In his *Elegies* Samīh al-Qāsim presents us with an example of a modern prophet, one from the earth who passes judgments and condemns, who gives glad tidings and also warns, who uncovers and lays bare hidden secrets, and who establishes in the midst of all the lamentation and sorrow a new world. In that world, John the Baptist, rising up from the people's wounds and the necks of the slaughtered, will begin to preach and will move all around the area of the Jordan repeating the baptism of repentance for the forgiveness of sins.

Hātim Muhammad Sakr. *Al-Ādāb*. Aug.,
1974, pp. 61–62†

AL-RĪHĀNĪ, AMĪN (1876–1940)

LEBANON/UNITED STATES

The essence of al-Rīhānī is to be found in the writings in his *Rīhāniyyāt*, but not for the lofty and original thoughts they contain, since they contain none; they were written before he had reached full maturity and his ideas had crystallized. Nor does this essence lie in the profusion of their subject matter, since it is not profuse. The reason is rather that they indicate a pattern for thought that tends toward close research and justification for everything described; things are analyzed in detail, from their basic structure to their elementary parts to the way these various parts join together easily and without complication. It is sufficient to note that the style used in his essays is easy to follow and beautifully structured. . . .

The collection *Song of the Sūfīs* [included in the *Rīhāniyyāt*] shows us al-Rīhānī as a poet talking through the recurring waves of his thought patterns and the beats of his heart. . . . The collection contains thirty-one poems, some long, some short, some rhymed, others unrhymed. In my view, the best poems are those that betray a certain amount of emotion, such as "The Wanderer," "Libānūs," "Prayer in the Desert," and "Hymn of Rain." . . .

In "Prayer in the Desert," for example, we hear a language that may seem less familiar to western ears than it does to eastern. Someone who lives in the desert prays for "just a little rain": 'O Lord, gives us some of Your rain!' The poet embodies through this prayer and in a most graceful style some aspects of the intense faith, devoutness, and recourse to the Creator in all things that are a part of the Eastern soul. In much the same way, "Hymn of Rain" is a poem of thanksgiving to the sender of rain from people who attribute every good thing on earth to Him. [1923]

Mīkhā'īl Nu'ayma. *Al-Ghirbāl* (Beirut, Dār Sādir,
1964), pp. 164–65, 166–67

The poetry contained in the four parts of the *Rīhāniyyāt* shows all the music of an inspired poet and a deeply felt yearning. There is not the slightest artificiality about it. Rather, [Amīn al-Rīhānī's] poems are cries of a soul in torment, one that can find no relief save in the arms of nature, which sometimes coddles its children but at other times treats them brutally. Music is also an integral part of Amīn's prose poetry, something that his own rebellious sensibilities compelled him to create even before he emerged as a great reformer. . . .

I have to admit that I am unable to comprehend what it is that Amīn al-Rīhānī is stating as his beliefs in the two prose poems "Mistress of the Valley," and the one he wrote as an elegy for his little nephew. In the first of these, he seems to emerge as being older than material substance itself; perhaps he sees himself as a contemporary of God Himself, a school colleague of His, as it were, so that they moved together over the face of the deep when the earth was without form and void. He has existed and will exist for all time. . . . The second poem, about his nephew, also contains some of these riddles and puzzles, but you can begin to understand what is being said after some intense examination. In this poem, we hear the intense emotion of a great poet who is expressing himself in a splendid and ornamental fashion, thus effortlessly rendering the memory of the young child immortal. . . .

Al-Rīhānī's style overflows with a poetic sensibility, although one has to admit that it is sometimes spoiled by trite and forced diction. Sometimes, too, there are sentences that make you die of laughter, so poor and flat is the use of language. The *Rīhāniyyāt* contains literature of two types: one (which incorporates the majority of the works) is overwhelmingly concerned with sorrow and lamentation, lending it a prophetic tone; the second shows a great deal of magic, and that is the more genuinely poetic side of his output.

Mārūn 'Abbūd. *Amīm al-Rīhānī* (Cairo, Dār al-Maʿārif, 1953), pp. 48, 70, 81–82†

One of the most prominent features of prose poetry which evokes wave-like rhythm is parallelism. Like Whitman's, al-Rīhānī's technique depends usually on a parallelistic presentation of ideas which unfolds the theme of the poem in a gradual manner, treating one motif at a time with detailed and analytic dispensation before moving on to the next. . . .

Al-Rīhānī's technique makes use also of repetition. Words or phrases of special importance are repeated several times in a poem, sometimes as part of a refrain, to emphasize an idea while evoking the rhythm of waves and imparting an incantatory tone that adds to the harmony and the unity of the poem. Rhyme, which is condemned by Walt Whitman, is a device used by al-Rīhānī for the same purpose, though more in his earlier (1907–1910) than in his later (1913–1935) prose poems. . . .

Al-Rīhānī's prose poems, like Walt Whitman's, were poems of ideas rather than of sentiments. In fact he was against the mawkish, sentimental poetry that was being written in the Arab world. In the spirit of Walt Whitman, his subjects ranged from meditations on nature with philosophic overtones, to criticisms of Arab society clinging to rigid traditions and religious customs, to denunciations of tyranny and despotic rule, to sympathy with the poor and lowly, to a celebration of freedom and democracy, and a hopeful outlook on the future of the Arabs. Even when he writes elegies, be they to a nephew, to a sweetheart drowned in the Amazon, to Jubrān, to King Faysal I, or on the occasion of Good Friday, al-Rīhānī never loses the dignity of positive thought, cheered up by hope, optimism, and a healthy joy in life.

However, the intellectual element in his poetry is so dominant that his poem becomes more like a ratiocinative essay than a poem. This feature of his prose poetry was somewhat reduced in the posthumous collection *Cry of the Valleys*, not only by the elimination of whole poems or the shortening of several of those republished, but also by the omission of conjunctions, and other particles of logical relationship, the removal of forcibly argumentational phrases, the dropping of redundant and prosaic terms, the weeding out of useless repetitions, and the refining of images.

Issa J. Boullata. *Al-'Arabiyya*. Spring–Autumn, 1976, pp. 30–31

[Another] service rendered by al-Rīhānī to modern Arabic poetry is his introduction of prose poetry. His resort to this kind of poetic expression may have been the result of an urge to express himself poetically, while hampered by his inability in the usage of Arabic metres. This inability could be due to a deficient early education in Arabic poetry, which should help to inculcate the rhythms of the Arabic metres in a young student, as well as to a lack of sensitivity to Arabic metre. His early access to Whitman's prose poetry, which he declares to have imitated, helped to some degree by his reading of the Bible . . . and probably of the Quran, must have inspired him with the idea. In fact there is a marked influence of the Quran in several of his works, in the strongly worded phrases, short rhymed sentences, invocations and typical Quranic repetitions. The easy flow of the Biblical style, its longer sentences, its melodious undulations so apparent in Gibrān's work, are also to be found. His choice of style for a work may have resulted naturally from the subject matter.

Al-Rīhānī's prose poetry, despite its direct Whitmanian background, was never able to outshine the deep influence of Gibrān's work. Despite some occasional linguistic and grammatical mistakes, Gibrān's mastery of the rhythm of the language was unequalled. However, it is possible that Gibrān . . . was influenced by al-Rīhānī's pioneer attempt, but one feels, nevertheless, that Gibrān would have found his own way to the particular kind of poetic expression he used even without al-Rīhānī. Al-Rīhānī's attempt probably influenced later generations in the Arab East, who were to use the same kind of structure. This consisted in the unity of theme; the division of the piece into shorter or longer stanzas; the use of short sentences, repetitive phrases and invocations, and of images and metaphors taken from nature; and the attempt—often less successful—at charging the piece with emotion. It is impossible, however, to trace with any accuracy his influence on other poets, but the first two volumes of *The Rīhāniyyāt* (1910, 1911) received an enthusiastic reception, thanks to their originality and freshness.

Salmā al-Jayyūsī. Trends and Movements in Modern Arabic
Poetry (Leiden, E. J. Brill, 1977), pp. 89–90

AL-RĪHĀNĪ, NAJĪB (1891–1949)

EGYPT

Kish-Kish Bey was the suggestive name given by al-Rīhānī to a fictitious Egyptian village elder or *'Umda*—always interpreted on the stage by al-Rīhānī himself—who passed through various misadventures and whose small talk (in the colloquial Arabic of Egypt) reflected the common-sense attitude of the simple man to all matters concerning world developments, state affairs, social conditions and morals. Kish-Kish Bey related his adventures and gave free, unasked-for advice to everyone. In this al-Rīhānī followed in the steps of his master, 'Azīz 'Aid, and drew his materials from the French vaudeville. However, he changed the material almost completely, by dubbing all his characters with Egyptian names and adapting most of it to treat satirically of matters and conditions more or less known to his audience. Among the most frequently used subjects one finds everyday incidents, mishaps of the simple-minded, the cheating of naïve villagers coming to the city, tit-for-tat, the behavior of the flirtatious woman, the spending of public funds (by the village head) on women, and the like. The show was further enlivened by airs, many of which became hits overnight. In this way, he was the real creator of the Egyptian vaudeville, in the teeth of the highbrow attitude of the local critics, who (although unable to dislike al-Rīhānī) scoffed at this sort of entertainment being called art. He was often imitated, hardly ever equaled; and the popularity of this new genre remains secure today even though its creator has been dead for several years.

Jacob Landau. Studies in the Arabic Theater and Cinema
(Philadelphia, University of Pennsylvania Press,
1958), pp. 87–88

Al-Rīhānī's plots were generally pirated, and the personality he used when he appeared on stage was but a poor distortion of Charlie Chaplin. So what, then, was there about Al-Rīhānī's work that can be considered authentically Egyptian? In what does his humor lie? He made a particular point of using childish gags that are generally characteristic of all shallow, bad art. For example, the characters in his plays are given names that are supposed to make people laugh; we find names like Mr. Parsley and Madame Onion, silly things that any connoisseur of genuine art would find repulsive. . . . A second cheap trick he uses along the same lines in order to create an artificially amusing situation is that all his characters have their own rigid and unchanging mold; they are supplied with an easily recognizable appearance that never alters from one play to the next. So we find the spendthrift son of well-to-do parents, the imbecilic rich man, the scheming servant . . . and so on. Each one has his particular attributes and is given no others because the audience liked that character just as he was the first time he appeared in a play. Henceforth, al-Rīhānī's plays had to be presented in accordance with the prerequisites established by these characters. . . . Hardly any play by al-Rīhānī is without the character of the old Turkish woman so that people can have a good laugh at the way she garbles Arabic. This is another patent and easy trick to play. A Turk also comes into the plays in the personage of the Egyptian Pāshā, who swears by God every other word. . . .

But then, why should we blame al-Rīhānī alone? It would probably be fairer to characterize his works as symptoms of a bygone age in which values were confused, one in which the Egyptian people found themselves beset by a monumental amount of swindling and trickery.

Yahyā Haqqī. Khatawāt fī al-naqd (Cairo, Maktabat Dār al-
'Urūba, n.d. [1961]), pp. 130–33†

Al-Rīhānī had particular gifts as a comedian, and it may be for that very reason that, of all people involved in Arabic comic theater, he was the most able to make the very fullest use of realistic situations and borrow from them to the extent that his own education would allow, not to mention his own views of society. After all, al-Rīhānī was presenting his plays to a particular audience, and a restricted one at that. This audience he would always refer to as the gentry, that is, those from the upper classes. He disliked the members of the lower classes and had no desire to appeal to them, not so much because he disliked crowds or preferred peace and quiet, but rather because all his own aspirations resided within the sphere of this gentry class. This may have been the hidden reason for the building of the Ritz Theater, which would accommodate only a small audience so that high prices could be charged for admission. . . .

Al-Rīhānī's works show two odd contrasting features. He championed the downtrodden in his works and showed sympathy for such people because they were often unlucky and their efforts went unappreciated by the wealthy, who were born with silver spoons in their mouths and who showed little concern for them. He was thus trying to imitate as much as possible the "philoso-

phy" of Charlie Chaplin. Actually, however, he was only offering a defense
of one particular subgroup from that larger group of the downtrodden, namely
the civil-servant types who were often not helped by fortune in their attempts
to join the gentry. . . .

Even *Hasan, Morcos and Cohen*, his greatest play, whose portrayal of
the social milieu has a great deal of authenticity, is basically derivative, and
only embellished with Rīhānī-esque additions. . . . Al-Rīhānī was content
merely to skim over the surface of society rather than to involve himself in it
to the full. His major interest was in borrowing ideas from others, in pro-
pounding his own myopic social views, and in restricting himself to an audience that would of necessity be in accord with his views and aspirations: the
rich gentry and their ilk.

Nu'mān 'Āshūr. Al-Kātib. June, 1962, pp. 98–99†

With the dawn of the thirties and the surging tide of Egyptian national self-
consciousness, Rīhānī realized that at last the time was ripe for the fruition of
Egyptian high comedy. In the absence of native playwrights, French sources
continued to provide him with the structure, techniques and often the story-
lines of his new comedy. Like so many of his contemporaries in Egypt at that
time, he looked to Paris for inspiration. He visited Paris frequently, went to
all the performances of the Comédie Française when they visited the Cairo
Opera House, and he subscribed to the monthly French journal *La petite illustration*, which provided him with the texts of the latest hits in Paris. But in
basing his plays on French sources, Rīhānī did much more than simply translate or "Egyptianize." He did more than just move the scene from Paris to
Cairo or "metamorphose" John into Mahmūd, and Mary into Fātma. He married Egyptian scene and character together with an authenticity which had
never been attempted before in the comic theatre.

To achieve realism, he had to struggle against almost every form or
genre that the modern Egyptian theatre had known since the 19th century. He
had to struggle against shadow theatre, against literal translations of French
farce, against operettas and the intrusion of music, and against his own com-
mercial successes. To Rīhānī, the realistic style which he finally succeeded in
imposing on Egyptian comedy, meant much more than just illusionism. To
him realism was truthfulness. . . .

His plays were "original" in the same way that Molière's were. They
bore the artist's stamp unmistakably. They were "unoriginal" only insofar as
they imitated the story-line, the structure, and technique of the French source.
Nonetheless, even though his mature comedies have far greater logical coherence than his earliest farces, by Western standards they are bulky and ram-
bling. The final form of a play depended very much upon the responses of the
audiences. If the public disliked or did not respond to a certain passage, it was
eliminated. If it responded enthusiastically to another passage, more in the

same vein was added. Time does not matter in the Egyptian theatre so long as the audience is kept laughing. Thus the plays are often twice as long as their French models. Retaining just the bare outlines of the plot of his source, Rīhānī created original Egyptian situations which he placed in realistically conceived settings. His plays, which sometimes ran for four hours, were also full of his own brand of repartee, dialogue, and jokes.

L. Abou-Saif. Journal of Arabic Literature. 4, 1973, pp. 6−7

AL-RUBAY'Ī, 'ABD AL-RAHMĀN MAJĪD (1939−   )

IRAQ

During the 1960s a number of writers initiated experiments in the short-story genre and have continued to do so, albeit with different enthusiasms and talents, to the present day. Among them, 'Abd al-Rahmān Majīd al-Rubay'ī occupies a distinguished position both for his considerable productivity and for the amount of time he has devoted to the short story.

The Sword and the Ship was his first collection, and was followed by *Shadow in the Head* and *Aspects of a Journey of Toil*. The novel *The Tattoo* is a culmination of the varied experiments and different treatments of material to be found in these collections. All these works represent a first phase in al-Rubay'ī's production as a narrative writer. In these works he tends to observe and portray the dark aspects of intellectual decline and psychological angst. A groveling servility toward a vicious external world emerges—a posture that results in the fragmentation and dashing of all the aspirations of the characters involved.

Other Seasons is the beginning of a second phase, which continues with *Eyes in the Dream* and *Memory of the City*. Here the author tends toward a greater realism and chooses characters of a different type who doggedly pursue their journey of struggle in life and persevere until they achieve eventual victory and triumph. [1976]

Kazim Jihad. Introduction to 'Abd al-Rahmān Majīd al-
Rubay'ī, Al-Khuyūl [The Horses] (Beirut, Al-Mu'assassa
al-'Arabiyya li-al-Dirāsāt wa-al-Nashr, 1979), pp. 6−7

Ever since al-Rubay'ī's first novel, *The Tattoo*, came out, it has provoked a good deal of critical comment whenever the subject of the modern novel in Iraq has been raised. The points most frequently mentioned are the work's new formal techniques and its fresh approach to the use of narrative and the association of ideas. As we noted earlier, al-Rubay'ī's constant quest for change and his attempts to discover new types of novelistic structure have brought him into the cultural arena under the banner of originality rather than blind imitation. It may be precisely this impulse that led him to bring out a new novel, *The Rivers*, which is quite different from *The Tattoo*. Actually, *The Rivers* is the story of political struggle in Iraq as seen through the diaries of Salāh Kāmil, who makes every effort to record events in a realistic fashion. Indeed, his portrayal of them comes very close to being reportage. I am firmly of the opinion that these diaries are a faithful picture of the Iraqi people's history during a crucial decade, a time when the country was going through a period of revolutionary ferment before the storm finally broke. . . .

The Rivers does not rely on one single character as its pivot, but instead makes use of a number of characters. The protagonist of the work thus becomes a whole collection of people who contribute to the establishment of a world with its own particular features: the world of politics, of love, and of danger.

'Abd al-Ridā 'Alī. *'Abd al-Rahmān Majīd al-Rubay'ī bayn al-riwāya wa-al-qissa al-qasīra* (Beirut, Al-Mu'assassa al-'Arabiyya li-al-Dirāsāt wa-al-Nashr, 1976), pp. 57, 60†

The fate of the petite bourgeoisie in the wake of the 1967 defeat is neither as grim nor as overwhelming as that of Karīm al-Nāsirī, the hero of al-Rubay'ī's novel *The Tattoo*. He makes a mistake and in an instant finds himself at the bottom of an abyss. Throughout the novel he is to suffer a variety of internal and external tortures and the prying looks of the outside world, which is full of condemnation and contempt. Karīm al-Nāsirī (like the protagonists of several other novels) comes to the realization that he cannot bring about political change. He chooses to withdraw within himself as a means of release and resorts to sex as a way of compensating for political failure. From the point of view of individual sentiment, *The Tattoo* records the life of an unknown quantity in Arab history. His name is Karīm al-Nāsirī: an intellectual who goes to prison and cannot withstand the tortures he suffers at the hands of his jailors. Eventually he breaks down and "confesses." Later, proclaiming his innocence in the newspapers as a way of getting to breathe the real air of the streets outside, he emerges from the whole experience as a disbeliever in society, political parties, and all the old ideas he dreamed of fulfilling.

The novel does not tell us anything about his childhood, but through the stream-of-consciousness technique we manage to deduce the early beginnings of Karīm's sense of commitment. From an early age he is aware of injustice in his village, and later on he becomes aware of the fact that his job in the city does nothing to weaken his sense of belonging to his own people, starving and deprived as they are. This incipient commitment is genuine enough then, but as the story proceeds we come to feel that Karīm al-Nāsirī is not really serious about his sense of commitment. In his case, belonging to a political party is not so much a process of becoming part of the societal "melting pot" but primarily a question of self-realization. Karīm al-Nāsirī is a hero with no heroism, since throughout the novel he is too preoccupied with himself to worry about anyone else.

Shukrī ʿAzīz Mādī. *In ʿikās hazīmat Hazīrān ʿalā al-riwāya al-ʿArabiyya* (Beirut, Al-Muʾassassa al-ʿArabiyya li-al-Dirāsāt wa-al-Nashr, 1978), pp. 109–10†

Al-Rubayʿī is constantly in search of new form of expression in his early short stories. He is never satisfied to stick to a single mode. In this way his efforts show many similarities to those of other writers of the same period. Al-Rubayʿī's collection *The Sword and the Ship* is marked by a certain obscurity, while the heroes display both existentialist and nihilist characteristics.

The issue of the author's unwillingness to stick to a single format and his constant search for what is new represents a question that is as legitimate as it is essential. It has to be the primary concern of every artist who respects his own work. As the poet Nizār Qabbānī puts it, creativity does not involve "drinking from the inkwells of others." We have to create our own language, something that will belong to us and clearly bear our own stamp. "Style is the man."

The fact that al-Rubayʿī's early attempts at story writing have elements in common with other writers of his generation points to the obvious fact that they all lived within a similar set of political, cultural, and social circumstances. They were thus situated within a single common creative environment.

Al-Rubayʿī has been accused of being excessively subjective in his early stories; it is said that he is unable to break out of the straitjacket that leads him into an exaggeratedly self-centered posture. When talking about the despair of contemporary man, he means himself; in referring to his hero's total boredom with the routine of daily life, he implies his own nonacceptance. . . . Even so it seems reasonable to ask whether al-Rubayʿī is the only writer to show such subjectivity in his first works and indeed whether such a personal involvement was not a predominant feature of cultural life in his country during the 1960s.

ʿAbd al-Khāliq al-Rikābī. *Al-Ādāb*. Sept. 1978, p. 52†

SĀLIH, AL-TAYYIB (1929–)

SUDAN

Season of Migration to the North is a fertile and authentic mixture of the virtues of the traditional novel, with its subtle and profound presentation of characters and a truly enjoyable story that holds your attention to the very end, and the virtues of the modern novel, which concentrates more on the portrayal of dreams and man's interior world. Al-Tayyib Sālih has used all the techniques and styles most appropriate to each of these features in an artistic mixture that is sound, fertile, and totally authentic. Thus, we are left at the end with the sense of a novel that is contemporary from one point of view but that from another point of view exudes an authenticity and evinces a direct link with the narrative heritage not merely of Arab fiction but of world fiction as well. In other words, it is an evolutionary Arabic novel, one that represents a new stage in our modern literature, indeed, one that opens to a new and brilliant page in the history of the Arabic novel. It is in every sense of the word a monument within our modern literary tradition.

This novel may well find itself severely criticized by certain more conservative literary groups because certain parts talk about sex in a very frank way. While the novel would retain most of its value if these sections were omitted, it would most surely lose something quite essential, namely, its genuineness and fire, not to mention its searing and bitter tone. In spite of its frankness and boldness on this particular topic, the novel deals with sex as an integral part of its structure and its artistic and humanistic spirit. It is this feature that gives the novel the right to remain exactly as it is without anyone attempting to alter it, including the author himself.

Rajā' al-Naqqāsh. Udabā' mu'āsirūn (Cairo, Al-Maktaba
al-Anglo-Misriyya, 1968), pp. 138–39†

The tendency to avoid the use of a simple chronology of events in the modern novel and to replace it with a structure that relies on the gradual revelation of events which are known in advance can be seen clearly in al-Tayyib Sālih's novel Season of Migration to the North. The murder of Jane Morris and Mustafā Sa'īd's trial are two incidents known to the reader from the second chapter, and yet we learn nothing of the relationship between these two people until the ninth chapter. The same thing applies to all the other incidents and information concerning the life of Mustafā Sa'īd. . . . But there is another story as well, namely that of the narrator and his relationship with the other characters on the farm estate, and particularly with Mustafā Sa'īd and thereafter his widow. That story follows an unswervingly chronological time frame and is interwoven with the first story. . . . But why does the author choose to combine these two structures in one novel? The truth of the matter seems to be that he believes that the former technique is more artistic. He uses the same method—though with a certain amount of caution—in The Wedding of Zayn. In fact, this technique is little more than a development of the flashback, and from that starting point the author can proceed to make use of a method somewhere between the two extremes. . . .

What is undoubtedly true is that al-Tayyib Sālih has been able by this method to present the character of Mustafā Saʿīd to his readers, along with all the character's contradictions, in a more effective way than would have been possible if he had adopted the more traditional approach. The narrator and his story show no such contradictions; they are basically uncomplicated and therefore suffer no harm from the more straightforward presentation they receive.

Shukrī ʿAyyād. *ʿĀlam al-fikr*. Oct.–Dec., 1972, p. 647†

In *Season of Migration to the North* al-Tayyib Sālih shows his tremendous narrative gifts and the way he can attract and hold the reader's imagination from the very first page until the last. The novel deals with a subject that has often attracted writers who have lived in the West and experienced that sense of fragmentation, the clash between Western civilization and their own roots and Arab nature. The novel is a profound and dramatic investigation of this experience in that it operates on the most intensely intimate levels. It represents the tragedy of a violent spirit torn apart by an overpowering thirst or a fundamental malaise; the main character is the victim of an uncontrollable, undefined ferment within himself. If this novel derives some of its power from the skill with which the events are presented and the way in which the reader is surprised, the same does not apply to the author's latest novel, *Bandar Shāh*, in which the author has no need to rely on such devices.

In this work, he presents us with a modern fable that derives its background, if not its overall plan, from the world of rituals and Sufi practices in the Sudan. A stranger with no memory arrives at flood time, the period when a marriage takes place between the all-encroaching, eddying waters and the firm, retentive earth. The stranger makes himself at home and teaches the peasants new skills. He marries, he has children. But then he disappears just at the time when the waters meet the dry earth once again, and then begin to ebb. Around this symbolic framework a number of problems are brought together, chief among them the clash between different generations in the Sudan. Strange echoes envelop the whole scene, lightning-like flashes in the light of which can be seen specters of the remote past, flashes that give everything a sense of antic magic. Through these works al-Tayyib Sālih has certainly injected some new blood into the Arabic novel nurtured in the West.

Khālida Saʿīd. *Mawāqif*. Summer, 1974, pp. 84–85†

In *The Wedding of al-Zayn*, al-Tayyib Sālih sits down on the ground with his own people and talks to them. And he is not satisfied just to talk to them; he actually becomes one of them in every sense of the word. He knows all their customs, he is aware of their inner feelings, he sympathizes with them in their sorrows, and he understands their hopes.

But he criticizes them, too. His status is that of someone involved but neutral, as we say in critical parlance. His vision comprises both good and bad characters, and he gives each one his due. Through his essentially artistic vision, however, we get a clear view of how bad the bad characters are and how good the good ones are. . . .

The author's vision of both people and things is a penetrating one; he affirms that behind what we see with our eyes there lies a whole series of other things. Change is brought about in two opposite ways: by material means and by the power exerted by the spiritual dimension, the hidden world that manages to involve itself in our own material world and sometimes even to overcome it, even though we do not give it the attention we should. . . .

Al-Tayyib Sālih makes use of this progressive mystical view to look at people, earth, fields, and all living things. From all of them he extracts his moral values, his artistic creativity, and his intellectual point of view. In a word, life is something wholesome for those who choose to make it that way; for others who would destroy it or work some kind of mischief against it, it is anathema. . . .

The Wedding of al-Zayn emerges as one long paean to life itself, a love song sung by an author who is both magnanimous and knowledgeable. But perhaps his greatest and most significant talent is that he has at last succeeded in breaching that unseen barrier that has separated the artist from his own people, however great his love for them may have been.

> 'Alī al-Rā'ī. In Ahmad Sa'īd Muhammadiyya et al., eds.,
> *Al-Tayyib Sālih: 'Abqarī al-riwāya al-'Arabiyya* (Beirut,
> Dār al-'Awda, 1976), pp. 102, 111–12, 117†

The problem of individual marginality, uprootedness, banishment from community, and suicidal defiance are reflected accurately in the works of the Sudanese novelist al-Tayyib Sālih. The first page of *Season of Migration to the North* (1966) announces the rejoicing of a major character at leaving the coldness of Europe and returning to the warmth of his tribe in a small village at the bend of the Nile. His tongue almost slips to say "warmth of womb," revealing a great desire to seek roots in the past and childhood. Back in the net of intimate relations, it is not long before he feels "as though a piece of ice were melting inside" him. Like Muhsin in Tawfīq al-Hakīm's *Return of the Spirit*, the narrator romanticizes village life. . . .

Yet the similarities in concepts do not really spring from the same vision. While the narrator and Mustafa Sa'eed in Sālih's novel suffer from the existential problem of relating to the universe, Muhsin (the protagonist of al-Hakīm) suffers from the emotional problem of relating to his girl friend. In the last analysis, Mustafa Sa'eed in particular is a highly sophisticated and unusual character whose relationship to the West is one of defiance and a need to avenge the colonization of the East. He purposefully establishes sexual relationships with several European women, kills one of them and possibly causes the suicide of three others. The women he entices to his bed include girls from the Salvation Army, Quaker societies, and Fabian gatherings. Even while being tried in court, Mustafa Sa'eed has a feeling of superiority towards Europeans. He wants to spite them, perhaps in revenge for their invasion of Africa and in particular for what they did to persons like Wad Ahmed, who was brought in shackles to Kitchener and had to listen to this arrogant English invader interrogate him. . . .

Though al-Tayyib Sālih far surpasses al-Hakīm in vision and artistic treatment, his major characters still resort to individual rebellion and defiance rather than revolution. When they fail in Europe, as expected, they seek personal rather than societal salvation in the warm relationships of the village. In the long run, of course, they fail to adjust to village life and traditional culture. Mustafa Sa'eed dies or commits suicide, it is not clear which. The narrator gradually develops a sense of disappointment at politics, traditional values, and the lack of change.

Halīm Barakāt. *Visions of Social Reality in the*
Contemporary Arab Novel (Washington, D.C., Center
for Contemporary Arab Studies, Georgetown University,
1977), pp. 26–27

Like every great work of art, al-Tayyib Sālih's novel *Season of Migration to the North* operates on multiple levels of meaning and can be approached from various angles. For example, the impact of colonialism, modernism, and Western ideas on a traditional rural community pervades the novel, and a discussion of this theme would be particularly pertinent in light of the fact that, on several occasions, the character Mustafa Sa'eed seems to imply a causal relationship between his distorted emotional relationships with English women and the economic, cultural, and psychological violence perpetrated by British colonial rule.

However, in the overall structure and meaning of the novel this theme plays only a supportive part. Much more central is the mythic, archetypal, and psychological significance with which the characters and events are invested. The psychological makeup and development of the two major characters, Mustafa Sa'eed and the narrator, and the complex relation between them, provide the most reliable index to the novel's inexhaustible thematic and stylistic suggestiveness. The novel subtly and powerfully contrasts the personalities of the two men and the struggle each wages to master his fate through comprehension of his unconscious being. The one fails, the other succeeds; the one succumbs to the dark unrealized side of his personality, the other, awakened from his illusions by the sufferings of the man he cannot ignore, becomes a whole self, an integrated being, through the process of individuation, and faces the world without fear or deluded hope.

Muhammed Siddiq. *Journal of Arabic Literature.*
9, 1978, p. 67

Daw al-Bayt in *Bandar Shāh* reminds us very much of Mustafa [in *Season of Migration to the North*], though he is very different from him. Daw al-Bayt, whose story, like Mustafa's, occurs as a flashback, is a white wounded soldier. He is driven by the waves of the river to the doors of the village of Wad Hamid, whose inhabitants discover that the soldier has forgotten his past. He does not know his name, his family, his religion or his country. In short, he has no roots. He is fed, cured, and later converted to Islam, given a name, circumcised and given in marriage to the girl who had nursed him. Like Mustafa, he is welcomed by the village of Wad Hamid and accepted as a member of the society. "You came to us like Allah's destiny from we do not know where . . . However, we have accepted you among us as we accept heat and cold, life and death." Both Mustafa and Daw al-Bayt get married to girls from the village; they work on their plots of land, and participate in the development of the village. Mustafa plays an important role in the Agricultural Project Committee, and Daw al-Bayt introduces new crops to the village of Wad Hamid. In summer he travels with caravans and returns with new kinds of clothes, perfumes and a variety of pots, food and drinks never known in the village. Both men disappear in the Nile during the flood season. The description of the villagers' search for both men is almost identical. In Mustafa's case, "the whole village, carrying lamps, combed the river bank, while some put out in boats, but though they searched the whole night through it was without avail." . . .

But the similarities between the two men should not obscure the differences between them. Mustafa, having no roots, comes to Wad Hamid in quest of his origin and of the religious beliefs; whereas he fails in his quest, Daw al-Bayt, the white foreigner, identifies with the society. While Mustafa's life-story and his disappearance have strengthened the narrator's belief in popular Islam, Daw al-Bayt's appearance, stay in the village, and subsequent disappearance have a parallel effect not only upon one individual but on the whole village. Though a white man, he learns how to read and write Arabic and to recite parts of the Qurān by heart in a very short time. He miraculously cultivates summer crops in winter and winter crops in summer. During his stay, the mosque is rebuilt, enlarged and adorned with rugs. His marriage is described in a way that reminds us of al-Zayn's [in *The Wedding of al-Zayn*]. On his wedding day Daw al-Bayt renews his Islamisation and recites a certain *sūra* from the Qurān entitled "The Brightness (of the Morning)," some verses of which apply to his case. God has taken care of him, guided and enriched him. His death is reported in mystical terms by the two men who were repairing the water-wheel with him on the night of his disappearance and who were miraculously saved. One of them says that he "glanced at Daw al-Bayt as if he, Daw al-Bayt, was suspended between sky and earth surrounded by a green light." No wonder then that one of the villagers said, "Allah has sent him to us as a carrier of goodness and blessing." Daw al-Bayt lived among them like a vision and went away like a dream, leaving behind him a son whose face is black like his mother's and whose eyes are green like his father's. Daw al-Bayt's son, Bandar Shāh, as some flashbacks indicate, seems to be more interested in authority.

Ahmad A. Nasr. *Journal of Arabic Literature.* 11, 1980, pp. 100–101

AL-SAMMĀN, GHĀDA (1942–   )

SYRIA

The collection *Your Eyes Are My Destiny* contains sixteen stories, of which fourteen have women as their main subject, while two have men. This shows clearly enough that the major subject of the collection is woman herself. Even so, that subject has a number of different aspects, in that the writer can deal with the problems of women in general or with problems of Arab women in particular vis-à-vis their social situation and inner feelings. . . .

The style the author uses suits the peculiarities of the characters very well. We cannot reasonably expect a character who is extremely excitable to speak in a slow or relaxed fashion. As anyone will perceive in real life, emotional people tend to speak in an abrupt way without using the normal connectors of the language. Ghāda al-Sammān realizes this fact, and deliberately omits connections between phrases and sentences at points in the story that portray rising excitement. In fact, she even hurls the sentences at you in a rough and frenzied fashion to a degree that you the reader have no time to take a breath while reading. . . . She makes very little use of dialogue (and then it is interior) because it would lessen the intensity of the situation and would not suit the nature of such emotional characters. . . .

Not all the stories in this collection are of the same level of excellence. Some of them are genuinely brilliant, others are mediocre, and one is a failure, namely "The Baby with Burning Cheeks." . . . Each incident in the story is a separate story, a complete subject in its own right; what we have is actually three stories in one. There is no real link between the events in the story . . . and the use of dialogue between the inner and outer selves of the character makes the story confused and disjointed and spoils the overall effect. . . .

In general, however, this collection succeeds in showing that its author has considerable talent and possesses a considerable command of the short-story genre. This emerges first in the appropriate use of character types and their reaction to events, in other words, in the understanding of "situation." Second, the author will begin with an idea or an event, and then, instead of making it develop naturally or simply continuing with it, we see her leaping forward to a second idea, then a third—leaps that are a particular feature of excitable imaginations. . . . Third, there is a subtle observation of emotions with all their variations, so that each character appears before our eyes as a living tableau.

Muhammad Haydar. *Al-Ādāb*. June, 1962, pp. 31, 34†

In a newspaper interview the author of this collection, *There Is No Sea at Beirut*, declares that she gave it this title because it conveys the ultimate sense of rejection, doubt, and anxiety and an insistence on the need to create new values that we can use as new bases for our society, values that cannot lose their authenticity or be hampered by apathy and inertia. . . .

The book itself certainly contains some excellent, even original, imagery, but it does not fit into the context; it is usually far more than is required. It frequently becomes a goal in itself. The style exhausts and dulls all the symbols and images, and makes them lose most of their significance. Rarely will you find a noun without one or even two adjectives. All this turns the pen into a bellows, while the experience of the book as a whole becomes a gaudy balloon being stretched to the point of bursting. Within all this there moves a single female organizing all the different versions of the experience. She lies, and knows it. She makes herself believe she is playing with her own values, and knows that too. She is convinced that she is being torn apart, and that delights her. She is forever on the move so that her illusion will not dissipate; all the while her eye is on the external world. When she falls into the abyss of her own psychological loneliness where the genuine experiences would begin, she leaps out to the external world once more, beating the drums for yet another tale of banishment. Her relationships with men are merely escapades of a pen filled with ink, set in a bourgeois atmosphere that shows not the slightest trace of rejection, doubt, anxiety, and so forth. In order to attract the reader's attention to these features, she sets up worlds, erects characters, injects events, sleeps with the language, and breaks the nerves of the very words themselves. . . .

Perhaps it is features such as these that have made *There Is No Sea at Beirut* such a successful collection. As an expression of the generation of rejection which is formulating the revolution in the Arab homeland at the moment, it is one hundred percent accurate and realistic. This is indeed a document that reveals with great clarity the revolutionary hot air filling the minds of our revolutionaries and all the ranting and raving with nothing of any worth beneath it.

Hānī al-Rāhib. *Hiwār*. 10, 1964, pp. 133–34†

Ghāda al-Sammān's literary output is actually a product of the fascination the poetic person feels toward subjects involving the self and society, and also of her tremendous sense of sound and music in language. The primary feature of her writing is the headlong and boisterous outpouring of genuine feelings and sensibilities and the daring ideas that are poured onto the page, sometimes easily within the reader's grasp and own emotional outlook, at other times shrouded and remote. These ideas are packed full of metaphors and symbols, and also are evidence of an overflowing imagination. . . .

To Ghāda al-Sammān the story is a poetic vision, a psychological screen, a sociological "find," a collection of psychological and social tableaux. It is the poetic vision that validates the artistry of the narrative. The different hues of that artistry occur in its structure and shape, in its descriptions, its analyses or its style. . . .

Above all, her work contains no colloquial usage at all, not even in dialogue between representatives of various classes of people. . . .

This latest collection, *Night of Strangers*, undoubtedly represents new horizons in the cultural exploration of the Eastern personality, both male and female. She has, no doubt, drawn her inspiration from the occasions when she traveled abroad to get her higher education and came into direct contact with Western society. . . . Other stories go into detail about the questions of commitment and experiences with the homeland, the people, and friends. . . . Still others are bold exposés, on both the individual and social level, of matters relating to sex, love, contemporary life, family life, married life, and so on. Certainly, some of these subjects in which she explores society and states her views on commitment can be considered new in her output . . . while others can be found in her previous collections.

But what is new in her artistry and represents a big leap forward is the conscious and unconscious association of ideas, coupled with solitary conversation, overt interior monologue, and even at times a tendency to use the "absurd" style and symbolism.

ʿAdnān ibn Dhurayl. *Al-Ādāb*. March, 1967, p. 41†

In her latest stories, Ghāda al-Sammān seems to be setting sail in the ship of her own personal feelings toward the further shores of revolutionary rejection, of commitment to the problems of the Arab homeland and the anxieties of the poor. . . . In so doing, she puts a distance between herself and the usual type of flashy slogans and the falsities of bourgeois society, and with persistent fidelity searches out her true Arab identity, and at the same time her real situation as a human being. She utterly rejects the usual and traditional in order to try out new experiences. She is genuinely authentic in her originality and her veracity. . . .

With all the skill of a great surgeon, Ghāda uses the scalpel that is the Arabic language to make incisions in the body of the Arab homeland. She is soon able to reveal where the malignant tumors are to be found; from the districts of Yemen to the streets of Vienna and even the cafés on Hamra Street in

Beirut, we find ourselves afloat in the uncharted regions of the Arab soul. And this is not restricted to place alone. In five out of the six stories in *Leaving the Ancient Harbors*, the story is told from the viewpoint of a girl of bourgeois background and upbringing who continually rejects her situation and aspires to achieve selfhood without guile in a merciless world. But we always come to realize in the end that her fidelity is a societal one, and that the sole solution is a conscious freedom and a revolutionary rejection of all the factors that lead to frustration, despair, and defeat. Ghāda, then, begins with a woman but finishes with mankind; from the individual she moves to the homeland as a whole. This is a genuine "departure" for Ghāda al-Sammān in these new stories, as opposed to her earlier works, such as *Your Eyes Are My Destiny* and *There Is No Sea at Beirut*. This aspiration to undertake a new journey may have represented the furthest stage of the personal despair and exile to be sensed in *Night of Strangers*.

Riyād 'Ismat. Al-Ma'rifa. Dec., 1975, pp. 94–95†

What distinguishes Sammān's writing is her obsession with identity and loss of self. Indeed, even before the [1967] war, she had written of identity fragmentation. In the first of her *Incomplete Works*, "Time of the Last Love," this fragmentation is limited to complete identification with another: the lover, whose voice comes out of her throat, whose cigarette smoke comes out of her lungs. Already there is the suggestion that the individual is no more than the sum of a number of points that only become a line, a thread of continuity, in retrospect . . . in a flashback? She is in constant anguish about her direction, for wherever she goes she is assailed by roads, cars and worlds whirling around her madly. Indeed it is as though she were on an LSD trip and her mind had entirely dissociated itself from the burden of her body. As she runs through life her disintegrating body is abandoned along the wayside only to take root in the asphalt and to sprout up as plants in the spring.

This early work is often obscure, sometimes brilliant but unfailingly violent and protesting. With the war has come concentration and perhaps direction. Protest, which, before the war, had been the main reason for writing, has changed into a challenge. The social protest that she had indulged in until well into the 70s has become an anchronism. The time for "flower-power" whining has passed, now is the time to shout and scream, to defy Death by living fully. And it is this call for life that distinguishes the works of all these writers. No longer is tomorrow dreaded as a dull repetition of today, no longer are we living in an Osborne-type hell. This hell is different and, for its difference, it is better. For now tomorrow is ever different, bringing the hope for some of peace and order, for others of danger and excitement.

Miriam Cooke. Journal of Arabic Literature. 13, 1982,
pp. 127–28.

In *Beirut '75*, al-Sammān deals with many of the issues discussed in her earlier works, such as discrimination, the sexual oppression of women, the concept of honour in modern Arab society, injustice, political corruption, and tribal revenge. In this novel, however, she deals with these issues as they relate
directly to the state of Lebanese society in general and that of Beirut in particular just before the Lebanese Civil War erupted. The novel may almost be described as prophetic, in that its characterization and setting lay bare the complex roots of the ongoing strife. It is to be noted that women's issues are not
an overriding concern here, but are taken up by al-Sammān only to the extent
that they impinge on the condition of society as a whole. . . .

Al-Sammān's novel is composed of contrasts from beginning to end. She
contrasts dreams and reality, life and death, all of which she uses to fore-
shadow the events and destinies of the characters as they develop in the novel.
The dreams of the characters are emblematic of different kinds of death,
whether psychological, spiritual, or physical. Yāsamīnah, for instance, un-
dergoes a dual death, at once psychological and spiritual, once she indulges in
sexual gratification and neglects her poetic talents. And she is of course faced
with physical death (murder) at the hands of her brother. While Yāsamīnah's
dream becomes a reality, Farah struggles to realize his own. Once he trans-
forms the dream into reality, however, he finds that he has lost his manhood.

In general terms, al-Sammān in *Beirut '75* deals with three distinct issues: politics, sex, and death. These three issues are interconnected throughout the novel, and she skilfully balances all three of them in her characterizations and settings for the action of the novel. We see, for example, how her
political commentary is presented through glimpses of the social and sexual
events in which the characters participate and her descriptions of the environment in which these take place. What is not clear, however, is whether she intends to commit herself to a specific political ideology; she allows us faint
glimpses and insights, but there is no possibility of discerning the precise outlines of her creed.

Al-Sammān also makes the reader very much aware of time and place
in her novel. Beirut is a wise choice as the focal point of the novel's intrigue. . . .

Perhaps, where al-Sammān is concerned, Beirut is the Arab world in
miniature, a microcosmic arena in which Arab society wages civil war on itself; it would be less a city than a symbol of Arab division. Many things she
says about Beirut suggest that this is the view she takes of it. But whether this
is so or not, it must be admitted that she has done a masterly job of conjuring
up a vision of a city that is nothing if not unique in the long annals of human
civilization.

Al-Sammān is also very successful in her technique of writing. Narration, description, monologue, soliloquy: she demonstrates unquestionable
competence in the handling of all of these. She is also impressively competent

in her use of the complex "stream-of-consciousness" device, and in effect admits that she stands in debt to James Joyce and Virginia Woolf. Her choice of characters is, of itself, very significant, in that it tells us a very great deal about the kind of people who have shaped her opinions concerning Arab society. Finally, it is characteristic of her writing at this stage in her career that it is marked by a certain inconclusiveness in the unravelling of the plot, as if she meant to suggest that the fiction writer cannot hope to arrest time and must shape his intrigue accordingly.

Hanan Awwad. *Arab Causes in the Fiction of Ghadah al-Samman, 1961–1975* (Sherbrooke, Quebec, Éditions Naaman, 1983), pp. 95, 108–9

SĀYIGH, TAWFĪQ (1923–1971)

PALESTINE

When Tawfīq Sāyigh's collection *Thirty Poems* appeared, it did not receive the dissemination throughout the Arab world that it deserved. But then, that may be part of the nature of things; free verse, after all, has few friends and many enemies. Even Professor Mārūn 'Abbūd, normally a critic who looks out avidly for new talents and tries to encourage them, proceeded to analyze the collection in two lengthy articles and then declared that he could not consider this type of writing as poetry, although he did confess that if Tawfīq Sāyigh's work had possessed both rhyme and meter he would definitely have placed it at the very pinnacle of Arabic poetry.

In future years, however, we will no doubt see free verse overcoming the reluctance of critics to acknowledge it. This particular collection will then establish itself as one of the most daring and profound pieces of poetry ever published in Arabic. Daring because of its use of language, its innovations, its use of words in ways the reader least expects. The profundity occurs in the concepts behind these words; they seem like precipices on which anyone may slip. The reader may be taken up with the struggle between the human soul and God, the soul and love, or the soul and aspects of rejection and arrogance, but Tawfīq's poetry constitutes a revolution not only against the rules of poetic composition and the canons of sound stress but also against traditional poetry's total lack of reference to the experience of modern man. If you wish to innovate, you never do it purely for its own sake but because you have something to say that cannot be said without innovation. If you do innovate, carried forward by your own concepts and discoveries, then you are committed to discarding all that is old in a complete and irreversible fashion.

Tawfīq Sāyigh does all this in turning his back on all the poetic conventions to which we are accustomed. He takes a different type of clay in his hands and proceeds to mold it in a new way, thereby producing images our eyes have never encountered before. All we have to do is to readjust our eyes in order to appreciate these images. This is what innovation means; this is what discovery entails. Tawfīq's discoveries have no connection with the familiar and hackneyed. How can there be the possibility of discovery within *that* framework? His poetry is a penetration into "the sea of gloom (the Atlantic)," a passage into the arcana of the human soul, in a way totally unfamiliar to poets writing in Arabic.

> Jabrā Ibrāhīm Jabrā. *Al-Hurriyya wa-al-tūfān* (Beirut, Dār
> Majallat Shiʻr, 1960), pp. 43–44†

We should correct the misapprehension that states that the use of prose in the process of poetic composition cancels the effect of the poetic flow; the liquid remains, as it were, while the alcohol evaporates. Paul Valéry noted this fact in observing that "the most beautiful poetry in the world becomes trivial and unbridled as soon as the harmonies in it begin to clash and its melodic essence is spoiled. . . ." Many people would maintain that Tawfīq Sāyigh, by abandoning the meters of al-Khalīl [ibn Ahmad, d. 791] and avoiding rhyme, is now left with none of the harmonic momentum and melodic essence of which Valéry speaks. But that would be wrong. The free metrics in his poetry are arranged into verses that have a specific structure, something generated from within rather than through some borrowed set of metrical rules. They interact and fuse together; some evoke echoes of others. They respond to one another, their voices are numerous, and they are far removed from the single strain from which Arabic poetry has suffered so much for so long. . . . Once in a while, the movement of the free verse may disappear from view, but it is always there for the ear to hear. Then again, this poetry is something new; it represents a complete and final break with the embellishments and double-entendres of the rhetorical style. It opens up new vistas, just as though the whole of the wide universe were its sphere, rather than some tiny garden with a hedge around it. . . .

The tragic aura that pervades the entire collection *The Muʻallaqa of Tawfīq Sāyigh*, seems to be destiny itself. Thus, the movement sometimes slows down and at others speeds up. However, it never comes to a complete stop, as though it exists in some kind of eternal time frame. We could hardly be further removed from that pessimism which the more superficial critics have chosen to identify in Tawfīq Sāyigh's works.

> Rawād Turbayh. *Hiwār*. No. 5, 1963, pp. 116–17†

Tawfīq Sāyigh's poetry neither cossets the ear nor tempts the imagination . . . . There is a firm connection with the intellect, but still more of a tie with experience. For that reason, he demolishes the metrical structure without erecting on the debris a symphonic structure of another kind. On the other hand, he is eager to have some harmonic design for his ideas. Tawfīq does not demolish the traditional Arabic metrical system by accident, nor does he do so on purpose either. In his poetry, the connection between letters and words is not the result of a musical consideration of the phonetic correspondences in the construction of lines, the molding of phrases, or the derivation of tropes. Nor does the relationship depend on some architectural plan prepared in advance that places parallel, corresponding, and opposing segments into some kind of neat pattern so as to elicit a perfect symmetry between different parts in relationship to the whole or the whole picture in itself.

The harmony Tawfīq Sāyigh craves with an almost mad passion is achieved by ideas in their generative and creative sense, rather than through any predetermined plan, skill, or subtlety in building up equations. When the idea becomes a cerebral reflection of the incredible effort involved in any experience, then the word turns into a fuel to light an eternal spark in the soul of mankind. There is no recourse here to the place occupied by the letters nor to the time consumed by the sound; poetry here is no longer the product of dimensions and computations, since it is derived from the very core of experience with both time and place. The poet's own experience lives above the level of mere history. There is no longer any hope of experiencing the poem via the pipelines of meter and stress (or what some people mistakenly term the "prose poem"); by its very nature poetry rejects any designations that try to hoodwink or threaten it or else to shut out the light so that it cannot see.

Ghālī Shukrī. *Shiʿrunā al-muʿāsir: Ilā ayn?* (Cairo, Dār al-Maʿarif, 1968), p. 84†

In his collection *Thirty Poems*, one third of the poems are inspired by the sweetheart. We do not know who she is or even whether she is only one lover. But we enjoy reading about a sweet love of short duration. . . .

However, when we read Tawfīq's second collection, *The Poem of K*, published in 1960, we are faced with another sort of love, and I believe it is another sweetheart. Of the collection's twenty-five poems, only three are directly inspired by the sweetheart, but her influence runs powerfully in almost all the others. Perhaps that is why the poet gave the collection the name of this sweetheart, Kay, by enigmatically using the initial letter K. He never refers to her by name; but in his "Muʿallaqa," first published in *Shiʿr* magazine in 1961 and later in a book in 1963, he refers to her by using the English initial letter K in his Arabic text. . . .

Tawfīq's experience of the homeland and the experience of the sweetheart coalesce as his love intensifies; the Zionist settlers in Palestine who were given the shore and the hills, only to evict the Palestinian Arabs eventually, come to the poet's consciousness as his sweetheart to whom he opens up his innermost depths turns out to be a similarly invasive woman. The love of this woman stands in the poet's consciousness to be contrasted with that of his mother: Kay's love is destructive, that of his mother is protective; one is hell, the other is heaven. He had thought that he could replace the one by the other. It was too late when he discovered that they clashed and he was the battlefield.

These thoughts, coupled with the poet's religious feelings of sin, set against a background of exile from the homeland and alienation in the modern city, were the subject matter of his greatest poem, one which when published in No. 20 of *Shi'r* magazine in 1961 he entitled "The Last Poem" but which when published in book form in 1963 he entitled *The Mu'allaqa of Tawfīq Sāyigh*.

In this long poem of over 750 lines of free verse, the poet epitomizes his experience of life in four parts that are like the four movements of a symphony, and the sweetheart is referred to in all the four parts by the English letter K.

Issa J. Boullata. *Journal of Arabic Literature*. 4, 1973,
pp. 83–84, 87

In Tawfīq Sāyigh's images there is nothing wasted or superfluous. They probably lack the spontaneity of al-Sayyāb's, but they remain apt and structural to the poem. Sāyigh's prose poetry is based primarily on precise meaning supported by images that help to bring out its basic clarity. He often follows up an extended image much as al-Bayyātī does in *Broken Pitchers*, although there does not seem to be any mutual influence between them. In an essay on *The Poem of K* the present writer described the nature of Sāyigh's images as follows:

> The poem is usually a chain of concrete and highly accurate pictures referring to abstract meanings or hidden feelings which the reader would not have been able to understand except through images. Often these . . . images, which resemble miniatures, are units in a complete [and extended] image which rules the poem. . . . Images in Tawfīq's poetry surprise us with their originality. It is clear [moreover], that this poet has an amazing consciousness of the world around him for he does not take his images from the realm of abstract fancy, [but from life around].

Sāyigh must be remembered as a man of precision, wit and originality. Probably the taste for his prose poetry has to be an acquired one, but even those who do not enjoy his writing should be able to appreciate his particular approach and technique. Much can be learned from the way he handles images and from their precision and congruity. It is never safe to try to assign an original talent to any particular school or tradition. The only general description one can give to Sāyigh's work is that it is more inspired by the English modern tradition than by any other. His precision and clarity of purpose show

Eliot's pervasive influence which, however, is too subtle to admit a direct
analogy except with difficulty.

> Salmā al-Jayyūsī. *Trends and Movements in Modern Arabic*
> *Poetry* (Leiden, E. J. Brill, 1977), pp. 702–4

AL-SAYYĀB, BADR SHĀKIR (1926–1964)

IRAQ

Al-Sayyāb's collection *Song of the Rain* has three different aspects to it: first,
that of tradition; second, of development; and last, of maturity. . . . In the first
case, it is the epic spirit that predominates, placing reliance on a poetic sensibility that scoops up mud and thorns along with the clear water, thus making it
less than transparent. The poetry is merely a lump of substance; if it were not
for the title, you would have difficulty knowing what its purpose was. . . .

The term "development" with regard to the second aspect is not being
used in a chronological sense, but to imply innovation; in other words, it is
being applied to those poems that are somewhere in the middle, between the
fully mature poems and those that evidence the older form. This can be seen
clearly in long poems [included in *Song of the Rain*] such as *The Blind Prostitute*, *The Grave Digger*, and *Weapons and Children*. . . . Here the vehemence
is softened somewhat, particularly in *Weapons and Children*, and this soften-
ing has allowed the image to come to the fore; it is now more pronounced,
raised above the hue and cry, and also has greater freedom. . . .

Maturity reaches its greatest heights in two poems, "Jaykur in the City"
and "Song of the Rain." In these poems the pivotal factor is vision; through
the choice of a certain symbol, vision is expanded both horizontally and verti-
cally. . . .

A few words should be said about al-Sayyāb's expressive technique in
this collection. In this regard, the following features can be pointed out:

First, there is verbal expansion, by which I mean the broadening of the
source from which the poetic vocabulary is drawn. The source is taken from
the very root soil of life itself, far from any notion of abstraction. It contains a
number of words drawn from the colloquial, which affords a greater earthi-
ness and dynamism.

Second, there are numerous meters. Each poem may have more than
one meter; this metrical variety is occasioned by a variegation in melodic
movement, which in turn comes from the content. This makes the whole
poem symphonic in its movement. Frequently, too, there is no rhyme, in that
rhyme hampers the melodic flow.

Third, we find a translucency; even though the words may be compact and the letters shrouded in darkness, they are not closed off. They form a spring reaching from the bottom of the well to touch the very sky itself.

The fourth and final feature is that of ramification. Al-Sayyāb will use various devices in order to moderate the inner cohesion of the poem, for example, by using various words that introduce similes: "like," "as though," and so on. . . .

Al-Sayyāb is the greatest poet dealing with civilization and culture who is affiliated with the Arab people in this generation. But additionally, he has gone beyond purely cultural boundaries with a powerful élan that helps him to discover new realms for poetic adventure.

Fu'ād Rifqa. Shi'r. Winter, 1961, pp. 163–65, 167–68†

The Blind Prostitute, al-Sayyāb's superb epic poem, shows us that the poet was a pioneer in a number of different fields: the depiction of the human tragedy in general and of the realities of life for Iraqi women in a bygone age; the portrayal of both the provinces and city in those times, and of our general Arab reality at that time; in showing our sense of loss; in establishing his own cultural awareness and in depicting his experiences with his own reality; in illustrating the beginnings of his own personal rebellion and of his own sense of loss (something that was "pleasant to begin with but thereafter became unpleasant"). This is a social poem as much as it is a realistic one about humanity or a nationalistic one.

The blind prostitute, Sabāh, is one of the victims of the imperialist, feudal, bourgeois [sic] system in Iraq in former times. Her interior monologue presents her whole story; in fact, it is precisely the tale of Iraq in those days. . . .

The woman in this poem is a simple peasant woman whose father kills the feudal overlord for whom he works. She is thus forced to become a prostitute in order to keep herself alive. Al-Sayyāb talks in this poem about the world of women—about Iraqi women in general and Arab women as a whole—by giving a lengthy description of the prostitute, with her regrets, dreams, hopes, griefs, and ideas, all of which are expressed through her interior monologue, which has great psychological dimensions. The things that happen to her are also of primary importance to the impact of the poem.

In all this al-Sayyāb is completely successful, even though there may be some small points of disagreement over the content and a comment or two about the form of the poem.

Jalīl Kamāl al-dīn. Al-Shi'r al-'Arabī al-hadīth (Beirut, Dār
al-'Ilm li-al-Malāyīn, 1964), pp. 269–70, 283†

For al-Sayyāb the poem is an encounter between one form that is in the process of disintegration and another that is in the process of emerging for the first time. This poem-encounter allows the poet to discover a symbol for his own life and for poetry at one and the same time. This symbol is embodied in the voice of an Oriental sage in "The Poem and the Phoenix" [in *The House of Slaves*]: the poem and poet exist only when they are cleansed of the accumulated mass of custom, burning up in its fire and rising once again in its ashes. In that way the past percolates into the moment of the present and there is renewal. The poem is born.

To al-Sayyāb life itself is a poem; it too decays and renews itself constantly. Forms spring up as part of this life because life involves the disintegration of forms too. Like poetry it is a form. The form is not a diachronic or synchronic representation; rather it is an exterior space which contains an interior one and which reveals its dimensions via its contents. . . .

Badr Shākir al-Sayyāb shows in his poetry the birth of a new kind of content and of a new form of expression. He refuses to differentiate between expression and life, form and content. Form is not some kind of receptacle for content or a piece of clothing it has to put on; nor is it an exemplar or a rule. Rather it is life on the move, ever changing within a world that moves and changes. The world of form is therefore a world of transformations.

However, the experiment with form did not achieve total independence with al-Sayyāb; it is as though he was tied from behind while he kept pushing forward. Tradition still lurks in many of his poems, and for that reason it cannot always be said that al-Sayyāb is producing something new. He reached the very edge of the old world, but he did not cross the threshold; instead he retained his ties with tradition. Artistically, he was not comfortable living on the edge that would separate him from what had been before and would hurl him into the abyss of what was to follow.

Adūnīs. *Al-Ādāb*. March, 1967, p. 2†

Al-Sayyāb makes full use of stories derived from religious sources in his poetry, but he does not confine himself to them. He reads Babylonian and Assyrian, as well as Greek myths and legends. We find in his poetry a great number of references to figures such as Tammuz, the god of fertility, and Ishtar, the goddess of love and fertility, both of them derived from ancient Babylonian myth. And then there is Sisyphus and other figures taken from ancient Greek sources. Al-Sayyāb does not use these myths for the purpose of some kind of superficial cultural review. Like all the greatest poets, he uses them to add depth to the artistic work and to give it more than one dimension. Thus, we discover that a poem is made up a numerous levels; each time one of them is revealed, a more profound, brilliant, and suggestive one emerges from it. Hence the poem is not like a lump of sugar, which quickly melts and vanishes altogether, but rather a living entity, which never surrenders everything it has easily. Its secrets are not to be discovered in some rapid, passing glance; the reader must contemplate the poem, devote some time to it, and indeed read it several times so that he can get closer to it and comprehend its magic and beauty. Al-Sayyāb's poetry brings with it a complex enjoyment, not one that is easily obtained and soon gone. . . . Nor is Al-Sayyāb merely content to make use of these varieties of different cultures. Of all our poets, he is one of the most cognizant of popular folklore, especially that of Iraq. However, he does not superimpose this knowledge of folklore on his poetry. Instead, it emerges as an integral part of the structure of his poems, giving them a special flavor and an authentic popular aura. . . .

In the poem "City without Rain" we find a wonderful and delicate use of the myth of Tammuz, the god of fertility. The poem speaks of the city from which Tammuz is absent. So everything is desiccated; there is no rain, and so there are no crops. . . . The people implore the god of fertility to have pity on them and bring them rain so that life may be restored to both crops and people. . . . Tammuz and Ishtar respond to the pleas of the young; spring returns to the city, bringing with it rain, wellbeing, and life. The poem has, of course, a political purpose in that the poet's aim is to portray Iraq during the period of Nūrī Saʿīd, when the country lived in a state of wretchedness and misery. Al-Sayyāb may also be alluding, through the return of spring and life to the earth, to the Iraqi revolution of 1958.

Rajāʾ al-Naqqāsh. *Udabāʾ muʿāsirūn* (Cairo, Al-Maktaba
al-Anglo-Misriyya, 1968), pp. 283–86†

Badr Shākir al-Sayyāb was a poet endowed with enormous gifts; in fact his gifts surpass those of his contemporaries in spite of their different intellectual and artistic levels, people like Salāh ʿAbd al-Sabūr, ʿAbd al-Wahhāb al-Bayyātī, Nāzik al-Malāʾika, Buland al-Haydarī, Adūnīs, Ahmad ʿAbd al-Muʿtī Hijāzī and so on . . . During his life which only lasted for a mere thirty-eight years he produced a colossal output. . . .

Al-Sayyāb's poetry in its two guises, classical and free, is one of tremendous profundity, overflowing with both authenticity and novelty in numerous instances. This ability has afforded him a unique position among Arab poets as a whole. His command of classical Arabic poetry and the way in which he was able to assimilate and respond to it are largely responsible for the success which his classical poetry has had. There are numerous examples of this in his first two collections, *Faded Flowers* and *Myths*. I certainly must disagree with Lewis ʿAwad, who says that the poetry in *Faded Flowers* is bad; there are numerous examples in this collection which show an excellent maturity and which are characterized by their artistic originality. . . .

During the course of his painstaking artistic journey, Badr Shākir al-Sayyāb made use of all the various possibilities with regard to rhyme. Sometimes he used a single rhyme scheme throughout the poem, as in the early collections mentioned above. On other occasions, he divided the poem into sections and used a single rhyme within each of these sections. In this technique he utilized the earlier experiments of our romantic poets, and in particular of ʿAlī Mahmūd Tāhā in Egypt. . . . As regards free verse, he tried using a

repeated rhyme to provide a harmonic unity between successive lines in a
poem but without there being any requirement that the rhyme last for a specific number of lines; he also tried a system where the rhyme alternates and
the rhyming syllable is the same in, say, the first and third lines. . . .

Hasan Tawfīq. Al-Majalla. Jan., 1968, pp. 35, 40, 42†

The trend of resurrection in al-Sayyāb's poetry culminated in "Christ after
Crucifixion," in which he makes a remarkable reconciliation between the subjective aspect of his work and the objective one insofar as the theme of his
poem goes. He incorporates and fuses the pagan ideas of the ritual of vegetation and the Christian theme of crucifixion. Moreover, while he expresses sincerely his personal experiences, he fully succeeds in making them impersonal. And, although the poem is analogous to the political persecution in
which the poet and his generation suffered immeasurably, al-Sayyāb transcends his experiences to a universal level. And thus, as in most of his poems,
al-Sayyāb brings to a focus the cultural and the individual dimensions in the
human condition. . . .

Al-Sayyāb's poem "Christ after Crucifixion" is a case in point. The
Christian background of the poem is evident, although the poet employs the
crucifixion's theme analogically to its human aspect. The Muslims believe
that Jesus Christ has not been crucified. He was uplifted to heaven and he will
come back again. It can be seen that al-Sayyāb in the poem suggests the crucifixion of Christ. . . .

Christ "the logos" as in "Ash Wednesday" and "Four Quartets" does not
exist in al-Sayyāb's verse and that of his contemporaries. The suggestions of
Christ as a symbol are mostly of heroic nature. He is Man who becomes divine and not divinity incarnated in Man. He is humanity laid on the cross.
However, the religious attitude of the modern Arabic poet does not vanish
completely. Simply, he switches from one level to another. In other words,
the center of his beliefs and sentiments is transferred from the metaphysical to
the human realm and by necessity from God to mankind. . . .

Undoubtedly both Eliot and al-Sayyāb seem of moral nature. However,
the fusion of pagan and Christian themes and symbols is a borrowing from
Eliot. But applying them to a social or revolutionary situation is evidently of
socialistic source. Simultaneously, still Christ as far as the poem is concerned
functions as a saviour, but from drought, hunger and thirst. In fact, he bears
striking resemblances with Tammuz. They both renew life by death. The
poem echoes Tammuzian reminiscences in Christ and recasts the myth of
Tammuz in Christian terms.

Nazeer al-Azma. Journal of the American Oriental Society.
Oct.–Dec., 1963, pp. 676–78

The images of al-Sayyāb are drawn with sensitivity from a myriad of things
perceived by the senses or by the mind. They are original for the most part

both in themselves and in their allegorical or symbolic usage. Sometimes it is their disarming simplicity, sometimes it is their shocking unexpectedness, but always it is their power of surprise and their gushing effusion that keeps al-Sayyāb's poems alive. In cases of deficient structure, al-Sayyāb's imagery is a saving element that absorbs attention with its richness and colour.

His awareness of life as a tension between being and becoming is projected in his imagery in which conflict plays a major part, keeping his good poems integrated and balanced. The conflict between good and evil, between love and hatred, between freedom and oppression, between fertility and barrenness, between life and death in which he was personally engaged and in which he conceived of himself as an embodiment of his country, the Arab world and humanity at large—found expression in his imagery as well as his themes. For there are many poems in which a certain counterpoise between two sets of images may be detected, though cleverly interwoven into the fabric of the poem, such as in *Weapons and Children* or "Darkening" and many others. In a few poems, even the prosody of the poem is affected by this contrast, notably in his poem "Port Said," where the movement of thought and the imagery dramatically pass through alternate phases of traditional metre and free verse.

Al-Sayyāb's interest in imparting symbolic meanings to his images grew steadily in the 'fifties. The forces of good and life and fertility were symbolized by rain, bread, light, poppies, the river, the village and other similar terms that evoked ideas of happiness and plenty. The forces of evil and death and barrenness were symbolized by fire, gold, rock, darkness, the city and a host of other terms suggesting pain, exploitation and misery. His insistence on themes of salvation made him use death-transcending symbols such as the cross, the grave, resurrection and other soteriological terms.

Issa J. Boullata. *Journal of Arabic Literature.* 2, 1971,
pp. 108–9

Badr Shākir al-Sayyāb showed a tremendous yearning for his homeland, even when he was actually within its borders. When, for example, he was either in London or Kuwait, he could sense the pounding of the Arabic letters contained in the letters sent to him by his wife. These letters were the only gleam of light in his world through the long night of sickness and exile in London. . . .

Warmth was the one element al-Sayyāb lacked through his prolonged journey on the train of pain, sorrow, and death. He kept trying desperately hard to achieve it through the juxtaposition of images of the body and woman . . . . For him, rain always signified aspiration and served as a symbol for spring and hope, for the future that al-Sayyāb wished so much would be Iraq's. For al-Sayyāb, rain was a powerfully suggestive symbol of hope for a future in which al-Sayyāb envisaged a better life for everyone and which would see both himself and other innovators achieving a state of genuine integrity. . . .

Al-Sayyāb, then, loved his homeland dearly and wished it well. He also loved himself and wanted always to be in love. Echoes of his love occur frequently throughout his poetry. For example, in the collection *The Submerged Temple* alone we find the majority of tableaux are concerned with his love for his own city of Basra. It is as though he were asking other people to give it their own love unadulterated and thereby to share that love with him. At that time—1962, when the collection came out, and thereafter—he was an exile in Basra too, kept away from his job sometimes by reason of illness and at other times for political reasons. . . .

But in spite of all this, his fervent voice will always remain with us, powerful and effective; the sound of his poetry will keep coming back in future generations and will affect everyone.

Muhammad al-Jazā'irī. Al-Ādāb. March, 1971, p. 24†

The poems entitled "Elegy of Jaykūr," "Elegy of the Gods," and "From the Vision of Fu Kai" (those three representing a single project that al-Sayyāb termed an "epic"), may well be the poems that show the most cogent connection with the influence of Edith Sitwell, in that they evidence a subtle classicism and an independence within the realm of that very classicism. . . .

"Elegy of Jaykūr" is separated from the other two poems, but that is merely the way they were arranged when the three poems were published in a collection. We have to look at these poems as a unit. "Elegy of the Gods" comes first . . . , then "From the Vision of Fu Kai," and lastly "Elegy of Jaykūr." The poet decided not to regard these poems as a complete unit when he felt he was unable to produce an epic poem that would be coherent and uniform. Even so, a certain amount of the overall plan does seem to emerge from these three sections, at least according to the arrangement I have presumed above: The first poem deals with the absence of the image of the deity from human existence—a deity that in past ages man would create; and the way in which man has deified power and money in the modern age under new names.
. . . The second poem shows the effect of the atom bomb on Hiroshima through the vision of Fu Kai, the secretary in the Jesuit mission there, who is driven mad by the sheer horror of what he witnesses. . . . And when al-Sayyāb feels that his poem will end with a tremendous sense of void, he adds a third poem, "Elegy of Jaykūr," to complete the picture of destruction. To him Jaykūr represents everything he loves. If it, too, is subject to destruction, then the world in his view is at an end. . . .

When we take a second look at the poems of Jaykūr [al-Sayyāb's own village], we feel that the village has become the focal point for the understanding of the dualities in life: in other words, Jaykūr or the city (on the spatial plane), those two realities that are at their most tolerable whenever they are encountered together. For they come to represent on the one hand a return to childhood, and on the other perseverance with the struggle, death for the sake of rebirth or death for its own sake, mother or wife, spiritual values or material ones, the past or the present, faith or atheism. Most of the time, the poet sides with the former group of values, but he comes to feel that both he and they are being swamped and overcome. There is just one occasion when he feels that Jaykūr has expanded to encompass everything, and its verdant lushness has permeated the whole of existence: that is when he hears his young son, Ghaylān, calling him "Daddy, Daddy!" Then he feels that Ishtar has poured flowers and fruits into the whole of Iraq, that the very word "Daddy" has the hand of Christ within it, and that Tammuz has brought back the ears of grain so that the wind can play around them.

Ihsān ʿAbbās. Badr Shākir al-Sayyāb (Beirut, Dār
al-Thaqāfa, 1972), pp. 258–59, 262, 325–26†

It is in the relatively shorter poems which he began to write around 1953, poems such as "A Stranger on the Gulf" and "Hymn to Rain" [i.e., "Song of the Rain"] (and others included in the volume *Hymn to Rain*) that al-Sayyāb attained the full height of his creativity. In such poems he managed to fuse together in the heat of the imaginative act the most disparate elements of his experience, so that it is impossible to disentangle the individual predicament of the suffering poet from the commitment to a social or national ideal. In them we find an emotional complex of elements related to the man who since early childhood has been yearning for a mother's love and who has therefore been nostalgically looking back to the happy days of his early childhood in his native village with its river, its shells and its palm trees, the emotionally starved young man who seems to be constantly suffering from unrequited love, the committed Marxist dismissed from his job as a school teacher, hunted by the police in an authoritarian state and forced into exile for long periods of time in Iran and Kuwait (where he earned his keep by washing up dishes and doing domestic chores). A good example is "Hymn to Rain." The poem describes al-Sayyāb's feelings as he watches rain falling on the Arabian Gulf in Kuwait where he is a political exile. The mood alternates between nostalgia for the poet's childhood and homesickness for his country, between grief over the present situation in Iraq and hope for the future. Rain is life-giving and results in flowers and crops, but in Iraq it brings only hunger for the people. However, despite the prevailing sadness of the poem it does not end on a pessimistic note. . . .

But the exact identity of the person the poet is addressing is never explicitly disclosed and from the progress of the poem and the nature of the rich imagery used, it seems that what we have here is a composite figure: it is both the lost mother and the missing mistress, the idealized village of the poet's childhood, Iraq itself and even nature at large. Hence the apparently contradictory nature of the profuse imagery: when the eyes smile "vines turn green and lights dance," the eyes are compared to "moons reflected in the river": they are dark but "in their depths stars pulsate". . . .

Mustafa Badawi. *A Critical Introduction to Modern Arabic Poetry* (Cambridge, England, Cambridge University Press, 1975), pp. 252–53

Many of the mythological themes used by al-Sayyāb arose from inner necessity, or at least were particularly appropriate to the circumstances of his life. For instance, the theme of Persephone taken into the underworld clearly struck deeply into his consciousness as a reflection of the death of his beloved Wafīqa in his early youth. . . .

Basically the same is true of the images and themes which he adopts from the Middle East, namely that they correspond to his inner necessity. In the period of his illness, for example, he speaks of himself as Job, and as a Lazarus hoping for a saviour, desperately yearning for a cure. . . .

Other mythological themes correspond closely to the popular beliefs of the people. The chilling gaze of the Medusa, for example, is another representation of the *jinniyya* whose fiery eyes have the power to stun those who behold her. Such presentation of familiar themes in a new garb shows a further aspect of the poet's genius for transforming and renewing archetypal beliefs buried deep in the unconscious mind of the masses. . . .

A striking feature of al-Sayyāb's poetry is that it is suffused with emotion. This sets him apart from the dry and cryptic poetry referred to above. In "Testimony of a Dying Man" (which is an obvious allusion to the situation and statement of Abū Bakr when he gave his last testimony to the Muslim community, appointing 'Umar to be his successor), al-Sayyāb says: "I am dying: dead people don't tell lies: I disbelieve in meanings if they spring from any source but the heart." It is the complexity and richness of his feelings that lead him to employ a number of techniques that, together with other features of his poetry, serve to express his genius.

M. A. S. 'Abd al-Halim. In R. C. Ostle, ed., *Studies in Modern Arabic Literature* (Warminster, England, Aris and Phillips, 1975), pp. 72–73

Among avant-garde contemporary poets, the poetry of al-Sayyāb shows a more harmonious resolution of the struggle between the Classical and the modern. His language is clearer, more immediate, and invested with more emotion than the language of Adūnīs, though it is less varied and original. However, he excels in the choice of the precise word which reveals an inevitability, as though each word were the only one to fit the context. His imagination derived its inspiration from the primeval elements of the Iraqi countryside, from its scenery as well as its sounds. [The Iraqi critic Ibrāhīm] al-Sāmarrā'ī was quick to notice al-Sayyāb's strong auditory imagination and the way he feels the sounds he describes. And indeed, when reading his poetry, one is infected with the experience of this auditory sensibility. Poets mostly use visual imagery. Sound images are usually less developed in people, poets included, but once transmitted are perhaps more easily received and remembered. A poet who has a particular sensibility to the sounds of life, and can portray them in auditory images, is always at an advantage.

Al-Sayyāb's love of the Iraqi countryside is linked always with human experience, for he shrank from the vague Romantic beauty of nature, and it was his abhorrence of vagueness that enabled him to be always so precise in his language and imagery. Alliteration is also an important technical feature. His adjectives, which he uses with caution, are usually very telling and never dull, but at the same time they do not show that search for the rare epithet which is seen in some of al-Malā'ika's poetry. Their inevitability, one feels, stems from the necessity to describe faithfully a picture born in the poet's mind from the immediate fusion of idea and image at the moment of poetic creation.

Salmā al-Jayyūsī. Trends and Movements in Modern Arabic
Poetry (Leiden, E. J. Brill, 1977), pp. 670–71

Anyone looking at al-Sayyāb's poem "A Stranger in the Gulf" will find that the title allows the reader to identify the sources of the poet's imagination, almost as though they were a logical result of its content. The imagined world revolves completely around the ideas suggested in the title: exile, water, and the Gulf itself. The first section of the poem is evidence of how true this statement is . . . of al-Sayyāb generally, and of this poem in particular, we can state that the use of imagery is both a structural and dramatic element, in that he is not satisfied to establish just one relationship within each image; we get the impression that for him the image is very rich and that the sources of the imagery and the links it helps to establish are of such variety that they can lend the image movement and a sense of life. Readers of al-Sayyāb's works may differ in their interpretations of the symbols he uses or in their understanding of his images, but it is undeniable that the authenticity of the liveliness and sincerity of his imaginative gift remains a distinctive feature of al-Sayyab's art.

Something else to which we should draw attention is that the musical stress in the poem is subordinated to the meaning the poet is striving to convey and to the various poetic devices that are needed to convey the thought and feeling of the poem.

Tāhā Wādī. Jamāliyyāt al-qasīda al-muʿāsira (Cairo, Dār
al-Maʿārif, 1982), pp. 19–20†

AL-SHĀBBĪ, ABŪ AI-QĀSIM (1909–1934)

TUNISIA

The primary support on which the style of al-Shābbī is based is a neatness of expression coupled with firmness and authenticity. The style is also marked by being far removed from any kind of superficial tendency to the prosaic, that being a fault frequently criticized in many poets of the modern school, and especially those who belong to the Émigré School in North America. Al-Shābbī's style flows along with a spontaneity and gentle simplicity; it is that of someone who is well aware of the impact of words and the extent of the force which they can have both as images and as music. This is so to such a degree that, whenever the thrill of composing gains full control over him, his poetic genius plunges ahead with a liberality and ease of which the reader is almost completely unaware. The poet feels the same sensation as when a river is rushing toward the sea and he comes to be aware of the power of the source from which it has sprung. This is a characteristic that can apply only to someone who lives with the meaning of words and who senses the emotional reserves hidden within them. There is no reliance on simply the oral sensations of the word that can beguile the ear; rather, the poetry is based on burning emotions that pierce to the very core of human feeling. . . .

The force of al-Shābbī's style does not lie in his use of words, even though he is a skilled practitioner and can use colorful and harmonious phrases with all the innate skill of a great painter or musician. The real power lies in his emotional sensibility. His is a style you feel before you really come to understand it, since the spirit flowing through it stands in your way and fences you in; as a result, it is difficult to pinpoint where the force actually lies. It is the power of this sensibility that is everything in his art and poetic genius.

Khalīfa Muhammad al-Tilīsī. *Al-Shābbī wa-Jubrān* (Beirut,
Dār al-Thaqāfa, 1957; 2nd ed., 1967), pp. 101–2†

The poem "Prayers at the Temple of Love" arises from the opposition in the poet's soul between light and darkness, or perhaps between the ideal and reality. Thus, we see his despair of ever achieving happiness and his anger at the realities of this vanquished world. . . . Gentle, sweet, harmonious beauty, with all the delights of nature and the virtues of the soul contained within it, is what consoles the poet in the face of bitter reality. It helps him turn away from the attractions of despair and nothingness and strive instead to embrace happiness, truth, and God, who bestows His love on creation through beauty. Beauty is love, beauty of soul and body. And love is redemption.

This poetic experience is emotionalism at the very point of bursting forth. It feeds on hope and benefits from the experiences of the poet with both the soul and nature. . . .

It may well be that the process of including a large number of adjectives in a poem is a feature of the romantics in that the meaning is colored with the hues of emotion and thereby achieves a level that cannot be reached by a single direct phrase. The romantics, qua primitives, place a great stress on adjectives in their poetry, since they are carried away by the ardor and frenzy of the words they are using. . . . There is no point in counting the number of epithets, since they occur in almost every line in the poem. What can we say is that, in general, they occur either as the rhyme word or else near the end of the line, either by themselves or else repeated; it is almost as though they betray a certain facility in the craft of verse composition and a shortage of word formulations in the poet's own self and in his use of expressions. For al-Shābbī is certainly no pioneer in the realm of the finely honed phrase and the taut and refined expression. His own agonizing sufferings deprive his art of the quality of relaxation and fun and do not permit his artistic goal to be restricted to itself. . . . Al-Shābbī's poetry is born after a period of difficult labor involving tears and anguish. Other poets can make use of their untrammeled minds to play around with words and then polish, trim, and correct them as they wish.

Īliyyā al-Hāwī. Abū al-Qāsim al-Shābbī (Beirut, Dār
al-Kātib al-Lubnānī, 1972), pp. 85, 89–90†

The influence exerted by the literature of the Émigré School in North America on al-Shābbī and his writings almost surpasses any other such influences. This stems from his earliest schooldays, when we hear that al-Shābbī used to read a great deal of poetry by the North American Arab poets and memorize much of their verse. There can be little doubt that the greatest influences on the human mind can occur during one's youth. . . . Al-Shābbī was not yet fifteen when he read the works of poetry written by Arabs in America; that is an age of great importance when it comes to the development of thought, behavior, and habits, a time when the adolescent mind finds itself beset by numerous strange images, marvelous and attractive varieties of fantasy, love, and dreams. . . .

In everything he wrote, al-Shābbī was a torch that served to light the paths of life and the trails of glory, for revolutionaries, the vengeful, for those who aspire to the heights and who work to found a youthful glory and an eternal literature.

That is the way al-Shābbī was, and such was the effect that the Arab literature from North America had on him; it induced in him a liveliness and radiance, a purity and magic. However, there are other factors as well that had a clear effect on al-Shābbī and his thought. The most important, in my opinion, are the following three: first, translations of Western literature; second, the style of Tāhā Husayn and al-ʿAqqād together with the ideas of both; and lastly, classical Arabic literature.

Among the classical poets we should mention al-Maʿarrī, Ibn al-Fārid, Ibn al-Rūmī and al-Khayyām. He also read as much translated Western literature as he could lay his hands on, even though he could read no foreign language himself. He admired the great Western poets and was particularly fond of Goethe and Lamartine. . . .

When we read al-Shābbī's poetry, we can see that in his expression, his imagery, his ideas, there are clear lines to show what their basic source is. To that he himself adds a forcefulness of expression, an excellent presentation and use of imagery, a firmness of style, a breadth of language, a powerful imagination, a beauty of construction, and a brilliance in simile and metaphor; all these features certainly serve to ensure that al-Shābbī will be remembered as one of our few genuinely great poets.

Abū al-Qāsim Muhammad Karrū. Abū al-Qāsim al-Shābbī
(Tunis, Al-Sharika al-Tūnisiyya li-al-Tawzīʿ, 1973),
pp. 97–99, 101†

Much of al-Shābbī's nature poetry is influenced by his unrealistic dream of an idyllic solitary life in the enchanting forest (e.g., "The Bonds of Dreams"; "The Forest"); but this self-indulgence by the poet does not detract from the striking effect of some of his descriptions of nature. In "A Morning Remembrance," he pictures the countryside awakening in the morning, a magical, breathtaking vision, a worthy testimony to the glory of God. He cries ecstatically to his feelings to bind him to the holy beauty of this morning awakening, for in that bondage he will find artistic freedom.

In "The Sad Evening," the pastoral beauty of rural life settling for the night is set as a foil for the poet's hope, which alone is unable to find repose. Tortured by paroxysms of despair, he nevertheless sees in well-ordered nature the promise of a new dawn, after the darkness.

Sensual love is an important element of al-Shābbī's world of beauty. He writes about a childhood sweetheart who died ("The Stream of Love"; "Paradise Lost," etc.). This experience, along with his more mature reflection on love, led him to an appreciation of the spiritual quality of human affection. He warned of the deception of mere physical passion divorced from abiding spiritual elements ("Sought-after Beauty"). Love is dangerous, for it can be a curse as well as a blessing ("O Love"); it can either ignite the flames of sorrow or extinguish them ("The Sorceress").

In "Prayers in the Temple of Love," we find al-Shābbī's supreme tribute to love. In the beautiful woman and in love for her, he discovers the grandeur of God, so she becomes for him an altar where he, a devoted priest, offers worship.

The sources of al-Shābbī's poetic inspiration are no mystery. His verse throbs with sentimental music, recalling Musset, Lamartine and Hugo. His great teachers were the Lebanese writers of the Mahjar (emigration to the New

World), of whom Jibrān Khalīl Jibrān (d. 1931) and Amīn al-Rayhānī (d. 1940) were among the most illustrious representatives.

Al-Shābbī shows the same predilection for freedom, love, revolt against reaction, high humanistic ideals, veneration for nature, intense feeling and complete simplicity of expression that Jibrān the Christian reveals in his novelettes and prose poems. Al-Shābbī, the singer, is a Tunisian "Jibrān." This fact in itself is not particularly surprising. What is remarkable, and what helps to give our poet his independent stature, is that he is a Tunisian *Muslim* "Jibran" who had no other language than Arabic.

R. Marston Speight. *International Journal of Middle East Studies.* April, 1973, pp. 183–84, 186

Al-Shābbī is one of the most brilliant minds to appear on the poetic stage in the first half of this century. There are occasional structural weaknesses and linguistic mistakes, but they do not spoil the overall effect. They are caused not only by the fact that al-Shābbī's poetic training in Tunisia was not able to provide a Classical mastery of expression which alone was able at the time to invest the poetic structure with strength, but also because of his inclination towards Romanticism. He aimed at writing poetry on a contemporary level and he had to experiment first of all, with language, and to eliminate, as much as possible, the traditional use of stock words, phrases and images. . . .

The poet, faithful to the Classical tradition, talks *ex cathedra* as a wise man or prophet, and naturally the style in such poems acquires the old Classical dogmatism, the rhetorical tone and the all-knowing attitude. Compared with his greater poems of experience, these poems remain flat and cold, pointing to the presence of two conflicting sensibilities, a traditional, and a much stronger and more authentic sensibility. However, the traditional sensibility was never completely conquered in al-Shābbī, for, even up to the end of his short career, his fascination with abstract ideas persisted, and he wrote several poems in this vein which, in their prosaic, analytic style and their lack of charged emotions are among the least interesting of his productions.

His themes are diverse, and side by side with poems treating abstract ideas such as the glorification of poetry, of childhood and motherhood, or those revolving around introspective meditations and Romantic reveries, stand his great poems of personal and communal experience, of exuberant love and angry political and social rebellion. . . .

Poetry at his hands seemed free to be applied to almost any situation. This he was able to achieve more through a change in tone, imagery and emphasis than through radical alterations of the form of the poem. Most of his poems, in fact, keep to the conventional pattern of two hemistichs, coupled with monorhyme. Other forms were the couplet, some three verse stanzas, quatrains, and other stanza forms including *muwashshahs*.

Al-Shābbī's poetic idiom is often new and fascinating, but is not always sure, as we have seen. What characterizes him most is his youthful energy. His poems have a simple lyrical charm, and, in their more successful examples, there is hardly any rigidity. One merit of his poems, though not in the main those with a direct social content, is the fact that, despite their clarity, they are open to multiple interpretations. When he discusses more personal topics, a new level is achieved. His idealistic, rather sentimental treatment of the theme of Nature is often superseded by a tragic tone stemming from the realization of the incongruities and absurdities of life around him.

> Salmā al-Jayyūsī. *Trends and Movements in Modern Arabic
> Poetry* (Leiden, E. J. Brill, 1977), pp. 416–17, 422

AL-SHARQĀWĪ, ʿABD AL-RAHMĀN (1920–)

EGYPT

We can sense the injustices, the sufferings and the suppression of freedoms that capitalist-based imperialism is still able to impose upon a number of peoples. We are particularly sensitive to it since we have only recently escaped from such a fate ourselves; indeed it may be said that we are still suffering from some of the aftereffects in many aspects of our life. Thus, when we see these same injustices and crimes overwhelming a sister Arab country, our sense of tragedy is even more profound and sharp.

This theme is the solid base on which ʿAbd al-Rahmān al-Sharqāwī builds his play *The Tragedy of Jamīla*. He does not merely present a record of this courageous Arab struggle; nor is he satisfied simply to present scenes from the heroic fight put up by the people of Algeria. He has also managed to project a picture of man in his nobility thwarted amid so much evil, injustice, and wrongdoing. . . .

While it is true that verse drama has almost died out by now, there still remain attempts to revive it. There is, of course, a firm connection between tragedy and poetry. The most crucial element that attracts our interest in a tragedy is the human emotions it portrays; poetry always has been and will be the most accurate mode by which to express such emotions. ʿAbd al-Rahmān al-Sharqāwī has certainly benefited from his predecessors in this genre [such as Ahmad Shawqī, ʿAzīz Abāza, Muhammad Farīd Abū Hadīd, and ʿAlī Ahmad Bākathīr], but he has also added a new dimension in this new production by the use of modern poetry. Even if this were all *The Tragedy of Jamīla* had achieved within our modern literary development, it would be a great deal. . . . All this is not to claim that the whole play consists of beautiful poetry. There are a number of lines in it that have only meter and stress to connect them with poetry in any way. . . . Perhaps the nature of dramatic dialogue has imposed this on the author, added to which is his obvious desire to simplify his use of language and thus bring it nearer to his mass audiences. In this latter goal he has succeeded to a large extent without depriving the language of its structure or the beauty of its cadences.

Fu'ād Duwwāra. *Al-Majalla*. April, 1962, pp. 62–63,
66–67†

The Egyptian revolution of 1952, the Algerian war of independence, and the ferment in Syria and Iraq helped to make the 1950's a decade of radicalism in the Arab world and set the stage for the contemporary political novel. The strong social pressures generated by these events forced writers to seek commitment to and involvement in the political issues of the time. As one post-revolutionary author, 'Abd al-Rahmān al-Sharqāwī, has said, "A writer in this age cannot be just a writer. He must adopt a message. His message should be to defend life, the future of mankind, and the spiritual heritage of our civilization."

When Sharqāwī's first major work, *The Earth*, appeared, it was hailed by the new literary establishment as a model of revolutionary literature. It dramatized the dormant potentialities, suppressed aspirations, and usurped rights of the peasant. Above all, it expressed the possibility that the peasant, if he were only given a chance, might be capable of heroic acts. Sharqāwī's style became known as "critical realism." . . .

Following *The Earth*, Sharqāwī wrote *Back Streets*, the story of Shukrī 'Abd al-'Āl. An Egyptian army officer, Shukrī was forcibly retired in 1925 following an argument with his superior, a British officer, over Shukrī's refusal to open fire on Egyptian street demonstrators. The events of the story take place in 1935. Shukrī, now a widower, lives quietly with his two daughters on 'Azīz Street, a back street of Cairo. He is suddenly recalled to active duty and reinstated in his previous rank, but his primary interest continues to be with the people who live on 'Azīz Street. He solves their problems, reconciles their differences, protects the weak, and finds jobs for the unemployed. He eventually organizes the inhabitants of the street into an effective action group that participates in the 1935 uprising against the British.

George Sfeir. *Daedalus*. Fall, 1966, pp. 953–55

The novel *The Peasant* actually sheds even greater light than *The Earth* on the extent of Sharqāwī's commitment to the recording of historical reality, a commitment that sometimes carries preciseness to extreme limits. . . .

In *The Peasant* Sharqāwī finds himself caught between two poles: at times, we find the problems of *The Earth* solved, while at other times they are not solved yet; sometimes the problem is one of honor and freedom, and at others it concerns exploitation. In this situation, the author's vision loses the relative clarity that can help him to put it into shape. Furthermore, as a work of art it loses its coherence. When a storyteller can no longer put his vision into a convincing narrative form, the work becomes instead a collection of speeches and articles interspersed with events that are described and commented on by the author in exaggerated terms. . . . In *The Peasant*, Sharqāwī's village is on the move, but in a direction that has no clear guidelines. The movement seems to have lost orientation. The distinction between the subjective and objective becomes obvious and the subjective element imposes itself on the story once again, defining the course of events. . . .

The author tries to make the characters in *The Peasant* an extension of those in *The Earth*. Since the gap in time between the two is so large, he cannot achieve his goal in a direct fashion. Instead, he tries indirectly by creating substitutes for them and changing their names, altering the behavior of some of them in the process and introducing some new characters as demanded by the new circumstances of the village. These substitute characters have helped the author to present ready-made characters with psychological traits that are familiar to us from before. This situation absolves the author from the need to reveal any physical or psychological features of his characters through the development of the events in the novel, since he has fulfilled that function already. . . .

In the novel, the village as a whole, with all its petty officials and students, comes to accept the peasant ʿAbd al-ʿAzīm as leader and carries out his orders with respect and affection. The author does not mention any straying from the revolutionary path in the village, except that a small number of students are keen on soccer and that a few officials are somewhat hesitant. It is very hard for us to believe that revolutionary characters can really be a group with similar features to such an extent as this. That a character is "revolutionary" should mean that he is superficial or dull.

In *The Peasant* Sharqāwī is still trying to give a subjective portrayal of the village, to record its spontaneous activities and to treat the peasants as human beings. However, the opaqueness of that vision has prevented him from producing a successful work of art. This novel and *The Earth* are really one and the same thing.

ʿAbd al-Muhsin Tāhā Badr. *Al-Riwāʾī wa-al-ard* (Cairo,
Dār al-Maʿārif, 1971), pp. 159, 162, 177–78, 184–85†

It was not the plot, however, that gave Sharqāwī's novel [*The Earth*] such a distinctive place in the history of the Arabic novel. It was rather the fact that the Egyptian "fallah" became truly articulate in this work of fiction. Sharqāwī's rural characters are now deeply imprinted on the imagination of Arab readers. They have even become such familiar types that it is rather difficult not to trace their likenesses in the work of other writers and in the later work of the author himself. The author was conciously trying to debunk the romantic image of the countryside given in Haykal's *Zaynab* and other novels. His

heroine, Wasifa, is the village beauty as Zaynab had been, but it was not frustration in love that rendered her life a misery, but rather worry over an empty
larder, her father's imprisonment, the curfew imposed on the village because
of their resistance to government officials, the terror of the Black Camel
Corps sent to impose the curfew, and the constant threat of falling into the
abyss of the landless poor who "serve" on the Pasha's land or join gangs of
unskilled labourers at the mercy of one contractor or another. . . .

The rich gallery of characters includes the schoolmaster, the shop-
keeper, the shepherd of Bedouin origin, the treacherous headman of the village, the village Imam who calls the peasants to prayers, contracts marriages
and reads the Koran at the village wakes. He lives on presents from the villagers, but allies himself with the landlord and the authorities, calling up the
peasants to "obey God, His Prophet and the Authorities."

Sharqāwī's peasants wage a desperate struggle for land; it is not just their
means of livelihood but it means dignity. "A landless peasant has no dignity,
no honour," say the characters of the novel, written when the revolutionary
government was introducing agrarian reform on a wide scale for the first time
in the Arab world.

Fatma Moussa-Mahmoud. *The Arabic Novel in Egypt*
(Cairo, Egyptian General Book Organization, 1973),
pp. 41–42

Al-Sharqāwī's later novels have unfortunately lost the grandeur of *The Earth*
and degenerated into pure propaganda. What makes them readable is the dialogue alone, which is still close to the speech of the people. Their interest lies
in the indication they give of the way al-Sharqāwī's views on his country have
developed. *Empty Hearts* suffers from the fate of many second novels in trying to be a repetition of its successful predecessor, at least in some respects.
But its subject has none of the epic quality of *The Earth*; it is the record of the
faits divers of a student's vacation, marriages, petty scandals, romantic longings, the state of the crops, combined with certain events which have a wider
significance. The idea to which the author pays most attention here is that of
peasant morality, because of which Ghanim, the nearest to a central character,
gets involved in most of his quarrels. . . .

Empty Hearts is one of the few novels which give any prominence to the
foreigners living in Egypt. The local representatives of this group, Maria and
Panayoti, are spiteful and dishonest, trying to sell Ghanim's straw with their
own, and instrumental in getting him arrested. Panayoti makes propaganda
for the Axis powers, although it is one of the minor inconsistencies of the
book that a man with a Greek name should support the occupiers of his own
country and earn the description of pro-Italian. The occupying troops are felt
to have a corrupting effect on morals, and so they earn the Egyptians' dislike,

to such an extent that actions which would normally be frowned upon are approved when they are perpetrated against foreign soldiers.

This aspect of the novel can be justified generally, by the peasants' belief that their society is being corrupted by Europeans, and particularly by the events of 1956. The fact that the book was published soon after the Suez invasion also explains the muted tone of its political message. On the one hand there was a situation of national emergency which necessitated support for the existing government, on the other the Communists were not going through a period of repression and must have felt that with the beginning of Soviet aid their position was strengthened. The plea for democracy is there, but it has lost its ringing tone for the moment.

Hilary Kilpatrick. *The Modern Egyptian Novel* (London,
Ithaca Press, 1974), pp. 133, 136

The Earth does three main things. First, it tells the story of the animosity of a great part of the Egyptian people towards the oppressive and iniquitous governments that succeeded each other during the first half of the 1930s. More specifically, it tells of the struggle of the farmer-owners in a certain Egyptian village against those governments; secondly, it presents character portraits of some of the villagers. Thirdly it gives us an inside view of the village's milieu.

. . . The book is not a piece of concentrated drama: it offers a rich, closely observed picture of village life. It shows some indebtedness to Haykal and Tāhā Husayn. But, unlike them, Sharqāwī concentrates on the village itself and not on his own life, and he is more prepared to take the village on its own merit rather than on the terms of one of its urbanized or even cosmopolitanized sons. Moreover, the interest in *The Earth* is more socio-political than "cultural" (in a broad sense of the word) as it is in those parts of *Zaynab* and *The Days* that concern themselves with village life. But in the portrayal of character, and evocation of memories of village life, their influence shows very clearly in *The Earth*. Still, Sharqāwī proves his own intimate knowledge of the Egyptian countryside, and his own powers of evocation are evident. He shows us his village with its traditions, its small and close community, the solidarity of the villagers as well as their infighting and jealousies, their idiom, and samples of their songs and the roughness of their speech that has little of the niceness of town speech.

The author makes it his business to observe the villagers' speech habits and he uses it to augment the illusion of reality in his novels. Thus he conveys to us the roughness of the villagers' way of expressing themselves even when they are being friendly or affectionate. . . .

The novel is full of vivid, well-realized characters and partially or sketchily drawn vignettes. The author's characterization is given in the common form of direct descriptions of a character's appearance and some of his or her mental or emotional qualities, gradually augmented, in the case of more fully realized characters through dramatic presentation.

A. B. Jad. *Journal of Arabic Literature*. 3, 1976, pp. 88–90

AL-SHĀRŪNĪ, YŪSUF (1924–   )

EGYPT

The Five Lovers is a short-story collection that takes as its focus a single topic, even though the reader may notice differences in both characters and incidents within the stories. This topic is the wave of anxiety that has taken hold of the twentieth century as a result of progress in civilization and of the dominance of the machine first over human thinking and then over the emotions and whims of mankind. Yūsuf al-Shārūnī believes that this world of ours is a single unit, one in which any incident that may occur in the remotest corner of this globe will have a corresponding echo closer to us; any trend in culture, thought, or the development of civilization in its most general sense will undoubtedly have an effect on the world as a single, indivisible collectivity. Mankind goes back to a single origin, and from that premise it follows that the elements and inclinations of the human soul show no differences of a major or minor kind from one area of the world to another. . . .

In this collection of stories, al-Shārūnī has as his aim to portray the darker side of the life of mankind in this, the twentieth century. That does not imply that al-Shārūnī thinks there is any other side to life apart from this one, although we do detect within this work a glimmer of hope that the affairs of the world may settle down in a more peaceable manner. Even so, the prevailing philosophy behind this collection is a fatalistic and materialistic one above all else. . . .

We should also deal with another important point discussed by the author, the relationship between men and women and the connection that relationship has with the underlying philosophy behind this collection. That philosophy reflects the anxiety prevalent throughout the world that is a direct result of the clash of modern civilization with ideals and morals, or, to be more precise, the clash of science with the unknown. In much the same way, the sexual aspect, which is the most vital one as far as mankind is concerned, has been affected in no uncertain terms by this trend. It can be seen very clearly in some of the stories in the way the sexual urge is mingled with a sense of sin, since the conservative society in which the characters live has imposed restrictions on that urge. . . .

In my view, this collection represents a new vista in the modern Arabic short story in that the author has succeeded in ridding himself of the restraints of time and place and also of the traditions which have held sway over Arab writers in the modern period. He has emerged into a more public and comprehensive arena where he can take a look at those minor incidents in life, those general human issues, that we all have to face.

'Ādil Salāma. *Al-Adīb*. Feb., 1956, pp. 60–62†

One of the most skillful aspects of Yūsuf al-Shārūnī's artistry is that he does not restrict himself to the mainstream of the story, but chooses to append a whole series of ancillary details which may seem merely unnecessary frills to the reader who makes a hasty judgment but which actually afford the text an element of freedom and candor; as a result, the atmosphere of the story gains its full share of liveliness and impact. In "The Man and the Farm," for example, we find a great deal of detail about the doctor who comes to attend the wife's delivery. Through this extra description we are allowed to enter the house, experience its atmosphere, and be with its owner during his hours of stress. These additions to the basic story are the result of a carefully studied approach. They remain in the background of the general picture, but nevertheless can possess a life of their own and an ability to convey their impact to the reader. . . .

The reader cannot avoid feeling that Yūsuf al-Shārūnī is an extremely sensitive craftsman who is both shy and tolerant. One gets the impression that he is optimistic and honest, and that it is his own shyness rather than any principles involving the story that account for his avoidance of pushing himself into the story or allowing himself to make the slightest comment on the action. He may even go to excessive lengths in this regard. It is this modesty that seems to deprive his style of any humor, not to say sarcasm. . . .

I have gone through this latest collection [*Letter to a Woman*] page by page and line by line and can say that it is almost devoid of similes, except for one that describes a woman as being as white as cream and as fat as a duck. In spite of their simplicity, these two examples emerge like gleaming pearls in the midst of such a wasteland, and I relished them both. There are also some metaphors, but they are few and in any case hackneyed, with nothing new about them. I am well aware of the pitfalls of having too many similes in Romantic writing . . . but I believe very strongly that a well-chosen simile is one of the most effective means that can be utilized in good writing. Through the process of choice, the author gives us a glimpse of his own philosophy as he combines disparate things together into a unity with its own particular purpose; it is the way the author may bring the worlds of the material and spiritual closer together. . . . Yūsuf al-Shārūnī is a veritable Scrooge in his use of similes. I wish he would tone down his modesty and honesty a little so that his style would have a little more color and we could feel the pulse of life in his stories. That, after all, is the purpose of all really great art.

Yahyā Haqqī. *Khatawāt fī al-naqd* (Cairo, Maktabat Dār
al-'Urūba, n.d. [1960?]), pp. 275–78†

In the majority of cases, the action of the stories in the collection *The Crowd* takes place in buses or trains; it is almost as though the author is in the habit of riding one or the other mode of transportation on a regular basis, and that feature of his life permits him to get to know the popular characters from close up, to chat with them, to probe their ideas and innermost thoughts, and then to portray them in his stories in such a subtle and effective fashion.

It is precisely in buses and trains that the crowding is at its worst, and so it comes as no surprise that the author chooses to portray the phenomenon; sometimes the vehicle is so stuffed full of passengers "that it would be impossible to get any more on." . . . Hence comes the title of the first story, "The Crowd," which gives its name to the whole collection. However, the crowd does not occur only in buses . . . but finds itself everywhere that Fathī 'Abd al-Rasūl, the bus conductor, goes or stays. Where he lives the rooms are packed close together. Inside the rooms themselves the bodies of men and women are packed close together too; "and every time the darkness of night brings them together, they breed like rabbits." Fathī 'Abd al-Rasūl is terrified of these crowds and has been ever since his father took him as a young boy to a religious festival, forgot him there, and left him; he would have lost him forever if one of the men of the village had not come to his rescue. . . .

The personality of the author can be detected in this and all the other stories in the collection. This sense of crush is present in, and in fact almost overwhelms, every story, every expression, and every image. He even makes the time when his stories occur the very hottest days of summer so that the stench of the crowd can be inhaled and the total impact can be at its most effective. . . .

The author presents his stories in a sarcastic and jocular style. This atmosphere of jocularity can even be seen in his most tragic and shocking tales, a trait that can be noted in the titles and the similes used, the phrases and sentences, the names of people and places, and even in the mode of presentation.

You read Yūsuf al-Shārūnī's stories from beginning to end for pure enjoyment; they make you want to laugh. They tend more toward a classical approach than to anything else. The author seems to be someone who is well read in the great writers of short stories in world literature. What the stories lack, in my opinion, are concentration, a firm grasp on structure, and a connection between incidents within the story.

Tūmā al-Khūrī. *Al-Ādāb*. April, 1970, pp. 71–72†

If we take a close look at the treatment of character in Yūsuf al-Shārūnī's first two collections, *The Five Lovers*, and *Letter to a Woman*, we can see quite clearly that a radical change has occurred in the way in which he builds up his characters. In *Letter to a Woman* he has abandoned to a large degree the tense and nervous treatment of character found in the first collection and now relies instead on a more relaxed and composed approach, content merely to make detailed observations. Facets of this realistic characterization are clearly visible in the second collection and serve to replace the more frenetic and subjective expressionist characters whom we encountered in the first collection.

In *Letter to a Woman* al-Shārūnī puts things into a tangible realistic framework. Even that particular village in *The Five Lovers*, where one could find an effusion of nervous words and activities, is now enveloped in a realism that gives us all the details of daily life. . . .

In this second phase of al-Shārūnī's technique of characterization, the characters have only a limited number of features. They have a particular and restricted existence within the framework of the story itself. . . . They come into contact with external influences, and it is through them that the dimensions of the characters themselves are revealed to us. . . . Furthermore, while the al-Shārūnī character in this second phase can be termed realistic, it is also a character in a state of flux, one that constantly has two aspects to it. Through this double-faceted character, al-Shārūnī is able in several stories to realize that link between two parallel worlds in which the character lives and between which he commutes. This he achieves most especially through the use of the interior monologue, which explores a particular situation of tremendous personal importance to the character and which thus reveals his innermost emotions and throws his whole life open to scrutiny. . . . This use of a metaphorical style enables Yūsuf al-Shārūnī to make the building of his characters both broader and deeper in his second collection, *Letter to a Woman*.

Naʿīm ʿAtiyya. *Al-Ādāb*. March, 1974, pp. 26–27†

SHUKRĪ, ʿABD AL-RAHMĀN (1886–1958)

EGYPT

In looking over the collections of poetry by Shukrī we find that he manages to combine aspects of the work of his two colleagues, al-Māzinī and al-ʿAqqād; in al-Māzinī, it is the aspect of emotion and complaint, defiant and pessimistic; in al-ʿAqqād, it is the intellectual feature, which is such a hallmark of his poetry, full of a conscious intention. It seems that each of these poets took from Shukrī the particular facet that suited his own temperament.

Shukrī maintained both facets but allowed one to dominate the other; and it is from that dominance that the tragedy of his life stems. He is actually a sensitive poet of emotion, but he gives his mind full control over his feelings and emotions, over all his pent-up desire and yearning. Thus, he can be classed neither as an emotional poet nor as an intellectual one. Rather his poetry has its own particular stamp, one that can best be described as poetry of contemplation or introspection.

Introspection is a philosophical method well known in classical psychology, consisting of a process whereby the mind contemplates the human soul and attempts to analyze its various elements as a way of becoming acquainted with that soul. . . . The problem with this method is that it can afflict the people involved in it, especially if they are writers and poets with excitable temperaments and sensitive feelings. . . . It is precisely this danger that has actually afflicted Shukrī. Introspection has taken him so far that he has even gone beyond the stage of certain fictional characters such as Hamlet. . . . We can, in fact, deduce such conclusions from a reading of his *Book of Confessions* if we can take time enough to analyze this work, which is really a psychological study of Shukrī, carefully enough. But, in spite of everything, we can establish that 'Abd al-Rahmān Shukrī does indeed stand alone among contemporary poets through this unique and particular facet of his poetry, that of contemplation and introspection.

Muhammad Mandūr. *Muhādarāt fī al-shiʿr al-misrī baʿda Shawqī* (Cairo, Matbaʿat Nahdat Misr, n.d. [1955–58]), Vol. 1, pp. 99–102†

The most frequent theme encountered in the first two parts of Shukrī's diwan [*Collected Poems*] is that of melancholic unrequited love, the pangs of which he endures patiently and stoically. All this is linked with the general sadness, dissatisfaction, and injustice he encounters in life. Not only is there nothing new about such themes in Arabic poetry, but the manner in which Shukrī expresses them is highly traditional. . . .

There are certain detectable changes beginning with the third section of Shukrī's diwan (the third section being where the first of his prefaces appears); but this is not a dramatic or radical process, and it results mainly from his concentration on certain limited themes—particularly himself. It should be recalled that Shukrī advocates, in the voice and terms of Hazlitt, the primacy of the imagination and the passions. But he also insists on the variety and contrasts in these passions, using the Arabic meaning of "'atifa" to include opposites like love and hatred, hope and despair, jealousy and contentment, joy and sorrow, terror and tranquillity, and so on. This variety of contrasts is seized upon by Shukrī, who becomes so obsessed by the vicissitudes of fortune, by the bitter-sweet nature of life, that the bulk of the remainder of his poetry takes a positively schizophrenic tone. Throughout the hundreds of pages of the succeeding sections of his diwan, it is quite rare to find a moment of pure, sustained joy or of happiness unspoiled by some cloud of gloom or tragic recollection. In all his brooding gloom at the lack of lasting felicity, he retains his attitude of what he considers heroic endurance, bravely bearing all the injustice of his fate.

Robin Ostle. *Comparative Literature Studies.* 7, 2, 1970,
pp. 359–61

Shukrī expresses feelings of bitterness and despair in some of his poems, but you will not be able to find a sufficient amount of such feelings in all his eight collections to fill a single volume! Thus, it seems entirely inappropriate to focus all our attention on that one aspect, thus ignoring the spirit of optimism about mankind, the desire to promote lofty values as a model for imitation, and the steadfast resistance to evil and terror, all of which emerge clearly from other poems. . . . The poet will inevitably portray the various moods of the human soul in different situations, and so he will give a picture of both the lighter and darker sides of that personality as he sees it and comes into contact with it. Were he merely to concentrate on one aspect, he could not possibly give his readers a satisfactory or complete picture. . . . If, at one particular moment, the poet finds himself projecting his own sense of despair, this does not mean that he is indicating a lack of confidence in the future of mankind. It is merely the verbal expression of a passing emotion, which will be overwhelming for an instant but will then dissipate just like a cloud. . . .

There is an optimistic note to be detected in many of his poems, but even that is not meant to be a basis for a discussion about hope, truth, goodness, and beauty. The impetus comes from a general theory of humanity. If, as several commentators have claimed, he was really inclined toward a pessimistic view, then he would presumably have put a distance between himself and such talk. As it was, he aimed, perhaps unconsciously, to put his own smiling and optimistic notions into words, something which in itself establishes that such feelings were active deep down inside him.

Muhammad Rajab al-Bayūmī. *Al-Adīb.* May, 1970,
pp. 35–36†

There are perhaps too many poems about the theme of idealized love in Shukrī's work, and their cumulative effect tends to be rather monotonous, especially as the tone is generally solemn and unrelieved by any humour. Furthermore, they are mostly in the first person: there is not enough variety in them which could have been achieved if the poet had made a greater use of the narrative and dramatic poems. Not that Shukrī's poetry is entirely lacking in formal variety. He uses the narrative and the dramatic monologue, deriving his material from well-known pre-Islamic Arabic stories and legends, or from more modern sources. . . .

Stylistically, too, despite the profound influence of English Romantic poetry on him, Shukrī's style remains in many respects traditional: the vocabulary is still quite difficult, requiring a glossary, and the verse does not flow smoothly enough for the particular themes it tries to express. As has already been mentioned, Shukrī addresses the beloved in the traditional masculine form, and occasionally uses conventional love and desert imagery. He has an unmistakable tendency to express himself in generalizations, sentiments and moral precepts in the manner of traditional gnomic verse. Once or twice when as a young man he talked about his great ambition he struck the note of traditional boastfulness (*fakhr*). He sometimes complains of his times in the manner of Mutanabbi, and even in a poem expressing *ennui*, a specifically modern disease, we hear verbal echoes from Mutanabbi's verse. It is true that Shukrī can attain a high degree of lyricism, as in his most accomplished poem "The Bird of Paradise," but this does not happen frequently enough. On the contrary, he can easily descend to the level of what is largely poetry of mere statement, even in a poem about a Romantic theme, as "The Ideal," which is an unabashed defence of the infinite inner world of dreams and the imagination against the drab and limited external reality.

Mustafa Badawi. A Critical Introduction to Modern Arabic
Poetry (Cambridge, England, Cambridge University Press,
1975), pp. 104–5

In 1909 'Abd al-Rahmān Shukrī published his first *dīwān* entitled *The Light of the Dawn*. In this *dīwān* he wrote an unrhymed poem of 162 verses which he labelled "A Poem in Blank Verse" and entitled it "Words of the Emotions." . . . There are narrative, romantic and meditative poems dealing with life, love, the soul, and other romantic subjects. He also versified some thoughts on love, life and emotions in two verses or more, such as "Sadness and Happiness," "The Way of Love," "The Twilight," etc. The same is the case with his second *dīwān*, entitled *Pearls of Thought* (1913). It does not contain any strophic verse, but there are four unrhymed poems. . . .

In the preface to his fifth collection, *The Notions* (1916), Shukrī discussed his new understanding of poetry. He argued that the field of poetry is to become aware of his emotions and to express what affects his spirit, and that the poet writes to the human intellect in every generation, and not to certain people, or to a particular nation. He must be intelligent and widely educated, in order to be able to create a public which can understand him. Shukrī also criticized the conventional idea that poetry must resort to falsehood and fancy. He argued that fancy (*tawahhum*) is a superficial, trivial and ephemeral activity which does not clarify reality, while the imagination (*takhayyul*) is an affirmation, and does illuminate eternal facts, the relationship between the subject and its simile, the right combination between character and object. Moreover, simile has to be evocative and inspiring, and used for clarifying external reality, not for its own sake. He also distinguished conciseness of style (*matāna*), rare words (*gharīb*) and pallor of style (*rakāka*). He preferred conciseness in simple style. He also called for the organic unity of the poem, and the unity of emotion and thought.

However, Shukrī's blank verse remained conventional. The verse of two hemistichs remained the unit in the poem, with no overflow of sense or real organic unity in the poem as a whole. Many of his poems are moral criticism of the upper class. Their tone is lyrical, melancholic, and [they] strike bitterly at his targets.

S. Moreh. *Modern Arabic Poetry 1800–1970* (Leiden,
E. J. Brill, 1976), pp. 66–67

The influence of the English Romantic school on Shukrī is apparent. Here is a new and idealized attitude towards poetry, similar to that of Gibrān. The poet's place in life is described as lofty and distinct from that of the ordinary person. "The true poet sees that poetry is the most glorious thing he can do in life and [believes] that he was born for it and that it is not a complement to his life but its very essence." Every poetic genius is worthy of being called a prophet of nature sent to this world to enhance men's souls and move their spirits, illumine and set them aflame. He is God's greatest creation and he penetrates deep into the soul and strips it of its secrets. However, there is little in Shukrī's poetry to show that he was able to penetrate deep into the realms of the soul and express its emotional and spiritual conflicts. Much of it remains on a rather superficial level, and although he did manage to express feelings and experiences of a subjective nature, and to establish some link with the human heart, he rarely went beyond this. The contrast in this respect between his poetry and his creative prose works, such as *Book of Confessions* and *Satan's Memoirs*, is significant. It was in prose that Shukrī felt free to depict the explosive elements felt in society, bringing to the fore his dark impressions, hatred, revulsion, despair and final condemnation in a way he was never able to do in poetry. This is again a proof that the poetic tools were not sufficiently flexible in the hands of the poets of the time and could not be used to the best advantage. Although most of Shukrī's poetry revolved around the love theme, nearly all of it followed the traditional pattern of love poetry in Arabic (the playful or plaintive tone, the play of words, the pseudo-fascination with "purity," the repetitive and limited experience); his power of introspection was limited and in his expression of personal experience, he was rarely able to achieve real emotional veracity.

Salmā al-Jayyūsī. *Trends and Movements in Modern Arabic
Poetry* (Leiden, E. J. Brill, 1977), p. 158

SURŪR, NAJĪB (19??–197?)

EGYPT

Even though the play's title carries the names of *Yāsīn and Bahiyya* and tells their story, the author is not so much concerned with the fate of the individual as with the era itself and the fate of the community as a whole. Epic drama takes as its topic the objective social world and its moving forces; it is concerned with conveying a sense of this world to the audience. In this particular play the basic situation involves the relationship of man to society. It is true that Yāsīn and Bahiyya are individual characters in their emotions and in their love story, and that this love story shows the distinctive aspects of the characters—their feelings, thoughts, and passions—but even so, the prominent position given to emotion serves basically to deepen our awareness of the objective reality, as we watch personal feelings clash with social and economic circumstances. In the same way, the fact that the characters express their sense of contradiction between their own private world and the external factors governing it serves to elucidate the way they are overwhelmed by their environment. Through such a concentration on the components of the social environment in depicting characters, the stereotypical aspect emerges clearly without causing any loss of individuality. Furthermore, the two principal characters are closely linked to a group of peasants through common emotional bonds; they all have a sense of their oppression and the common destiny that unites them. Thus, the narrator starts by telling us that he will be telling the story of "the Beys" and "Yāsīn and Bahiyya"; this word order gives precedence to the Beys, the oppressors of society in general. . . .

This linkage in the presentation of societal destiny is seen in the connection between the three levels on which the events of the play operate; on the first, we find the narrator and the crowd; on the second, a group of peasants in dire straits; and on the third, the family of Yāsīn and Bahiyya. The first level tends to be narrative in function, while the other two are dramatic. Characters and events are usually described and analyzed through narrative, which gives the work a narrative quality that is a feature of the epic drama (even though it is somewhat exaggerated in this instance). Even so, the poetic images are visual and tactile, taking shape in the imagination as physical images; such is also the case on the other two dramatic levels in a structure that unifies the narrative and the dramatic approaches. This linkage among the three different levels makes the movement from one level to another smooth and easy.

Amīn al-ʿAyūtī. *Al-Masrah.* Dec., 1964, pp. 81–82†

In his play *O Night, O Moon!* Najīb Surūr has used the folktale of Yāsīn and Bahiyya to tell the story of the struggle of the Egyptian people from the time when the peasants were oppressed by the Turkish Beys until the period before the revolution of July 23, 1952. By the end of the play the author has made a firm connection between the Egyptian people's struggle against imperialism, represented by the British occupation, and a similar struggle against exploitation in the form of feudalism and capitalism. The two struggles are really two aspects of one movement. The two predominant elements in the play reflect the author's vision of reality and govern the essence of all popular movements: the first is the idea of renewal and continuity; the second is the victory of the will to live over death. Each is essential and complements the other. . . .

In the printed text the author terms the play "a poetic tragedy in three acts." I cannot agree with that description. The play is neither tragic nor poetic. . . . The Arabic word for tragedy refers to the traditional form that began with the Greeks, developed in the hands of many writers through the ages, and has now assumed its contemporary form in the works of such dramatists as Ibsen and O'Neill. In spite of its continual development, however, tragedy has maintained its principal feature, namely, that it shows an organic growth from beginning through middle to end; the conflict in a play must also take its course from start to finish. Such criteria cannot be applied to *O Night, O Moon!*

To say that this is a poetic play only scratches the surface, but does not indicate a deeper exploration of its nature. The language, which varies from colloquial metrical verse to a kind of rhymed prose, is evidence of a basic poetic form. Style, however, here represents the means, not the end in itself. It is a necessary consequence of the epic structure, which implies a specific vision that comprehends reality in all its intricacies and contradictions; such a mature view of reality absolutely requires the use of a poetic style, which can tolerate dissimilarities and enables the writer to explore ambiguities. . . .

With a rare talent for both drama and poetry, and through his genuine love for Egypt and its people, Najīb Surūr has offered us through this play a superb work of art that is valuable in itself but that also marks a turning point in modern Egyptian drama. Since his vision of reality is in accord with the one that forms the basis of epic drama, he has succeeded in grasping the epic dramatic form and molding it to the exigencies of artistic expression as they emerge from the Egyptian environment and personality. He has thereby provided Egyptian drama with a form that has everything it needs to carry on into the foreseeable future.

Latīfa al-Zayyāt. *Al-Majalla*. April, 1968, pp. 38–39, 43†

The title of this play, *Where Shall I Get People From?*, Najīb Surūr's fourth verse drama, derives from folklore. To those who are familiar with the previous works of this dramatist, the title comes as no surprise. His artistic temperament combines within itself drama and song, and he has been able to blend these two elements successfully, which many others have failed to do.

In this play, however, there is no doubt that the song element has over-whelmed the dramatic movement.

The first thing we notice is the title itself; . . . it is a sentence derived from a folk song of Adham al-Sharqāwī . . . and Surūr is drawing our atten-tion to the fact that folk songs will form a major artistic medium in this lyrical drama. . . . The title also indicates that our cultural heritage has exerted a con-siderable influence on the playwright: the Pharaonic hymns to the dead; cer-tain concepts derived from the Koran and the New and Old Testaments; the poetry of al-Maʿarrī [d. 1057], particularly his *Luzūmiyyāt*; the poetry of Ahmad Shawqī; and the popular verse of Bayram al-Tūnisī. The play's con-tent also shows the strong influence of popular songs. . . .

The subject of the play is derived from the tale of Hasan and Naʿīma. . . . However, Surūr begins where that story ends. Hasan the singer has been mur-dered, and his faithful beloved, Naʿīma, wanders from one village to another in search of his body (just like Isis in the Pharaonic myth). . . .

Because of the way the play is put together, the manner in which the con-flict is set up, and the temperament of its poet-author, it seems inevitable that it will be sung throughout and will constitute a lyrical drama. If it is to be pre-sented on stage, I would strongly suggest that a great deal of song and expres-sive dance be used and that copious use be made of lighting effects and changes of scenery so that the play may be seen in a manner that accords with its own special artistic format.

Tāhā Wādī. *Al-Kātib*. April, 1976, pp. 110–13, 115†

Najīb Surūr was a poet and director of great talent. All his plays possess a haunting beauty, being expressed in a poetry of great musicality and vivid-ness. His version of the Hasan and Naʿīma story takes place after the murder and is entitled *Where Shall I Get People From?* (1976). Naʿīma wanders through Egypt in search of the body of her beloved and meets all kinds of peo-ple. She discusses with them the oppression under which they all suffer; the general atmosphere is a pessimistic one and within this framework the figure of Hasan comes to represent resistance. To my knowledge, this play has yet to be performed on stage, and bearing in mind the characteristics of Surūr's dramatic oeuvre and the difficulties in staging his previous plays, that is per-haps not surprising. His first play, *Yāsīn and Bahiyya* (1963), was described by one critic as "a long dramatic poem." Critics were unanimous in declar-ing that the transfer of the play to the stage, in spite of the obvious attempts on the writer's part to incorporate all manner of Brechtian devices—the use of a narrator and chorus, for example, in order to provide the element of distancing—created problems. The direction was entrusted to Karam Mu-tāwiʿ, one of the most brilliant of the younger generation of directors, and the play was performed in the more intimate surroundings of the Masrah al-Jayb (Pocket Theatre). The love story of Yāsīn and Bahiyya is set in an Egyp-

tian village in pre-revolutionary days. Yāsīn is deprived of his land by the local pasha, but he gradually learns to resist, and before being killed, he leads
the peasants of the village in a fierce revolt against feudalism. The story is
continued in a second play, *O Night, O Moon!* (1967), in which Bahiyya has
married Yāsīn's aide, Amīn, and they are living in Port Saʿīd at the time immediately before the Egyptian Revolution of 1952 when Egyptians were fighting the British army stationed at the Canal. Amīn is killed in the fighting, and
Bahiyya is once again a widow.

All of Surūr's plays use the dramatic mode to highlight the most important events within the particular tale which is being related; there is no illustration of the development of the situation. This lends them many of the features
of a tableau. The element of distancing provided by the narrator and chorus
and their comments constitutes a further challenge to the ingenuity of the director of such works. The very beauty and musicality of Surūr's poetry en-
courages the use of both music and singing in productions, and all those
which have occurred have made generous use of these media to aid the forward movement of the play and to popularize the otherwise stark and static
presentation. It seems fair to say that these plays were interesting experiments
in dramatic techniques and in the possibilities of utilizing Egyptian lore in advancing the cause of drama, but critical and popular reaction suggests that
most of the theatre-going pubic were not prepared for such radical attempts.

Roger Allen. *Edebiyat.* 4, 1, 1979, pp. 112–13

TĀHĀ, 'ALĪ MAHMŪD (1902–1949)

EGYPT

There are some people who accuse Tāhā of "westernizing" poetry. For my
part, I applaud this tendency and regard it as a means of honoring Arabic poetry and of educating Eastern tastes and developing the Arabic language, provided that both are prepared to accept things that have never been done before. If I could criticize the poet for anything, then it would be for the way his
own stance serves to confuse the reader; we do not know whether his encounter with his Eastern and Western colleagues has come about purely by chance
or whether it is the result of a deliberate effort on his part. . . .

Let me add that I find the style of his poetry to be pleasant and the diction
eloquent; he chooses his words with great care. His language and his ideas
have a most attractive luster to them that prompts the reader to ask for more.
There is also a music in his poetry that is rarely encountered in the works of
many modern poets. To a large degree, Tāhā has succeeded not only in blending grace of language and of thought, but also, in the brilliance, beauty, and

purity of his style, in reconciling modernism with traditionalism. All this is
evident in his collection *The Lost Mariner*, and I would cite as exceptions to
this rule only the poems that were recited on public occasions, where the inspiration does not spring from the soul of the poet. Our poet is an interpreter
of nature, and also of mankind, whenever he is in communion with nature and
loses his way in its wilderness or amid the fascinations of its beauty. But he is
not a person to deal with groups, either as a poet or interpreter. Instead, he is a
singer whose personality is stronger than his environment, rather than a storyteller whose environment is more powerful than he is.

At this point I should express my annoyance to him . . . in that, while he
pays great attention to the music of his words (something that is necessary and
for which we owe him thanks), he focuses more on the music of meter than of
rhyme, and I find his use of rhyme objectionable in several instances. . . . Another thing for which I would criticize him is that on occasion his syntax and
idiom is deficient; he would no doubt be able to find people belonging to one
school or another who will suggest that such and such an anomaly is possible,
but I dislike seeing serious and excellent poets resorting to such excuses.
[1945]

Tāhā Husayn. Hadīth al-Arbiʿāʾ (Cairo, Dār al-Maʿārif,
1957), Vol. III, pp. 146–48†

ʿAlī Mahmūd Tāhā was a disciple of Khalīl Mutrān, and in following Mutrān's school of ardent emotion, he was much aided by his French education.
He described nature through his own consciousness, breaking loose from the
restrictions imposed on Arabic verse during the classical period and turning
from old genres such as eulogy and raillery to new, universal themes. The
subject matter of his poetry differs in its essentials from the older lyrical poetry and shows a greater intensity and involvement. There is also a marked
change in imagery and invention in his verse; they are complex and cannot be
conveyed merely by linguistic niceties such as similes and metaphors. The
range of the image is greatly expanded, particularly in regard to nature. . . .

Tāhā was especially influenced by French literature and the luminaries of
the Romantic school in France, such as Lamartine and Alfred de Musset.
Tāhā's collections are full of emotional poetry that devotes all of its energies
to the expression of the personal feelings that distinguish the poet from other
people. And that is the essence of inventiveness in literature. . . .

A veritable cloud of grief, despair, and alienation seems to hover over
Tāhā's early poetry. . . . This is precisely the same tendency to melancholia
that predominated in the writings of the Romantics in Europe as a result both
of their failure to achieve their aspirations in their poetry, of their conflict with
the bitterness of reality, and their revolt against so many of the customs that
fettered society. . . .

Anyone reading his later poetry cannot fail to notice that the shadows caused by this melancholy gradually disappear until they are almost invisible. This may be because once he had achieved glory, fame, and fortune, he devoted himself more to the sensual pleasures of life in the belief that life is short and should be enjoyed as much as possible. . . .

Tāhā was influenced not only by the French Romantics . . . but also by the English members of that school as well. For example, he translated Shelley's well-known poem "To a Skylark" into Arabic. . . . He expressed his personal experiences and feelings in his poetry, using such Romantic images as sunlight, the waves of the sea, sand dunes, the call of the nightingale, and the cooing of doves.

Jamāl al-dīn al-Ramādī. Khalīl Mutrān (Cairo, Dār
al-Ma'ārif, n.d. [1960]), pp. 315–16, 318, 321, 323–24†

One of the features of 'Alī Mahmūd Tāhā's poetry is that he only rarely makes use of imagery. It might seem to some that a poem without any images will be stripped bare and deprived of a great deal of its beauty and authenticity. However, we soon come to realize that in Tāhā's poetry the fact that there are few images does not detract in any way from it, since it manages to retain a great deal of beauty and brilliance. The reason for this peculiar situation is that the poet possesses a special and remarkable ability to create a suggestive and fascinating radiance that blinds us to the fact that there are few images. Tāhā thus emerges as a poet of atmosphere, not one of imagery, and as such, he differs from other poets like Nizār Qabbānī, Mahmūd Hasan Ismā'īl, and Badr Shākir al-Sayyāb, who rely more on imagery than on atmosphere and rarely succeed in creating an ambience rich enough to lend significance to the poem itself. . . .

In many of Tāhā's poems we also find him using symbols to illustrate ideas that he does not express explicitly. . . . We should immediately point out however that these poems do not place Tāhā in the ranks of the Symbolist school as it was known in France and then Europe as a whole in the nineteenth century. Tāhā's symbolism is that of an Arab poet, in the literal sense of the word "symbol." A symbol is a means of alluding to something and even of clarifying it. It gives the poem profound dimensions that stimulate thought and give the aspirations of the imagination room to move. . . . All Tāhā's symbolic poems number among his most excellent works. . . .

Nāzik al-Malā'ika. Muhādarāt fī shi'r 'Alī Mahmūd Tāhā
(Cairo, Ma'had al-Dirāsāt al-'Arabiyya al-'Āliya, 1965),
pp. 156–57, 164–65†

In Tāhā's second volume, The Nights of the Lost Mariner, a significant change [from melancholic idealized love] takes place. It is true that in it we still find a poem such as "The Statue," which is a dramatically moving and somewhat allegorical work, representing the loss of hope at the approach of old age. This poem however, is not typical of the general mood of the second volume, any more than a poem like "She," in which the poet expresses regret at having defiled his spirit by indulging in carnal pleasures. *The Nights of the Lost Mariner* celebrates the pleasures of the flesh in a manner that is perhaps new in modern Arabic poetry. It represents the poet's liberation from the narrow teachings of a puritan society, mainly as a result of his exposure during his travels to Europe in which he found not only a different kind of landscape of breathtaking beauty, consisting of lakes and mountains hitherto unfamiliar to him, but also a way of life that is colourful and gay. . . .

Tāhā is chiefly a lyric poet, although two of his seven volumes represent interesting excursions into fields other than that of lyrical verse. *Spirits and Shades* is a long dramatic poem of about 400 lines, a dialogue between various characters, a hotch-potch, in fact, of many figures from Greek mythology and the Bible. The theme of the poem is the conflict between body and soul, represented in man's relation to woman, and the style used is highly evocative, relying heavily upon sheer profusion of imagery. Similarly, *Song of the Four Winds* is a dramatic experiment, based upon a fragment of an ancient Egyptian song in which a sailor makes an unsuccessful attempt to capture four maidens, representing the four winds, by luring them to his ship. Around this Tāhā weaves a dramatized story, pointing out the unhappy end met by a dissolute and lecherous Phoenician pirate given to the pursuit of illicit earthly pleasures. With the exception of a number of poems in the last volume, *East and West*, which deal with political and nationalist themes, the whole output of Tāhā concerns the poet's personal experiences. These he managed to express in a highly musical verse in which he evolved a very skilful strophic form based on *muwashshah*, and made a successful use of the quatrain, especially to convey philosophical meditations in poems of unusual length. His achievement encouraged a whole generation of younger men among his admirers throughout the Arab world to imitate him, often in a facile and derivative manner. This is true of his hedonistic themes and images no less than of the other aspects of his own brand of romanticism which combines a fondness for sensous pleasures and a tendency to suffer from vague metaphysical doubts.

Mustafa Badawi. *A Critical Introduction to Modern Arabic Poetry* (Cambridge, England, Cambridge University Press, 1975), pp. 141, 144–45.

The imagery in 'Alī Mahmūd Tāhā's poetry, bursting with life and rich in meaning, uses every human sense—sight, hearing, taste—and even contemplation. The poetry also evinces a blending of essence and nature, of the material and the spiritual, and of delicate sensitivity and an awareness of the realities of life. . . .

Another thing to note about the aesthetics of Tāhā's work is that he is considered among his generation of Romantic poets as one of the foremost preservers of the traditional Arabic poem, both in regard to rhyme and meter and to the correctness and appropriateness of diction. He also shares with [Ahmad] Shawqī a certain kind of objectivity, that is, his works display the public personality of the poet. Tāhā worked hard on matters of general concern to the people of his country and religion. It is not surprising therefore that in his writings we find what is termed occasional poetry on two levels, the local Egyptian one and the pan-Arab one. . . .

Many of Tāhā's poems can serve as illustrations of his preservation of the traditions of the Arabic poem. Even so, they also show that, in spite of his sometimes conservative tendencies, he was at the same time one of those poets of his generation who were assiduous in trying to achieve a unity of idea within the poetic structure and to tie the content and style of the poem together into a single harmonious and unified creation.

ʿAlī Mahmūd Tāhā will remain one of the luminaries among our modernist poets and the second of the two great poets of the Apollo Group, the other being Ibrāhīm Nājī.

> Tāhā Wādī. *Jamāliyyāt al-qasīda al-muʿāsira* (Cairo, Dār al-Maʿārif, 1982), pp. 174–75†

TĀMIR, ZAKARIYYĀ (1931–   )

SYRIA

This collection of short stories by Zakariyyā Tāmir, *The Neighing of the White Horse*, should really be called a long ode to mankind, to man as a lover, as a good person, as a picture of sorrow, as a revolutionary; both compassion and fervor radiate from him. Lively, tangible images emerge, but there is also a tragic, poetic sense of human failure. Abundant life-giving rain will fall on the stony ground covered with thorns, and the artist will bring about his own adjustment to the process of creation. His aim is to grasp the dark thorn, squeeze it, and extract from it the seeds of beautiful flowers. . . .

Tāmir is a master of the world of the tragic imagination. He lays bare the material dimensions of images and gives them terrifying witches wings, just like the witches in *Macbeth*, who bring Macbeth tidings of murder and kingship at the same time. Although Tāmir uses sensory imagery in the way he portrays hunger in the stomach, hunger for sex, and hunger for honor and love, he still presents us with dark visions, in which lurk the transformation through art of thorns into roses that will never have an existence of their own, will never exude their gorgeous perfume, and will never reveal their glorious, flirtatious spring blossoms. . . .

The reader comes to realize that every story in this remarkable collection is, in fact, a project involving the construction of magical worlds that have no point of contact with reality. In fact, these magical worlds end up destroying that reality for the sheer pleasure of rejection and arrogance. The stories emphasize the idea that the world of the inner self has its own value, without any recourse to the concrete.

Mutāʿ Safadī. *Al-Ādāb.* Dec., 1960, pp. 37–38†

In Zakariyyā Tāmir's collection *Spring in the Ashes,* love transcends sex and deprivation and brings us to a fabulous, magical world, to a world of creative love that uses childhood, the sea, travel, and dream-making in forests to fashion its familiar and matchless flowers. . . . And when it is clothed in the superb poetic language that distinguishes Tāmir's style, love shines forth, delicate and incandescent, far removed from the traditional atmosphere of union and separation. Love here is a necessity for other worlds, which draw sustenance and comfort from it. . . .

Tāmir's stories are filled with rich characterizations; each one is a living world pulsating inside a small segment of prose. In these stories the heroes suffer from all kinds of problems. Loneliness, lack of freedom, and bitter disappointment rain blows on them mercilessly, as, for example, in "The First Face" and "The Crime," in the second of which the author paints us a picture of the underworld, the world of sinners and of divine retribution. . . . The reader is shocked by the realization that the author, in a most striking fashion, places the protagonist, Sulaymān al-Halabī, in one world, and his brother and parents in its opposite. . . .

Saniyya Sālih. *Hiwār.* No. 5, 1964, pp. 119–20†

The story "The Face of the Moon" attempts to capture the first moment of awareness of sexual desire in the depths of a young woman. It is a pure psychological story and the writer would consider himself successful to have put this experience in any concrete form. His protagonist, Samīha, does not represent a common phenomenon or a general problem; she is true to her own experience. But through her individual experience we come in touch with the larger problem of sex in the Arab East. So, at one and the same time, Samīha represents her own problem and that of her kind. For an oriental woman, sex is—and has been for many ages—a vague experience in which illumination, even after marriage, is precarious. Without the help of circumstances of the sort that this story illustrates, an oriental woman may marry, give birth to a dozen children, tell her grown-up daughters about marriage and instruct them in the minimum of sexual techniques necessary to please their husbands and die without having gone through any genuine sexual experience—as we gather from some brief hints in the story. . . .

It is not easy to grasp the idea of the story from a quick reading, but one is inclined to feel after the first reading that what can be called the ambiguity of the story is of that kind which arouses the reader's curiosity and makes him read it more carefully. From the beginning one feels that the story has something to say: what it says about the world of the senses is interesting but it is mainly concerned with the inner world of the character. Vagueness, then, is not the fault of the story; it is rather the reflection of the vagueness of the inner world, which cannot be explained in any definite, clear vocabulary. In fact the writer has no choice but to resort to the objective correlative to express the inner movement of the psyche. . . .

In such a story it is not easy to differentiate between content and style in the classical sense. The story forms an integral unity. The images, for example, cannot be spoken about in terms of rhetoric; they should be understood as substitutes for particular feelings which cannot be put into direct, ordinary language. Their value lies in their suggestiveness. Sometimes they do not appeal to the reader aesthetically, but they are able in most cases to communicate the mood. . . .

The sentences also reflect the movement of the story. At the beginning they flow at ease, and are of normal speed and length. But gradually they grow shorter and quicker with the growth of emotional movement inside Samīha. The writer relies heavily on the short verbal clause beginning with a verb in the past tense and advancing with gradually accelerated rhythms. These clauses are in the past tense only in grammatical terms; in the story they have the living power of the present. This is exactly what is wanted in the style of the short story.

H. al-Khateeb. Journal of Arabic Literature. 3, 1972,
pp. 100–101, 103, 104–5

Zakariyyā Tāmir has published three collections of short stories: *The Neighing of the White Horse* (1960), *Spring in the Ashes* (1963), and *Thunder* (1970). In addition he has written a large number of stories that are not included in the three collections, even though some of them were both written and published before the appearance of the second collecton and the majority were in print before the publication of the third collection. There are, in fact, so many of them that they could easily make up two further collections of the same size as the ones already published. These facts lead us to make our initial observation about Tāmir's world of the short story. For each of his collections he is eager to produce a harmony and a sense of completeness in style and content; hence, the collections seem to be a wide-ranging storytelling experience involving a variety of voices but an integrated vision. There may be a large number of themes, but they are not incompatible, and the characters, while they share features, are not repetitious. The situations vary, but there is no sacrifice of the total structural and ideational unity that brings together all these themes, similar characters, and varying locales and situations. In my opinion, it is for this reason that Tāmir has left some of his best stories out of his published collections, a view corroborated by the fact that many of the omitted stories present the reader with a world that is a unity in itself. . . .

An important aspect of Tāmir's world, which coincides with our discussion of his vision of the world through the eyes of children, is the fact that he is extremely involved in the world of children; as an artist he is one of the most expert at making use of this feature in his stories. I am not talking about children as little beings who need love and sympathy from grown-ups, who have to be talked down to. Rather I mean that children constitute another world with its own rules and its special potential for unrestrained liberties. It is characterized by an intelligence higher than that of adults and by an ability to imagine in a way that even the greatest poets are unable to match, a world with its own logic, more genuine and coherent than that of older people. . . . Tāmir knows all the secrets of this remarkable world; he makes his way there and devotes some of his time to its logic, almost as though he has himself become a child again, a child who has managed to break away from the tedious world of grown-ups. In all this he shows a wonderful awareness of the magical, frightening world of the young.

Sabrī Hāfiz. *Al-Ādāb*. Sept., 1973, pp. 32, 38†

Zakariyyā Tāmir's work is a splendid example of the maturity of the expressionist school. . . . His stories are characterized by their liveliness, spontaneity, and authenticity; they are a combination of innocence and madness. Tāmir is an exemplar of the struggle between these two tendencies in his own artistic career. At various times, one or the other of these tendencies has the upper hand, but he achieves the highest level of artistic success when he manages to blend the two together and make the most of both.

The influence of foreign narrative tradition is much stronger in his earlier collections than in the more recent ones. In fact, we may go further and say that a number of the more recent stories represent an attempt to lay new foundations for the story genre without depriving it of its connection with reality or of its intense contemporaneity. In his early work Tāmir was not writing about some imaginary utopia; his early efforts tended to be more universal and traditional than his later ones. As time has passed, his style has become simpler and more compact, and his mode of expression has gained in intensity and power. The basis of comparison, however, rests on the fact that Tāmir still writes his stories within the framework of the "story-tableau"; in other words, the formal elements give it a symmetry and precision, thus providing a musical rhythm and design. . . .

Initially, and especially in *The Neighing of the White Horse*, Tāmir's concerns were general and on a universal scale. The stories could have been about any place or person; had they been translated into a foreign language, there would have been no way of perceiving their Syrian or Arab identity.

Nonetheless, he has been making one attempt after another to establish

the Syrian short-story tradition with a lively, contemporary form. This becomes very clear in his most recent collection, *Damascus of the Fires*, where
the prolonged struggle between tradition and modernity can been seen. That
struggle is finally focused within stories that are solid, compact, and authentic, stories that express realistic social concerns stemming from this country
and this age. However, they are also stories that transcend the boundaries of
regionalism to express the crisis of mankind as a whole.

Riyād ʿIsmat. *Al-Maʿrifa.* Nov., 1975, pp. 58–59†

TAYMŪR, MAHMŪD (1894–1973)

EGYPT

Taymūr maintained a steady output of stories of a very high standard. It is to
be admitted that, in these earlier years, he leaned heavily upon western patterns and was strongly under the influence of such men as Maupassant and
Chekhov. This imitation of western models is a trait which ran throughout Arabic writing in this early period, as these authors were seeking to discover
new forms of literary expression. That it should be so with the short story is
not surprising. It may be observed, however, that from the very beginning
Taymūr sought to present situations and characters which are typically Egyptian. It is this local color, both in scenes and in personalities, which makes the
Taymūr story what it is and, especially as he gained his own confidence of
method and style, constitutes the essential originality of his work. In fact, one
could hardly find a better source of material for the understanding of the common man of Egypt than stories from the pen of Taymūr. He is a keen observer
of human situations and of individual personality. His psychological understanding of the motives of these people is remarkable; and he is able to set
down accurately and vividly the individual traits of these men and women
whom he found in the common walks of Egyptian town and village life. He
portrays them in his stories with all their weaknesses and follies as well as the
touch of genuine goodness which is ever present, though often deeply hidden
by poverty and despair. These stories, it must be admitted, do not always appeal to western taste. This is often due to the fact that they are studies of situations so thoroughly foreign to our mode of living; but nowhere do we have a
better insight into the subtleties of human motives as they apply to the men
and women who constitute the main mass of Egyptian society. He shows the
rivalries and intrigues, the pettiness and meanness or even the depravation of
character which exist in the rough struggle for existence in the less favored
districts of the Egyptian city. He also pictures the simple beauty and basic integrity which are to be found in this lowly life of the peasant or city laborer.

We may further characterize Mahmūd Taymūr's short stories by saying that they are less stories of plot than of situation and the portrayal of character. They range over a wide variety of types; the fantastic story, the romantic tale, sketches of social situations and studies of personalities, both peasant and urban.

Kermit Schoonover. Muslim World. Jan., 1957, pp. 40–41

Rightly considered as one of the leading Arabic story-tellers of our times, Mahmūd Taymūr has made himself a name among the playwrights in a remarkably short period considering that he has been publishing plays only since 1940. Like Tawfīq al-Hakīm, Taymūr takes his subjects and characters out of all the strata of Egyptian life, from both village and town. Although the ideas for some of his plots were inspired by that excellent French publication of plays in periodical form, *La petite illustration*, the results were purely Egyptian. Then, again, even though the example of Maupassant may be felt in his treatment of various characters, these are none the less real. Indeed, one of the great causes of Taymūr's popularity is the lifelike nature of his types, many of whom seem copied *in toto* from everyday society in Egypt. . . .

To a great extent, Taymūr succeeded so well because he concentrated on comedy-writing: his historical plays are rather artificial, while his dramas are good only when they verge on comedy (e.g. *Shelter No. 13*). By concentrating on the kind of dramatic composition most suitable to his temper and talents, he improved upon it. The satire, in his comedy of manners and his comedy of character—at both of which he is a master—is less veiled than al-Hakīm's. His readers or his audiences can thus understand him more readily, subtlety being the prerogative of the enlightened few. In this way his satire, when bent on some social reform or other, can carry further with the masses. . . .

Taymūr's literary Arabic is often mixed with idioms borrowed from the colloquial, while his colloquial Arabic often employs expressions of a purely literary character. This, at least, is a new and original approach to the language problem, so baffling to all Arab playwrights. A mixture of the literary and colloquial Arabic may be a solution of this difficulty.

Jacob Landau. Studies in the Arabic Theater and Cinema
(Philadelphia, University of Pennsylvania Press, 1958),
pp. 152–53

Salwā Blown in the Wind is not the novel of Taymūr I admire the most. It takes second place to *Young Boys and Girls*, one of the finest novels I have ever read. . . . Taymūr excels in stories that have some connection with his own life and high social class, in that he can portray the characters from the inside. When he deals with characters from other classes of society, his portrayal comes from the outside. . . . We will often find Taymūr indulging almost in a diversion by portraying a character for whom there is no real sense of emotional involvement; the portrayal may give you a certain amount of enjoyment, but that human pulse so essential to the portrayal of character almost comes to a standstill. . . . *Salwā Blown in the Wind* belongs to the first of these two categories, that of description from the inside. While Salwā herself may not be a member of the aristocratic class, she has lived her life and experienced her anxieties in such a milieu and has tied her own life to it. The other characters are either aristocrats or else hangers-on. . . .

Mahmūd Taymūr uses the brush of a master in character painting, whether it be portraits from the inside, which deal with the environment he knows so well, or pictures taken from public life seen from the outside. . . . In this novel his "interior" portraits are both subtle and skillful. He has presented his readers with a series of perfectly formed human figures, such as the nurse Shīrīn, a good and loyal woman who devotes herself to the service of her mistress and who is the personification of goodness. Taymūr makes good use of her to reflect the deceit that Salwā shows toward her friend.

ʿAbbās Khidr. Qisas aʿjabatnī (Cairo, Dār al-Fikr, 1961),
pp. 109, 112†

Six years after completing his novel *Rajab Efendī*, Taymūr produced his second novel of the period between the two World Wars, namely *Ruins*, which the author describes as being an Egyptian story. It seems that in this work Taymūr lost interest in depicting the common people. The passage of time seems to have lessened his enthusiasm for the portrayal of such people, which had been fired by the 1919 revolution. [*Ruins*] takes place within the aristocratic palaces of the Turks, and it is from this milieu that he chooses his characters. Artistically speaking, this second novel adds nothing new to *Rajab Efendī*. It involves the history of the life of one of Taymūr's peculiar and sickly characters and is narrated by the protagonist as he describes the various stages of his life from childhood to adolescence. . . .

From the artistic point of view, *Ruins* is inferior to *Rajab Efendī*, although both are concerned with much the same topic, namely a survey of the life of an odd personality. If *Rajab Efendī* deals with the dangers involved in being victimized by swindlers, then *Ruins* is content merely to present a peculiar character. As Taymūr narrates the story, he proceeds to talk about a number of details that may be diverting but that actually add nothing to the novel. It is very difficult for the reader to understand what Taymūr's purpose is with this novel or to see clearly what its major focus is. . . .

It seems, therefore, that in *Rajab Efendī*, Taymūr's aim was to give his readers some excitement through a series of frightening situations. In *Ruins* he is quite clearly trying to arouse sexual fantasies in the reader's mind, and he shamelessly exploits the illicit relationship between the hero and his brother's wife for that purpose. The protagonist goes to see his beloved dressed in women's clothing, and she can be sexually satisfied only when she is beaten and whipped and when she sees both her own and her beloved's blood flowing. . . . The whole situation is made worse by the fact that the narrative is purportedly put into the mouth of the protagonist. Of course, the events of the story should *not* have been told from the author's point of view but rather indeed from that of the protagonist. However, the author has placed the behavior of the hero during his childhood and adolescence on exactly the same level as that of his later years of discretion and increasing consciousness. The reader is left with the impression that the person presenting the story is Taymūr himself and not the hero at all.

ʿAbd al-Muhsin Tāhā Badr. *Tatawwur al-riwāya
al-ʿArabiyya al-hadītha fī Misr* (Cairo, Dar al-Maʿārif,
1963), pp. 258–60†

The realism in Taymūr's novel *Salwā Blown in the Wind* does not always aspire to things greater or broader than itself; in fact, it sometimes descends the "literary ladder" several rungs to the photographic level or something very close to that. We can see a good example of this tendency in the descriptions Taymūr gives of the countryside as the car proceeds, sometimes at high speed, other times more slowly, taking Salwā, Saniyya, and the nurse on a trip to the pasha's estate. Here the author insists on presenting to his readers pictures of the country road that have nothing original or profound about them, quite apart from the fact that they are packed full of trivial details and have no organic connection with either the events in the novel or the characters who are involved in them. . . . In his depiction of reality, the author relies heavily on such external views of his subject matter without offering any hint of the emotions or ideas that might justify the presentation of such pictures and that might add a certain profundity to them. To a large degree, they show what I mean when I say that in this novel, realism sometimes descends to the level of naturalism. The only significance this picture of the countryside can have is the most direct and superficial one. . . .

In spite of all this, however, we should note that Taymūr succeeds in depicting the struggle that goes on in Salwā's soul between her actual situation and her aspirations. While this success is not exactly consistent (indeed, the author falters occasionally, when Salwā pretends that she cannot understand herself and has no idea of what she wants), even so, Taymūr does give us a good portrait of Salwā herself, providing her with a lively personality. Our interest in her does not flag, whether she is up on the heights or down in the depths, when she shows her true intelligence or when she seems perplexed and stupid.

ʿAlī al-Rāʿī. *Dirāsāt fī al-riwāya al-Misriyya* (Cairo,
al-Muʾassasa al-ʿĀmma li-al-Taʾlīf wa-al-Tarjama wa-
al-Tibāʿa wa al-Nashr, 1964), pp. 208–10, 220–21†

Among Taymūr's stories that are particularly concerned with the portrayal of character is "Shaykh Jum'a," which gives its name to his first collection of stories. It is a faithful portrait of a provincial man who is happy in his faith, who relishes his own flights of imagination, and who is quite content with his own simplicity. Another story of this kind is "'Amm Mitwallī," the title story of his second collection. This is a portrait of a good and simple man who is turned by internal delusions and external suggestion into a "saint of God." This peddler of peanuts and melon seeds eventually becomes the long-awaited Mahdī [Muslim Messiah] himself. All this happens, of course, within his own deluded imagination and that of some simple folk of his ilk.

Both these stories show a strong sense of sympathy toward the protagonists—the decent peasant and the naïve peddler. In the second story this sense of sympathy is amplified by the presentation of the dangerous results that can be brought about by the popular imagination. The author deals with this same theme in his story "Shaykh Sayyid al-'Abīt," too, where we also detect a strong sympathy toward the hero. This, the title story of his third collection, portrays a good peasant who is injured in an accident that also makes him lose his memory. Initially, people regard him as someone possessed and as a holy man, but as his condition deteriorates and he becomes truly mad, some people get hurt and they begin to regard him as the devil. . . .

Among the salient features of Taymūr's stories is his concern with structure and the skillful way he makes use of the techniques of realism. . . . From the point of view of language, it can be observed that Taymūr writes in a beautiful, simple, and subtle style. When the dialogue demands it, he can lean a little toward the colloquial; this happens in his earlier stories (at that time, this was something of an experiment), whereas later on he changed his mind and used the classical written style in dialogue as well, becoming in the process a fervent opponent of the use of the colloquial in literature.

Ahmad Haykal. Al-Adab al-qasasī wa-al-masrahī (Cairo,
Dār al-Ma'ārif, 1971), pp. 57–59†

Mahmūd Taymūr's novel *The Call of the Unknown* appeared in 1939. The novel is a clear example of a romantic work, yet even in the nineteen forties in Egypt ideas about the exact meanings of Western literary terms were vague, and it is perhaps for this reason that such a knowledgeable critic as Dr. [Muhammad] Mandūr, for instance, was able to refer to the work as "a well-defined specimen of realistic literature." To demonstrate this, he discusses the minor characters in the novel, not taking into account the fact that "minor figures in most stories are presented in only one aspect as 'flat,' 'thin,' 'disc' characters," and that therefore they tend to seem superficially realistic whether or not they appear in a realistic work. . . .

It is obvious that such a story is far from complying with the simplest principles of realism, and reminds us rather of the kind of novels which had been written before [Haykal's] *Zaynab*—and indeed are still being written. The setting is an imaginary one outside of Egypt, the plot of the novel has an element of the fantastic about it, and of the principal characters only one is Egyptian, all these being features commonly found in earlier novels, which were often improbable, romantic tales involving non-Egyptian characters in a non-Egyptian setting. It seems that here Taymūr was attempting to break away from the realism of his short stories, which portray the life of the Egyptian lower classes and were particularly rich in local colour, and was trying to give his work a more universal quality. However, one feels that the novel, while having no well-developed plot or profoundly realized characters, at the same time has no universal significance which would justify this approach.

Hamdi Sakkut. The Egyptian Novel and Its Main Trends 1913–1952 (Cairo, American University in Cairo Press, 1971), pp. 28–29

One of Taymūr's distinguishing features is that he has rewritten a significant number of his short fictional works. This is usually explained by linking this phenomenon with the problems of the written language. But the revisions Taymūr made in his works of fiction cannot be explained merely on the basis of his changes in style. . . .

Fathī al-Abyārī attributes the revision of certain stories to the fact that the Arabic Language Academy gave Taymūr a prize for his writing in 1947. The prize was awarded for his stories in the classical written language alone, which is to say, Taymūr's other stories, written entirely or partially in the colloquial, were ignored. Such an explanation seems far from the whole truth. When we look at the works revised after Taymūr won the prize, even the sketchy comparison that al-Abyārī himself makes between *Ruins*, first published in 1934, and its later version, *Young Boys and Girls* (1951), seems to make it abundantly clear that references to the problem of language use alone are simply not sufficient to explain the process of revision. In fact, such an explanation can only be a partial one. The difference between the two versions of the story to a large extent transcends the bounds of the language problem.

[Taymūr himself] expounds on this subject, and it is clear that the revision process involves two elements: style and treatment. Since the term "style" comprises the sense of "language," we should expect that the revision process will reveal features of the author's development in this area . . . and that is precisely what has happened. The use of language in the revised stories shows a tendency to take the traditional written language and make its usage more precise, and these revisions were made before Taymūr was awarded the Language Academy prize! But style is not restricted to these considerations. The author intends something of much broader scope, something we might term the "rhetoric of the story," as Wayne C. Booth (in *The Rhetoric of Fiction*) calls it. . . .

The aim of the author in this revision process was to improve his stories. He came to feel that his early works were not successful enough and looked for a way to raise the standards of his output. We can well understand the author's feelings toward some of his works when it becomes clear to him that, after all his efforts, they are going to be failures. . . . [Taymūr's own statements on that subject] make it clear that this is the principal reason for his decisions to rewrite some stories.

M. Peled. *Al-Uqsūsa al-Taymuriyya fī marhalatayn* (Tel Aviv, Tel Aviv University and the Arabic Publishing House, 1977), pp. 1–4†

AL-TIKIRLĪ, FU'ĀD (1927–   )

IRAQ

In the first part of his long short story "The Other Face" [in the collection of the same name] Fu'ād al-Tikirlī deals with a character called Muhammad Ja'far, who is seen on his morning walk to work, at his job in a government office, and during his conversations with other civil servants. His wife is pregnant and about to give birth, but he does not have any money to send her to the hospital. She keeps on asking him to take her back to her own family so that she can give birth to their first child at home, but he refuses because her family is so poor. Muhammad Ja'far lives in the midst of a maelstrom of problems that reach a climax when his baby is born dead and his wife is struck down by childbed fever. He soon gets bored with her and abandons her after falling in love with Salīma, the daughter of the landlady of the house where he lives. In her warm body he finds what it was he was missing in the body of his wife. Muhammad Ja'far, then, represents the generation of Iraqi youth wandering aimlessly in the wake of the 1948 war. . . .

The author paints his scenes clearly and without any ambiguities or obscurities; they are realistic and vivid, full of life and movement. They encourage the reader to involve himself in the action, since they continually evoke a world he lives in and recognizes. His portrait of the blind wife is particularly brilliant, as, for example, when she cries and screams out in anguish on hearing that Salīma has put on some of her jewelry. The frenzied movement of her fingers evokes a similar feeling of grief in the reader's mind. . . .

Most of al-Tikirlī's characters are round, three-dimensional; they have all the opinions and ideas need to enter into the struggle with existence and society. Muhammad Ja'far, for example, refuses to die like an imbecile with his blind wife, even though he was the cause of her being blind; he refuses to save a man close to death, he refuses to listen to the advice of Ismā'īl, in fact he refuses to do everything save for himself. . . .

The story's style draws most of its features from the author's nature and temperament. It is neither dry and austere, nor loose and flabby, nor artificial and heavily ornamented. Instead it is concentrated and lively, encouraging the reader to continue; the author achieves a balance of heaviness and emotional intensity and of poetic sensibility and abstraction. The style is both realistic and profound.

ʿUmar al-Tālib. *Al-fann al-qasasī fī al-adab al-ʿIrāqī*
al-hadīth (Al-Najaf, Matbaʿat al-Nuʿmān, 1971),
pp. 319, 321, 323, 327†

One of the features of the stories of Fu'ād al-Tikirlī is his own particular brand of realism. It sets him apart from other short-story writers in Iraq, who . . . tend to deal with general problems of society and politics, so that we get hardly any picture of the private, interior world of the protagonists or of the petty concerns that form the fabric of their daily lives. . . . In al-Tikirlī's stories, on the other hand, we are presented from the outset with an internal world bursting with emotions and anxieties. It is in this sphere that the storyteller's pen goes to work, and only on rare occasions does it leave it. It is a rich and fertile world, sorrowful, pessimistic, forever trying to assert its own identity so as to create its particular values. As a result, most of the heroes tend to be defiant; they reject the accepted values and traditions of society and sometimes even more, so that it seems that the values and traditions of Iraqi society are presented within the framework of these stories only in order to be rejected, and so that it can be made quite clear how much change is needed. The way these characters reject the reality of Iraqi society may not be immediately obvious, but everything about their behavior is an embodiment of that spirit of defiance. . . .

The other feature we should note about his stories is their construction. For, while the premises governing his notion of what a short story is involve specific rules (he seems closer to the restraint of de Maupassant than to the freedom of Chekhov), his way of presenting stories also reveals that he has taken conscious advantage of the potential of the modern story genre in its various guises. This not only involves what the stories of de Maupassant and Chekhov have to offer, but also more modern examples, such as those of James Joyce and Katherine Mansfield. . . . His particular style of story structure is evident in the choice of events, the endings, the technique of rendering atmosphere, and the language. To clarify the point, we can say that he is trying most of the time to express the content of his stories through the consciousness of the principal character.

ʿAbd al-Ilāh Ahmad. *Al-adab al-qisasī fī al-ʿIrāq mundhu*
al-harb al-ʿālamiyya al-thāniya (Baghdad, Dār al-Hurriyya
li-al-Tibāʿa, 1977), pp. 291–94†

"The Oven" (1973/4?) is a monologue, a character's imaginary self-defence in a law court. He goes over several versions of what happened—"the truth" —in succession, and it is for the readers to work out which one, if any, is in fact the truth, or piece together what really happened from clues inadvertently dropped by the speaker.

This way of presenting, or not presenting, the facts is a self-confessed experiment on the part of the author, an elaborate ironic artifice, part of whose purpose is to demonstrate the extent to which incest is taboo: the narrator cannot bring himself to talk about it, even to himself, and speaks ferociously about the lesser taboo, adultery.

More seriously, it is an indictment of a certain attitude to the truth, an attitude which involves a failure to be self-critical. The terms in which the narrator sees himself—as a "noble savage," irrational and intellectually disorganised in a way which is defensible, because it has an attractive simplicity, and yet a "poetic," even spiritual, mystery—smack of exoticism and borrowed conceptualisations.

The narrator's saving grace is that his love, or passion, for Halima appears to be genuine, and he is more anxious to defend her (presumably the actual murderess) than himself. He is on the whole an unpleasant character, although the author's concern is not with him personally as much as with his attitudes and ways of "reasoning." He has some ambition and much self-interest, having taught himself to read and write, reached a respectable rank in the army and taken it upon himself to advise his brother-in-law not to contravene the government's directives concerning agricultural reforms.

These details, conveyed in passing, make his central statements psychologically believable, although the idiom is obviously not intended to be naturalistic. One of the rare occasions when we feel sympathy for him is when he says simply, at the beginning of his defence: "Honour is precious, and a person doesn't know when he should tell the truth." In general his language is clumsy, half-formal, grandiose, fraught with passive verb forms as he self-consciously accepts a fatalistic view of life in order to exonerate himself.

Ominously he speaks like a fundamentalist, even a fanatic—"Honour is indivisible whether it's a question of adultery or any other disgrace"—although this must make ironic reference to his own real "sin." While seeking leniency for himself for his avowed crime, which is in fact much more honourable than the real one, he adopts an unequivocal stand against the sins of others, which are not to be discussed or categorised, merely punished and purged.

Catherine Cobham. *Azure*. No. 8, 1981, p. 29

The increasing belief in freedom is bound to work, aesthetically, against the despotism of the omniscient narrator. But faced with radical changes that sap the very foundations of tradition and belief, writers also find in multiple voices a way out, leaving it to the reader to formulate his own personal conclusions and views. Revealing in this sense is the Iraqi writer Fu'ād al-Tikirlī's *Echo from Far Away*. In an old house in a typical district in Baghdad lives a family comprising three generations (grandparents, parents and nephews). Focusing on the aspirations and distresses of this family during the last days of Qāsim's reign in Iraq, 1962–63, the novelist delves into their very private lives and manners. While placing the action in a solid frame of logical motivation and time sequence, he achieves access not only to the three principal characters' accounts, but also to each character's levels of consciousness through a series of flashbacks, double-shots, aside from the stream-of-consciousness technique. But whether working through monologues, multiple voices, or other channels of expression and action, the writer's purpose is to capture every moment of rapture, distress, and every lapse of mind, enveloping the whole paradoxical life of aspiration and frustration in a thick, and at times stifling, atmosphere. The chatterings of the old, the shrieks of children, the unpredictable outbreaks of the drunk, religious sermons, political speeches, recollections from the past and expressions of love blend with the noise of heavy bombardment and furious outbreaks of rowdyism.

Although al-Tikirlī's novel is based on the love which the two brothers Karīm and Midhat feel for their cousin Munīra, the writer is realistic enough to doubt the possibility of a thriving love-affair in an uncongenial milieu. Social malaise brings about sterility and death rather than love. It is in such an atmosphere that the nephew 'Adnān rapes his aunt Munīra, a development that provokes more disequilibrium in an already exploding scene of internal strife, disintegration and civil war. The omniscient narrator has no role in a novel of this complexity and richness and instead use is made of multiple voices, interior monologues and cinematic techniques that leave the reader overwhelmed with an overall impression rather than anything specific.

Muhsin Jassim Ali. Journal of Arabic Literature. 14, 1983,
pp. 72–73

TŪQĀN, FADWĀ (1917–   )

PALESTINE

This new collection has no introduction; the poet is content merely to preface it with an extract from the title poem, "I Found It." It is this poem that gives the collection its spiritual core. The poet proclaims that she has discovered the way to her inner self, and she announces this discovery with all the joy of Archimedes on the day he discovered the solution to his problem. She cries out, "I found it!" with all the enthusiasm of a child who has discovered a treasure he has dreamed about for a long time and about which he has heard many tales, with the ardor of a long-lost wanderer who suddenly finds the road again. . . .

Tūqān has discovered herself through her poetry; her personality is crystallized in it. Through poetry she has broken out of prison, namely, tradition. Through her poetry she lifts the voice of womanhood and breaks out of that prison as she embraces life with a new élan. Through poetry she can experience the achievement of some meaning in her existence; neither the dust of neglect nor the gloom of incarceration can blot it out. . . .

In *I Found It* we see a new Fadwā Tūqān. The one who was forever *Alone with Days* has found companionship. She has set sail and ventured forth on a long journey in search of love. After a long period of wandering and alienation, she has now discovered the way to selfhood under the guidance of poetry and love. Whereas before, her voice groaned, now we hear it powerful and free. In so doing, she leaves her place among the poets of pain and takes up a middle position between them and the love poets. In this new collection the predominant psychological experience is that of love; sometimes it is forbidden, other times it makes her fearful of the future, at still other times it fills her with happiness. . . .

As with other poets, she has rid herself of the constraints of traditional meter and rhyme and writes in a contemporary fashion; her verse is simple, devoid of complexities and ornamentation, and sweetly cadenced. . . . From the point of view of content, she is still in the caravan of romanticism, addressing herself to the distant beloved, dreaming of a meeting with him and recalling her memories, as she simply and sincerely complains of her loneliness, her grief, and the departure of her beloved.

Khuzāmā Sabrī (Khālida Saʿīd). Shiʿr. Autumn, 1957,
pp. 103, 105–6†

It is impossible to talk about Fadwā Tūqān's latest collection, *Give Us Love*, without making some reference to the two previous volumes, *Alone with Days* and *I Found It*. Her latest collection is simply a further chapter in the continuing love epic this sensitive poet has been writing throughout her career.

Love, then, is the principal topic of these three collections. Her first collection contains some poems in which you will find some mystical reflections, intimate conversations with nature, and some discussion of the poet's soul, yet her heart seems hardly to open to the first thrill of love. Eventually, however, she finds her place and a means of expressing the way she feels personally about love. It is, of course, inconceivable that the Palestine tragedy could touch a sensitive Palestinian poet without shaking her and arousing her innermost feelings. Thus, toward the end of this collection there are five poems on that subject. *I Found It* has two such poems: one, "Call of the Earth," is almost a narrative, while the other, "Dream of Remembrance," mingles memories of her brother, who died fighting for the Palestinian cause, and an exploration of the problem itself, which led him to fight. There is also another

poem, "Torch of Freedom," dedicated to Egypt for its struggle against the tripartite invasion of 1956.

This latest collection, *Give Us Love*—with the exception of the remarks
made above with reference to the first two collections—is also monopolized
by the subject of love; there are pictures of various situations, and of their
emotional impulses and the human attitudes involved. . . . This collection
also shows the poet's continuing interest in nature as she produces images
pulsating with its rhythms and steeped in its perfume. . . . Her feeling for nature is a perfectly authentic one even though she chooses to make use of it in
the service of love, to the point that this feeling almost assumes the status of a
mystical experience.

Malik ʿAbd al-ʿAzīz. *Al-Ādāb*. Jan., 1961, pp. 33, 36†

It is to be noted that [Fadwā Tūqān] stays away from the kind of poetry that
offers advice and spiritual guidance; she does not adopt the role of preacher or
moral guide who relies on the vocabulary of valor to instigate revolution and
anger. She has abandoned the editorializing style; we do not find words like
"kill," "revolt," "destroy," words that die as soon as the event itself does. She
speaks quietly and with a clear logic that allows her words to reach both heart
and mind. This is because she tells a heartbreaking story in which she describes the sufferings of the displaced refugees. In much of her poetry she
paints eloquent and humane portraits of such people, portraits that arouse
deep sympathy. One such story occurs in the first poem of *I Found It*. Even
though the style is quite close to that of prose and is not as purely poetic or
well polished as that of some of the leading modern Arabic poets, the poem
treats its subject through vivid imagery and reveals its ideas with great elo-
quence. Her poetry can stand with the best in world literature in that her imagery forces people to share and participate, and that is better than poetry of
valor that glorifies war, fighting, and destruction. While poetry of valor may
serve a purpose sooner or later, Tūqān's poetry penetrates people's hearts and
prepares people to deal with the issues logically. . . .

Our poet has tasted the bitterness of loneliness, spiritual deprivation, and
social angst. She has given a beautiful portrayal of the tragedy, and in [*I
Found It*, *In Front of the Closed Door*, and *Give Us Love*] the diligent reader
can find evidence of this pain and the political, social, and intellectual tragedies involved. Her personal poems have been more numerous than poems
about her homeland, but once her homeland was occupied by the Israelis, she
began to write more about it. Three of her poems are both the most beautiful
and the most accurate portrayals of the occupation ever written by a poet.

Yūsuf ʿIzz al-dīn. *Fī al-adab al-ʿArabī al-hadīth* (Baghdad,
Dār al-Basrī, 1967), pp. 312–13, 317†

Were we to use the topics of the poems in *In Front of the Closed Door* as our
only gauge . . . we would consider it to be almost a personal collection whose

focal point consists of the memories and sorrows of the poet and her family. The first poem is about a Palestinian from Jordan living in England; there is one dedicated to William Faulkner, followed by a large number of poems about her dead brother. Then we find a poem by another woman poet, Salmā al-Jayyūsī, along with a poem by Fadwā Tūqān dedicated to her; a poem to Tūqān's friend, "Y," in which she talks about her experience in love; and so on. . . .

In some of the poems in this collection Tūqān succeeds in escaping from the confines of the self so that she can come to grips with reality, but on several occasions she tends to resort to traditional visions or to indulge in excessive introspection. . . . Her vision of love is a traditional one, as is her view of death. When a poet turns inward and his sense of his own self assumes large proportions, he is unable to be sensitive or sympathetic to others and resorts to condemning them; the problems he deals with cannot be seen in their full dimensions. For this reason, Fadwā Tūqān prefers friendship to love, since she feels she is the only one who knows the real meaning of profound love and hence cannot establish any love relationship with anyone else in this world. . . .

Judging from the titles and subject matter of her poems written after June 1967, a radical revolution seems to have taken place in her poetry, or at least a complete change, from one opposite to another. The titles assume a new tone, one in which Tūqān abandons all introspection and faces the issues head on. . . . A general perusal of these poems shows that each of them has a distinctive tone. It is as if some entity wanted to assume some form so that it could take on a new guise, yet is as yet unable to settle on the particular guise to use. The poet is trying to rid herself of the old world, and these poems show us clearly the difficulty she is having in tearing herself away from it. All this shows that changes in literary tone do not happen suddenly, but need a prolonged and painful gestation. Thus, we cannot give a general picture of the poems she has written since June 1967, because what we are hearing is a number of melodies rather than a single one. Some of them remind us of the old Fadwā, while others come close to having an entirely new sound, which we all hope will be used by her to its fullest extent.

ʿAbd al-Muhsin Tāhā Badr. *Al-Ādāb*. March, 1969,
pp. 20, 136–37†

AL-ʿUJAYLĪ, ʿABD AL-SALĀM (1918–   )

SYRIA

We should really start by talking about al-ʿUjaylī's highly regarded short stories; he is a storyteller with few peers. . . . However, as a poet he is merely one among many. It may be his own appreciation of this fact that leads him to say in the introduction to his collection *Nights and Stars*: "I believe that the covers of this book contain some beautiful poetry, but I am equally convinced that they are not enough to sing a paean of praise for a real poet."

You are right in your verdict, Doctor, and you have confounded the sage who declared that it is very difficult for a man to know his own self. However, this poetic bent, which will not erect a house for you in the city of poetry, has built one as good as that of the famous poet al-Farazdaq [640–729] in the world of the short story. For that I thank the verdict of the heavens. Anyone who has no instinct for the poetic will never be a really successful story writer. . . . All the best storytellers have, like you, begun with poetry, but they went even less far than you have with it before turning away and becoming story writers. . . .

Dr. 'Ujaylī is a doctor of medicine, not literature; this is evident more in his stories than in his poetry. His analytical powers are excellent, and logic always plays a role in both his verse and prose works. This tendency may actually be detrimental to his poetry while benefiting his prose. . . . Why do I say that he is so good at logic? It is because I consider him extremely successful at formulating ideas and then presenting them with such a total command of organization that, when you read one of his poems, you get the impression that he is writing a research paper, not composing a poem. For this very reason, the musical element, which has always been regarded as so important in Arabic poetry, is very weak. Al-'Ujaylī himself characterizes this exactly when he says at the conclusion of his introduction: "These poems are the conversation of my soul, the story of my own feelings and sensibilities. I have simply put them between the covers of a book and called them *Nights and Stars*."

Mārūn 'Abbūd. *Dimaqs wa-urjuwān* (Beirut,
Dār al-Thaqāfa, 1966), pp. 197–98†

The settings of the majority of the stories in this new collection, *Horses and Women*, are Europe and Bedouin campsites. In these stories the author is trying to put into concrete form the human element behind the activities and behavior of his characters. He ignores one crucial point, however, and that is that the human element behind the behavior of mankind is not something absolute, nor does it depend on considerations of time and place. It is conditioned by specific historical and social circumstances.

It is from this viewpoint that the author presents images and scenes relating to the ethical values governing the life of the Bedouin in the desert. However, he makes no attempt to probe into the inner core of reality in order to discover the way these ethical values are linked to the living conditions of the Bedouin. What he does is to present various aspects of Bedouin behavior and then leave it to the reader to form an opinion on the subject. . . .

In this collection the author continues to use his old techniques, even though he has published many collections of short stories. In my opinion, every writer should continue to be innovative in his content so as to keep pace with the cultural progress of his own people. A corollary of this is that he must keep developing the forms of artistic expression by which he conveys the content of his stories. However, a rapid glance at the stories in this collection is sufficient to show that the author is still utilizing the old forms for this genre, forms that have been well known in the Arabic short story since the early days of its modern history.

Mahmūd Shuqayr. Afkār. Aug., 1966, p. 122†

Dr. 'Abd al-Salām al-'Ujaylī's novel Bāsima in Tears tells of the tragedy of this generation, victims of the crisis brought about by the bitter contradictions between the values of the old society and the social relationships arising out of the new society. The author portrays all his characters according to this basic plan. Sulaymān, for example, is a young lawyer who dabbles in politics by giving speeches and writing; he is a genuine symbol of the youth of an entire generation. Bāsima, too, represents a particular aspect of Arab womanhood, leading a life of bewilderment and perplexity between the heaven of her ideals and the earth of hard reality. Hiyām represents another aspect of womanhood: she is content to live in her own dream world, far removed from the strange events of reality, from the problems for which no one has solutions. . . .

Through these characters—hewn from the solid rock of our own reality—the author has succeeded in presenting us with a superb tableau, a valuable document revealing the wounds suffered by this generation, even though the tableau itself may be confined to lines and colors. It does not offer us a narrative thread in which a series of minor events are put together and gradually develop until the author is able to achieve his major purpose in the grand dénouement. The sexual relationship between Bāsima and Sulaymān, the spiritual relationship between Sulaymān and Hiyām, and his earlier relationship with the nightclub dancer—these relationships are all as unstable as gelatin; there are no particular circumstances to set any one of them apart or to justify their existence.

Even though the author portrays his characters in a totally realistic way, the narrative thread binding them together is tenuous and weak, and indeed does not create a narrative structure at all. The first big revolt in Bāsima's life, for example, which could be a major event in the novel (in that she rebels against her husband, family, and society) is simply summarized in a very rushed fashion. . . .

In this way, the author does not allow us the opportunity to become fully acquainted with the historical phase through which Syria is now passing; it is almost as though the country is isolated from the world, even from the Arab region itself. By "historical phase" I am not referring to any temporal chronology, but rather to the historical aspect, which cannot be separated from the social and psychological aspects of a literary work.

Ghālī Shukrī. *Al-Riwāya al-'Arabiyya fī rihlat al-'adhāb*
(Cairo, 'Ālam al-Kutub, 1971), pp. 158–59, 162†

Al-'Ujaylī's art as a storyteller emerges at its most enjoyable and forceful in his short stories, which, for all their large number and variegated topics, are tied by a single thread or, perhaps, a single vision, to the affairs of life, and, I might almost add, of the universe too. And when that vision is a single one, as it is with every truly original author—and al-'Ujaylī is such an author—then it must of necessity be personal and distinct, and the author must be able to convey its special nature to others. . . .

We are prepared to say that al-'Ujaylī's vision is a single one because it springs from a single source and finishes its course at a single outlet, however varied the bends in its course may be. I say that it is both distinct and personal because al-'Ujaylī's face looks down on us, clear and discreet, with well-defined features that bear no resemblance whatsoever to any other visage in modern Arabic literature.

This vision starts its course in *The Witch's Daughter*. . . . All the stories in this collection can be regarded as being scientific, or, to be more precise, medical. The characters are doctors or patients, the themes diseases and cures. Even so, there is no suggestion in them of determinism or scientific causality, the kind of theory that for every symptom posits a causational factor that is within the grasp of the human to investigate and examine. It is precisely because the stories in *The Witch's Daughter* do not conform to the rules of science and causality and instead attempt to prove that these laws are either faulty, useless, or wanting, that the term "vision" as applied to al-'Ujaylī's works seems appropriate.

Jūrj Tarābīshī. *Al-Ādāb*. March, 1971, pp. 49–50†

WAHBA, SA'D AL-DĪN (19??–   )

EGYPT

In *Al-Mahrūsa* [an epithet for Egyptian cities, lit., "protected by God"], realism was carried to such excess that the play was swamped by details. But in his next play, *The Caboose*, Wahba has managed to rid himself of some of the more tedious details as well as some of the flesh and blood realism. The vision in the two works is very similar, yet the significance of the vision in the two plays is very different. *The Caboose* is not just more mature from the dramatic point of view (because of its reliance on a unified, cohesive plot), but also considerably richer, in that it makes use of multilevel symbolism.

In *The Caboose* destiny is no longer something that reaches its tentacles into every sector of society. It has now become embodied in a clear and forceful symbol, one that gathers firm threads around it, then pulls them together with great skill and thereby develops them into a unified, interlocking fabric.

The bomb in the play may be destiny itself, or perhaps destiny has dropped it on this particular town; then again, the bomb may be the rebellion against destiny, ready to explode at any moment and destroy the corruption that lurks beneath the fabric of society. . . .

On the realistic level, the play uncovers the corruption of the entire societal apparatus and the falsity in every member of the society, from the policeman, Fathī, at the bottom of the scale, to the Superintendent at the top. On the symbolic level, the situations in the play suggest that people have an overwhelming sense of waste and a loss of confidence. This is not merely a loss of confidence in the societal order and everything arising from it, but a loss of confidence in oneself and those nearest to one, and a complete shattering of those close ties that bind a husband and wife together.

Muhammad Muhammad 'Inānī. Al-Masrah. July, 1964,
pp. 52–53†

What issues are raised in *The Road to Safety*? In fact, is it Sa'd al-dīn Wahba's intention to deal with specific questions, or does he mean to present us with a new experiment in drama, with its own new artistic vision? . . . When we listen to the dialogue involving Samīha Ayyūb, one of the characters—"This is the road to safety; this one is the road to remorse; and this one is the road from which there is no return for anyone who takes it"—we of course understand that the play is involved with these different roads and choosing among them. However, we leave the theater at the end of the play without seeing any one specific road advocated. In fact, quite to the contrary, the play presents to us a series of characters in a car who have lost their way. Each character has a road different from that of the others. No one road predominates. They are all roads along which the characters have traveled, and now these people describe these roads on the stage through a discussion of the crisis that confronts them: the car has broken down, and as a result, everyone's life is threatened.

If this play does not present us with a series of roads to choose from, then are we to suppose that it gives us a series of human stereotypes that symbolize, for example, the kind of life we lead, the society in which we live, or human society as a whole? . . .

From the point of view of dramatic structure, there can be no objection to the author's choosing to give us an experimental play with no single plot or climax in the normal sense of the word. However, in this play it is particularly noticeable that the characters and events do not change in any dramatic way, that is, as a result of dramatic conflict. One of the faults of the play, in fact, is its lack of dramatic conflict. As a result, we have no sense of the dramatist's trying to deal with the circumstances the work purports to address; in fact, we get no real impression of the circumstances themselves. We emerge from the theater asking ourselves what the author's intention is; does every author inevitably have to deal with specific problems? This play does touch on some issues, but only in a sketchy and superficial way. The dialogue jumps back and forth among the characters with no sense of focus or clarity.

'Abd al-Fattāh al-Bārūdī. Al-Thaqāfa. March, 1965,
pp. 29, 31†

The problems of society with which the theater deals have their roots in the history of that society. Thus, the drama can play an important role in the life of the people and in developing their way of thinking. This is exactly what Sa'd al-dīn Wahba tries to do in his plays.

The first thing we notice in his plays is that he concentrates on portraying the lives of the poorer classes of people and on showing the cruelty, injustice, and exploitation to which they are exposed. The playwright does not set his scenes in palaces, but rather places the action in humble locales. In Al-Mah-rūsa he chooses a police station in a village somewhere north of Cairo; in The Caboose he directs his attention to another village in the same region; and Kafr al-Battīkh [lit., "melon village"] is set in "any Egyptian village provided it is in the north." . . . The characters are chosen from among the common people so as to show the hard life they lead and the treachery with which they have to deal. There are both wrongdoers and wronged, barbers, peasants, guards, policemen, village headmen, agricultural inspectors, grocers, teachers, health inspectors . . . and he portrays the relationships among all these different types, whether they number among the forces who live at the expense of others weaker than themselves or whether they belong to those groups who have to submit to all the exploitation and injustice. . . .

It may be Wahba's attention to a broad spectrum of people that forces him to do without any pivotal characters. His entire concern is with developments on a societal level, not an individual one. Through this process we find that attention is never focused on a single person, someone with whom we are supposed, qua audience, to identify. Instead, Wahba disperses the audience's attention over a whole group of characters. The concentration is on the intellectual and emotional content of the play.

Amīn al-'Ayūtī. Al-Masrah. July, 1965, p. 32†

The Nails has managed to break the terrifying silence that has fallen on literary and theatrical life while our writers busy themselves with the process of "responding to experience"—a phrase that has become an excuse for apathy, for fear of taking the initiative, and for turning a deaf ear to the call of clear imperatives. I am not for a single moment suggesting that the entire blame rests on the shoulders of writers alone; all the cultural and press organizations share the blame. . . .

The Nails shows the correct way a writer should conduct himself during the challenging and dangerous situation we are all facing at the moment. In his plays his words are spoken courageously and with artistic skill; he thus proves that art and candor are not necessarily incompatible. In my opinion, *The Nails* is the best work Wahba has written since *Al-Mahrūsa*, in that we come to feel through this play that same pulse of simplicity and spontaneity that characterized the earlier play and made it such an exceptional work of art. . . .

In this play Wahba makes his points about politics and human nature not through bald, direct statements but through the inner logic of the work. The action of the play is clearly constructed and well focused. The most significant events are presented in a sequence in such a way that their inner meaning emerges as an intrinsic part of the structure; there is no further need for comment or explanation. . . .

It must be said, however, that certain events and situations in the play encroach upon the natural development of the drama at certain points. . . . When this excess padding is removed as part of the process of producing it on stage (which will happen soon, we hope), the play will definitely be a success. It is an excellent work that has come at exactly the right time.

Bahā' Tāhir. *Al-Kātib*. Oct., 1967, pp. 122–23, 126–27†

Wahba has not perhaps been such an innovative figure as some other playwrights. . . . However, his often bitter comedies, combining accurate vignettes of Egyptian provincial and urban "types" with symbolic representation of some of the more pressing problems of his homeland, drew large audiences during the 1960's. Several of his plays display these tendencies, but of them all *The Caboose* is probably the most successful from the various perspectives of dramatic production.

The play is set in the village of al-Kūm al-Akhdar. The events unfold in chronological sequence through three acts, and the author describes the setting for each scene in considerable detail. At the beginning of the play we learn that one of the village policemen, Sābir, has discovered a bomb. The news has been reported to the provincial authorities, and various investigators, both local and provincial, are on their way to start inquiries. Throughout the play, Wahba makes excellent use of the privileges of rank within the police force and the perks which are presumed to come with such a position, to criticize the venality of much of the system of justice in Egypt before the Revolution. The village police are in the process of cleaning up the station in preparation for the arrival of the investigating team when the shattering news reaches them that the bomb has disappeared. In a panic, Sergeant Darwīsh instructs Sābir to place a lead paperweight from the station desk at the spot where the bomb had been discovered. . . .

This play then gives us a lively and accurate portrayal of the realities of Egyptian provincial life before the 1952 Revolution. The antics of the police and detectives are depicted with a biting humor, while the symbolism of the bomb—the latent revolutionary force demanding change and justice—is skillfully woven into the essentially realistic treatment of a provincial village and its various strata. The work is expressed in a colloquial language which is at once pungent and witty, thus lending a further touch of realism to the presentation.

Roger Allen. *Edebiyat.* 4, 1, 1979, pp. 114–15

WANNŪS, SAʿDALLĀH (1941–   )

SYRIA

The play *The Elephant, O King of All Ages* (1971) is a popular tale both in its original version and as used by the author here, no more and no less. I heard it from a neighbor as a child, and later on went back to it to understand fully what its import was. That is precisely what Wannūs has not done. Most people regard the tale as an example of cunning, of a lucky escape from a tricky situation, and of the ability of a person to turn a situation to his own advantage. The tale is also viewed as an example of the way people feel uncomfortable in the presence of authority figures and find themselves dumbstruck. Here, however, the playwright (who is presumed to be both aware and intelligent) presents the play simply as it is, without any interpolations of his own. By relating the tale in this way he seems not only to condone individual opportunism but goes even further by consciously condemning the masses, those poor, oppressed, downtrodden folk.

Any research into history will suffice to squelch such an attitude toward the populace. Furthermore, sociology can easily show the playwright to be in error. People select intellectuals and thinkers to act as their spokesmen. History and sociology both tell us that it is the intellectual class that betrays the cause of the people through its opportunism; the people never betray themselves, especially when there is someone among them to make them fully aware of the issues they are facing. In this play the hero, Zakariyyā, tries to make everyone aware and to organize protests against the way the elephant is allowed to roam around the city. He would have to speak in the presence of the kind even if the populace abandoned him as their spokesman. . . .

All these comments are concerned with the question of attitude and its

historical and intellectual consequences. As far as the question of dramatic development in the context of a popular tale is concerned, what is the point of
simply transferring it to the stage in exactly the form in which people tell it to
each other? Of what use are all the efforts of the dramatist if he is satisfied
merely to adapt and not to write something new? Where is all that ability to
create characters, to build the action to a climax so that it finishes with the
tragic martyrdom and death of the hero? Would it not have been better for the
dramatist here to have taken a second look at the senses of responsibility
among the protagonists in such a way that the hero would emerge either as a
martyr—a victim of the people's fear—or else as an opportunist who betrayed the people who entrusted their fortunes to him? Had he done so, the
tale would surely have developed into a drama of either comic or tragic proportions, one with a political content in either case.

Muhyī al-dīn Subhī. Al-Mawqif al-adabī. May, 1972,
pp. 29–30†

We can say without reservation that *An Evening's Entertainment for the Fifth
of June* is the richest play written about the trials and tribulations of the 1967
defeat; it deals not just with present-day situations but with the entire consciousness of the Arabs and with Arab governmental systems in general too.
We may also claim without reservation that it is one of the richest plays in the
entire corpus of Arabic drama, in both its structure and content. In the face of
our current sick Arab reality this play emerges as a cry of criticism, of exposure, of protest, one that shows everything with clarity, sincerity, tremendous
seriousness, and skill. With this play we do not become absorbed in some dramatic fantasy or attend a performance of a work of art that merely mimics reality. We attend reality itself, with all the accompanying brutal tensions, the
reality of our disaster, our suffering, our defeat, our doom-haunted conscience. . . .

In this play there are no symbols or allusions; it points and it speaks with
a terrifyingly direct clarity and a realism that is absolute and crude in its impact. However, in spite of the directness of the impact and the crudity of the
message, we never lose touch with the sense of art, of poetry, because we remain in touch with candor and truth. Things never degenerate into mere chatter; instead we live reality itself within a clearly focused framework, in the
essence of the essence as it moves and careens in front of us, around us,
through us, in us. The dialogue cascades downward like so many cataracts;
the events pile up until they heave mountains of sheer disaster on to our shoulders; the characters emerge from us, take us with them, and tell our story.
That is why we hardly have time to catch our breath during the play; it also explains why it was not possible to chop it up into two or three acts. We would
not have been able to loiter in the lobby waiting. Such a powerful happening

overwhelms us because it emerges from our own living reality with all the violence, cruelty, and roughness that come with it. . . .

This is indeed a distinguished work of art from the point of view of both form and content. It displays the intellectual daring of its author, as well as his expressive powers and his artistic authenticity. Our Arab drama should look forward to seeing many artistic treasures emerge as a result of his creative talents.

Mahmūd Amīn al-ʿĀlim. *Al-wajh wa-al-qināʿ* (Beirut,
Dar al-Ādāb, 1973), pp. 209–11†

The play *The Adventure of the Slave Jābir's Head* can take place in a café or anyplace else suitable for listening to popular folktales told by a well-known storyteller . . . . The predominant atmosphere at the beginning is one of languor; smoke rises from the water pipes and there are inane conversations between the customers and the café waiter, who rushes around carrying the fire [for lighting the pipes] or tea and coffee throughout the play. The point at which the play starts is optional and depends on an estimate of the amount of familiarity that has been built up between the audience and the people on the stage. From that point we can grasp the basic issues the play is going to raise: the circumstances of the very people who are watching the work itself, who are part of the equation of the tale the play sets out to tell; or the moral of the fable the storyteller is narrating; or, lastly, the posture of the writer toward history and contemporary reality and the extent of his success in applying the theoretical bases he has proposed for the significant experiment in the theater of "politicization."

It might be best to start by talking about the storyteller, Old Mūnis. This type of character is well known in the works of Brecht (such as *The Caucasian Chalk Circle*). However, with Wannūs it assumes a rich and distinctive flavor. The storyteller here is not merely a means of communication, but rather a symbol of history itself . . . and when the customers ask him to tell them the saga of al-Zāhir Baybars, his response is: "Stories are tied to each other; one cannot come before the other. The Baybars saga will come all in good time, but only after we have finished with the earlier stories we have started to tell." In this way history, in the form of Old Mūnis, instructs us that nothing ever happens accidentally without forewarning or specific conditions. . . .

Wannūs here exposes in a remarkable way the deadly diseases of defeatism and opportunism that are the hallmarks of life in the contemporary Arab world. In this he is helped by his fine choice of story—the way it is appropriate to our way of life—and his ability to capture the audience's attention and be convincing. To a large degree Wannūs also manages to adhere to the principles he sets out in his theoretical statements and introductions, and in that he is aided by the excellent way he makes use of modern techniques. . . . Last of all, *The Adventure of the Slave Jābir's Head* provides a living model of the theater's potential as a school for revolutionizing the masses.

Bū ʿAlī Yāsīn and Nabīl Sulaymān. *Al-adab wa-al-idīyūlūjiya fī Sūriyya* (Beirut, Dār Ibn Khaldūn, 1974), pp. 355–56, 363†

In his fascinating play *The King Is the King* Saʿdallāh Wannūs uses with tremendous artistic skill one of the tales from *The Thousand and One Nights*, telling how Hārūn al-Rashīd became exasperated one night and decided to take his minister out with him for a walk around the city. They hear a man saying, "Oh, if only I were king, I would make sure people were just to each other, and I would do this and that. . . ." And so the caliph decides to take the man to his palace and make him caliph for just one day. Wannūs also utilizes another tale, which tells how Hārūn al-Rashīd goes out with his minister in disguise looking for some good company. They discover a man dressed exactly like Hārūn al-Rashīd, even to the extent of having a minister and an executioner with him. He can perform this role so well that no one can tell him apart from the real thing.

In my view, *The King Is the King* represents the most effective adaptation yet by a modern Arab dramatist from the heritage of *The Thousand and One Nights*; more than any other previous work, it succeeds in making use of these tales by bringing them out of the frozen past and placing them squarely within the lively, bustling atmosphere of the present, in the process conveying a political message. In Wannūs's play, the king becomes exasperated and decides to play tricks with his people in order to relieve his boredom. He is an autocrat and a tyrant, sure that his throne is secure, his guards are well armed, and his people are under his thumb. As a result, he despises everyone, his own minister included. . . .

In this wonderful play Wannūs has managed to make use of all his old theatrical ideas in an organic way and to incorporate them into a version of a popular tale, with its special atmosphere. . . . I think that this is Wannūs's most subtle and successful composition to date. . . .

The play contains an obvious political lesson: changing individuals does not mean changing systems. Systems have to change their basic principles before everyone can feel really comfortable and happy.

In this regard Wannūs does not stray far from the improvisatory drama he obviously adopted eagerly in *An Evening's Entertainment for the Fifth of June* in that the whole play begins with a group of people trying to organize themselves and assuring the audience that what they are going to see is just a play. . . .

Here, then, we see the popular theater—at last—finding a writer who can make full use of its style, its special devices, and its ability to attract the masses. From it he manages to make a play that can be acted and that people can thoroughly enjoy, while at the same time giving us a work that is undoubtedly a fine piece of literature.

ʿAlī al-Rāʿī. *Al-masrah fī al-watan al-ʿArabī* (Kuwait, ʿĀlam al-Maʿrifa, 1980), pp. 194–95, 197, 199†

WATTĀR, AL-TĀHIR (1936–   )

ALGERIA

Al-Tāhir Wattār's story "The Snow-Covered Cap" [in *Smoke from My Heart*] is about a young girl shackled by traditions and the bonds of society; she is afraid to mix with young men and comes to feel that anytime she comes close to a young man she is committing a terrible sin. . . .

What is new in this story is the use of interior monologue, or stream of consciousness, from start to finish. This method of presenting events and portraying character gives the work a greater liveliness and provides a new depth and sense of dimension. . . . The author of such a story, however, needs a good deal of ingenuity and inventiveness, since this narrative technique can sometimes burden a story with a sense of monotony that will cramp it and prevent the development of the events in a straight line, as is the case in this particular story. This is even truer when the stream-of-consciousness technique demands constant repetition of a particular image. In this case the image of the footfall of the young man as he pursues the girl is repeated no fewer than seven times during the course of the story; it falls flat because it does not fit well into the sequencing of the events, and its repetition shows no sense of artistry or timing. . . .

Other stories also show this same tendency toward a romanticism steeped in a subjective awareness of the self: "Desert Forever," "Dawn of the Days," and "Smoke from My Heart." They all involve a young boy or girl living in perpetual deprivation and going through an emotionally charged adolescence. Love involves merely looking at a picture, or else it may come about through the mediation of a schoolmate or friend; it may even be limited to an exchange of glances with one of the girls next door, with no possibility of really meeting. The result, however, is always the same: a continuing sense of failure.

ʿAbdallāh Khalīfa al-Rakībī. *Al-qissa al-qasīra fī al-adab al-Jazāʾirī al-muʿāsir* (Cairo, Dār al-Kātib al-ʿArabī, 1969), pp. 189–90†

The Algerian novelist al-Tāhir Wattār has recently published a novel called *The Fisherman and the Palace*. Wattār has previously given us historical coverage of the course of the Algerian revolution, from its beginnings as a war of liberation right up to the most recent societal changes, in three novels: *Al-Lāz*, *The Earthquake*, and *Mule's Wedding*. Through these works the reader is able to make out the winding path of Wattār's career.

Although *Al-Lāz* was still essentially classical in form, it was, nonetheless, a work of considerable importance. *Mule's Wedding*, on the other hand, is regarded as a great leap forward in Wattār's work from the point of view of both form and content. . . . Now comes *The Fisherman and the Palace* to confirm the view that Wattār is a significant realistic novelist. He has tried to make use of a number of different styles to convey the ideas of a progressive and has remained unabashed in the face of critical attacks on him for his use of direct political reportage in some of his works.

'Alī, the fisherman in the novel, is a simple man who learns from a friend that the sultan has just escaped from death after three knights have tried to assassinate him. No one is sure that he has survived, however; some say he has, while others say that he did in fact die. 'Alī the fisherman decides to give the sultan the biggest fish he can catch as a symbol of his joy at the sultan's survival and starts off for the palace. Part of his dream comes true when he catches a huge fish, which he proceeds to carry on his shoulders as he heads for the palace. To get to the palace, he has to pass through seven villages and then seven royal guard posts. . . .

We cannot survey the entire novel in this brief space, but we must point out that there is a lack of focus in the principal organizing element on which the novel is constructed, namely, the atmosphere of fable. In some of the villages the reader finds himself confronted with lessons and consciousness-raising and with the slogans of opposition. . . . The so-called village of the enemies follows the road of communism in that "everything in this village of ours is distributed in equal shares." . . .

In spite of some problems, this novel, with its fablelike ambience, its political content, and its distinctive style, is the most important experiment yet undertaken by al-Tāhir Wattār.

Anon. Al-Yasār al-'Arabī. June, 1981, p. 32†

The struggle for national liberation and its aftermath are treated with more subtlety in the works of the Algerian novelist, al-Tāhir Wattār, and no more so than in *The Earthquake*. The particular focus of this work is agricultural reform, and the author manages to convey postrevolutionary attitudes with great clarity and force by using the figure of Shaykh 'Abd al-Majīd Bū-Arwāh, a landowner and teacher who returns to his home town in order to dispose of as much of his land as possible to his heirs before the reform law takes effect. The "earthquake" of the title refers both to the physical transformation of the earth's crust (and the city of Constantine where the novel is set lies on such a fault line), but also refers to a quotation from the Qur'ān (Sūra XXII, 1) which is repeated by the Shaykh throughout the novel. As he makes his disgruntled way around the city, he notices the changes which the revolution has brought about and discovers to his dismay that all his descendants to whom he is hoping to bequeath his land have in one way or another become reconciled to the realities of the revolution. Here, too, there is much discussion of current societal and political issues, but in Wattār's work it is conducted within the framework of the Shaykh's internal monologue as he quotes the text of the Qurʾān, curses Ibn Khaldūn for his theories of civilisation, and hopes for the physical or societal earthquake which will eradicate all the revolutionary changes which have so radically altered his lifestyle and surroundings. This novel represents a most successful manipulation of the narrative point of view, since the achievements of the Algerian revolution attained after a great deal of social upheaval and bloodshed are seen through the eyes of a character whose attitude is totally antagonistic.

Roger Allen. *The Arabic Novel: An Historical and Critical*
Introduction (Syracuse, N.Y., Syracuse University Press,
1982), pp. 74–75

WORKS MENTIONED

Listed here, author by author, are works mentioned in the critical selections. Each writer's works are arranged alphabetically by the literal translation used uniformly throughout the book. (If a title is given in Arabic rather than in translation, it is a personal or place name.) Following each literal translation in parentheses are the Arabic title and the date of original publication. If a published translation of a work exists, its title, together with the city and year of publication, is given after a colon.

Because of space limitations, only full-length, separately published volumes—novels, plays, collections of short stories, poetry, and essays, and book-length nonfiction—are included. Individual short stories and poems are not listed, even though mentioned in the critical selections. However, when available, titles of collections of an author's poems or stories in English translation that do not correspond to one particular Arabic collection are given at the end of the list of the author's works. Many translations of short works may also be found in various journals cited in this volume, particularly the *Journal of Arabic Literature*. In addition, translations of modern Arabic stories, plays, and poems appear in the following general anthologies:

Abdel Wahab, Farouk, ed. *Modern Egyptian Drama*. Minneapolis and Chicago: Bibliotheca Islamica, 1974.

Arberry, A. J., tr. *Modern Arabic Poetry*. Cambridge, England: Cambridge University Press, 1967.

Aruri, Naseer, and Edmund Ghareeb, eds. and trs. *Enemy of the Sun: Poetry of Palestinian Resistance*. Washington, D.C.: Drum and Spear Press, 1970.

Boullata, Issa J., tr. *Modern Arab Poets 1950–1975*. Washington, D.C.: Three Continents Press, 1976.

Johnson-Davies, Denys, ed. and tr. *Arabic Short Stories*. London: Quartet Books, 1983.

———, ed. and tr. *Egyptian Short Stories*. London: Heinemann, 1978.

———, ed. and tr. *Modern Arabic Short Stories*. London: Heinemann, 1974.

Khouri, Mounah A., and Hamid Algar, eds. and trs. *An Anthology of Modern Arabic Poetry*. Berkeley: University of California Press, 1974.

Kritzcek, James, ed. *Modern Islamic Literature*. New York: New American Library, 1970.

Manzalaoui, Mahmoud, ed. *Arabic Writing Today: The Drama*. Cairo: The American Research Center in Egypt, 1977.

———, ed. *Arabic Writing Today: The Short Story*. Cairo: Dār al-Maʿārif and the American Research Center in Egypt, 1968.

ʿABD AL-HAKĪM, SHAWQĪ

The Blood of Yaʿqūb's Son (*Dam ibn Yaʿqub*, 1967)
Hasan and Naʿīma (*Hasan wa-Naʿīma*, 1965)
The Hider (*Al-Mustakhbī*, 1964)
King Maʿrūf's Birthday (*Mawlid al-malik Maʿrūf*, 1965)
Peasant Literature (*Adab al-fallāhīn*, n.d.)
Shafīqa and Mitwallī (*Shafīqa wa-Mitwallī*, 1964)
The Sorrows of Noah (*Ahzān Nūh*, 1964)

ʿABD AL-SABŪR, SALĀH

I Say to You (*Aqūlu lakum*, 1961)
Laylā and Majnūn (*Laylā wa-Majnūn*, 1971)
People in My Country (*Al-Nās fī bilādī*, 1957)
The Tragedy of al-Hallāj (*Maʾsāt al-Hallāj*, 1965): *Murder in Baghdad* (Leiden, 1972)

ABŪ MĀDĪ, ĪLIYYĀ

The Brooks (*Al-Jadāwil*, 1927)
The Collected Poems of Īliyyā Abū Mādī (*Dīwān Īliyyā Abū Mādī*, 1919)
The Thickets (*Al-Khamāʾil*, 1940)

ABŪ SHABAKA, ILYĀS

Ghalwāʾ (*Ghalwāʾ*, 1945)
The Lyre (*Al-Qīthāra*, 1926)
Melodies (*Al-Alhān*, 1941)
The Serpents of Paradise (*Afāʿī al-Firdaws*, 1938)

ABŪ SHĀDĪ, AHMAD ZAKĪ

Ardshīr and Hayāt al-Nufūs (*Ardshīr wa-Hayāt al-Nufūs*, 1928)
The Gods (*Al-Āliha*, 1927)
Groans and Echoes (*Anīn wa-ranīn*, 1925)
Ihsān (*Ihsān*, 1928)
Poems of Egypt (*Misriyyāt*, 1924)
The Spring (*Al-Yanbūʿ*, 1934)
The Weeping Twilight (*Al-Shafaq al-bākī*, 1926)
Al-Zabbāʾ; or, Zenobia, Queen of Palmyra (*Al-Zabbāʾ; aw, Zanūbiyā malikat Tadmur*, 1928)

ADŪNĪS

The Book of Metamorphosis and Migration in the Regions of Day and Night
(*Kitāb al-tahawwulāt wa-al-hijra fī aqālīm al-nahār wa-al-layl*, 1965)
First Poems (*Qaṣā'id ūlā*, 1956)
Leaves in the Wind (*Awrāq fī al-rīh*, 1958)
Songs of Mihyār of Damascus (*Aghānī Mihyār al-Dimashqī*, 1962)
Stability and Change: An Investigation of Classicism and Creativity among the
Arabs (*Al-Thābit wa-al-mutahawwil: Bahth fī al-ittibā' wa-al-ibdā' 'inda
al-'Arab*, 1974)
The Stage and the Mirrors (*Al-Masrah wa-al-marāyā*, 1968)

The Blood of Adonis (Pittsburgh, 1971)

AL-'ĀNĪ, YŪSUF

The Cost of Medicine (*Fulūs al-dawā*, 1957)
I'm Your Mother, Shākir (*Anā unmak yā Shākir*, 1955)
The Key (*Al-Miftāh*, 1968)

AQL, SA'ĪD

Cadmus (*Qudmūs*, 1944)
The Daughter of Jephtha (*Bint Yafthāh*, 1935)
The Magdalen (*Al-Majdaliyya*, 1937)
More Beautiful Than You? No! (*Ajmal minki? Lā!*, 1960)
Rindalā (*Rindalā*, 1950)
Yārā (*Yārā*, 1963)

AL-'AQQĀD, 'ABBĀS MAHMŪD

The Dīwān: A Book on Criticism and Literature (*Al-Dīwān: Kitāb fī al-naqd wa-
al-adab*, 1921)
Gift of the Plover (*Hadiyya al-karawān*, 1933)
The Inspiration of Forty (*Wahy al-arba'īn*, 1933)
Morning Wakes (*Yaqzat al-sabāh*, 1916)
Passerby (*'Ābir sabīl*, 1937)
Sāra (*Sāra*, 1938)

'ARĪDA, NASĪB

Despairing Spirits (*Al-Arwāh al-hā'ira*, 1946)

'ĀSHŪR, NU'MĀN

The Female Sex (*Jins al-harīm*, 1959)
The Flour Mill (*Wābūr tahīn*, 1962)
The Middle-of-the-Road Family (*Al-'Ā'ilat ad-dughrī*, 1963)
The Movie's a Mess (*Sīmā awanta*, 1958)
The People Downstairs (*An-Nās illī taht*, 1956)
The People Upstairs (*An-Nās illī fawq*, 1957)

'AWWĀD, TAWFĪQ YŪSUF

The Loaf (*Al-Raghīf*, 1939)
The Mills of Beirut (*Tawāhīn Bayrūt*, 1972): *Death in Beirut* (London, 1976)
The Tourist and the Guide (*Al-Sā'ih wa-al-turjumān*, 1964)

AYYŪB, DHŪ AL-NŪN

Doctor Ibrāhīm (*Al-Duktūr Ibrāhīm*, 1939)
Empty Glory (*'Azama fārigha*, n.d. [after 1940])
Hand, Earth, and Water (*Al-Yad wa-al-ard wa-al-mā'*, 1947)
Prophets of Culture (*Rusul al-thaqāfa*, 1937)
The Toilers (*Al-Kādihūn*, 1939)
The Tower of Babel (*Burj Bābil*, 1939)

BA'ALBAKKĪ, LAYLĀ

Disfigured Gods (*Al-Āliha al-mamsūkha*, 1960)
I Live (*Anā ahyā*, 1958)
Spaceship of Tenderness to the Moon (*Safīnat hanān ilā al-qamar*, 1963)

BARAKĀT, HALĪM

The Return of the Flying Dutchman to the Sea (*'Awdat al-tā'ir ilā al-bahr*,
    1969): *Days of Dust* (Wilmette, Ill., 1974)
Six Days (*Sittat ayyām*, 1961)

AL-BAYYĀTĪ, 'ABD AL-WAHHĀB

The Book of Poverty and Revolution (*Sifr al-faqr wa-al-thawra*, 1965)
Broken Pitchers (*Abārīq muhashshama*, 1954)
Fire and Words (*Al-Nār wa-al-kalimāt*, 1964)
Glory to Children and the Olive (*Al-Majd li-al-atfāl wa-al-zaytūn*, 1956)

Love Poems on the Seven Gates of the World (*Qasā'id hubb 'alā bawwābāt al-'ālam al-sab'*, 1971)

Words Which Do Not Die (*Kalimāt lā tamūt*, 1960)

DARWĪSH, MAHMŪD

Attempt Number 7 (*Muhāwala raqm sab'a*, 1974)

I Love You or I Do Not Love You (*Uhibbuki wa-lā uhibbuki*, 1971)

A Lover from Palestine (*'Āshiq min Filastīn*, 1966): *A Lover from Palestine, and Other Poems* (Washington, D.C., 1970)

Sparrows Are Dying in Galilee (*Al-'Asāfīr tamūtu fī Jalīl*, 1970)

Selected Poems (Cheadle, England, 1973)

DIYĀB, MAHMŪD

Harvest Nights (*Layālī al-hisād*, 1967)

Shade on the Other Side (*Al-Zilāl fī al-jānib al-ākhar*, 1964)

The Storm (*Al-Zawba'a*, 1964): *The Storm*, in *Arabic Writing Today: The Drama*, ed. Mahmoud Manzalaoui (Cairo, 1977)

FARAJ, ALFRED

'Alī Jannāh al-Tabrīzī and His Follower Quffa (*'Alī Jannāh al-Tabrīzī wa-tābi'uhu Quffa*, 1968)

The Barber of Baghdad (*Hallāq Baghdād*, 1964)

Pharaoh's Fall (*Suqūt Fir'awn*, 1957)

Policeman and Thieves (*'Askarī wa-harāmiyya*, 1966)

Prince Sālim (*Al-Zīr Sālim*, 1967)

Sulaymān al-Halabī (*Sulaymān al-Halabī*, 1966)

FARMĀN, GHĀ'IB TU'MA

Another Child (*Mawlūd ākhar*, 1955)

Five Voices (*Khamsat aswāt*, 1967)

Millstone Harvest (*Hisād al-rahā*, 1955)

The Palm Tree and the Neighbors (*Al-Nakhla wa-al-jīrān*, 1966)

AL-GHĪTĀNĪ, JAMĀL

The Events in the Za'farānī Quarter (*Waqā'i' hārat al-Za'farānī*, n.d. [1976?])

Ground to Ground (*Ard . . ard*, 1972)

Remembrance of What Is Past (*Dhikr mā jarā*, n.d. [1978?])
Al-Zīnī Barakāt (*Al-Zīnī Barakāt*, 1974)

HABĪBĪ, EMĪLE

The Peculiar Events Surrounding the Disappearance of the Ill-Starred Saʿīd the
Pessoptimist (*Al-Waqāʾiʿ al-gharība fī ikhtifāʾ Saʿīd abī al-nahs al-muta-
shāʾil*, 1974): *The Secret Life of Saeed, the Ill-Fated Pessoptimist: A Palestinian Who Became a Citizen of Israel* (New York, 1982)
Sextet on the Six Days (*Sudāsiyyat al-ayyām al-sitta*, 1969)

AL-HĀJJ, UNSĪ

Never (*Lan*, 1960)
The Past of the Days to Come (*Mādī al-ayyām al-ātiya*, 1965)
The Severed Head (*Al-Raʾs al-maqtūʿ*, 1963)

AL-HAKĪM, TAWFĪQ

Boss Kandūz's Building (*ʿImārat al-muʿallim Kandūz*, 1950)
Courtly Love (*Al-hubb al-ʿudhrī*, 1950)
The Deal (*Al-Safqa*, 1956)
Diary of a Provincial Public Prosecutor (*Yawmiyyāt nāʾib fī al-aryāf*, 1937): *The
Maze of Justice* (London, 1947)
Equilibriumism (*Al-Taʿāduliyya*, 1955)
The Flower of Life (*Zahrat al-ʿumr*, 1943)
I Want to Kill (*Urīdu an aqtula*, 1950)
King Oedipus (*Al-Malik Ūdīb*, 1949): *King Oedipus*, in *Plays, Prefaces and
Postscripts of Tawfīq al-Hakīm*, Vol. 1 (Washington, D.C., 1981)
The People of the Cave (*Ahl al-kahf*, 1933): *The People of the Cave*, Act 1, in
Modern Arabic Literature 1800–1970, ed. John A. Haywood (London,
1971)
The Predicament (*Al-Warta*, 1965)
Pygmalion (*Pigmāliyūn*, 1942)
The Return of the Spirit (*ʿAwdat al-rūh*, 1933)
Scheherazade (*Shahrazād*, 1934): *Shahrazad*, in *Plays, Prefaces and Postscripts
of Tawfīq al-Hakīm*, Vol. 1 (Washington, D.C., 1981)
Shams al-Nahār (*Shams al-Nahār*, 1965): *Princess Sunshine*, in *Plays, Prefaces
and Postscripts of Tawfīq al-Hakīm*, Vol. 1 (Washington, D.C., 1981)
The Sultan's Dilemma (*Al-Sultān al-hāʾir*, 1959): *The Sultan's Dilemma*, in
Modern Egyptian Drama, ed. Farouk Abdel Wahab (Minneapolis and
Chicago, 1974); *The Sultan's Dilemma*, in *Arabic Writing Today: The
Drama*, ed. Mahmoud Manzalaoui (Cairo, 1977)
Theater of Society (*Masrah al-mujtamaʿ*, 1950)

The Tree Climber (*Yā tāliʿ al-shajara*, 1962): *The Tree Climber* (London, 1966)

Plays, Prefaces and Postscripts of Tawfīq al-Hakīm, Vol. 1 (Washington, D.C., 1981)

HAQQĪ, YAHYĀ

Antar and Juliette (*ʿAntar wa-Jūliyat*, 1960)
The Lamp of Umm Hāshim (*Qindīl Umm Hāshim*, 1944): *The Saint's Lamp, and Other Stories* (Leiden, 1973)
Leave It to Allah (*Khallīhā ʿalā l-Lāh*, 1959)
People in the Shade (*Nās fī al-zill*, 1971)
Slept Well! (*Sahha al-nawm*, 1955)

HĀWĪ, KHALĪL

The Flute and the Wind (*Al-Nāy wa-al-rīh*, 1961)
River of Ashes (*Nahr al-ramād*, 1957)
The Threshing Floors of Hunger (*Bayādir al-jūʿ*, 1965): *Naked in Exile* (Washington, D.C., 1984)

AL-HAYDARĪ, BULAND

Dialogue across Three Dimensions (*Hiwār ʿabra al-abʿād al-thalatha*, 1974)
Footsteps in a Strange Land (*Khutuwāt fī al-ghurba*, 1965)
Journey of the Yellow Letters (*Rihlat al-hurūf al-sufr*, 1968)
Songs of the Dead City (*Aghānī al-madīna al-mayta*, 1951)
Songs of the Dead City, and Other Poems (*Aghānī al-madīna al-mayta, wa qasāʾid ukhra*, 1957)
The Throb of Clay (*Khafqat al-tīn*, 1946)

HAYKAL, MUHAMMAD HUSAYN

Egyptian Stories (*Qisas Misriyya*, 1969)
She Was Created Thus (*Hākadhā khuliqat*, 1955)
Zaynab (*Zaynab*, 1913)

HIJĀZĪ, AHMAD ʿABD AL-MUʿTĪ

Aurès (*Ūrās*, 1959)
City with No Heart (*Madīna bilā qalb*, 1959)
Elegy on the Handsome Life (*Marthiyyat al-ʿumr al-jamīl*, 1973)
There Remained Only Confession (*Lam yabqā illā al-iʿtirāf*, 1965)

HUSAYN, TĀHĀ

Adīb (*Adīb*, 1935)
Beyond the River (*Ma warā' al-nahr*, 1976)
The Call of the Plover (*Du'a' al-karawān*, 1942)
The Days (*Al-Ayyām*, 3 vols., 1929, 1939, 1972): *An Egyptian Childhood* (London, 1932); *The Stream of Days* (Cairo, 1943); *A Passage to France* (Leiden, 1976)
Dreams of Scheherazade (*Ahlam Shahrazād*, 1943): *The Dreams of Scheherazade* (Cairo, 1974)
The Tortured on the Earth (*Al-Mu'adhdhibūna fī al-ard*, 1949)
The Tree of Misery (*Shajarat al-bu's*, 1944)

IDRĪS, YŪSUF

The Black Soldier (*Al-'Askarī al-aswad*, 1962)
The Cheapest Nights (*Arkhas layālī*, 1954)
The Farfoors (*Al-Farāfīr*, 1964): *The Farfoors*, in *Modern Egyptian Drama*, ed. Farouk Abdel Wahab (Minneapolis and Chicago, 1974); *Flipflap and His Master*, in *Arabic Writing Today: The Drama*, ed. Mahmoud Manzalaoui (Cairo, 1977)
Isn't That So? (*A-laysa kadhālik*, 1957)
The Language of Screams (*Lughat al-ay-ay*, 1965)
The Sin (*Al-'Ayb*, 1962)
The Taboo (*Al-Harām*, 1959): *The Sinners* (Washington, D.C., 1984)
The Terrestrial Comedy (*Al-Mahzala al-ardiyya*, 1966)

The Cheapest Nights (Washington, D.C., 1978)
In the Eye of the Beholder: Tales of Egyptian Life from the Writings of Yūsuf Idrīs (Chicago, 1978)
Rings of Burnished Brass (Washington, D.C., 1984)

ISMĀ'ĪL, ISMĀ'ĪL FAHD

The Light Swamps (*Al-Mustanqa'āt al-daw'iyya*, 1971)
The Other Shores (*Al-Difāf al-ukhrā*, 1973)
The Rope (*Al-Habl*, n.d. [1972?])
The Sky Was Blue (*Kānat al-samā' zarqā'*, n.d. [1970?])

JABRĀ, JABRĀ IBRĀHĪM

The Closed Circuit (*Al-Madār al-mughlaq*, 1964)
Cry on a Long Night (*Sarākh fī layl tawīl*, 1955 [written 1946])
Hunters on a Narrow Street (*Sayyādūn fī shāri' dayyiq*, 1974 [written in English, published 1960])

The Ship (*Al-Safīna*, 1969): *The Ship* (Washington, D.C., 1985)
The Search for Walīd Masʿūd (*Al-Bahth ʿan Walīd Masʿūd*, 1978)
Tammūz in the City (*Tammūz fī al-madīna*, 1959)

JUBRĀN, JUBRĀN KHALĪL (KAHLIL GIBRAN)

Broken Wings (*Al-Ajniha al-mukassara*, 1912): *The Broken Wings* (New York, 1957)
Nymphs of the Valley (*ʿArāʾis al-murūj*, 1906): *Nymphs of the Valley* (New York and London, 1948)
Processions (*Mawākib*, 1918): *Processions* (New York, 1958)
Spirits Rebellious (*Al-Arwāh al-mutamarrida*, 1908): *Spirits Rebellious* (New York, 1947)
A Tear and a Smile (*Damʿa wa-ibtisāma*, 1914): *Tears and Laughter* (New York, 1949); *A Tear and a Smile* (New York, 1950)

IN ENGLISH:
Earth Gods, 1931
The Forerunner, 1920
Jesus, the Son of Man, 1928
The Madman, 1918
The Prophet, 1923

KANAFĀNĪ, GHASSĀN

Men in the Sun (*Rijāl fī al-shams*, 1963): *Men in the Sun* (London, 1979)
Returning to Haifa (*ʿĀʾid ilā Hayfā*, 1970)
Umm Saʿd (*Umm Saʿd*, 1969)
What Is Left for You (*Mā tabaqqā lakum*, 1966)

Palestine's Children (Washington, D.C., 1984)

AL-KHĀL, YŪSUF

The Deserted Well (*Al-Biʾr al-mahjūra*, 1958)
Herodia (*Hirūdiyā*, 1954)
Poems at Forty (*Qasāʾid fī al-arbaʿīn*, 1960)

AL-KHARRĀT, EDWARD

High Walls (*Hītān ʿāliyya*, 1959)
Hours of Arrogance (*Sāʿāt al-kibriyāʾ*, 1974)

LABAKĪ, SALĀH

Disgust (*Sa'm*, 1949)
From the Depths of the Mountain (*Min aʿmāq al-jabal*, 1945)
The Moon's Cradle (*Urjūhat al-qamar*, n.d.)
Promises (*Mawāʿīd*, n.d.)
Strangers (*Ghurabā'*, 1956)

AL-MĀGHŪT, MUHAMMAD

The Hunchback Sparrow (*Al-ʿUsfūr al-ahdab*, 1967): *The Hunchback Sparrow*,
   in *Arabic Writing Today: The Drama*, ed. Mahmoud Manzalaoui (Cairo,
   1977)
Room with Millions of Walls (*Ghurfa bi-malāyīn al-judrān*, 1964)
Sadness in the Moonlight (*Huzn fī daw' al-qamar*, 1959)

MAHFŪZ, NAJĪB

Bayn al-Qasrayn (*Bayn al-Qasrayn*, 1956)
A Beginning and an End (*Bidāya wa-nihāya*, 1949)
Black Cat Tavern (*Khammārat al-Qitt al-Aswad*, 1968)
Chatter on the Nile (*Tharthara fawq al-Nīl*, 1966)
Children of Our Quarter (*Awlād hāratinā*, 1959): *Children of Gebelawi* (London,
   1981)
God's World (*Dunyā Allāh*, 1963)
Honeymoon (*Shahr al-ʿasal*, 1971)
Al-Karnak (*Al-Karnak*, 1974)
Khān al-Khalīlī (*Khān al-Khalīlī*, 1946)
Love in the Rain (*Hubb tahta al-matar*, 1973)
Midaqq Alley (*Zuqāq al-Midaqq*, 1947): *Midaq* [sic] *Alley* (Washington, D.C.,
   1974)
Miramar (*Mīrāmār*, 1967): *Miramar* (London, 1978)
Modern Cairo (*Al-Qāhira al-jadīda*, 1945)
The Mockery of the Fates (*ʿAbath al-aqdār*, 1939)
The Quail and Autumn (*Al-Summān wa-al-kharīf*, 1962): *Autumn Quail* (Cairo,
   1985)
Story with No Beginning and No End (*Hikāya bilā bidāya wa-lā nihāya*, 1971)
The Thief and the Hounds (*Al-Liss wa-al-kilāb*, 1961): *The Thief and the Dogs*
   (Cairo, 1985)
The Trilogy (*Al-Thulāthiyya*, comprising *Bayn al-Qasrayn*, 1956; *Qasr al-Shawq*, 1957; *Al-Sukkariyya*, 1957)
Under the Bus Shelter (*Tahta al-mazalla*, 1969)
The Vagrant (*Al-Shahhādh*, 1965)

God's World (Minneapolis, 1973)

AL-MALĀᵓIKA, NĀZIK

The Bottom of the Wave (*Qarārat al-mawja*, 1957)
Life's Tragedy (*Maᵓsat al-hayāt*, in *Dīwān Nāzik al-Malāᵓika*, 1970)
Lover of the Night (*ᶜĀshiqat al-layl*, 1946)
Problems of Contemporary Poetry (*Qadāyā al-shiᶜr al-muᶜāsir*, 1962)
Song for Man, I and II (*Ughniyya li-al-insān, I, II*, in *Dīwān Nāzik al-Malāᵓika*, 1970)
Splinters and Ashes (*Shazāyā wa-ramād*, 1949)

AL-MAᶜLŪF, FAWZĪ

Collected Poems [of Fawzī al-Maᶜlūf] (*Dīwān Fawzī al-Maᶜlūf*, 1957)

AL-MASᶜADĪ, MAHMŪD

The Dam (*Al-Sudd*, 1955)
Sindbad in Quest of Purity (*Sindbād wa-al-tahāra*, n.d.)

AL-MĀZINĪ, IBRĀHĪM ᶜABD AL-QĀDIR

Carry On! (*ᶜA-l-Māshī*, 1937)
Ibrāhīm Again (*Ibrāhīm al-thānī*, 1943)
Ibrāhīm the Author (*Ibrāhīm al-kātib*, 1931): *Ibrahim the Writer* (Cairo, 1976)
The Magic Box (*Sundūq al-dunyā*, 1929)
Spider's Webs (*Khuyūt al-ᶜankabūt*, 1935)
Starting All Over Again (*ᶜAwd ilā badᵓ*, 1943): *Return to a Beginning*, in *Al-Māzinī's Egypt* (Washington, D.C., 1983)

Al-Māzinī's Egypt (Washington, D.C., 1983)

MĪNA, HANNĀ

Blue Lamps (*Al-Masābīh al-zurq*, 1954)
Fragments of Pictures (*Baqāyā suwar*, n.d.; 2nd ed., 1978)
The Sail and the Storm (*Al-Shirāᶜ wa-al-ᶜāsifa*, 1966)
The Snow Comes In through the Window (*Al-Thalj yaᵓtī min al-nāfidha*, 1969)
Sun on a Cloudy Day (*Al-Shams fī yawm ghāᵓim*, 1973)

MUNĪF, ᶜABD AL-RAHMĀN

East of the Mediterranean (*Sharq al-Mutawassit*, 1977)
Endings (*Al-Nihāyāt*, 1978)

Race of the Long Distances: A Journey to the East (*Sibāq al-masāfāt al-tawīla: Rihla ilā al-Sharq*, 1979)

The Trees and the Assassination of Marzūq (*Al-Ashjār wa-ightiyāl Marzūq*, 1973)

When We Abandoned the Bridge (*Hīna taraknā al-jisr*, 1976)

MUTRĀN, KHALĪL

Collected Poems of Khalīl (*Dīwān al-Khalīl*, first vol., 1908; 4-vol. ed., 1948–49)

NĀJĪ, IBRĀHĪM

Behind the Clouds (*Warā' al-ghamām*, 1934)
Cairo Nights (*Layālī al-Qāhira*, 1951)
Collected Works (*Dīwān Ibrāhīm Nājī*, 1973)
In the Temple of Night (*Fī maʿbad al-layl*, 1957)
The Wounded Bird (*Al-tā'ir al-jarīh*, 1957)

NUʿAYMA, MIKHĀʾĪL

Fathers and Sons (*Al-Abā' wa-al-banūn*, 1916)
Job (*Ayyūb*, 1967?)
Marginalia (*Hawāmish*, 1965)
Murmurs of the Eyelids (*Hams al-jufūn*, 1945)
Notables (*Akābir*, 1956; 2nd ed., 1963)
Once Upon a Time (*Kāna mā kāna*, 1937)
The Sieve (*Al-Ghirbāl*, 1923)
___
A New Year (Leiden, 1974)

QABBĀNĪ, NIZĀR

The Brunette Told Me (*Qālat lī al-samrā'*, 1944)
Childhood of a Breast (*Tufūlat nahd*, 1948)
Darling (*Habībatī*, 1961)
Drawing with Words (*Al-Rasm bi-al-kalimāt*, 1966)
Poems (*Qasā'id*, 1956)
Samba (*Sambā*, 1949)
You Are Mine (*Anti lī*, 1950)

QĀSIM, 'ABD AL-HAKĪM

The Seven Days of Man (*Ayyām al-insān al-sab'a*, 1968)

AL-QĀSIM, SAMĪH

Blood on My Hands (*Damī 'alā kaffī*, 1967)
Elegies of Samīh al-Qāsim (*Marāthī Samīh al-Qāsim*, 1973)
The Fall of Masks (*Suqūt al-aqni'a*, 1969)
Songs of the Alleys (*Aghānī al-durūb*, 1964)

AL-RĪHĀNĪ, AMĪN

Cry of the Valleys (*Hutāf al-awdiya*, 1955)
The Rīhāniyyāt (*Al-Rīhāniyyāt*, 4 vols., 1922–24)
Song of the Sufis (*Unshūdat al-Sūfiyyīn*, 1921): *A Chant of the Mystics* (New York?, 1921)

AL-RĪHĀNĪ, NAJĪB

Hasan, Morcos, and Cohen (*Hasan wa-Murqus wa-Kūhīn*, 1943)

AL-RUBAY'Ī, 'ABD AL-RAHMĀN MAJĪD

Aspects of a Journey of Toil (*Wujūh min rihlat al-ta'ab*, 1966)
Eyes in the Dream ('*Uyūn fī al-hulm*, 1974)
The Horses (*Al-Khuyūl*, 1976)
Memory of the City (*Dhākirat al-madīna*, 1975)
Other Seasons (*Al-Mawāsim al-ukhrā*, 1970)
The Rivers (*Al-Anhār*, 1974)
Shadow in the Head (*Al-Zill fī al-ra's*, 1968)
The Sword and the Ship (*Al-Sayf wa-al-safīna*,1966)
The Tattoo (*Al-Washm*, 1972)

SĀLIH, AL-TAYYIB

Bandar Shāh (*Bandar Shāh*, 1971)
Season of Migration to the North (*Mawsim al-hijra ilā al-shimāl*, 1966): *Season of Migration to the North* (London, 1969)
The Wedding of al-Zayn ('*Urs al-Zayn*, 1966): *The Wedding of Zein* (London, 1968)

AL-SAMMĀN, GHĀDA

Beirut '75 (*Bayrūt '75*, 1975)
Incomplete Works (*A'māl ghayr kāmila*, 1979)
Leaving the Ancient Harbors (*Rahīl al-marāfi' al-qadīma*, 1973)
Night of Strangers (*Layl al-ghurabā'*, 1966)
There Is No Sea at Beirut (*Lā bahr fī Bayrūt*, 1963)
Your Eyes Are My Destiny (*'Aynāka qadarī*, 1962?)

SĀYIGH, TAWFĪQ

The Mu'allaqa of Tawfīq Sāyigh (*Mu'allaqat Tawfīq Sāyigh*, 1963)
The Poem of K (*Al-Qasīda K*, 1960)
Thirty Poems (*Thalāthūn qasīda*, 1954)

AL-SAYYĀB, BADR SHĀKIR

The Blind Prostitute (*Al-Mūmis al-'amyā'*, 1954)
Faded Flowers (*Azhār dhābila*, 1947)
The Grave Digger (*Haffār al-qubūr*, 1952)
The House of Slaves (*Manzil al-aqnān*, 1963)
Myths (*Asātir*, 1950)
Song of the Rain (*Unshūdat al-matar*, 1960)
The Submerged Temple (*Al-Ma'bad al-gharīq*, 1962)
Weapons and Children (*Al-Asliha wa-al-atfāl*, 1954)

AL-SHĀBBĪ, ABŪ AL-QĀSIM

Songs of Life (*Aghānī al-hayāt*, 1955)

AL-SHARQĀWĪ, 'ABD AL-RAHMĀN

Back Streets (*Al-Shawāri' al-khalfiyya*, 1958?)
The Earth (*Al-Ard*, 1954): *Egyptian Earth* (London, 1962)
Empty Hearts (*Qulūb khāliya*, 1957?)
The Peasant (*Al-Fallāh*, 1967?)
The Tragedy of Jamīla (*Ma'sāt Jamīla*, 1962?)

AL-SHĀRŪNĪ, YŪSUF

The Crowd (*Al-Zihām*, 1969)
The Five Lovers (*Al-'Ushshāq al-khamsa*, 1954)
Letter to a Woman (*Risāla ilā imra'a*, 1960)

SHUKRĪ, ʿABD AL-RAHMĀN

Book of Confessions (*Kitāb al-iʿtirāf*, 1916)
Collected Poems (*Dīwān ʿAbd al-Rahmān Shukrī*, 1960)
The Light of the Dawn (*Dawʾ al-fajr*, 1909)
The Notions (*Al-Khatarāt*, 1916)
Pearls of Thought (*Laʾāliʾ al-afkār*, 1913)
Satan's Memoirs (*Mudhakkirāt Iblīs*, n.d.)

SURŪR, NAJĪB

O Night, O Moon! (*Āh, yā layl, yā qamar*, 1967)
Where Shall I Get People From? (*Min ayn agīb nās?*, 1976)
Yāsīn and Bahiyya (*Yāsīn wa-Bahiyya*, 1963)

TĀHĀ, ʿALĪ MAHMŪD

East and West (*Sharq wa-gharb*, 1947)
The Lost Mariner (*Al-Mallāh al-tāʾih*, 1934)
The Nights of the Lost Mariner (*Layālī al-mallāh al-tāʾih*, 1940)
Song of the Four Winds (*Ughniyyat al-riyāh al-arbaʿ*, 1943)
Spirits and Shades (*Arwāh wa-ashbāh*, 1942)

TĀMIR, ZAKARIYYĀ

Damascus of the Fires (*Dimashq al-harāʾiq*, 1975?)
The Neighing of the White Horse (*Sahīl al-jawād al-abyad*, 1960)
Spring in the Ashes (*Rabīʿ fī al-ramād*, 1963)
Thunder (*Al-Raʿd*, 1970)

TAYMŪR, MAHMŪD

The Call of the Unknown (*Nidāʾ al-majhūl*, 1939): *The Call of the Unknown* (Beirut, 1964)
Rajab Efendī (*Rajab Efendī*, 1928)
Ruins (*Al-Atlāl*, 1934)
Salwā Blown in the Wind (*Salwā fī mahabb al-rīh*, 1939)
Shaykh Jumʿa (*Al-Shaykh Jumʿa*, 1925)
Shaykh Sayyid al-ʿAbīt (*Al-Shaykh Sayyid al-ʿAbīt*, 1926)
Shelter No. 13 (*Al-Makhbaʾ raqm thalāthata ʿashara*, 1941)
Uncle Mitwallī (*ʿAmm Mitwallī*, 1925)
Young Boys and Girls (*Shabāb wa-ghāniyyāt*, 1951)

AL-TIKIRLĪ, FUʾĀD

Echo from Far Away (*Al-Rajʿ al-baʿīd*, 1980)
The Other Face (*Al-Wajh al-ākhar*, 1960)

TŪQĀN, FADWĀ

Alone with Days (*Wahdī maʿa al-ayyām*, 1955)
Give Us Love (*Aʿtinā hubban*, 1960)
I Found It (*Wajadtuhā*, 1957)
In Front of the Closed Door (*Amāma al-bāb al-mughlaq*, 1967)

AL-ʿUJAYLĪ, ʿABD AL-SALĀM

Bāsima in Tears (*Bāsima bayn al-dumūʿ*, 1958)
Horses and Women (*Al-Khayl wa-al-nisāʾ*, 1965)
Nights and Stars (*Layālī wa-nujūm*, 1951)
The Witch's Daughter (*Bint al-sāhira*, 1948)

WAHBA, SAʿD AL-DĪN

The Caboose (*Al-Sibinsa*, 1966)
Kafr al-Battīkh (*Kafr al-Battīkh*, 1963?)
Al-Mahrūsa (*Al-Mahrūsa*, 1965)
The Nails (*Al-Masāmīr*, 1967)
The Road to Safety (*Sikkat al-salāma*, 1965)

WANNŪS, SAʿDALLĀH

The Adventure of the Slave Jābir's Head (*Mughāmarat raʾs al-mamlūk Jābir*, 1970)
The Elephant, O King of All Ages (*Al-Fīl, yā malik al-zamān*, 1970)
An Evening's Entertainment for the Fifth of June (*Haflat samar min ajl al-khāmis min Hazīrān*, 1968)
The King Is the King (*Al-Malik huwa al-malik*, 1977)

WATTĀR, AL-TĀHIR

The Earthquake (*Al-Zilzāl*, 1974)
The Fisherman and the Palace (*Al-Hawwāt wa-al-qasr*, 1980)
Al-Lāz (*Al-Lāz*, n.d.)
Mule's Wedding (*ʿUrs baghl*, 1978)
Smoke from My Heart (*Dukhān min qalbī*, n.d.)

COPYRIGHT ACKNOWLEDGMENTS

INDEX TO CRITICS

Names of critics are cited on the pages given.